*The situla from Vače excavation site (6th century B.C.), Hallstatt period,
preserved at the National Museum of Slovenia in Ljubljana.
One of the many situlas found in Slovenia.*

VENETI

First Builders of European Community

Tracing the History and Language
of Early Ancestors of Slovenes

Jožko Šavli, Matej Bor, Ivan Tomažič

Editiones Veneti
A–1080 Wien, Bennogasse 21
Austria
Co-published by Anton Škerbinc
Boswell, British Columbia, Canada

Canadian Cataloguing in Publication Data

Šavli, Jožef, 1943-

Includes bibliographical references and index.
Translation of: Unsere Vorfahren die Veneter.
ISBN 0-9681236-0-0

1. Veneti 2. Venetic language. I. Bor, Matej, 1913- II. Tomažič, Ivan., 1919- III. Title.
DG225.V3S2813 1996   937'.3   C96-910543-6

Typesetting by Warren Clark
Printed and bound in Canada by D. W. Friesen and Sons Ltd.

Distributed by:
Anton Skerbinc
Site 1, Box 17, R.R. #1
Boswell, BC V0B 1A0 CANADA

Canada $34.00 CAD
USA, Australia & Other Destinations $29.00 USD

Contents

PART TWO

PART THREE

Introductory Foreword

By Professor Dr. Tareq Y. Ismael

That this book has since 1988 seen publication in German, Slovene, and Italian should speak of its importance in the field of Central European history. It has earned considerable recognition already among scholars and laymen in Europe in a field which is marked by ideological strictures and a tendency for current politics to overwhelm historical accuracy, and try to force historians, linguists, and archaeologists into the service of regimes.

The study of history developed a strongly nationalistic trend in the latter half of the last century. The goal of the field was no longer to document the development of culture and history through new and improved methods, but rather to create history that would assure cultural prestige and even superiority. Uncovering historical truths was of secondary importance.

These ideological foundations remain to the present day in the minds of many scholars and even entire schools of thought and method. Most studies on history and linguistics of Central Europe have been suffused with these nationalistic attitudes, with historians guided by predetermined aims. Their primary concern has often been to maintain the belief that Slavs are not indigenous to Central Europe. With the tragic events in the region since 1990, the debate has become increasingly polarized, with little hope of real progress in developing a true history of Central Europe that serves no agenda.

The principal aim of this work is to draw attention to the need for a new attitude and a new vision of the early history of Central Europe, and hopefully to promote unbiased research methods. It is a plea for more openness and honesty, as well as recognition of the common heritage of the peoples of Central Europe regardless of nationality, language, and religion. While there will be considerable opposition to these goals, we can only hope that the reader will be impressed by scholarship rather than ideology, and give this work the consideration it is due.

In Part One, contrary to traditional views, the author argues that the West Slavs are indigenous to Central Europe, and that it was the West Slavic Veneti or Wends who were, through the Urnfield culture, one of the first disseminators of a major cultural complex in Central Europe. Through their migration originating circa 1200 BCE, they spread over a large area of the continent, including present-day Austria, Slovenia, eastern Switzerland, and northern Italy.

In Part Two, the author interprets Venetic and Old-Etruscan inscriptions with the help of the Slovene language and its surviving dialects and other Slavic languages including Old Church Slavic. He makes a strong case that his findings indicate that the Veneti were a Proto-Slavic people, whose language is preserved in the roots of modern Slovene to this day.

In Part Three, the main areas are reviewed and further elucidated by the author with a variety of studies and commentary. His submissions strongly emphasize the work's originality of approach.

Special mention must be given to the efforts of Anton Škerbinc in the translation of this work. In the academic field, it is no mean task to try and convert both the style and the substance of an author into another language, yet these efforts are absolutely necessary if an important work such as this is to be shared with the world's scholarly and lay community.

The main concern of this work is to contribute to peaceful coexistence among the nations of Central Europe, all of whom, according to the authors, share to some degree in the cultural heritage of the Veneti.

Tareq Y. Ismael
University of Calgary
Alberta, Canada
May 1996

Translator's Notes

A pronunciation table of those Slovene letters which are unfamiliar to the English speaker is included; hopefully it will be of some value to the reader:

c **ts** as in ca**ts**
č **ch** as in **church**
g **g** as in **g**et
j **y** as in **y**es
š **sh** as in **sh**op
z **z** as in **z**enith
ž **zh** as in plea**s**ure

In Part Two, there are many Old Church Slavic and Russian words which were transcribed in Slovene orthography, but two graphemes from the Cyrillic alphabet were also used. They are: ь, which indicates palatalization of the preceding consonant, and ъ, which indicates nonpalatalization.

The process of translation followed the original Slovene text as closely as possible; only some minor changes were made for the sake of clarity. Care was taken to spell all foreign words correctly, and names of historical personalities, regions and cultures were adapted to English usage. To facilitate the reader's perusal of this volume I created an index of all names.

My gratitude to all who in any way assisted or encouraged me in this lengthy task. Special thanks to Betsy Brierley, for her meticulous and patient editing.

Anton Škerbinc
Boswell,
British Columbia, Canada
May 1996

Foreword

The solving of the mystery of Venetic and Etruscan inscriptions with the help of the Slovene language places before us the still open question regarding the initial formation of Indo-European languages. But before we examine this problem, we must recognize that the Venetic and Etruscan languages have to be included in this group. The Etruscan has till now been denied this right.

How and why did Indo-European languages develop? We can say that they formed from a language widely distributed in central Europe. The reasons are unknown but we can draw some conclusions from the later development of Latin based languages; the internal and external causes creating these languages are known to us. We can infer that Indo-European languages also formed as a result of specific internal and external circumstances. The internal conditions of the time are unknown; however, we have some understanding of the extraordinary influence of the invasion and domination of a warring people from the area of the Caucasus in the Late Stone Age (Neolithic) between 3000 and 2000 B.C. Their Battle-Axe culture imposed itself on the predominantly agricultural indigenous peoples. These new circumstances demanded new, improved communications which meant new languages. The change first unfolded in Europe itself, and then because of migrations spread eastward to Persia and India. The dawning of the Indo-European era was the first major turning point in the historical development of Europe.

There is also the question of the original language in Europe which served as the base for the first Indo-European languages. Among these we must count the Venetic and the Illyrian. I would venture to say that it was the Proto-Slavic language. A number of substantiations are presented later in this book.

In the Middle Stone Age (Mesolithic), European people already had important material cultures with correspondingly well-developed languages. Among archaeological remains of the Vinča culture—the middle Danubian area during the 6th to 4th millenniums B.C.—the Etruscologist professor Dr. Radivoje Pešić found all letters of the Etruscan alphabet. Obviously their language was already relatively advanced. The Ice Man from the Tyrolean glacier, dating back to 3300 B.C., provides evidence of an important, orderly society existing in that area. Also in the excavations at Abensberg on the Danube in Bavaria there are strong indications of life in well organized settlements. The thousands of flintstone (Feuerstein) mines found there, dating from 5000 B.C., indicate a prosperous culture based on trade with this "steel of the Stone Age" and the production of a variety of tools.

From the symbiosis of the old indigenous cultures and the new Battle-Axe culture, new societies and new languages formed. Around 1500 B.C., the Únětice (Aunjetitz) culture was known in central Europe. Within it the Indo-European components dominated, including the Kurgan or Mound-grave burial. There was a change around 1300 B.C. when the famous Lusatian culture established itself. Within this culture ancient indigenous elements prevailed; it was here that cremation of the dead and the burial of ashes in urns originated. This burial custom marks the beginning of the Urnfield culture, which spread its religious message with great speed through much of Europe.

The important question at this point concerns the bearers of this culture. Who were they? And who were the first people in central Europe, or possibly all of Europe, who outgrew the narrow constraints of tribal community and developed a higher level of social organization? Until the Second World War researchers identified the people of the Urnfield culture as Proto-Illyrians. More recent archaeological and historical data have led them to the conclusion that these people were Proto-Veneti, since it is known that the Illyrians never occupied the region of central Europe.

Numerous settlements of Urnfield people dating from 1200 B.C. were found around Ljubljana, Slovenia. We may conclude that the Veneti moved from this area farther south to Italy, a hypothesis that corresponds with the findings of the Italian scholar, Giuseppe Sergi, who presented evidence that the Veneti came to Italy from the north in the Bronze Age. It was this group of Veneti, inhabiting the territory between the Alps and the upper Adriatic, who founded the Este culture. Through this culture we are today best able to discover their identity and through them the identity of their predecessors.

The Veneti were a Slavic people; that is, they were the earliest known Slavs in the new form of the Indo-European reality. As the Urnfield culture spread, so did the Venetic (Slavic) language. The most authentic components of the ancient Venetic language have been preserved by the Slovenes who are still living in the region of the Este culture.

The aim of this book is to present evidence that will lead to fundamental changes in the contemporary views of European history.

In the first part of this book Dr. Jožko Šavli presents a survey of the prehistory of central Europe. He then takes us on a journey through the remains of the Venetic culture and language, especially in the Alpine region and northern Italy between the Po River and the Alps. Hundreds of names of mountains, valleys, rivers, and villages still exist today in this region and witness the past presence of Veneti—a nation living on in its descendants, the majority of whom have lost the Venetic language.

In the second part of the book, the mysteries of the Venetic and Etruscan inscriptions are unveiled. These inscriptions belong to the oldest monuments of written language in Europe. Scholars had not been able to decipher them until linguist-academician Matej Bor found in the Slovene language the key to their translation. Although the Venetic inscriptions are more than 2000 years removed from contemporary Slovene, the similarities between the two languages are such that these important cultural monuments can still be understood.

These surprising discoveries have attracted not only admiration and approval from scholars and laymen, but also sharp criticism from those who cannot accept the fact that they made wrong decisions in the area of historiography and archaeological legacy.

The third part of the book was written as an answer to these critics, with the goal of dispelling false theories which have until now surrounded the Veneti and their identity.

We would like to break the barrier of silence which surrounds the Venetic culture and to present the reader with an unobstructed view of the ancient past of Europe, which is to some degree still reflected in the Slovene nation.

The reader will notice that this book was written at a specific time in the history of the Slovenes—before their independence. This is the reason for some sharp polemics, provoked especially in connection with entrenched ideological and historical views. We think the importance of the data presented speaks for itself. We also think that the book transcends all ideological positions. Needless to say, every effort was made to scrupulously avoid nationalistic motives.

The principal purpose of this book is to determine those elements of material culture and historical events which link the nations of central Europe with their predecessors, the Veneti, regardless of the different languages involved.

We would like to contribute to mutual understanding and recognition among the nations of Europe, to strengthen peace and friendship, especially among the nations living in the Alpine region, once the cultural and national centre of the Veneti.

Ivan Tomažič

PART ONE

In the Footsteps of Veneti

Jožko Šavli

Introduction

Historical sources, especially the Fredegarii Chronicon (7th century) often use the name Veneti or variations such as Wenedi or Winidi and even Vandali to refer to the Carantanians or Slovenes in general. Since the Middle Ages and into the present century, the Slovenes have been called by their German neighbours "Windische" and by the Hungarians "Vendek"—corresponding closely to the older names Veneti or Wends.

Until now linguists and historians have not concerned themselves with the question of why the Slovenes are called Veneti or Wends. The usual explanation is that in the writings of the Middle Ages, many peoples and regions were given names which were already in use during Roman and pre-Roman times.

This simple explanation is in some cases correct, but not in the naming of the Carantanian Slovenes as Veneti or Wends. The region of the eastern Alps where Slovene Carantania appeared in the early Middle Ages was previously called Noricum. Before the presumed arrival of the predecessors of Slovenes in the 6th century, a Romanized people lived there and before them the Celts (as we are told by official historians). Accordingly, the Carantanians would have been called Norici or Noricans, not Wends or Veneti. Moreover, we cannot connect this naming with the Roman province Venetia (present-day Veneto), as the presumed colonization of the eastern Alps by the Slavs in the 6th century never extended that far.

The Veneti are known to us in history books as the ancient, pre-Celtic inhabitants of Venetia. Although they are often cited in historical source-material, the researchers did not give them particular attention until the Second World War. During the years following the war, however, research into early European history has repeatedly occupied itself with the Veneti, whose appearance brought about such important cultural changes as Europe seldom experienced before or after.

In recent decades an equally significant change has resulted in a new understanding among some linguists. This change can be best represented thus:

The Veneti were the Proto-Slavic people. They were the bearers of the Urnfield culture and the Urnfield migration, which originated circa 1200 B.C. in central Europe (Lusatian culture) and spread over much of the European continent.

This statement completely invalidates all previous conceptions about Europe's prehistory, the early Slavs and their native land, as well as their presumed first appearance in central Europe in the 6th century A.D. This latter assumption was developed by German historians toward the end of the last century and was later repeated by Slavic and other historians.

According to this view, the original home-base of the Slavs would have been the Pripet swamps behind the Carpathian Mountains. From there the Slavic tribes spread out through Europe in all directions shortly before the 6th century A.D.

The position of the autochthonists appeared in this context in a new light at the end of the last century and even later. They considered the early inhabitants of Europe to have been Slavs. Among the Slovenes who supported this view was Davorin Trstenjak. His writings on this topic were published before the turn of the century, most notably in the *Matica Slovenska Yearbook* in Ljubljana, Slovenia. The well-known Slovene scholar, H. Tuma, who specialized in Alpine toponymy and the Alpine herdsman's customs and culture, also advocated this viewpoint.

After the First World War, in the area of historiography and linguistics the official and predominant view remained in the entrenched position: the Slavs originally resided behind the Carpathian Mountains and from there migrated to other regions in the 6th century. This view has not been proven or substantiated from a scientific standpoint. It was developed and maintained for political and strategic purposes by nationalistic ideologies, above all by the pan-Germanic, the pan-Slavic and later, the South Slavic Unitarianism.[1] The latter, the roots of which go as far back as the middle of the 19th century, became especially influential after the First World War in the newly-formed Yugoslavia.

The Slovenes had to merge into the strong nation of Yugoslavia in order to protect themselves from the dangers of assimilation by Germans and Italians. This was particularly urgent, since it concerned a situation that existed in past

---

[1] Important sociological studies were carried out after World War Two regarding the use of ideologically distorted information and its effect on public opinion. As expected, the results of these studies were not utilized either by historians or linguists. These two groups of researchers continued to apply the older, outdated models, which resulted in systematic exclusion of all areas of study that did not serve their nationalistic interests. Even the most admirable elements of a culture which they wanted to denigrate were deliberately repudiated or ignored. Historic events were, and still are, portrayed in distorted images that never existed in reality. In this way the ideologues were able to create conditions that were protective of the interests of those who held privileged positions in society...A. Burghardt, *Allgemeine Wirtschaftssoziologie/* A General Study of Sociology in Economics; München, Pullach 1974.

centuries; i.e., relentless encroachment on their ethnic territory.

The theory that the Carpathian hinterland was the native land of all Slavs and that they migrated in the 6th century A. D. remained as an unwritten ideological taboo. As a result, no fine distinctions were made, but ideologically-driven generalities were repeated: The South Slavs came to the Balkan peninsula and some of them settled in the eastern Alps during the same period. Any other interpretation in regard to Slovenes would have been politically untenable. The search for and discovery of other historical roots for the Slovene nationality would have been considered destructive to Yugoslav unity; consequently, historians came to no new discoveries regarding the ancestry of Slovenes. However, repeated attempts were made after the Second World War to discover the true origin of this nationality.

In his work, "Essays on the Slovene Language," (Ljubljana 1969) the respected Slovene linguist, France Bezlaj, attributed much older roots to Slovenes and their language than what had previously been acknowledged. He found that the meanings of many Slovene words coincide with those in Baltic languages—an indication that the Slovene cannot be included in the South-Slavic language group.

Western historians in general, but especially those of German and other Anglo-Saxon background, maintained the older view of the origin of the Slavs. Their independent research in this field is hindered by a lack of knowledge of Slavic languages; they are usually limited to one Slavic language, which is simply not enough for this study.

New inroads in the search for the origins of Slavs were made after the First World War by Polish scientists who proposed that the bearers of the Urnfield culture were the Veneti, a Proto-Slavic people (Lehr-Spławiński). After the Second World War, some Italian linguists also acknowledged the Veneti—irrespective of their origin—as the bearers of the Urnfield culture (G. Devoto). In addition, German linguists (e.g. H. Krahe) concluded at the beginning of the 1960's that during the pre-Celtic era central Europe had belonged, not to the "North Illyrian" but rather to the Venetic branch of languages. Even the thesis about the ancestral land of the Slavs in the far reaches of the Pripet swamps has been recently discarded by Russian scholars, according to O. Trubachov.

In the present study we discover that the Slovenes, whose settlement in the eastern Alps in the 6th century A.D. is totally undocumented, are direct descendants of the ancient Proto-Slavic Veneti or Wends.

During the early Middle Ages, historical writings used the names Veneti, Winidi or Wends to designate only the West Slavic group, including the Slovenes. The South Slavs, who settled in the Balkans in the 6th century A.D., were called

Sclabenoi by Byzantine authors, clearly showing the difference between the West Slavic Veneti and the South Slavs.

When the Slovene edition of this work came out (Ljubljana 1985), it aroused much criticism in Slovenia as well as in Yugoslavia but it also received much recognition, especially after the well-known Slovene poet, Matej Bor, Slavist and member of the Slovene Academy, published his interpretations of the Venetic inscriptions with the help of Slovene and other Slavic languages. His monumental work forms the second part of this book. It represents a major breakthrough in the study of Venetic heritage.

In regard to the name Veneti, Matej Bor gave us an explanation that is at once understandable as it is historically accurate:

"As much as we can tell, the original designation must have been *Slovent*, from this *Slovenc*, pl. *Slovenci* (Slovenes); i.e., people who understand each other (*slovo*—word). The ancient Greek authors, Homer and Herodotus, called them *Enetoi* simply because in Greek the prefix *slo-* and the sound *v* did not exist. The Romans adapted this term to Veneti, while the Greeks during the Roman era used the form Uenedai (Ouenetai)."

A variety of new findings from the periods following the First and Second World Wars were the basis for this study.

The Supposed Settlement

*No author tells us when and from where the
Slovene people came into the land they
today inhabit, nor how they settled there
and subdued the soil they still cultivate.
(H.Tuma)[2]*

The so-called Alpine Slavs, the ancestors of the Slovenes, allegedly settled in the eastern Alps in the second half of the 6th century, after the Langobards had migrated to Italy in the year 568. The Slovene settlement would have encompassed present Carinthia and Styria, Carniola and the coastal area of the Adriatic Sea, the Slovene littoral; in the north it spread as far as the Danube, and in the west as far as the Traun River. This means the area that is today Upper and Lower Austria was included.[3]

This theory, maintained by historians, is taught in all history books. What very few people know is the fact that the colonization of Slavs in the Alps during the above time period cannot be authenticated by any historical source. It represents a fabricated, fictitious view that is repeated without critical examination.

Newer official interpretations of this question give us some additional facets of "information" that were lacking in earlier explanations. The Alpine Slavs settled in the Eastern Alps in two waves, one from the north and the other following after from the southeast moving upward along the Alpine rivers.[4] The northern-wave theory was developed in an effort to make the migration of the Slovenes from the southeast more believable. Meanwhile, linguists have discovered fundamental differences between the Slovene and South Slavic languages, which simply do not allow a unified South Slavic language group that would have included the Slovenes in the 6th century.

---

[2] H. Tuma, *Krajevno imenoslovje/*Regional Toponymy, *Jadranski almanah*, Trst (Trieste), 1923, p. 128.

[3] M. Kos, *Zgodovina Slovencev/* History of the Slovenes, Ljubljana, 1955, pp. 46–7. B. Grafenauer, *Zgodovina slovenskega naroda/* History of the Slovene People, Ljubljana 1964, pp. 287–289.

[4] B. Grafenauer, ibid., pp. 288–289

The Slovene language owes its origin to the West Slavic branch; however, this fact is incompatible with the official theory of the colonization of the eastern Alps by the South Slavs. The reference to a preceding wave of a West Slavic colonization does not lend greater credibility to a unitary South Slavic ancestry. We will gradually dispel this confusion as we proceed.

If we analyze what has been written by the Slovenes themselves about their present settlement area, something interesting becomes apparent; viz., that no historical source reports knowing when and how, or if at all, the Slovenes or their ancestors colonized the eastern Alps. In addition, the documented departure of the Langobards to Italy in the year 568 offers no basis for the conclusion that the Alpine Slavs moved into the Alps at that time. The Langobards, moreover, did not live in the eastern Alps but rather on the western edge of the Pannonian plain; i.e., in the area leading to the Alpine region.[5] Their migration to Italy should not be seen as an evacuation of the eastern Alps. This area was therefore inhabited by another people. The obvious and so far officially unanswered question is: Who were these people?

Because the Langobards lived far to the north of the Alpine rivers Drava and Sava prior to their migration to Italy, they could not have blocked the supposed route to the Alps for Balkan Slavs living in the area of these rivers. Consequently, there was no reason for the Slavs to wait for the migration of the Langobards in order to move into the Alps.

Since the Langobards did not settle the eastern Alps, the question arises: Was this territory left without a defence after the fall of the Roman Empire and the dissolution of the ensuing Eastern Gothic and Byzantine occupations? In such a case the Baiuvarii/Bavarians would have occupied the eastern Alps as they occupied the central Alps and the plains north of the Alps half a century earlier.

Another question arises: What would have driven the Slavs living on the Balkan peninsula into the Alps? According to prevailing views, they had just come out of the Russian plains or the Trans-Carpathian swamps and were therefore largely unaccustomed to mountain life.

The arrival of Slovenes in the eastern Alps thus remains open to debate. Related to this is the unanswered question about the earlier inhabitants and what happened to them after the presumed arrival of the Slavs. On this subject, Slovene historians hold totally contradictory views without being able to substantiate them. *They are all tuned to the German and Austrian theory about the "Einbruch der Slawen"—the invasion of the Slavs—a theory that was designed to facilitate*

---

[5] Around 490 A.D. they occupied the territory of the Rugians in Lower Austria. See Brockhaus Enzyklopädie, Wiesbaden 1970 (Langobarden).

and justify the expropriation and denationalization of the West Slavs, and particularly the Slovenes.

F. Kos: "We can say with complete justification, that the Slovenes, after their arrival in Pannonia and Noricum, in contrast to the Goths, Langobards, and other Germanic tribes, had acted in a much more bloodthirsty and cruel manner....Indeed they usually exterminated the inhabitants of the countries they occupied."[6]

M. Kos: "Apparently we will have to consider more seriously the capacity of Slovenes to assimilate. Upon their arrival in the eastern Alps and on the Karst, they apparently assimilated the indigenous inhabitants. These original settlers, who survived in fairly large numbers, were a Romance people, the descendants of former rulers, the Romans, speaking a heavily muddled Latin. There were also remnants of the Celtic and Illyrian tribes, who communicated with each other partly in Latin, and probably also in their own languages."[7]

B. Grafenauer: "The difference in the situation in the territory that had been occupied by the Slovenes on the one hand and by the Landgobards as well as the Bavarians on the other, is more understandable than the documents from Roman times indicate; that is, the later Slovene Noricum had to a large extent been Romanized, in contrast to Bavaria and the mountainous Rhaetia....This situation is difficult to explain other than by the fact that the Romance people and the Romanized inhabitants of Noricum had fled in considerable numbers into the western Alps and Friuli."[8]

The boldness displayed by these Slovene scholars is amazing; lacking any data from historical source-material, they arrived at such diverse conclusions about the fate of the ancient inhabitants of Noricum after the presumed arrival of the Slavs. Equally amazing is the repeated revision of original statements about the extermination of the native population, statements that were obviously too drastic. A massacre of that magnitude would certainly have been recorded, at least in a list of Christian martyrs. Incidents of much lesser importance than this presumed event are recorded. But the documents are silent in regard to the slaughter of the inhabitants of Noricum—a slaughter which would have happened if there had been an assault by the Slavs on this territory.

The explanation that the Slavic newcomers assimilated the original inhabitants is more desirable, more reasonable; yet, this admittedly milder theory is also questionable. The process of assimilation takes decades, sometimes centuries. History tells us that Romanized nations, among which the people of Noricum are mistakenly counted, were on a higher level of culture and were able to assimilate

---

[6] F. Kos, *Zbrano delo/*Collected Works, edited by B. Grafenauer, Ljubljana 1982, p. 79.

[7] M. Kos, op. cit., p. 71.

[8] B. Grafenauer, op. cit., p. 308.

even their conquerors. The Romans assimilated the Goths and Langobards as well as the Franks, who represented a much greater military power in comparison to the so-called Alpine Slavs. But this does not explain why the Slovenes were not assimilated.

Thus, it seemed more convenient for scholars to develop the supplementary theory that the presumed Romanized people of Noricum fled to the west, into Rhaetia and Friuli, to the Bavarians and Langobards. Moreover, it was noted that the latter could not have been as barbaric as they once were, since they had been influenced for a long time by Roman culture.[9] Yet, according to the same scholars, remnants of the indigenous inhabitants in the eastern Alps were to have decisively enriched the Slavs and their culture.[10] In other places, they allege that inside the territory settled by the Slavs, traces of Romance people were extremely weak.[11]

All arguments that support the settling of Slovenes in the 6th century are found to be mutually contradictory; hence, they cannot be seriously considered. A critical investigation shows that historians base their conclusions solely on the assumption that the Slovenes are South Slavs who advanced into the eastern Alps after they settled the Balkan peninsula.

Theories about the migration of the Langobards to Italy and the supposed destruction, assimilation and flight of the indigenous people of Noricum were developed in such a way as to fit within the framework of the South Slavic hypothesis which leads unavoidably to predetermined conclusions. The principal function of this ideology is to emphasize anything that will corroborate and promote the idea that Slovenes are South Slavs and belong to Yugoslavia. Included in this collection of unsubstantiated views which have survived in the Balkans to this day, is a claim that the Slovenes were in 7th century Carantania not yet an independent people separate from other South Slavs (B. Grafenauer);[12] also that they were until the 9th century "of the same race and blood" (M. Kos),[13] and that they were living as their South Slavic neighbours in extended family communes (Serbian: *zadruga*), at least until the 8th century. The dependability of these methods of substantiating one hypothesis with another will be left to the reader's judgment.

The basis for the social structure among the Slovenes has always been the farming town or village community (Slovene: *soseska, sosenja*) with the village

---

[9] B. Grafenauer, ibid., p. 309.

[10] B. Grafenauer, loc. cit., p. 309.

[11] B. Grafenauer, op. cit., p. 307.

[12] B. Grafenauer, op. cit., p. 325.

[13] M. Kos, op. cit., p. 34.

elders, village judges, and the *župan* (mayor) at the head. The Slovene *župan* was mentioned in historical source-material in the year 777.[14] This is a clear indication that the Slovenes did not live in a proto-structure (extended family) in the 8th century. Any trace of this structure is lacking in Slovene history.

During this period a clear distinction between the Slovenes and the South Slavs can be seen in the use of the names **Veneti or Winedi**, which appear in historical documents, designating the Carantanians as "Venetii" and "Vinidi" or even "Vandali" and "gens Wandalorum".[15] These names have always been used only for the West Slavs and never for the South Slavs. As well, Carantania was consistently called "**marca Winidorum**".

From this we can conclude that the settling of the Slovenes or their ancestors in the 6th century could have originated only from the region of the West Slavs, that is, from the north; but there is no documentation for this move. The principality of Carantania appears in the 6th century in the eastern Alps with its inhabitants referred to in documents as "Sclavi coinomento Winidi". The same records, as well as archaeological finds, say nothing about their settlement during this period.

The settlement and presence of the Slovenes in the eastern Alps has proved to be a contentious question from the standpoint of current and still accepted historical writing. This debate, as noted earlier, has seemingly been resolved through the conclusions of the pan-Slavic or South Slavic ideology, but never scientifically.

But resolving the problem through a process pervaded with ideologies does not lead to a fundamental solution, and if we do not accept the proposition about Slovenes being part of the South Slavic "one race and blood", we are left with but one single hypothesis; namely, **the Slovenes were, in their present homeland, the original, indigenous inhabitants!**

When official historians speak of the people who lived in the eastern Alps before the 6th century A.D., they call them the "original inhabitants". When they speak of the same people after that date, they call them "the Slavs" although they know that the rural population in the eastern Alps never changed after the arrival of Veneti in the 12th century B.C., and that the Slovenes are their most direct descendants.

In their desperation, historians grasped at anything that seemed a solution, using every possible explanation including the invention that the pagan Slavic settlers subdued the indigenous Christian inhabitants, thus "confirming" the ex-

---

[14] B. Grafenauer, op. cit., pp. 341–342, 349.

[15] F. Kos, *Gradivo I/* Papers on the History of the Slovenes, Numbers 151, 164, 190, 194.

istence of the latter. Yet, all these efforts have very little significance in light of later discoveries and admissions.

Before the First World War, the autochthonists again advocated their old position that the origin of the Slavs, including the Slovenes, was to be found in central Europe. However, as a result of limited research in linguistics and archaeology carried out at that time, and above all due to ideological pressures, their position was not sustainable. Nevertheless, thanks to newer findings, conceptions about the origins of Slavs and Slovenes were to some extent altered. It was possible to think that the indigenous people of the Alps were neither Celts, as was originally believed, nor Illyrians, as was believed later. Were they not, therefore, Slavs?

In light of this possibility two questions arise: In what time period should the beginning of the Slavic people be placed, and where was their original homeland?

Traditional explanations about the Slavic native land appear "perfectly clear". Before the migration in the 5th and 6th centuries, the Slavs supposedly lived behind the Carpathian Mountains; yet, in the preceding century different Germanic tribes, mainly the Goths, had occupied this same territory.

Consequently, German historiography took care of this detail in the last century and designated only the marshy territory in the upper part of the Pripet exclusively as the Slavs' native land. As proof they cited among other things the notion that the Slavs adopted the term "bukev" Ger. Buche—beech tree—from their Germanic neighbours only after they settled in their new homeland. From this we would "clearly" see that the Slavs lived in the swamps where the beech tree does not grow. Older Slovene authors (e.g. Ložar),[16] who rely on German "precision", still accept such meaningless proofs and explanations.

Even today official German historians persist in putting the original Slavic homeland in the Trans-Carpathian swamps.

As is obvious from the study of living conditions at that time, only a few tens of thousands of people could have lived in the Pripet swamps, which does not correspond with the number of Slavs after their purported migration, considering the enormous area they settled.

For this reason, some Slavic historians have attempted to provide a larger dimension for the hypothetical native land. According to the Polish scholar, Lowmiański, in the period from the 1st to the 5th centuries, around 0.9 million Slavs could have lived behind the Carpathian Mountains in an area of 500,000

---

[16] R. Ložar, *K teoriji o skandinavskem izvoru Slovencev/* Notes on the Theory of Scandinavian Origin of the Slovenes, Most, Trieste, 1981, pp. 13–18.

square km; whereas, at least 1.25 million could have lived in an area of 750,000 square km—in the largest possible dimension for this hypothetical homeland, equal to the present-day Ukraine.[17]

The numbers impress us as being very scientific, but life and history are not mathematics; history is more readily determined by geography. Within the largest possible extension of this fictitious homeland, the ancient Slavs, Goths and other Germanic tribes would have crowded each other out, again leading to the old theory of the enslaved Slavs. But today this theory is entertained by neither the German nor the Austrian historians, who instead remove the Slavs to the Pripet swamps where they do not stand in anyone's way.

It is interesting how official historians can build theory after theory, and never consider that their speculations may be completely unrealistic. Are they not capable of brushing aside political considerations and looking at the evidence in a simple, unbiased way?

The idyllic leitmotif of the ancient Slavs living behind the Carpathian Mountains dancing the circle dance also turned out to be pure fantasy. It had been influenced by the poetic fervour of German romanticism in the last century (see J. G. Herder). Among the Slovenes, the popular writer F. S. Finžgar brought this to its emotional culmination with his novel *Pod svobodnim soncem*. In his work everything is present: the circle-dance, games, the fight for freedom, youths with sheepskin garments bound around their hips, girls in homespun linen. Everything is healthy and natural—one big happy family of Slavs.

These are, of course, nothing but naive, childish conceptions. Yet, this is how the Slovene public even today imagines the ancient Slavs, without knowing it is simply an ideological front. The linguistics of today distances itself from all this, although it has accepted such views for decades. It has determined that differences in dialects had already come about in the ancient Slavic homeland and that the Slovenes cannot be counted with the South Slavs in regard to their language (see F. Bezlaj). *There are also no archaeological finds from the region behind the Carpathian Mountains that could prove the existence of an ancient Slavic cultural entity*. This point cannot be stressed enough, yet it is systematically avoided by most historians.

The origin of the Slovenes is much older than what has hitherto been accepted by historians and explained with the help of various ideologies. The migration of the Slavs almost certainly took place in prehistoric times. The arrival of the South Slavs on the Balkan peninsula could only have been their last migratory move.

---

[17] B. Grafenauer, op. cit., p. 233.

Since a clear dividing line exists between the Slovenes in the Alps and the South Slavs on the Balkan peninsula in the areas of language, history, ethnology, and social structures (village, as opposed to the extended family commune), and because the migration of the Slovenes in the 6th century cannot be substantiated, it is obvious that we must look deeper into history and prehistory for the origin of the Slovene people. The starting point of this research must be the region inhabited by the Slovenes, their ancient village life, and farming culture. We must examine in detail whether the Slovenes themselves—since they were and, in some instances still are, called Winidi or Windische or Wends—could be the descendants of the ancient Veneti who were (as many linguists now agree) of Slavic origin.

The Names Testify

The inhabitants of the northern (i.e., Salzburg) side of the Hohen Tauern gave the name "Wendenberge" to that part of the mountain range which divides it from the southern valleys where the Slovenes lived. (L. Steinberger)[18]

The settlement area of Slovene ancestors in the eastern Alps is estimated by historians to be around 70,000 square km. Accordingly, historians determined that from around 150,000 to a maximum of 200,000 people could have lived in this territory.[19] Thus, the corresponding population density on average amounted to two or three inhabitants per square km. The Slavic settlement was to have at first encompassed the valleys and valley-basins, where the settlers were to have taken up their abode on already cultivated land left behind by the previous inhabitants.[20]

Such conclusions with respect to geographic data are understandable if we imagine the Slovene ancestors, the so-called Alpine Slavs, as a primitive race who lived from agriculture and knew nothing about livestock-raising and still less about commerce. Goods would have been produced solely for their own needs; there was no importing or exporting of anything. The Slovene ancestors would have been at that time only a part of the South Slavs, who came with the migration wave of ancient Slavs over the Carpathian Mountains to the Balkan peninsula. The Slovene historian L. Hauptmann, who relied on the Byzantine historian Maurikios, gives the following questionable description about the nature of the Slavs:[21]

"They lived among dense forests, inaccessible swamps and lakes. Neverthe-

---

[18] L. Steinberger in the *Zeitschrift für Ortsnamenforschung/* Periodical for Place Name Research, VIII, 1932, p. 254.

[19] B. Grafenauer, *Zgodovina Slovenskega naroda/* History of the Slovene People I, Ljubljana 1978, op. cit., p. 315.

[20] M. Kos, op. cit., p. 70.

[21] L. Hauptmann, *Staroslovenska in staroslovanska svoboda/* The Old-Slovene and the Old-Slavic Freedom, Čas, Ljubljana 1923, p. 209.

less, they were in continual fear, and therefore, hid themselves in secluded areas. In their huts they made several exits to be able to flee at any moment. In an emergency they jumped into the water like frogs and breathed through reeds, until the enemy had disappeared. They carried only simple weapons. Because they were incapable of organizing themselves, they lurked about as thieves waiting in ambush for victims. They did not have fighting troops. They also did not want to fight on open flat ground. Yet when they found themselves engaged in a battle they would go forward screaming at the enemy. If by this he became intimidated, they charged courageously after him. If not, they would turn around and seek refuge in the forest."

And so the term "forest Slavs" appeared in German and Austrian historiography. Maurikios had described the South Slavs from the standpoint of the highly developed military strategy of the Byzantines. As a matter of fact, the ancient Slavs or the South Slavs in the Balkans were, because of their guerilla tactics, a serious opponent even for the Byzantines.

In light of Hauptmann's description, one would expect to find similar tendencies among that segment of South Slavs that had presumedly advanced upward along the Alpine rivers into the eastern Alps.

However, this group, the so-called Alpine Slavs, had a totally different character. They did not dwell in swamps and forests, for them secure ground. Rather, they settled on hills and sunny sides in full view of their potential enemy. They had an already advanced level of agriculture and a totally different social structure from that of the South Slavic commune (zadruga). If we accept the official history, the Slovenes progressed within one generation to a governmental system and founded the Duchy of Carantania. They even conducted foreign policy, joining the alliance of Slavs north of the Alps, a kingdom under the leadership of King Samo. Even the most devoted followers of the official line have to recognize that to advance this much in one generation is simply impossible.

Samo's kingdom was not a mere "tribal union" of Slavs, as historians allege, but rather a powerful confederation which was capable of defeating the Franks advancing from the west. In the east it was able to stand against the pressures of the Avars, who at that time were a superpower intimidating all of southeastern Europe, including Byzantium.

As many sources cite, King Samo was a Carantanian. Hence, in his kingdom, Carantanian Slovenes occupied the leading positions.

It is fairly obvious that the ancestors of Slovenes in the eastern Alps conducted themselves quite differently from the South Slavs, with whom they were supposedly "of the same race and blood". [The recent events in former Yugoslavia shed some light on these differences]. Tr.

Historians were aware of these contradictions, and in order to extricate themselves they developed one more convolution; i.e., some of the original inhabitants remained in the eastern Alps and in a decisive way influenced the culture of the Slovenes. These native residents were supposedly Romanized Celts, the Ladins (Slov. Lahi, Vlahi), whose presence should be proved by a few topographical names of Romance and Celtic origin. In contrast, there are countless toponyms throughout south central Europe that are presumed of Illyrian origin. Many of these names are compounds of common expressions still in daily use in the Slovene language; many are also derivations from Vend, Windisch, clearly showing that Slovenes lived here in pre-Celtic and pre-Roman times.[22]

If the unusually swift cultural development of the Alpine Slavs—as compared with that of the Balkan Slavs—were to be traced to the influence of the Romanized original inhabitants, then these ancient inhabitants must have been very numerous. But the rarity of topographical names of Celtic origin points to the fact that, in the area under consideration, the major part of the original population must have been of different descent, from the pre-Roman and pre-Celtic period. They could only have been the Veneti/Wends, who were until recently included among the Illyrians by historians.

If the older "Illyrian" population influenced in crucial ways the culture of the newcomer Slavs, then we would expect to find a substantial number of Illyrian words in the Slovene language, especially in the area of agriculture and social structures. Instead, the Slovene language is lacking even in traces of Illyrian, as well as Romance word groups. The farming terms are indigenous, that is, Slovene, which means the majority of indigenous inhabitants in the region of the Alps were pre-Celtic Veneti; i.e., the ancestors of Slovenes. In that case they could not have settled in the Alps as late as the 6th century A.D. They must have already been there before the Romans and Celts. Let the historians ponder these things and make some refreshingly simple discoveries.

Arguing in favour of the Slavic origin of the Veneti, who inhabited the eastern Alps, and at the same time supporting the indigenous status of their descend-

---

[22] The name of the plateau Banjščice near Gorica, and the names of its villages Bate and Baske, originate according to B. Grafenauer (op. cit., pp. 305–7) from the old Illyrian term "venti"—dwelling place, and some terms from the herdsman's vocabulary still in use today: tamar, medrje, buša, vardevati, are presumed to be leftovers from the Illyrian that passed through the Vulgar Latin. More to the point is F. Bezlaj, *Eseji o slovenskem jeziku/* Essays on the Slovene Language, Ljubljana 1967, p. 87: "Even place-names Banjščice, Bate, and Baske derive from the ethnicon Venti, which is closer to old Veneti than to the South Slavic Antes."

15

ants, the Slovenes, is also the following evidence: Pasture and mountain names of Slovene origin are preserved in upper Alpine levels, although the alleged settlement of the Slavs in the 6th century would not have included those areas. These names are evidence of a lively Alpine culture: dairy-farms, cleared woodlands, fields and meadows, highly specialized local knowledge such as weather conditions and daily routine of the mountain dwellers—all these would have been unfamiliar to South Slavs coming from plains and swamps.

The South Slavs also had no need to advance into the Alpine highlands to find homesteads for themselves; there was more than enough land in the valleys for all their needs. In fact, the feudal lords, who arrived much later, were able to settle Bavarian farmers in many uninhabited regions.

The homesteads in remote Alpine valleys, with numerous pastures and small mountain fields which are still there today, are of a prehistoric origin. They have provided sustenance and shelter from their enemies for the inhabitants and their herds from time immemorial.

The mountain names have ancient origin; note the specific terms used for diverse surface formations and bodies of water, names from the plant and animal world, as well as designations for particular rocks, mountain peaks, gorges, valleys, springs and streams. Such names could not have been left by a transient people, but are rather a bequest from permanent residents of the mountain region.

They needed these names to designate where they could pasture or mow, what paths were to be crossed, in which places one could rest, over which mountain ridge the storm would approach, behind which mountain peak the sun rose, on which mountain the first snow would fall, and so on.

One is obviously dealing with an indigenous mountain culture that the alleged Slavic newcomers could not have had or been suited for. They would have to adopt not only the culture of the original residents but also the necessary terms and names. As already mentioned, expressions that should be of Celtic and Illyrian origin are missing in the Slovene language. *The nomenclature and terminology from the domain of Alpine culture are Slavic, actually Slovene.*

The Slovenes themselves have not dealt with the social, national, and economic history of Alpine culture in any significant way. A number of papers and articles have been written by Tuma, who decidedly supports the view of Slavic ancestry for the Alpine herder. After the Second World War, V. Volk, R. Badjura and others had published in the Slovene language interesting professional travel books and topographical papers. Apart from these, nothing of importance has been published in Slovenia on the subject.

Mt. Triglav—*There are cases when a name reveals more than merely the morphological characteristics of a particular natural formation or land area. Such a name is certainly that of Mt. Triglav 2,869m, literally "Three-headed", the highest peak of Slovenia.*

This mountain actually does not have three peaks (heads). We think the origin of the name is in mythology, and derives from the pre-Christian period, carrying on an ancient tradition of the Sacred Mountain, often found in the mythology of ancient peoples.

Three-headed or three-bodied creatures originated in the Mediterranean religions of pre-Indo-European time, and are not rare in Greek mythology (Geryon, Typhon, Hecate). They belong to the world of night and evil.

In the Indo-European world, triplicity was understood in a positive sense, reflecting the universal, natural and vital phenomena—The Roman Capitol Triad for example, and the Indian Trimurti.

The three-headed statues found all over the ancient territories of Gaul, Germany, Italy, and the Slavic countries confirm that once triplicity was a conceptual expression of the Universe. Aristotle stated in 4th century B.C.: "Natura perfecit omni ternaria numero."

In the ancient region of Thrace (Bulgaria), four stones with a three-headed rider profile have been found. One of the stones carries a Greek inscription: "To the god of the Universe." Mt. Triglav (Three-headed) is in all probability related to this concept of the god of the Universe.

But Triglav as a deity, like other Old-Slovene deities, cannot be traced historically due to the early influence of Christianity (early 8th century). Consequently, it fell into oblivion and was not recorded.

However, in 12th century A.D. the existence of this deity has been confirmed in the territory of other Western Slavs, particularly the Pomeranians who still live in northern Poland along the Baltic sea. Considering that the Slovenes are also West Slavs, descendants of the ancient Veneti, the right of the god Triglav to the Old-Slovene Pantheon can be confirmed.

There is mention in 12th century sources of the god Triglav as the chief deity of Szczecin, the capital of Pomerania.

According to historical records of the time, there were three hills in the city where the Triglav's temple was located. His three-headed image was made of gold. The pagan explanation of the image was that he was the ruler over the three worlds: the sky, the earth, and the netherworld. A black horse of admirable disposition, flashy and high-spirited, was consecrated to Triglav. His guardian was one of the four temple priests. The Triglav statue was destroyed by St. Otto, the Bishop of Bamberg, during a missionary expedition among Pomeranians.

In Carinthia (the territory of the once Roman province Noricum, the later Slovene Medieval state, Carantania), some traces of Triglav worship have been found. On Mt. Štalen (Magdalensberg), where the capital of Noricum was located, a stone tub

(2nd century A.D.) was found bearing three heads: a young man, an older bearded man, and a woman. In Millstatt, a small town near Spittal, there was a pagan temple of mille statuae (a thousand statues). On top of three columns were placed three heads—the lion, the wolf and the goat—symbolizing the sun and the sky, the winter and darkness, and the earth and fertility.

Mt. Triglav became the symbol of the Slovene homeland. It is visited from spring to fall by many climbers, who desire to enjoy the beautiful panorama from its summit and perhaps, as in ancient myths, to experience the timeless union with nature and the universe.

In the Hohen Tauern and Beyond

A graphic example of how the original names survived after the Slovene language had long been forgotten, even in remote regions, can be drawn from the names in Hohen Tauern and neighbouring mountain groups.[23] These names are original and not borrowed. They later found their way into the German language in forms that clearly reveal their Slovene (Venetic) origin. Had they been Celtic, Illyrian, or Romance they would have been carried over in one of these languages first into Slovene and afterwards into the German language. However, to this day, they have retained their Slovene form with very little change.

We will use a number of expressions, which will help us understand how Alpine toponymy formed. Let us start with the term **lanež**. In Slovene it means a difficult-to-cross, snow-covered, shady mountain slope or its buttress. In the terminology of the Hohen Tauern this term is contained in the names Lanisch Kees, Lanisch Seen, Lanisch Eck 2935m, Lanisch Scharte 2883m, and Lanisch Hafner 2940m. In this area most fit the criterion of being a shady place.

The term **klin** (wedge) is used to designate an angular, sloping mountain crest situated between two rift valleys. In the German variation this term is found as Lin Alm, Gling Spitz (Artal), Kling, Klingspitze, and so on.

We also come across numerous variations of **rt** (spit of land) and **nart**, which are found in compound names with Ort-, Rett-, Ritt-, Reit-, Ritter; also in names such as Ardning, Irdning, Rittolach, as well as in the Italian terminology, Ardegna and Artegna.

A rock projection or an elongated knoll and similar forms are called in Slovene **krmol.** This term appears in the German variation as Gramul 3271–3055m at the foot of the Grossglockner.

---

[23] R. Badjura, *Ljudska geografija/* The Geographic Terms in Local Dialects, Ljubljana 1953 (The Toponymic Index).

The Slovene **preval** (pass) is expressed in the following names: Perwald, Prewald, Präwali, Präwald, Prevaling. We find also the related **predol** (pass valley), for example by the Hochschwab in the following names: Pretalhöhe 1069m, Hohe Pretal; whereas **predel** (mountain or border crossing) can be found in the Predlitz 922m on the Salzburg/Styrian border along the Turracher Predlitzbach, *Bach* (stream, brook); Predlitz, from *predelca* (stream flowing from *predel*).

The word **kompolje**, the end of a field before a slope, is translated into German as Gumpold and similar names. Among the most frequent topographical terms is **holm**, and in Slovene dialects generally as *hom, hum, kum*—a solitary hill or mountain; in mountain names translated as Chulm, Kulm, Helm, as well as Kahlenberg. The common **kuk**, actually *kolk* (hip), in Slovene terminology means a peak standing at the end of a mountain chain; in German variations it is found as Guk, Gugu, Kuku (derived from the Slovene locative *na kuku*—on the Kuk).

In the name Grossglockner 3798m, formerly Kleckner, the Slovene **klek** is reflected; i.e., a mountain visible from a distance, a peak with a peculiar form. On the Grossglockner stretches the glacier, Pasterze (Slov. *pastirica*— shepherdess).

A very common name in the Alps is **peč** (wall of rock, cliff or boulder), the other meaning of *peč* is oven, which is never used in this context, often incorrectly translated into German as *Ofen* (oven), and into Italian as *forno* (oven). This name is also used unchanged, and is found in forms like Pötsch, Pötschach (from the Slovene locative pl.) *v pečeh* (in the cliffs), Pötschenwald (outside of Salzburg) and Pötschen (above Hallstätter lake).

The Slovene term **golica** stands for a dome-shaped grassy mountain and is expressed in such mountain names as Golling, Hoch Gall, Hoher Göll, Hochgolling, Gol Sp., Golz Alpe, Golitsch Sp., Golzhöhe, and so on.

The horseshoe-shaped end of a valley, wedged into walls of rock, is in Slovene **krnica** and is found in the names Karnitzen, Garnitzen, Garnitz. And **sleme** (ridge, the ridge of a hill) in the names Zlem and Zlaim.

We find the frequent word **dol** (hollow, small valley) in the names Tull, Tul, Duller, Dolling. There is also **mel** (slope of rubble, rock-debris), pl. *meli*, and *melci* dim. in names as Melzen, Melach, Melitz Sp., Melitzbach, Melschütz Bach, Mulitz Bach, Preiml, Möll River (Mela).

The equivalents to the word **klanec** (ascent or descent on a road) are Glanz, Glanitzen, etc. Similarly for the word, **strmec** (precipice, waterfall) we find under the Dreiherrnspitze and also under Grossvenediger, Stürmitzer Alm, Stermetz.

In several mountain names appears **tesen** (the narrow part of a valley):

Dössener Tal, Dössener See, Dössener Winkel, Dössener Scharte, Dössener Törl, Dössener Sp. 2897m, Desenköpfl. And also **deber** (gorge, trench with steep sloping sides dug out by water): Daber Tal, Daber Alm, Daber Sp. Motschendaber, etc. The related feminine form **debernica** appears as Dabernitz Kees, Dabernitz Höhe, and Dabereck, as well as Dober, Doiber, Daba, Tober, Tobring, Tüffer.

The forms of mountain peaks often resemble the shape of a chair, in Slovene **stol**, in the diminutive *stolec* or *stolc*. These appear in such names as Stolzkogel, Stotz Kogel, Stolzalpe. Those names derived from **lonca** (summit): Lonca Höhe, Lanzwiesen, Lanzen, Lanzenboden. And derived from **sedlo** (a pass), in the diminutive *sedelce,* are: Zeduz, Zedöling, Zedelach, Zdelacher Alm, Hochsedl, Karsedl. The word **guge** (a horizontal fold on a mountain) is characteristic in the name Huggach K. 2340m, from the Slovene locative, *na gugah* pl. (on the...).

A hot spring, Slovene *toplica,* usually in the plural, **toplice,** occurs in the names: Toplitz, Tauplitz, Töplitz, Dobel, *topla* (the warm f.). A forceful spring is called **kropa,** from which comes the name, Kaprun. A standing, or dammed-up water is called *kal;* an example is found in the name Kals (Kalsertal, at the foot of Grossglockner).

These expressions and terms concern real, original designations of mountain formations and natural phenomena of which we could list many more.

The strikingly accurate descriptions of mountain forms and natural manifestations—through the Slovene idiom—in the Alpine region that have never been affected by the 6th century South Slavic settlement wave, unequivocally show that the original inhabitants were of Slovene (Venetic) ancestry. These indigenous people have preserved on their Alpine homesteads since prehistoric times a culture based on animal husbandry. It should be noted that the place-names on the plains outside the eastern Alps are also of West Slavic origin. This is one more example which strongly negates the assumed move of the South Slavs into the Alps.

Sometimes the names in the Alps somewhat correspond with those in the Balkans. However, if the South Slavs came from the forests and swamps beyond the Carpathian Mountains, they were unfamiliar with mountain life. That is why they did not settle in the Balkan highlands and did not leave their names there. Those names most likely come from the older inhabitants of the Balkans, the Illyrians, indicating that the Illyrians were Slavs and that there could have been migratory streams from the Balkans into the Alps and possibly farther into central Europe in prehistoric times. This was assumed by historians and archaeologists until a few years ago.

The language of the ancient Illyrians could thus be connected with Slovene. At the same time, this would indicate a relatively close relationship of the Slovene

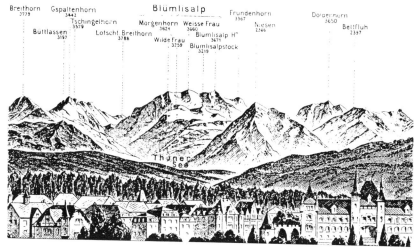

Breithorn 2779 Gspaltenhorn 3442 Blümlisalp Frundenhorn 3367 Doldenhorn 3650
Buttlassen 3197 Tschingelhorn 3579 Morgenhorn 3624 Weisse Frau 3660 Niesen 2366 Bettfluh 2397
Lotschf Breithorn 3788 Wilde Frau 3259 Blümlisalp H° 3671 Blümlisalpstock 3219

The city of Bern; above it, the Blümlisalp with its winding ridge (see footnote 54).

(Venetic) and Illyrian languages to the Indo-European. Linguists and archaeologists have observed that the people of the eastern Alps developed, in spite of Illyrian influences, a strong national characteristic in their material culture and language.

Also bearing witness to this are the names Winidi, Veneti, Windische, Wends, which source-materials use to designate only the Slovenes and Slavic people north of the Alps and never the Illyrians or the South Slavs.

The Venetic or Wendian name has also been kept by **Grossvenediger,** 3674m, the largest if not the highest mountain in the Hohen Tauern in the eastern Alps. In this region there are almost fifty mountain peaks over 3000m high, with numerous glaciers—a veritable kingdom of high mountains. One finds in German literature often incorrect and even comical explanations about the name Grossvenediger; e.g, that from its peak one can see Venice, which is rather unlikely, considering the distance. However, the researchers acknowledge that the mountain has been so named because it is the highest in the Venetic or Wendian, i.e., Slovene territory.[24]

During the pre-war years, the well-known Slovene mountain climber, J. Mlakar, relates the following in a description of his Grossvenediger climb: "The Venediger inherited its name from Slovene predecessors, the Wends or Veneti,

---

[24] V. Volk, *Grossvenediger,* in *Planinski vestnik,* Ljubljana 1959/7, p. 305.

21

who lived at its base."[25] Already towards the end of the 17th century, J. Resch mentions that the mountains to the north of Lienz had been named "**montes Veneti**" after the Slavs living there.[26] This was also the opinion of L. Steinberger before World War Two.[27] Testifying to these inhabitants in the surrounding area of the Grossvenediger are numerous Slovene (not Illyrian) names, such as Bobojach (*povoje* or *povodnje*—flood plain), Prägraten (*pregrade*—boundaries); Isel, locally Islitz (*izlivnica*—the one that pours, runs); Welitz (*belec*—white head); Stermetzkopf (*strmec*—cliff top, precipice); Zapotnitzenbach (*sopotnica*—noisy stream full of waterfalls). At one time, the ancient path led near the Sonnblick from the southern to the northern side of the Hohen Tauern, over the **Windische Scharte** 2727m, now renamed great Zirknitzscharte. There is a second Windische Scharte 2306m in the Niederen Tauern, east of Windsfeld.

The ancient Venetic (Slovene) names appear very frequently in the region that at one time belonged to Carantania. However, we can still attribute those to the alleged South Slavic settlers who were supposed to have founded Carantania, although this does not explain names outside this region.

In any case, these names reach north of the Hohen Tauern, westward through Tyrol and into eastern Switzerland. They are also found in Bavaria and in Swabia. In no way can these be connected to the alleged South Slavic migration model.

North of the Hohen Tauern range, running parallel to its summit, is the wide valley of the Salzach (a derivation from *Zalica,* the diminutive of *Zala* which is a known Slovene river and stream name*).* From the southern side, the Mühlbach flows into the Salzach Valley. Above its slopes stands the Planitzer Berg 2562m. In Slovene language, the term *plan* dim. *planica,* pl. *planice,* means a grassy slope without trees. That is why the mountain peak above it is called Planitzer Berg (mountain). Near Zell am See there opens a wide crevice into the Saalach— *Zala* Valley. Near Salzburg lies the Gugen Valley (*guge*—horizontal fold). South of the city rises the Hohe Göll 2522m (*gol*—barren, i.e., barren mountain); below it there is Golling (*golnik*—barren treeless place). In the Hochkönig Range we find the Lam Kogel 2831m; *lom* refers to a high ledge, a step on a slope, and the peak above it carries this name. Near Hallein lies Götschen 930m (*kočna* from *kotčina*—end of the valley, i.e., the mountain above it). The list goes on.

In the province of Salzburg, as well as in Bavaria and Swabia, there are many compound place-names with Zell-. These names could derive either from the "*cella*" of the monasteries in the Middle Ages, or from the Slovene term, *sela* pl.,

[25] J. Mlakar, *Izbrani planinki spisi I/* Selected Alpinistic Papers, (Grossvenediger), Ljubljana 1938, p. 200 op. cit., V. Volk, ibid., p. 304.

[26] V. Volk, op. cit., p. 308.

[27] Cf. footnote num. 18.

for a settlement, hamlet, its locative pl. *iz sel*—out of the hamlet. The original meaning is similar in both cases.

There are also many compound place-names with Reut- which can be derived from both the German *Gereut* (to make arable) as well as from the Slovene *rut* or *rovt* from *ruvati* (to pull out roots); hence, in both cases, a woodland cleared for cultivation.

The Venetic or Slovene root is recognizable in place-names as Göggingen (*guge*—horizontal fold on a mountain) near Augsburg, or the name Ravensburg (*raven*—flat, level). The same is true for the compound place-names with Strass-(*straža*—guard, watch); for example Strassburg on Rhein. We should also not overlook the neighbouring town, Wendenheim.

Pointing to Slovene or Venetic origin are place-names with the ending -**ach.** These can be derived both from the German *Ache* (stream), as well as from the ending -ah for the Slovene locative pl., *v Selah, v Rovtah,* etc. The same is seen in the case of place-names with the ending -**au**, in Slovene -ava, as in *Donava* (Danube), *daljava* (distance, remoteness), *tokava* (stream bed), *nižava* (lowland, plain) among others. In German word formation the ending -au is otherwise not used. It is explained in the official nomenclature as a derivative from the *Aue*, which is seldom the case. Also the ending -**ing** in place-names (Straubing, Platting, Assling) corresponds to the Slovene -*nik* (m.), -*nica* (f.). All the above-mentioned endings still have their meaning in Slovene word-formation; in German on the other hand, they are already obsolete. Due to ideological pressures German grammarians usually place these endings together with Latin and Celtic examples.

The fact that the already mentioned place-names can be traced in their meaning to Slovene (Wendian) archetypes proves that at one time the Wends must have lived in Bavaria and Swabia, for both regions constituted the Roman province of **Vindelicia.** More about this later.

Furthermore, the Slovene origin of the ending -**itz,** in Slov. -*ica* (f.) or -*ice* (pl.) cannot be denied. The place-names with this ending appear most frequently in the region that reaches from lower Bavaria northward to Franconia, into the area of the Pegnitz and Regnitz Rivers. East of Bayreuth is the city of **Windisch Eschenbach.** The region with these place-names stretches farther to Thüringen, Saxony, into Lusatia and over Brandenburg toward Pomerania and Mecklenburg. Their density, in any case, shows that the Venetic people survived in this area for a relatively long time. This is also expressed in the German word, **Wenden,** for the Lusatian Slavs.

Some place-names in this area are Ölsnitz (Olšnica), Chemnitz, (Kamnica) near Leipzig (Lipsko), Imnitz, Reudnitz, Connewitz. South of Berlin are also Teuplitz, Wellmitz, Tschernitz, Beelitz. In Mecklenburg, Strelitz and **Wendisch**

Baggendorf, and on the island of Rügen (Rujana), Sasnitz. To the east on the Baltic coast there are Stepenitz, Dölitz, Sageritz, Bublitz, as well as Stargard and Belgard. This territory lies east of Oder and Neisse and is today Polish.

The Name Veneti is Our Guide

Along with those names already mentioned, there also appear numerous Wendian and Wend- compounded place and province names such as **Wedel** and **Wentorf** near Hamburg; **Wendisch Evern** near Lüneburg; **Wenden** near Siegen, east of Cologne; **Winden**, east of Koblenz; **Wendelsheime**, southwest of Mainz; **Winden**, northwest of Karlsruhe; **Wendlingen** and **Winnenden**, near Stuttgart; **Winden**, northeast of Freiburg i. Br.; **Winden**, near Ansbach; **Bad Windsheim**, west of Fürth; **Wendelstein**, near Nürnberg; **Windsbach**, southwest of Nürnberg; **Windischletten**, near Bamberg; **Windischbergerdorf**, near Cham, east of Regensburg.

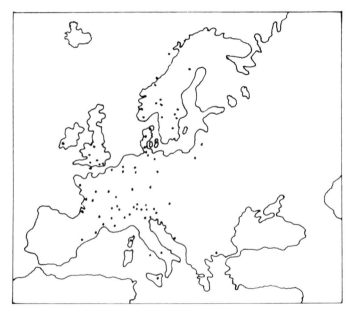

The names of Veneti in Europe. Their distribution coincides with the settlement of the Veneti after the 12th century B.C.

Wendian, Venetic place-names often encompass whole regions, as for example the **Wendland** on the Elbe River east of Lüneburg; **Wedemark**, i.e., **Wendenmark** near Hannover; **Wendeburg** and the area surrounding Braunschweig; **Windeck**, i.e., **Windeneck**, east of Bonn; and **Windorf** (Windischdorf) on the Danube, northwest of Passau. There is even a mountain, the well known **Wendelstein** 1838m, south of Rosenheim.

Outside of central Europe the Wendian/Venetic names are much more scattered, though not rare. A place called **Wenduine** lies on the coast of Belgium. There is also **Weddel** and similar places in Friesland in the Netherlands and near Allenstein in East Prussia is **Wenedien**; even in Lithuania and Latvia there is a **Venta** River. At the top of Jutland is **Vendsyssel**; in Sweden **Vanern-See**; in Norway **Vindsvik**, south of Bergen. Also the name of the Scandinavian nationals, the **Vandals,** who could only be Germanized Wends, i.e., Veneti, must be included. The historical source-material mentions in the 10th century the Wendian trade city **Vineta** at the mouth of the Oder River. Its exact location has until now not been determined. Farther south we are reminded of the Wends at the eastern foothills of the Alps by the Roman encampment **Vindobona**, the present-day Vienna.

In Brittany, the former Armorica, Veneti lived separate from their Celtic neighbours during the conquest of Gaul by the Romans. Off the coast of Brittany is the island Belle Ille, which is called **Vindilis** in historical documents. The neighbouring province of **Vendée** carries its name after the Wends to this day. Even in Britain we can find Venetic names, such as **Ventnor** on the Isle of Wight or **Windsor** near London; also the historical land of **Venedotia** (Celtic Gwineth, Gwined), today Gdwynedd as well as Gwent, on the northern and southern coasts of Wales, where ore and coal deposits are found. This coincides with the mining skills of ancient Veneti.

At the southernmost location we find **Venetico** in Sicily, near Milazzo, where significant finds of the Urnfield era have been discovered.

The Central Alps

Names such as "Jamtal, Jamspitze 3175m, Jamjoch, Jamtalhütte" are important witnesses testifying that at one time the Slovenes and their influence reached as far as the Dreiländerspitze 3212m between Switzerland, Austria, and Italy. (R. Badjura)[28]

In the area of central Europe, the Venetic (Slovene) place-names have been most densely preserved in the Alps. Numerous names in the areas, which are today Germanized or Italianized, testify that in the past the people in the Alps spoke a language that was identical with or closely related to present-day Slovene. From a certain standpoint this is admitted by the official historiography, geography and toponymy as well, but only for the eastern Alps, presumably in order to conform with the limitations imposed by the imagined 6th century settlement of Slavs from the Balkans.

However, the territory with Venetic (Slovene) names continues far to the west, over the entire Tyrol and eastern Switzerland. This means that it covers areas never reached by the presumed settlement.

Who were the people who left us all these Slovene names in the central Alps, and when?

The official historians offer no answer. Worse, they systematically ignore the obvious facts in order to bypass the contradictions created by their settlement theory, including the idea that it extended only as far as Hohen Tauern. Clearly, as long as they use such disorderly methods, there can be no true answers.

The high density of Slovene names in the central Alps could have originated only from an older Slavic settlement.

The acknowledgment of these names is the key that will allow a view above and beyond the ideological models of official historiography and linguistics. It will bring us to the very roots of the Slovene people, to the times of ancient Veneti or Wends, who were their distant forebears.

L. Purtscheller, a mountain-climber and researcher around the turn of the

---

[28] R. Badjura, op. cit., p. 192.

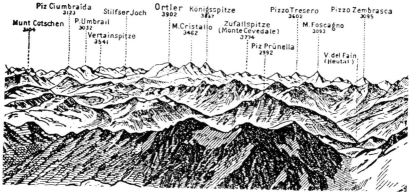

*A view of Ortler 3902m, which has a form of an **rt**—a projection—as seen from the summit of Piz Languard above Engadine.*

century, a famous name in classical Alpine climbing, has demonstrated in his research into the origin of Alpine mountain names that at one time the Slavs not only lived in the Puster Valley (as far as the source of Drava River), but also in the Inn, Ziller, and Wipp Valleys in Tyrol. Numerous names of places, mountains, Alpine meadows and streams, as well as house names and family names remind us of this today.[29]

Thus, at the entrance to the Ziller Valley we come across the village Strass (*straža*—guard, watch); farther along the valley also Zell am Ziller (*sela*—hamlet or settlement). At the end of the valley are characteristic names: Kainzen Kees or Kainzenhütten 1564m (*konec*—end, the end of a valley). The road above Innsbruck leads over the Scharnitz Pass (*čarnica*—border post) towards Bavaria. In west Tyrol on the Lech River is the city Reutte (*rovte*—clearing). In neighbouring Bavaria there is near Garmisch-Partenkirchen again a village called Kainzenbad (*konec*—end) and south of Munich, Bad Tölz (*dolec, dol'c*, dim. of *dol*—small valley). Such similarities with Slovene terms also appear in other parts of Bavaria.

There are several place-names of Slovene origin also around Munich—Pullach, Pullenhoffen, Pulling, and so forth—which are derived from *polje* (field). Also representative are Jedenhoffen, Jetzendorf, Etzenhausen, Jedelstetten, from

---

[29] L. Purtscheller, *Zur Nomenklatur der Venediger-Gruppe/* Concerning the Toponymy of the Venediger Mountain Chain, in the Zeitschrift des DÖAV, 1883, pp. 511–522, op. cit., V. Volk, op. cit., p. 309.

jedlov'ca abbr. (spruce forest); also Jesenwang, Jasberg, from *jasa* (clearing in the forest); Lüss, from *luže* pl. (ponds); Dolling, from *dolina* (valley) and so on.

North of the Hohen Tauern in the Salzburg part of Pinzgau, we find numerous Slovene names. At times we also find seemingly German names which are really nothing more than poor transliterations of the original Slovene. Let us look at the Katzenkogel 2533m, above the small Winkel Valley, *Winkel* (angle, corner), in Slov. *kot* and dim. *kot'c* (end of a small valley); this becomes after common vowel change, *kat'c, Katz* in German, which is unrelated to cats, as the German form would indicate. Kogel derives from Slov. *kog* or *kopa* (rick)—in other words, the rick-shaped peak above the end of the valley. The same is true of the Hundskogel 2402m, wrongly translated from Slov. Podsinji, *pod* (under, below); *sinji* (blue), a mountain with a blue background, sky or forest. In dialect this is "Psinji", same as the adj. of *pes* (dog), which translates into German as Hunds—dog's. The Slovene village Podsinja ves in Carinthia, Austria, in this way became Hundsdorf. Needless to say, the original Slovene name is not related to Hund or dog.

In Tyrol

Above the wide Inn Valley there rises near the city of Imst the Tschirgant 2372m, i.e., *čer* (cliff) above the *konta* (rocky hollow, chasm).[30] Farther in the direction of Landeck stands the **Venetberg,** 2513m over the Inn Valley; on its slopes are two pasture areas called **Venet Almen.** In the neighbouring Pitz Valley is a small market town **Venns**, and also a place called Jerzens (*jezerca*—pools or ponds), dim. of *jezero* (lake). The nearby Ötz Valley ends in several side valleys, among them also the **Ventertal** with the small town of **Vent**[31] and above this area towers the Ramolkogel 3549m (*kramol*—rocky overhang). Under Landeck, on the west side of the Inn Valley rises the Gatsch Kogel 2947m (*gače*—prominent formation lower than the main peak).

---

[30] The German spelling of Tschir indicates the Slovene term *čer*—cliff, Gand, *konta*—a rocky hollow, chasm. Cf. H. Tuma, *Slovenska imena v ladinskem in bavarskem narečju/ The Slovene Place Names in the Ladin and Bavarian Dialects, Planinski vestnik,* Ljubljana 1926, pp. 159, 161.

[31] The names with the root Venet- found in Tyrol do not belong to German toponymy; the latter came into the Alps at a much later period, cf. K. Finsterwalder: Die Namen Venetberg, Venediger, Vent, Venns, Vorrömische und Deutsche Wortbildung in "Venetername." In Natalicium Carolo Jax septuagenario...oblatum, Innsbrucker Beitr. zur Kulturwiss. III, Innsbruck 1955, pp. 254–60, op. cit., in G.B. Pellegrini and A.L. Prosdocimi, *La lingua venetica II*, Padova 1967, p. 329.

In South Tyrol the Venetic names become more concentrated, especially in the upper Etsch Valley; i.e., in Vintschgau above Meran.[32] This entire area has the Slovene name (Windischgau) to this day.

Near the city of Meran, before the entrance to the Vintschgau, there are names telling us of the former inhabitants, the Veneti: Perval, Perfl, Pirbl (*preval*— pass); Kanzen, Kanz, Konz, Kunz (*konec* or *kon'c*—end of the valley); Troier (Ladin *troi,* from Slovene *utro*— commons or ground well beaten down by cattle); Tel, Toll (*dol*—small, narrow valley); Loch (*log*—wet meadow, or alluvial ground); Kuchalberg (*kukla* or *čukla*—large, solitary rock); Lazins (*lazne, laze* pl.—field on steep slope that is worked with a hoe); Laner (*lanež*—snow-covered shady mountain slope); Gande (*konta*—rocky hollow, chasm); Gatsche (*gače*—prominent formation below the main peak); Taber (*tabor*—camp, fortress or *deber*—ravine); Pöntsch (*peč*—rock wall); Marling, until 1290 Mernig (*mernik*—bushel); Ursinig, until 1380 Virsinic (*vr.šič*—high point or peak); Tisens, until 1259 Tisana (*tesna*—narrow pass); Laas (*laz, laze*—field on a steep slope); Zocha, until 1580 Zouch (*suha*—dried-out bed of a mountain torrent); Tamasseg, until 1560 Tamerseg (*tamarček,* dim. of *tamar*—shelter, corral); Brizsche since 1311 (*brišče,* abbr. for *brdišče*—knolls, hillocks).

In Vintschgau above Meran we also come across the following names: Laatsch (*loče, loke*—valley meadows); Plaus (*plave*—waterway used for running logs or a valley where logs are transported in this way); Voran (*vereje,* abbr. for *medvereje*—fold, corral);[33] Tartsch (*tamarč,* dim. of *tamar*);[34] Tschars (*čeri*— cliffs); Volan Ital. Foiana (*poljana*—level field); Vlatschberg 3257m (*vlačiti*—to drag, to skid, *vlače, vlake*—hay sleigh or stone-boat, area used for dragging or skidding); Kortsch (*koritca* pl.—basins or pools in a small river); Lana (*plana*— grassy slope without trees); from this, *planina* Alpine meadow); Matsch (*močila* pl.—swampy meadow); Mals (*meli* pl.—rubble slope).

On the south side of the valley rises the Ortler 3899m (*rt, ort*—formation extending out from the main body). In the upper Etsch, opening toward the west

---

[32] H. Tuma, *Slovenska imena/* Slovene names, op. cit., pp. 160-161, Hof und Burgnamen in Meran, by Tarneller.

[33] H. Tuma, *Imenoslovje Julijskih Alp/* Toponymy of the Julian Alps, Ljubljana 1929, p. 23.

[34] R. Badjura, op. cit. p. 275–East of Ortles is found also Cima Sternai, in Ger. Hintere Eggenspitze 3443m (from the Slovene dial. *sterm*—steep) and the Passo di Soi, in Ger. Soy Scharte 2888m, i.e., sunny, exposed to the sun (Slovene *soj*—shiny or light); and there is also the summit of Hasenöhrl, in Ital. Oreschia di Lepre 3257m, another case of wrong translation, in this instance from the abbreviated Slovene word *p'zeči, polzeči*— slippery, to *zejčji*—hare's.

is the rift valley called Rojen (*roje*—small stream), Carinthian Slovene *roja* (storm, or spring run-off). The crossing into the Inn Valley has the name Reschen Pass 1504m, Ital. Resia (*reža*—crevice, fissure).

East of Reschen Lake rises the Rabenkogel 3391m, which derives its name from *rob, rab* with a common vowel change from o to a (edge, precipice or brink) or *robje* pl. (indented cliffs or rocks) and is not related to crows, (Germ. *Raben* pl.). There is also a Rabenstein 1419m at the end of the Passeier Valley.

In the Dolomites

Going from Bolzano in northeasterly direction we arrive in the Eisack Valley, Ital. Isarco (*izaro, jezernica*—stream with pools). On the eastern side rises the large rocky mass of the Schlern (Sciliar in Italian), with the peak Petz (*peč*—rock wall). Upward along this valley on the same side appears the Grödner Valley. At its entrance lies the town Laien, until 1914 Loien (*loje, poloje* pl.—gentle slope). At the end of the Grödner Valley we find a town called Plan and above it the peaks: Tschierspitzen 2592 (*čeri* pl.—sharp-edged cliffs), Puez 2673m (*peč*—rock-wall) and Sellajoch 2218m (*sedlo*—pass). On the north side of the Grödner Valley rises Raschötzer Alp (Rascieza in Italian) up to a height of 2308m (*rasica*—flat area). The next side valley is called Villnos (Funes in Italian), where we find such names as Crnidoi (*čarni dol*—defendable narrow valley); Got (*kot*—corner or end of a valley); Gost (*gozd*—forest); Praprot (*praprot*—fern); Trebe (*trebež*—newly cleared land).[35] Also, just above Brixen (*brišče*—knolls) stands the mountain Plose 2514m (*polože* pl.—gentle slope) as well as *plaze* pl. (avalanche of rock debris).

In the neighbouring Puster Valley lies the town of **Vintl;** its name reminds us of the former presence of the Wends. Above it rises the Stollberg 1835m (*stol*—chair), a common Slovene mountain name. The same is also true for the Obersteiner Holm 2452m (*holm*—dome-shaped hill or mountain) north of Bruneck, which was not even transcribed into the German *Kulm.*

An oddity in this area are the mountain names Knapphenne 2456m, and Henne 2480m. These are not related to what the German names indicate, i.e., *Henne* (chicken). They originate in the Slovene name *Golina,* in dialect *Galina* (a barren, treeless mountain or tract of land). Under the Romans it was transcribed as *Gallina* (chicken), which became the German *Henne.* Such and similar wrong transcriptions are common. Numerous Slovene names are also found in the Do-

---

[35] H. Tuma, *Slovenska imena/*The Slovene Names, op. cit., p. 160. Do not confuse *čarni*—rocky, abrev. *črni*, with *črn*—black. Au.

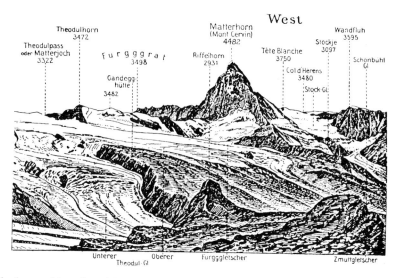

The famous Matterhorn/Mont Cervin 4482m. From the top of Gornergrat, it looks like a giant čer—cliff.

lomites and in the Venetian Alps, handed down in Ladin and Veneto-Italian dialects.[36]

Above Vicenza extends the highland of **Assiago** (Sette Comuni). Here we encounter towns Rotzo (*roče* pl.—small mountain ledges); Roano (*ravne*— relatively flat mountain terrace); Ronco (*ronek*—base, or foot of a mountain); Baita (*bajta*—hut); the Alp Fratta (*frata, fratje*—clear-cut area); Mt. Nos 1630m (*nos*— nose); Val di Miele (*meli* pl.—slopes of rock debris); Porta Leposse (*lopoč*— pool); Col Schiavo 1243m, (Slavic summit); also appearing often is Cocco (*kolk, kuk*—peak at the end of a mountain-chain).[37] Eastward from the Assiago highland rises Mt. Grappa 1779m (*grapa*—rift valley); i.e., the mountain above the

---

[36] H. Tuma, Krajevno imenoslovje/ Regional Toponymy, op. cit.

[37] The word *frata* means the vegetation growing in a deforested area (the same word is sometimes used to describe a hillside which has in the course of years become free of any growth other than grass). The young branches are harvested and dried (called frodel in Slovene), and used as forage for sheep and goats; this practice dates back to very remote times. The meaning of the word frata is the same in Friulian, found in the dictionary Il nuovo Pirona (Udine 1967): "localita disboscata di recente"—a recently deforested area. The Slovene word *bajta* is an ancient term spread also in the southern part of the Alps as far as Piedmont. The word *lopoč* means a watering hole on an Alpine meadow.

grapa. The word *grapa* also means an ugly, non-descript narrow valley.

A peculiar mountain group is made up of mountains with the name **Pale,** *polica* (terrace-shaped grassy areas). The highest peak among them is called Pala di S. Martino 2996m; indicative of the ancient presence of Veneti is also Pizzo Miel 2774m, *mel* (slope of rock rubble). Northwards from this group rises the lofty Cimone Pala 3168m. In the Marmolada mountain group are Pala Verde and even Pala Rabiosa, probably the translation of the Slovene *Zelene police* (green terraces); i.e., grassy terraces, and *Hude police* (difficult-to-climb terraces).[38] Numerous names with Pala are to be found in the vicinity of Cortina d'Ampezzo, in the Cardini mountain group. The name Cortina itself seemingly derives from *korito* (trough-like deep valley). Not far from here, south of Cernera 2657m (*čer*— cliff) and west of Andrazzo, we again meet Cernadoi (*čarni dol*—defendable narrow valley). Above the Livinallongo Valley towers the Col di Lana 2426m (*lanež*—shaded snow-covered mountain slope).

Among the most frequent mountain names in this region is **Lasta** (*lašta*— rock ledge). There is a Cima di Lasta 2573m in the Marmolada mountain group, in the Lagorai group Laste (pl.) delle Sute 2615m; east of Pieve di Cadore again the Cima Laste 2555m, as well as in the diminutive *laštica,* Lastizza 2071m. [39]

Through Veneto, Trentino, and Lombardy

In many areas due to the relatively long existence of the ancient Venetic people, the Venetic field-names become noticeably more frequent. Thus we encounter for example around Agordo names like Mt. Tamar 2564m (*tamar*—corral, fold);[40] Mt. Celo 2083m (*čelo*—forehead, gable); Col Bel 1936m (*bel*—white,

---

[38] In Friulian, the word *pala* means a sloped surface in the high mountains which is suitable for mowing and not for pasture. Cf. Il nuovo Pirona, cit.—In the Ladin language this word also means a sloped mountain meadow. Cf. A. Walde, J.B. Hofmann: *Lateinisches etymologisches Wörterbuch*/ Latin Etymological Dictionary, Heidelberg 1938.

[39] The word *lasta,* which has its correlative in the Latin *plastrum*, is an Indo-European term existing also in the Russian and means a flat surface. Cf. H. Tuma, *Krajevno imenoslovje*, cit. p. 46. This word is quoted by C. Battisti as being used in the province of Trentino, plural form "laste"—piani leggermente inclinati di roccie nude—a gentle slope of flat rocks. The word has the same meaning in Slovene. It is often translated incorrectly, as for instance the Slovene name in plural Lastavice 1908m found in the mountain group of Višarje (Lussari), which is translated in German as Schwalbenspitzen and in Italian as Cime delle Rondini. Interestingly, the word *lastavica* (singular) in Slovene language indicates both a swallow and a rock slab.

[40] The word *tamar* stands for a hut of simple construction, with a fenced area used by

white summit); Mt. Pala 1505m (*polica*—ledge); in the vicinity of Belluno, Mt. Piz 1609 (*špik*—peak). Above Longarone also Mt. Certen 1882m (*črten*—cleared land), and even Cima dei Preti 2703m, incorrect translation of *frata* pl. *frate* (clear-cut areas) as Priest—Ital. *frate, prete,* pl. *prerti.* On the Piave there is the village Mel (*mel*—slope of rock rubble). Near Forni di Sotto also Pic Mea 2207m (*meja*—border, boundary or edge of a forest).

In the mountains west of Triento there are numerous Venetic (Slovene) names, as in the **Adamello** mountain group: Mt. Cercen 3283m (*črče*—deforested area, clearing);[41] Lobbia Alta 3159m and Lobbia Bassa 2958m (*lob, lobanja*—skull, head); again Mt. Frati 3283m. In Val Ledro there are places such as Molina (*melina*—stream carrying rock debris) and Locca (*loka*—valley-meadow). In Val Giudiccari Breguzzo (*bregec* dim. of *breg*—slope, bank); Roncone (*ronek*—base or foot of a mountain), and Mt. Melino 1433m (*meli*—slope of rock rubble).

Field-names like **Tamar**, **Črče**, and also **Laze** tell us of the farmer's and herdsman's culture handed down from antiquity, and at the same time define the origin of the people to whom this culture belonged. The preservation of the Slovene meaning of these names through millennia is a strong indication that the bearers of this prehistoric culture were the Veneti, the predecessors of the Slovenes.

It may seem surprising that the traces of this ancient culture, revealed through place-names, are to be found not only in the Alps but also in the whole of the Apennines, even as far as Sicily. The name **Frata**, as a clear-cut area with young brushwood used for small livestock, is found in the southern Italian provinces of Rome, Potenza, and Messina. The name, **Medrje**, abbr. for Medvereje, the enclosure where livestock are kept overnight, is seen in names like Mandria, Mandra, Mandriola, and so forth; it appears in the provinces of Ravenna, Bologna, Naples and Palermo. Frequently one finds the name **Polje** (*polje*—field) or **Poljana** (*poljana*—flat field) in forms such as Poiana, Pogliana, Poiano, Poia, Foiana;[42] among them also the name of the territory, Apulia, Ital. Puglia, le Puglie.

---

herdsmen. This type of structure was used from prehistoric time and was moved from pasture to pasture together with the herd. The Slovene verb *tamariti* describes the moving of a *tamar*. The term is mentioned as a place name by Pliny and also by Strabo, Tomarus in Epirus. In southern Italy we find a Tammaro, Foggia, and in the Basilicata a Timmari, in the vicinity of the prehistoric site of an urn-burial field. Cf. G. Sergi, *Italia—le origini*; Turin 1919, p. 383. The word is of pre-Indo-European origin, a relic of the ancient Afro-European pastoral culture.

[41] The Slovene word *črče* or *krče*, a deforested area, a clearing, from *krčiti*—reducing in size; reducing the size of brush-land or forest.

[42] H. Tuma, *Krajevno imenoslovje*, op. cit., pp. 137, 140, 148.

Besides the names that indicate earlier forms of agriculture and pastoral life, there are in the Apennines also numerous area names whose basic meaning is still understood among modern Slovenes. The most frequent among them is **Kuk,** *kolk* (a peak at the end of a mountain chain). In upper Friulian Carnia there are eighteen mountain names derived from *kolk*; in the province of Ravenna there are five. There are name variations such as Cuccu, Cucco, Cuccuzzo, Cuccolo and Cuccara in the western Italian provinces of Genoa, Parma, and Cuneo; also in central Italy in the provinces of Bologna, Arezzo, Pisa, and Perugia, then in the southern provinces of Bari and Catanzaro, as well as in Sicily and Sardinia. Often appearing is the name, **Ronek,** (the base or the foot of a mountain, where the slope turns into a plain) and the name **Roce**, abbr. of Roncine, same as ronkine (mountain ledges); there are also name variations as Ronco, Rozzo, Ronzino, in the southern provinces of Catanzaro and Palermo. Also characteristic is the nationality name, i.e., **Schiavi** (the Slavs). In the Marmolada mountain group we find the Cima Schiavoni 2570m, and near Lorenzago above the Piave, Mt. Schiavoni 2317m. The name variations, Schiavoni, Schiavi, or Schavo appear also in the southern provinces: Rieti, Naples (three times), Benevento, Foggia, Potenza, Lecce, Catanzaro, Messina, and Palermo.[43]

The usual explanation for this is that the names originate from Slavic refugees, who came from the Balkans during the time of the Turkish wars and settled in the Apennines. But this is incorrect. Slavic refugees did found some villages in central Italy (Molise); however, they settled neither in the Alps nor in the whole of the Apennines from the plains of the Po to Sicily. The indigenous inhabitants named the regions after the Slavic Veneti, wherever Venetic linguistic enclaves within the non-Slavic provinces were able to survive for a long time. In all probability, the initial settlement wave of Veneti (as is conveyed by the field-names) had encompassed only certain tracts of land and formed enclaves. This would be especially true for the southern Apennines.

Into the Engadine

In comparison to the Apennines, the Alps represent a retreat area for Venetic culture. The Venetic (Slovene) place-names even today appear in high numbers in this region, and testify to the indigenous rural culture. They give the area through the entire Tyrol and eastern parts of Switzerland the characteristic sense of an ancient presence.

---

[43] H. Tuma, op. cit., pp. 441–442, 149, 150.

34

On the Austro-Swiss border we find the lofty mountain range of the **Silvretta,** where numerous peaks still carry old Slovene names.

On the Austrian side of this range, there is the high valley of Jamtal (*jama*—cave, mine, or depression surrounded by mountains), which leads to the Jamjoch, topped by the Jamspitze 3175m. In this mountain group there is also the Lobspitze 2890m (*lob*—skull), Bieler Hohe 2046m, the summit above the *Bela* (whitewater stream), Versail Sp. 2459m (*vršaj*—ground deposited with silt), Kops (*kopa*—dome-shaped mountain), Matschauner K. (*močivni vrh*—peak above a damp slope), Gontschetta Thälchen, Romance dim. of *konta,* (small hollow or chasm), Medje Thali (*med*—between, the between-valley), Piz Roz 3115m (*roč, roče*—small mountain ledge or ledges). On the southern side of this mountain group tower the Roggenhorn 2897m (*rog*—horn, a tautology) and the Piz Cotschen 3034m (*kočen, kočna*—end of a glacial valley), with the observation outpost Muot de Hom 2334m (*holm*—solitary dome-shaped hill or mountain). Below passes the Val Tasna (*tesen* or *tesnice* pl.—narrow part of a valley), at its end the Val Urschaj (*vršaj*—ground deposited with silt) and the Val Urezzas Joch 2815m (*vratca* dim. of *vrata*—door, passage) and Piz Champatsch 2925m (*kambač* from *kambast*—with rounded sides; *kamba* or *kvamba* is in Slovene the rounded, U-shaped part of an ox yoke which passes under and around the neck of the animal).[44]

South of Silvretta in the **Lower Engadine,** there is the wide valley of the Inn, in which small towns have the following names: Crusch (*kruše*—rock formation crumbling away), Scuol (*skol, skala*—cliff, rock), Susch (*suše*—dry place). Suggestive of the ancient Venetic presence are also the names of some side valleys: Val Zeznina, likely from *zareznina* (carved-out valley), Val Saglains (*zaglajen*—valley with noticeably even floor). South of Engadine tower the lofty peaks of Piz Pisoc 3147m (*pesek*—sand, sandy slopes or formations), Montpitschen 3162m

---

[44] A. Schorta and R. von Planta: *Rätisches Ortsnamenbuch, Bd. 2, Etymologien/* Directory of the Rhaetian Toponyms, vol. 2, Etymologies, Bern 1964. The authors of this work derive the name *Gams* or *Gems* from the German Gams—chamois. In reality this word originates in the Venetic/Slovene word *kamen*—stone, a stony or rocky formation. The common Slovene toponyms like Kamnik or Kamnica were in earlier times written in German as Gamming and Gams. The Slovene linguist F. Bezlaj *Etimološki slovar slovenkega jezika I/* Etymological Dictionary of the Slovene Language I, Ljubljana 1976, interprets the root "leb" as face, skull, head. Similar explanation is found in the Rätisches Ortsnamenbuch for "lobia" (Felskopf—a rock head, boulder-like formation). The following names have unconvincing explanations: Urezzas, from aura—breath; Cotschna, from *coccinus*—summit, peak; Roz is included in the group of names of unknown origin.

Labels on panorama:

Weisshorn 4512 · Barrhorn 3633 · Bruneggh? 3849 · Gr.Combin 4317 · Hot Belalp 2137 · M.Blanc 4810 · Aig Verte 4127 · Rothlaunhorn 3155 · Schilth? 3128 · Gisigh? 3182 · Sparrhorn 3026 · Belgrat · Nesthorn 3820 · Fusshorner 3106 - 3626 · Rothhorn 3701 · Sattelhorn 3746

Aletschhorn and its massive glacier, viewed from the summit of Eggishorn. It presents an image of a kleč—craggy reef-like formation.

(*špičen*—sharp or pointed) and Piz Lischanna 3105m (*lisa*—bald or bare area). Some of these designations may not be accurate any longer, since the weathering conditions could have changed the original appearance of these land forms.[45]

Crossing from Lower to Upper Engadine, we find a strategically important

---

[45] In the Rätisches Ortsnamenbuch, op. cit., only the toponym Plavna (open valley) is explained sensibly. Totally unacceptable are explanations of names (still understood in Slovene and clearly of Venetic origin) like Crusch from the Latin crux (cross) and Zeznina, from the Lombardic *zazza*—a tuft. F. Bezlaj refers to Indo-European *kreus* (to break, to carve) for the Slovene *krušiti*; the Old Slavic *lys* and the Slovene *lisa* (a clearing, a bare place) correspond to Lischanna. A. Walde, J.B. Hofmann, op. cit., in connection with the Latin *piscis,* the Indo-European *pitsya*—slippery, Slov. *spolzek*. W. Meyer-Lübke, *Romanisches etymologisches Wörterbuch/* Romance Etymological Dictionary, Heidelberg 1911, attributes to the Greek verb *encharassein*—make a cutting. The meaning of the name Zeznina may well originate in the Slovene *zareznina*—cut, jagged, notched; the name Saglains corresponds well with the Slovene word *zglajen* (smooth, even) a valley with a noticeably even floor, and Mt. Pitschen is like the Slovene *špičen*—pointed, sharp.

36

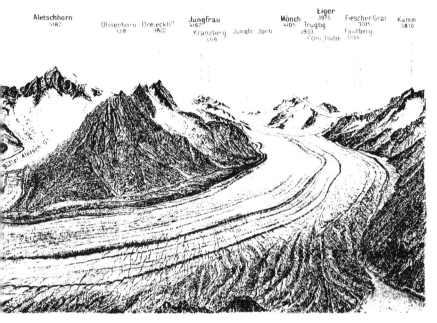

locality appropriately called Zernez (*čarnica*—guard-post). Here the road branches off from the main valley and continues eastward into the Vintschgau, over the Pass dal Fuorn 2149m, Oven-Pass, incorrect translation of *peč* (wall of rock). Above this pass rises the Piz Tschierv 2969m (*čeri*—cliffs). Just below the Pass dal Fuorn there is on this road the hill, Crastatscha, from *krasta* (scar, rough area), or *krastača* (toad).[46]

Southwest from Zernez runs the **Upper Engadine.** In the middle of this valley lies Zuoz (*zvoz* or *zvože*—place where things are taken to, farm products, firewood, etc.). Above St. Moritz rise the peaks, Piz dell 'Ova Cotschna 2710m (*kočna*—end of a glacial valley), Piz Rosatsch (*rosač*—cleft, fissure, mountain with these features), Piz Staz 2995m (*stol'c,* dim. of *stol*—chair). Near the ski region of Silvaplana, there are two hamlets with names Fratta (*frata*—clear-cut area) and Plaz (*plaz*—rock-debris avalanche). North of here towers the Piz Polaschin 3122m, and below is a small lake called Tscheppa 2624m (*čepa* or

---

[46] The name Zernez corresponds to the old Slovene or Venetic term *čarnica,* this could be also inferred from the position of the locality Scharnitz between Tyrol and Bavaria where since time immemorial a frontier post has been maintained. W. Meyer-Lübke, op. cit., derives the name Tschierv from the Latin *cervix* (nape), and F. Bezlaj thinks the meaning comes from *červen*—bright red; i.e., a red mountain at sunset.

Bernina—its skyline from the summit of Piz Languard is a chain of "knolls" or "hillocks", Slovene brda, brdnina.

kepa—rounded mountain). At the end of the Engadine is the Maloja-Pass 1815m (*mel*—steep slope of rubble), and nearby is the Alpine pasture with the name Aira della Palza (*polica*—shelf or terrace).[47]

On the south side of the Upper Engadine rises the high mountain-chain of the **Bernina** with the highest peak of the same name 4049m.

The name Bernina most likely originates in the word *brdnina*—knolls, hillocks. In spite of its great heights, the skyline of this mountain chain gives a knoll-like impression.

Also in this mountain group are several peaks with Slovene names: Piz Tschierva 3546m, Piz Palu 3912m, Piz Chaputschin 3391m, La Sella 3587m, Piz Cambrena 3604m, Piz Scerscen 3967m, Piz Led (*led*—ice), Crastaguzza 3872m (*krastovica*—scarred peak), Piz Corvatsch 3458m (crooked peak), Piz Roseg 3943m, Piz Morteratsch 3754m, etc.[48]

---

[47] Cf. the name Zuoz from the Slovene *zvoz* or *zvoze,* originating in the common verb *zvoziti*—to transport things together by means of wagon or sleigh; see R. Badjura, op. cit., pp. 271, 276. In the Rätisches Ortsnamenbuch we find the following explanation for the name Rosatsch: it comes from the pre-Roman root *rosa*—a glacier, torrent, land-slide; the name Polaschin on the other hand they derive from the Latin *polex*—thumb; it probably comes from Slovene *položen*—moderately sloped. This is a wrong interpretation in our opinion in regard to name Staz from *statio*, and of Palza from *pausa* (calm, pause) probably from Slovene *polica*—ledge, or terrace.

[48] The name Bernina seems to be an abbreviation of the Slovene term *berdnina* or *brdina*—a mountain with spurs. The word *brdo* could only be a correlative of the Latin *vertex* with similar meaning. In the Rätisches Ortsnamenbuch we also find: Caputschin, from *cappucia*—hood; Roseg, from *rosa*; Morteratsch, from *mortarium*—mortar. There is no explanation for the name Led from *led (*ice) in Slovene. The following derivations are also doubtful: Corvatsch, from *corvus*—crow; Scerscen, from *circinus* (circle), and

The Mountainous Graubünden

On the north side of the Upper Engadine lie the Rhaetian Alps, and beyond them stretches a mountain landscape which slopes down into the upper **Rhine Valley.** From Engadine into this area run high mountain passes, among which is the Julier/Guglia Pass 2288m, an important route since Roman times. This pass runs in the direction of Chur/Cuera, the capital of canton Graubünden. In this area we again find Slovene names: Crap la Pala 2152 (*pala*—mountain terrace), Piz Platta 3386m (*plata, plat*—level area, ledge), Fuorcla da Tschitta 2922m (*čita* or *kita*—plait or braid). Above the Albula Pass 2312m, towers the Piz Uertsch 3273m (*vršič*—top of a mountain). On the other side of this pass lies Latsch (*loče*—a valley-meadow), above it Cuolm da Latsch 2268m (*holm*—rounded hill or mountain). Not far from here is Crep della Rescha (*reža*—fissure or crevice). In the vicinity of Chur there is Tschiertschen (*črče*—clearing), the well-known health resort. Above the health resort Arosa, rises over a side valley the Tschuggen 2023m (*čukla, kukla*—large boulder). Over the Strela Pass 2353m (*strela*—a lightning bolt) we arrive at Davos. Northeast of Davos near Klosters, we find one more Cotschna 2267m (*kočna*—end of a glacial valley).[49] North of Strela Pass there is a summer cottage settlement named Strassberg (*straža*—guard, watch).

West of Chur, the Hinterrhein branches off from the Rhine Valley in a southerly direction; there the ancient road leads to the Via Mala canyon (*mela*—stream

---

Palü, from *palus*—marsh. The latter corresponds to the Slovene word *polica*—a terrace or ledge. A. Walde, J.B. Hofmann quotes the word *kamb* (to fold, to bend) to explain the name Cambrena; cf. also the Slovene term *kamba* or *kvamba*—the U-shaped part of an ox yoke. W. Meyer-Lübke derives from the Latin *sarcelum,* root *sars* (Hacke) *hoe*; this is also present in the Slovene term *sršen* (a large European hornet), and explains the name Scerscen.

---

[49] We find in the Rätisches Ortsnamenbuch: Tschitta, from pre-Roman *ciuttare*, Rhaeto-Romance *tschuttar*—to observe, to watch; Platta, from Rhaeto-Romance *platt* (slab, flat rock), *plata* in dial. Slovene; Tschuggen *čukla*—a large boulder or solitary rock. There are no meaningful explanations for the following: Uertsch from the Lombardic *dverh*—slanted, crooked; Rescha, from the Latin *resia*—resin, pitch; Strela, from Rhaeto-Romance *striga*—witch; Tschiertschen, from the Latin *circinus*—circle; no explanation is given for Latsch. R. Badjura, ibid., p. 201, uses *kočna* (same as Cotschna) with the Slovene root *kotjina* (the name for the end of a glacial valley; this name was eventually transferred to the mountain itself. H. Tuma, *Krajevno imenoslovje/* Regional Toponymy; op. cit., p. 151, explains the toponym Tobel with the Slovene word *duplja*—a gloomy glen.

carrying rock-debris). In that area we find the Tschappina (*čepina,* from *čepa*—mountain with a rounded top) and Reschen (*reža*—fissure, crevice), Krogs 1531m (*krog*—round, circular), Piz Grisch 3043m (*griž*—place with rubble), Piz Tschiera 2632m (*čer*—cliff). On the upper course of the Hinterrhein appears a valley basin named Rheinwald just under the St. Bernardino Pass. A road leads to the Splugen/Spluga Pass 2113m; beyond here lies Val Loga (*log*—swampy meadow or alluvial ground). In the west the Rhine forest ends with the Zapportgrat; the Zapporthorn 3149m is the highest peak, *zapora* (barrier), *zaprt* (closed, locked).

In this mountain chain there is also a Vogelberg 3220m (*vogel*—corner, sharp formation), and of the same derivation is the mountain name Pizzo Ucello 2716m, near the St. Bernardino Pass. Neither of these two mountains are related to the word "bird", Italian *uccello,* German *Vogel.*

The main valley of the Rhine, called Vorderrhein, runs from where the Rhine branches off westward to the Via Mala, past the Illanz/Glion (*glina, ilo*—clay), and as far as Surselva, in the direction of St. Gotthard. On the north side of this valley we find Piz Grisch 2902m, Tschep 2943m (*čep, čepa*—rounded top) and several Tobel (*duplo*—hollow, cave). At the end of the valley lies Milez (*melec*—slopes of rock rubble) and the surrounding peaks: Piz Medel 3203m (*medel*—snow-capped); Piz Valatscha 3110m and Plaunca Cotschna 2770m (*kočna*—end of a glacial valley), followed by the Oberalp Pass 2044m, above which is Gams Stock 2965m. Gams is from *kamen* (stone, rock, rocky peak) and Piz Prevol 2860m, the peak above the *preval* (a pass).[50]

North of Chur in the wide Rhine Valley there are Zizers (*črče*—clearing*),* and Igis (*ig, igo*—yoke, yoke-shaped), and at the entrance to the side valley Prättigau, also Grusch (*gruž*—gravel, coarse sand). Across from the railway junction, Sargans, rises the Guschaspitze 1105m (*golša, guša, govša*—projecting part), lower on the Rhine one finds the town Gretschins (*grčine*—gnarled-looking),

---

[50] Tschappina is in the Rätisches Ortsnamenbuch inferred from Latin *cippina* (in upper Rhine Valley—brushland, deforested area), dial. *tschuppina* (in Breil area—a parcel of land divided into lots); cf. Slovene *čep*—a picket, a sighting stake, and *čepina*—a parcel of land marked by pickets, which coincides with Tschep, from the Latin *cippus*—boundary post, frontier *cippus.* The name Spluga/Splügen should derive from the Latin *spelunca* (cavern, grotto), but it seems to be closer to the Slovene verb *splužiti*—to clear from snow; the noun *spluga*—a route cleared of snow. The name Reschen is not explained; it corresponds to the Slovene *reža*—a crevice. The name Ilanz/Glion is shown as of unknown origin, but was explained by F. Bezlaj with the Slovene root *il*—clay, and *glina* with the same meaning. The names Grisch and Medel derive from family names, but we find in Slovene also *griže* pl.—a heap of stones; this is a frequent toponym on the Karst around Trst.

and again Gams (*kamen*—stone, rocky ledge) and Salez, a compound of *za* (other side, beyond) and *les* (forest, i.e., the other side of the forest). By Bad Ragaz, the Tamina (*temina*—stream from the mountain ridge) flows into the Rhine. Nearby is a hill called Tabor 843m (*tabor*—camp, fortress), and in the neighbouring mountains there is **Vindels** 1650m (probable derivation from Vend). From Sargans the wide Seez Valley with its swampy floor leads in a westerly direction to Lake Walen. Located here is the village Flums (*flum*—clay). Above Lake Walen runs the mountain chain called Churfürsten with the peaks of Kaserrug 2266m, Hinterrug 2309m, Zustoll 2239m, and Scheibenstoll 2238m, compound words from *rog* (horn) and *stol* (chair).

South of here, in the canton Glarus, we find under the Gemsfayrenstock the slope Grisi (*griži*—rock-debris). In the direction of the canton Schwyz lies the Klöntal Valley (*klon*—incline). In the Toggenburg is a village called Kappel (*kapla*—gateway), and in the Santis mountain group a dairy area called Kraialp (*kraj*—edge).[51]

The Lake Constance/Bodensee Area

In the broad countryside south of the Bodensee are numerous compound place-names with *Zell-*. This region was first settled during the Early Middle Ages and therefore these place-names could be derived from the Latin *cella*—settlement. The Bodensee itself had at the time of the Romans two names, Lacus Brigantinus, and **Lacus Venetus** (Pomponius Mela, De Corographia III, 24—around 44 B.C.). The Roman Brigantium was on the shore of this lake, as is the Austrian city Bregenz (*bregec* diminutive of *breg*—shore). On the Bavarian side is Lindau.[52]

---

[51] There are a few more names in the Rätisches Ortsnamenbuch: Salez, from *salictum*—a pasture overgrown with bushes; Flum, from the Romance *flumen* (also quoted by Meyer-Lübke). Some questionable explanations: Guscha, from the Rhaeto-Romance *gusche*—small load of hay; cf. the Slovene *goša* or *gošča*—brushwood; Grusch (wood chips or wood splits), the Slovene *grušč* (gravel) is obviously more to the point; Gretschins, derivation from a family name, in Slovene *grčine*—gnarls. The meanings of the names Rug and Stoll fit the Slovene *rog*—horn, and *stol*—chair, cf. R. Badjura, op. cit., pp. 135–6, 275, and that of *klon*—incline, slant, see F. Bezlaj, op. cit. The name of Tabor, like Mt. Tabor in Palestine, is explained as a fortress, and seems to be another Afro-European relic. It appears all over central Europe and also frequently in Slovene territory where it means a fortification, usually around a church on high ground, a refuge for people at times of danger.

---

[52] The name Lindau could not be inferred from the German word Linde (linden tree) but from "linda" which F. Bezlaj explains as: an area in front of the house still under the

In the region west of the Bodensee there are many place-names with the ending *-ach*. As already mentioned, this ending is not necessarily German. A special study and an appropriate explanation of the individual place-names should be undertaken. The Venetic root shows in place-names such as Wyden (*viden*—observation post) or Lausen (*luže*—pools) near Sissach. In the name Zürich, Rom. Turicum, the term *turje* (steep mountains) is recognizable. Near Brugg the ruins of the large Roman camp, **Vindonissa** (present-day Windisch, i.e., Slovene) are still preserved; this place-name supports our claim of earlier presence of Slavic Wends or Veneti in the area. On the open Swiss plateau west of here, the Wendian names become more infrequent indicating that in this region the Wends could not hold out very long among the newcomers. However, even on the German/French language border lies a city called Laupen (*lipa*—linden tree) that still has a linden tree on its coat of arms.

The Bernese and Valais Alps

Venetic names are to be found again in the area around Bern, thus, Konitz (*konec*—end of a valley) and south of here is Guggisberg (*guge*—mountain with a horizontal fold), and they become more frequent, especially in the highlands of Bern. This region rises into the Bernese Alps with the Jungfrau 4158m being the highest peak.[53]

On the north side of this mountain group are found peaks with names such as Lobhorn 1570m (*lob, lobanja*—skull); Tschuggen 2523m (*čukla*—boulder); Tanzboden 2136m, incorrect translation taken from *ples* (dance) instead of *pleša* (bald piece of ground) and *plešivec* (treeless mountain); Grutschlap 1490m (*griž*—rock debris); Pletschen Alp (*pleča*—shoulders); Guggi-Gletscher (*guge*—hori-

---

roof; an even better explanation is given by E. Bernecker (I, 722): *überhängender Teil des Daches*—the projecting part of the roof. It also conveys a general meaning of a refuge or haven, a natural harbour, which this place is. An incorrect interpretation of this word is given by Miklošič who derives it from the "line" in Middle High German.

[53] The name Jungfrau (maiden, in Ger.) appears as an incorrect translation of the old name Devin. The name is West Slavic (see Czech verb *divati*—to watch) meaning a summit with a broad panorama suitable as an observation post, the sentinel, but also a mountain that is seen from far. In central Europe we find this name in several areas: Devin (Bratislava), Theben in German; Devin (Prague); Devin (Trieste), Duino in Ital.; Duin 1772m in the Dolomites; Tour de Duin 563m above Rhone near Bex, Switzerland; Thebes Greece, and even Thebes in Egypt.

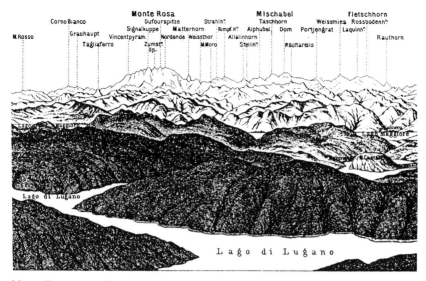

Labels on the panorama:
M.Rosso · Corno Bianco · Grauhaupt · Monte Rosa · Dufourspitze · Signalkuppe · Vincentpyram. · Tagliaferro · Zumst. Sp. · Nordende Weissthor · Strahlh? · Matterhorn · Rimpf.H? · M.Moro · Mischabel · Taschhorn · Alphubel · Allalinhorn · Stellih? · Dom · Portjengrat · P.Bottarello · Fletschhorn · Weissmies Rossbodenh? · Laquinh? · Rauthorn

Laghi Maggiore · Lago di Lugano · Lago di Lugano

*Monte Rosa, a view from Monte Generoso above Lugano Lake, Slovene **raza**—fissure.*

zontal fold on a mountain) glacier; Trugberg 3933m, from Strugberg (*strug*—gully cut by water); Tschingelhorn 3599m (*čela* pl.—foreheads). On the north side of this same mountain group flow streams with names like Weisse and Schwarze Lütschine (*lučina*—brightness). Southward runs the Lötschen Valley (*loke, loče*—valley-meadow) with the Lonza River (*lonca,* dim. from *lona*—summit; i.e., the river coming from the summit). In this valley one finds the village Blatten (*blata* pl.—bogs).[54]

The wide Rhone Valley with its side valleys form the canton **Wallis/Valais,** which is German in its upper part and French in the lower. On the south side there are the Walliser Alps, where once again several Venetic names appear. In their

---

[54] The Rätisches Ortsnamenbuch explains the names Gütsch or Grütsch as follows: a roundish hill, summit, a rocky overhang, same as in Slovene. The meaning of the name Trug resembles very closely the Slovene word *strug*—a cleft or channel formed by water, cf. R. Badjura, ibid., p. 218. The word *lučina* is derived by F. Bezlaj, from the Indo-European *leuk*—to shine; Lutschine is therefore a river or place out in the open, full of sun and light. The name Tschingel, from Rhaeto-Romance *tschengel*—a terrace with rocky face—is same as the Slovene names *čengla, čela.* The Blümlisalp does not derive from flowers—die Blumen; it is but an incorrect translation of the Slovene *svitje* (a twisted or winding crest) which may sound in dial. as "cvietje" and was therefore mistaken for "cvetje"—flowers. Such linguistic flourishes appear also in the mountains of northern Italy; for instance Campo di Fiori 1226m, above Varese.

43

western part, as seen from the south, just above the Aosta rises the huge Grand Golliaz 3238m (*goljač*—treeless, barren). The well-known Matterhorn 4478m is called Cervino (*čer, ker*—cliff) on the Italian side; perhaps also from *červen*, crimson in Old Slovene, sunburnt in Czech. In the Mt. Rosa group, there is a glacier named Loccie and also a Colle delle Loccie 3353m (*loka*—meadow, mountain over the valley-meadow). Above the resort area, Arolla, there is Mont Dolin 2976m (*dolina*—valley, a mountain above the valley). On the north side of the Walliser Alps is the Eivisch Valley (Vall d'Anniers) and above it is Pas de Lona 2767m (*lona*—high summit). In this valley are names such as Grimentz (*kremenica*—place of flintstone), also a place made defendable, from *kremenit* (sturdy, strong); Vissoie (*visok*—high, elevated place); Gradetz (*gradec*—fortification); Vergoppa (*vrh kope*—top of a rounded summit); Czernec (*černec*—place of frontier guard), and so forth.[55]

In the Wallis we also find Brig (*breg*—slope); this valley then gradually climbs to the Furka Pass 2431m. Below lies Gletsch (*kleč*—crag).

North of Furka there are numerous high peaks, and just above the Engelberg the Titlis mountain group with the following Wendian names: **Wendenstock 3044m, Wendengletscher, Wenden-Alpe, Wendenbach**, *Bach* (creek). This creek runs through the mountain valley called Urat (*vrata*—door, gate, gorge), evidently not by chance. The original Wendian (Slovene) inhabitants must have held on much longer in this region, which is why the Germanic neighbours preserved these names.

Canton Ticino

Southward from the St. Gotthard Pass 2108m stretches the Italian canton of Ticino, Ger. Tessen (*tesen*—canyon, or narrow part of a valley). Its capital is Bellinzona, Ger. Bellenz (*bela, belenca*—white-water stream). Nearby is the castle,

---

[55] The name Monte Rosa denotes a massif of eroded rocks. See W. Meyer-Lübke, op. cit., 3rd ed. 1935, who quotes the verbs *rasare (*to carve) and *rosicare*—to gnaw. The name Lyskamm characterizes a smooth ridge; cf. the Slavic expression *lis*—smooth. F. von Velden noted some hundreds of Slavic words in the French-Swiss dialect; see *Das Patois der Westschweiz als Zeuge völkergeschichtlicher Vorgänge*, published in Politisch-anthropologische Revue 1910/11, No. 9, 10, pp. 457–470, 527–536. His observations were rejected by L. Gauchat and J. Jeanjaquet in the *Bibliographie linguistic dela Suisse romande*, vol. II. Neuchâtel 1920, p. 29.—A friendly response from the Institute Glossair des patois de la Suisse romande (Neuchâtel), with the letter of Dec. 5th. 1983. This question is calling for a new examination and comparison with the Slavic languages.

Suitto 310m, in Ger. Schwyz.[56] East of here, above Grono, we find Alpe de Mea 1856m (*meja*—border, timber line). In the west our attention is drawn to the big Lago Maggiore, Ger. Langensee; the Romans called it **Lacus Verbanus** (*vrba*— willow, willow trees may have grown by the lake); compare this with *Vrbsko jezero* "Willow lake"— Wörther See in Carinthia.

By Lago Maggiore lies the well-known holiday resort, Locarno, Ger. Luggarus (*log*—swampy meadow), or *loka* (meadow by a body of water). To the north of the lake lies Val Verzasca with the Forcella di Cocco 2137m (*kuk*—peak at the end of a mountain chain). In the neighbouring Val Lavizzara is a village called Peccia (*peč*—wall of rock). On the east side of Lago Maggiore rise the peaks, Mt. Tamaro 1967m (*tamar*—shelter, corral), and Mt. Gradisca 1018m (*gradišče*— castle hill, fortification). In the valleys of Centovalli and Vigezza east of Locarno flows a stream named Melezza (*melica*—rubble-carrying water, stream running under rock rubble). By the same lake we find the holiday resorts, Pallanza (*poljanca* dim. of *poljana*—level field), and Ronco (*ronek*—foot of a mountain). Farther to the west is Lago d'Orta, and the village Orta (*rt, ort*—spit of land, projection); a spit of land reaches into the lake at this location. Still farther in this direction is the industrial city of Biella (*bela*—white-water stream). In the mountains north of the city we find Frate di Mea 2812m (*frate* pl.—brushland, *meja*— border) and again a Cima Cucco 1288m (*kuk*—peak at the end of a mountain chain).

In the Ossola Valley there are places like: Albo (*lobje*—skull); Pallanzeno (*poljance*—small field); Noga (*noga*—foot); Ronco and Rencio (*roče*—small ledges); Cellio (*čelo*—vertical formation); Locarno (*loka*—valley meadow); and Colma (*holm*—rounded hill or mountain). Above the valley are Monte Cerano 1702m (*čer*—cliff); Pizzo Camino 2148m (*kamen*—stone); Moncucco 1896m (*kuk*—end of mountain chain and Monte). We should not forget Monte Camino 2391m (*kamen*—stone, i.e., the rocky mountain).

For the majority of names given, the meaning is clarified only through the

---

[56] The name Switto has the same origin as the Slovene word *zvito*—twisted, crooked. The name of Mt. Torrione 1984m and similar names found in this area originate from *turra* which means a heap of earth, stones or even sheaves of grain according to W. Meyer-Lübke in Romanic languages. He thinks it is originally from Celtic, and denotes a rise or a knoll. He does not accept derivation from the Latin *taurus,* but presupposes a yet more distant origin in a common pre-Indo-European language extending through France and Italy. This word could also be a relic of the Afro-European language once spread out in the Mediterranean area and western and central Europe. See also other similar words and names, as *turje* in Slovene, and Taurus, Tauern, Tauromenium (Taormina) in Sicily, the mythological Tura Mashe (Mountain of Salvation) in Syria and so on.

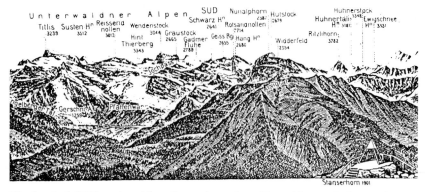

Wendenstock 3044m, viewed from Stanserhorn above Vierwaldstätten Lake near Luzern.

Slovene and no other language. Old Greek may be of some help because of its closeness to ancient Indo-European language. However, this would apply only to Greek colonies in coastal areas and not to the Alpine region.

In numerous instances we have also the proto-names preserved in Slovene Carinthia, which is the area that has most recently been annexed to the German language block. Above all, many of these names are still common in Slovenia. Moreover, the majority of the meanings are still in common daily use in the Slovene language.

Regrettably, this has been only an overview of the Slovene topographical names on Swiss soil and the surrounding area. A more detailed investigation of field, house, and family names could not be undertaken because of the size of the project and the difficulty in assembling the highly specialized source material.

When we consider what has already been said, it does not surprise us that so many names of the Swiss Rhaetia have modern Slovene endings; e.g., **-ec** (Zernez), **-ica** (Crastaguzza), **-čina** (Lütschine), **-čen** (Piz Cotschen), **-nina** (Bernina), **-avna** (Val Plavna), **-ača** (Crastatscha), **-ič** (Gritsch), **-ač** (Rosatsch), **-je** (Plattje, Vissoie), and so forth. In the Rhaetian directory of place-names, these endings are mostly explained from Romance, Latin, and sometimes German models; thus, for instance, *-atsch* from Lat. *-aceu*.[57] The comparison with the Slovene endings indicates much older Venetic derivation. Also the Italian endings like *-asca, -o* (Val Verzsca, Bergamasco) or *-eza* (Rascieza) totally correspond to the Slovene *-ska, -i,* (slovenska, tirolski) and *-ica (rasica)*.

---

[57] In a courteous letter of Sept. 1st, 1983, from the Institute Dicziunari Romantsch Grisun in Chur/Cuera: "There is a variety of opinions in regard to the affinity of the Rhaeto-Romance language with other languages distant in space and time."

46

The analogous forms, especially between the Slovene and Rhaeto-Romance place-names, as well as word endings, allow us to presume the existence of synonymous word groups in both languages. Casually looking through the pages of the Rhaeto-Romance directory of place-names we find entries like:

tana—wilderness camp, in Slovene *stan*—room in a cabin; **trogio**—footpath; in Old Slovene *tropa*—footpath; **sterna** *štirna*—water reservoir; **ciucca** *čok*—log; **brenta** *brenta*—a wooden container for carrying grapes; **braita** *brajda*—cultivated area in grape growing region; **brig** *breg*—slope; **dota** *dota*—dowry; **drögh** *draga*—a narrow valley; **fetta** *feta*—slice; **gassa** *gasa*—lane; **junicia** *junica*—heifer; **tschoffa** *čop, čuf*—tassel; **latta** *lata*—railing; **piccare** *pikati*—to pierce; **planca** *planja*—Alpine meadow; **pusch** *buša*—cow, in child language; **resch**—ploughed area, Slov. *rez, razor*—irrigation ditch; **sala**—river, Slov. river names Zala, Zila *zlivati*—to pour; **bulla** *bula*—bump; **broia**—a tank for collecting spring water, Slov. *broja, brojnica*—a forceful spring.

The above word pairs in Rhaeto-Romance and Slovene cannot be a mere coincidence as they appear too frequently. Their meaning becomes fairly clear when we consider that in the distant past the Slavic Veneti or Wends lived in the central as well as the eastern Alps. As is evident from linguistic comparisons, they were closely related to the Slovenes, or were even one and the same people.

Another detail that may seem surprising is that the Wendian/Slovene names in the central Alps exhibit idiosyncrasies of western Slovene dialects; for example the change of consonants **k** to **ch**—*kukla/čukla, kepa/čepa, kita/čita, skera/ ščera* or the vowel modification of **o** to **a** *lonce/lance, lob/lab, loje/laje* and the following abbreviations—*kon'c/konec, dol'c/dolec, stol'c/stolec* and so forth.

Such dialect peculiarities in the nomenclature of the central Alps, where the alleged 6th century Slav settlement did not occur, point to an older origin of the Slovene language and hence of the Slovene people, much older than what is allowed by the official theory regarding their settlment in the eastern Alps.

As we move on, we would like again to submit two important questions, the same questions that have been asked before. Who were the indigenous inhabitants in the Alps, and did the ancestors of the Slovenes really arrive only in the 6th century A.D.? If we agree on the time of settlement (i.e., after the migration of the Langobards into Italy, year 568), and agree on the officially prescribed settlement area in the eastern Alps, then how are we to explain the presence of countless Slovene topographical names in the central Alps?

Before we again raise the issue of the settlement problem of the Slovene ancestors in the Alps, we will make a detailed inquiry into the research and findings of the archaeologists and consider them in relation to our study.

Prehistory

The name "Veneti" belongs in history only to the people designated as the bearers of the Urnfield culture. (G. Devoto)[58]

Permanent settlements of people in central Europe became evident during the neolithic age, around 3000 B.C., effecting a turning point in the life of prehistoric Europeans, particularly in regard to economic and domestic activities and social structure. Community life gave rise to new cultural forms which came to expression especially in the making of earthenware and the ensuing domestic life. During this time pottery production experienced an exceptionally fruitful development; archaeology refers to this early stage of civilization as "The Age of Ceramics".

Around 2000 B.C., man had already found copper in central Europe, but this did not bring about substantial change in the life of people during the neolithic age.

Then around 1800 B.C., with the discovery of bronze, Europe once more experienced a major advancement. Tools and weapons made of bronze were much stronger. The Bronze Age lasted until 900 B.C. when Europe entered the early Iron Age.

The Bronze Age was the era when the proto-groups gradually formed into tribes, a development that occurred under conditions that were dependent on geographic factors, the nature of the soil for use as pasture and cultivated fields, and trade with neighbours. Each proto-group and the resulting tribal units developed on the basis of the level of civilization and their own conditions of life. Archaeology is now able to give us a fairly clear picture of these ethnic groups through their economy, domestic life, use of weapons and tools, and how they worked and waged war.

Based on ritual objects, especially ornaments and symbols discovered on vessels and other artifacts, researchers were able in some measure to determine the beliefs of these groups.

During this era, each ethnic group distinguished itself particularly through

---

[58] G. Devoto, *Origini indoeuropee*, Florence 1962, p. 194.

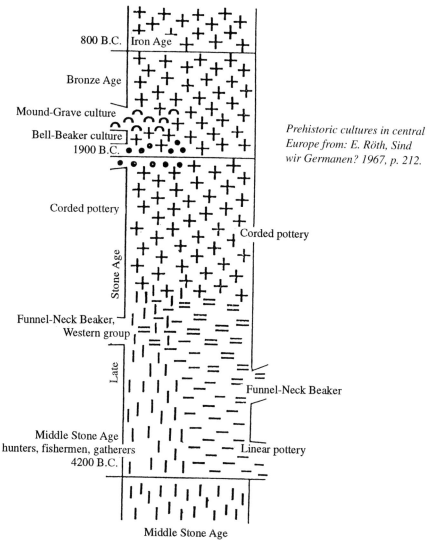

800 B.C. — Iron Age

Bronze Age

Mound-Grave culture

Bell-Beaker culture
1900 B.C.

Corded pottery

Stone Age

Corded pottery

Funnel-Neck Beaker,
Western group

Late

Funnel-Neck Beaker

Middle Stone Age
hunters, fishermen, gatherers
4200 B.C.

Linear pottery

Middle Stone Age

*Prehistoric cultures in central
Europe from: E. Röth, Sind
wir Germanen? 1967, p. 212.*

various furnishings, including armaments and jewellery found in the graves of its members. Each group developed in its sphere of existence its own dialect which gradually became an independent language and thus separate from the neighbouring groups. Linguists surmised that in the neolithic age in Europe extensive language regions had come into being, but they gave most of their attention to the language family of the Indo-Europeans. Considering the origin of the lan-

49

guages of prehistoric humanity in Europe, archaeologists cautiously limit their comments to general statements.[59]

The various cultural units in Europe around 2000 B.C. could not as yet be considered Proto-Indo-European; they were at best the cells from which new groups and communities emerged. The leading element of these groups was evidently the "Funnel-Neck Beaker culture", followed in central Europe by the "Bell-Beaker culture". In the Bronze Age after 1800 B.C., central Europe could already be designated as the territory of the Indo-Europeans; nevertheless, a division of individual Indo-European tribes had not yet taken place.

However, the preparations for such division could already be recognized, as for example in the differences between the **Mound-Grave culture, Lusatian culture,** the Nordic "bronze age", early Hungarian metallurgy (lower Don region), and the **Greek Pit-Grave culture**. Behind all these cultural forms were established communities, yet it is not possible to assign to them historical, individual tribes; they merely contained the basic tendencies for future development (e.g. R. Pittioni).

There is a great diversity of opinion as to what a unit of people actually is. As viewed by archaeologists, a culture group based in a relatively well developed internal organization is without a doubt much younger than a language group; i.e., a people with the same language. For this reason, linguists settle the beginning of Indo-Europeans (and in central Europe that of Veneti and Illyrians) in the period of the Linear-pottery culture, around 4000 B.C. (E. Röth, 1957). This moves the origin of Indo-Europeans as a linguistic group yet further into prehistory by a full thousand years or more.

The Indo-Europeans

For a long time Central Asia was considered the origin of Indo-Europeans. Later, eastern, central and northern Europe were seen as Indo-European core regions during the neolithic age. In the broad territory between the Rhine and the

---

[59] Compare R.Pittioni, *Italien, Urgeschichtliche Kulturen/* Italy, Prehistoric Cultures; in Real-Enzyklopädie der classischen Altertumswissenschaft, suppl. Bd. 9, (1962), pp. 352–354. The author quotes also other papers: R. Pittioni, *Alteuropäische Sprache und Urgeschichte/*The Old-European Language and Prehistory; Anzeiger, Vienna 1959, p. 203 passim; H. Krahe, *Sprachliche Aufgliederung und Sprachbewegungen im Alteuropa/* The Linguistic Division and Language Movements in Ancient Europe; Abh. Akad. Mainz Phil. sozialwiss. Kl. 1959, No. I.

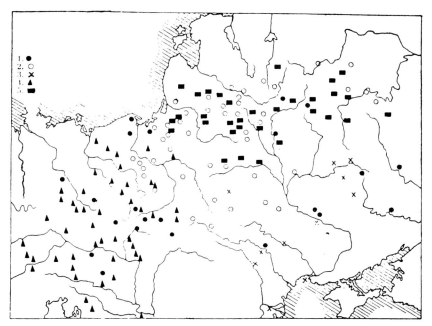

The linguistic origins of some geographic names in Europe. The symbols mean: 1. pre-Indo-European 2. Ugro-Finnish 3. Iranian 4. Venetic (earlier: Illyrian) 5. Baltic names. (source: V. Polák, Vznik a počátku Slovanu 1, 1956, 24). In this drawing there is a clear division between the groups of Balts and Proto-Slavic Veneti (West Slavs).

Volga, groups appeared that could be seen as the bearers of Indo-European cultural foundation. These people engaged in agriculture and bred livestock, especially bullock, sheep, pigs, goats, and horses. Recent ethno-genetic theories, which take into account historically demonstrable relationships, consider central Europe (H. Krahe, P. Thieme) and eastern Europe (E. Wahle, A. J. Bryusov) to be the ancestral territory of Indo-Europeans.

Moreover, there exists the view of the "double ancestral homeland". Not yet divided, the Indo-Europeans moved from a central eastern location to the west; from there they migrated to the historical territories. Archaeologically viewed, their expansion phase is characterized by **Battle-Axe culture** (Corded-pottery culture). Around 1800 B.C. these neolithic cultures were confined to eastern, northern, and central Europe; their bearers belonged predominantly to European racial stock.[60]

---

[60] Brockhaus Enzyklopädie, Wiesbaden 1970 (Indogermanen, Indoeuropäer). Also J. Filip, *Enzyklopädisches Handbuch zur Ur- und Frühgeschichte Europas/* The Encyclopedic

After considering the relationship of the traditional languages in Europe, we come to the conclusion that Indo-Europeans were once a unified nation. As a result of archaeological discoveries, the existence of those cultural groups is proven but their kinship is today unknown. Horses and war chariots made it possible for Indo-Europeans to rapidly penetrate the European and Mediterranean area. Their invasions were recorded in the east around 1760 B.C. in the chronicles of Mesopotamia. In the 16th century B.C., Indo-European Hittites founded their empire in Anatolia, which was destroyed around 1200 B.C. by Indo-European Phrygians. A strong migration wave of Indo-European Aryans pushed into India towards the end of the second millennium B.C.

The name "Aryan" is probably the original designation of the so-called Indo-Europeans. In Sanskrit (the classical Old Indic literary language) arya means noble, which is what Indo-Europeans presumably considered themselves in relation to the indigenous inhabitants of India. The meaning of the word itself refers, seemingly, to agriculture—*arare* (Latin); *orati* (Slovene) to plough—and thus suggests the farming origin of the Aryan people.

In the middle of the second millennium B.C. two predominant linguistic groups had already developed in the spacious Indo-European territory. The division is still accepted today—the western group of kentum (centum) languages and the eastern group of satem languages.

The western group is characterized by (voiceless) velar plosives (**k**) where cognate words in the eastern group have sibilants (**s, z**). To the latter group belong the Indian, Iranian, Baltic, and Slavic languages.[61] Both groups may have had their origin in the dialects that emerged after the first Indo-European migration.

The use of bronze in Europe between 1700 and 1300 B.C. brought about an advancement of material culture as never before in this region. The **Mound-Grave culture** (1500 to 1300 B.C.) emerged, represented by diverse groups north of the Alps from the Rhine to within the Carpathian basin. This culture possibly marks the division of the original core of Indo-Europeans into the succeeding language groups, such as Illyrian, Thracian, and probably also Germanic.

Bronze weapons and tools from this era were varied and strong, therefore highly valued in trade. This fact played a decisive role in the development of domestic life and the economy, reaching its high point in the middle of the Bronze

---

dic Handbook of the Prehistory and Early History of Europe; (Streitaxkulturen), (Schnurkeramische Kulturen).

[61] Brockhaus Enzyklopädie, op. cit., (Indogermanische Sprachen). Encyclopaedia Britannica, Chicago 1982.

*Urn from Late Bronze Age
and its grave.*

Age in the **Lusatian culture** (1300 to 1100 B.C.). The culture had its focal point in Lusatia (Lausitz), and later spread over a region that reached from the central basin of the Oder River and the Bohemian/Slovakian mountain ridge, to the east as far as the Ukraine, and in the north to the shores of the Baltic Sea.

The densely settled region of Lusatian culture is characterized in its development by particular ceramic, bronze, and later iron articles: knives, spearheads, sickles, and particularly well-made axes.

The economic basis of Lusatian culture was for the most part agricultural. Several kinds of grain and leguminous plants, three kinds of wheat, millet, rye, broadbeans, peas and vetch were cultivated, accompanied by livestock breeding, hunting, and fishing. The settlement areas were in most cases founded near flowing waters. The fortified settlement had assumed a special status.

The dead were cremated and the ashes placed in urns, *then interred in extensive burial-fields; thus the designation "Urnfield culture".*[62]

As is known through excavations, Lusatian culture reveals a strong social and military structure, which was probably the main reason for developing their own language. Through its language, a culture group expresses its nationality; that is, it becomes an ethnic group. This brings us to the logical question: What ethnic affiliation could be attributed to the bearers of the Lusatian culture?

The experts are of divergent views on this topic. Lusatian culture has been linked with Teutons, Thracians, Dacians, and Illyrians. There were also tendencies to consider the bearers of this culture as Proto-Slavs (J. Kostrzewski). The

---

[62] J. Filip, op. cit., p. 686 (Lausitzer Kultur).

53

theory of an Illyrian origin for Lusatian culture has evoked polemics and lively contradictions (e.g., P. Kretschmer 1943, V. Milojčić 1952, K. Tymieniecki 1963). J. Pokorny, one of the original advocates of this theory, changed his position after the Second World War when he defended the thesis that the language of bearers of the succeeding (and according to him) kindred Urnfield culture, must have been closely related to the Baltic languages (1950–53). There were also arguments claiming that the bearers of Lusatian culture were an Indo-European tribe of unknown name which had an important role in the history of Europe (J. Böhm 1941); or that the bearers of this culture participated in development of the historical Slavs, Celts, Illyrians, and other ethnic communities. The view, which finds in the bearers of Lusatian culture the foundation from which the historical Slavs were formed (J. Filip 1946), is also very close to the view which states: *Lusatian culture must be equated with the culture of the Veneti* (P. Bosch-Gimpera 1961).[63]

In the ensuing Urnfield culture during the late Bronze Age, cremation and the use of urns as the means of interment mark a major change for most European people of the time in regard to their earthly existence and life after death. The oldest urn graves belong to the end of the neolithic age—the German Schönfeld group and the early Bronze Age of Anatolia. In Europe urn graves are characteristic of Lusatian culture, and through its Urnfield migration they spread through most of Europe. The Urnfields are most heavily represented in central Europe where the following areas can be differentiated: the Lusatian culture, the so-called Southern German Urnfield culture, and the Central Danubian Urnfield culture.[64]

The Urnfields

The Urnfield migration occurred in the 13th century B.C. and fundamentally changed the cultural and linguistic nature of Europe. The bearers of the Urnfield culture settled the entire territory from the Baltic southwards over the Alps to the Adriatic Sea and the Apennines. Their migrations also reached other parts of Europe.

Archaeologists find that the Urnfield migration contributed in a major way to Indo-Europeanize the regions as far as the Apennines.[65] There is, however, no

---

[63] J. Filip, ibid., pp. 688–689.

[64] Brockhaus Enzyklopädie, op. cit., 1947 (Urnenfelderkultur). J. Filip, op. cit., p. 1555 (Urnenfelderkultur).

[65] R. Pittioni, op. cit., p. 354/60.

consensus among them nor among linguists concerning the ethnic affiliation of bearers of the Urnfield migration. The predominant view until the Second World War was that Lusatian and Urnfield cultures were to be attributed to the Illyrians. This view found acceptance into the 1960s, when it was finally rejected by linguists.[66] Afterwards, the following finding was widely accepted: *The bearers of the Urnfield culture were Veneti or Wends.*

Their language was the common Indo-European language from the 2nd millennium B.C. While Greeks, Hittites, Iranians, and Indians developed their separate ethnic characteristics, the tradition of the Veneti reflects the unchanged old ways (G. Devoto).[67]

As already observed, the term "Venetic" as the linguistic characterization of the Veneti, and "Illyrian" (as used in earlier identification) in the term "North Illyrian" refer to the same people in the region from the north Adriatic to the Baltic Sea. The name Veneti appears in the south as well as in the north of their designated linguistic territory (W. Meid).[68]

Not all of the migration and settlement movements that took place in Europe during the Urnfield period can be attributed directly to the Veneti. In the regions where they conquered, settled, and flourished, which are outside the area between the Adriatic and Baltic Seas, the Veneti are revealed only by a few historical records and archaeological finds, and mainly by their place-names. In historical literary sources their presence is attested to as far as Asia Minor, Brittany, the shores of the Baltic Sea, and other regions.

Even the Vandals, originating in Scandinavia, bore the Venetic name and came from the original Venetic Urnfield migration. They were only later Germanized. In the vicinity of Uppsala, Sweden, there is a place called Vendel, where many lavish graves were discovered, although from a later period (7th–10th century A.D.). A group of Veneti remained by the Baltic Sea until Roman times. Hence, the Russians were called Venäjä (from Venädä) by the Finns; the Pomeranians were called Vindr and their land Vindland by the Scandinavians.[69]

During the Urnfield migration the Veneti or Wends moved from the core region of Lusatian culture in present-day Poland and eastern Germany, in a strong

---

[66] J. Pokorny and R. Pittioni designated them as Illyrians as late as after the Second World War; however, due to justified criticism they both abandoned this position. Afterwards the latter designated the Veneti as Proto-Illyrians. Cf. R. Pittioni, op. cit., p. 355/20.

[67] G. Devoto, *Origini...*op. cit., p. 194.

[68] W. Meid, *Beiträge zur Namenforschung/* Contributions to Toponymic Research, XV, (1964) pp. 112–113, see G. B. Pellegrini, A.L. Prosdocimi, *La lingua venetica* II, Padova 1967, pp. 248–249.

[69] See G.B. Pellegrini, A.L. Prosdocimi, op. cit., p. 239, from: Collinder, *Die urgerma-*

migration towards the south, over the Alps into northern Italy, the Po Valley, the Apennines and to some extent as far as Sicily.[70] As already considered in the opening chapter of this paper, place-names, especially those that refer to agricultural and herdsman's lifestyles, tell us of their presence in this region. The meaning of such names can still be explained by the vocabulary of the old Slovene village culture. Even names such as Apennines, *apno* (lime, limestone mountains) and Padana (the plain under steep mountains) are in this way made understandable to us, and are another indication of the Slavic origin of the Veneti.

The culture groups that arose out of the neolithic age in the Apennines, namely, the late *Belverde-Cetona culture* (after 1200 B.C.), were to some extent shaken by the arrival of the Veneti in their territory. The discoveries in burial places of Castelfranco-Lamoncello in the Fiora Valley in Tuscany indicate conflict between the Veneti and the indigenous population. The finds show the resistance of native inhabitants especially in the southern Apennines. This was so perhaps because the Veneti had brought a new spiritual and cultural orientation, as indicated by urn graves as early as 1000 B.C. in Timmari, *tamar* (shelter, corral) near Matera in the Basilicata or in Milazzo, *melec* (a slope of rock rubble) in Sicily. Around 750 B.C. the first Greek colony had been founded in Cumae (Kyme) near Naples, followed by numerous colonies on the south Apennine coast. The Greek colonies had a major cultural and linguistic influence on the southern Apennines and southern Italy in general, through which national characteristics of the Italians or Latins were formed.

In the central Apennines along the Adriatic coast in the provinces Marche and Abruzzi, the Novilara culture, attributed to the Picentian people, developed and expanded after the 8th century B.C. Urn graves in Pianello near Ancona support the idea that there was a preceding Venetic influence.

The Territory of the Veneti

In the region along the Tyrrhenian coast the Veneti had become the ruling class for a definite period of time (according to discoveries in the burial grounds).

---

*nischen Lehnwörter im Finnischen/*The Old-Germanic Loanwords in the Finnic, Uppsala 1932, p. 14. F. Bezlaj, op. cit., (Venice).

[70] G. Sergi, *Le prime e le piu antiche civilta/* The First and the Oldest Cultures, Turin 1926, pp. 262–3. G. Sergi, Italia–*le origini*, Turin 1919, pp. 306, 383, 405. H. Tuma, Krajevno imenoslovje, op. cit., p. 154. The latter quotes G. Sergi and designates the urn-grave of Forum Romanum discovered in 1902 as Slavic.

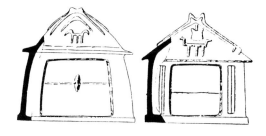

Urns from 10th to 9th century B.C. found in Rome (in Foro Romano), with house signs, ancient marks of ownership.

The graves show the indigenous burial and also the presence of Venetic urns. Afterwards, inhumation burial rites gradually became predominant, indicating the merging of two ethnic elements and the beginning of a new, apparently Etruscan, culture group.

This course of events is also confirmed by the excavations in Rome and its vicinity.[71] On the Palatine, remains of *round, elliptical huts* were discovered. Remains of settlements from the 10th or 9th century B.C. were discovered on the Esquilin and Quirinal Hills and also in the Forum Romanum. The graves show burials in oak coffins as well as in urns. Of special interest in this find is an "urna capanna" (house-shaped urn) from a Forum grave.

In the neighbouring Alban Hills—Colli Albani in Italian—more urn and inhumation graves were found, originating from the succeeding era and characteristic of the culture in the central Apennines and of the Etruscans. This culture is named by Pittioni[72] after the place of discovery, Marino, in the Alban Hills.

The **Marino culture** (800 to 500 B.C.) encompassed an area that reached from the Alban Hills to north of Tarquinia. It revealed a continuation of the unification process of indigenous and Venetic population elements and attained its culmination after the 7th century B.C. The high point of Etruscan culture is especially reflected in the spacious and elaborate chamber graves or tombs that are preserved to this day. In the warrior-grave (tomba del guerriero) from around 720 B.C. in Corneto, Tarquinia, Greek pottery of late-geometric design was found. The typical fayence vase (painted and glazed pottery) from the same grave confirms Etruscan trade with Phoenicians.

Etruscan culture was marked by Mediterranean as well as central European influences, and yet it was already original and self-made. Archaeological finds reveal the persevering character of these people. Their link to Mediterranean

---

[71] G. Sergi, *Italia*...p. 130. R. Pittioni, op. cit., p. 288/20.

[72] G. Sergi, *Gli Arii in Europa e Asia/* The Aryans in Europe and Asia, Turin 1903, p. 49. R. Pittioni, op. cit., pp. 257–258, 287/20, 355/30.

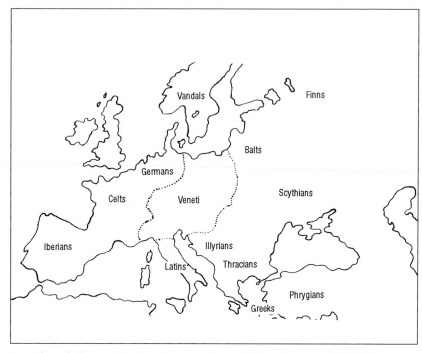

Densely settled area of the Veneti after the Urnfield Migration, circa 1200 B.C.

cultures enabled them to develop excellent stone-working skills, and they were capable of building technically as well as artistically impressive structures. During the same period, Venetic people in central Europe developed an exceptionally strong social and military structure that was based on a new religion and its spiritual power. These two trends decidedly influenced the rise of Etruscans and their culture, which was later adopted by the Romans.

Here we have the question of the Etruscan language, handed down in numerous inscriptions, engraved for the most part on tombstones, yet not deciphered on the basis of Mediterranean languages. Considering the invasion of the Slavic Veneti into the central Apennines, it would only be natural to include Slavic languages in this research. Incidentally, Anton Berlot[73] was able to read and translate a large number of Etruscan and Rhaetian inscriptions using the vocabularies of Slavic languages, especially that of the Slovene, which is the oldest Slavic

---

[73] A. Berlot, Eine Studie der Sprache der Rassenen oder Etrusker/ A Study of the Rasennian or Etruscan language, Zürich 1966.

language and has best preserved its Proto-Slavic roots. He uncovered among other things the "dual", a grammatical peculiarity of Slovene. While deciphering the Etruscan tablets from the city of **Pyrgi** (circa 500 B.C.) he noted a reference, perhaps the earliest, to the name **Sloveni**, "Cluveni", which shows that the Veneti in all probability used this name for themselves. The unusual circumstance of two names still exists; the Slovene people are also called "Windische" and "Vendek" by Germans and Hungarians respectively.

* * *

Lusatian culture in central Europe persevered in its development, even after the Urnfield migration. From its nucleus new cultural groups were formed, which fell under the influence of the Celtic La Tène culture during the conquest movement of the Celts in the 5th century. Out of these circumstances there arose during the 2nd century B.C., in present Poland (according to Polish archaeology), the **Venedic culture** which survived into the 6th century A.D.[74] In spite of many influences and attacks from outside, the original people, the Proto-Slavic Veneti/Venedi, maintained their national identity within this culture.

As expected, the ethnic affiliation of the Venedic culture still represents a point of dispute between Polish and German researchers. German scholars attribute it for the most part to the Germanic tribes, especially the Vandals, whose territory was to have extended from Vendsyssel, Jutland, into Poland. Polish researchers, however, regard Venedic culture to be a successor to Lusatian culture (J. Kostrzewski), sustained by Proto-Slavic tribes. Vandalic discoveries on Jutland are to a large degree related to those from the Venedic culture (J. Werner).[75]

Farmer with hook-plough. Representation on situla Certosa, Bologna (Villanova culture).

---

[74] J. Filip, op. cit., p. 1059 (Polen).
[75] J. Filip, ibid., p. 1100 (Przeworsk-Kultur).

Este—Situla Benvenuti,second half of 6th century B.C. (Museo Nazionale Atestino).

We get much closer to the solution of the problem if we assume that the Scandinavian Vandals, with their Venetic name, descended from the Urnfield culture and were Germanized afterwards.

According to Polish research, two main groups are distinguished within Venedic culture:

In the north, where the Lusatian culture was succeeded by the Pomeranian culture (extending over the coastal region from the mouth of the Oder to the mouth of the Vistula) there developed a group called *Oksywie.* If the Lusatians and the succeeding East Pomeranian culture and the group Oksywie were, as we think, Slavic, then the present-day Pomeranians or Kashubians must be seen as their descendants. In reality this ethnic group has to this day kept the Proto-Slavic name, Slovincians.

The southern parts of present Poland were encompassed by the *Przeworsk group.* Here, archaeology recognizes major Celtic influences. In the 2nd century B.C., the Celts arrived in southern Poland through Moravia and formed a weak, insignificant ruling class. In central Silesia they developed a dense settlement, but by 1st century B.C. Celtic elements merged with the indigenous population.

The present nation of the Poles (who are in dialect still called by their German neighbours—Lechen) developed on the cultural foundation of the Przeworsk group. In German dialect the Celts were generalized with the name Lechen (Welschen). Thus, the Celtic element left behind its name in the Polish nation.

In German science, the Oksywie group is attributed to the Burgunds and the Przeworsk group to the Vandals.

In Bohemia and Moravia other local culture groups formed after the Urnfield migration. Nevertheless, in the 5th century B.C., Celts invaded this region and prevailed with their La Tène culture.

The areas of present-day Austria, Bavaria, Swabia, eastern Switzerland, and northern Italy, as well as Slovenia, were all conquered and settled by the Veneti during the Urnfield migration. Their language and culture attained dominance and the indigenous population merged in a relatively short time with the Venetic newcomers. In the upper Po Valley, Italy, the indigenous Terramare culture, which also included the especially strong Polada, was totally eradicated. A new epoch had begun in the development of central Europe.

In the Alps and in the neighbouring regions there arose, after the 10th century B.C., several new cultures.[76] The movement that was sustained by the Urnfield culture stood in the forefront; it took part in the creation of the outward form of the culture of this period. This means that there was no massive decline of the pre-Venetic population, either in a biological or in an intellectual sense. Through co-operation with the original inhabitants there developed a new reality. The Venetic ruling class would have been numerically too weak on its own to bring about a new cultural development with enough intellectual and spiritual energy to shape the future, namely, the cultures belonging to the Late Bronze and Early Iron ages.

South of the Po River, in the present provinces of Emilia and Romagna, was the region of the **Villanova culture** (1000 B.C.), whose golden age occurred during the 7th and 6th centuries B.C. One of the important elements of this culture was cremation of the dead and interment in the noted Villanova urns. Inhumation, as the burial rite, was practiced in isolated cases only. But by the beginning of the 5th century B.C. it already predominated. This indicates that by then Villanova culture was under the influence of Etruscans; yet, this Etruscanization from the last third of the 6th century B.C. encompassed only centres like Felsina, Marzabotto, and Spina. The country-side remained unaffected. The invasion of the Celts into the Po Valley and then into Rome (around 390 B.C.) brought about the end of this culture. The capital, Felsina, was conquered by Celtic Boians and from that time on has been called Bononia (Bologna).

Among the rich cultural bequests of Villanova culture are the situlas with

---

[76] R. Pittioni, op. cit., pp. 292–352. G. Sergi, Italia...op. cit., pp. 122–3.

lids. The art of situla-making originated in the Villanova culture and was later adopted by neighbouring cultures. It reached its perfection at the beginning of 5th century B.C., as seen in the *Certosa situla* and also, at the end of that century, the *Arnoaldi situla*. The close relationship of representations on the Certosa situla with the life of the Villanova people is clearly presented: the parading of troops, two horsemen, musicians with a listener. Especially noteworthy is a farmer with a hook-plough on his back driving a pair of oxen. On the Arnoaldi situla is, among other things, a war chariot pulled by two horses.

In the upper Po Valley, in Piedmont and Lombardy as far as Liguria, spread the **Golasecca culture** (800–150 B.C.). Because of its relatively dispersed character, it lacked internal uniformity but had an active relationship with neighbouring cultures. During the 5th century B.C., Greek wares entered its territory, black-figure pottery came through Villanova and red-decorated pottery through Marseille. Cremation and urn burial was predominant in this culture; in the Ligurian region a stone box (*casetta*) was also used for burial. An interesting find from this era from the beginning of the 7th century B.C. is the ritual waggon (*carrettino*), from the grave in Ca 'Morta. Especially rich in additional objects are two warrior-graves of the 4th or 5th centuries B.C. from Sesto Calende.

From the time of the Celtic invasion, Golasecca culture exhibited Celtic La Tène influences. Rock-drawings in Val Camonica, with representations of warriors and horses, originate from this time.

The farming people of Golasecca culture remained separated, resisting all foreign influences. As is evident from farm and homestead related names that

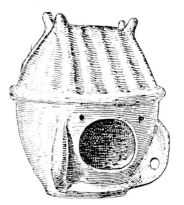 

*Representative urns from the Hallstatt period: **house-urn** (from Saxony), which reflects the belief that the deceased must be given a dwelling that is similar to his home in life; **face-urn** (from Pomerania), that would give the ashes human form again.*

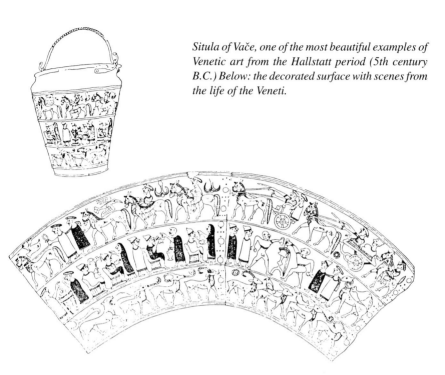

Situla of Vače, one of the most beautiful examples of Venetic art from the Hallstatt period (5th century B.C.) Below: the decorated surface with scenes from the life of the Veneti.

have survived in the Alpine and fore-Alpine regions, they had already specialized in livestock-raising and the utilization of Alpine meadows.

During this period there evolved in southern Tyrol, Vorarlberg (Austria) and the canton Graubünden (Switz.), the **Melaun culture** (800 to 100 B.C.), named after the excavation site near Brixen. With the *Fritzian group* it is also represented in northern Tyrol. The older **Crestaulta culture** appears to have merged into the Melaun, as shown by the excavation site Cresta petschna in Engadine.[77] Cremation was also generally practised. In the pottery from this era the Melaun handle is predominant. Characteristic also are numerous hill settlements and walled-in strongholds.

In the 6th century B.C., Este situla-making became known and was incorporated into the creative process of Melaun culture. Motifs on Melaun situlas show once again riders and men with horses; there is also a boxing or wrestling match. After the invasion of the Celts, La Tène influences from the Po Valley are detectable; however, settling of Celts in the Melaun area has not been proven. No La Tène grave has been found in southern Tyrol.

---

[77] J. Filip, op. cit., p. 248 (Crestaulta).

The provinces of Veneto and Friuli were the core region of the lively and tenacious **Este culture** (800 to 180 B.C.), named after rich grave discoveries southwest of Padova. Cremation was practised generally; inhumation was rare even in later periods. Within this culture, attention should be given the **Lucia Group** (Most na Soči, Slovenia) where many artifacts from around 700 B.C. were discovered.

The Situla—*After 600 B.C., that is, in the second half of the Hallstatt period, an outstanding artistic development appeared among Veneti in the area of the central Alps, the lower Po Valley and the upper Adriatic. The creative aspirations of Veneti were encouraged by contacts with Greeks and Etruscans, but they gave their artistic production a feature of their own, so that apart from Greek arts, Venetic art works became the most important in the early historic period in ancient Europe.*

This artistic activity was spread in a relatively small territory in which cultures already mentioned in this chapter (Villanova, Este, Melaun, Eastern Hallstatt) began to flourish. These cultures had their own characteristics, but they also reveal some common elements; one of these is the production of bronze vessels bearing beautiful decorations made in the toreutic technique.

We are speaking of a small festive vessel called the **situla** *which was used for ritual drinking. In its composition the situla essentially differs from Greek and Etruscan vessels. For this reason archaeologists and art historians gave its production and diffusion a separate name to set it apart from other types of production; they named it "The Art of Situla".*

Among all the situlas which have been excavated and preserved till now, that of Certosa near Bologna (Italy) enjoys the reputation of being the most beautiful. Its features and decorations reflect influences of the Etruscan artistic and spiritual world; for example, the sphinx and other winged animals unrelated to Venetic mythology. This fact is in full agreement with the Etruscanization of the final phase of Villanova culture, as established by archaeology. A more Venetic outward form and symbolism distinguish another very fine situla originating from an unknown location and conserved now in Providence, Rhode Island (U.S.A.).

Many beautiful situlas were also excavated in Slovenia, mainly south of Ljubljana in the Lower Carniola. A world-famous situla was found there in the village of Vače and is the pride of the Slovene National Museum in Ljubljana, where it is now preserved.

In situla art, the situla of Vače represents a very fine example. It deserves our attention not only for its original "northern" flavour, reflecting the vigorous Venetic spirit, but also for its illustrations which are a document of Venetic social life.

Illustrations on the frieze of this situla are depicted in three tiers. In the first tier the horse is the dominant figure. He appears being held on the bridle, put to the carriage or mounted by a rider. The second tier shows scenes from the life of a Venetic prince. Presented are details from his life: drinking, music, inhalation of fragrances. The prince wears a head covering still known and used nowadays which is called the Phrygian cap. The third tier shows animals, mostly deer, marching in a row. Some of the deer are eating plants.

The wavy line which usually divides the tiers is lacking. It appears, however, in other illustrated scenes. As a symbol of life it is depicted on the decoration hanging from the helmet between two wrestlers, the helmet being presumably the award for the winner. It is also on a leaf held in the beak of a bird.

The composition of decorations on this situla does not bear winged beings or other oriental symbols. Even the geometric elements, like meander, are absent. What is even more noticeable is that, in the overall sense, the Venetic art of situla was uninfluenced by the mighty spiritual and artistic world of the Greeks. The influences came only from the neighbouring Etruscans, who were spreading into the Po Valley.

With the end of the Hallstatt period, after 400 B.C., Venetic situla art died out. The following La Tène period was carried by the Celts, who brought their own artistic and cultural contributions.

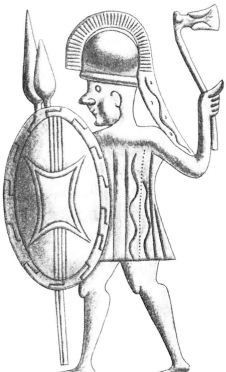

Hallstatt warrior—On a belt buckle from discovery site Vače, Slovenia, 7th century B.C. (Source: F. Stare, Situla I/1960, Supplement).

The Celts occupied the Po Valley but did not conquer the neighbouring Venetic plains nor the Alps where the Veneti survived till the arrival of the Romans and beyond. Why Veneti in the meantime did not continue the production of the situla is still an open question. The likely explanation is that with the end of the Hallstatt, the supply of specialized materials used in the production was no longer available, or else the customary routes of delivery of such materials were disrupted. In any case the end of situla production was probably drawn-out rather than sudden.

The art of situla-making reached its climax in the Este culture. An example is the *Benvenuti situla*, which has motifs showing the spiritual and temporal life of the Este people: mythical beasts, a bird, a horse, a dog, an ox being driven by a man, a man blowing a horn, a man with lances, a war chariot. Among the many animal figures, the horse is predominant, showing the importance and appreciation of the animal within Este culture.

The Celtic invasion was not able to change the core of this culture; only very sparse evidence of Celtic presence is indicated. Even Romanization took place very gradually.

The predominant urn graves and ensuing demonstrable superiority of Veneti in the northern Italian and Alpine cultures do not reveal anything about their Slavic language, especially after the invasion of the Celts around 390 B.C. Ultimately, language is the medium through which the ethnic affiliation of a people survives and is transmitted to successive generations.

If the Venetic language prevailed even in Etruria, where the indigenous population played a decisive role in its cultural development, we would have to assume that Venetic was the dominant language also for the cultures of the Po Valley (Villanova, Golasecca and Este). With the Celtic invasion, however, the situation had changed so that (with the exception of Este culture) the Celtic language predominated in the ruling class, while the Venetic language continued to be spoken among the rural population, surviving into the Roman era. The Venetic (Slavic) toponyms preserved in this region also confirm this course of events.

The name "Veneti", along with the Este culture, survived into Roman times and has been recorded. This name must also be applicable to the cultures of Villanova and Golasecca. Only in the Ligurian Golasecca, i.e., among the people of Liguria, does the presence or absence of Veneti still remain an open question.

The bearers of Melaun culture were the Rhaetians, who also spoke a Venetic language and probably preserved it during the entire Roman period, as demonstrated by the frequency of Venetic names in this region. As we find with the Este Veneti, the Rhaetians also had seven variations of the Etruscan alphabet. It

66

cannot be said with certainty that they borrowed it from the Etruscans, for it may well be that it is simply a case of traditional Venetic characters having developed into an alphabet.

Finally, it is necessary, when examining a culture, its language, and other details to include a study of the farming population. That portion of population that is engaged in farming can often be as high as ninety percent, but that reality is seldom taken into consideration when evaluating a culture; consequently, the researchers convey an incorrect image.

The Hallstatt Period

The strongest expression of the early Iron Age (after 9th century B.C.) in central Europe is represented by the **Hallstatt culture** (800 to 400 and declining until its demise in 15 B.C.). It encompassed an extended area in the plain north of the Alps and eastern Alps, including Alsace, northern Switzerland, Swabia, Bavaria, Austria and Slovenia, the eastern arm reaching Moravia, Pannonia, and Transylvania.[78] The effects of Hallstatt culture on other regions were so strong that the entire early Iron Age in Europe has been designated by archaeologists as the "Hallstatt Age". The territory of this culture is divided into two regions: the western Hallstatt, closely connected with the formation of the Celts, and the eastern Hallstatt, which shows a relationship to Illyrian tribes in the Adriatic area. The excavation site of Hallstatt in Austria, where the name originates, lies approximately on the border line between the two regions.

Hallstatt culture emerged from Urnfield culture and belongs to the Veneti. In its development, however, it received important impulses from the southeast, and during its golden age had connections with Este and Etruscan cultural spheres. There were also trade relations with Scandinavia.

In Hallstatt culture there was wide-ranging production of pottery and bronze vessels, as well as a flourishing goldsmith trade known for great detail and fine workmanship. In the area of ornamentation, the eastern region preferred figural motifs, which often turned into more or less precise geometrical patterns. Among other economic activities of significance is the extraction of salt and the resulting trade. Iron works, though, play the leading role in this culture. Iron from the eastern Alps (later Noricum) was known throughout Europe into the late Roman era, as "Norican iron" valued especially for its hardness and durability.

---

[78] J. Filip, ibid., p. 258 (Hallstattkultur).

Pruning hook, scythe, shovel and fork from the discovery site Idrija pri Bači, Slovenia. Late La Tène period. Tools of this kind are still in use today and corroborate the continuity of farm culture in the eastern Alps.

Out of the original tribe of Veneti, there arose in the Hallstatt culture period two ethnic groups whose names later appear in Roman literature: the *Vindelici* (the western region) and the *Norici* (the eastern region).

The bearers of Hallstatt culture, as already shown, come from Venetic Urnfield ancestry. They were not Illyrians, as German authors assumed up to the 1960's. The Vindelician group, formed in the western region, was settled predominantly in what is today Swabia and Bavaria. After the 5th century B.C., they succumbed to the Celts advancing out of western Switzerland and eastern France. Though merging with them in some degree, the Veneti kept their identity and name into Roman times.

Illyrian cultural influences are detectable among the Norici in the eastern region, though the Illyrian settlement area did not include even present Slovenia. The Latobics in Lower Carniola, Slovenia, were considered by Slovene historians to belong to the Illyrian language group; however, this has never been proven. A great deal of confusion prevailed among historians simply over the question of the expanse of Illyrian territory—a good example is J. Pokorny, who tried to derive the name "Illyrians" from the Bavarian Iller River, inhabitants on the Iller.[79] In this way, the Vindelicians were also able to become an Illyrian ethnic group.

As with the Celts, Illyrians developed an independent cultural identity. Characteristic for them was burial in mound-graves, as we see from the most significant Illyrian discovery site, Glasinac near Sarajevo. The study of these mound-

[79] A. Stipčević, *Gli Illiri*, Milan 1966.

graves allows us to assume that Illyrians, like Teutons, Thracians, Dacians, and others must have already separated at the time of the Mound-grave culture (after 1500 B.C.) from the Proto-Indo-European formation. For a very long time their social organization was the commune and, like the Celts, the Illyrians, compared to the Veneti, were a substantially younger culture group.

At a later time Illyrians too adopted the practice of cremation and urn burial. Their culture was also under the influence of the Greeks who, since the middle of the 8th century B.C., had founded colonies on the Adriatic coast. Illyrian influence moved northward into Slavonia, Croatia, and to the eastern edge of the Alps and Pannonia, where Hallstatt Val culture and its bearers, the Pannonians, held out longer than the Illyrian element.[80]

During the Hallstatt era there were, according to grave discoveries, invasions by Crimeans and later by Scythians from the eastern European steppes, especially into Pannonia. To what extent the Pannonians were able to maintain their own national character as a result of these invasions and Illyrian influences cannot be determined, though it is presumed that the Pannonian/Venetic farming class remained intact into the Roman era. Before the First World War several Slovene linguists concluded that, on the basis of Latinized place-names in Pannonia, the ancient Pannonians were of Slavic lineage.

The La Tène Period

The dividing line between the Early and Late Iron ages in Europe is represented by the migration of the Celts around 400 B.C. This destroyed the cultural framework of the Hallstatt era north and south of the Alps, and thereby disrupted the extensive network of trade connections. Northern Europe, that is, the territory on the North and Baltic seas as well as Scandinavia, became isolated from central Europe.

With the Celtic migration begins the Late Iron Age, or the La Tène period, widely represented by La Tène culture (400 to 15 B.C.). The discovery site of the same name is on Neuchâtel Lake in western Switzerland. The bearers of this culture are Celts, and the influence of La Tène culture was very strong. Its effects were felt even in regions that had never been reached by the Celtic migration; hence the reason the La Tène finds are not always dependable evidence of Celtic presence in the corresponding discovery areas.[81] In central Europe the settling of

---

[80] J. Filip, op. cit., (Illyrier, Ungarn, Bosnien, Kroatien). R. Pittioni, op. cit., p. 355/20.

[81] R. Pittioni, op. cit., p. 328.

Celts is proven in those regions where it was relatively easy for them to advance. They reached out-of-the-way areas and mountainous regions only when there was a good reason to do so; e.g., salt-mines or other prospects.

During the Late Bronze and Hallstatt ages, the population in the Alps was thus able to survive undisturbed until their Romanization. (R. Pittioni).[82]

This is why there were within the Alps, or eastern Alps in particular, relatively few finds from the La Tène period; moreover, they are mixed with Hallstatt finds.[83] For the Alpine people who held their own during the La Tène period, the following Roman era did not necessarily mean Romanization.

The Alps are to be excluded from the theory of Celtic occupation. They have never in a general sense become Celtic. Not even areas like Bavaria, Bohemia, Po Valley, which were conquered by Celts, were completely Celtic. Even in these regions there are numerous Venetic (Slavic), non-Celtic place-names, a clear indication that the older Venetic population persevered and survived Celtic rule.

Concerning the region of Este, available data is not sufficient to allow us to estimate with certainty the relationship of the Veneti to the Celts, and to the succeeding Romans. Latin inscriptions on containers from late Este graves do not furnish any evidence as to the language of the population. They are only a sign of stylistic change, just as are the Celtic names on Este tombstones. This probably means that after the Celtic invasion, Este parents tended to give their children fashionable Celtic names.[84] It seems we are left mostly with unanswered questions regarding this period and the succeeding Roman period.

We cannot completely rule out the possibility that the Celts may have been linguistically quite close to the Veneti, if not actually part of the same ethnic group. They too started on a new road of advancement, developing a strong military organization and exceptional skills in metallurgy and trade. Contact between the older Veneti and the younger Celts was quite remarkable. There was no warfare between them. From all known instances of interaction between the two groups, we see that there was friendly co-existence, this being especially true and obvious in Vindelicia and Bavaria.

We know of the presence of Celts through archaeological finds, but there are no toponyms or place-names of Celtic origin—with the exception of a few compounded from Lahi, Welschen (Ladins), pointing to the presence of Romanized Celts. The names preserved to this day are Venetic (Slavic) in origin. When they are compared with present-day Celtic language on the Atlantic coast, there is

---

[82] R. Pittioni, ibid., p. 328/60.

[83] B. Grafenauer, *Zgodovina...*op. cit., p. 133.

[84] R. Pittioni, op. cit., p. 360.

almost no similarity; in a few instances some common meaning is detected through Indo-European roots. From this we can deduce that the Celtic language in Brittany is actually the language of the pre-Venetic, pre-Celtic population. Later arrivals, the Veneti and after them the Celts, were both absorbed linguistically into the indigenous population—showing the vitality and strength of their culture, which had already in the Late Stone Age (around 2000 B.C.) expressed its creative power by raising the extraordinary dolmens and menhirs.

Just as the Celts before them, the Romans maintained forts and fortified settlements, from where they were able to control strategically important roads and bridges. The Veneti were free to conduct agriculture and to raise livestock as before; that is, after they had turned over to the occupying forces the prescribed quantity of their products. The Romans also had good reason not to burden the farmers excessively, for fear they might revolt or move to other regions, which would have resulted in great difficulties for the settlements and the army.

The Roman culture started with the Roman occupation, confining itself first to towns and gradually moving outward, but even the city of Aquilea (Slovene— Oglej) in Friuli must have had a predominantly indigenous population, since their municipal god Belin (Belenus) was also the sun-god of the Venetic Carns and the Norici.

The Romanization of the Empire proceeded gradually, first in those areas where the army, civil service and Italic colonies were established. It happened in the province of Venetia as well as Vindelicia, Pannonia, and later in Rhaetia. To what extent Romanization was successful and when it was completed is uncertain. In some areas it occurred through Christianization as late as the early Middle Ages. Only Noricum met with another fate.

The Veneti

The West Slavic group (the Veneti) retained its ancient, Proto-Slavic vocabulary, while the ancestors of the East and South Slavs underwent new stages of development.

(C. Verdiani)[85]

In the region extending from the Baltic Sea to the Adriatic, the Po River region and farther south into the Apennines, numerous Slovene or Slavic names aroused the attention of linguists and other researchers during the last century. Today their statements appear to us in a new light, mainly because archaeologists have shown that the bearers of the Urnfield culture came from Lusatia and were, according to linguistic research, Proto-Slavic Veneti or Wends. Included in this research is the study *Staroitalia slavjanská/* The Slavic Ancient Italy by Jan Kollár (Vienna 1853).[86] The author was without doubt inspired by a romantic Pan-Slavism which is apparent in his other papers. His work must be viewed critically, but should not be overlooked.

We are once more confronted with the problem of ideology and its influence on scientific research, whereby historical interpretations serve national or political goals. The history of central Europe has been marked since the last century by two ideologies with recognizable official status: German nationalism and Pan-Slavism.

The History Schools

In the first half of the last (19th) century, the universities in Europe established History Schools, which developed their own specialized methods of work and research. Their general intention was to research the historical past, but they also examined deeply the history and culture of their own nations. This study was until then neglected by Latin and Church oriented sciences.

---

[85] C. Verdiani, *Il problema dell' origine degli Slavi/* The Question of the Origins of the Slavs, Florence 1951, p. 77.

[86] Not even the Yugoslav Encyclopedia (Zagreb 1962) indicates this study under Jan Kollár. The Brockhaus Enzyklopädie (Wiesbaden 1970) states among other things, that Kollár

In the latter half of the last century, the History Schools received a strong nationalistic stamp. Their intention was no longer to discover the history and culture of their own nations with the help of new, improved methods, but to *create* the kind of history that would assure prestige or even superiority. Uncovering historical truths became of secondary importance.

The ideological foundations established in the last century by the History Schools have remained with us to this day. The writing of Slovene history was influenced primarily by the German and Czech Schools, through the Universities of Vienna, Graz, and Prague. The Slovenes never developed their own, independent History School.

The principal contribution of the **German History School** was the development of the work method used in their research. This method was deeply permeated with nationalistic spirit and was soon applied to linguistics, law and history. The three disciplines were considered as one unified science; major contributions were made during the second half of the last century under K.F. Eichorn and F.K. Savigny. It continued to intensify and set the tone around the turn of the century with the "settlement archaeological method" developed by Gustav Kossinna. His so-called "lex Kossinna" had a profound influence not only on ensuing German historiography, but on European history-writing in general.

According to the Kossinna school, ancestors of the Germans were the Indo-Germanic people, who were to be equated with Indo-Europeans. Only the Celts, Romans, and Germanic people were seen as the bearers of European culture. Slavs, on the other hand, who came out of the Pripet swamps in the 6th century, and consequently were at an amazingly low level of civilization, could have adopted their culture only from the central European culture-bearers.

Under the pretext of bringing culture and progress to the "unhistorical, primitive" Slavs, the Germans justified their nationalistic eastward expansion and the so-called bridge to the Adriatic.

The negative effects of the Kossinna school have not been totally overcome. The "Indo-Germanic" theory has left its jargon in a large number of books, dictionaries and encyclopedias, which serve as reference material for new works, especially in Western Europe and North America. The reader who is unfamiliar with Slavic languages, and cannot independently study opposing points of view, will be seriously misled by the above books and materials.

---

was the founder of romantic pan-Slavism and an author of pseudoscientific works. The Lessico Universale Italiano (Rome 1973) mentioned the study with the observation that the author "discovered" evidence of Slavs in northern Italy.

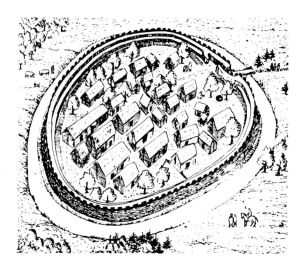

Lusatian fortified settlement from the beginning of the Iron Age, at Zly Komorow/Senftenberg. (Reconstruction).

In the historiography of Slavic nations the **Czech History School** was predominant until the First World War, advocated by such well-known names as F.J. Šafařik, J. Dobrovsky, and especially L. Niederle, whose work met with strong approval. His views regarding the period when the Slavs emerged as an ethnic group were put forward in his principal work *Slovanské starožitnosti/* Slavic Antiquity, Prague 1902-24. Based on anthropological, linguistic, ethnological, and historical data, he placed the original homeland of the Slavs in the broad area that reached from the Elbe River in the west to the Dnieper in the east. Within this territory of the ancient Slavic homeland several regions could be considered, including present Poland or the southern part of Byelorussia as far as Kiev and Podolia. He placed the ancient Slavic homeland in the Carpathian hinterland and stated that they settled in the region which they occupy today in the 2nd or 3rd, or even in the 1st century A.D. (see H. Tuma).[87]

Niederle's interpretations resulted in repudiation of the autochthonists (especially among the Austro-Slavs), who saw in the ancestors of Slavs the original inhabitants of Europe. The Slavs' settlement area was to have extended from the Urals to the Atlantic; thus Etruria (Kollár), the seven hills of Rome and the cultures of Scythians and Sarmatians were Slavic. This means the Slavs were equated with the Indo-European people in regard to language, as should be the case today, since Slavic nations can be linguistically traced directly to Indo-European roots. Other ethnic groups in Europe have already greatly distanced themselves

---

[87] H. Tuma, Krajevno imenoslovje, op. cit., p. 128.

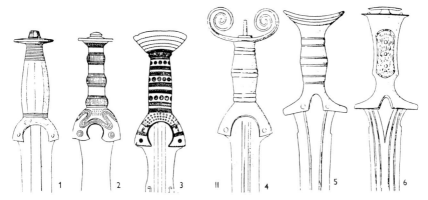

Full-handle swords from the Urnfield period in the region between the Baltic and Adriatic Seas: 1. Riegsee type 2. Liptov type 3. bowl-shaped type 4. antennae type 5. Moringen type 6. Auvernier type (Source: J. Filip, Enzykl. Handbuch z. Ur- und Frühgeschichte Europas, 1969).

from this original position. It is a theory which has not been seriously examined by linguists.

The **Russian History School,** represented by such prominent names as I.I. Barsov, I.P. Filevič, and A.I. Pogodin, had similar interpretations to those of Niederle. This school assumed that the Germanic people had indeed settled west of the Vistula River. Later, the views of A.A. Shachmatov became prevalent. He had placed the ancient homeland of the Slavs much farther to the north; i.e., the upper basin of the Nemen River and West Dvina, to the Wolchov River and Ilmen Lake. Later the ancient Slavs were to have moved westward into the area of the Vistula, where they found their second homeland, abandoning the first to the Baltic people.

After the Soviet Revolution in Russia (1917), J. Marr founded a new History School and thereby brought about new theories based on Marxist views. According-ing to his interpretations, the Slavs were an autochthonous people who had not come to Europe from anywhere; rather, they had developed from tribal and lan-guage groups which lived in the area from the central part of the Dnieper River, westwards as far as the Elbe and from the Baltic sea southward to the Carpathians. After the Second World War, Soviet historiography changed Marr's views; the older thesis about the original homeland of the Slavs being in the Carpathian hinterland was again accepted.[88]

---

[88] See B.A. Rybakov, *Yazichestvo drevnih slavyan/* Paganism of Ancient Slavs, Moscow 1981, pp. 222–223.

Russian and Soviet interpretations about the Slavic homeland agree with German views on this question, though for different reasons. Russia wants to be known as the cradle of all Slavs who advanced from there into the Balkans and hence into the eastern Alps.

At the time of the First World War, this position became the foundation of Pan-Slavism and South Slavic unitarianism, while German nationalistic circles persistently sought to emphasize the cultural inferiority of Slavic people. The real purpose of this view was to facilitate the German advance into Slavic lands, and at the same time represent it as a culture-bearing mission. Pan-Slavism, too, set up far-reaching goals. A common nation of South Slavs united with the greater family of Slavs from Trst (Trieste) to Vladivostok was portrayed to the Austro-Slavic people as salvation from the German yoke. History was expected to confirm that a greater family of Slavs with its core in the Carpathian hinterland—in Russia—had once existed.

After the First World War, this concept took on a more or less obvious form of Yugoslav centralism—a form of overriding ideological necessity. The search for the historical roots of the Slovenes, who do not belong to the South Slavic but rather to the West Slavic nations, is therefore represented as something politically suspicious (separatism) and cannot expect to merit scientific criticism.

After the First World War the **Polish History School** began to examine, beyond prescribed ideological boundaries, the question of the origin of Slavs.

The founders of the Polish School were J. Kostrzewski and L. Kozłowski (early history), J. Czekanowski, and K. Stojanowski (anthropology, ethnology) and T. Lehr-Spławiński (comparative linguistics). In 1922 this school took as its starting point the assumption that *Lusatian culture constituted the foundation of historical development of the Proto-Slavs.* The Polish researchers conducted lengthy investigations involving M. Rudnicki (linguistics) and K. Moszyński (ethnology). Lehr-Spławiński coordinated, compiled, and published the results of this research after the Second World War (1946–48).[89]

These Polish scholars were undoubtedly guided in their research by national pride but, with the exception of a few ideas that may seem extreme, they were more consistent than their German or Russian counterparts. The assumption that Slavs already existed between the Oder and the Vistula around 2000 B.C. is pos-

---

[89] Cf. C. Verdiani, *Il problema...*op. cit., 31–33, where he quotes the works of Lehr-Spławiński *O pochodzeniu i praojczyznie Słowian/* The Origins and Ancient Homeland of the Slavs, Poznan 1946, and *Zagadnienie pochodzenia Słowian w świetle nauki polskiej i rosyjskiej/* The Problem of the Origin of Slavs in the Light of Polish and Russian Research, Warsaw 1948, and other works.

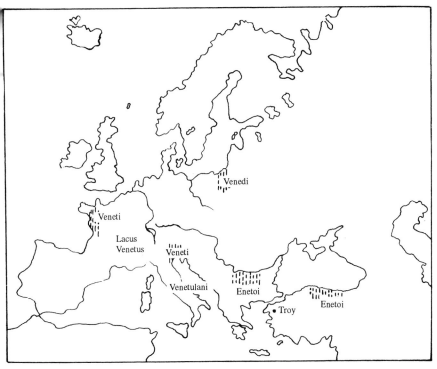

The areas for which Greek and Latin writers mention Veneti. The earliest historic reference is to Enetoi in Asia Minor, Paphlagonia; they are mentioned as allies of Troy by Homer (9th century B.C.).

sibly one of those views. Their thesis on Slavic beginnings in the Lusatian culture was, as expected, persistently rejected by German historians and is therefore generally not accepted by historians in the West.[90] It is also disregarded by Pan-Slavic circles, which still hold to the theory of the ancient Slavic homeland in the Carpathian hinterland; i.e., Russia.

Polish authors (e.g., Lehr-Spławiński)[91] first of all refer in their discourse to historical documents in which the Proto-Slavs can be presumed. The Neurs in the region of the upper and central Dnieper, the northwestern neighbours of the Scythians (mentioned by Herodotus in the 5th century B.C.), as well as the

---

[90] Brockhaus Enzyklopädie, op. cit., 1970 (Lausitzer Kultur).

[91] C. Verdiani, op. cit., pp. 42–53.

Veneti—Vinidae, Uenedai—(mentioned in the first to second century by Pliny the Elder, Ptolomy, and Tacitus), were Proto-Slavs. On the basis of comparative linguistics, prehistoric archaeology, and original river names, Polish researchers give us the following results of their combined studies :

The Corded-pottery culture (Battle-Axe culture) appeared in central Europe during the last third of the neolithic period (2000–1700 B.C.). Its bearers migrated east over the Oder River into the region of the Comb-marked-pottery culture, which was common among Finno-Ugric tribes.

As a result of this meeting of the two cultures in the region between the Oder and Vistula Rivers, there emerged another culture within which the Proto-Slavs developed. East of here, as far as the Volga and Oka, where the original Comb-pottery culture had succumbed to the stronger Battle-Axe culture, a culture and language group developed in which the Proto-Balts are recognized. After 1700 B.C. new ethnic groups migrated eastward giving momentum to the Únětice culture (in Bohemia). From this developed the Lusatian culture (latter Bronze Age, 1300–1100 B.C.) within which the language and ethnic identity of Proto-Slavs were conclusively formed.

Lusatian culture at no time extended in the east over the anthropo-geographical boundary on the Bug River; thus resulted a gradual breakdown of language unity between the Proto-Slavs and Proto-Balts. The bearers of Lusatian culture were Proto-Slavs, historically known as Veneti or Wends.

With Horse and Sword

Polish science gives its attention in further studies predominantly to the area of present Poland and neighbouring regions. In spite of unanswered questions in many areas that are still under review and in need of detailed clarification, the generally ideology-free Polish archaeological and linguistic studies have confirmed two fundamental points of departure for this present study. They are:

1) *Lusatian culture is to be regarded as the foundation on which the development of Proto-Slavs or Veneti took place; and*
2) *the Veneti or Wends are to be regarded as bearers of the ensuing Urnfield culture, which spread outward into the different areas of Europe, including the Mediterranean region.*

The ruins of fortified settlements in the area of Lusatian culture show that its bearers possessed a strong military organization and often battled with neighbouring Scythian and Germanic tribes.[92] Through archaeological discoveries in eastern central Europe, i.e., in the area of Lusatian culture, we have evidence of the heavy, **full-handle sword** made of bronze (15th to 13th century B.C.)[93] and the domesticated horse.[94] Both of these were very useful in battle. Such equipment made it possible for the bearers of Urnfield culture, the Veneti, to quickly advance into the broad expanse of European territory.

The Greek, Euripides, (Athenian tragic dramatist) mentions in his work *Hippolyt*, 5th century B.C., that the Veneti were exceptionally **skilled horse-breeders**. In the Venetic cultures of Villanova, Golasecca, Este, and Hallstatt the horse was the most frequently represented animal. Heavy work horses and even race horses from Noricum (eastern Alps) were well known during Roman times.[95]

To what extent the Veneti initiated military campaigns and mass migrations during the Urnfield age cannot be exactly determined. Bearers of the Urnfield culture are to be found in a region that extends from Iberia to Britain, from the Apennines to Scandinavia, and not just in central Europe where they had a dense settlement. Archaeological discoveries bear witness to the invasions of Aryan tribes during the 13th century B.C., incursions that had shaken the ancient civilizations of the Mediterranean area. In this way the prospering late Minoan culture on Crete was destroyed. Full-handle swords, similar to those of central Europe from this period, have been unearthed there. Troy was also destroyed (archaeologically Troy VII). The advancing Phrygians brought an end to the Hittite empire in Anatolia. The Egyptian Pharaoh, Ramses III, struck down the attack of Aryan Philistines who later settled in Palestine (1190 B.C.). Their specialty was iron-smithing.

Several place-names in the east could derive from these military and settle-

---

[92] Brockhaus Enzyklopädie, op. cit., (Lausitzer Kultur).

[93] The Encyclopaedia Britannica (Europe, Ancient). J. Filip, (schwert) citing: H. Müller-Karpe, *Die Vollgriffschwerter der Urnenfelderzeit aus Bayern/* The Full-handle Swords of the Urnfield Period from Bavaria, 1961. After having stated the finding places (Riegsee–upper Bavaria, Milavče–Bohemia, Baierdorf–Lower Austria), the archaeologist considers the Riegsee sword as the oldest of the bronze swords with full handle originating from the eastern part of central Europe, approx. in the 13th century B.C. The shields used at that time were made of bronze and wood, cf. J. Filip, ibid., (Schild).

[94] J. Filip, ibid., (Pferd). The excavations carried out in central Europe tell us about the importance of the horse in the Lusatian culture where it was used not only for riding but also for pulling implements. Its domestication is supposed to have been carried out on the steppes of Central Asia in the Late Neolithic.

[95] G. B. Pellegrini, A. L. Prosdocimi, op. cit., p. 327. R. Pittioni, op. cit., p. 312. E. Polaschek, Paulys Real-Encyclopädie, op. cit., (Noricum), p. 1044.

ment campaigns; e.g., Tabor (*tabor*—a fortress, camp) in Palestine, or Suez (*zvez*—connection, road). They indicate that the language of the invading Aryans in the Near East and the languages of the modern Slavs or Slovenes in particular are related.

After the Urnfield migration, the Veneti preserved their ethnic unity and for the most part their language for a whole millennium. Greek and Roman authors quote their names along with those of other peoples in numerous lands:[96]

1. **The Veneti in Paphlagonia** *(northern coastal area of Asia Minor), mentioned in the 9th century by Homer in the Iliad (B 852). Philemon from the race of the Eneti (Enetoi), leader of the Paphlagonians, rushed with a platoon to help besieged Troy. All Greek and Latin authors who mention Veneti in their writings more or less directly rely on this report. Since there was no* v *in Greek, they also wrote Heneti; the letter* h *here stands for the* digamma, *a sound between* b *and* v.

2. **The Veneti in Illyricum** *were the Veneti on the lower Danube, referred to by Herodotus (I, 196) under the name Enetoi in the 5th century B.C. His record served historians until recently by identifying the Veneti with Illyrians; after the Second World War linguists determined that these were two different language groups.*

3. **The Veneti on the upper Adriatic,** *also mentioned by Herodotus (V, 9). The Latin authors call them Veneti. They repeat the story of this Venetic group, taken by their legendary leader Antenor into the region on the upper Adriatic after the destruction of Troy.*

4. **The Veneti in central Europe,** *mentioned by Tacitus (Ger., 64) as well as by Pliny the Elder (IV, 97) as Veneti, Venethi or Venedi and by Ptolemy (III, 5) as Uenedai. In the 2nd century A.D. Ptolemy cited the Venetic Bay (near Gdansk) and Venetic Mountains (in Masuria, northeastern Poland).*

5. **The Veneti in Gaul (Brittany),** *mentioned by Caesar, Pliny the Elder, Strabo, Ptolemy and Casius Dio. This Venetic group also founded their settlement called Venedotia or Gwynedh in Britain.*

6. **The Lacus Venetus** *was the name given by Pomponius Mela (III, 24) in the first century for Lake Constance/Bodensee. The possibility that this name could be derived from "vanam" (water), or meaning light blue, does not detract from the historical significance of the above designation (Giovani Battista Pellegrini); however, it is much more appropriate to derive "Boden" from "vode" (waters) still used in the Slovene language.*

7. **The Veneti in Latium,** *who are referred to by Pliny the Elder (III, 69) under the name "Venetulani." Archaeology confirms the presence of an Aryan people (G. Sergi) in the Alban Hills and in Rome.*

---

[96] G.B. Pellegrini, A.L. Prosdocimi, ibid., pp. 237–240.

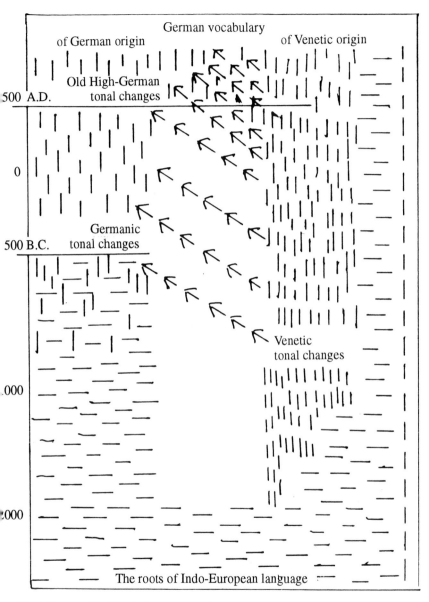

The influence of the Venetic language on the German language, whose vocabulary is only one third of Germanic origin. (E. Röth, Sind wir Germanen?, 1967, 264).

In the 1960's German linguists (H. Krahe, H. Kronasser) also recognized Venetic as an independent language, after they had insisted for almost a hundred years that central Europe had been inhabited by the Illyrians during the pre-Celtic era. They were to have been the bearers of Urnfield and Hallstatt cultures.[97] There are no known relics of Venetic language other than inscriptions found in northeastern Italy and Slovenia. These had been much studied but never deciphered until the Slovene linguist and academician Matej Bor discovered the method and deciphered many of them. Italian linguists believe that they have found Venetic roots for word groups in the Latin language; however, they did not compare them with Slavic vocabulary, which is closest to the Indo-European. Thus, they were not able to determine the original meaning of the words. This work method prevailed because of the preferred position that Slavs developed as the last language community in Europe. When a comparison with Slavic languages is unavoidable, they customarily use the term "Indo-European"; thus it was possible to bypass the Slavic origin of the Veneti. In other words, it was a heavily politicized work-method.

The Veneti as Slovenes

With a study based on a more scientific method, it will be difficult to avoid recognizing that the name Veneti refers to the Proto-Slavs, and that the terms "Indo-European" and "Proto-Slavic" are closely related.

"The ethnic name 'Veneti' had spread over a broad area, coinciding with the finds of Urnfield burials....In the Germanic world the name 'Veneti' is used to designate the neighbouring Slavs as well as Balts....The appearance of the Veneti is equated with the time period of the 'conquerors, organizers'....Wherever we find the name Veneti, there we find organized people, with the Indo-European language tradition, who, in comparison to other ethnic groups, must be designated as 'victorious.' The nationality of Veneti held its ground in the centre of the region and drove out to the periphery of the Celtic and Indo-European area the older designation, 'Aryans'...". (G. Devoto).[98]

---

[97] G.B. Pellegrini, A.L. Prosdocimi, ibid., p. 248, citing H. Krahe, *Von Illyrischen zum Alteuropäischen, Methodologische Betrachtungen zur Wandlung des Begriffes "Illyrisch"*/ From the Illyrian to the Ancient European, Methodological Observations of the Changes of the Concept "Illyrian", Indogermanische Forschungen LXIX (1964), pp. 201–212, and particularly: H. Kronasser, Illyrier und Illyricum, Die Sprache XI (1965), pp. 155–183.

[98] G.B. Pellegrini, A.L. Prosdocimi, ibid., p. 243, citing G. Devoto, *Gli antefatti del latino*

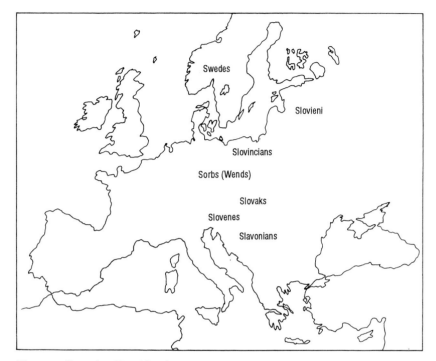

The name Sloveni or Veneti has been preserved in various forms only by their direct descendants, the West Slavs.

One more point should be made regarding the present-day situation: "The West Slavs and their dialects derive from Proto-Slavic ancestry." (C. Verdiani).[99]

There have been many attempts to explain the name "Veneti". It has been derived, for example, from "to be victorious" *vincere* (G. Devoto). Another meaning ascribed to it is "great nation" (Lehr-Spławiński). Some want to explain it through *vendere*—to sell, or through Proto-Slavic *veti*—greater, or Celtic *uindos*—white. None of these makes much sense, but the derivation from Slovenci is logical and direct. The original name, Slovenet(c)i, was changed to Veneti by

---

Venus ei problemi delle omofonie indoeropee/ The Early History of the Latin Venus and the Problems of the Indo-European Homophony, in *Studi...*Schiaffini, Rome 1965, pp. 444–452.

[99] C. Verdiani, *Il problema...*op. cit., p. 258.

other ethnic groups for linguistic reasons, as will be explained in detail by Bor at another place in this work.[100]

It is surprising how both names, "Sloveni" and "Veneti", coincide from a historical and geographical standpoint. Both names have remained only among West Slavs, who had originated from Proto-Slavs and are both preserved in the following forms: Slovenci (Slovenes), Slavonci (Slavonians in Croatia), Slováci (Slovaks), Slovincians (Pomeranians), also Wends (Lusatian Sorbs), Slovieni on the Ilmen Lake and near Novgorod in northwestern Russia, who were mentioned in the beginning of the 12th century by Nestor in his chronicle.[101]

On the western periphery of the Slavic world, from the upper Adriatic to the Baltic sea, the names "Veneti" and "Wends" appear even today. The West Slavic languages in this region have preserved certain ancient peculiarities; e.g., the characteristic **Proto-Slavic consonant pair tl and dl,** as in the Slovene dialect of the Zilja Valley (Gail) in Carinthia: *šidlo*—awl, *močidlo*—damp field, or the common Slovene word *dleto*—chisel, *pletla je*—she knitted or braided. The same consonant pair is retained in the northwest Russian dialect of Pskow; i.e., in the region of the "Slovieni" (Nestor).[102] Archaeologists have also determined that the ancestors of the "Slovieni" had come into this region in the 2nd and 3rd century A.D. from the area of the Venedic culture in central Poland (Przeworsk group).[103]

Thus the original name "Sloveni" accompanied the Veneti from the beginning. In the Middle Ages they were differentiated very clearly from other Slavic peoples. Their settlements in the river basins of the Regnitz and the Main in central Germany were called "Ratenuuinida" and "Moinuuinida", whereas the neighbouring Czechs were called "Beouuinida". This name has survived among Germans, as did the distinction between the *Beheim* (Czechs) and the *Vint* (Slovenes),[104] showing that the Czech people developed from two ethnic or culture groups—the Celtic Boians and the Proto-Slavic Veneti.

The ancient name, *Slovenec* (from Slovenet), is derived from **slovo**, which means in the Slavic languages "word". Thus, Slovenec means the person whose word or language is understandable to me. The derivation with the meanings

---

[100] Z. Golab, *The Oldest name of the Slavs,* The Journal of the Indo-European Studies, 1975.

[101] C. Verdiani, op. cit., p. 92.

[102] F. Ramovš, *Kratka zgodovina slovenskega jezika/* A Short History of the Slovene Language, Ljubljana 1936, p. 93.

[103] C. Verdiani, op. cit., p. 93.

[104] G. B. Pellegrini, A.L. Prosdocimi, op. cit., p. 239.

"sons of Slava" (using "word" to mean honor, or a supposed Slavic deity), or "inhabitants on a Slova River" in some ancient homeland, have no foundation.[105] As already mentioned, it is incorrect to refer to the inhabitants on the Iller River as Illyrians.

On their western boundary the Slavs were encountering a people whose language they did not understand therefore calling them Nemci (Germans); this designation is related to the word *nem*—mute, incomprehensible. Considered from the historical standpoint, we cannot say how old it is but it must have been in use since prehistoric times, as it is found in all Slavic languages. However, in historical source-material the name "Germani" is to be found first.

The well-known German archaeologist, Kossinna, associated the origin of the Germanic people with the "Aryans" (Indo-Germanic people) in the 2nd millennium B.C. His views of early history were entirely subservient to German nationalistic goals. His teachings were intensified by his followers and when they later divided prehistoric culture groups strictly along Kossinna's ethnic models, they fell into sharp disagreement with Polish researchers after the First World War. The German side particularly rejected the affiliation of Lusatian culture with the Proto-Slavs.

The first culture that can most probably be archaeologically attributed to the Germanic people is the Jastorf culture, a collective term for various groups represented in the area west of Hanover and on the sea coast, dispersed over the central Elbe region and as far as Mecklenburg, Schleswig-Holstein, and Jutland. Its development since the early Hallstatt age occurred parallel to La Tène culture in western and central Europe. It arose primarily from an older, indigenous culture, which was strongly influenced by Urnfield culture. Gradually Jastorf culture adopted more La Tène tendencies and became predominantly Celtic. The initial extended family or commune form of internal organization remained longer in force among German tribes than among those European peoples who had earlier contact with the southern cultural environment. Since La Tène period, the economic and social development of the Germanic people progressed along a rapid course.[106]

As we can see from the example of Germanic tribes, the course of development of an emerging people can be rather drawn-out. The language was formed already through differentiation within related tribes; but we can speak of a people only when the group has developed its material and intellectual culture to a level of unity, when it is able to act outwardly in a coherent and independent

---

[105] F. Ramovš, op. cit., pp. 4–5
[106] J. Filip, op. cit., (Jastorfkultur), (Germanen).

manner. This is possible without a separate language; what is important is the sense of belonging to a given group. In certain cases, this is still so even today (for example, the Germans in Alsace are French).

Language and Nations

Around 2000 B.C., Indo-Europeans presented themselves in their proto-form as the oldest people of central Europe; i.e., as Vinidi or (according to older terminology) Illyrians. They were well organized as is evident from the graves of their leaders—the aristocracy of the time. Linguists think that it was probably at this time that the division of dialects and later languages began, forming the kentum (centum) and the satem languages. This division is clearly a result of great distances on the far-flung European continent and the influence of Finno-Ugric Comb-pottery cultures.

The split within the satem Balto-Slavic language group occurred about 1700 B.C., resulting in the Proto-Baltic and Proto-Slavic language groups. In the domain of the Proto-Slavic group, there arose during the second half of the Bronze Age in Bohemia the Únětice culture, which merged after 1300 B.C. with Lusatian culture. The latter is not only the linguistic but also the material and intellectual foundation of the strong social structure of Vinidi or Veneti. A strong military organization had been developed as a result of a need for defence. Archaeologists have discovered in central Europe traces of frequent invasions from the east European steppes dating to approximately 1500 B.C. For the first time, domesticated horses appeared and were used to a great advantage in defence against these invasions.

The raising of horses during early history meant a major change in the life of tribal groups. The attackers could cover great distances in a relatively short time, and those under attack were forced to build fortifications, assemble supplies of food and other provisions necessary for defence or counter-attack; here, too, the horse and sturdy weapons, especially swords, were necessary. These developments were prominent in Lusatia and afterwards in the Urnfield culture.

The Vinidi or Veneti or Sloveni that developed out of the above-mentioned cultures represent the trunk from which other Slavic groups branched out. These do not necessarily represent new language groups; rather, they indicate new culture groups. Such a group was from 700 to 400 B.C. the *Vysock culture* widely distributed on the upper Dniester and central Dnieper.[107] The people of this cul-

---

[107] C. Verdiani, op. cit., p. 87 passim.

ture, mentioned by Herodotus in the 5th century B.C., were the Navari. From 400 to 100 B.C., they were displaced by the Przeworsk group, which afterwards, in the 2nd to 3rd centuries A.D., spread northward into the swampy Pripet, and united there with the *Zarubincy culture* (probably Proto-Slavic). Out of this developed the present-day East Slavic language group.

Archaeologists inform us that the Slavs invaded the Balkan peninsula as early as the 2nd century A.D. In the 4th century, the Huns penetrated this area after having already destroyed the empire of the Goths. In the middle of the 5th century, the power of the Huns was shattered. There followed a large Slavic settlement movement coming out of two directions into the Balkans: from the east over the Carpathian Mountains, along the Tisa River, and through the plains of Wallachia, and also from the north across Pannonia into the western Balkans. The dividing line between the two settlement waves is still unresolved.[108] After they crossed the Danube and entered the Byzantine Empire, their advance onto the Balkan peninsula is well documented. During the reign of Justinian I (527–565) Byzantium had been threatened by the Slavs, who advanced as far as Greece and even settled on the Peloponnesus and several Aegean islands. Out of this settlement movement the South Slavs gradually evolved.

The Gothic historian Jordanes, writing around 550 about the origin and exploits of the Goths (Getica, 34–35), mentioned three ethnic groups which can today be recognized as Slavic: **Venedi**, as a general designation as well as the ethnic group occupying the broad region as far east as the Vistula River; **Sclaveni**, the group occupying the territory from the mouth of the Sava River to the Danube delta; **Antes**, those living between the Dniester and Dnieper Rivers.[109] This description coincides closely with the present classification of the West, South and East Slavs.

At this time the ancestors of the Slovenes could not have moved out of the settlement area of the South Slavs in the Balkans into the eastern Alps. Neither documentary sources nor archaeological discoveries report such move.[110] The relatively close relationship of Slovene with South Slavic languages, especially with Kajkavian, (the old dialect of the Slavonians—north Croatia) reflects the

---

[108] J. Filip, op. cit., (Slawen, Südslawen).

[109] C. Verdiani, op. cit., p. 66.

[110] The Byzantine historical sources report battles with the Balkan Slavs. These reports were applied by German as well as Slovene historians to the Carantanians, the ancestors of Slovenes. Needless to say, those events had no connection with Carantanians in the eastern Alps. Carantanians were not an extension of South Slavs; they are descendants of the West Slavic Veneti and had a separate and different historical development.

influence of the West Slavic, Slovene language on the development of Kajkavian, and in a lesser degree on other South Slavic languages. Out of these conditions apparently arose the Koszthely culture (6th–8th century) in West Pannonia, which cannot be ascribed to the Avars since it came about from the merging of Romanized tribal remnants and South Slavic newcomers. As a result of the settlement movement of the Shtokavian dialect group (Serbian) from the east, beginning in the 14th century, the Kajkavian dialect was pushed back to the edge of Slavonia (Croatia).

From the foregoing we can represent development of the Slavic nations in the following manner:

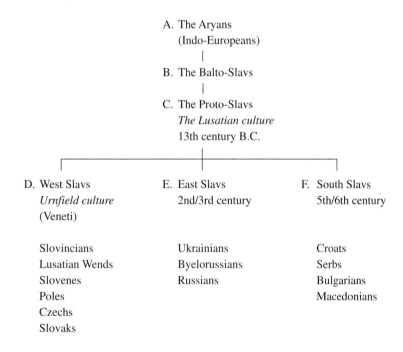

A. The Aryans
   (Indo-Europeans)

B. The Balto-Slavs

C. The Proto-Slavs
   The Lusatian culture
   13th century B.C.

D. West Slavs	E. East Slavs	F. South Slavs
Urnfield culture	2nd/3rd century	5th/6th century
(Veneti)		
Slovincians	Ukrainians	Croats
Lusatian Wends	Byelorussians	Serbs
Slovenes	Russians	Bulgarians
Poles		Macedonians
Czechs		
Slovaks		

The relationship C-D is certain, as shown by the common developmental line of the ethnic groups. "The obvious relationship of their languages in the area of grammatical structure and vocabulary is not found in any other Aryan group of languages."[111]

---

[111] C. Verdiani, op. cit., p. 21.

The Slovene Language as a Testimony

The **Slovene language** belongs to West Slavic languages; that is, to the Proto-Slavic Veneti. It retained the Proto-Slavic foundation for a very long time. As can be clearly seen from the Brižinski Spomeniki/ Freising Manuscripts representing the Slovene language of the early 10th century, it was not substantially different from the Proto-Slavic (Toporišič).[112] The South Slavic language group, on the other hand, developed in its new homeland in the Balkans.[113] The Slovene language distinguishes itself from South Slavic languages through preservation of Proto-Slavic characteristics, and even through its lexical relationship with Baltic languages.

"There is more than enough evidence to convince us that the basis of the Slovene language is of the North Slavic type (i.e., West Slavic, author), which from the very beginning has developed under South Slavic influence." (F. Bezlaj).[114]

"When searching for the meaning of a Slovene word that has no Slavic affinities and no corresponding Romanic, Germanic, or Hungarian connection can be found, I develop the most probable Proto-Slavic reconstruction, then transfer this into Proto-Baltic and thence derive the modern Lithuanian or Latvian; it is no surprise to me when I find that the result corresponds with the meaning in the Slovene language...". (Bezlaj).[115]

Besides the lexical relationship with the Baltic languages, Slovene exhibits still other Proto-Slavic characteristics: the **dual**, as with the Wends in Lusatia; **the supine**, as with the Czechs; **the genitive in the negative form**, as found in the Balto-Slavic group.[116] The large number of dialects, forty-six altogether, revealsthe great age of the Slovene language, as is not the case with any other

---

[112] J. Toporišič, *Slovenski knjižni jezik I/* The Slovene Literary Language I, Maribor 1965, p. 39.

[113] F. Ramovš, *Kratka zgodovina...*op. cit., p. 95.

[114] F. Bezlaj, *Eseji o slovenskem jeziku/* Essays on the Slovene Language, Ljubljana 1967, p.122.

[115] F. Bezlaj in the magazine *Naši razgledi* (Ljubljana, 20th Oct. 1980, p. 588) and ibid., about the political repression: At a Belgrade congress, where I spoke about the importance of the Slovene Studies (not the Slavic Studies), I was told to see the president, Aleksandar Belić. His statement to me was, that there would be serious consequences...When I got home to Ljubljana, the Serb dominated department tried to open a disciplinary inquiry against me...They also sabotaged my lectures at the University of Ljubljana, Slovenia.

[116] C. Verdiani, op. cit., p. 36.

Slavic language; Slovene distinguishes itself in this respect from South Slavic languages which, being much younger, exhibit in comparison relatively little change from region to region. Then too, there is the **stress on the penult** which, compared with South Slavic languages, gives Slovene a completely different melody. And finally, the "r" in the Slovene words kdor, kar, kakor, odkoder and nikamor, is not found in South Slavic languages and points to its northern origin. In Slovene, all the reflections of the ancient Proto-Slavic have been preserved.[117]

The dual—*As mentioned earlier, the Slovene language preserved the ancient grammatical form of* **dual** *to indicate the number that is positioned between the singular and the plural signifying two persons or things. Nouns and adjectives as well as verbs have a distinct form to indicate the dual.*

In Slovene we say: hiša (house), hiši (two houses), hiše (three or more houses). When the adjective lep (nice) is added we have: lepa hiša, lepi hiši, lepe hiše, respectively. The present indicative of the verb, biti (to be) is conjugated as follows:

jaz sem (I am)	*midva sva (we two are)*	*mi smo (we are)*
ti si (you are)	*vidva sta (you two are)*	*vi ste (you are)*
on je (he is)	*onadva sta (they two are)*	*oni so (they are)*
ona je (she is)	*onidve sta (they two are f.)*	*one so (they are f.)*

The origin of this form goes far into prehistory. It is found in the Sanskrit of the Vedas. The most ancient Rig-veda contains it. It is also preserved in the ancient Persian text, the Avesta.

Both the Vedas and Avesta go back to the first millennium B.C. In modern Indian languages the dual has already disappeared, and it is not present in modern Iranian except in the dialect spoken by the Jagnobi of the northwest Pamir region (Tadzikistan).

In Europe the dual is to be found in ancient languages only, particularly in the ancient Greek of Herodotus's time (5th century B.C.). It was used in the conjugation of verbs (except in the 1st person) and in the substantive declension. But it soon disappeared, first in declension leaving its place to the plural, and then also in the conjugation.

In Latin we only find a few reminders of the dual, as in expressions like "duo" or "ambo", which do not appear later in Romanic languages except in Italian.

The Slavic languages lost the dual in the last millennium, except for Slovene and Lusatian Wendish. The latter preserved it in the conjugation of the imperfect verb and the aorist.

Among Baltic languages, Lithuanian is unique in having preserved a certain form of the dual; in Germanic languages it is found in the ancient Gothic, but only in a certain limited use in the declension of personal pronouns.

---

[117] F. Bezlaj, *Eseji...op. cit.*, p. 113.

In Basque, the unique pre-Indo-European language existing still in present-day Europe, the dual has also been lost.

Outside of Europe, the dual is still present in Semitic languages, above all in Arabic, while it has nearly disappeared from modern Hebrew. Hamitic languages (Egyptian, Coptic, Berber) do not possess the dual; neither do Chinese, Korean, and Japanese.

But it is to be found in the ancient tongues of Australia and Melanesia in which, besides the plural, the forms of three or four persons appear.

The ancient peoples of Siberia such as the Samoyeds and the Innuit have preserved the dual in their languages. This is also true of many Indian languages in North and South America.

The Slovene language is a speech island in central Europe. It preserved the dual, while surrounded by nations speaking languages without this ancient grammatical form (Latins, Germans, Hungarians, and other Slavs). This unusual phenomenon has attracted the attention of a large number of linguists; their various studies will eventually, we hope, include a close examination of the factors which allowed the preservation of this grammatical form in a well-defined territory for such an extraordinary length of time.

According to Bezlaj,[118] "The vocabulary of the Balto-Slavic archaisms and lexical parallels in the Slovene tell us of its great age as an independent language, reaching back to the times when vowel gradation was still in its creative stage, at least to the 4th century A.D.; one cannot say for certain whether this had already occurred in the ancient homeland or whether a Slavic settlement wave into the south had appeared several centuries before the officially recognized date. Both of these are theoretically possible."

In reality, only Bezlaj's second proposition is possible: a settlement wave from the ancient Slavic homeland in Lusatia spread into the south at least one and a half millennia before the settlement movements of South Slavs in the 5th to 6th century A.D. As is already apparent, archaeological discoveries detailing the expansion of the Urnfield culture from Lusatia, around 1200 B.C., and findings of the linguists confirm that the bearers of this culture were the Veneti (G. Devoto), in reality the Proto-Slavs or the present-day West Slavs (C. Verdiani). In addition there are no archeological discoveries, for the time period from 1200 B.C. to the 6th century A.D. and beyond, that would suggest movement of any Slavic people between the Baltic and upper Adriatic.

There is also the question of development that should be considered. After settling in the Balkans, why did the South Slavs undergo a different social and linguistic development than the Slovenes in the Alps?

---

[118] F. Bezlaj, *Eseji...*ibid., pp. 122–123.

*Belin (Belenus), sun god of the Carns and Norici. The statuette was unearthed at Gagliano near Cividale/Čedad (1870). His name has been preserved in the name of the church **S. Bellino** on the hill S. Pantaleone e Orzone (see A. Tagliaferri, Coloni e legionari nel Friuli celtico, Pordenone 1986, 228). A reminder of the sun god is the place-name **Beligna** near Aquileia/Oglej. In the upper Soča Valley a folk tale has been preserved about Belin and his miraculous keys that return the light to the eyes.*

The ancient western movement of the Slavs (Veneti) and the later eastern movement of South Slavs met on the Balkan peninsula, resulting in the development of a new Slavic language group. Did this process include borrowings from the Illyrian and Thracian? If so, can we determine the extent of these borrowings? If the ancient Illyrians and Thracians had been Latinized or Grecized, there would have been preserved in South Slavic languages some of the Latin and Greek vocabulary; also, we cannot imagine that, as the Slavs advanced, both established ethnic groups collectively ran and took refuge behind the walls of the coastal cities or disappeared in the "sea" of Slavs. On the contrary, the native inhabitants remained in their places and merged with the newly-arrived Slavs. The fact that Thracian and Illyrian vocabularies are not clearly distinguishable in present South Slavic languages can be explained by the probability that Proto-Slavic as well as Thracian and Illyrian were still very close to Indo-European, which means they were related to each other. Only the Albanian language is different; it was exposed in a large measure to Greek and later to Turkish influences.

If the vocabulary of the Illyro-Thracian population does not stand out conspicuously in the languages of South Slavs, other traditional features of these cultures are clearly and powerfully represented and expressed. Balkan cultures distinguish themselves very strongly from those of the Slovenes and other Slavs. The special features are to be attributed to the heritage of Illyrians and Thracians.

When comparing to the South Slavs, we find that the Slovene language and ethnic culture reveal separate historical development. The Slovenes belong, as already mentioned, to the Proto-Slavic family of the West Slavs, which settled in the Alps during the Urnfield migration and has survived until today mainly in the eastern Alps through diverse stages of culture: Hallstatt, La Tène, Noricum under Rome and Carantania in the Middle Ages. If these facts were utilized free of ideological interference, they would represent a very good starting point for further historical research.

Historians in Slovenia found themselves under a variety of ideological pressures, but historians in other countries did just as poorly. They had more freedom

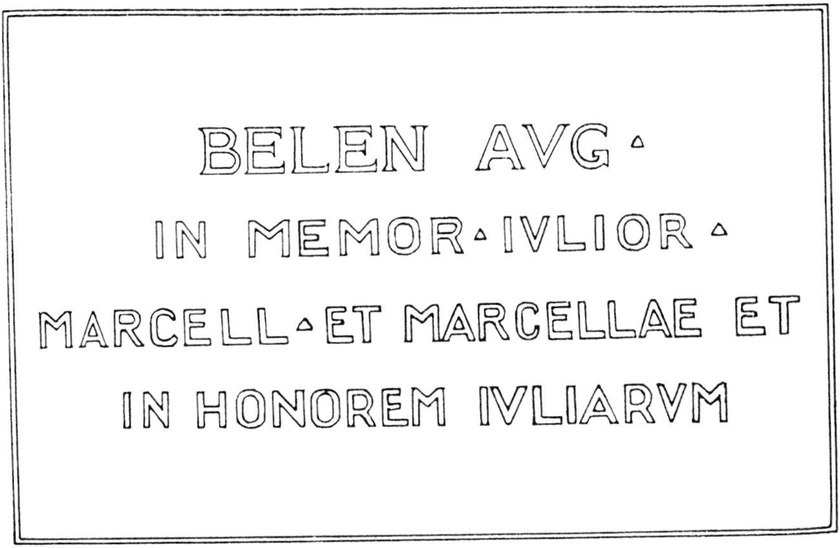

BELEN AVG ·

IN MEMOR · IVLIOR ·

MARCELL · ET MARCELLAE ET

IN HONOREM IVLIARVM

Aquileia (Oglej)—A votive inscription on an altar dedicated to god Belenus; Roman period.

but were generally ignorant of the Slovene language and culture, and hence unable to formulate an independent outlook. However, there are exceptions. Some very valuable contributions have been made; for example, Pellegrini made a highly significant statement regarding the Veneti: *"After the breakdown of the concept 'Illyrian' (which we retained mostly for the sake of convenience), the Venetic language and its territory should have their place in linguistics reassessed, and the question of non-Celtic Indo-Europeans in Noricum and Pannonia must be examined 'in primis'."*[119]

Polish authors, who presented strong arguments against German monopoly regarding prehistory, did not particularly concern themselves with the origin of the Slovenes, although they had prevailed to a considerable degree in the scientific world with their views about the ancient homeland of the Slavs. It is time that the Slovenes begin independent research into the roots of their nationality, regardless of ideological difficulties.

---

[119] C.B. Pellegrini, A.L. Prosdocimi, op. cit., p. 258.

The Roman Period

...iuxtaque Carnos quondam Taurisci
appellati, nunc Norici. His contermini
Rhaeti et Vindelici, omnes in multas
civitates divisi. (C. Plinius Secundi Nat.
hist. III, 133)

New culture groups were formed in central Europe after the 10th to 9th centuries B.C.; that is, during the late Bronze Age and early Iron Age. They were built on the foundation of Urnfield culture which the Veneti disseminated from Lusatia in the 13th century B.C. The Veneti were the bearers of these cultures in the territory which extended uninterrupted from the Baltic sea to the Adriatic. In the central and eastern Alps, as well as in bordering regions (which are of particular interest to us in this study), culture groups flourished on the traditions established by the Veneti. The already mentioned cultures of Villanova, Golasecca, Este, Melaun, and Hallstatt were named after their most significant discovery sites.

In the lower Po River region the influence of the Etruscans on Villanova culture became ever stronger until the latter succumbed towards the end of the 6th century B.C. Its centre, Felsina (Bologna), became one of the most important Etruscan cities.

In the beginning of the 4th century B.C., the Celts advanced into the Po region, also conquering Felsina and thus ending the Etruscan period of Villanova culture. Golasecca culture in the upper Po region also met its end during the Celtic assault. Archaeological discoveries and numerous place-names in the Po River basin around the major lakes, as well as in the lowlands (e.g., in the province of Ravenna) demonstrate that the Venetic people in rural areas were able to survive, following the time-honoured occupations of farming and animal husbandry, through the period following the Celtic conquest and subsequent Roman rule.

The Celtic invasion had very little effect on Este culture on the plains of Venetia and the neighbouring Alps; this culture survived intact into the Roman era. Excavations at their latest stage, Este IV, have produced only a few finds from Celtic La Tène culture. Typical statuettes of naked warriors with La Tène helmet, sword, shield, and spear (discovery site Lagole)[120] are indications of a Celtic ruling class who worshipped the national goddess, Hecate, along with the indigenous population.

The presumed Celtic stratum of the population, with its La Tène artifacts (if they were not the result of trade), gradually merged with the Veneti. The Celts who were present in the region of Este culture do not seem to have been the occupying forces but, rather, allies. Even Celtic names on monuments of the later Este period could only be the outward expression of a spirit of unity and not one of Celtization.

Venetia

In the year 225 B.C., the Romans defeated the Celts near Telamon on the Etruscan coast, which meant a gradual decline of the Celtic stronghold in the Po region. Consequently, in 192 B.C., the Romans conquered Bononia, (Felsina), today Bologna, the centre of the Celtic Boians. In 183 B.C., they also occupied the region of Este culture and named it after its inhabitants—**Venetia**. This name has remained to the present day: Veneto for the province, and Venice (Ital. Venezia) for its capital city.

The Roman name, Venetia, is in itself a very strong evidence that at the time the Romans arrived, the ancient Venetic population and their language still dominated this region. Numerous Venetic (Slavic) words have survived in the dialects of Venezia, Padova, and Mantua, exhibiting word forms and meanings related to modern Slavic languages. They remind us that Venetic culture was of Slavic origin.

The Proto-Slavic origin of the Adriatic Veneti, was advocated a century ago in the writings of the Slovene scholar, Trstenjak.[121] He based his findings on numerous Slovene expressions in the dialects of the present province of Veneto. His detailed studies were categorically rejected by the Slovene historian, Kos (1896), who did not deny the existence of Slovene words in these dialects, but

---

[120] R. Pittioni, op. cit., p. 337/20.

[121] A review of D. Trstenjak's writings has been published recently in the Collected Works of F. Kos (by B. Grafenauer, cf. footnote No. 6), pp. 63–64. Cf. also the writings of Trstenjak in the *Letopisi/* Annual Reports of the Matica Slovenska 1870–77, as well as the booklet *Slovanski elementi v venetščini/* Slavic Elements in the Venetic language, Ljubljana 1874, where the author notes his perusal of the dictionary of the Venetian dialect, *Dizionario del dealetto veneziano* (Boerio), Venice 1867. He also used in his research words found in the dialects of Padova (Patriarchi) and in those of Mantua

found a totally meaningless explanation for this occurrence. The following paragraph is a good example of his unprofessional attitude:

"Trstenjak has compared in his studies the Venetian dialect with Slavic languages and is convinced that the Venetians are using numerous expressions that are to be found among Slovenes, constituting for him a proof that the ancient Veneti were of Slavic origin. This conclusion is incorrect in my opinion. Some linguists could find in the dialect of Gorica (Gorizia) Slovenes numerous Italian expressions. Should we then conclude that Slovenes from Gorica were actually Slovenized Italians?"[122]

Kos has forgotten the geographical reality; he should have known that Italians in the area of Venice, Padova, and Mantua do not and never have shared a common border with present-day Slovenes, a circumstance which would have allowed them to borrow Slovene or other Slavic words for daily usage. (Author).

There are some records (we cannot examine here how true they are) that the Adriatic Veneti originated in Paphlagonia, Asia Minor, that they came to help the besieged Troy, and after its fall, ostensibly under the leadership of the legendary Antenor, reached the coastal region of the northern Adriatic. Relying on Greek sources, Latin writers also repeat this story; as for example, Pliny the Elder (who cites Cato as his source) as well as Cornelius Nepos, Livy and others. Archaeologists have so far not been able to provide us with an answer.

We have no dependable data telling us when the indigenous Venetic (Slavic) language became extinct in the province of Veneto. The Romanization of the ancient Veneti could not have taken place suddenly (R. Pittioni, ibid., p. 337/30). In all probability, the language was able to survive for many centuries among the farming population before the Italic language finally took over. Judging from the toponyms in the Venetian Alps, the Venetic language prevailed longest in these remote regions.

Carnia

In the year 181 B.C., a large Roman military camp was established in Aquileia (Slov. Oglej) in the eastern part of the Roman province of Venetia, present Friuli. It was in this region before the arrival of the Romans that the meeting of Este and

---

(Cherubini). The thesis regarding the Slavic origin of the Adriatic Veneti was supported also by Schlötzer, Surowiecki, Mannert, Šafařik, Springsguth and others, later also by the German scholar Contzen, in addition to the Russian Gilferding and the Slovene Linhart.

[122] F. Kos, *Zbrano delo*, op. cit., p. 68.

Hallstatt cultures produced the people called Carni; the territory was named after them—**Carnia**. At present, Carnia includes northern Friuli and the Carnic Alps. Of the same origin are other names that have been with us since the Middle Ages or longer: *Carantania* (Carinthia, Ger. Kärnten, Slov. Karantanija, Koroška or Korotan), *Carniola* (Ger. Krain, Slov. Kranjska, Gorenjska). The term Karst originates from the same source (Slov. Kras, Ital. Carso). Jan Kollár[123] derives the name "Carni" from "gorni", in modern Slovene *gorani, gorjani* (mountain dwellers).

The land in lower Friuli was at that time still swampy and overgrown, which is probably why, according to historical documents, the Carni inhabited the surrounding hills and mountain valleys including the lower part of Carinthia, Upper Carniola and Karst. Their trade centres were the cities of Oglej (Aquileia), Gradež (Grado), and Trst (Trieste), this last derived from the Latin Tergeste and from the original Venetic Terg, modern Slovene *trg*—market town. Also belonging to Carnia were the Forum Julii, Čedad (Cividale), after which present-day Friuli is named, as is Concordia (near Portogruaro). Above Tolmezzo we find the Carnic centre of Julium Carnicum (today Zuglio). Pliny the Elder (Nat. hist. III, 133) identifies the Carni with Taurisci and Norici in the eastern Alps.

The identity of Carni and Norici is confirmed by their close ethnic relationship with other Venetic groups, and by the fact that they all worshipped a deity of the same name, the sun-god Belin (Belen, Belenus) who was identical to, or on the same level with, the Roman god Apollo.

The Carnic or Noric Belin was also the municipal deity of Aquileia, which means that in spite of the presence of the Roman army and the fact that the Latin language dominated public life, this city was still predominantly Carnic, i.e., Venetic (Slovene).

The Roman writer, Tertullian, described Belin as a Norican god (*Noricus Belenus*—Apol. adv. gent. 24, 7; ad nationes II, 8). Inscriptions preserved from this period, as for example, *Belino sacr* on the Ostrovica (Osterwitz) castle and *Belino Aug. sacr.* from the Celovec (Klagenfurt) suburb of Cigole (Ziggulin), show that this god had been venerated in Noricum. Belenus had his temple in Julium Carnicum as well as inscriptions dedicated to him in Concordia, Altinum, and Venice, meaning that he was venerated in Venetia as well as Noricum.

Additional Belenus inscriptions are in Rimini, Tivoli, and Rome (Latinum); also near Burdigala (Bordeaux) in Gaul and on several Gallic coins (Belenos).[124]

---

[123] J. Kollár, *Staroitalia Slavjanska/* The Slavic Ancient Italy, Vienna 1853, p. 59.

[124] Paulys Real-Encyclopädie...op. cit., 1899 (Belenus). G.B. Pellegrini, A.L. Prosdocimi, op. cit., p. 240.

Finds from Hallstatt, after which the old Iron Age in Europe is named. The bearers of this culture were the Veneti, Wends. The distinctive figurines of bull and horse on various items reflect the military and farming character of this culture. (Source: J. Filip, ibid., p. 457).

Hallstatt

The name Belin or Belenus is certainly not Celtic. It is a reflection of Belbog (*bel*—white; *bog*—god), the ancient Slavic god of sun and light. His name appears everywhere the Veneti are found. Belin was also known in the region of Villanova (Rimini) and in Latinum where, according to Pliny the Elder (III, 69), Venetulani still lived, and in Gaul where during the arrival of the Romans in Armorica (Brittany) there was an uninterrupted region inhabited by the Veneti. It could only have been from the Veneti that several Celtic tribes adopted this god.

In Friuli, Italy, almost nothing has been discovered from La Tène culture, and the old toponyms or place-names do not provide any evidence of Celtic settlements before the appearance of the Romans. In spite of all attempts by present Friulian separatists to base the character of Friuli on Celtic origins, and despite forced derivations of many Friulian place-names from Celtic, almost all these names, including those that derive from "Sclavoni", originated with the Venetic (Slavic) Carni of pre-Roman and pre-Celtic times. This description is for the regions where the Slavs or Slovenes were never supposed to have been (according to historians).[125] The large number of Slovene words in the Friulian lan-

---

[125] Cf. G. Frau, *Dizionario toponomastico friulano*, Udine 1978. The explanations are not completely accurate, but numerous toponyms are unquestionably Slovene—as for example along the Tagliamento River the names of Belgrado, Gorizza, Gradisca, Goricizza,

A woman's diadem made from gold from a princely grave in Stična, Slovenia, Hallstatt period, 6th century B.C. In the centre is a stylized sun and the tree of life in the form of an arrow. (Source: J. Kastelic, Situla I/1960).

guage[126] can also be traced to a certain extent to the ancient Carni and not to the close proximity of Friulians and modern Slovenes.

It is of interest that Friuli, in contrast to the province of Veneto, had not been Romanized. Latin was predominant in the cities, in commerce, and in the Roman army—it was the official language.[127] Only after the Christianization of these regions does Latin appear to have gradually reached the Friulian people in the countryside, and only in the late Middle Ages did the neo-Latin Romance dialect become prevalent in the Friulian villages.[128]

---

and Grizzo above Pordenone, some mountain names in Carnia, and so on. Such toponyms are also found in the province of Veneto where we find near Vicenza also Schiavon and Schiavi and near Este, Schiavonia.

[126] See G. Marchetti, *Lineamenti della grammatica friulana*/ An Outline of the Friulian Grammar, Udine 1967, pp. 41–44.

[127] Besides the Friulians, the neo-Latin is used by the Ladins in the Dolomites (central Alps) and by the Rhaeto-Romance people in southern Switzerland. The Italian linguists distinguish the Romanic (Italian) dialects from that of the neo-Latin. Cf. Tullio de Mauro, *Storia linguistica dell' Italia unita*/ The History of Languages of the United Italy, Bari 1963, pp. 25–26.

[128] According to historian Nicoletti (d. 1596): "the principal language in the Friulian vil-

Raetia, Vindelicia

The large area of the central Alps, especially Tyrol and the canton Graubünden, was the home of Melaun culture during pre-Roman times. Its inhabitants, the Rhaetians, were first mentioned by Polybius (Strabo IV, 209) in his writings, telling of one of the four Alpine passes leading through the territory of the Rhaetians, via Raiton. **Raetia**, the name of the province, was first mentioned by Velleius (II 39, 104).[129]

The Rhaetian people were made up of numerous scattered communities in the Alpine valleys. Their names were carved into the victory monument, *Tropaeum Alpinum* (7th century B.C.), and Pliny the Elder (III, 136 ff.) refers to them as the "gentes Alpinae", among whom are the **Venostes** in Val Venosta/Vintschgau and **Venonetes** in Valtellina whose names still reveal the Venetic form. At the time of Pliny the Elder (III, 47. 134) there were still several Venetic groups in the valleys around the upper Po region, such as the **Veneni** in the Stura Valley (province of Cuneo), where even today we find the village of *Vinadio;*[130] also the *Lepontii* in the upper Val Lepontina and *Salassi* in the Aosta Valley, who are mentioned by Cato (Pliny the Elder III, 134) as the *Tauriscae gentis*. From this we can conclude that a relationship had existed in the eastern Alps, with the Taurisci who were also called Norici and Carni; this relationship is also indicated by old place-names. The distribution of various forms of Venetic names in this area shows that we are looking at *fragments of the same tribe* (H. Hirt).[131]

The above-mentioned tribes were not Celtic and were certainly not Celticized. The Roman writer Livy (V, 33) even reports that the Rhaeti were descended from

---

lages during the Aquilean Patriarchate was the Slovene, because the Friulian was at that time still undeveloped and had an unpleasant and harsh sound." Compare also G.F. Palladio de gli Olivi who tells us that: "Il linguaggio schiavo nelle ville per l'ordinario si praticava, e l'idioma foroguiliese nelle citta haveva l'uso."—The Slovene language was used in the villages and the Friulian in towns; in Historia prov. Friuli II. Udine 1660, pp. 3–5, cf. M. Premrou, *Monumenta Sclavenica*, Ljubljana 1919, p. 35

[129] Paulys Real-Encyclopädie...op. cit., 1914 (Raeti, Raetia).

[130] Paulys Real-Encyclopädie...op. cit., 1955 (Veneni). North of the mentioned village rises the characteristic summit Rocca la Meia 2831m, *meja*—frontier; above the Valle Varaita there is Mt. Viso 3841m, *vis* (high) and in the same neighbourhood there is the Cima delle Lobbie 3015m pl. of *lob*—a peak in the form of a skull.

[131] H. Hirt, *Trümmer eines einheitlichen Stammes/* The remnants of a homogeneous people; Die Indogermanen I, 1905, p. 127 passim. See Paulys Real-Enzyklopädie... op. cit., 1955 (Venedae).

the Etruscans and had retained the Etruscan language, albeit not unchanged. Pliny the Elder (III, 133) and Pomponius Trogus (Just XX, 5) were of the same opinion; both came from the region of the above-mentioned tribes. The language of the Etruscans, as well as that of the Rhaeti, originated from the Venetic; i.e., Slavic. Thus, it is not surprising that A. Berlot[132] was able to decipher the Rhaetian inscriptions on the basis of modern Slavic languages. As already mentioned, there are numerous names in this region whose meaning can be understood through Slovene and other Slavic languages; and numerous discoveries verify the presence of pre-Celtic cultures that were still flourishing in many regions until finally incorporated into the Roman Empire.

The Venetic or Rhaetian territory extended in the west as far as central Switzerland. The Celtic Helvetii and Raurici lived to the west. **Vindelicia** was located north of the Swiss Alps and Lake Constance (Lacus Venetus) in present Swabia and Bavaria. Its inhabitants developed in the western region of Hallstatt culture and afterwards merged with the new-comer Celts. Nevertheless, the original Venetic ancestry is reflected in the name of this country and its inhabitants.

Roman writers do not make a clear distinction between Rhaetia and Vindelicia and mention both together; e.g., Velleius (II 39, 3) in the year 30, citing that Tiberius had acquired numerous lands for Rome, among them *Rhaetiam et Vindelicos*. Vindelicia proper, situated north of the Alps, belonged since the early La Tène period to the settlement area of the Celts (5th century B.C.). In contrast, inhabitants of Rhaetia or the central Alps were exposed to only minimal Celtic influence as shown by excavations and river and field-names reaching as far as the valley basin near Bolzano. It is for this reason that several researchers were emphasizing at the end of the last century, that the inhabitants of the Alps were in reality Veneti and not Celts or Illyrians.[133]

Despite massive Celtic intrusion in the northern Alpine foreland, the Vindelicians of that region were not a totally Celtic or Celticized people. This is evident from Roman rule, as many graves have been found with non-Celtic objects. There were also Romanized yet non-Celtic names of cities: *Celio* (Kellmünz), *Febiana* (at the mouth of the Iller River), *Foetibus* (Füssen), *Parthanum* (Partenkirchen), and *Scarbia* (near Mittenwald); in addition, there are river names:

---

[132] A. Berlot, *Raseni so spregovorili/* The Rasennes began to speak, in *Itd* (18 Feb., cap. VII), Ljubljana 1977.

[133] Paulys Real-Encyclopädie...op. cit., 1961 (Vindelici). R. Pittioni, *Stand und Aufgaben der urgeschichtl. Forschungen am Oberetsch/* The Position and Tasks of the Prehistoric Researches in Alto Adige; Beiheft VI zum Jahresbericht für Gesch., Kultur und Kunst, Bozen 1940, p. 60 passim.

Inn, Lech or *Partnach,*[134] and also *Iller* and *Traun*. We can conclude that, in the case of Vindelicians, a Celtic upper class and possibly a ruling class existed; but, this does not necessarily mean a subordination or subjugation of the Venetic Vindelicians, although such a relationship could be imagined after the Celtic invasion. The following period, however, did result in the merging of the two groups, undoubtedly accelerated if the languages of the two groups were related.

The Romans subdued the Rhaeti and Vindelicians in the year 15 B.C. Their commander, Drusus, defeated the Rhaeti on Isarcus and then advanced over the Brenner and Seefeld passes towards Vindelicia. His comrade-in-arms, Tiberius, attacked from out of Roman Gaul and decisively overthrew the Vindelicians on Lacus Venetus (Lake Constance). From the conquered region of the Alps and the lands north of the Alps, the Romans created the province of Rhaetia with the administrative centre and army camp in *Augusta Vindelicum* (Augsburg). This camp was connected to Italy by way of the ancient road along the Fern Pass 1210m, into the Inn Valley, then over the Rechen/Resia 1508m, into the Vintschgau and on to Merano, Bolzano, Trento, and farther south into the Po Valley. West of Lake Constance the Romans founded, near the present city of Brugg, an enormous camp called Vindonissa (today Windisch) and also built *limes* (border fortifications) in the north along the Danube.

After the invasion of the Marcomans in the year 166 A.D., the Romans changed their defence of Rhaetia and Vindelicia several times. The command was moved to camp Castra Regina/Regensburg. For reasons of defence and agriculture, numerous colonists had settled in the region immediately north of the Alps. Through his administrative reforms, Emperor Diocletian (284–305) divided the province of Rhaetia into two new provinces: *Rhaetia prima* (Rhaetia) and *Rhaetia secunda* (Vindelicia). The latter could not be defended for very long. From the middle of the 4th to the middle of the 5th century, the Roman defence remained limited to that of Alpine Rhaetia.

In the meantime, the indigenous (i.e., Venetic and Celtic) population of Vindelicia almost totally disappeared. Right after the conquest of this territory, the Romans carried off a large number of young men for the Roman Army. Subsequently, Roman troops were brought in, along with predominantly Germanic colonists. For this reason there are relatively few Venetic place-names in the region of former Vindelicia, presently Swabia and Bavaria, but they appear frequently in the territory of former Rhaetia, presently eastern Switzerland and Ty-

---

[134] R. Reinecke, *Der bayerische Vorgeschichtsfreund* IV, 1924, pp. 27, 30, 38, 42; 1926, p. 41, cf. Paulys Real-Encyclopädie...op. cit., 1961 (Vindelici). Nevertheless, this archaeologist considers the Vindelici of Celtic origin. Au.

rol, where traces of Roman civilization and city development are absent (with the exception of the city of Curia/Chur).[135] At the end of the 5th century, the Alemanni settled to the north and south of Lake Constance, while the Baiuvarii/ Bavarians settled to the east. Nevertheless, the Venetic or Wendian language must have survived for several centuries among the farming population in the central Alps.

Noricum

The eastern Alps were the focal point of Hallstatt culture. It greatly influenced the entire central Europe. At its centre was the archaeological site, Hallstatt, from which its name is derived. Under Hallstatt influence other culture groups formed in bordering regions: *Knovíz, Bylany,* and *Milavče* in Bohemia, the *Velatice* and *Baierdorf* in Moravia and Lower Austria, the *Chotín* in western Slovakia, and the *Vál* in western Pannonia. During the same period we can see in the surrounding area (present-day Slovenia) Illyrian influence among the Hallstatt discoveries.[136] In the 6th and 5th centuries B.C. there were many invasions by the Crimeans and Scythians from the east. Grave excavations show burial of both rider and horse with harness, etc., as was customary among the plains inhabitants. This type of grave was found in the area that extends on the eastern periphery of the Alps from Lower Austria and Slovakia over the western part of Pannonia to Slovenia. The invasions from the east were seemingly not detrimental to Hallstatt culture in the eastern Alps.

The primary contributor to the prosperity and strength of the eastern Hallstatt region was the mining industry. During the late Bronze Age, before the Urnfield migration, the province of Salzburg was a major mining district with rock-salt works and copper mines, with smelting furnaces and farms to provide the miners with their daily necessities. There was also a network of mule-trails where copper and bronze articles were transported over high Alpine passes toward the south.

---

[135] R. von Planta, *Das alte Raetien/* The Old Rhaetia; 1872,p. 211 passim., cf. Paulys Real-Encyclopädie...op. cit., 1914 (Raetia), p. 53. J. Filip, ibid., (Raetia), p. 1118.

[136] The Slovene archaeologist S. Gabrovec (Germania 44/1966) thinks that in Slovenia the Hallstatt culture represents not only the Urnfield culture, but also an influx of new elements from the Balkans. Cf. by J. Filip, op. cit., p. 1325. This interpretation is useful to the relatively recent unitaristic Yugoslav ideology, but quite meaningless in every other respect. Another Slovene archaeologist T. Knez states: "The Slovene Hallstatt is in its essential characteristics expressly connected to the Alps." Cf. *Arheološki vestnik* XXIV, Ljubljana 1973, p. 323.

Coin from Noricum—The Norici minted their own coins from the first half of the first century B.C. onward. Characteristic were their large silver coins of two types: those from west Noricum's mint at Štalenska gora (Magdalensberg), and east Noricum's mint at Celje, Slovenia. On the obverse side of these coins was Belin's (Apollo's) head and on the reverse, an image of a horse or a horseman. The Venetic inscription VOKK found on some means the Norican king (rex Voccio). In the picture is the obverse side of a silver coin from the treasury discovered at Lemberg near Celje. (From P. Kos, Celje Museum III, Numismatic exhibit, Ljubljana 1982).

On the eastern periphery of the Alps ran the **Amber Road,** which led from the area east of the mouth of the Vistula on the Baltic coast in a southwesterly direction, outflanking the Alps and continuing on to the Adriatic, mainly to the city of Aquileia, which was the greatest market for amber. This road was in operation from the Bronze Age onward, through the ancient settlement area of the Veneti. From this we can conclude that they were the bearers of the amber trade. To prehistoric man, amber was a precious substance. It was used in the manufacture of a variety of objects, among them amulets for children. In the central Apennine cultures of Marino and Novilara and also later in the Roman culture, the use of amber in handicrafts reached its high point.[137] For our forefathers amber was not just the substance that we moderns use for jewellery; it was a "substance of the sun", endowed with mystical powers. It was as precious as gold and was sought after by both the barbaric north and civilized south.

Around 700 B.C. the **iron industry** came to occupy a dominant role in the eastern Alps, with iron works near ore deposits in upper Carinthia and upper Styria. The iron from the eastern Alps was of very high quality, reaching the hardness of steel, and since that time its production has been the most important source of economic stability of this region. Rock-salt extraction was also of major importance; the salt beds ran along the north side of the Hohen and Niederen

---

[137] J. Filip, cit., (Österreich). *Lessico Universale Italiano*, Rome 1968 (ambra). Brockhaus Enzyklopädie, op. cit., 1967 (Bernstein).

Tauern (Hallstatt, Hallein). Strong economic centres developed mainly in the valley basins of Vienna, Graz, Klagenfurt, and Salzburg, as well as in Burgenland and Lower Carniola (Vače group).

A highly developed mining and metal processing system required a well-functioning organization, the division of labour into separate groups—in short, an organized community under the direction of a ruling class. That such a class existed in the eastern Alps can be concluded from the presence of **princely graves**, known to exist in Europe since the Stone Age. Besides those found in Etruria, the graves of the "nobility" in Hallstatt culture represent considerable magnificence, both in the western as well as the eastern region. Especially known for their opulence in the eastern region are the Travnik (Wies) group in central Styria, near Lipnica (Leibnitz),[138] with the most significant discovery site located in Klein-Glein.

Advancing from the west in the 5th century B.C., the Celts did not settle in the eastern Alps. Celtic graves, however, provide evidence of their presence around eastern Alpine economic centres. Yet Celtic finds within the eastern Alps from the La Tène period are either extremely rare or are mixed with those of Hallstatt culture or are totally absent.[139] These finds, therefore, are generally to be attributed to trade with the Celts.

Celtic graves in the eastern Alpine economic areas do not in themselves provide any basis for a conclusion that the Celts forced themselves as the ruling class upon the Hallstatt Veneti. This is maintained by German and Austrian historians, and this same assumption is accepted and repeated by other western scholars. We can expect that a Celtic stratum did exist in these economic areas but consisted mainly of Celtic miners and, still more likely, Celtic craftsmen and merchants. After the Celts had conquered all the regions around the Alps, European trade, on which the eastern Alpine iron industry was also dependent, came under their control. This is clearly seen in Celtic coins and other finds. The coins originate from the 2nd century B.C.; there are also several Venetic coins from the same period that were found in Gurina in the upper Zilja (Ger. Gail) Valley below the Pleke Pass, 1360m (Ger. Plöcken).

Some historians are convinced that by the end of the 3rd century B.C., the presence of Celts in the eastern Alps had increased, which meant that by then (if not earlier) the Celts had conquered that region. Historians support this conclusion with the following record:

---

[138] J. Filip, op. cit., (Fürstengräber).

[139] B. Grafenauer, *Zgodovina slovenskega naroda* I, op. cit., p.133.

A woman from Noricum's Roman period (2nd century) is portrayed on a gravestone now on the wall of the church of St. Jacob at Dhovše (Lendorf) near Celovec (Klagenfurt). The woman belongs to the upper class and represents Noricum's Roman culture with its costume and rich jewelry.

In 225 B.C. the Romans defeated several Celtic tribes in a decisive battle near Telamon on the Tyrrhenian coast, whereby the Taurisci, supposedly a Celtic tribe, came to the aid of the Celts (Polybius II 28, 4. 30, 6). After their defeat, the Taurisci withdrew into what is now northwestern Carinthia, where we find Celtic rule over the native "Illyrian" population from the 2nd century B.C. onward.[140]

in Tauriscis Noricis

It is quite certain that only the Taurisci from the western Alps could have participated in the battle near Telamon, which is explicitly implied in Polybius' passage. The Taurisci were also described by Polybius (115, 8) as being inhabitants of the places that face the plains,[141] and by Cato (Pliny the Elder III, 134) as *Tauriscae gentis* in his mentioning of the Leponti in Tessin and Salassi in Aosta. The earlier-mentioned tribes were, however, not Celtic but Venetic remnants (Golasecca culture), even if they were under the rule of northern Italic Celts. The Roman city, *Julia Augusta Taurinorum* (Torino), was named after them, that is, after the western Taurisci. A third tribe in northwest and northeast Pannonia called Taurini is recorded by Ptolemy (III 8, 3).

In documentary sources that make reference to this time period, no name is found for the inhabitants of the eastern Alps. Greek and Latin authors report that,

---

[140] P. Reinecke, *Der bayerische Vorgeschichtsfreund* VI, p. 39, see Paulys Real-Encyclopädie, op. cit., 1934 (Taurisci). B. Grafenauer, op. cit., p. 133. E. Polanschek, op. cit., (Noricum), p. 972/60.

[141] M. Fluss, in Paulys Real-Encyclopädie, op. cit., (Taurisci), p. 2/30, 40.

at the beginning of the 2nd century B.C., tribes which they describe as Gallic (i.e., Celtic) again intruded over the Alps towards the south. These reports, however, originate from the beginning of the Christian era. In 181 B.C., the Romans built the powerful military camp, Aquileia, to defend against these invasions, and in 170 B.C. they were already maintaining diplomatic relations with these same people.

Livy informs us about the "Alpini populi" (XLIII 5, 1) describing them as Gauls; Strabo does the same (VIII 293, 313). Livy also refers to their rulers as "rex Gallorum Cincibilius" and the succeeding "regulus Gallorum Balanos" (XLIV 14, 1), whereby he must have had in mind a kingdom, a state in the eastern Alps.[142]

Livy's verbatim report: "...rex Gallorum Cincibilius nomine Alpinorum populorum, sociorum." It was "rex Cincibilius" who sent a protest to the Roman senate through his brother. The Latin term "populus" means a people organized in a state (populus Romanus). This refers unquestionably to the "populi Alpini", who were their allies "socii".

The name of the people in the eastern Alps is revealed to us for the first time in the middle of the 2nd century B.C. by Polybius (XXXIV 10, 10—in Strabo IV, 208) where he writes that **in Tauriscis Noricis**—in the territory of the Noric Taurisci—abundant gold deposits were discovered. The Taurisci drove away Italic merchants and took over the gold trade. As a result the price of gold in Italy fell by one third, which led to an intensification of relations between Rome and the Taurisci.

The Taurisci were defeated by the Romans in 129 B.C., as the Carni were soon afterwards. Yet, as the Germanic Cimberians laid siege to the Noric capital, *Noreia*, the Romans rushed to the aid of the Taurisci only to suffer defeat themselves (113 B.C.). After the Cimberian danger had passed, a friendship treaty was agreed upon between Romans and Taurisci that was to last almost one hundred years.

The kingdom of the Taurisci or Norici in the eastern Alps was relatively large during pre-Roman times, extending in the north as far as the Danube, in the west as far as the Inn River beyond the Alps, and to the Tyrol/Salzburg watershed. South of here it encompassed the Rienz Valley as far as Brixen; from there the border ran again eastward along the Dolomite mountain chain and Carnic and

---

[142] Paulys Real-Encyclopädie, op. cit., 1936 (Noricum), pp. 973–974, ibid., 1934 (Taurisci). Regarding the names and ethnic affiliation of various groups, we consider Polybius (ca. 205–126 B.C.) more reliable than the later Livy (59 B.C.–17 A.D.) or Strabo (63 B.C.–19 A.D.).

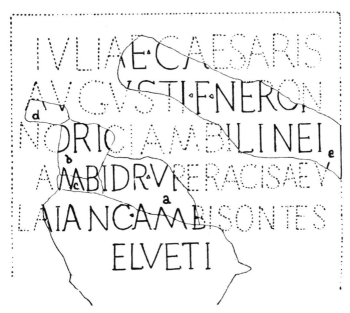

Štalenska gora (Magdalensberg) Carinthia—A tablet dedicated to Julia, daugther of Emperor Julius Caesar.

Julian Alps as far as Nauportum and Emona/Ljubljana. Also belonging to it was Lower Carniola and Lower Styria with the two cities of Celeia/Celje, Poetovio/ Ptuj, and the Pannonian cities of Savaria/Szombathely, Scarbantia/Sopron and Carnuntum/Petronell.[143] The **Amber Road** passed through these cities.

According to German historiographers, the kingdom of the Norici is to be considered Celtic, although such a conclusion cannot be extrapolated from available source-material, archaeological discoveries or surviving toponyms.

Even in the open region of western Pannonia, where the Celts exercised uncontested dominion, archaeological discoveries have established a continuous presence of the original Venetic (J. Filip—Illyrian) people into late Roman times. Excavations in Bohemia show that even after the invasion and settling of the Celts and the ensuing development of their rule, the original Hallstatt Venetic population continued even though in a subordinate position; La Tène culture was accepted only slowly by this segment of society.[144]

---

[143] E. Polaschek, in Paulys Real-Encyclopädie, op. cit., 1936 (Noricum), p. 977.

[144] J. Filip, op. cit., (Ungarn), p. 1547, (Tschechoslowakei), p. 1504

Archaeological finds show that the province of Salzburg had the strongest Celtic presence in the eastern Alps; but even this does not give us any basis for presuming Celtization and Celtic dominion over Noricum. The *Eastern Noric culture* group (Styria), founded on the Hallstatt Venetic base, survived to the end of the La Tène period. As mentioned earlier, Venetic coins were found at Gorina in Carinthia and in neighbouring Vremje, bearing inscriptions in the Venetic alphabet and script. In addition, not far from here, there was during Roman times a village called Loncium (Itin. Ant. 279); i.e., Lonka or Loka (*loka*—valley meadow).[145]

Numerous researchers see in the Taurisci, who were supposedly the Celtic ruling class in the eastern Alps, merely the first-recorded name of the Norici.[146]

Pliny the Elder (III, 133) writes:...*iuxtaque Carnos quondam Taurisci appellati nunc Norici* (like the Carni, formerly called Taurisci, now Norici) and ...*Tauriscis Noreia* (III, 131).

The names "Taurisci" and afterwards "Norici" dominate when the form of government in the eastern Alps is considered. Consequently, historians assume that the leadership role passed from the first to the latter; i.e., from the alleged Celtic upper class to the indigenous "Illyrian" population. Pliny the Elder thinks otherwise: he says that we are dealing in both cases with the descendants of the same people, who had developed in the eastern region of Hallstatt culture. We can conclude from passages in the source-material that eastern Alpine tribes (to whom others were affiliated during Roman times) originally consisted of four groups living in the following regions: *Taurisci* in western Carinthia and the valleys of the Hohen Tauern, also on the Salzburg side; *Norici* in central Carinthia and the region of the Niederen Tauern; *Carni* in the valleys of the Carnic and Julian Alps as far south as Karst; *Latobici* in Lower Carniola, Lower and central Styria as well as in the Carinthian Lavant Valley.

The fact that there are no geographical or time divisions mentioned in the source-material for these tribal regions supports the premise that these are one and the same people. Thus, according to Pliny the Elder (III, 131), the Hrušica

---

[145] The name Gurina, or Gorina is Slovene and means elevated, high. The name Loncium mentioned in *Itinerarium Antonini* the linguists derive from the Balto-Slavic *lanka* or *lonka*, cf. G.B. Pellegrini/ A.L. Prosdocimi, op. cit., pp. 607–608. In Slovene language *loka,* arch. *lonka,* means a meadow along a body of water.

[146] See R. Egger, *Frühchristliche Kirchenbauten 2/* Church Construction in the Early Christian Period, Paulys Real-Encyclopädie, op. cit., 1934 (Taurisci), p. 3. M. Fluss, the author of the term "Taurisci", ibid., affirms that the ruling Celtic Taurisci were lost within the common population of the Illyrian (now Venetic, Au.) Norici. Later he falls into a contradiction with himself, defining the Norici and their kingdom as Celtic.

Pass (Slovenia) and Sisek in Croatia (*Carnis Segesta et Ocra*) also belonged to the Carni; however, according to the same author (III, 148), the Taurisci came as far as Skordiscia near the Slavonian mountains—Croatia (*mons Claudius, cuius in fronte Scordisci, in tergo Taurisci*).

Alpine inhabitants were able to withstand Celtization mainly because of the mountainous terrain which did not suit the Celts, but allowed the indigenous Venetic people to defend themselves successfully. A decisive factor was the high level of culture of the Alpine people, especially their farming culture, which cannot be attributed to Celtization. Approximately one thousand years earlier, as the Veneti settled in the Alps during their Urnfield migration, Alpine inhabitants of that time, because of their primitive level of culture, quickly merged with the Veneti (e.g., Crestaulta culture in the Engadine).

regnum Noricum

The kingdom of Noricum was mentioned in the 1st century B.C. by Julius Caesar (Commentarii de bello Gallico I, 5, 4) as **ager Noricus.** There he writes that the Celtic Boians were driven from Bohemia (Boiohaemum) by Marbod, king of the Marcomans. The Boians then advanced into Noricum and laid siege to Noreia, attempting to conquer it, but they were instead defeated. This particular turn of events clearly shows that *the Norici were not a Celtic people*, otherwise they would have come to the help of the Boians in their battle against the Marcomans, or at least would have accepted them into their land. Instead they were besieged by them.

In addition, the Norici were allied with Germanic Suebians. According to Caesar's report (bell. Gall. I 53, 4), the second wife of Ariovist, the king of the Germanic Suebians, was the sister of King Voccio of Noricum (*Norica, regis Voccionis soror*).

King Voccio must have been a man of considerable political importance at that time. He was able to repel the attacks of King Burebista, the powerful leader of Dacians. These attacks were directed over north Pannonia against Noricum, the capital of which was afterwards transferred from Noreia, on the Styria-Carinthian border east of Neumarkt, to Mt. Štalen (Magdalensberg) north of Gospa Sveta (Maria Saal).

Štalen became Noricum's centre for trade, which was mainly directed at Aquileia; Aquileian merchants established permanent agencies at Štalen. The Norican economy was based primarily on mining, agriculture, livestock, forestry, and apiculture.

Mentioned among trade items brought to the market in Aquileia are: resin, cattle, pitch, firewood, wax, honey, and cheese (Strabo V, 208), as well as wool, woolen cloth, and leather (Vergil, Georg. III, 474 ff.) The export of metals and metal products, such as lead, zinc, copper, and especially iron, extended much farther. **Norican iron** was famous far and wide for its hardness; swords made of it were of the best kind and were simply called *ensis Noricus* (Horace, epod. XVII, carm. I, 16, 9). In Rome there was a Norican *statio*—trade representative station.

Religion occupied an important place in the Norican national and governmental identity. We first encounter Norican deities[147] during the Roman Empire, when there was also veneration of Greek gods and even Egyptian Isis Noreia alongside Roman state gods and Caesar himself. The great profusion of foreign gods did not, however, crowd out indigenous gods.

In Noricum we also come across the ancient Euro-Asian belief in two fundamental deities: light (the sun, heavens) and earth (fertility). From the union of the two elements issues vegetation and, thereby, life.

There were in Noricum during the Roman Empire two basic deities: the sun-god, *Belin* (Belenus) and *Noreia,* the state-goddess, the goddess of fertility, the giver of abundance.[148] In addition, there was the war-god *Latobius,* identical with the Roman Mars.

There were during the Roman Empire also city deities, like Celeia, Teurnia. Epona and Albiona, among others, tell us of the presence of the Celts. The state Noricum was represented by *genius Noricorum,* the guarding spirit of Noricum, who had residential rights in the forum in Virunum as well as in the "statio Noricorum" in Rome.

The presence of Roman civil servants and several cohorts of soldiers left behind numerous inscriptions dedicated to Greco-Roman deities. The Mithras cult which, it seems, entered Noricum through Aquileia became particularly widespread.

After the Romans subjugated Pannonia, the Norici were no longer able to maintain their independence, and in the year 15 B.C. joined them. As an ally of long standing, the Norici were able to maintain as **regnum Noricum** the status of limited self rule for the next half a century; only under Emperor Claudius

---

[147] See Vera Kolšek, *Pregled antičnih kultov na slovenskem ozemlju/* A Review of Ancient Cults in the Slovene Territory, *Arheološki vestnik* 19, pp. 282–283.

[148] The story about Belin (Belenus), who cures the eyes (returns the light from the sunny deity) with his miraculous key, has been preserved in the upper Soča Valley and is certainly of pre-Roman origin. Cf. *Guida del Friuli* V, Udine 1931, p. 85. We find the same Belin also among the Adriatic Veneti, while the goddess of the earth and mother of their country was Rhaetia. Cf. R. Pittioni, op. cit., p. 311.

Štalenska gora (Magdalensberg) Carinthia—Provincial Assembly "conventus Noricorum"
built after the year 15 B.C. (Roman era).

(41–54 A.D.) did Noricum become a House province and later under Marcus Aurelius (161–180) a regular Roman province. The cities on the southern and eastern periphery of Noricum—Emona, Poetovio, Savaria, Scarbantia, and Carnuntum—were separated from Noricum under Roman rule and joined to Pannonia; only Celeia remained. Noricum was not a subjugated land even after it ceased to be an independent kingdom; when it had the status of a House province it was headed by an imperial administrator (procurator) and when it became a regular province, by an imperial governor (legatus).

In contrast to other provinces in the Empire, the position of Noricum remained special. In the city on Mt. Štalen (whose name is still unknown to us), the foundation of an assembly hall was excavated. It is presumed that the Norican **conventus** (provincial legislature) met here. Under Emperor Claudius the following Norican towns received the status of a Roman city, i.e., *municipium*: Virunum (from this time on the capital of the province), Teurnia (near Spittal), Aguntum (near Lienz), Celeia (Celje in Slovenia), and Juvavum (Salzburg).[149]

---

[149] Pliny (III, 146): omnia Claudia sc. municipia. Noricum enjoyed a special position in the Roman Empire if compared with Rhaetia where only Cambodunum became a Roman colony, and in comparison with Pannonia where only Scarbantia, the town of the Roman colons, occupied such position. Only later did Savaria receive the same status.

113

Around the year 70 A.D. Flavia Solva (near Leibnitz) also became a *municipium*, and in the following century, Ovilava (Wels) and Cetium (St. Pölten), and later Lauriacum (Lorch). These were centres where, during pre-Roman times, a stratum of Celtic craftsmen and merchants was present. After that, they became Roman administrative and civil service centres.

ius gentium

More than ninety percent of the population of Noricum was of indigenous stock;[150] i.e., Veneti. That is why they left behind a far greater archaeological legacy (as well as place-names) than did the Celts,[151] whose stratum of craftsmen and merchants in the cities was Romanized. Under the Romans the cities were still small and their population was at least half Venetic (Slovene).

According to Roman law the majority of Noricum's inhabitants were "peregrini" (foreigners), since they did not have Roman or Latin citizenship; however, they were granted the status of a nation and internal rule according to indigenous legal customs. In contrast, the "peregrini dediticii", whose community life was destroyed after subjugation by the Romans, no longer possessed their own legal customs.

Another factor contributing to Noricum's social and economic stability and affecting the rural population in particular, was the ownership of land. Arable land was in private possession and pasture land was held communally even at that time. A land tax was levied by the occupying forces. Until the middle of the 2nd century A.D., there were no Roman latifundia in Noricum, but they were a dominant feature in neighbouring Pannonia.[152] Farming tradition and lifestyle on small land-holdings in Noricum had evidently not been interfered with during Roman rule. We should add that there were no appreciable numbers of Italic colonists, and it is known that only one Roman legion was stationed on Mt. Štalen (Magdalensberg); its command was in Poetovio/Ptuj. The northern border of the Empire along the Danube was more heavily fortified by Roman troops.

Noricum's predominantly small farms belonged to indigenous inhabitants. Fields were cultivated by the farmers themselves who were united in village

---

[150] F. Glaser, *Die römische Stadt Teurnia/* The Roman City Teurnia, Klagenfurt 1982.

[151] B. Grafenauer, op., cit., pp. 174–175.

[152] B. Grafenauer, ibid., pp. 174–175.

communities,[153] the **civitates peregrinae**.[154] In Roman provinces, large estates generally displaced small farmsteads. Noricum was apparently spared this fate by virtue of its special standing in the Empire; only in the latter part of the 2nd century can some "villae" (that is, administration buildings for the latifundiae) be shown to have existed in this country.

civitates

Village communities in the eastern Alps outlived the Roman Empire in part because of the *Constitutio Antoniniana* (212 A.D.), through which Emperor Caracalla abolished all differences between foreigners and other inhabitants, thus giving Roman citizenship to all free people. As a result the Norici, who were ninety percent indigenous, became Roman citizens. Of course, they had to pay taxes and were subject to military conscription but they now had rights and were, in comparison to other peoples subdued by the Romans, a free nation.

Were the Norici Romanized? Latin predominated in the cities as the official and commercial language, but there is no documentary evidence that Noricum became Latinized or Romanized. It is even impossible to say that the cities were (apart from the Italian immigrants) Romanized in spite of the prevailing Latin language.

Historians who were influenced by German nationalist or Pan-Slavistic ideologies tenaciously repeat the theory that Norici were Romanized. The reason for this is very simple. In order to set the stage for the invasion of Slavs about a century after the departure of the Romans, historians moved the "Romanized" indigenous population westward and in this way made the entire Inner Noricum ready for the Slavs.

After the 3rd century, the crisis within the Empire became ever more noticeable, resulting in insurrections, emergence of new religions and a general weakening of defence. For that reason Emperor Diocletian (284–305) reformed Roman administration. Among other changes, he divided Noricum into two prov-

---

[153] Cf. B. Grafenauer, ibid., p. 175.

[154] *civitates* (the village communities) prevailing in the Alps and on the Danube, cf. Paulys Real-Encyclopädie, op. cit., Suppl. I, 1903 (Civitas). The same conditions existed in Noricum because this kingdom was inhabited by Veneti who had a social structure based on village communities acknowledged also by the Romans (ius gentium). Noricum could not have been organized on the Celtic model, whose society was formed into kinship communes, *Sippe* in German.

inces, the northern half reaching as far as the shore of the Danube: *Noricum ripense* (Outer Noricum) and *Noricum mediterraneum* (Inner Noricum). The border between the two followed the mountain ridges of the Hohen and Niederen Tauern. The capital of the former was Ovilava (Wels) and that of the latter, Virunum. The military command was at Lauriacum (Lorch) headed by a *dux* (duke).

After Christianity became the state religion of the Roman Empire under Emperor Theodosius (381), bishoprics were established in Norican cities and were subordinated to the patriarchate in Aquileia. Christianity in Noricum remained limited to the cities.

At the beginning of the 5th century, Germanic tribes began to invade Outer Noricum. The Vandals and Alans moved westward on the road along the Danube in the year 401; at the end of 406 came another large wave of Alans, Vandals, and Suebians. In 451, the Huns led by Attila travelled through the area on their way to Gaul and back, and around 472 came the Alemanni, Thuringians, and Heruli.[155] After King Odoacer of the Heruli invaded Italy and deposed Emperor Romulus Augustulus (476) of the Western Roman Empire, he relinquished Outer Noricum to the Germanic tribes in 488.

Inner Noricum still remained allied to Italy at this time. King Odoacer was overthrown in the year 493 by Theodorik, king of the East Goths, who was sent by the Byzantine Emperor, Zenon. The East Goths were thereafter rulers of Italy and **Inner Noricum.** Archaeological discoveries show that they were able to maintain their occupation of many areas in the eastern Alps; for example, the East Gothic settlement in Kranj, Slovenia. However, in 535, the East Goths were defending themselves in Italy against the Byzantines and had to relinquish all of Inner Noricum to the Franks. The East Gothic kingdom in Italy finally fell in the year 555 and the Byzantine Governor Narzes advanced from Italy into Inner Noricum, where he established Byzantine administration in 561. Thus the country came under Byzantine rule.

In 568, the powerful Langobards moved out of northwest Pannonia in a southwesterly direction into Italy. They destroyed Byzantine strongholds in northern and central regions except for the cities of Ravenna and Rome and their environs. The Langobards established their new kingdom in Italy, which did not include Inner Noricum.

We have thus reached the crucial thirty-year period after the Langobard migration out of Pannonia; that is, the time when according to official history the Slavs migrated into the region of the eastern Alps and founded their state,

---

[155] E. Polanschek, in Paulys Real-Encyclopädie, op. cit., 1936 (Noricum), p. 1013.

Carantania. This group of Slavs, the so-called Alpine Slavs, are assumed to be the ancestors of present-day Slovenes.

No historical source-material gives any indication about such settlement in the Alps at that time. But we have good reason to believe that the Adriatic Veneti as well as the Carni in the Alps were Slavic speaking people. A number of post-antiquity writers were of this same understanding, depending in their research on the old toponyms, at least in part (D.E. Springsguth 1772).[156]

The Byzantine author Constantine Porphyrogentos, writing in the 10th century A.D., mentions in his work *De Administrado Imperio* (27, 84) that the ancient Veneti built various fortified places on islands in the Venetian Lagoon. Among the names of these new settlements we find the following: "Congradum, Rhibalenses, Boes, Pristena, Bronium". According to Springsguth, these names are of Slavic origin and have familiar Slovene meanings: *grad*—castle; *ribiški kraj*—fishing area; *boj* or *bojišče*—place of battle; *pristan*—harbor, port; and *bran* or *utrdba*—defended area. Livy (XLIV, 26) speaks of a place, **Bylazora** in Dalmatia, and Ptolemy (lib. II) mentions **Curieta**; these two names are undoubtedly Slavic.

Many Roman names of places in Slovenia and in the wider Venetic region have no meaning in their Latin form, either morphologically or topographically, although place-names are commonly structured in this way. However, as soon as the names are considered to be of Slavic, i.e., Slovene origin, they acquire a meaning that accords very well with their natural surroundings. **Tergeste,** Trst, Trieste—*terg* or *trg* is still a common word in Slovene for a market place or town where a market is held regularly; **Timavus** (Timava, Timavo) contains the etymon, or primary meaning of *tema*—darkness—which is very appropriate as the course of this river is in greater part underground; **Loganticus** (Logatec), *log*—a meadow by a body of water.

In Roman times, the very important road from Aquileia to Noricum, called **via Beloio,** ran along the river that is to this day called Bela—white (water) river, a very common Slovene name for a stream or river in the mountainous region, Ger. Fella. At its source, there was the **statio Bilachinium** near the town of Santicum, now Beljak; also its Ger. name Villach is derived from the original Slovene meaning. In the same area there was **Meclaria,** today Meglarje, Ger.

---

[156] D.E. Springsguth: *"Quae fuit gens Adriam accolens nempe Veneti quam Polybius, Strabo, Livius memorant nec Latino nec Graeco nec Gallico sermone usam fuisse,"* pro anno 1772. This means: "Who were the people living on the Adriatic? Certainly the Veneti recorded by Polybius, Strabo and Livy and who spoke neither Latin nor Greek nor Celtic."

*Village linden tree at
Vrba, Slovenia.*

Maglern, from *medgorje*—the passage between two mountains; **Teurnia,** *turje*—steep mountains; **Tamasicum** Ger. Tamsweg *tamar*—shelter, corral.

The place-name **Ocra mons,** on the ancient road from the Adriatic to east central Europe, was later called **Ad Pirum** and yet later in the Middle Ages in German writings, Birnbaum; both names mean pear tree (*hruška* in Slovene). The original and topographically correct name comes from *krušica* or *hrušca,* meaning easily-broken rock (shell). Today the place is called Hrušica—a good example of how the original name was corrupted by the translation of an incorrect word which had only a resemblance to the original.

The ability to expound these names on the basis of the Slovene language has been excluded in advance by official linguists and historians, although research in toponymy based in Slovene expressions still in common use clearly presents the origin and meaning of these and many other place-names presented in this study.

Carantania

...Qui mox cum exercitu in Sclaborum provinciam introiens, patrata victoria, ad solum proprium cum maxima praeda remeavit. (Pauli diaconi Historia Langobardorum)[157]

The preceding chapters tell us that the Venetic people had survived to a considerable degree in the central and eastern Alps and in the mountain valleys around the upper Po region after the arrival of the Romans. These are the areas where we now find many Venetic (Slovene) place-names as well as historically proven variations on the name of the once-unified Venetic people, such as Veneti, Venoneti, Veneni, Venosti, and Vindelici. Archaeologists have determined that in those regions where these Venetic names appear, pre-Celtic cultures like Golasecca, Melaun, and especially Este and Hallstatt, had existed in part until the arrival of the Romans.

In spite of the fact that the Celts had occupied all regions around the Alps, they settled in the Alps only in small numbers. The great majority of the Celtic La Tène discoveries in the Alps are to be attributed to trade and not to the Celtic presence.

We can be fairly certain that there were some Celtic merchants and miners, but this does not mean that indigenous Veneti remained only farmers; they had been active in mining and trade much earlier.

The ideologically oriented historians continue to tell us that before the arrival of the Romans, the Celts made up the leading social stratum in the Alps. *Neither archaeology nor toponymy gives us any evidence to support such a conclusion.* A number of Roman authors (for example, Livy) do in fact report that in the eastern Alps there existed a kingdom of several Celtic (Gallic) tribes, but they were writing about events of at least 200 years earlier. Seen in relation to archaeological discoveries and toponymy, these reports confirm for us what was presented earlier: *the presence of Celts in the cities, but not the Celtization of indigenous Venetic people of rural areas of the Alps.*

---

[157] F. Kos, *Gradivo* I, op. cit., no. 112.

Considering the arrival of the Romans in the first century B.C., a natural question develops at this point: Did the indigenous Alpine people, erroneously seen by many as Illyrians, become Romanized during the following centuries?

institutio Sclavenica

In regions where Italic merchants, craftsmen, and colonists settled during Roman times, Romanic dialects were accepted and Romanic languages are used to this day. Those regions that were not Romanized in this manner were Latinized through the presence of Roman civil servants and troops and later also through Christianization. Strong evidence lies in the Ladin territory, until a few centuries ago a unified region which extended from Friuli over the Dolomites as far as Swiss Rhaetia. Another detail we must keep in mind is that countries that were conquered by Romans in battle were not allowed to keep their own legal systems. Their inhabitants were classified as foreigners without rights (peregrini dediticii). Rhaetia was such a territory. In contrast the situation in the eastern Alps, in Noricum, was very different.

In the beginning the status of a kingdom was maintained. Later, for the duration of a century, Noricum was an Imperial House province and, in the latter half of the 2nd century A.D., attained the status of a regular Roman province. In the beginning of the 3rd century under Emperor Caracalla, the Norici (who did not belong to the class of "foreigners without rights"), became Roman citizens, and at the end of the 3rd century the indigenous legal system, the *ius gentium*, was accepted as equal to Roman Civil Law—*ius civile*.[158]

Noricum had been an ordinary Roman province for only thirty years when its inhabitants became Roman citizens. All of Noricum's major cities were *municipia* from the first century A.D., while the people in the countryside were organized in *civitates,* that is, village communities.[159] Because of Noricum's special status, we cannot consider that its rural people were foreigners.

The recognition of the "ius gentium" implies the existence of an indigenous

---

[158] Paulys Real-Encyclopädie...op. cit., 1937 (Peregrinus), p. 655.

[159] G. Ankershofen, *Urkunden-Regesten zur Geschichte Kärntens/*The Document-Register on the History of Carinthia; Archiv für Kunde österr. Geschichtsquellen I, 1848, 3, Heft No. LXXXIV, p. 38. From the second half of the last century the historians, like A. Jaksch and Ankershofen, have for ideological reasons left out the "Slavica lex" when quoting this source. F. Kos, in his *Gradivo* III. See also J. Šavli, Institutio Sclavenica, in *Slovenska država Karantanija*, Editiones Veneti, Vienna 1990.

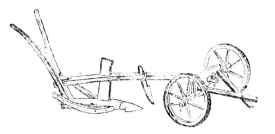

Plough on two wheels from the area of Carinthia and Lower Styria. Its form originates in the first century A.D.

ruling class in Noricum, especially since there is no documentary or archaeological evidence that Noricum had been Romanized or Latinized. After the partitioning of the country during the reign of Emperor Diocletian, Outer Noricum was defended against invaders by Roman border troops (limitanei) in addition to the regular Roman army (comitatenses). This continued until the weakening of the Roman government at the beginning of the 6th century, which allowed various Germanic tribes and finally the Bavarians an opportunity to advance into Outer Noricum as well as into Rhaetia and Vindelicia.

We must ask at this point the unavoidable question, because most of the ongoing inquiry will depend on the answer: **Why did the Bavarians not occupy Inner Noricum at that time?**

The mountains of Inner Noricum could not have been an obstacle for them, just as the central Alps were no obstacle in their occupation of Rhaetia. Then why would they have waited for the Slavs to come and settle in Inner Noricum before their very eyes?

There is only one logical answer: Inner Noricum had resisted the attacks of other Germanic tribes and it also resisted the Bavarians. The resistance could have been administered only by a native people who were neither Latinized nor Romanized. If they had been Romanized, the circumstances in Inner Noricum would have been the same as in other provinces: when the Roman army and state administration collapsed and withdrew, Inner Noricum would have been overrun by Germanic tribes.

There is no doubt that events at that time developed very much along the lines as indicated above. Inner Noricum's population was ninety percent native Venetic and was well capable of defending its home territory. Historians suggest: "There are two facts to be noted; i.e., the eastern Alps were, at the time of the mass migration of barbaric people, mainly Romanized and Christianized."[160] It would have been much closer to the truth if they had said: The eastern Alps were mainly not Romanized or Christianized.

Following the decline of the Western Roman Empire, various Germanic kingdoms sprang up in its territory. Roman laws "leges Romanorum" still applied to Romanic and Romanized inhabitants of these kingdoms, whereas Germanic inhabitants were subject to so-called Barbarian laws "leges Barbarorum".

The latter were translated into Latin and issued as codes of law as early as the 5th and 6th centuries. Visigoths in Spain had their Lex Visigothorum, Ostrogoths in Italy their Edictum Theodorici, Langobards issued Edictum Rothari in the 7th century, and Alemans or Swabians had Lex Alamannorum. In the 8th century Lex Baiuvariorum was issued for Bavarians and, in the beginning of the 9th century, Lex Saxonum for the Saxons after they had been defeated by Charlemagne.

Franks gradually took over Western Europe after the downfall of Roman rule. In the beginning, they had a number of minor kingdoms. Later these evolved into two larger units: Neustria under the rule of the Meroving family, and Austrasia under the Carolingians. Neustria was subject to Lex Salica, written around 490, known particularly for its rule of agnatic descendancy, where women were excluded from ascension to the throne (as distinguished from Lex Visigothorum), while Austrasia was subject to Lex Ripuaria, which was essentially a common law written as late as the 7th century. Somewhat modified, these codes of law were applied into the Middle Ages.

In Carantania (previously known as Inner Noricum) the old local law from the Roman period was retained. This was actually the old pre-Roman common law, preserved as a legal custom—consuetudine—valid for statutory legal occasions and social organization of Carantania. At the time, when Carantania was first mentioned in historical sources, this law was not specifically cited. Only as late as the beginning of the 11th century was it designated by historical reports as:

Institutio Sclavenica
communis omnium Slavica lex

that is, *the Slovene legal system*, or *general Slovene law*, which is derived directly from Noricum's "ius gentium". The Norici and Carantanians who followed

---

[160] B. Grafenauer, op. cit., p. 201.

these laws were the same people: they have always been a "natio" which means a recognized community in terms of jurisprudence.

The social organization of Carantanians differs from that of Germans, who were organized along the old clan blood-related Sippe (commune), as was the custom among the Franks. Carantanian society was organized and based on the village—Slovene *vas*—meaning a community and a settlement with divided fields and common pastures and forests. The Slovene word *župan* (mayor), a village head, is the only remnant of the old *župa* or clan-related commune. *Historical sources fail to report any clan or commune system in Noricum or Carantania.*

Each village had its own territory; several villages were connected geographically into a district, headed by a leader (princeps), whose abilities were mostly military. The *princeps* was also responsible for communications with the central government, headed by the duke. The duke and leaders of districts represented the nobility which was still very close to the common people.

In regard to decision-making, the common people had the final say. At the village level they met in an assembly called *sosednja* or *sosečka*—neighbourhood gathering. At the district level this gathering was called a *pojezda*—a riding gathering—where usually a high-ranking regional or national representative was present, having arrived on horseback; sometimes it was the duke himself. At the national level this gathering was called *veča,* which elected a new duke, either directly or indirectly through representatives, the so-called "good people". A newly-elected duke was invested on the Prince's Stone by the people through their representatives.

We are acquainted with these details of the Carantanian state from later writings only. There is no doubt, however, that they existed from the very beginning and only later, in the Middle Ages, merged with feudal elements into the mediaeval feudal system of Carantania. There are a few more particulars from the old Slovene legal system: *rota,* oath taken at certain places called "rotišče"; witnesses were of two kinds, *svidok,* the one who saw (testis oculatus), or *posluh,* the one who heard (testis auditus). A community is called *občina,* communal work is *robota,* internal unrest is *kramola,* premeditated murder is *razboj.* Only sometime in the 10th century was another legal form adopted, which was testified by means of "professio juris".

The Carantanian woman—as distinguished from the Germanic woman—had the same rights and avails as a Carantanian man in regard to property and legal capacity and position; Carantanian noblewomen were able to make major property transfers. **St. Hema** was a Slovene noblewoman from Carantania who founded monasteries and built many churches—possible only because she was subject to Carantanian law, which related to the person and not to the territory.

In the absence of a male heir, a Carantanian woman had full rights to inheritance. Inheritance and succession laws fully included female descendants and applied even in regard to the ruler—examples are Duke Arnulf of Carantania (9th century), son of a noble Carantanian woman, and the Frankish Prince Karlman. A good example of family inheritance law was the family Spanheim which took its name from a son-in-law from the Rhine Valley who married Rikarda, heiress of a Carantanian noble family. The ruling class in Carantania remained native—Slovene.

The social organization and law of Carantanians could only have been derived from their ancestors, the natives of Noricum, considered a "natio" under the Romans; that is, a nation with a recognized legal system and statutory rights. Only under such conditions could they have preserved their legal customs, their culture and traditions.

The Ideology of Settlement

Claims about Romanization and Christianization in the area of the eastern Alps, although without historic foundation, are of key importance for the continuation of official history-writing. If the population of this area had been Romanized and Christianized earlier, and pagan during the later Slavic period, then it would be clear that the old population moved away, and the area was taken over by pagan Slavs. This presentation regarding the settlement of Slavs in the Alps during the 6th century becomes fairly convincing.

But if the population of the eastern Alps was neither Christianized nor Romanized, then we have to find out who these people were and what language they spoke. The answer is arrived at easily because all evidence is clear: the Norici spoke Venetic (Slovene), just as did their neighbours the Rhaeti; this is obvious from Slovene place-names throughout the eastern Alps and as far west as eastern Switzerland. Historians silently pass over this evidence.

In spite of all efforts made by official historians to get the Slavs into the Alps in the 6th century—though only as far as the Hohen Tauern and not beyond—there is enough evidence to contradict this theory. Slovene place-names go much farther to the west, much beyond the official demarcation line. There is another indisputable fact which should be repeated: **No documentary source tells us about the settlement of Slavs in the eastern Alps at the end of the 6th century.** It is difficult to imagine a settlement wave of such magnitude going unobserved. Numerous Germanic invasions, leaving no significant after-effect, were recorded in historical documents. The Slavs, on the other hand, are supposed to

Carantania in the 7th century; its boundaries were almost the same as those of Inner Noricum.

have occupied all of Noricum without arousing the attention of even one ancient writer?

This question was temporarily resolved before the First World War on the basis of the South Slavic model. Slovenes were South Slavs in regard to language and every other detail; that established, there was no difficulty with the rest of the projected image. They arrived in the Balkans along with their kinfolk and proceeded into the Alps. The majority of linguists and historians agreed there could be no better solution; they liked the "clear-cut" explanation for a seemingly unsolvable problem. Some of them did everything possible to ensure success for this politically-inspired theory; one of those scholars was the Slovene linguist, V. Oblak, who was convinced that South Slavic languages, including Slovene, were but a series of closely related dialects. He too had to do something with the indigenous population of the Alps, insisting that whoever they were, they could not have been Slavs.[161] In his efforts to develop a solution to this relatively minor problem, he created more and more confusion:

"The presumed indigenous people of Noricum, the ancestors of Slovenes, must have been a very large group to be able to withstand the countless barbarian assaults, and if they were such a numerous people, how could they have vanished without a trace? There should be in upper Styria and northern Carinthia something to remind us of these people, possibly some place- names. However, such do not exist."

About that time many articles were published in the Slovene press regarding Slavic, that is, Slovene names in the Alps, so it is even more confusing to hear Professor Oblak insist that there is nothing to indicate an indigenous Slavic population in the Alps prior to the arrival of the South Slavs.

It is very unlikely that Oblak was ignorant of the presence of countless names of Slovene origin throughout the Alps, or that he was unable to connect the various probabilities into a sensible conclusion. His problem was the one that most Slovene scholars had: their tenure was always dependent on goodwill from Vienna or Belgrade. They had to toe the line or lose their jobs.

F. Kos, the otherwise praiseworthy Slovene historian, also tried very hard to get the Slovenes into the Alps from the Balkans. He was plainly unable to shake off the South Slavic model, and at the same time he made an effort to develop some of his own (though erroneous) ideas on the subject:[162]

"The South Slavic and West Slavic people: the Bulgarians, Serbs, Croats, and Czechs had not settled in their present-day places until the 6th century A.D. From this we can conclude that at the same time also the Slovenes had settled in their present territory by the Sava, Drava, Mura, and Soča Rivers, and not a thousand years earlier.

"The Avars gained Pannonia and the land of the Gepids under the terms of a treaty, whereas Noricum still had to be conquered, and apparently the Slovenes carried out this task.

"The Slovenes probably destroyed the city of Tiburnia or Teurnia...they apparently at the same time also destroyed the city of Aguntum...additionally, it is

---

[161] V. Oblak, *Eine Bemerkung zur ältesten südslawischen Geschichte/* An Observation on the Earliest History of the South Slavs; Archiv für slawische Philologie XVIII, pp. 228–234. See F. Kos, *Zbrano delo*, op. cit., 1982, p. 102/2 (1896).

[162] F. Kos, *Zbrano delo*, op. cit., pp. 100, 105, 107, 108, 113, (1896, 1901).

presumed that they tore down Emona.... The Slovenes settled in Noricum and the bordering regions, by moving up the river valleys."

This simplistic—though politically correct—theory about the Slovene settlement in the Alps is disqualified by those linguists who recognized that the Slovenes do not linguistically belong to the South Slavic group. This has been repeatedly pointed out by us; viz., *the Slovenes/Veneti/Wends are West Slavs, and their settlement in the Alps did not coincide with the settlement of the South Slavs in the Balkans.*

Since it was impossible to just pass over these facts, the historians have made an attempt to supplement the initial theory about the move from the Balkans into the Alps by stating: "The eastern Alps were around the year 550 already taken over by a Slavic settlement wave from the north; that is, from the present- day Moravia and the region south of the Carpathian Mts. (B. Grafenauer)."[163] We are told that from this particular settlement wave came the following words in Slovene dialects: *šidlo, močidlo, sedlo*, and so on. However, archaeology confirms that this settlement wave from the north moved over western Pannonia into the Balkans. What we have here is simply an attempt at rescuing the invention that the Slovenes came into the eastern Alps from the Balkans, an attempt that rescues nothing.

The official historians are desperate to establish the settlement of Slavs in the eastern Alps in the 6th century on a predetermined model along Germanic and Pan-Slavic ideological lines, but they are also aware of the frailty of this position. That is the reason every effort was made, citing countless papers, literature, and names of academically respected scholars to secure this view in the minds of the public. Secondly, historians wanted to establish that, after the fall of the Western Roman Empire (which was brought about by the Germans), the social and economic structures had not been destroyed in the former Roman provinces. However, in the eastern Alps, after the departure of the Langobards to Italy (568), these structures disappeared. From such inconclusive evidence the experts came to the "logical" conclusion that Roman social and economic structures were destroyed by the Slavs who, according to documentary sources, were discovered inhabiting the eastern Alps in the following century, therefore "proving" that they had just arrived in the eastern Alps.

The Slovene historian, B. Grafenauer, produced numerous studies and essays about the presumed cessation or marginal continuation of the ancient Roman culture and social structure in the eastern Alps. In the process, he carefully avoided

---

[163] B. Grafenauer, op. cit., pp. 267–269. The citing of the year (cir. 550 A.D.), without indicating the source, is highly presumptuous on his part.

a number of studies which examine the continuation of pre-Roman social elements (which several Austrian authors try to interpret as Celtic remnants). Here are a few excerpts from his writings:[164]

1. Carantania's Slavic period, from the end of the 6th century to the beginning of the 9th century is, in regard to its economic and cultural structure, sharply differentiated from late antiquity; this structure was not destroyed by the Eastern Goths during their occupation; the [later] ashes of the Norican cities were a symbolic testimony of this (R. Egger, J. Klemenc).

2. The settlement area already in existence from the time of Hallstatt culture remained the same during Carantania's Slavic period, thus proving that the newcomer Slavs settled in the areas occupied by the previous inhabitants, on the lands that were suitable for agriculture and already cultivated (M. Kos, E. Klebel, R. Egger).

3. In the ancient Carantanian realm the indigenous inhabitants, the Lahi (Romanized Celts), were sparsely represented, as can be seen from place-names that have their roots in antiquity (M. Kos). Some of these Romanized Alpine people moved westward when the Slavs arrived. The name Noricum is supposed to prove their past presence in this region.

4. No traces of Roman field division are to be found during Carantania's Slavic period. The medieval method of field division (i.e., of permanent private ownership of fields) was supposed to have been fully developed only under the Franks (B. Grafenauer, S. Vilfan). Also during this period the Carantanians would have adopted the improved two-wheel version of the Rhaetian hook-plough, Slov.—*ralo* (S. Gabrovec).

5. The social structure of the extended family (zadruga), ruled by a chieftain and assumed to be typical for the above-mentioned Carantanian period, was characterized by a common hearth, undivided arable land, small settlements, clans sharing pasture lands. This kind of internal organization is considered to have been of Slavic origin and does not stem from antiquity. The chieftains (Slov.—*kosezi)* were a form of Slavic military personnel (Ukrainian družiniki) accountable to the prince (B. Grafenauer).

6. The Christianization of Carantania was, we are told, accomplished relatively quickly because of the presence of a remnant of Christianized, Romanized Celtic population in the country.

These statements are to prove that there was a complete break between antiquity and the Middle Ages; that there was, in other words, no continuation from one period to the other. It all sounds fairly convincing, but can it be substantiated?

---

[164] B. Grafenauer, *Die Kontinuitätsfragen in der Geschichte des alt-Karantanischen Raumes/* The Problem of Continuity in the History of the Early Carantanian Territory, Alpes Orientales V, Ljubljana 1969 pp. 55–79.

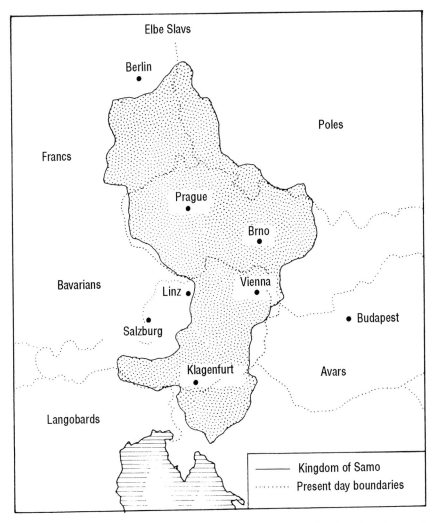

Kingdom of Samo (623–658) united into one state: Slovenes... Czechs, Moravians and Elbe Slavs (Polabians).

Town and Countryside

The ruins of Noricum's cities do not in themselves prove that the Slavs arrived at that time and started burning. The Slovene historian F. Kos was aware of this, and wrote very cautiously, "...it seems that the Slavs had done this."

It is fairly accurate to say that, with the destruction of Noricum's cities in late antiquity, its culture perished; but we must be careful to recognize that what perished was the Roman system, the city culture, and not the rural farming communities, where nine-tenths of the population lived. The rural population was organized into communities, "civitates", with their own legal system at least nominally intact and ownership of small parcels of land. Pliny the Elder (III, 133) mentions that the Rhaeti and Vindelici lived in numerous "civitates", which could only have been villages, not cities (municipia). For the Carantanian period around 670, Anonymus Ravennas (Cosmographia IV, ch. 19) lists for Carnia and Carniola names of twenty-five "civitates" which could not have been cities but rather villages or large villages. The basis of Carantanian (Slovene) social structure, as was earlier the case under Roman occupation, was **the village with its accompanying hamlets;** i.e., the village community, Slov. *sosednja, sosečka,* or *srenja.* Place-names consisting of the word *vas* (village) are to this day characteristic of valley basins and heavily populated areas.[165] A smaller yet independent village is in Slovene called *selo;* an older form is *sedlo* (hamlet, settlement) and belongs to the village community, whereas the word, *zaselek,* refers to a part of a village. All of these signify established settlements which form one land-registry unit.

The village and village community are the foundation and structure of Carantanian society, as opposed to the extended family commune of the South Slavs, which B. Grafenauer wishes to attribute to the Carantanians during the early period of their independent state. For good measure he is also assigning to them (on the Ukrainian model) the "družiniki", as the armed attendants of the Carantanian duke. Needless to say, all of these are only products of his imagination.

If we assume that the settlement of the Slavs in the eastern Alps occurred at

---

[165] M. Kos, *Vas in selo v zgodovini slovenske kolonizacije/* The Village and the Hamlet in the History of the Slovene Colonization; Razprave SAZU, Ljubljana 1966, pp. 80–82, 92–96. The word "vas" is of very ancient origin: Sanskrit *vastu*—dwelling, house, from *uas*—to stay, to dwell; Arabic *ma'uan*—lodging-place, night resting-place; Semitic *A-u-i.* (Au.). Cf. H. Möller, *Vergleichendes indogermanisch-semitisches Wörterbuch/* The Comparative Indo-European-Semitic Dictionary, Göttingen 1911, p. 20

the same time as that on the Balkan peninsula, then such parallels between the eastern Alps and eastern Europe would make some sense. Such argumentation, however, turns the methodology upside-down, for the alleged result is presented as the reason for its cause!

Bearing in mind that the Alpine Slav settlement in the 6th century is unproven, and that all other components presented in support by official historians are also unproven, we are left with but one conclusion in regard to Noricum's cities.

After the Langobards had overthrown Byzantine rule in Italy and established their own kingdom there, Noricum was cut off administratively. Without fear of consequences, the indigenous population, non-Celticized and non-Romanized Veneti or Slovenes, were able to burn and destroy the cities, the centers of foreign administration and exploitation. There is some logic in this, but after a more detailed examination, the proposition is questionable.

If these cities were really destroyed by Slavs, there must have been major battles, but official historians tell us that the inhabitants fled into Italy and Bavaria. If the cities were deserted, why would the advancing Slavs burn them? Because they were barbaric and did not know the value of ready-made accommodation? Very unlikely. Many armies of invaders passed through Noricum; precisely who destroyed its cities is not known. One thing is certain and it needs to be repeated: **The destroyed cities of Noricum do not prove the arrival of Slavs at that time**.

After that, the power in Noricum could only have been taken over by the indigenous population, which lived in village communities and possessed the constitutional legal system. Part of the Romanized population must have stayed in the country and later contributed to the relatively speedy Christianization of the rest of the Norici (Carantanians).

Village and Hamlet

Among the most important "proofs" of a Slavic settlement in the eastern Alps is field division, which is totally different from that of the Romans. The continuation of Roman field form is archaeologically proven only in Georgenberg near Micheldorf in Upper Austria.[166] If landed property in the Roman Empire was divided into squares, then even the fields would have had a square shape; but

---

[166] H. Vetters, Der Georgenberg bei Micheldorf, Oberösterr. Heimatblätter 8, 1954, p. 23 passim (see B. Grafenauer, *Die Kontinuitätsfragen*...op. cit., p. 69).

there was no such division in early Carantania. The Roman square measurement system was based on the *iugerum*—2520 square meters, Slov. *oral.*

However, this does not presuppose a widespread system of square field division. The archaeologically proven example of a quadratic field shape in Upper Austria cannot be extended to all of Noricum for the period of Roman rule; it represents but an isolated case established in late antiquity by Roman colonists in Outer Noricum.

Arable land in Inner Noricum adjusted itself to the terrain, whether flat, rolling, or sloped. The fields usually had an elongated shape. Although the surface could be measured in Roman squares—and it probably was for tax purposes—this does not presuppose a square shape or division of fields or pastures; that would have been quite impossible in mountainous Inner Noricum. From time immemorial the customary method for measuring fields in Inner Noricum was pacing, and the most important element regarding ownership was who cleared the land and who cultivated it.

If the land was not taken from the indigenous people, we cannot expect a Roman type of field division in the region, and that is why we find no such traces during Carantania's early period. We are told that Roman field division was destroyed by the Slavs, but this is obviously another desperate attempt to establish the otherwise unproven settlement of Slavs at that time.[167]

Plough and Hook-Plough, Bees...

Another unsuccessful endeavour to prove this Slavic incursion involves a farm implement, namely the plough. The plough belongs among the most important of agricultural tools; we can estimate historically the growth of agriculture by examining the developmental stages of the plough. The well-known Slovene

---

[167] The Slovene (Carantanian) social structure with the village community based on the divided arable land can only be derived from Noricum's rural society. This social structure is also in the later period sharply differentiated from that found among the South Slavs; these were the results of the research carried out by V. Bogošić in the last century. See also: *Zbornik sadašnjih pravnih običaja u Južnih Slavena/* A Codex of Current Juridical Customs of the South Slavs; vol. I, Publications of JAZU, Zagreb 1974. Another statement regarding this was given by the Slovene scholar S. Vilfan, who discovered that no traces of the South Slavic *zadruga*—the extended family with common arable land—were found among the Slovenes. Cf. S. Vilfan: *Pravna zgodovina Slovencev/* Law History of the Slovenes, Ljubljana 1961, p. 54.

Carantania—Brooches with the image of a panther (9th century) from several discovery sites: Bohinj, Bled, Mengeš, and Brunn. The panther became the coat-of-arms of the Duchy.

archaeologist, S. Gabrovec, discovered (after he had classified the excavated plough-shares from the La Tène period to late antiquity) that the eastern Alps had become the centre of agricultural progress during the Roman Empire.

He also took into consideration historical evidence that in this region the original simple plough (improved version of hook-plough) was lifted onto two wheels.[168] Ploughing was made easier, since the plough no longer dug too deeply into the ground. Pliny the Elder (XVIII 18, 48) informed us of the two-wheeled plough from Rhaetia, using the word "plaumorati".[169]

After the Slavs settled in the eastern Alps, they allegedly did not adopt the use of the two-wheeled plough, but rather continued to use the primitive *ralo* (hook-plough)—supposedly proven by excavations in Carinthia where, for the time period from the 6th to the 9th century, corresponding finds of the improved plough were not present to confirm the change-over. Even the word *plug* (plough) is considered to be a foreign word in Slovene, supposedly adopted by Slovene newcomers, from the Romans or Germans, who got it from the Celts (plovum). Nevertheless, the Slavs in the eastern Alps are believed to have acquired longhorn cattle and several breeds of horses from the indigenous inhabitants and to have

---

[168] S. Gabrovec, *Predzgodovinsko gradivo za preučevanje rala na Slovenskem/* The Prehistoric Materials for the Study of the Hook-Plough on the Slovene Territory; *Slovenski etnograf* 8, Ljubljana 1955. See also B. Grafenauer, op. cit., p. 182.

[169] The word "plaumorati" is closely linked to the word and meaning in the Slovene language: *plaum, plovum*, in Slovene *pluti*—to navigate, to furrow, indicative (1st person); *plovem*, and *orati*—to plough. Cf. G. Krek, in the magazine *Kres*, Klagenfurt 1884, p. 104 passim. The German word "Pflug", in Slovene *plug* (plough) derives from the Rhaetian according to the recent interpretations. Cf. Mackensen, *Deutsches Wörterbuch*, Cologne 1983, p. 1217. The Rhaetians were of Venetic ethnicity. Au.

133

brought poultry-raising and bee-keeping from their homeland.[170] These conclusions seem accurate, but they are all contradictory.

First of all, the allegation that the word *plug* could not be indigenous to the Slovene language is unfounded.[171] Also without basis is the statement that the Alpine Slavs adopted the Celtic or Roman term for plough but not the implement itself. Even if archaeologists had not discovered finds corresponding to Carantania's so-called Slavic period, that is no proof, since finds cannot always be lined up and classified according to periods. They often simply did not survive.

We are told that the previous inhabitants carried with them two-wheeled ploughs as they were fleeing the Slavs, while on the other hand they left behind for the newcomers horses and longhorn cattle. This sounds rather naive. If these ploughs were left behind in the eastern Alps, then the Slavs would not have known what to do with them, but would have continued to use the primitive hook-plough. Were these backwoods folk really so ignorant and inept? Probably not.

In contrast, recent research by German and Austrian folklorists gives us a different picture. Even before World War One, K. Rhamm[172] did not dispute the Slavic plough in the Alps (1908). After the Second World War, H. Koren[173] established that Alpine Slavs were indeed in possession of the plough in regions which were never cultivated by Bavarian settlers. Also noteworthy is Koren's statement that the older, supposedly typical Slavic *ralo* (hook-plough) is known in all of South Tyrol and also in parts of northern Tyrol; these are the areas not settled by Slavs in the 6th century, according to official theories. As shown earlier, these findings relating to the plough are in agreement with surviving Venetic (Slovene) place-names through Tyrol and as far as central Switzerland.

The assumption that the Slavs brought with them from their homeland poul-

---

[170] J. Korošec, in *Zgodovinski časopis* XII–XIII, 1958–59, pp. 75–109, op. cit., by B. Grafenauer, *Die Kontinuitätsfragen...p. 69.

[171] The assumption that the word "plug" cannot be of Slovene origin is based on a lack of knowledge of other Slavic languages. In the Slovene we also find the verb *plužiti*—to pull a snowplough.

[172] K. Rhamm, *Ethnographische Beitrage zur germanisch-slawischen Altertumskunde/* The Ethnographic Contributions to the Study of the German-Slavic Antiquities, Bd. II, p. 964, Note 2; Braunschweig 1908, op. cit., by H. Koren, see footnote 173.

[173] H. Koren, *Pflug und Arl: Ein Beitrag zur Volkskunde der Ackergeräte/* The Plough and the Hook-Plough: A Contribution to the Ethnography of Farm Implements; Salzburg 1950, p. 268. The Slovene word *ralo* from *oralo*, and from this the German word *Arl* from *aralo*, are ancient terms for the hook–plough; they coincide with the Latin *arare*— to plough, and *aratrum*—a plough. According to F. Bezlaj, "ral" derives from the metathesis: or-ra, oralo—ralo—ral. In German with apophony, o-a the *Arl*.

try production and bee-keeping coincides with nationalistic German views of the enslaved and culturally inferior Slavs. Jan Peisker, Professor of History at the University of Graz, developed an interesting theory in connection with these views (1905).[174] According to his speculations, the Turko-Tartars and Germanic neighbours subjugated the Slavs and did not allow them to raise cattle. This may be so, but the idea of the Slavs carrying geese, ducks, chickens and beehives on their backs over the Carpathian mountains is questionable. Cattle are certainly the most important means of subsistence for a people during migration. It is hard to imagine who would travel in this manner to a new and very distant land— probably only those people created in Peisker's imagination.

Prehistoric bee-keeping was indigenous to the Alps. Thus, there are among Slovenes no technical terms to bring to mind the forest bee-keeping of the Slavs in the north and east.[175] And another surprise: **the traditional Slovene beehive**, called "kranjič" (i.e., the Carniolan hive), was widespread even into this century in Styria, Carniola, the coastal areas of the northern Adriatic, throughout Carinthia, over the Puster Valley into the Eisack Valley, and over the areas of Brixen, Bolzano, and Merano into the Vintschgau, farther west through Val Venosta, the Engadine and elsewhere in canton Graubünden.[176] Throughout the eastern Alps we have to this day the Slovene bee, **Apis mellifica carnica**. Does the appearance or the wide distribution of the Slovene beehive coincide only by chance with numerous

---

[174] J. Peisker, *Die älteren Beziehungen der Slawen zu Turkotataren und Germanen und ihre sozialgeschichtliche Bedeutung/* The Early Relations of the Slavs with the Turko-Tartars and Germans and their Significance in Social History, Vierteljahrschrift für Sozial und Wirtschaftsgeschichte III, 1905, see J. Mal, *Nova pota slovenske historiografije/* New Ways of the Slovene Historiography, in *Čas*, Ljubljana 1923, p. 188. For J. Peisker, one proof of slavery of the Slavs is the word *mleko* (milk) which is in his view of Nordic origin; according to Peisker, the Slavs did not have this word because their strange masters would not allow them livestock-raising. The theories about the supposed slavery of the Slavs which served to sustain the German national-istic ideology were first fabricated by L. Gumplowicz at the University of Graz, Aus-tria. S. Vilfan, *Wirtschaftsgeschichte und Rechtsgeschichte/* The History of Economy and the History of Law; in Kl. Arbeitsreihe zur europ. u. vergl. Rechtsgesch., Heft 17, Graz 1985.

[175] Cf. S. Mihelič, *Sodobno čebelarstvo/* The Modern Apiculture, Ljubljana 1958, p. 62. The old Russian word *bort* as well as the Czech *brt* and Polish *bart* indicate a beehive that was originally made from a tree trunk and was used for exploitation of wild bees. In the Slovene language the beehive is called *panj* which corresponds to the word *bugno,* which had wide distribution in the territory of the Adriatic Veneti.

[176] L. Armbruster, *Die alte Bienenzucht in den Alpen/* The Ancient Apiculture in the Alps, Neumünster 1928, op. cit., by S. Mihelič, op. cit., pp. 50, 58. L. Armbruster believed

135

Slovene names in the Alps? Did the Slovene bee spread only by chance in the territory to coincide with Slovene place-names? Probably not. There is too much evidence to the contrary. These facts show us that at one time the territories in question were peopled by the ancestors of modern Slovenes—the ancient Veneti. During Roman times **Alpine pastures** were held as common property, as they are today.[177] From among Slovene authors, Tuma must be mentioned in regard to Alpine dairy activity and the Alpine economy in general; he made an important contribution in this field even before the First World War. His detailed studies strongly emphasize the Slovene character of Alpine life since prehistory.

The findings of Tuma were disputed by the Slovene folklorist, V. Novak.[178] He based his study on the authority of German etymological dictionaries and made the following presentation: "The Slavs had adopted the ways of Alpine living from the previous inhabitants, the Ladins—the Romanized Celts." He qualified his conclusions with the suggestion that many expressions of Slovene Alpine vocabulary were taken from other languages; for example, *medrje*—fold supposedly from Ital. *mandria*—herd, *tamar*—shelter, pre-Roman, *hlev* from the Gothic *hlaiw*—barn, *bajta*—log cabin, *pinja*—churn, *skuta*—curds, *trnač*— cheese stirrer, supposedly from Celtic root *tar*, also *konta* supposedly from the Ital. *cunetta,* and so on. In any case, Tuma has a much more realistic explanation for all these terms, taking into account wide-ranging historic realities and findings of other researchers in this field (e.g., Dietz, Hehn, Battisti).

Considering the ancient agricultural and shepherding culture of the Veneti, and the relatively late development of the Romanic people, it is obvious that the above-noted Alpine technical terms travelled in the opposite direction, as already observed by Tuma.[179] Moreover, it is doubtful that the South Slavs would want

---

initially that the well-known beehive called "the Carniolan" was spread in the Alpine region by the Roman colonists; later he changed his mind and dismissed his own theory of the Roman origin of this beehive.

[177] B. Grafenauer, *Zgodovina...op. cit.*, p. 182.

[178] V. Novak, *Die Stellung des Alpwesens in Slowenien zwischen dem germanischen und romanischen Raume/* The Position of Alpine Life in Slovenia Between the Germanic and the Romanic Areas, Alpes Orientales II, Graz 1959, p. 123 passim.

[179] According to H. Tuma, the term *medrje* from the Alpine herding vocabulary in the Julian Alps did not derive from the well-known Italian word *mandria* (a herd of cattle) but is rather an abbrev. of the Slovene word *medvereje*—fold, enclosure where the cattle were kept overnight. Both of these words, *medrje* and *mandria,* derive from a pre-Indo-European theme and can be considered as remnants of a very ancient pastoral culture. Cf. H. Tuma, *Naše planine/* Our Alpine Pastures; in *Jadranski almanah*, Trst (Trieste) 1924, pp. 92–94.

pastures in the high Alps when there was more than enough room for pastures and fields in the valleys. They had just arrived from the plains of eastern Europe, had no knowledge of life in the Alps, and were not accustomed to high altitudes. At that time an estimated 200,000 people lived in the eastern Alps as opposed to the present 3.5 million.

The *legend of the* **Mountain Man** (Slov. *Gorni mož*), who was to have taught people the art of cheese-making, is still known in areas from the eastern Alps westward as far as canton Uri,[180] wherever we have a concentration of Slovene place-names. As we review the old elements of rural culture that have been preserved to this day, we find the idea of settlement from the Balkans into the Alps even less believable.

Gavazzi, the well-known folklorist,[181] observed that the location of ethnic culture indicates that cultural influences had proceeded from the Alps into the neighbouring Balkan regions and not the reverse. The customs, farm implements, building methods and folk traditions that one encounters in the eastern Alps coincide with village customs and traditions of neighbouring Slavonians in northern Croatia. We recall the young men's societies, the parading of the plough on Ash Wednesday, the carrying of branches on the feast of St. George, the bonfires at Easter and summer solstice, grain-sheaf harps or racks (Slov. *kozolec*), the oven fork (Slov. *burkle*) a specialized tool used for moving pots, and firewood within the big bread oven, hand-split shingle roofs, painting on glass, and so on.

In spite of the variety of these discoveries, official historians continue to cling to their ideological biases and the notion of the Slovene migration from the south. These biases are passed from book to book provided with copious footnotes in order to appear scientific; yet, at the same time relevant evidence is not taken into account. Consequently, the Slovenes are assumed to have settled in the eastern Alps in the 6th century, regardless of whether it makes any scientific sense or not.

The geographical settlement area itself and the rural culture that descended from prehistoric times have an uninterrupted presence. We can add here a few items from archaeological finds of the Hallstatt period that have relevance to rural life: bronze sickles from Loga ves (Augsdorf), Carinthia, above Wörther

---

[180] I. Grafenauer, *Zveza slovenskih ljudskih pripovedk z retijskimi/* Similarities Between the Slovene and Rhaetian Folk Tales; *Slovenski etnograf* XI, pp. 49–68. Cf. V. Novak, ibid., p. 130.

[181] M. Gavazzi, *Die Reichweite der alpinen Kultureinflüsse auf die Benachbarte Gebiete Südosteuropas/* The Range of the Alpine Cultural Influences on the Neighbouring Areas of Southeast Europe, Alpes Orientales II, Graz 1959, pp. 9–16.

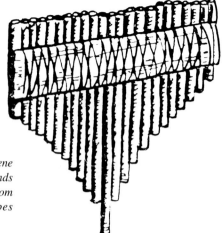

Panpipes have been preserved in the Slovene Alps to this day. They are seen in the hands of the musician portrayed on the situla from Vače, Hallstatt period. (Source; Alpes Orientales V, 119).

See (lake) and bronze crampons from Trovavska ves (Treffeldorf) at the foot of Mt. Štalen (Magdalensberg), Carinthia. The discoveries from the late La Tène period in Idrija pri Bači, Slovenia, include iron forks, shovels, pruning knives and iron scythes; they tell us of aspects of agricultural work that have survived using the same tools for two thousand years, and in a limited way to this day.

Carantania—provincia Sclaborum

After the Langobards had broken the power of the Byzantines, which included Inner Noricum in the eastern Alps, there appeared quite suddenly in this area the medieval state called Carantania in documentary sources. As historians themselves had to concede,[182] **the region of Carantania coincided almost completely with the borders of Inner Noricum.**

The reader may wonder why the Slavs or Veneti, if they were already living in Noricum during the Roman occupation, are not mentioned by their own name in documentary sources of that time.

In Roman reports the Veneti and tribes with similar names were cited for different regions; however, these various Venetic groups also had other names as an expression of their separate development, as we can see from the names Rhaeti and Norici. Groups of Celts likewise had different names: the Boians, Scordisci, and so on. The same is true even today with Germanic people and

---

[182] B. Grafenauer, *Zgodovina*...op. cit., p. 220.

Urn from a Roman grave (2nd century) from Zloganje near Škocjan, Novo mesto, Slovenia. Saltcellars of the same shape are still made in Slovene Pannonia.

other language groups including Slavs. It is fairly certain that indigenous Veneti referred to themselves as Sloveni regardless of what others called them. It is also very likely that they called their country Carantania or Gorotan before the Roman occupation and continued to do so after the Roman departure.

Roman writers refer to Noricum in their accounts and speak of cities which were partly Latinized and influenced by Roman culture. Inscriptions from Noricum are Latin; monuments which belong to the urban population are engraved with representations of Greco-Roman mythology. On the other hand, farming people did not write historical accounts or build stone monuments. Only after the fall of the East Gothic and Byzantine occupations, when the rural population took control, did it draw the attention of historians. Since that time it is clear that we are dealing with Veneti/Wends, the forebears of modern Slovenes.

Latin remained the literary language in all of Europe, which does not mean that European nations were Latinized during the early Middle Ages. Even so, the Latin language and Roman culture in Noricum's cities in no way indicate the Romanization of the Norici, who were also not Celticized.

The Roman name "Noricum" is also used for Carantania during the Middle Ages. In 973 Pope Benedict VI presented to the Salzburg Bishop Friedrich apostolic jurisdiction over all of Noricum—*in tota Norica provincia*.[183]

---

[183] F. Kos, *Gradivo* II, op. cit., No. 446.

Grain-sheaf drying rack (kozolec) in Slovenia. These are found outside the Alps only in Scandinavia and along the Baltic Sea; that is, in the old Venetic areas.

The supposedly Romanized indigenous inhabitants, said to have fled before the advancing Slavs, had obviously not taken the name of their homeland with them to Bavaria. The name Noricum remained (as did the people) the West Slavic Veneti, who have resided in the Alps since prehistoric times.

The Langobard historian, Paulus Diaconus, first mentions in his *Historia Langobardorum* in 595 the independent Slovene state in the eastern Alps. During the same year the Bavarians invaded the land of the Slovenes—"in Sclaborum provinciam..." and returned with much loot. The following year they repeated the invasion, but were defeated by Slovenes who now had the help of the Avar kaghan.[184] This occasion is used to prove that the Slovenes settled in the eastern Alps under the protection and authority of the Avars.[185] Such a conclusion would make sense only if Slovenes came into the Alps from the southeast at that time, as there was then Avar rule on the Balkan peninsula. However, since there are no

---

[184] F. Kos, *Gradivo* I, op. cit., No. 112 (Historia Langobardorum). Paulus Diaconus, second half of the 8th century.

[185] F. Kos, *Prvi nastop Slovencev v zgodovini/* The First Appearance of Slovenes in History in *Zbrano delo*, op. cit., pp. 103–104, 114–118.

Typical Carinthian farmstead with a clear division of residential and other functions, common to this day in the area of former Noricum and Carantania (Kozenn Atlas, 1972).

archaeological finds from the eastern Alps that can be attributed to the Avars,[186] we can conclude from the report by Diaconus that Slovenes and Avars were allies at that time.

The Avars lived in Pannonia and Transylvania and from there periodically attacked Byzantium with the help of the South Slavs, who were at that time subservient to them. This makes it clear that these activities are not related to the Carantanians (Slovenes) in the Alps.

For ideological reasons, historians have counted Slovenes among South Slavs and at the same time insisted on their subservience to the Avars. Thus, they are able to build the theory that Slovenes could have settled in the Alps only under the rule and protection of the Avars. This theory also "proves" that Slovenes were incapable of self-rule. This position was and still is advocated by all leading Slovene historians including F. Kos, J. Gruden, L. Hauptmann, M. Kos, and B. Grafenauer.

There is no historical connection between the Veneti (Slovenes) in the Alps and the South Slavs who took part in the clashes with the Byzantines, regardless

---

[186] B. Grafenauer, *Zgodovina*...op. cit., p. 179.

what our historians say, who built their careers on this fallacy in the past and continue to do so now.

It is recorded that, in the year 603, the Avar kaghan sent Slavs (Sclavi) to help the friendly Langobards, who were besieging the city of Cremona.[187] These Slavs could only have come from the Balkan peninsula, then controlled by Avars, and not from the eastern Alps. The ideologues are making every effort to prove that the medieval Carantanians (Slovenes) were a subservient people, but the above attempted explanation falls short of their aim.

The Avar/Langobard friendship did not last very long: in the year 610 the Avars invaded northeast Italy and defeated the Langobards. Slavs are not mentioned in documentary sources in connection with this event.[188] In the following year (611) near Aguntum, without the help of the Avars, the Slovenes defeated the Bavarians, who quickly regrouped and drove out the Slovenes. In the same year the Slavs invaded Istria.[189] Also from this account we cannot infer Avar domination over the Slovenes.

The independence of the Carantanians in the eastern Alps is undoubtedly indicated by the term "provincia",[190] which Diaconus uses in reference to their country. In addition, the existence of this "provincia" or state affirms the indigenous status of the Slovenes. Two things from this period should not be forgotten: first, it is impossible to think that the supposedly backward Slavs who had "just arrived" from the Pripet swamps could establish themselves so quickly in a totally unfamiliar Alpine setting; secondly, that it was the Slovenes in the Alps who among all Slavs first founded their own state in the Middle Ages. Other Slavic groups (in the lowlands) did the same two to three hundred years later.

This can be explained only by the fact that the Slovenes were indigenous inhabitants, as already established. In addition, since they were already resident

---

[187] F. Kos, *Gradivo* I, op.cit., No. 140 (Historia Langobardorum).

[188] F. Kos, *Gradivo* I, ibid., No. 145 (Historia Langobardorum).

[189] F. Kos, *Gradivo* I, ibid., No. 147, 148 (Historia Langobardorum).

[190] According to the Slovene historian F. Kos, the words "in Sclaborum provinciam" prove that the Slovenes were at that time already well acclimatized in the territory which had become their possession (Gradivo I, No. 112). This does not confirm the theory of settlement at that time; according to official view the Slovenes came from the swamps and flatlands of Trans-Carpathia and adjusted themselves in record time to a totally new environment. This rather strengthens the idea that they were an indigenous Alpine people. Au. The term "provincia" as was used by the Langobard historian Paulus Diaconus means a kingdom, as it is the same term used by themselves for their own kingdom in Italy. This indicates that Carantania was an independent state on the level of a kingdom.

in the eastern Alps during the Roman Empire, the Christian faith was not unknown to them; it is for this reason that Slovenes were, from among Slavic peoples, the first to accept Christianity.

If the Norici, i.e., the Veneti or Slovenes, were still pagan during Roman rule, that is in itself nothing unusual. Pagans were not considered opponents of the Empire even after the Emperor himself became a Christian, simply because the entire structure of the Empire was based on pagan traditions.

The medieval state, on the other hand, was founded on the Christian worldview, whereby the state was seen as an institution of God and the sovereign authority as a commission for which the king was responsible before God. The principal duty of the state at that time was to spread Christianity. Thus, zealous missionary work was being carried out in Carantania. The people who opposed Christianity were seen as representing a danger for Christian Europe and action was taken against them.

The Christianization of Europe was no small task; it continued for centuries. Attempts at proselytizing the Veneti (Slovenes) were already in evidence at the beginning of their independence. According to documented evidence around the year 612, St. Columban wanted to set out on a mission. But the devout man had seen in a dream that the people of this Venetic or Slavic land—**"termini Venetiorum qui et Sclavi dicuntur..."** the land of Veneti who are also called Slavs—were not yet ready for the Christian faith; hence, he dedicated himself to other regions. With similar intentions St. Amand (circa 630) crossed the Danube, making his way to the Slovenes. His mission was without success.[191]

Besides the fact that documentary sources mention the same people (Slovenes) under two names, Veneti and Slavs, the expression "termini" (which describes a defined geographic area) strengthens the contention that there was a form of government, a state with distinct internal organization and not, as ideologically-biased authors allege, a tribe of extended families.

King Samo and the Name Carantania

The names Sloveni and Veneti—**Sclavos coinomento Vinedos**—are also found in the historical document which recounts the Slav revolt in 623 against the Avars, whose domination they could no longer bear. The insurgents were joined by a merchant named Samo who, because of his bravery, was chosen to be their king.[192]

---

[191] F. Kos, *Gradivo* I, op. cit., No. 151 (Vita St. Columbani), No. 162 (Vita St. Amandi).

[192] F. Kos, *Gradivo* I, op. cit., No. 154 (Fredgarii Chronicon).

There is nothing in this report to suggest that the Slavs in the eastern Alps were subjected to the Avars. In the document the name Veneti referred also to the Elbe Slavs, Lusatians, and Moravians (Slovaks). The centre of the revolt against the Avars was Moravia and Bohemia.[193]

King Samo (623–658) was originally a merchant in the Frankish province of Senonago, the location of which is no longer known. The document, *Fredegarii Chronicon* (around 658), includes Samo among Frankish nationals (natione Francus), which does not mean that he was also of Frankish extraction (genere Francus). At his court Slavic customs were the rule and the envoy had to change into Slavic attire before he could be presented to King Samo. Would the Slavs have chosen a man of Frankish origin to be their king? The later document *Conversio Bagoariourum et Carantanorum* (circa 873) clearly shows that Samo reigned in Carantania.[194] The *Excerptum* of this document presents him as the first Duke of the Carantanians.

Samo's residence could only have been in Carantania, south of the Danube, which St. Amand had to cross in order to reach his court. Missionaries were required first to present themselves before the king in order to receive consent for their mission.

Among all Slavic countries Carantania had the best governmental structure and, because of its mountains, was the most secure.

The assumption that the seat of Samo's court would have been in Unhost near Prague is historically unproven. The assumption was propagated by Czech historians in order to give more credence to Bohemia's history, and has since been repeated in history books of other Slavic nations.

In the year 631 near Wogastisburg, "Sclavi coinomento Vinidi" under Samo's leadership defeated the Franks, who were under the command of King Dagobert I.[195]

In the same year, the Slovene state in the eastern Alps is referred to as **marca Vinedorum**, the land of Veneti. Its ruler was Prince Valuk (Wallucus dux

---

[193] B. Grafenauer, *Zgodovina* I, ...op. cit., p. 328.

[194] F. Kos, *Gradivo* I, op. cit., No. 154 (footnotes 3, 4 and 5), No. 163... *Temporibus gloriosi regis Francorum Dagoberti Samo nomine quidam Sclavus manens in Quarantanis fuit dux gentis illius* (from Conversio Bagoariorum et Carantanorum).

[195] H. Kunstmann from the University of Munich, Bavaria, published years ago his studies concerning the place of those battles. According to him, the historic castle Wogastisburg should be in the district Burk of Forchheim on the Regnitz River in Franconia. There is an old tradition that King Samo had the title "poti byl otec"—the father of our way. Later, the Frankish settlers twisted this into "Ponzius Pilatus" and handed down this nonsense for centuries. See Erlanger Tagblatt 24/25 Nov. 1979.

Winedorum).[196] Carantania had its own prince, but was undoubtedly incorporated into Samo's Kingdom. The designation "marca", as earlier "provincia, termini", refers to a defined area and does not in itself mean that the Carantanian nation was not independent.[197] In reality, it appears most certain that King Samo ruled from Carantania, which was as a government base stable, strong, and protected by mountains, as opposed to other less stable Slavic principalities.

The name Carantania is mentioned in historical records around 670, which does not preclude its previous existence. The name "Carantania" is first mentioned by Anonymus Ravennas (Cosmographia IV, C. 37) wherein he cites that Italy's territory borders on that of Carantania—**inter Carontanos**—among the Carantanians.[198]

To this day linguists and historians disagree over the origin of the name *Carantania*. Thus, E. Kranzmayer, the Carinthian name researcher, derives it from the Celtic word "carantos" (men, friends). The Slovene historian, B. Grafenauer, on the other hand, finds the answer in the French language, thus relating it to the word "karanto" (Charenton) based on the supposed pre-Indo-European "kar" (rock). He also observes that it could not be of Slavic origin and was not brought by the Slavs into the Alps.[199]

The latter is correct, since there were no Slavs who moved from Trans-Carpathia into the Alps in the 6th century. Carantania's name is, therefore, indigenous just like its Venetic people.

Historians and linguists who base their work in German nationalistic or Pan-Slavic ideologies hold fast to their notion of a late formation of Slavs and,

---

[196] F. Kos, *Gradivo* I, op. cit., No. 164 (Fredegarii Chronicon).

[197] B. Grafenauer (*Zgodovina*...p. 333) thinks the term "marca" does not indicate an independent state. At the same time he also tells us that Carantania in that period was not subjugated by the Avars, Bavarians or Langobards. According to him, Carantania was only a vaguely delineated area of the Slav tribe called Vinedi. A very strange situation: Carantania was not subjugated by any of the neighbouring nations and at the same time it was also not independent. Yet, the Carantanian leader bore the title dux, which unquestionably belongs only to a sovereign. The term "tribe" used by Grafenauer for Carantanians (Slovenes) is not appropriate for a nation organized in its own state. Dealing with Slovenes as if they were a subject race from pre-historic times (e.g. J. Peisker) serves but one purpose; i.e., that of German nationalism which, through centuries of brutality and forceful assimilation, has denationalized a large segment of the Slovene people.

[198] F. Kos, *Gradivo* I, op. cit., No. 182.

[199] B. Grafenauer, *Zgodovina*...op. cit., p. 337, and in *Glas Korotana* 6, Vienna 1978, p. 3, taken from: C.Rostainge, *Les noms de lieux*, 1958, p. 27 passim.

consequently, of Slovenes, and do not accept an older origin of the Slovene language as compared to other Slavic languages. The word "kar" is preserved in a number of combinations among Slovenes, *kar, karn, karnele* (also črnele), meaning a steep, fragmented, rocky mountain. The related word "gora" in Slovene also stands for a high mountain or rocky peak, as contrasted to anything lower, such as hill, knoll or mound.

The name "Carantania" existed in the form *Korotan* as well as *Goratan* among the people of Carinthia into the last century. The first variation is attested to by the Carinthian national poet, Drabosnjak, and even before him by O. Gutsmann (1777), while the second variation is associated with the word "gora" (mountain, peak) by the Slovene author A. T. Linhart (1791).

Along with the name variations *Carantania, Korotan, Goratan* and *Koroška,* i.e., Ger. *Kärnten* (Carinthia) are *Karawanke* and also *Carniola* (Kranjska) and *Carnia,* which are derived from the same root word "kar" (rock, mountain). The latter two name variations even appear in much older documentary sources; for example, Pliny the Elder (III, 131) who equates Carni with the Norici (III, 133).

Is it a chance occurrence that Carinthia (Carantania), Carnia, and Carniola are neighbouring lands and exhibit the same root form in their names; that they were settled in the course of history by the same people who in part inhabit them today? And if in the same region names such as Vindobona (Windisch, Venetic), Carnuntum, or Carnium (Kranj) appear, Carantania can only be a new form of the ancient name Carnia, a Latinized variation of the name Korotan or Goratan.[200]

The name Korotan or Goratan undoubtedly contains, besides the root form "kar" (rock, mountain, peak), the proto-Aryan word "stan" meaning residence (comp. Slov. *stanovati*—to reside; *stan*—residence, dwelling-place). It appears in the wider area as far as India (Pakistan, Hindustan). Korotan or Goratan (from it Carantania) is therefore derived from "gora(s)tan" (mountainous region).

The name Carantania can only be a newer form of the name Carnia, which is a Latinized form of Korotan, Koratan, or Goratan; however, no matter which one we choose, it tells us of the indigenous nationhood of Carantanians (Slovenes) in the eastern Alps. That the Latin name *Carantanum* is derived from the Slovene

---

[200] Cf. G. Ankershofen, *Prüfung der verschiedenen Ansichten über die Herleitung des Namens Kärnten*/ The Examination of Various Views Concerning the Derivation of the Name Carinthia; Archiv für vaterl. Geschichte und Topographie I, Jg. Klagenfurt 1849. The author is convinced that the Latin form Carantanum (Carantania) can be only from the Slovene term *goratan* from *gora*—mountain. He rejects every attempt made by linguists to attribute this name to Celtic origin, as it could not have survived through the five centuries of Roman domination.

Korotan (mountainous region) was claimed by the well-known Carinthian historian Ankershofen in the last century.[201] He rejected a Celto-Romanic origin of this name.

While we are considering the various elements associated with Carantania's earlier period, we must not forget a number of symbols. The **panther** is one of these; it appears on Roman stones in Noricum from the 2nd century. In the Carantania of later centuries the image of the panther was used on its banner and coat of arms.

Another emblem is the **linden tree**. Its veneration was common throughout the region where the Veneti once lived and left behind their name, from the Alps to the Baltic.[202] The linden tree had also been engraved on the Roman stone from Noricum (2nd century) found in Jedlovca (Ettendorf) in the Lavant Valley; it is a small tree with three roots.[203] Later in the Middle Ages the sprig of a linden tree was frequently used as a symbol representing the tree of life.

The Veneti (Slovenes) have survived from the time of prehistory until this day. At first this may seem to be a miracle, but in a relative sense they had a good system of defence. They withstood the attacks of the Scythians, Celts, then the occupation of the Romans. Later they accepted Christianity; in the Carolingian Europe of the early Middle Ages this implied the acknowledgment of and right to an independent national life.

As with other people of prehistoric roots, we encounter among Slovenes the same model: the basis for their existence was a **farming culture**. A rural lifestyle with a developed agriculture, cattle breeding, and a defense organization are all in evidence in this case from the time of Lusatian culture.

This ancient culture was symbolically represented in Carantania on the occasion of the duke's enthronement: the stone (the Prince's Stone), representing an ancient symbol for God; the ox, representing the field and cattle; the horse and sword symbolizing the military, and finally the life-sustaining elements, water and fire. Thus we have economy, defence, and religion as the basis for a social organization on the level of a nation.

The Prince's Stone — *When the last of the occupation armies left Inner Noricum leaving behind ruined cities, the indigenous population of Veneti (Slovenes) was able*

---

[201] J. Šavli, *Črni panter/* Black Panther; in *Glas Korotana* 7, Vienna 1981. J. Šavli, *Black Panther, Coat of Arms of Carantania,* The Augustan Society, Omnibus, Book 11, Torrance 1990.

[202] J. Šavli, *Lipa drevo življenja/* Linden the Tree of Life, *Glas Korotana* 8, Vienna 1982.

[203] Cf. Carinthia I, Klagenfurt 1978, p. 23.

to reestablish its own rule. The name of the new state Carantania was formed from Slovene roots and was probably in use in same or similar form before and during Roman occupation. The Carantanians enthroned their own princes in the Slovene language in a ceremony centred around the **Prince's Stone** *until it was discontinued under German pressure in the year 1414. Below is a summary of the investiture ceremony of the dukes of Carantania by the people. It became well known in Europe at the time, and was recorded in several historical sources in Latin and German languages. Centuries later it was examined in detail by the French political theorist Bodin in his Les Six Livres de la Republique (Paris 1576). This work was one of the sources used by Thomas Jefferson when he wrote the American Declaration of Independence.*

The earliest known historical source recording the ceremony is the Conversio Bagoariorum et Carantanorum written circa 870. It describes with great precision the ongoing right of the Carantanians to elect their ruler. We read in this document that after the death of Duke Borut, the Carantanians asked for his son Gorazd (being held in Bavaria) who was returned by order of the Frankish king (in 751), whereupon they made him duke, "eum ducem fecerunt". And again in 752 after Gorazd's death, they received in like manner his cousin Hotimir and gave him the dukedom, "ducatum illi dederunt".

Carantanians had preserved the right to accept the proposed duke or to reject him if they so chose. Thus, in the eleventh century, they prevented the appointment of three dukes nominated by the Emperor because they were unrelated to the Carantanian (Slovene) nobility (not even on the mother's side), and therefore not indigenous in the sense of the Institutio Sclavenica (Slovene law).

The Duke of Carantania was the Master of Hunts in the Empire. No one could install a duke except the freeholders of Carantania, represented by the "homines boni" (good men); these elected from among themselves a deputy, and he in turn asked those assembled whether the ducal candidate whom the Empire had given them was acceptable. If he was not acceptable to them, the Empire was obligated to give them another lord and duke. If, however, he was acceptable, then he was given a warm and respectable welcome.

The installation of the duke took place on a hill named Krnski grad (Karnburg), a few miles north of Celovec (Klagenfurt). There, not far from the church of St. Peter, in a meadow, is the Prince's Stone. The ceremony unfolded as follows:

The new duke arrives on the hill surrounded by nobles and knights and the Carantanian banner. With one hand he leads a black and white bull and with the other a horse of the same colours. He puts aside his precious vestments, the people dress him in a grey coat, and gird him with a red belt from which hangs a red hunting bag such as is suitable for the Master of the Hunts. He is given a hunting horn bound with red straps and they also put shoes wrapped with red thongs on his feet. He is then draped in a grey cloak and a grey Slovene hat with a grey cord is placed on his head. A free peasant is now sitting on the Prince's Stone. This office belongs to him by right

148

of succession, hereditary in his family. The duke carries in his hand a staff and comes forward. Alongside him walk the Count Palatine (the king's representative) and other nobles.

The peasant sitting on the Prince's Stone asks in the Slovene language: "Who is he that is approaching?"

All those assembled around him answer: "He is the prince of the land." After this, he asks: "Is he an upright judge, is he seeking the well-being of the country, is he freeborn and deserving? Is he a defender of the Christian faith?"

All answer: "He is and he will be." The peasant then asks: "By what right can he displace me from this seat?"

The people reply: "He will present you sixty denarii and give you the two animals and the peasant clothes that he is decked with, and he will make your house free and without tribute."

Whereupon the peasant, after giving the duke a gentle stroke on his cheek, proffers him the seat. The new duke now steps on the Prince's Stone and, drawing his sword, turns in all directions in order to show that he will be a righteous judge to all.

The duke then takes a drink of cold water from a peasant hat so that the people, seeing this, will not crave for wine but will be content with what the native soil produces to sustain life. Finally they lift him onto a horse and conduct him around the Stone three times to indicate that he has now taken possession of the Land. At the same time all sing a hymn in Slovene, praising God for having been given a new ruler in accordance with His will. [This last detail became part of the ceremony only after the introduction of Christianity].

After the ceremony at the Prince's Stone, the duke and his escort descend the hill of Krnski grad and cross the field to the cathedral of Gospa Sveta (Maria in Solio); there the bishop or another outstanding prelate celebrates the liturgy and blesses the duke.

*Following the church service, the duke and his escort proceed to the **Ducal Throne**. This is a two-seat stone throne standing in the field not far from the church. The eastern seat belongs to the duke from where he performs the first duties as the sovereign, pronouncing judgments and rendering justice to all; he also bestows fiefs and privileges associated with the lands and properties and other jurisdictions now belonging to him. The western seat is occupied by the Count Palatine, the king's representative. His duty on the seat is supplementary to that of the duke; he resolves problems that are not satisfactorily dealt with by the duke.*

The ceremony on the Prince's Stone was last performed in 1414 on the occasion of the enthronement of Duke Ernst of Iron, from the Leopoldine line of the Habsburg family, who ruled Inner Austria, i.e., the old Carantania. Thereafter, the presentation ceremony continued at the Ducal Throne till the year 1651, as before in the Slovene language. From that time on until 1728 the presentation continued in Slovene at the State House in Celovec (Klagenfurt). After that the Carantanian legacy, the "institutio Sclavenica", was incorporated into the Austrian Constitution.

Through the centuries, the ceremony of enthronement aroused the curiosity of numerous social theoreticians and writers. The enthronement of Carantanian dukes was a sovereign act on the level of the nation and has no comparison. The Slovenes have preserved it for many centuries with remarkable vitality and constancy.

Ethnic Culture as Evidence

*La civilisation préromaine a eu
peu de chances de survivre dans ces
villes.... Au contraire, à la campagne
on ne peut pas traiter cette question sans
tenir compte de la différence entre
centres urbains et campagne.*
(S. Vilfan)[204]

The rural culture in the Alps constituted the basis for the existence and survival of Veneti or Wends, the ancestors of Slovenes—clarified by archaeological excavations and in a large measure by place-names.

This study would not be complete without citing the results made public by folklorists of all ethnic groups in the eastern Alps, members of the independent research group "Alpes Orientales",[205] during their regular meeting in 1967 in Slovenj Gradec, Slovenia.

The theme of the conference was survival of the ethnic culture in the eastern Alps, from the time of late antiquity up to and including the Middle Ages, and in part until the present day. The conference represented the first international gathering of this kind to examine the topic that was and still is in all countries of the area, more or less banned. As was expected, the participants did not distance themselves from ideological premises. There was no questioning the supposed incursion of the Slavs into the eastern Alps in the 6th century and there was no consideration of the possibility that Slovenes were an indigenous people. However, the discussion itself of ethnic culture brought about a radical change from previous investigations into historical problems of the eastern Alps area.

---

[204] The pre-Roman civilization had little chance of surviving in the cities...In the country it is the opposite. We cannot consider the question of Romanization without taking into account the difference between the city and the country. S. Vilfan, *Le problème de continuité sous trois aspects: habitat, communications, droit,* Alpes Orientales V pp. 88–89 Ljubljana 1969.

[205] *Alpes Orientales* V, published by the Institute for Ethnographic Research by the Slovene Academy of Sciences and Arts, Ljubljana 1969.

Members of the conference were aware that the results of their research would represent only the first step towards the solution of a number of complicated questions. But their findings are of great value just the same, showing that the rural culture of the eastern Alps had continued from prehistory and in many ways has survived to this day. We would like to present them here as a supplement to this study, but will preface them with a few more remarks regarding historians. Their opinions appear especially contradictory in light of the findings of the folklorists.

The Presumed Break With Antiquity

The leading Slovene historian, B. Grafenauer, uses every means at his disposal to prove that there was a complete break between antiquity and the so-called Slavic period in Noricum. This position is very important to him, because his other pet theory depends on it; i.e., the settlement of Slovenes in the 6th century. He worked very hard to please his superiors for whom he had undying admiration; however, this great devotion to the official policy (which earned him recognition) has made him intellectually insensitive. Needless to say, his presentation along Serb-dominated Yugoslav lines is totally unrealistic; the imagined unity of Slovenes with South Slavs can never reconcile the cultural and linguistic differences between Slovenes in the Alps and Yugoslavs in the Balkans. Dr. Grafenauer could have distilled finer results if it were not for his devotion to the Marxist dialectic.

He hoped to strengthen his position on the presumed break with antiquity and the cultural difference between antiquity and the so-called Slavic period in Noricum by stating: "In the making of pottery and metal jewellery, the classical forms were partially continued, though in a new, substantially worse state of workmanship."[206] This statement was intended to vindicate his obsession with his settlement theory, but when examined critically, it yields just the opposite; i.e., it is specifically the continuation of the production of pottery and metal-ware by village craftsmen—which was of lower quality than the products made by city professionals—that show us that in the rural culture there was no break with antiquity.

These details suggest that we must examine the rural life and culture of antiquity separately from that of the Romanized city. It is true we have very little knowledge of rural life at that time, but ninety percent or more of the population of the eastern Alps lived in the rural areas, indicating that the countryside held an

---

[206] B. Grafenauer, *Die Kontinuitätsfragen...* Alpes Orientales V, p. 55 passim.

important position in the economic and political life of Roman Noricum. This should not be overlooked. The rural culture and its preservation into the Middle Ages suggests an entirely different turn of events at the fall of the Empire, than if we consider Noricum only from the position of the Romanized cities.

The following summary from the conference "Alpes Orientales" shows us to some degree that in rural culture there was no break with antiquity, even during the so-called Slovene period of Carantania.

The Slovene expert in the field of social history, Sergij Vilfan (Ljubljana),[207] writes:

"There are numerous hypotheses concerning the prehistoric, that is, pre- Roman origin of several types of houses in the eastern Alps; for example the **smoke-room** (Slov. *dimnica)* is one of them. It is probable that most building types in the eastern Alps conceal prehistoric elements and components which have not been researched until now.

"The **Roman roads** (frequently built on the existing pre-Roman Venetic roads) continued to exist, although they lost their former economic and military importance. Only through the salt trade did they retain their earlier significance.

"The pre-Roman legal system was more noticeably maintained in the pasture lands, principally the **Alpine meadows**, than in the grape-growing land use."

But also in this area there is need for more research.

The Slovene Region

Concerning the building art of the eastern Alps, the Slovene art historian, Emilijan Cevc (Ljubljana),[208] states that in the early Middle Ages certain peculiarities survived which are still characteristic of the Slovene landscape, especially numerous **mountain churches**—in many cases of pre-Romanesque or Romanesque origin (Romanesque style of architecture of western Christendom, 8th to 12th century). The first parish churches were built on former places of pagan worship. Writing about Slovene mountain churches in his book *Des Österreichs Wallfahrtsorte/* Austria's Places of Pilgrimage, Vienna, 1913, A. Hope emphasizes the following very interesting observation:

"Wherever nature provided a prominent and pleasant hill, the devout Slovene

---

[207] S. Vilfan, *Le probleme...*op. cit., pp. 87–101.

[208] E. Cevc, *Das Problem der Kontinuität im Kult und in der bildenden Kunst in Slowenien/* Problem of the Continuity of Cults and Visual Arts in Slovenia; Alpes Orientales V, pp. 103, 106–107.

built a church." And about this distinctive trait of the Slovenes to erect churches as places of pilgrimage, he also adds that "only the Slovene people were able to translate this intention into reality, for they indeed possessed an unswerving inclination to build churches on high mountains...".

The place of pilgrimage called Svete gore (holy mountains) above Sotla River in lower Styria offers the most interesting and beautiful example of the continuation of an ancient place of worship: pre-Romanesque characteristics in the chapels of St. George and St. Martin; an embossed plate with the representation of a sitting figure and ornamentation in Celtic tradition; and characters which strongly resemble the Venetic alphabet.

The Slovene intellectual world, traditions, and customs reach into the distant past. They reveal a certain trait of lyricism and enjoyment of the picturesque.

The Linden—*The ancient people knew and valued the linden tree, which was to them not only a symbol of vegetation related to their surroundings, but sometimes also a source for food and other uses, and thus directly linked to the welfare of the people. It was a symbol of the nation's life and prosperity, a relic of the original religion of man in which the tree is an embodiment of the Spirit.*

Since time immemorial, the linden has been considered the Tree of Life among Slovenes. It occupies an important place in their popular traditions. The ancient Slovene village cannot be imagined without a linden tree growing in the middle of it. Until the present century the village assembly or sosednja, composed of householders under the leadership of the župan (the mayor), met beneath the linden in accordance with old tradition to consult and to pronounce decisions concerning their common affairs.

The linden tree was also the centre of social life for village people; their meetings and dances took place there. Every year they held under the linden the first dance for the village youth. In the villages of the Zilja Valley (Gailtal), in Carinthia, the dance has been preserved. It is still called "the dance under the linden" (rej pod lipo—in Slov.). Boys and girls decked in traditional costumes and flowers, dance their first dance which symbolically admits them into adult life. Their bouquets are composed of the three traditional plants: carnation for love, rosemary for faith, and the leaves of the aromatic geranium for hope; this is the traditional Slovene bouquet or boutonniere.

In popular Slovene legends the linden is presented as a tree giving refuge to righteous people; it is also viewed as the Tree of Life. The linden is mentioned in a large variety of songs and poems; it appears in many religious songs and narratives, and especially in the passages about the Blessed Virgin. It gives cooling shade to Mary and Child. Under the linden tree rest the apostles, and there is the little golden house of Jesus.

The linden is also present in the King Mathias legend. Mathias is the personification of Slovene history, reflecting popular thinking about life and final redemption. Mathias was a good but pagan king. He was a powerful ruler and victorious over all adversaries; his success led him to become haughty and even rebellious against God. For punishment his army was defeated on the battlefield. The king was left with only as many soldiers as could find refuge in the shade of a linden tree, and finally a mountain covered them all. Since that time they have been sleeping in a cave in the mountain.

However, the time will come when a linden will grow in front of this cave and bloom at midnight on a Christmas Eve. King Mathias will then wake up and rise and unsheathe his sword and wake his soldiers. They will fight against the enemy monarchs; the linden scent carried by the warm wind will encourage the warriors and cure the injured at the same time. King Mathias will be victorious in this battle and, after victory in the field, the combatants will make peace under the linden tree with seven trunks (which after all this passage of time have dried up).

On this linden tree Mathias will hang his shield and the tree will become green again. Then there will follow the Golden Age for all humankind.

In this story we find, besides the linden tree itself, other symbols: the linden shade as grace of God; the southern warm wind as the symbol of the Holy Spirit which dissolves all wrong and sinful attitudes; the shield as defence of faith, at which the arrows of temptation are striking in vain....

The linden is a symbol handed down from the pre-Indo-European culture (before 2000 B.C.). On the other hand, the oak tree was adopted as the national symbol in areas where the Indo-Europeans prevailed in central Europe, .

The linden tree does not appear only in Slovene villages, but is present all over central Europe where the ancient Veneti resided in the distant past.

The entire region of the Alps is a land of folkloric relics where ancient cultural elements and traditions were able to survive as in a kingdom isolated from other cultures.

The noteworthy Croat folklorist, Milovan Gavazzi (Zagreb),[209] described for us several elements of ethnic material culture whose prehistoric and early historic origin is proven:

"Among the contrivances and implements stemming from prehistoric times, we should mention first the **dugout canoe** (Slov. *kopanja, drevak*). It has survived among the Slovenes and is linked with the distant past, that is the period of Lake or Pile-dweller culture in the Ljubljana Moor district. Also of undeniable prehistoric origin is the use of animal teeth, especially from wild boar and bear, as pendants.

---

[209] M. Gavazzi, *Vor- und Frühgeschichtliches in der Volksüberlieferung im Ostalpenraum/* Prehistory and Early History in Popular Traditions of the eastern Alps, Alpes Orientales V, pp. 113–122.

"The prehistoric or early historic **plough** (Slov. *plug, drevo*) is of great importance in this study. We are here considering the finds of ploughing tools in the eastern Alps, dating from Roman era in most cases.

"Among these finds were ploughs with symmetrical shares and coulters. The coulter makes a vertical cut in the soil and facilitates the work of the ploughshare itself. It is characteristic of the Slovene area and is still in use in Slovenia— a reminder of the distant past.

"Also well documented through prehistoric finds is a **baking-bell** (Slov. *pekva*), a vaulted lid or cover which is used for baking bread in a relatively short time on a preheated open hearth.

"In Slovene Pannonia (north of Mura River), there are pottery **saltcellars** produced to this day. They are egg-shaped with a vertical opening and a rooster ornament on top. These salt containers are modeled on the "house-urns" that were in use as burial urns from 50 B.C. to 250 A.D.

"In the easternmost region of the Alps the **Pan-pipes** (Slov. *orgelce, trstenke* or *piskulce*) are still made on a small scale and used as a folk instrument to this day in eastern Slovenia. They may well be a direct descendant from the Pan-pipes in the hands of the musician on the situla from Vače, originating in the Early Iron Age, about 1000 B.C. (Hallstatt culture)."

In the eastern Alpine area there are cultural elements from early history, which can still be found in widely separated regions. Although often originating in locations with great distances between them, they have identical characteristics, in spite of the fact that there were no population movements between these regions in historical times.

We are considering here similar or same forms of certain cultural elements in the eastern Alps, Scandinavia and the Baltic region. At the same time we should keep in mind that only after the Urnfield migration and during the time of Hallstatt culture had there been a continuous territory (between the Alps and Scandinavia and the Baltic) occupied by the same people—the Veneti. This unity was consequently broken up by the incursion of Celts into central Europe.

Among similarities found in Slovenia, Scandinavia, Byelorussia and Lithuania is the characteristic **grain sheaf drying rack** (Slov. *kozolec).* Another is the interesting **diagonal fence** (Slov. *plot* or *ograja),* the railings of which are laid diagonally to the ground and held in place by posts of small diameter and wooden loops made from spruce boughs. Also found in Scandinavia and Slovenia is a primitive type of **ski** (Slov. *smuči),* which in both cases exhibit the same structural features.

A very important remnant of prehistoric architecture is the **herdsman's cabin** (Slov. *pastirski stan* or *bajta).* The example is from Velika planina in the Kamnik

Alps, Slovenia, and is described by Anton Cevc (Ljubljana).[210] The cabin itself, or the herdsman's quarter, is a log structure of squared logs, surrounded by an oval stone enclosure which serves as cattle shelter. The cabin and enclosure form one unit which is covered by an oval roof of hand-split shingles of spruce. This is the original *tamar*.

Since the Roman remains in the eastern Alps are only rectangular structures, we must place the beginning of the herdsman's cabin in the Hallstatt or La Tène period, even earlier if we compare it with remains of oval shelters in Rome from the 10th or 9th centuries B.C.

Folk Traditions, Music

Folk traditions in the eastern Alps, whether in Slovene, or in present Germanized or Italianized areas, demonstrate ancient origin. Among Slovenes this is not at all well researched. In the area of **folk medicine** certain practices have been preserved from antiquity to modern times. From among a diversity of traditional conceptions of diseases and popular methods of treatment, at least one example should be mentioned; it is the supposed transfer of diseases from people to trees, plants, and animals.

The cure was based on principles of the classical "Magia Naturalis" and was from the time of the Renaissance practiced among people; it was known and carried out by mediaeval medical practitioners as "Transplantation morborum". As can be concluded from the study by Elfriede Grabner (Graz),[211] the practice was prevalent in Styria. Another notion along the same lines was that bullfinches, yellow-hammers, crossbills, and canaries attracted jaundice.

The myth of the **Midwinter Woman** (Slov. *Torka* or *Pehtra baba*) has survived in Slovene mythology. According to the myth, the Midwinter Woman is the leader of souls as well as guardian of laws and morality. She is related to the Wild Hunt (Indo-European myth) that rages particularly on the eve of Epiphany; that is, in the middle of the winter. Her appearance may bring good or bad; she is either punishing or rewarding. A mythical female who is found in folk-tales and

---

[210] A. Cevc, *Vorgeschichtliche Deutung der Senngütte in den Kamniker Alpen/* The Prehistoric Implication Concerning the Alpine Herdsman's Cabin in the Kamnik Alps, Alpes Orientales V, pp. 125–136.

[211] Elfriede Grabner, *Kontinuitätsfragen in der Volksmedizin des Ostalpenraumes/* The Problems of Continuity in the Folk Medicine of the eastern Alps, Alpes Orientales V, pp. 257–265.

traditions as far as Central Asia, she appears in the same story also among Bavarians.

The Slovene ethnographer, Niko Kuret (Ljubljana),[212] determined that this myth represents the indigenous folk-tale tradition. The Scandinavian researcher, Waldemar Liungman, believes that the core of this Alpine tradition about Torka is to be found in the Carantanian area, in the vicinity of Celovec (Klagenfurt).

Slovene story-telling has preserved many elements from antiquity, which the ethnographer Milko Matičetov (Ljubljana)[213] considers to be of pre-Slavic origin. In his enumeration of the most significant examples, we present the following old tales:

"**The Legend of St. Matthew or St. Luke,** who killed his own parents, belongs to traditional legends of the Theban hero, Oedipus.

"**The Tale of the Wild Man,** who was made drunk in order to be captured, resembles the Phrygian story of Silen who was captured by King Midas in the same manner.

"**The Poem of the Musician,** who goes to purgatory to save his loved ones, resembles the myth of Orpheus and Eurydice.

"**The Legend of St. Anthony,** who brings fire from hell to warm the freezing people, is a Christian interpretation of the myth of Prometheus."

These apocryphal legends and tales cannot be considered as the heritage of Christianization. They could only have been adopted from Latin or Greek immigrants in ancient Noricum. At the same time they show us that the native Norici remained in their country. However, the legends could have had their origin in Indo-European or Venetic prehistory and been later remodelled.

The Goldenhorn—*Another Slovene legend which reveals old roots, perhaps reaching back into prehistory, and which has survived in oral tradition until recent times— that of the Goldenhorn—is of interest and will be presented here.*

A long time ago there was in the Julian Alps, in the sunny neighbourhood of Mt. Triglav, a mountain paradise. High above the Soča River and its tributary Koritnica and the picturesque little village of Bovec, there lived the white ladies (people still remember them with gratitude). They were gentle, kind-hearted beings ever ready to help. From time to time they descended into the valley to help a needy, poor person and, in particular, to assist in childbirth; such a child would then be for the rest of his life under the benign protection of the white ladies.

---

[212] N. Kuret, *Die Mittwinterfrau der Slowenen/* The Midwinter Woman Among the Slovenes, Alpes Orientales V, pp. 209–239.

[213] M. Matičetov, *Elementi preslavi nella narrative popolare slovena/* The pre-Slavic Elements in the Slovene Folk-tale, Alpes Orientales V, p. 208.

They instructed the shepherds about the powers of different healing herbs, and they also encouraged the growth of grasses and leaves among rocky crags so that the poor man's goats and sheep had needed pasture. The kind ladies avoided gratitude from people, and if someone came too close to their settlement he was turned away with threatening gestures. If anyone came by chance or knowingly too close to their dwellings, a terrifying hail storm or rock slide would force his retreat.

The white ladies kept a flock of white goats, which grazed on the steep slopes of their Alpine domain. The flock was led by a stately white buck called Goldenhorn, a fine looking male with shining golden horns. The white ladies made him secure against any injury; that is, if a hunter injured him, then regardless of where he fell, from his blood instantly grew a herb called the "miraculous balm" or Triglav flower. When the Goldenhorn ate but one leaf, he was at once made well no matter how serious the injury. There was one other very special thing about him: his golden horns were the key to the treasures of gold the white ladies kept inside Mt. Bogatin.

At that time there stood by the road in the valley an inn, and the innkeeper's daughter was the most beautiful girl in the area. Many young men were wooing her but she loved only the handsome young hunter from Trenta, the son of a blind widow. He was known far and wide as the best hunter; people also spoke of him as being under the protection of the white ladies. Every remote area in the mountains was known to him, as was every narrow footpath; he never had to worry about rock slides. When he returned from the mountains he would bring the most beautiful flowers for his sweetheart, so that the inn was always like a garden of mountain flowers.

One spring, a number of merchants from the south stopped at the inn. They admired the mountain flowers but they admired the beautiful young lady even more. When asked where she got such wonderful flowers, she told them about her young friend, the hunter.

"Oh him, well, he could have brought you something yet nicer than these flowers if he really loved you; he is, after all, friendly with the white ladies."

The curious girl wanted to know what could be nicer than the colourful mountain flowers.

"He could bring you the shiny horns of the Goldenhorn, or some of the treasure from Mt. Bogatin," they told her.

The girl laughed at this, but deep in her heart the poison of their words took hold. She was less and less friendly to the young hunter, eventually even turning down his flowers. This made him very unhappy. Finally, in his despair, he asked her what was wrong; why did she not love him anymore?

"It is not me," she said, "but you who does not love. If you really loved me, you would already have brought me the horns of the Goldenhorn; bring me those, then I will know that you really love me, and I too will be able to love you!" She went back to her chamber.

Before dawn next morning the hunter started out into the mountains. He was very sad, and yet hopeful that he would be able to prove his love to the innkeeper's daugh-

159

ter. When he climbed high into the mountains, the white ladies joined him and picked flowers that shone in the morning sun like diamonds and rubies, which he would take down into the valley to his girl to soften her heart.

"Don't kill our Goldenhorn," they begged him. "That will bring nothing but sorrow for all of us; the young lady will change her mind, sooner or later...".

But the hunter did not listen; his mind was elsewhere. High above, upon a rock he saw the magnificent Goldenhorn, whose horns were bright as the sun. The brilliant colour of the golden horns blinded him completely. Now his only thought was how to get the horns.

An uneasy silence pervaded the massive rocky formations and high cliffs. The white ladies had retreated and were nowhere to be seen. There was a distant rumble of thunder announcing a storm. The hunter climbed higher and higher and finally he discharged his weapon. Mortally wounded, the Goldenhorn fell to the ground. From his blood instantly grew the fire-red Triglav flowers. With his last strength he ate one of them and was instantly healed, and his powers were fully restored. With sudden, unexpected leaps, he threateningly approached the hunter on a narrow ledge. His horns were stunningly bright in the sun, and the hunter was overwhelmed by the sight. Right there in front of him was the magnificent Goldenhorn; behind rose an impassable rock wall and below him an immeasurably deep precipice. He lost his poise and balance and fell headlong into the abyss.

After that, there was a wild storm; rain came down in torrents, and lightning struck all around until the rocks were splitting and falling apart. The tempest lasted all night.

In the morning when the sun rose from behind Mt. Triglav, the sky was clean as if washed. The innkeeper's daughter went to the river to rinse her skeins of yarn. She saw something resembling a log floating down the river. When it came close enough, she recognized to her horror the body of her hunter friend, who clutched in his hand a bouquet of Triglav flowers.

The white ladies left their mountain paradise forever and with them went the Goldenhorn. When the shepherds came with their flocks of sheep and goats the next summer, they found instead of a paradise only rocky crags and cliffs. Gone were the lush meadows with the sweet grasses, for the Goldenhorn had in his rage destroyed everything. Even to this day you can see in the rocks the marks of his horns.

In this legend we find the elements of a very ancient mythology—that of the eternal struggle between good and evil. This is symbolized in the Indo- European area by the hunt of the sunny deer (A. Kuhn, 1869). The story about the miraculous healing flower was described by Aristotle (4th century B.C.) in his **Animalium Historia** (IX, 6). The Goldenhorn appears as a messenger of the god of light (white colour) and of the sun (golden horns) and he punished the man who dared to break the integrity of nature, that is, divine law.

The legend also suggests the continuation of the indigenous population from distant past to present day. The legend of the Goldenhorn was presented in a fine poem by the German poet, R. Baumbach (1877), and translated into other central European languages—Slovene, Polish, Czech, Wendish, and Italian.

* * *

The roots of Slovene folk music are very old. During the last century the peculiar rhythmic structure of some songs came to the attention of collectors and cataloguers of Slovene folk songs. Influenced by the then popular Pan-Slavic attitude, it was explained as a Slovene, i.e., Slavic specialty; however, after the First World War, there were some voices heard in opposition to this view, whereby greater emphasis was given to correct writing of the rhythm. Instead of the presumed 5/4 time, a continuous change between 3/4 and 2/4 time was revealed.

The Slovene musicologist, Valens Vodušek (Ljubljana),[214] conducted a comprehensive analysis of all available Slovene folk songs which have such a rhythm. The predominant stanza in these songs is considered to be the original one, and is known to musicologists as the **octosyllabe gallo-romain.** This rhythm is found mostly among Slovenes in the western region, particularly in the Rezija Valley (now in Italy), where it is the dominant feature in their folk dances. It is also present in the "first circle dance" (ta prvi rej), the ceremonial dance under the linden tree in the Zilja Valley (Gailtal) in Carinthia.

There is no other Slavic nation where this rhythm occurs in folk songs. Surprisingly, it is to be found everywhere in France; this fact indicates a genetic relationship between Slovene and French folk songs. The author of this study therefore suggests a common Celtic origin in both cases.

To conclude this partial presentation of contributions to the conference "Alpes Orientales", we add a few more details and at the same time ask the reader to bear with us a little longer.

France Bezlaj (Ljubljana)[215] presented his findings in regard to the name, Ture; the original name was **Turje**, which still has a common meaning in the Slovene language. Later German settlers changed it to Tauern. Urban Jarnik, the

---

[214] V. Vodušek, *Über den Ursprung eines characteristischen Volksliederrhythmus/* Concerning the Origin of an Unusual Rhythm in the Slovene Folk Songs, Alpes Orientales V, pp. 151–178.

[215] F. Bezlaj, *Das vorslawische Substrat im Slowenischen/* The pre-Slavic Substratum in the Slovene Language, Alpes Orientales V, pp. 2–4, from U. Jarnik, *Versuch eines Etymologikons der Slowenischen Mundart in Inner Österreich/* An Etymological Study of the Slovene Dialects of Inner Austria, Klagenfurt 1832, p. 107.

Carinthian Slovene recorder of folk traditions, listed the meaning in the last century as "stark ableitiger Hügel"—a steep-sided hill.

Related to this is the prehistoric name, *Taurisci,* for the earliest known people in the eastern Alps, who were later named *Norici* and yet later *Carni.* The name Taurisci is connected to steep mountains (*turje*—Ture, Tauern). The name Carni is also related to rocky mountains (*kar*—rocky wall, cliff). In both instances it means inhabitants of a mountainous region.

The name Norici coincides with the old Slovene word *nora (*cave, hollow—modern Slov. jama, votlina);[216] however, the terms "jama" and "nora" do not only mean cave or hollow, but also an enclosed mountain valley. The Norici were therefore inhabitants of mountain valleys, identical to mountain dwellers. Pliny the Elder (III, 133) thus rightfully equates the Taurisci with the Norici and Carni. They were the same people.

***

The cultural region from the Po Valley and the Alps to the Baltic and Scandinavia developed uniformly after the Urnfield migration of the Veneti. This unity was broken after the invasion of the Celts around 400 B.C.

The original elements of this culture have survived until today in isolated parts of the Alps, the Baltic and Scandinavia. Similarities of cultural characteristics in these regions have been studied in the last decades, and attempts have been made by such well-known folklorists as Karl Rhamm, Bruno Schier, Georg Graber, and Leopold Kretzenbacher to explain them. Generally speaking, they attribute these similarities to Germanic tribes who later merged with the Slavs.

These folk traditions are the remnants of the culture of Veneti, who represent the basis of all nations in central Europe from the Baltic to the Adriatic. The following statement by Bruno Schier, regarding this ancient, culturally defined territory is of some interest:[217]

"Based on numerous concurrences, a uniform sphere of culture can be observed in Scandinavia, central Europe and the Alps... The appearance of eastern

---

[216] F. Bezlaj, *Etimološki slovar slovenskega jezika/* Etymological Dictionary of the Slovene Language, vol. II, Ljubljana 1982.

[217] B. Schier, *Hauslandschaften und Kulturbewegungen im östlichen Mitteleuropa/* The House-type-areas and the Culture Movements in the Eastern Central Europe, Göttingen 1966, p. 9, op. cit., by F. Jeza, *O ključnih vprašanjih rane karantansko-slovenske zgodovine/* Concerning the Key Problems of the Early History of Slovene Carantania, Buenos Aires 1977, pp. 138–140.

and northern European building techniques in the Alpine countries is puzzling, but there must be a causal relationship between these regions and their unity of culture. The high level of their type of housing and its superiority to that of the west Germanic people, is particularly obvious in several instances: a two-structure farmyard plan, with its rigid division between living area and barns; the stone oven for cooking and baking; the bath chamber...".

By the term "eastern Europe", the ethnographer means eastern Germany and Poland, the ancient Venetic territory. The "Nordic" element found in Carinthian day-to-day living has been investigated by Georg Graber.[218] Here we find the Carinthian two-structure farmyard and also the square court farmyard with barns, the smokehouse, the plough, the beehive made from a tree trunk and the predominant horizontal beehive, "the Carniolan", made of spruce boards. He also found a series of customs, legends, and fairy-tale traditions.

Through this comparative research of folklorists it is obvious that the oft-cited break between late antiquity and Carantania's so-called Slavic period can only refer to the Roman culture of the cities, whereas the rural culture in its essence can still be felt and the original bearers of this culture could only have been the Veneti, the predecessors of modern Slovenes.

Closing Remarks

In this exploration of Veneti, the author had to limit himself to the Alps; that is, the region where the prehistoric rural culture of Veneti has survived to this day. This culture formed the basis for the existence and survival of the Venetic people, and represents together with their language the most important witness to their presence in these regions since prehistory.

Our attention must also be directed, at least briefly, to the insufficiently re-searched questions of prehistory, whose comparison with the Slovene language and ethnic culture would probably bring new insights to relevant, yet unanswered questions. The prehistoric element in Slovene cultural tradition has remained strong in spite of centuries of sustained effort to suppress it and to deny it its rightful place.

When we consider the Proto-Slavic origin of the Veneti and their eventual spreading out through much of Europe during the Urnfield migration, then pre-history and early history appear in a new light.

---

[218] G. Graber, *Volksleben in Kärnten/* The Rural Life in Carinthia, 1941, pp. 1–3, op. cit., by F. Jeza, ibid., p. 141.

Archaeology has discovered that during the late Bronze Age (around 1000 B.C.) a relatively large settlement wave of Alpine inhabitants moved into the Parisian basin[219] and beyond. During Roman times the Veneti were found in Armorica (present-day Brittany); we are reminded of them by a few names like *Vennes*, or *Rue du Thabor* in Rennes. This group of Veneti were good sailors and maintained active relations with Britain; the name *Ventnor* on the Isle of Wight is in all probability related to them.

The Veneti in this area had sustained relations with Alpine people. Evidence is found in Hallstatt discoveries from the mouth of the Loire River and from the south of England (around 600 B.C.).[220]

We are reminded of the Veneti in England by several historically transmitted names. Thus: Vennonis (Vennonae, Itin. Ant. 407, 4), today High Cross in Leicestershire; Venta Belgarum (Ptol., II 3, 28), centre of the Belgae, today Winchester; then, Venta Icenorum (Ptol., II 3, 21), centre of the Iceni, today Caistor St. Edmunds; and Venta Silurum (Itin. Ant. 458, 9), during antiquity the centre of the Solures, today Caerwent in Monmouthshire.[221]

These examples show us the need for a comprehensive study of the archaeological, historical, and linguistic peculiarities of these regions. Included should be a comparison of the nomenclature of the regions to that of the West Slavs and Slovenes in particular. There are also many place-names in France which call to mind the presence of Veneti in the distant past; e.g., place-names around Orleans, Tours, and Troyes—*Vendome, Vendoevres, Vendeuvre;* around Lyon—*Vendranges, Venissieu, Vienne;* near Toulouse—*Vendine;* around Marseille—*Venelles, Vinon; Venaco* on Corsica, and so on.

In southwestern France in the province of Gironde (the region of Bordeaux), urn graves have been discovered that are different from those ascribed to the Celts, and which show strong influences from central Europe.[222] Several inscriptions dedicated to the sun-god Belin were also excavated there; they are similar to those discovered in the provinces of Veneto (Italy), Carniola (Slovenia), and Noricum.[223] In addition, the place-name *Vendays* and numerous place-names ending with -*ac* (Calignac, Cadillac) call to mind the presence of the pre-Celtic Veneti. Also distinctive is the place-name *Belin* south of Bordeaux and river names *Vienne* and *Charente* near Limoges. North of Charente-Maritime is the province

[219] P. Merlat, Paulys Real-Encyclopädie, op. cit. 1955, p. 710 (Veneti).

[220] J. Filip, op.cit., p. 164 (Bretagne), p. 333 (England).

[221] Paulys Real-Encyclopädie...op. cit., 1958, vol. VII, A/2.

[222] J. Filip, op. cit., p. 42 (Aquitanien), p. 371 (France).

[223] Baumstark, Paulys Real-Encyclopädie, 1899, p. 200 (Belenus).

of *Vendée*. These details point to Veneti and the time before the Celts had developed as a people.

A strong Venetic group also settled in **Scandinavia** when, after the Ice Age (around 2500-800 B.C.), the conditions in the *Sub-Boreal* were very favourable for agriculture. It seems the Veneti carried Urnfield culture directly to Scandinavia.

From the Scandinavian Urnfield culture several rock engravings have survived, including representations of ploughing tools. They are in southwestern Sweden and in neighbouring Norway. The plough testifies to the developed agriculture of early history and coincides with the representation of the plough on the Certosa Situla from Villanova. The Nordic Bronze Age occurred at the same time as the Hallstatt period in central Europe, and Hallstatt discoveries in Scandinavia tell us of active trade relations between the two regions.

The cooling of the weather in Scandinavia around 800 B.C. strongly affected its flourishing culture. Archaeologists surmise that as a result an extensive migration of the population followed. The appearance of the Iron Age in this region in the 5th century B.C. reveals a strong influence of Germanic Jastorf culture in archaeological finds. However, this only signifies a gradual Germanization of the Scandinavian Veneti. Later, only the tribal name "Vandals" reminds us of them and of the people who appeared during the first two centuries A.D. in central Europe and later settled in North Africa.

The Vandals could have therefore been Germanized Veneti (Proto-Slavs). They most probably came out of the central part of Sweden today called Svealand, (as opposed to the south Swedish Gotaland). The name calls to mind the Slavs, and still more, the adjective *svensk* (Swedish), which is close to the abbreviation for *slovensk* (Slovene). This may seem farfetched but a comparison of the two words is not unusual.

Venetic names also appear in the Nordic area, as in the Swedish province of *Dalarna* (valleys), e.g., *Vintjarn, Venjan, Vinas*; in addition, the *Vanern Lake* and by it the town *Vinninga*. Then in Norway: *Vinstra, Venaseter, Venasen* in the region Gunbrandsdal, north of Oslo; and in the coastal area below the city of Trondheim: *Vinsternes, Vinje,* north of here *Vendesund.*

Along with names derived from "Veneti" that are found throughout Europe, there are other forms of Venetic origin. They are so numerous that we can present here only the most typical ones. However, just a few name types and their distribution give us a fairly clear picture of how the ancient Veneti or Wends designated various topographical features, conditions of the soil, arable land, strategic points, and so on.

Among the most widespread place-names in all of Europe is Holm. Its meaning in the Slovene language is, even today, a rounded peak or mountain summit which stands apart from its surroundings, especially on a plain.

In separate language regions the name *Holm* appears in various forms. In the German-speaking area, in place-names such as *Kulmbach, Kulmain, Helm, Homberg* and *Homburg, Colmberg, Chulm, Chamerau, Cham.*

In the Polish and Pomeranian areas are *Chelm, Chelmza, Chelmno;* in western Russia, *Chelm;* in Denmark, *Holm, Humlum, Humble, Lindholm;* in Norway, *Holmengil, Holmen, Holmedal, Hommelvik, Holum*; in Sweden, *Holm, Holmfors, Holmsund, Kumla, Stockholm, Norsholm, Katrineholm.*

These names appear often in France. Inasmuch as they do not stand for a field (champ), these names appear with *Cham-* in compound place-names: *Chamberet, Chambery, Chambilly, Chambord, Chambon, Chamboulive, Colmar, Combles.* In Great Britain are *Chelmsford, Holme, Holmfirth, Cumnock* and *Holmhead, Colmonell* and the county of *Cumberland.*

Also found scattered here and there in Spain are *Cumbres, Colmenar;* in Portugal *Cumieira;* in Italy, *Cuma, Cumiana, Comiso, Como;* in Greece, *Chelmos 2341m.*

In Slovenia the name Holm appears in several forms—*Holm, Hum* and *Kum*—as well as the diminutive *Holmec* or abbreviated *Homc.* There is moreover, the family name Humar; i.e., the inhabitant on the Hum or Holm.

The derivation of this word from the Latin *culmen* (peak) is incorrect, as is obvious from its distribution in regions which were not influenced historically by Latin language and culture, especially Scandinavia. We must add that place-designations with *Holm* are rare in typically Latin regions, for example in the Apennines, Italy. The name *Holm* is pre-Celtic, as the settlement wave of the Celts had not reached Scandinavia where the name frequently appears. However, Veneti or Wends did migrate that far.

Names derived from *Holm* occur most frequently in central, western, and northern Europe and thereby show the original settlement area of Veneti (Wends) after their migration out of Lusatia (12th century B.C.). In the regions where the term *Holm* occurs, there also appears in various forms the place-name Lom, which describes a fault, a quarry, an incline or gradation on a mountain slope. Compare these with the Slovene verb *lomiti*—to quarry, to break off. In Slovene speaking areas there is also the diminutive *Lomič* (sing.), and *Lomiči* (pl.); i.e., terraces, the gradation of a mountain slope.

In the nomenclature of various regions of Europe these place-names appear as *Lom, Lam,* and *Lim* and are found in Germany, *Lembruch, Lamsfeld;* in France, *Lamarche, Limay, Limoges;* in Denmark, *Lemvig;* in Sweden, *Lima;* in Norway,

Lom, Lomen; in Bohemia, *Lomnice;* in Poland, *Lomza;* in Spain, Portugal, Italy, *Lomello, Lama;* in Great Britain, *Lambourn, Lamlash;* in Romania and Greece, *Lambia, Lamia.* In Slovenia it is found as *Lom, Lam, Lomno, Lomnik, Podlom,* etc. In addition, there are corresponding family names: *Lomšek* and *Lomar.* We must mention the name Loka, in the older form *Lonka* or *Lanka.* This name is found already during Roman times in the Zilja Valley (Gailtal), Carinthia as "Loncium" (Itin. Ant., 2nd century). In Slovene it is still used today to designate a meadow by a body of water. It is found in Europe outside of Slovene and Slavic areas in general. In German speaking regions as *Laak, Lachen, Lachendorf;* in France as *Lacanau, Lacave, Lacq;* in Great Britain as *Lacock,* probably also *Lancaster;* in the Nordic area as *Lakselv, Lakatrask, Lakolk;* in Spain as *Lacunza;* in Italy as *Lanciano;* in Switzerland as *Locarno;* in Greece as *Lakka, Lakkion.* This name is often accompanied by the place-name Log, signifying a seasonally flooded area. In German names we encounter it in the form *Langen;* in French as *Longville, Longeau;* in Spanish as *Lugo* and *Longares;* in Italian as *Longo, Longarone, Lugano,* and in Greek as *Longanikos.*

The names with vowel mutations must also be taken into consideration. Thus, the name Lob (cliff, rocky knoll, hill) appears as *Alb,* as is shown by place- names in Italy, such as *Albano, Albenga;* or in France, *Albens, Albaron;* in Spain, *Albatera;* in Germany, *Albstadt.* The name Kar, also *Ker* (cliff), became Akra in Greece, where it means a cape, point, a spit of land. The name Rob, also *Rab* (precipice or brink) became *Arbe* and similar forms.

Among the names that mean land cleared for cultivation is the very common place-name Trebež (arable land, clearing). It is found in France, *Trebes, Treves;* in Italy, *Treviso, Trevi, Treviglio;* in Germany, *Trebel, Trebur, Trier;* and of course in different forms in Slavic countries. Uuncultivated land, on the other hand, is designated by the name Rod. We encounter these in Germany, *Rodach, Rodenkirchen;* in Norway, *Rodel;* in Great Britain, *Rodel;* in France, *Rodez;* in Spain, *Roda;* in Italy, *Rodi;* in Greece, *Roda, Rodia....*

Linked to the defence of ancient Veneti is the name Straža (guard, watch), which occurs very often in West Slavic regions; beyond this area it appears as: *Strass, Strassberg* in Austria and Germany; as *Strasbourg* in France, and *Strassa* in Sweden. Also related to these names is the Greek word *stratos* (army) and accordingly Greek names like *Stratoniki, Stratonion, Stratos;* and the English *Stratton, Strathaven, Stratford* and so on.

Although it is not possible to guarantee the meaning of each of these names, the very number of them tells us of the existence of the Venetic language during pre-Celtic times. The roots of modern Slovene, Lusatian Wendish (Sorbian), Slovincian, Czech, and Slovakian are to be found there. These names show us

167

that in the distant past there was a western Proto-Slavic language, the language of the Veneti.

Many examples of closely related expressions from Slovene and Swedish or Norwegian vocabulary were published by F. Jeza.[224] They refer above all to the ethnic culture and affirm the prehistoric relationship between the Alps and Scandinavia. The prehistoric bearers of civilization in these regions were not the East Germanic people, as Graber and after him Jeza assumed. These two experts were merely repeating the "scientific" expositions of Gustav Kossinna, who desperately wanted Scandinavia to be the original home of Germanic people, a theory which he traced all the way to the Stone Age. Scandinavian archaeologists have since disproved such interpretations.

Moving eastward, we find that from the standpoint of archaeology and toponymy, the area has not been researched regarding the appearance of Veneti in Asia Minor. According to Homer, those who settled in Paphlagonia were allies of Troy. Also, the appearance of Veneti in the lower Danube area, as reported by Herodotus, remains uninvestigated.

We do not know what ethnic affiliation to assign to the Dorians who advanced from the north into Greece around 1200 B.C. On Crete, for example, central European full-handle swords from this period have been found. From this we can assume that among the attacking hordes, who had destroyed the Creto-Mycenaean culture, were Veneti. Furthermore, were the Pelasgians, also allies of Troy (Iliad II, 840 ff.),[225] really a pre-Indo-European people or were they perhaps Venetic? And can we learn anything from the name of the Thraco-Phrygian goddess, *Zemele*, the Mother of Dionysos? The name is completely Slavic (*zemla* or *zemlja*—earth). The necessary research and comparisons are still lacking, particularly with respect to Slovene and other Slavic languages and traditions.

The most remote location with a name that may well be of Venetic origin is Vindhya parvata (Windian Hills) in India. At one time these hills constituted the dividing line between the Aryan north and Dravidian south. Was this name brought to India by the Aryans? Is the name India itself an abbreviation of Vindia? It is possible.

It was not possible to devote any time in this study to inscriptions left behind by the Adriatic Veneti. They were collected and classified by Pellegrini in his famous book, "La lingua venetica", but he was not able to decipher them. According to E. Vetter, these inscriptions originate in the 5th and 4th centuries B.C. The only Venetologist who has so far been able to decipher them scientifically is

---

[224] F. Jeza, *O ključnih...op. cit.,* pp. 158–81.
[225] F. Schachermeyr, Paulys Real-Enzyclopädie... op. cit., 1937 (Pelasgoi).

168

Matej Bor, whose extremely important study will form the second part of this book.

The characters of Venetic inscriptions coincide with those of the Etruscan and Rhaetian. Apparently it was from Etruscan characters that the Latin alphabet developed and was spread through the west by the Romans. The Greeks, on the other hand, acquired their writing from the Phoenicians (Herodotus V 58), who are today considered the inventors of the alphabet. The prevailing opinion in scientific circles is that the individual letters originally developed from hieroglyphics, first used in Egypt.

Linear characters appeared with Phoenicians between the 13th and 11th centuries B.C., when they were living in the land of Canaan. Significantly, this was during the time of Urnfield culture and Urnfield migration, which extended over the Aegean Sea encompassing Asia Minor and the Near East.

Is it possible then that the Veneti brought the alphabetic script to Etruria as well as to Phoenicia? The similarity between these writings is amazing, just as is their similarity with runic characters, which are generally assumed to be of Germanic origin. Although the earliest runic inscriptions date only from the 2nd century A.D., they are considered by most experts to be older. The Norwegian researcher, Marstrander,[226] is of the opinion that the runes have their origin in Etruscan characters. Although earlier runic inscriptions have not survived, it is likely that they are older than Etruscan writing itself. In support of this conclusion, we look at the name *rune*, from *roniti*—to deepen, to make incisions—as possibly Venetic, i.e., Slavic. There is also reason, in our opinion, to investigate whether the Veneti created or transmitted the basis for the modern western alphabet and individual sounds.

Another detail that speaks in favour of this possibility is house insignias or house marks; these are signs originating in prehistory composed of different patterns of incisions. They are in evidence in the Late Stone Age and have been preserved into this century, particularly in northern Europe and in the Alps. In Slovenia they are concentrated in the northwest area in the Alpine region. These marks had and still have names similar to the letters of Greek or Phoenician alphabets and the runes.

Just a few more words regarding the very things our critics love most, the earlier mentioned, possibly Slavic (Venetic) place-names in the Near East; for example, Tabor in Palestine, Suez, Golan. We will be told how naive or simpleminded we are for even considering such a remote possibility, but their objec-

---

[226] J. Filip, op. cit., p. 1177 (Runen).

tions do not help advance the research. Serious scholars (e.g., E. Meyer)[227] tell us of three invasions of Indo-Europeans into the Near East: the invasion of kentum Hittites before 2000 B.C. into Anatolia reaching the area of upper Euphrates; the invasion of satem Indo-Iranians around 1750 B.C. and the establishment of their Mitanni kingdom in upper Mesopotamia; around 1200 B.C. an invasion of "people from the sea", who were defeated by the Egyptians.

A number of scholars also say that Indo-European languages did not take shape only in the Late Stone Age or in the Bronze Age, but had already formed their basic delineations in the Old Stone Age—before 8000 B.C. We know there was a much closer connection between western Europe and North Africa; this also explains the considerable relation between Indo-European and Hamitic and Semitic languages in their composition as well as word structure. We should therefore not be overly surprised by, or discount, the possibility of finding Indo-European or Slavic word connections in languages or toponymy of North Africa or the Near East.

Considering the facts presented in this study, we can all recognize how inadequate and disproportionate has been the investigation of the ethnic and cultural roots of the Slovene people. Until now practically all research has been hindered by the falsehood of a Slovene migration from the Balkans into the eastern Alps in the 6th century.

The author of this study makes himself available for any criticism that is founded on facts and is not motivated by nationalistic ambitions.

Instead of customary servility to ideological dogmatism, there ought to be an honest and impartial investigation of history, and an objective reporting of facts and events. We hope that someday Slovene historians will dare to have their own independent point of view, and will be able to critically examine the question of political and ideological subservience.

---

[227] E. Meyer, *Die Indogermanenfrage/* The Problem Regarding Indo-Europeans; in *Die Urheimat der Indogermanen/* The Ancient Homeland of Indo-Europeans; Wege der Forschung Bd. 164, Darmstadt 1968, p. 281.

PART TWO

The Venetic Language and Venetic Inscriptions

Slavic Elements in the Etruscan Language

The Etruscan, Rhaetian and Yapodic Inscriptions

Matej Bor

The Key to the Venetic Language

The controversy surrounding the origin of the Slovenes has recently flared up again, but this is no surprise; the debate has been going on for more than a century. I too am preoccupied with this question, and have accumulated a considerable amount of material; however, I had decided not to publish my findings until I was able to do so in a larger book, where enough room would be available to substantiate the results of my research in some detail. But I have since changed my mind. Although my findings are of limited interest to the general public, I think it would be wrong not to publish at least part of them.

The Encyclopedia of the Lexicographic Institute in Zagreb contains the following information about the Veneti:

"Name by which several Indo-European tribes are known in antiquity:

1. The Celtic tribe on the Atlantic coast of northwestern Gaul (between the Seine and the Loire), which maintained active trade relations with Britain. It was subdued during the Roman conquest of Gaul. In the year 57 B.C. a revolt ensued which was put down by Caesar on land, and by Decimus Brutus at sea.

2. The inhabitants of Northern Italy on the Adriatic coast between the Po River and Istria. During the 2nd Punic War they came under the rule of the Romans who founded the colony of Aquileia in this region in 182 B.C. Their territory was at first incorporated into Cisalpine Gaul, and then, at the time of Augustus, it became together with Istria the 10th Italic province (Venetia et Histria). Under the Romans they retained their complete autonomy, and in the year 89 B.C. they obtained the 'ius Latinum'. They were commonly known to be skilful merchants, especially as traders in amber, which they transported from the Baltic Sea to the Adriatic by way of the so-called 'Amber Road'. The Venetic language belongs to the Indo-European language group; its only historical documentation is made-up of approximately 200 short inscriptions. This language was at first considered to be an Illyrian dialect; however, recent linguists place it among one of the independent languages close to the Italic languages. The letters of the Venetic inscriptions were borrowed from the Etruscans, but the Veneti also had several graphemes and phonetic values of their own."

What I already knew at that time about the Veneti and their language did not correspond with some of the statements in the encyclopedia. For example, the assumption that the Veneti in Brittany were a Celtic tribe is questionable. The statement that the Venetic language is close to Italic languages is also questionable, unless we include the Etruscan language among them. The Etruscans were neighbours and contemporaries of the Veneti. Furthermore, the information about the distribution of Veneti in Europe is very incomplete.

I studied the Venetic inscriptions partly by way of books, among them *La lingua venetica (LLV)* Giovani Battista Pellegrini and Aldo L. Prosdocimi, a particularly accurate work which far surpasses Michel Lejeune's *Manuel de la langue Venete,* although the latter includes the most recent finds; and partly by examination of actual specimens in northern Italian museums.

I looked at all inscriptions and compared them a hundred times, always with the assumption that I was dealing with a Balto-Slavic language which had left deep impressions on the Slovene dialects, particularly those spoken in the western part of Slovene ethnic territory, and of course also in the Slovene literary language. It was an exciting idea and yet a sense of doubt came over me. Perhaps I was right, I thought, but to prove it would be very difficult or even impossible. Although there are a considerable number of inscriptions available and new ones are being discovered, there are all the same too few of them for me to clearly show a recognizable language which I sense in the Venetic inscriptions, and which I would like to reveal.

What should I do—continue with my search or stop? I was uncertain; finally, I decided to leave the matter alone for a while and later, when I took it up again, I would see whether there was still the desire and joy for the Venetic adventure, which—in case it ended successfully—would prove what others have attempted to prove for a long time. The ethnogenesis of the Slovenes would be fundamentally altered and consequently also our view of our identity, where we came from and all the factors that have influenced our language, our character, and our conscious and unconscious mind. I therefore pushed aside the books on linguistics, the dictionaries and everything that I had written on the subject, and turned again to contemporary Slovene language and thus to literature. I wrote, among other things, the novel "Odloženi", which is unrelated to my Venetic adventure, except for a reminiscence of our American compatriot, an architect, Jager, who devoted some of his money and free time to the study of the Etruscan language. His efforts were not what could be called professional, but over the years he collected a considerable library on this subject, which still excites the imagination of research lovers. This imagination is often totally lacking among experts. He bequeathed his entire collection of Etrurological books to the Slovene Academy of

Sciences and Arts. I had the impression that by studying and investigating the unexplored origin of the language I was writing in, I would enrich myself if nothing more. Thus, many words that smelled of soil and the distant past became more friendly, more valuable and I in turn came closer to them. I sensed in them those expressions about which I had earlier known nothing. Even if I accomplished nothing else, the journey into the old Venetic mysteries would be reason enough. I would feel rewarded, and the time spent would not be lost. But aside from that it is always useful for a writer to occupy himself with a language in one way or other.

As my above mentioned novel was already on the way to the printers, I asked myself: what now? Should I begin another literary project? No, it would be premature. Let us wait until there is an indication of some kind. But since one has to make use of the time at hand, I decided to return to the Venetic language, as I promised I would do as soon as I had completed the novel.

I must admit that at first, something inside me was opposed to this. Why deal with a topic that is probably unsolvable or at least unprovable. Nevertheless, I almost instinctively placed the Venetic inscriptions on the table in front of me. I read and examined them again, as I had done many times before, only to come to a very similar conclusion. And probably this is how things would have remained had my eyes not stayed fixed one evening upon the reproduction of the tablets identified by the numbers Es 23 to Es 27 in the book *La lingua venetica.* The tablets are relatively well preserved, although in one place or other a small piece is missing, except for Es 23. However, since one is dealing with very similar and in part identical tablets, comparative analysis makes it possible—as had already been accomplished by previous Venetologists—to reconstruct and read all the inscriptions.

There I was then, sitting in front of these tablets, trying to decipher them. As usual, only the inscriptions fascinated me. That is why I did not spend nearly as much time on the part where other Venetologists saw the magic word **akeo.** Furthermore, I felt a disapproval for their interpretations, but I did not have a better one. However, this time something was different.

Let us first take a look at the Venetic inscription on the tablet **Es 24.**

I began straightaway by examining this **akeo.** First I noticed the shape of the letter O in the 5th row from the bottom. The letter O (majuscule) in Venetic is upright; it has this shape ◇. On this tablet (Es 24), and not only on this one, but on all except Es 23, these letters are on their side ◇. Horizontally strung together, they form a sort of border between the upper and the lower part of the tablet. Furthermore, those on Es 24 are also smaller than the other letters. So that the reader might better understand what had unexpectedly caught my attention

Es 24 (LLV)
Museo Nazionale Atestino

on that evening, he would do well to take a good look at the reproduction of the tablet Es 24. This should not be too difficult since the characters on this tablet, though partially damaged, are clearly visible.

However, in order to see it even more clearly, tablet Es 26 is represented as a drawing (instead of a photograph), as it is published in the book *La lingua venetica,* (p. 112).

Now that we have taken a look at these tablets, I can continue with the assurance that the reader will be able more easily to follow and check my comments.

As I already mentioned, the row of horizontal O's form a kind of border between the upper and the lower part of the tablet. One has an involuntary impression that it is of a decorative nature. And not only that, as everyone can see, the letters O on the tablet Es 24 are not connected with the lower characters; they have a separate existence. It would seem that those (as in *La lingua venetica*) who connect this O with the vertical letters to form AKEO are treating this detail rather unscientifically. They are especially unscientific if they do not see that

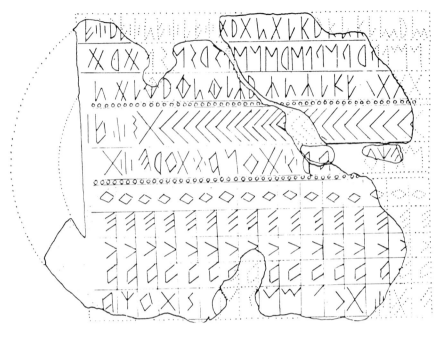

Es 26 (LLV)

under this AKEO there are other letters which are very clearly graphically linked with the vertical characters above, forming a whole.

The exception to the rule is the bronze plaque, or more exactly its fragment, which does not come from the shrine in Ateste, but was found in Vicenza. On this plaque fragment, one can see that there are no consonant groupings, but only the inscription at the top. On the other tablets where a series of derivations and forms of EKA are carefully inscribed, are here only superficially arranged. The letters in the vertical direction are not related to each other and several consonants in the bottom row are upside down. Also in respect to the graphics, the work is somewhat awkward compared with the tablets from Ateste. This suggests that the tablets were not only used for teaching purposes, but also had a magical character, though no longer being properly understood. This occurred presumably only in the latter period when the Venetic language was already replaced with Latin, and the original meaning of the tablets was lost.

As I became aware of this, there pressed upon me one more question: Who says that we have to read the letters on the tablets in the way Venetologists from Pellegrini to Lejeune and Vetter have done—from bottom to top? We could read them with much greater justification in the opposite direction. And if in the process we consider the already mentioned facts—that is, that the lower row is to be connected with the rest of the characters, and the row made up of horizontal O's is not to be included—we get a totally different picture. My reading of the letters follows the official Venetological scientific method. Instead of AKEO, which other Venetologists conjured up, there are on the **Es 24** the following groups:

$$
\begin{array}{ccccccccccc}
E & E & E & E & E & E & E & E & E & E & E \\
K & K & K & K & K & K & K & K & K & K & K \\
A & A & A & A & A & A & A & A & A & A & A \\
E & H & B & T & IS & R & \check{S} & P & J & D & V \\
\end{array}
$$

If we compare this tablet with other tablets, we can reconstruct the part that is damaged. We need not trouble ourselves here, since this has already been painstakingly taken care of by other Venetologists. The explanation for the symbol |✕|, the 4th letter from the right, will be dealt with later on. Missing are:

$$
\begin{array}{cccc}
E & E & E & E \\
K & K & K & K \\
A & A & A & A \\
N & M & L & K \\
\end{array}
$$

If we write them down starting from the left, we obtain the following: **ekae, ekah, ekab, ekat, ekais, ekar, ekaš, ekap, ekan, ekam, ekal, ekak, ekaj, ekad, ekav.**

If we consider that the Venetic language is very closely related to Balto-Slavic as attested by several other linguists (among them the recent and well-known Pokorny, or Prosdocimi, who thinks that the Veneti were probably of Slavic origin) are we then doing something very unscientific if we assume that a beginning **e** (being connected to the following consonant) is to be pronounced as **je, (ye** in yes) as in Russian, although it is written as **e** (*ego, jego*— Slov. *njega*— him). The result of our investigation will show that we were justified in doing this. Thus, let us write all of the above words one more time with the beginning **je,** as in Slovene or Serbo-Croatian: **jekaje, jekah, jekab, jekat, jekais, jekar, jekaš, jekap, jekan, jekam, jekal, jekak, jekaj, jekad, jekav.**

And now let us look at those words which are at the moment the most interesting. They are: **jekat, jekam, jekaš, jekaj, jekal, jekaje, jekah.**

Who would not be amazed at the appearance of these words which have been conjured up before our very eyes from the Ateste tablets?

The majority are still familiar to us today:

The women still today approach the grave crying (**jekat,** jokat).
The north wind howled (je **jekal**) around the corners.
Don't cry (**jekaj**) any more!
Such a whiny (**jekav**) voice!
Why are you crying (**jekaš**)?
I am crying (**jekam**).
They went away weeping (**jekaje**).

Only the form **jekah** is no longer used, since the Old Slavic aorist has been lost. However, it is still found in the Slovene dialect in Italy which exhibits the closest similarities with the Venetic, and of course in Serbo-Croatian. The word **jekat(i)**—to cry—is still found in Slovene dictionaries. Pleteršnik: **jekati, jekam**—to echo, to resound; **jeka,** f.—an echo; **jek, jeka** m.—sound, *Slovar slovenskega knjižnega jezika*/Dictionary of the Slovene Literary Language: jekati, -am. Examples: 1. To give short, sharp sounds: The bells in the tower resounded (jekali); the shots echoed (jekali). 2. To reverberate: His words echoed (jekale) from the cliffs. The song of young men resounded (jekala) from house to house. I am including the Russian form of the same verb *екать*—to produce a sharp, cracking sound.

Now let us take a look at those forms that do not exist in Slovene (I do not want to compare them here with other Slavic languages), though it is almost certain that they existed, but disappeared in the course of time. These are: **jekar, jekak, jekad, jekan.**

Venetic Grammar
in Light of the Word "Jekat"

Before we say anything more about these forms of the word **jekat,** we must ask ourselves: what is **jekat,** what does it mean? It is a short infinitive, as it occurs in most of the Slovene dialects, especially in the west, where in the mountainous region the Venetic tradition survived longest.

Its meaning was probably the same as the Slovene word **ječati** (to moan). Relatives and friends of the deceased mourned **ječali so** at the burial ceremony. They grieved and sang dirges. If my assumption is correct—and I believe it is— since so many Venetic inscriptions are somehow related to the cremation of the deceased, then the mourner(s) **jekar** was the person who either himself mourned or led the ceremony. Supporting this explanation is the ending -**ar,** which is still used in the Slovene language: **zvonar** (bell-ringer), **pisar** (copyist), **klicar** (town-crier), etc.

Similar to the word **jekar** is the derivative **jekak.** It is foreign to us, although we have more than enough words with the ending -**ak:** *junak* (hero), *učenjak* (scholar), *težak* (heavy), *bedak* (simpleton), etc. The word **jekak,** which was also indigenous to us, was changed to **jekač,** probably because of the two k's.

The third derivative in this group is **jekad.** Also here we find parallels: *divjad* (game, venison), *suhljad* (dead, dry branches). Less well-known is **zijat** (Pleteršnik, chasm). But why not mention the word that stands the closest to the Venetic **jekad?** I am thinking of **jekot** (Plet. booming or roaring sound). So it was not really correct when I said that the noun **jekad** no longer exists in Slovene. It is still here, though only in the form *jekot.* The same is true of the participle **jekan.** It does not exist any longer in Slovene, although from the perspective of its grammar and meaning it would be possible. **Jekan** means *objokovan* (being mourned), and *objokan* (mourned), which is very similar to it; *jek* and *jok* also have the same derivation. The root (j)ek- is found in the following Slovene words: *jekati, ječati, jek, jeka* (France Bezlaj, echo); also from the same root is **jok** (Franc Miklošič, a cry).

What about **jekab?** It could be a type of word such as *svarb* (itch), or *srab* (Plet.). In the Tolmin area the word *jekab* is still known.

From among the presently known derivatives of the verb **jekati, jekap** is the most distant from the Slovene and Slavic languages. It is difficult to say what it

Es 25 (LLV)
Museo Nazionale Atestino

is supposed to mean, although nouns ending in -ap are also found in Slovene, such as *kap* (drip line), *slap* (waterfall), etc.

Besides the forms dealt with so far, there are several more. On the tablet Es 25 in the last square from the right we do not find the vowel **e** as on Es 22, 24, but rather **ii** (II), and **a** on Es 26.

In the place of the participle **jekaje** we have the forms **jekaa** and **jekaji**. It is probably the aorist, 3rd per. singular, only here there is **aa**, since the **a** in the aorist was long or was pronounced twice, as in the Old Church Slavic (OCS) imperfect **delaaše**. However, it is not impossible that one may be dealing with the noun **jeka**, which is still used among us today, or the participle with -**a,** as often appears in the Venetic. **Jekaji** corresponds to our *jekaje;* it could however also be the active pres. part., **jekajij** *jekajoči*—crying in the existing form. Compare with Old Church Slavic (OCS) *znajej, hvalej*—he who knows, he who praises.

And now it is time that we learn more about the tablets where, to my amazement, I discovered a whole chapter of Venetic grammar. The majority of the forms are still in use, be it in the Slovene literary language or in the surviving dialects, which tells us a great deal about the nature and structure of the Venetic language.

These "alphabet tablets" were found in Este, southwest of Padova, which is at present a rather insignificant small town. However, a number of archaeological discoveries brought to light there give us a different picture; they give strong evidence that at one time Este was a very important center of Venetic culture. In Este, or Ateste as it was called during the Venetic period, there was a shrine dedicated to the god (or goddess), **Reitija**. The legendary shrine of the West Slavs, **Retra** (Lusatia) was almost certainly dedicated to the same god. Among the most valuable of the numerous finds which have been discovered till now, which include small bronze statues, various tools and weapons, vases, clasps, money are also the "alphabet tablets". An important component of this shrine or even its principal part was a school for writers or scribes (scuola dei scrittori), at least from the 6th to 5th centuries B.C. These were learned priests who also made these tablets. In Venetology they are called "alphabet tablets" (tavolette alfabetiche). Furthermore, we find on them, as can be seen here in the printed reproduction, the Venetic consonants and tautosyllabic consonant pairs, such as kr kn kl, tr tn tl, sr sn sl, mr mn ml, pr pn pl, zr zn zl, br bn bl, etc.

Nevertheless, Venetologists have till this day not noticed that besides containing a small segment on Venetic phonetics, these tablets also contain instruction on Venetic word form. The forms and derivatives of the verb **jekat** were not found just anywhere; rather, they were found precisely where they would be expected—on the grammar tablets (as I prefer to call them). This is a piece of evidence which clearly shows that we are dealing with a chapter from Venetic morphology. But since the verb **jekat** in its various forms is obviously Slavic, Slovene, we finally have a fairly clear answer to the question concerning the origins of the Venetic language.

Of course, this is no small matter, for it turns upside down the accepted approach to history and linguistics, and thereby opens a completely new perspective in the research of European history. The Ateste tablets with the Slavic/Slovene grammar substantiate the claims of all those who believe that the Slovenes arrived in their territory much before the 6th century A.D.

The school of the "scribes" was not concerned that their tablets appeared graphically harmonious or original; rather they developed a playful way of teaching grammar in addition to the standard visual method. The reader can see that the lowest row on these tablets represents Venetic consonants. Everything indicates that, in this particular case, they found a verb whose root would lend itself efficiently to various transformations by adding any vowel. Just such a verb was **jekat.** The majority of the forms that have come from this verb, as we have already seen, are still in common use in the Slovene language and/or its dialects.

It is not totally clear whether **jekat** is an infinitive or a supine. After examining the Venetic texts, I am convinced that it is a short infinitive. The Venetic language is nothing more than the western form of the Proto-Slavic, which had developed somewhat differently from the Proto-Slavic in the east. In recent years this has been postulated also by Dr. France Bezlaj, whose research is based on certain characteristics of the Slovene language, but he still does not equate Slovene with the Venetic language. The western, and above all the Mediterranean proto-Slavs lived, thought, and spoke faster, resulting very early in the so-called "modern" vowel-reduction as well as other changes: the 'akanje' (the tendency to change the unaccented **o** to **a**); a very strong diphthongization; betatism (the change of **v** to **b**); the prefix **vi** in place of **iz**, as in the upper Zilja Valley (Gailtal) where the words **vihnat**—to drive out, and **vibirat**—to choose are used, the velar h instead of g, which our western dialects have preserved since those far off days when the Venetic culture was at its height. There will be more discussion about this in the chapter in which I compare the Slovene dialects with Latvian and Breton. The Veneti lived in the areas where both of these languages are presently spoken.

Now let us return to our grammar tablets. If we look more closely at the bottom row, we see that the assumption that we are dealing only with Venetic consonants is not quite correct. The truth is, several vowels are found among them. On three tablets the letters **a, e** or **ii** are at the end. But since the learned scribes who wanted to give the letters a good appearance readily used the vertical lines (particularly the lines on the right of the squares for all letters with ascenders, which the reader can see for himself in the reproduction of the tablet Es 26) the question then arises whether these lines were also the symbol for the letter **i**. Tablet Es 24 confirmed my assumption on this point. Here the letters are not framed, therefore the use of the right line of the square for the letter i was not possible. And what did the scribe who composed this tablet do? He placed the letter **i** immediately before the **s**. Thus the bottom row has two vowels at the same time, an **e** and an **i**. Venetologists in such cases gladly avoid the problem by saying that it must be a mistake. One could agree with them if it were not for tablet Es 23, where a very clear **i** appears before the **s**. The right line of the square is placed a little to the left. Apparently the author wanted to point out that it is at the same time the symbol for the **i**.

Of interest is also the fourth square from the right. Here there are two crossed lines which are identical to the letter **t** but, according to Venetologists, they do not represent a **t**. They do not know what to do with this letter. Some call it simply a dead letter, although it is found occasionally in other inscriptions; others see in it a **th**.

Both of these explanations are unacceptable since |X| is nothing more than a **t** and the vertical lines of the square before and after are the letters **i**, consequently together **iti**. That this assumption is justified can be seen from the draw-

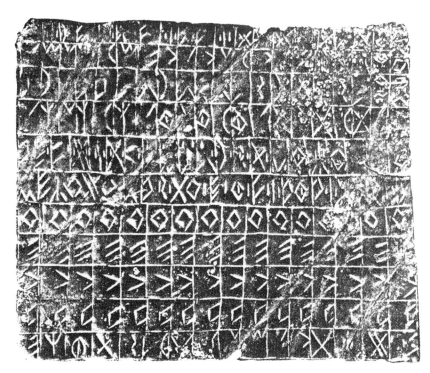

Es 23 (LLV)
Museo Nazionale Atestino

ing of the tablet Es 26 as well as the photo of the tablet Es 23 and the comparison between the 4th square from the left |X| and the 4th square from the right |X|. There is no difference between them, except perhaps in the latter the cross is a bit larger, which of course can be overlooked. At no time are all the letters of these inscriptions exactly the same; accordingly we find in the 4th column from the right still another form: **jekaiti;** however, in the 12th column **jekais.**

What do these two forms represent? Apparently **jekaiti** is the iterative infinitive of **jekat.** It is interesting how the **i** had not yet fallen away as in **jekat.** As concerns **jekais,** it is not difficult to see that it is the 2nd person pres. sing. In view of the assumption that it is an iterative, I would like to make reference to a comparison of the Slovene *dati, dajati*—to give, to give repeatedly. The difference is that in Slovene an **a** or **e**—*dajem,* is to be found in the place of an **i;** however, the idea that the already referred to **jekajij** is not a participle from **jekat,** but rather from **jekaiti** cannot be ruled out.

For what reason did these secondary details appear to me so important? I concluded from all that I had learned so far, that the bottom row was not only a list of consonants; it also had another significance. To make the study of grammar more attractive for the pupils, the teachers resorted to playfulness. The letters in the bottom row could be arranged in such a way to incorporate a riddle for the student to decipher. The letters thus form a complete sentence or more specifically, a saying, a proverb. Otherwise one cannot explain why vowels are added to the consonants. So that they could fill up the empty space? That could, if need be, explain the vowels at the end of the row, but in no way the distinct **i**'s before the **s.**

If I bear in mind what I have already said about the vowels in the bottom row, and at the same time also consider that the Veneti sometimes did as their neighbours, the Etruscans (they left out some vowels, especially those which were not accented or were reduced) then I could read the bottom row as follows:

VIDIJ TI K LIMIN PŠIRS T BGA
Videc ti ki tablice širiš tu boga

If we insert other vowels in addition to the **i,** it would change to this:

VIDIJ TI KI LIMINI POŠIRIS TU BOGA

In more readable Slovene: Vedež, ki tablice boga tu razširjaš.

In English: The seer (knowledge-bearer), you who are here distributing the tablets of god.

A number of explanations could be made in regard to the individual words, but we will limit ourselves to a few notes:

vidij—seer or knowledgeable person; Slov. *videc* or *vedec*. In Carinthia, this would be *videj*. *Videti*—to see, and *vedeti*—to know—come from the same root. However, it is not to be ruled out that **vidij** could be equal to the OCS *vetij*—rhetor, teacher of rhetoric—which would be an appropriate term for the learned priests who taught in the school of the scribes. Otherwise, though, **vidij** is the same form as **jekajij.**

ti—you; Slov. *ti.*

ki (k)—who; Slov. *ki.* Abbreviated from *kyjь;* Chakavian *ki;* OCS *kъ;* Venetic **k,** because the silent vowel was at times left out. We are therefore allowed to read **k** without **i,** just as is still done in various Slovene dialects.

limini—corresponds with the Lat. *lamina*—plate; but it could also be *limus*—

mud. If they made imprints in clay then this would be logical, and the Latvian *limenis*—level, surface—must also be considered.

pširs—you distribute; Slov. *(po)širiš*, e.g., *širiti božjo besedo*—to spread the word of God, to proclaim. The priests in the Rejtija temple proclaimed the news of their god in any way they could, including the writing of the tablets.

t—here; Slov. *tu*.

bga—of god; Slov. *boga*. There is on one of the tablets instead the **a** in *bga*, the **ii**, thus *bgji*, Slov. *bogji*, later *božji*, after the **g** had changed into a **ž**. However, on another tablet there is an **e**, *bge*, which could be a genitive as OCS *ime, imene*—name, and Slov. *dan, dne*—day. Interestingly in OCS the **o** is also often left out: *Bga, bže*, instead of *Boga, Bože* (Leskin).

One could also interpret it as the adjective, **bogje**, modifying **limini**, being read this way since the following line of the square could also be understood as an **i**. In this way the grammar tablets yield interest and variation. The teacher had the opportunity with **limini bogje** *lamine božje* to speak about the noun, adjective, plural, and their declensions. The fact that we encounter this **boga** in other places supports the correctness of my assumption.

The grammar tablets have still another part, the component at the top above the decorative border of **o's**. The first two parts, as we have seen, are devoted to phonetics, and the third part is concerned with phraseology and also syntax. This part further confirms what has already been found on the lower part of the tablet, namely, that there is a **similarity between the Slovene and the Venetic languages.**

Everything indicates that the bronze tablets from the school for writers in Ateste are, moreover, moulds which were pressed into clay or wax. The rather deep and thick incisions indicate that this was probably the case. There is an important detail we must mention in connection with this: in LLV the authors explain (p. 112) that the tablet Es 26 had been found in a layer of earth from which it could not be extricated without totally destroying it. Two symbols, ·|· and |X|, are only recognizable because of their imprints in the ground—probably clay. This proves that the tablets could have been used as plates or blocks for duplication and distribution. Even the so-called 'chiodi'—styles from the same school of writers probably served not only as writing tools, but also as moulds, since their bronze surfaces were incised with inscriptions.

The language and grammar disclosed by the tablets of Ateste are corroborated by all inscriptions. There are of course small dissimilarities among them, allowing for place and time differences.

Let us look at some examples. The imperative of **jekat**, as we were able to see, is **jekaj** There are many instances of this imperative form:

koljaj—split! Slov. *kolji* from *klati* (to split in two or more parts).

vantaj—swear (to)! Slov. *zagovori, ventaj!* In Bohinj this word is still used today in connection with evil spirits (see Tine Logar, *The Slovene dialects*). The word **vantaj** appears very frequently in Venetic inscriptions.

kantaj—bury! be buried! OCS *katati* from *konta* (Mikl.), Slov. *pokopati;* Bulgarian *ktam;* Ukrainian *kutaty*—to store, to deposit; Russ. *кутать;* Slov. *konta*—rocky hollow. It is fairly certain this word is of Venetic derivation.

st(e)naj—burn! Slov. *stenj*—wick; Slov. *tinjati*—to extinguish (Plet.).

jaj—travel! Latv. *jaju, jati*—to travel; Slov. *jahati*—*to ride, jaati* is found also in a Serbo-Cr. dialect.

These are only some imperatives of the form **jekat.** Of course, as a Proto-Slavic language the Venetic had developed other forms of the imperative. For example:

genej—hunt! banish! Slov. *ženi!* from *gnati*—to drive.

se boj—fear! Slov. is the same *se boj!*

torjoj—make your way! Slov. *torati*—*to carry, to drag,* (Plet.), Russ. *торить.*

omnoj—mention! remember! Slov. *omeni!*—mention! *pomni!* think about it!, OCS *мьпо*—I think.

nos—carry! Slov. *nosi!*

uherijoj—run! storm! Slov. *vihari!* arch. *viheri!* from *vihreti* (Plet.).

tišej—be quiet! Slov. *utišaj!* from *utišati*—to pacify.

nettijoj—burn! set on fire! Slov. *neti!* from *netiti,*— to ignite.

konjoj—finish! Slov. *končaj! *konaj!* from *konati*—to end (Plet.).

osti—remain! Slov. *ostani! obstoj!*

uvantijoj—swear (to)! Slov. *zagovori! zaklinjaj!* dial. *ventaj!*

We also find parallels for the noun **jekad:**

višad—height, high ground; Slov. *visota, višava;* Slov. arch. *viša;*

zijad—chasm; Slov. *prepad, zijat.*

Words in the aorist tense are very numerous:

kanta—had been buried; **nerka,**—had been buried; **r(e)ka**—said, hed said; Slov. *rekel, izrekel,* Rezija Valley *rkat;* **b(e)**—he was; Slov. *bil je;* **vierva**—had pulled out; Slov. *izruval je.* Prefix **vi** also Slov. Zilja Valley; **stiha**—he became silent; Slov. *utihnil je;* **konja**—he finished; Slov. *končal je.*

Participles:

viougonti—cremated; Slov. *ugonobljen, ugonobiti*—to annihilate, Rezija Valley Slov. dial. *ohnjewt, onjewt;* Latv. *ugunot*—to illuminate; **zgen**—burned; Slov. *žgan;* **virem**—place inside; Russ. *virat*—put in; comp. Slov. *zavirati;* **viremaj**—placed in the urn; **ur(e)klejoj**—sworn, decried; Slov. *urečeni, urekli* (dat. sing. fem.), Old Russ. *rkli, urькnuть.*

And here are some pronouns:

jego—him, acc., Slov. *njega;* **mego**—mine, Slov. *mojega, mego* arch. (as in the *Brižinski Spomeniki/* Freising Manuscripts; **ma**—my, Slov. *moje;* **jim**—to them, Slov. *jim;* **nijoj**—her, Slov. *njej,* Serbo-Cr. *njoj;* **ti**—you, Slov. *ti;* **s toju**—with her, Slov. *s to,* OCS *s tojo;* **taj**—this one, Slov. *ta;* **taj**—there, Slov. dial. *taj* lit. *tja;* **mu**—to him, Slov. *-mu.*

Long infinitives:

vesti—to behave, Slov. *vesti, vedem;* **molti**—to pray, Slov. *moliti;* **iti**—to go, Slov. *iti.*

This is probably enough. The reader has a fair idea now. I will in a detailed book closely examine each of the above mentioned words with the aid of test analysis from all possible perspectives, etymologically, morphologically, semantically and phonetically. Concerning the present study I would like to make the following remarks:

The discovery, if I may use this word, of the Slavic grammar on the tablets from Ateste is the result of my own research.

I am amazed that till now, as far as I know, no other linguist has made this discovery—a discovery that so plainly presents itself.

I believe there are two reasons for this. First, the Slavic linguists have ceded the Venetic language to western researchers, from among whom there is probably not one who has full command and intimate knowledge of the Old Slavic or the modern Slavic languages, and also of the surviving Slovene dialects which play an extremely important role in this undertaking. The second, and equally important reason is that only with modern technology has precise photographic reproduction become possible. The reproductions are now often much clearer than the originals in the museums, allowing the researcher to examine them, and discover the fine points of the Venetic language.

The Venetic Alphabet

One often hears that the Venetic letters are identical with the runic characters. This can in no way be correct. The first Venetic inscriptions appeared at about the same time as the Etruscan, ca. 500 B.C., if not earlier. The runic alphabet was used by the Germanic people almost a thousand years later; actually the oldest known runic inscriptions belong to the second half of the 2nd century A.D. It is true that the Germanic runes, which were also used by the Vikings and Goths, were influenced by the Etruscan and Venetic characters. This can easily be seen when they are compared.

The Adriatic Veneti did not have such a highly developed culture as their neighbours and contemporaries, the Etruscans; yet in comparison with their neighbours to the north they were on a higher level. For this reason it is not surprising that their culture spread towards the north, and also towards the east and west wherever their trade relations extended.

Where did the Veneti get their alphabet? In all probability from the Etruscans. But it also could be the other way around. In both alphabets the majority of the letters are the same and have the same meaning.

Let us now take a look at the Venetic alphabet. The most common letters are found in almost every inscription, regardless where it may have originated. The inscriptions or letters are generally read from the right to the left.

This alphabet has been assembled from the so-called "tavolette alfabetiche" (alphabetic tablets) and other inscriptions.

The symbol ⟩⟨ in the inscriptions is often difficult to distinguish whether it represents a **k** or an **ic.** If the line shows a larger space⟩|, the assumption of Venetologists that it is not to be read as a **k** but as an **ic** is justified, though perhaps both are correct when used in a word game that was very much enjoyed by the ancient Veneti.

The **t** before the silent vowels (e.g. in Tergitio—merchant) was read by the Veneti as **t', c** or **ć,** though they had their own letter for this, the ⟩ , which is like the Latin **c** facing left. The ancient Veneti, like the Etruscans, wrote from right to left, though often also from left to right.

As can be seen from the list, the letters are angular. This is simply because they are transmitted to us imprinted in bronze, stone or clay. They were probably also carved in wood; however, since wood is not so durable, there are no surviv-

Common Ateste Letters		Uncommon Letters	
A — ⊃		T — ◇	
E — ∃		T,D — ⟩	
I,J — |		H — ₿	
O — ◇		B,V — φ	
U — V		Č — »	
V — ⊣			
D — ⫢			
T,T' — X			
K — ⋊			
L — ⌐			
M — ᴧ			
N — ⋎			
P — ⌐			
Š,Ś — M			
R — ◁			
S,Z,Ž — ⟨			
B,V — ◇			
G,H — Y			
C — ⟩			

ing specimens. The angular writing was suitable for the methods used by the stonecutters and woodcarvers and others, and was for this reason preferred by the writers. We are only aware of capital (majuscule) letters in the Venetic (as well as the Etruscan) writings. We know nothing about lower case (miniscule) letters. The question arises: Did the Veneti know and use the lower case letters? They probably did, perhaps only on wax plates or other material with a much shorter life. It is also possible that the Veneti used parchment and papyrus, which perished in the course of centuries. We must consider yet another circumstance which even more adversely affected the preservation of ancient literature. It is common knowledge that the Romans destroyed every trace of the Etruscan culture and literature. The Veneti were probably treated in the same way. Only those things survived which were underground with the dead, and even those were not always secure.

There are still several comments I wish to make concerning the alphabet as presented above. I have studied it for many years and checked time and again to see if the meaning of the individual letters was correct. In the beginning, when I had not yet discovered the Slavic morphology on the "alphabetic tablets", I was of the opinion that ◁ should be read as **d.** Later, I became convinced that it was an **r,** except in some cases when Venetic began to be mixed with Latin writing. In the same way, I did not accept the symbol ⋇ as representing a **d** since it was borrowed from the Etruscan alphabet where it signified a **z.** Again, as a result of very strong arguments which are particularly evident in the Latin transcription of the word ⋇ ◇ Ψ ⌐ ⟩ ✕ ◇ **donasto,** I had to give way. Why had the Veneti adopted this symbol for the letter **d**? Probably because in Venetic there is in addition to the sound **d** also the sound **dz** which were both represented by the same symbol.

I have just cited two examples where, after thorough investigation of the inscriptions, I departed from my earlier opinion and had to concede that the Ventologists were right; however, there are elements in the interpretation of the individual letters that would today separate me from Venetologists. An example is the **e,** that was both **e** and **je,** similar to the case today in the Russian language. A classic example would be **ego**—*jego/*yego—him.

There is every reason to believe that the Veneti were rather uncertain about the pronunciation of several of the letters, as is the case today with the Slovenes in the coastal area of the Adriatic (Primorska). They easily confuse **v** with **b** (betatism); e.g. **vog** instead of **bog.** In a similar way they confuse **s** with **š,** from which an intermediate **ś** usually developed, as in Etruscan; that is why I too transcribe it as **ś.** Also the plosive **g** changed into a fricative γ (gamma) or **h,** as it occurs today in the western Slovene dialects. These are areas which were the closest to the Venetic core region or formed a part thereof. But the Venetic also had an **h** similar to the **h** in Slovene; e.g. in *hleb and hlev.* There was only one symbol Ψ for both, in some cases also ꝑ. Venetologists read the symbol ·|· as **h,** without a good reason, since the ·|· is not at all a letter, rather simply an I (i) with dots. We will discuss this in detail when we deal with the topic of punctation.

Even the plosive **k** was often confused with **h,** a habit which we encounter

Es 119 (LLV)
Museo Nazionale Atestino
First half of the inscription on the loom weight (see A Song at the Loom).

today in the Slovene language, when in certain cases an **h** is written and pronounced instead of **k;** e.g. *h komu*—to whom.

It is certain that the Veneti also had a **z** as we have in Slovene and in other Slavic languages. Moreover, it is almost certain that this sound, as well as the **s,** was expressed with the letter ⟨ , which is still the case in a number of alphabets. Even our "Bohoričica" alphabet (middle of 16th century), used the same letter for both **s** and **z.**

And **ž**? Considering the fact that the Veneti, similar to **s** and **š,** had often confused **z** and **ž,** one can assume that the letter for **s** and **z** was also used for **ž.** However, it is not impossible that the **ž** was not yet fully developed and constituted an intermediate **z,** similar to the **ś** between **s** and **š.**

Venetologists call the symbol |X| a dead letter. In reality, they are three already familiar symbols, together they are **iti** |X| , being very beautifully documented on the loom weight Es 119.

Finally, I must comment about the symbol |, with the dots ·|·, which seem to be very important to Venetologists. According to one theory, which is considered to be the only correct one, this symbol stands for two sounds, **j** and also **h**. However, when it appears after **v** it becomes digamma **vh**, which is a symbol for **f.** This would seem alright, if it were not for the Venetic texts and in particular the Ateste grammar tablets with their consonant pairs **kr kn kl, mr mn ml, pr pn pl, sr sn sl, tr tn tl,** etc. Only with the consonant **v** is there an exception, where between the **v** and the following consonant a **j** is inserted, so that instead of **vr vn vl,** we have **vjr vjn vjl.**

What does this mean? Nothing other than that the consonant pairs **vr vn vl** were not yet present in Venetic. This corresponds precisely to the development of the words of the type **vreti** (from *ver-*), **vnuk** (from *vunuku*), **vleči** (from *velk-*). The older form was, in my opinion, simply **ver ven vel.** However, since the **e** was pronounced as **je** (**ye** in yes), **ver ven vel** has to be read as **vjer vjen vjel,** and after the reduction of the **e** into **ǝ**: **vjr vjn vjl.** The difference between the spelling and pronunciation of **ver** in Slovene (*vera, vira*), is the same phenomenon as found in the Venetic language.

Consequently, **vh** is by no means an **f,** but rather a consonant pair similar to those presented above, only of a special kind. Perhaps at a more recent time, when the Venetic language was already under Latin influence, the **vh** had in fact become **f.**

Had the Veneti after their gradual Latinization really used the sound **f?** It is difficult to say. In my opinion this was not the case.

And why not? For the simple reason that as they adopted the Latin script, they also took along with it the letter **F.** This symbol was already Venetic; it did not mean **f,** but rather **v.** Since the Veneti did not know the **f** sound, they also did not need a letter to represent it. In Latin, on the other hand, there is no difference between the capital U and **V.** The letter **V** is used for both. As we can see from their phonetics the Veneti have retained the difference in the letters by using the capital **F** for **v** and the capital **V** for **u.** Thus, the assumption that the Veneti would have spoken **f ougon taj** instead of **v ougon taj** is unfounded.

This statement is of great importance. Venetologists want to show precisely by means of the letter **f** that the Venetic language is not related to the Balto-Slavic, since Slavic did not have a fricative **f** or used it only as modern Slovene does, in imported foreign words. Hans Krahe, a one-time proponent of the existence of a connection between the Adriatic Veneti and the Balto-Slavs, eventually distanced himself from this view, and used the unprovable Venetic **f** in order to show the opposite: that Venetic as well as Illyrian belong to another language group, namely, the Italo-Celtic where the **f** is found.

Those who wish to relate the Venetic with the Italo-Celtic language group have found another symbol in the Venetic alphabet, namely the **kv,** which they

192

take to be the Latin **q**. In view of the fact that **kv** is included in the consonant pairs, it is to be considered in this case as a consonant pair; i.e., the same **kv** as occurs in the Slavic languages. Analysis of the texts where the **kv** is found confirms this beyond question. In the Ateste tablets it is (along with **vj**) especially noted in order to show that it is to be considered a consonant group and not a sound that is equal with the Latin **q**. The Latin elements (e.g., syntagma, *libens merito*) which were already present on the Ateste tablets prove that this special emphasis was necessary, thus showing that the relationship between the two languages was already well developed.

One final point. When I explained earlier the letter Ɏ (g), I said that the plosive **g** was unknown in Venetic language; hence, there was no need for letter **g.** Consequently, the Ɏ was the symbol for γ (gamma) and **h,** depending on the word it was used in. During the Roman times the Veneti used the Latin **x** for the **h** (the Czech and Slovak **ch**). Since the sound **xi** was not known to them, they used this letter for the consonants for which they did not have their own symbols.

It is clear therefore, that I do not flatly reject the official interpretation of Venetic letters; rather I am amending it in the areas where I consider it necessary, based on the Venetic, as it is reflected in the Slavic languages. Finally, the Slavic languages had developed long before the first millennium A.D. in the broad regions of central and eastern Europe, and according to the most recent archaeological research by Prof. Dr. Radivoje Pešić, probably also in the lower Danube area. History itself tells us that the Veneti came as far as the Balkans and beyond.

The "Mystery" of Punctation

The Venetic inscriptions exhibit a special characteristic that is rarely found in the Etruscan. They contain a number of dots which have aroused the attention of linguists ever since they have been dealing with these inscriptions. In their attempt to find out just what these dots might signify, they have finally made the "discovery".

The Viennese Venetologist, E. Vetter, has proposed a rule according to which the beginning vowels of syllables and words are to be designated by dots (also the **i** and **u** with vowel meaning), and the consonants at the ends of words (and the **i** and **u** by falling diphthongs). Moreover, he discovered that many consonant

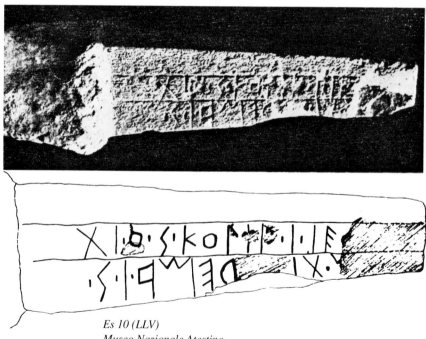

Es 10 (LLV)
Museo Nazionale Atestino
Example of punctation, particularly of letters S and I.

Ag 1 (LLV)
Museo di Belluno
In this inscription only one O has a dot, suggesting they were included by engravers at their own discretion.

groups, where the first symbol is not dotted, are to be considered as part of the next syllable—a rather complicated system; that is, if it were at all valid. But it was fortunate for the ancient Venetic writers and readers that it never was in use.

Then why are there so many of these peculiar dots? They were simply used to fill the empty space between the letters and also within the letters themselves. The scribes wanted to make the less conspicuous letters, such as I, S, L, T, N ·|· ⦚· ⅃· ·Χ· Ⲙ· easier to distinguish from other letters.

The following two inscriptions show very convincingly that this is indeed the case:

B ʘ V. Ð I L L V S and B O V D I L I V —

Both words are identical, one being without dots, the other having a total of three; i.e., in the middle of O and D and between the V and D. It is true that Holder includes these two words in his book *Altkeltischer Sprachschatz* among the Celtic words, for which, however, he has no grounds since they could just as easily be Venetic in Latinized form. In any case, as can be seen from our example, the dots do not have any particular significance. The ancient stonecutters, woodcarvers, and scribes used them in order to fill in the empty spaces. The same was done by the Etruscans, only not as often. Horror vacui, it would seem. There were also those writers who were not afraid of plain surface; one of these was the writer who wrote the word Boudilius without dots. The use of dots and eyelets was characteristic of the Lusatian and Urnfield cultures. They are also found on the relics of the Adriatic Veneti.

Punctation was used in many cases to better differentiate two letters from one another, or simply as a form of decoration. There are dots in O and D; there is also one beside the V. There are many such examples in Venetic; e.g. **Ag 1.** The inconspicuous letters such as **I** and **S** are more often punctated then other bulkier letters. Other letters have dots partly to fill the space and partly to divide the syllables; for example, with **a** and **o** which are prepositions in Venetic (Old Slavic **a, o**). Letters were also punctated if there was need to emphasize that they constituted separate syllables, for example **u.r.kle.i**. According to Vetter's rule, the **r** belongs to the first syllable. We would then have to read it as *ur-klej*. But analysis of the inscriptions shows that this is not so; we are rather dealing with a word which is still used today in the Slavic languages, namely, the participle (also adjective) **urekli,** which comes from the verb *ureči*. In the Slovene dialect which is called "venetic" (in northeastern Friuli, Italy), we come even closer to the ancient Venetic. There we find words like *rkao, rkovci;* in Slovakian *urknouti*; in Old Russ. *rkli, urьknutь*—to swear. See Miklošič, *Etymologisches Wörterbuch der Slavischen Sprachen/* Etymological Dictionary of Slavic Languages.

Vetter's rule, as you can see, cannot at all hold up under close examination. It is true that these inscriptions are written without spacing (in continuo) and do not tell the expert where one word begins or ends (except in some cases where the separation is clear), but this constitutes a problem only for those who are not equipped with the necessary knowledge of languages. *Those who do not have a command of Slavic languages, and especially the Slovene dialects, do not have the necessary knowledge.*

The reason why the Veneti had written in continuo, without spacing or separation of the words, may be found in their partiality for anagrams and palindromes. Such linguistic pieces of art could be much more easily formed if there were no spacing between words.

196

Who Were the Veneti?

Many historians, archaeologists and linguists have already dealt with this question. As expected, their opinions vary a great deal; more so than when any other group of people is being considered. It is certain that the Veneti lived during the first millennium B.C. and that even today, place-names in the most diverse regions of Europe still call them to mind. Historians from Herodotus, Polibius, and Strabo to Ptolemy, Livy, Pomponius Mela, Tacitus and Jordanes mention them, as do Greek and Roman writers, among them Homer, Euripides and Sophocles.

From them we learn that the Veneti had lived by the Baltic and the Black Seas, the Atlantic and the Adriatic. They resided also in the Balkans and by Lake Constance (Bodensee), which was during the Roman times called Lacus Venetus (the Venetic lake). Yet, all this information is incidental since these authors knew very little about other peoples; to them they were all barbarians, regardless whether they were Celts, Germanic people, Veneti or Scythians.

We learn most about the Veneti in Caesar's book, where he gives an account of the conquest of Gaul (De bello Gallico), yet this is from a later period when the Veneti in Italy were probably already Romanized and fought alongside the Romans. The Veneti in Gaul, on the coast of present-day Brittany, offered such resistance that Caesar was filled with considerable respect for them, although he was also infuriated by their stubborn independence. There was nothing else Caesar could do but thoroughly prepare himself for the battle. "The Veneti are by far the strongest tribe on this coast," wrote Caesar. "They possess the most powerful fleet with which they sail as far as Britain. Their knowledge and experience of navigation is far superior to that of other tribes. Since the coast there is exposed to the open sea there are few harbours, and they are controlled by Veneti, who can force almost everyone who sails in these waters to pay the toll."

Due to these factors Caesar was in serious trouble. "They had a powerful fleet, while we had no ships at our disposal; moreover, we were not well informed about the depths, harbours and islands of this coast where we had to fight. Sailing on the open ocean was something totally different than sailing on a protected sea, like the Mediterranean." It is interesting that other reports which we have about the Veneti represent them as exceptional seamen.

The earliest writer to mention their name was Homer, some 800 years before

Caesar. After Troy had fallen, the Enetoi, i.e. Veneti, who fought on the side of Troy, as Livy writes, were to have driven out the Etruscans and the Euganeis in Liburnia after a long sea voyage along the Illyrian coast and then settled as far as beyond Timava River. Many authors, among them the Slovene historian Linhart, are of the opinion that the Adriatic Veneti came later. It is possible that Livy, who was himself of Venetic descent from Padova, wanted to bestow on his ancestors some of the Trojan glamour, but there is of course no proof that this is only a legend, and we should not forget that legends at times contain important historical truth.

Livy reports that the homeland of the Veneti was Paphlagonia, on the south coast of the Black Sea. They also lived on the Baltic Sea in the north of Europe where, according to ancient writers, the prosperous Vineta, Urbs Venetorum (city of the Veneti), was located. It was a lively commerce center. This northern Venice was a thousand years older than the one on the Adriatic, similar to the Etruscan Spina at the mouth of the Po River. When we consider all these things, we wonder whether the Veneti on the Black Sea still had links with the Baltic from where they originally came. They were very skillful seamen, used to the rough waters of the Baltic Sea, and were probably also familiar with the rivers that flow into it; this means that if they sailed on the Oder, Vistula and Elbe, they were probably also attracted by rivers that flowed south. The source of the Dnieper was not far from the upper courses of some north flowing rivers. Tacitus and Ptolemy tell us about the Dnieper and the Veneti that lived there. Caesar had, as we know, a very high opinion of the boats and the sailing skills of the Veneti. Keeping this in mind we recognize that it would not be impossible to travel from the Baltic to the Black Sea. The later Vikings, also northern mariners, had probably built their ships on Venetic models and eventually settled on the Dnieper River, especially in Kiev. They had a lively commerce with Byzantium and served under its emperors. Their reputation as the best and most feared guards was well known. They came out of the Baltic area, traveling on the Russian rivers.

If the Vikings had chosen this route, why could the Veneti not have done the same much earlier? The reports about the Veneti around the Baltic, the Dnieper River, the Balkans and the Black Sea strongly support this assumption.

It is also probable that the Veneti sailed along the Baltic coast, around Denmark, and made their way through the North Sea and the English Channel, as was earlier maintained by the unjustly misunderstood and neglected Venetologist Davorin Trstenjak. It is not impossible that a part of the Veneti had arrived by this route at the coast of Brittany and settled there similarly as Antenor's Veneti had settled on the northern coast of the Adriatic after the fall of Troy.

We find them also in Central Europe. The prevailing view is that the Veneti were the bearers of the Lusatian Urnfield culture from about the end of the 2nd millennium B.C., and that this culture was connected with the similar culture of the Danube area. How did the Veneti get there? Or did they live there already from time immemorial? Or did they come this far in their ships? It is interesting that we find them there again on the water, though very far from the sea. They also lived on Lake Constance (Lacus Venetus). It was on this lake, separated from Italy by the Alps that, according to Schlötzer, there was the link between the Baltic and the Adriatic Veneti.

As one of the more interesting proofs supporting the connection of the northern and southern Veneti, I would like to mention Retra, the legendary shrine of several West Slavic tribes, about which a whole series of mediaeval writers report (Thitmar of Merseburg 1008–1018, Adam of Bremen, the chronicler Helmond and others). They tell us that the shrine was in the region of Lusatia, in the middle of a lake. Considering that the homeland of the Urnfield culture during the 2nd millennium B.C. was centered in that area, and that the Veneti lived there, it is certain that the Reitia of Ateste and Retra of central Europe are identical. The transformation of Retra into Reitia, or Reitia into Retra, is entirely possible. Perhaps archaeological findings from the northern shrine, its sacred vestibules and sacred groves with surrounding dikes, could complete our conception of the shrine at Ateste.

If this assumption is justified or even correct, then the cult of Retra must have lasted a long time, approximately from the middle of the first millennium B.C. to at least the year 955 when Emperor Otto I burned Retra to the ground. East German archaeologists who are conscientiously researching and working on the remnants of the ancient Slavic culture in present-day German territory have come to the conclusion that the Slavs (though much primitive animism can be found in their religion) had certainly come close to having a monotheism, representing an advanced form in the development of religion. (See also the contribution by Anton Janko in "Delo" May 31, 1983). Judging from the inscriptions which are readable, there was the same situation with the religion of the Adriatic Veneti—even more so. If we compare the various urn inscriptions, we see that the majority expressed the wish that the soul of the deceased would as soon as possible enter **van** or **rej** Slov. *raj*—heaven—without previously having to struggle with the spirits in the life beyond. One of them was called **Bukka**. It is interesting that in the ancient Icelandic language, the language of the Vikings, **Bokka** means apparition. And this word even has two "k's," just as the Venetic **Bukka.** The northern Russians, who also had contact with the Veneti, use this word as well. To them **Bukka** means an apparition—frightening to children and also to older people.

Everything points to the fact that the original homeland of the Veneti was in the area between the Baltic Sea and the Vistula, the Danube and the central Dnieper, where they are mentioned by Tacitus and Ptolemy as being a great nation.

No scholar who has studied early European history would in essence oppose this. The dispute begins only when the ethnicity of the Veneti is questioned.

It is common knowledge that the documentary sources of late antiquity first called the Slavs Veneti, Venedi, Winidi, etc. These names have survived till now. The Slovenes and the Lusatians are still called Windische and Wendische by Germans. The idea that the ancient Veneti were Slavs has not pleased the German historians. If Slavic ethnicity of Veneti could be proven, it would mean that Slavs were already in central and even western Europe as a civilized and developed people well before the Germans. *That is the reason why so much effort went into the theory that Germans were the original inhabitants of central Europe.* The Slavs were presented as the late-comers who first made their way to the west during the tribal migrations. These assumptions were designed to clear the way for the political powers to carry out Germanization of the West Slavs.

The Czech, and above all the Polish linguists, archaeologists and historians, from Šafařik to Niederle and Lehr-Spławiński, have rejected this interpretation of events and ethnic origin of the indigenous people of central Europe.

The Slavic origin of the Veneti was unacceptable to German historians, even though some of their own researchers (e.g., Kretschmer) considered the Veneti as bearers of the Lusatian (Lausitz) culture; he assigned to them the Alpine regions as well as northeastern Italy. At the same time Jokl had demonstrated the etymological connection between the dialects of northern Italy and Rhaetia and the Baltic and Slavic languages. There were also other German scientists who did not go along with the Pan-Germanic ideas; rather, they stated that the Slavs have from time immemorial lived in the territory between the Baltic and Adriatic Seas.

Helping the German nationalists out of this dilemma was the Berlin professor, Gustav Kossinna, who maintained that the Lusatian culture and consequently the area of eastern Germany had never been Slavic. According to him, the Veneti were not Slavs; nevertheless, when the Slavs came from the east and settled in the region of the Veneti, they also took over their name. Of course Slavs did not have to take over this name; it was given to them from time immemorial by the Germans. We can be sure that the Germans would not simply have adopted the alleged newcomers from the east and presented them magnanimously with the name of the conquered indigenous population.

Kossinna's hypothesis (for which he supplied no proof) was eagerly accepted by German historians, and the same is true of Slovene historians who studied in Vienna. They were so impressed and fascinated by Kossinna's intellectual "superiority" that they completely forgot to use some of their own intellects, or to break new ground regarding their own origin.

The discussion whether the Baltic Veneti and those living in east central Europe were Slavs is not yet over. Thanks to the untiring work of Polish and Czech historians, archaeologists and linguists, the discussion has developed in their favour, although the nationalist German ethnologists still want to place the homeland of their Slavic neighbours far to the east, among the Scythians. In this they are being supported by a segment of Russian scientists, who do not like to see the cradle of Slavs in central and east central Europe as presented by Polish historians.

Nevertheless, the position that the Lusatian culture was Venetic and that the Veneti in central Europe were Slavs is now relatively well established in the scientific world.

Not even all German authors disagree with this view at present. For example, Stöhr (*Lexikon der Völker und Kulturen* 1972) says that the Veneti mentioned by Ptolemy, Tacitus and Pliny were certainly descended from Slavs, which, however, has not been proved for the Adriatic Veneti.

It is true that there is still no conclusive proof regarding the Slavic origin of the Adriatic Veneti. At the same time we must bear in mind that the Veneti not only lived in what is now Slovene territory, but also in areas that were once Slovene and have long since been Romanized or Germanized. The territory of the Adriatic Veneti extended to Istria and Slovenia, even as far as Carinthia. Our first written words (inscriptions) were found in this area.

They can all be explained and understood with the help of the language which we have discovered on the grammar tablets from Ateste.

The Slovene historians view the inscriptions found in Slovenia as the heritage left by the Celts or Illyrians, but F. Duhn stated that these inscriptions can in no way be Celtic, since with unimportant exceptions, the alphabet is identical to the Venetic *Italische Gräberkunde* II, Heidelberg 1939. However, the Venetic alphabet is, as is commonly known, only the northern variation of the Etruscan. With respect to this, T. Mommsen included the Venetic inscriptions, found up till the middle of the last century, in his comprehensive study *Die nordetruskischen Alphabete auf Inschriften* 1853. C. Pauli also published them in his *Altitalischen Forschungen I* under the general title "north-Etruscan"; nevertheless, he classified and attributed them to the Veneti who are well known to various documentary sources. Furthermore, he discovered the consonant **f** in the inscriptions, for which the Italian Venetologists are very thankful. This discovery is without basis, as we have already stated in the chapter on the Venetic alphabet.

Julius Pokorny *Keltologie,* 1953, insisted on a connection between the Baltic and the Adriatic Veneti, maintaining that their language was closely related to the Balto-Slavic.

Pokorny did not stand alone in his convictions. Recently two well-known linguists have affirmed the same view. Lehr-Spławiński *O pohodzeniu i praojcyznie Slowian,* 1946, and in *Etnogenezy Slowian,* 1964, observed that the river names between the Oder and Bug exhibit parallels to those of the lower alpine-Adriatic region. And V. Georgiev *Issledovanji,* 1985, states that the tribes which lived between the Danube and the Adriatic had similarities with the Veneti living between the Oder and Vistula. Among the earlier linguists, A. F. Gilferding *Drevnejši period istoriji Slovian,* 1868, attempted to show that the Veneti and Norici were Slavs, and Contzen *Wanderung der Kelten,* 1861, tried to do the same for the Adriatic Veneti, wanting to show that they also remained Slavic after the Celtic invasion. A. L. Schlötzer, whom I have already mentioned, confidently explains in his *Allgemeine Welthistorie,* 1771, that Slavic tribes had from time immemorial settled the eastern half of Germany from the mouth of the Elbe River to the Adriatic Sea. One could quote many more authors but I would just like to mention Pavel Šafařik (a contemporary of the Slovene poet Prešeren), who insisted in his *Slovanske starožitnosti* 1837 that the whole territory of the Greco-Roman state as far as the Vistula and Danube was settled with Slavic tribes. The Vinds, the Corotans and Veneti were Slovenes.

Šafařik may have gone too far; nevertheless, his theory about the indigenous nature of the Slavs, which was later sharply criticized, is today confirmed by many. The grammar tablets from Ateste with their ancient Slavic morphology are one such confirmation.

The ritual verses from the upper part of the Ateste tablets were also found on some gravestone pedestals. A good example is **Es 64.**

MEGO DONASTO KANTE SVOTEJI
Jaz donašam dar, pokopavši svojce

O SA KUTS ŠAJNATEJ REJTIJAI
v ta kotec, šajnati Rejtiji.

English: I bring a gift, after burial of relatives
in this corner (of burial ground), to the shining Rejtija.

The Venetic text is so similar to Slovene, it needs very little explanation. We will examine only the following words:

kante—buried; Slov. *pokopavši;* OCS *(sъ)katati*—to bury. From *konta* (Mikl.), in many inscriptions **kanta;** here it is in the form of a participle.

202

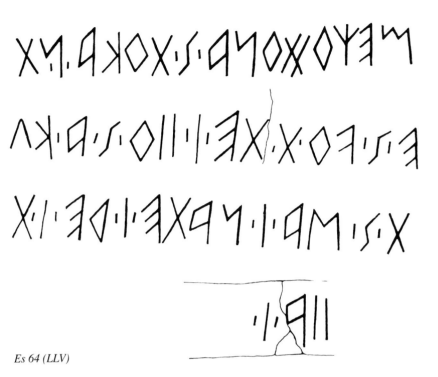

Es 64 (LLV)

svoteji—relatives; Slov. *svojta, svojec*—relatives, relative.

o sa kuts—in this corner (of the burial ground); OCS *kotьcь*—cell; Slov. *kotc*—corner, small room, cubicle.

Contemporary Venetologists such as Pellegrini and his student Prosdocimi (both from the University of Padova), the Indo-Europeanist Michel Lejeune (from the Sorbonne), and the German, Vetter—although they do not understand Venetic—have done a very good job with the representation of the Venetic inscriptions. Since the book *La lingua venetica* has been available, where the inscriptions are presented accurately and purposefully with reproductions of such high quality that every individual letter can be recognized, it is not necessary to visit museums to study Venetic inscriptions. (Of course there are some obscurities that necessitate a trip to the museum).

I have already said that the Italian linguists are very happy for each word or peculiarity that may suggest the relation of the Venetic language to Latin and which substantiates the Italic origin of the people who lived during the first mil-

203

lennium B.C. in northern Italy. Of course the Italian linguists cannot avoid the enormous evidence which shows that the Adriatic Veneti came from the north; that is, from the area of the Lusatian Urnfield culture around the year 1000 B.C., if not earlier. Their route led them across the Danube, Lower Austria, the eastern Alpine valleys, along the border of the Pannonian plain, then over present-day Slovenia, and on to northern Italy. The archaeological signposts are the urn graves of Southern Bavaria, Lower Austria, Western Hungary, Styria; in Slovenia they were found at Hajdina near Ptuj, Dobrava, Ljubljana, Križna gora near Lož, Sv. Mark near Gorica, Most na Soči (Sv. Lucija).

However, we must not exclude Livy's report entirely; there may be some truth to it. A part of the Veneti may have come to the northern Adriatic coast from the Black Sea, where they had lived in close contact with the people and culture of the Middle East. This may explain the oriental touch of the ornamentation on the situlas, but not very convincingly when we remember that their neighbours the Etruscans had strong artistic influences from Asia Minor.

Linhart was very critical in his *History*, but he finds this tradition believable. Yet, if the Veneti also arrived in Northern Italy and the eastern Alps from the Black Sea area, they would have encountered the Veneti who had come directly from the Baltic area. The two groups had the same origin and spoke a similar or even the same language. The fundamentals of this language are still found today in a form probably closest to the original, in the modern Slovene language and its numerous dialects.

Perhaps it was for another reason that our linguists were satisfied with Kossinna's hypothesis which maintained that the Slavs had received the name Veneti from the earlier inhabitants of the region whose territory they had occupied. The racist historians in Carinthia (Austria) tell us that the Wends (Windische) were not Slovenes, that their language was not Slovene, and that they were descendants of a people with whom they had no ethnic affiliation. The same was said by several Italian historians about the Slovenes in the westernmost part of our ethnic territory. As long as this was affirmed only by a few intolerant politicians, it could be overlooked. However, the matter got more serious when in the last century the well-known expert in the Rezija Valley dialect, Bauduin de Courtenay, came to the conclusion that because of its peculiarities this language was a relic of a dead language, a yet unknown Proto-Slavic language.

It is very clear to every Slovene who knows our dialects, that in spite of their peculiarities the Carinthian and Rezijan (Rezija Valley is now on the Italian side of the border) were just as Slovene as the dialect of Idrija or the Pannonic region. We did not have any dialectological studies or thorough and comprehensive analysis that would show and prove this, until Ramovš. After the tremendous work

204

accomplished by him and his students (above all Tine Logar), the inherent relatedness of the Slovene dialects from the easternmost Raba River region in Hungary to the Rezija Valley in Italy in the west is thoroughly clear now. The Veneti in northern Italy were Romanized, while the Veneti in the eastern Alps survived the fall of the Roman Empire. The modern Slovenes are their descendants. The only difference is that the Venetic influences, including the language, survived best among Slovenes in the west rather than those in the east. With the later settling of new Slavic tribes from eastern Europe there was some mutual influence which gave the Slovenes an unusual ethnogenetic identity.

I already mentioned that the western Proto-Slavic language, i.e., Venetic, had developed in many respects along a different path from the Slavic language in the east.

Dr. France Bezlaj, who counselled me years ago to study Venetic instead of the Etruscan language (for which I am very thankful, although I did not give up the Etruscan), was involved in a passionate discussion with me regarding the possibility that there may have been more than one ancient Slavic language. I did not feel at the time that he was exactly enthusiastic about this hypothesis, through which one could come closer to the Venetic and also the Etruscan languages. With this in mind, I was pleasantly surprised when I read several years later in the journal *Jezik in slovstvo*/ Language and Literature (1976/77, No. 2) that, during the work on the Slovene etymological dictionary, he felt compelled under the weight of evidence to change his basic views instilled in him by his Slovene and Czech teachers. "[There is a need to change our views] not only concerning the Slovene ethnogenesis," he writes, "and the position that the Slovene has among the Slavic languages, but also regarding the ancient Slavs from whom the Slovene lexical and grammatical forms originate. Miklošič and Ramovš [two important Slovene linguists] must forgive me and a whole series of my research colleagues, for presuming that there were several Proto-Slavic languages which had influenced each other during the tribal migration." At the end of his essay in which he substantiates his thesis with ancient Slavic unproductive synonyms "...which are most frequent in the Slovene language, and fewer in the Kajkavian and the Chakavian," he writes, "the West Slavic stratum was predominant in the Alpine Slovene. At the same time we must consider the influence of the Slavic newcomers from the east in the 6th century. The oldest stratum of the language we can only sense. Perhaps somewhere in central Europe a Slavic tribe was roaming around, having split off from its tribal unit around the time of the birth of Christ and later joined up again with the Slavic migrations?"

The grammar on the tablets from Ateste confirms Bezlaj's thesis, and at the same time it refutes it. The ancient Slavic people about whom he speaks did not just roam around; they were domiciled, spread throughout central Europe from the Baltic to the Adriatic, and also on the Atlantic coast. Between the Alps and the Adriatic they created the important Este culture. Much of what is attributed to the Celts or Illyrians is actually Venetic.

If the Etruscans had kindled the light, as Werner Keller writes in his best seller with the same title *Denn sie entzündeten das Licht,* 1970, then the Veneti carried this light throughout Europe, not as conquerors—this was already far behind them—but rather as merchants who had transported southern merchandise to the north, which at that time could not compare itself with the south. They traded wares from Mediterranean countries that had very advanced cultures. The Ateste school of writers indicates one such cultural advancement. Judging from the texts and other items that survived, the Venetic culture was not equal to that of the Etruscans, though it was not far behind. That fewer Venetic relics survived can be the result of two causes: The Veneti did not put as many objects into the graves of their deceased, above all not as many valuable ones as the Etruscans had done, since they were not as rich and had not been influenced to the same extent by the Orient; and secondly, probably because in their area of the Alpine foreland wooden construction was prevalent. The wood consequently rotted while the stone construction in the central and southern parts of the Apennine peninsula endured. The ruins at least endured. There is perhaps another cause. The Romans, as history tells us, had systematically eradicated the memory of the civilization and culture of the people, whom they had conquered, in some cases after century-long fighting and brutal extermination. The Veneti, though to a lesser degree than the Etruscans, contributed more to the Roman civilization than the Greeks, but were just the same ruthlessly suppressed. What has survived is that which has been found in the graves.

Regarding the question of where the Veneti lived at the time of the Celtic invasions and the Roman occupation, there is no ready answer on the basis of historical data. One source of information is the family names that have been preserved. Let us look at these names:

Verbic (Holder, *Altkeltischer Sprachschatz*), Bucic (A. Müllner, *Emona*), Mocianc, Babek, Buran, Nemnik, Peucinia, Suttich, Suadula (Jabornik, Kärnten's Römische Alterthümer, 1870), Volovic, Sporilla, Samuda, Pametus, Obilia, Mogianc, Goruna, Mira, Micha, Medu, Matico, Maro, Devva, Dumia, Covio, Conzia, Cocina, Castic(us), Bucia, Buccio, Butura, Babecc, Borio, Derva (Geza Alföldy, *Noricum*, 1974).

Among the names from the Roman period we find: Jabornik, also Gordiano, as well as the Latin translation Augusto (dat.) which is derived from the Old Slavic *grъdъ*—mighty, proud; Russ. *gordyj*; Serbo-Cr. Grdan, Grdana (names).

The meaning of this word among Slovenes during the Roman period remained magnificent, majestic (augustus). However, in the course of time it came to mean *grd*—ugly. Strange are the ways of words, but in them, the soul of a people is revealed.

Most of these names in their Latin or Celtic form cannot hide their Slavic origin. As a result we can conclude that the Veneti did not disappear. Neither did the Venetic language. When we consider that this language had very distinct diphthongs, vowel reductions, transformation of the accented **o's** into **u's,** and so on, we can say with relative certainty that the Venetic population had survived. If the dialectologists think I am wrong then they should correct me. But I have the impression that the diphthongization and vowel reduction are in direct relation to the distance from the former Roman centres. They tend to be present in the mountainous areas and represent local conditions.

It would become too involved if one wanted to deal with this question in detail; we should perhaps leave it to future researchers. I am convinced that there will be enough of them since the Slovenes have again become interested in their past. They would like to know where their roots are, the ancient roots which we still unconsciously feel within us.

Everything indicates that the influence of the Adriatic Veneti reached farther than some Venetologists assume; in the west it reached into the Alps, and in the east as far as the borders of Pannonia and along the eastern shore of the Adriatic. Perhaps the elements in Chakavian and Kajkavian which are also common in the Slovene language can tell us how far the Venetic influence reached. To be convinced of this, one only needs to read early authors from Dubrovnik or Zagorje, or discover these common elements in casual conversation with people from those areas.

To some degree we can also understand, from the names we know, how Dalmatia must have looked demographically during Roman times. All the names have a Latin or Greek form, written by people who did not know the Slavic language. The Illyrian names are undoubtedly predominant, but among them are names that show there was also a Venetic population here.

The nature of the Illyrian language is so far unknown in spite of the Messapian inscriptions in southern Italy, which are supposedly the only written documents of the Illyrian language. Noone can say with certainty what is and what is not Illyrian. For example, who can say that **Plaheniis** is an Illyrian name? The word **plah**—shy—exists in the Slavic languages as well as in Albanian. However, in Albanian this word is isolated; it is not used in forming new words. On the other hand, in Slavic languages and the OCS *plahъ* is very productive in creating derivatives. This is even more so with the word **Hoia,** this beautiful name which is still used for our girls. The name **Baiula** could derive from the Slavic *bajati*—to foretell—as well as from the Albanian *bajat*—tired, old. **Baraccio** could easily be the Latinized form of the Slovene *berač*—beggar or *vrač*—untrained health practitioner or a similar Albanian word. Women's names, such as Seio, Cato (Kato), Thana (Tana, Tanja) are even now found in Dalmatia.

There is yet more evidence showing that the Dalmatian population was mixed, namely Illyrian and Venetic; that is, non-Slavic and Slavic. For example the words in the Messapian inscriptions which are supposed to be Illyrian such as **molda** Slov. *mlada*—young, and **prevezivena** Slov. and Serbo-Cr. *prevesti*—to lead across, to transport—clearly have a Slavic character. This shows that Venetic had strongly influenced Illyrian during the first centuries of the first millennium B.C. Later, when the Veneti under Celtic and Roman occupation lost their independence in the region between the Alps and the Adriatic, they were in a possibly subordinate position in relation to the Illyrians, or at least numerically a smaller group. This does not necessarily mean that they were of a lower status; on the contrary, the Veneti were probably the less numerous ruling class. The preponderance of the Illyrian names on Roman monuments reflects this condition.

Of course these are only assumptions, but not completely without basis. The OCS documents in Glagolitic (the Glagolitic alphabet was used by Slavs in Dalmatia and Istria, but was soon displaced by the Cyrillic alphabet in the east, and in the west by Latin), show that there was a lively contact between the Veneti in Italy and Dalmatia. The Glagolitic alphabet made use of several letters which could have only come from Venetic or Etruscan, among them the left-facing E, G, P, S. One has the impression that there was an effort, by way of various changes, to blur their origin since the Etrusco-Venetic writing was by then in disgrace and banned.

The old dispute concerning who the inhabitants in ancient Dalmatia really were could in this way receive an answer that shows both sides to be right: those who maintain that they were not Slavic, rather Illyrian, and their opponents who deny this.

The controversy concerning the origin of the Slovenes has always engaged, on the one side, the amateurs who are not professionally occupied in a chosen field of research, and on the other side, the specialists who look disapprovingly on the amateurs, forgetting that we owe our gratitude precisely to the amateurs for a good part of the discoveries in all branches of science.

It is true that a characteristic of amateurism is that it is not always aware of the difficulties which are related to the question that is being examined, as Goethe said, who was himself a highly gifted amateur in many areas. It is also true that amateurs are prone to premature announcing of their unproven findings. Fortunately, there are also strokes of genius that can suddenly make clear what has been up till then surrounded by uncertainty. Thus, what has been written about the history of the Slovenes by amateur historians has, in spite of the errors and premature conclusions, something which often eludes the professional—courage and intuition. The amateur can make a mistake because he has nothing to lose; however this is not true of the professional, since he can lose everything—his reputation or his job or both.

This fear is the death of science. A science that looks with scorn on the amateurs as if they were just ignorant dreamers forgets that it often also waddles about rather clumsily.

Traces of the Venetic Language in Slovenia

The readers will probably be interested to know whether any traces of the Veneti have survived in Slovenia besides the toponyms. It would be odd if this were not the case, since at one time they lived on the land that the Slovenes now occupy. Traces have survived not only in those forms that are of interest to archaeology and ethnography, but also in the form of the written word. A number of inscriptions have been found in Slovenia on various objects: a bronze situla, several pottery urns, a bronze tablet, a number of bronze helmets etc.

I am amazed that from the time I first became fascinated by these inscriptions, no Slovene apart from a few amateurs had concerned himself with them. Nonetheless, they are the oldest written words found on Slovene soil, and south central Europe. Our language specialists are convinced that these inscriptions have nothing in common with the language they are researching, namely Slovene. But I think it would do them good to study the inscriptions, compare them with those of northern Italy, and discover for themselves how these ancient characters relate to the modern Slovene language and its dialects. They will be very surprised indeed.

To discover the true meaning of the various inscriptions, the meaning that goes beyond the alphabet and phonetics, we probably need more than just linguistic knowledge; we need something which I would, for lack of a better word, call intuition, especially when we are dealing with texts of a poetic character. To uncover the morphological meaning on the Ateste tablets or any other aspect of the Venetic language, one certainly has to keep one's eyes open. It may be that our researchers are lulled to sleep by the idea that Slovenes came to their present land much later, in fact a full 1000 years later than the origin of the Ateste tablets. Curiously, at that early period the scribes were engraving the tablets with words like: **jekal, jekam, jekaš, jekaj, jekaje, jekav,** etc., Venetic forms of words that have remained unchanged to this day in the Slovene language.

Someone may ask, how can it be that words and grammatical forms remain unchanged for so long?

The case is that some word forms and phrases change very little; they stay practically the same for an extremely long time.

Let us consider the following sentence: **Bože usliši molitvǫ mojǫ** (OCS). If we remove the nasal o's, the sentence is Slovene. The same is also true of forms such as **delaj, delaje, delal, delati, delan, delat** (supinum), which have remained in their original form in Slovene if we leave out the nasal sounds which have disappeared, and if we remember that the **e** is today pronounced as **e** and not as **je** (ye). *Delat(i)* belongs to the same class of words as **jekat(i)**.

If 1000 years ago the Slavs had spoken some words and phrases in the same way as we do today (i.e., they made words and phrases in the same way we do now), then why could they not have spoken the same words 2000 or more years ago? The Ateste grammar tablets have with one verb and its derivatives affirmed this hypothesis. These words are in the Slovene and other Slavic languages still in use today with only minor changes. That is why some words should probably be read as though they had the silent vowel **ә** as is still used in Slovene language or the soft consonants as represented in the OCS; e.g., "jekaль", by the soft-sign ь, (for the palatal or soft quality of a preceding consonant at the end of the word or before another consonant). This would correspond to the Etruscan reading of the consonants. Perhaps the **e** in **jekae** was a nasal sound, for they had no specific letter for these sounds. However, in my opinion we cannot rule out the possibility that at least in the later period—because of a faster pace of life and consequently a faster way of speaking—the Venetic language had separated itself from the softened suffixes, except for some verses which were written earlier when the softened consonants still existed. We will find some evidence of this when we analyze texts which are obviously set to a meter or rhythm.

The fear that the Ateste forms of the verbs are too modern is not justified.

I often recall a professor from India who once asked me, as we talked about everything possible, what the word **plavava** meant. I told him it was dual form of verb **plavati**—to swim. He was very surprised and expressed how extremely odd this was. **Plavava** in Sanskrit means exactly the same, first person dual. I asked him why he had become interested in precisely this word. He answered that he had heard it at a spa.

Some words are more stable than others, among them also **jekat(i),** along with most of its derivative forms, because they have pure vowels which are less subject to reduction; furthermore, they do not have any difficult-to-pronounce groups. Nevertheless, in the course of centuries and millenniums they also underwent minimal change. In Slovene for example, the aorist and the imperfect fell out of use, and are now very remote; for example *jekaahomь, jekaašete, jekaaho*. Did the Venetic still have these? They are not on the tablets from Ateste, perhaps though the aorist **jekaa**. The imperfect was not suited for this type of crossword-grammar because it was too long.

Other words and their forms have also survived, and if we compare them with Old Slovene we see that they have indeed remained unchanged to this day; that is, if we disregard the absence of soft consonants at the end of some words. For example: *vinograd, čuditi, čuti, čudo, jug, junica, jama, jasli, jahati, gubiti, pogubiti, znati, poznati, pol, mazati, pomazati, mesti, pomesti, pokoj, pojiti, napojiti, vpiti, vpisati, brati, begati, beda, bežati, bogateti.*

I could continue to list words which remain in the same form as when they were written down by the truly brilliant linguists, the holy brothers Cyril and Methodius (who established in Moravia in 862 their mission, which was soon destroyed by Germans, whereupon they worked in the Slovene Pannonia—future Hungary—under the protection of Slovene Prince Kocelj). They had invented letters for every subtlety which had not been taken into account by Veneti or Etruscans in their simple alphabets. Because of the exactness of the Cyrillic alphabet, we have a clear picture of how the Old Slavic sounded. I sometimes think they were too precise, above all with the palatalized and non-palatalized consonants which were probably by that time disregarded in several dialects, or not heeded as thoroughly as by these classically trained linguists.

Among the forms and derivatives of the verb **jekat,** found on the grammar tablets, there are those which undoubtedly correspond to present-day Slovene and Slavic phonetics in general. However, there are also those which are uncertain, for example **jekam;** is it first person singular or the first person plural? Both are possible. It may be that in Venetic, as said earlier, the m at the end of a word came into use very early. The OCS had this ending, though only in some cases: *датъ, jатъ, естъ, ветъ, iтатъ.* It became accepted because it could be more quickly pronounced, consequently resulting in the loss of those that took more time such as *delaio, jekaio, delam, jekam*—I work, I cry.

I would now like to examine several inscriptions taken from among the presently known finds of Venetic culture in the Slovene area.

The Inscription from Škocjan

The historian Sila mentions that Livia, the wife of Emperor Augustus, greatly valued the "vinum pucinum", a wine which was at her request provisioned from Devin near Trst (Trieste). The wine was to have received its name from Pečine (Slov.—wall-like rocks, cliffs) near Devin. The area was even during his childhood called Pečine.

If the wine from this area was of such high quality, it was only natural that it would also have been greatly valued during the time of the Veneti, even to the degree that the containers from which it was drunk were inscribed with appropriate Anacreontic epigrams. Just such an example would be the situla made of bronze which was found before the First World War, in 1911 to be exact, in the proximity of Škocjan, Slovenia, not far from Trst (Trieste).

Ts 1 (LLV)
Venetic language in Slovenia.

OSTI JAREJ
Stay young!

As can be seen, the inscription is to be read from left to right. Let us examine the two words:

osti—stay, remain; Slov. *ostani*; Serbo-Cr. *ostaj* (imperative). Old Slavic had two root words **sta** and **sti** (Miklošič). The imperative **sti** has survived in Slov. e.g., *oprosti!*—forgive me (Skok, Etim. rječnik).

jarej—young; Slov. *jar*—spring-like, new, e.g., *jaro žito*—spring grain. This word is in general use among Slavic people.

Osti has dots between the letters as is often the case with Venetic inscriptions, and are ascribed special significance by Venetologists. They are essentially decorating the smaller, less conspicuous letters such as ⸲ ·|· ; these dots are sometimes also used to separate syllables, as for example in our inscription.

In an effort to help the reader gain confidence in the accuracy of my translation, I would like to mention here two Venetic inscriptions from the Treviso museum which likewise contain the word OSTI. The first one is **Tr 3.**

OSTI JAKO USEDI ČA
Stay, just as you have sat (lain) yourself down there!

osti—stay, remain; Slov. *ostani* (see above comment), Serbo-Cr. *ostaj.*
jako—just as; Slov. *kakor;* OCS *jakъ*—just as, such as.
usedi—you have sat down; 2nd per., aorist, sing.; Slov. *usedel (si se), sedel si.* Compare Serbo-Cr. aorists and OCS *hvalihъ*—praise.
ča—there; Slov. *tja*, Chakavian *ča.*

It is a proverb wishing the deceased rest; that is, that he remain in peace, just as he had lain down.

Tr 3a (LLV)
Museo Civico di Treviso
Venetic language in Slovenia.

The second inscription, **Tr 1**, is similar:

MOLO ARVON KO S OSTI JAKO
Into the earth buried as you are, stay thus!

molo—soil, dative; Slov. *mulju (mulj*—a mixture of small particles, sand, clay), found in other Slavic languages in similar forms.

arvon—written **arbon,** but due to betatism (v to b) I consider it to be **arvon.** In the dative form this means: buried in the earth Slov. *mulju zarit, v mulj zarit.* The urns were buried in the earth or sand. Compare OCS *jama rъvena,* (Venetic **arvona**), and *rъvenikъ—puteus* (Miklošič) decomposing, rotting, buried. Both words come from the OCS *ryti, ryjo, ryvati*—to dig (Mikl.). Slovene *riti, (za)riti*— to dig into, to bury in the earth.

ko s—as you are; Slov. *ko si, kot si.* It is an abbreviation of *jako(s)*—just as. Slov. *ko, kot* is an abbreviation of *kakor*; *kos* is to be read in other cases as the Polish *ktoš*—whoever, Slov. *kdorkoli.* We could also read it here in this way, though **ko s** seems to me more correct.

Tr 1 (LLV)
Museo Civico di Treviso
Venetic language in Slovenia.

Both inscriptions confirm our transcription of the epigraph on the situla from Škocjan. The contextual meaning also corresponds to the transcription of other similar inscriptions which we are familiar with, from a later Christian period. We need only to think about the inscription on Shakespeare's gravestone which closes with the following: and curst be he that moves my bones.

Feast of the Earth in Idrija pri Bači

From among the most ancient documents of the Slovene language, I would like to comment on three which come from Idrija pri Bači, Slovenia. All three were found in 1850 along with the important discoveries of the burial place in Most na Soči, Slovenia. The graves themselves, as well as the various urns, kettles, bronze pans, clasps, pins and situlas call to mind the burial places in Ateste. The speculation that these could be remains of Celtic culture was rightly rejected by archaeologists involved in Venetic research. By way of these three inscriptions and their letters, which differ only marginally from the Ateste writing and

215

exhibit a slight Etruscan influence, it has finally been proven that these are Venetic finds. The observation that these graves could have originated in an earlier epoch during the first millennium B.C., when the Veneti were settled in our territory, is probably correct. The language of these inscriptions exhibits many characteristics of the Slavic languages which are much older than what Slavists maintain. These same indications are found in the Slovene dialects.

Is 3 (LLV)
Naturhistorisches Museum, Vienna
Venetic language in Slovenia.

The bronze tablet **Is 3** on which the inscription is engraved is 78mm long and 18-19mm wide. On the right side there is a hole which, because of rusting, has become larger in the course of centuries. The tablet apparently remained where it belonged, attached to an object with a nail probably on a wooden or ceramic container in which garden produce or perhaps a beverage was stored.

But what could lead one to such a conclusion? The inscription itself. According to my transcription it reads as follows:

LYK Z(E)MELIN K S
HAJI ČOS KA B

In Slovene: Kadar je ta praznik zemlje počivaj, pa naj bo karkoli.
In English: When there is this feast of the earth, rest, no matter what be.

The individual words:

lyk—celebration, dance, feast; OCS *likъ*—choir (Mikl.). Ukrainian *lykovati*—rejoicing, dancing (Mikl.). In modern Slovene the word *likati* belongs to farm tasks, for example removing the leaves from heads of corn or other similar tasks. This *likati* is a neighbourhood activity accompanied by song and even some drink, a custom that I experienced as a child. Also interesting are the additional meanings of *likati*: to swig, to sob, to peel (Plet.). *Likof* is in my opinion not borrowed from the German Leikauf (Litkouf), but rather the opposite; it is a Slavic loanword in German, as are many other words. Also, **lit**—a fermented fruit juice, is not a loanword from mediaeval German **lit**, but rather an original Slovene word, traced directly to the verb *liti*—to pour.

z(e)melin—of earth; the first **e** was left out (possibly because it was not accented) after the custom that came from the Etruscans, who received it from the Semites. This omission of vowels was in a small way practised also in the Venetic language (northern Etruscan according to Mommsen). Zemlja was not only the earth but also a goddess. Here we have an interesting connection. The name Zemele (consort of Zeus) obviously came from the Thraco-Phrygian name of the goddess of earth Dzemelo.

k—if, when; Slov. *ko*, in dial. *k*, which equals the Venetic **k**.

s—this one; Slov. *to, tu;* OCS *sь*.

haji—rest; Slov. *počivaj*, in dial. also *hajaj* and *haji*, from *hajati, hajam* (Plet.), Russ. dial. *hajatь*, and *nehaj*; also used in Slovene child language: *ajati, ajaj, aji*.

čos ka—whatever; Slov. *karkoli*, Czech *čos*—some.

b(i)—would; the Venetic silent vowel **i** was often left out. In colloquial Slovene we also often say *b* instead of *bi*.

In this inscription there is in all probability also the following anagram:

LYK Z(E)MELIN K S(I)
HAJI ČOS KA B(I)

In Slovene: Lik (podoba) zemlje, kot si, počivaj v miru, pa naj bo karkoli že!
In English: Image of the earth, as you are, rest (in peace),
no matter what (happens)!

lyk—*lik* means in Slovene also form or image. It is likъ] in OCS, and Slavic languages in general. Many words derive from it: *olika*—good manners, shape, *likati*—to smooth out, to iron, *slikar*—painter, etc. Everything indicates that even the Etruscan word *lukumon*—spiritual and worldly leader, shepherd, has the same origin. The Ukrainian word is *lyčman*—shepherd, the oldest among the shepherds. The Venetic language as the Slovene, does not distinguish between y and i, which is why both forms are written here with ∧, an upside-down u (V). Both words, *lukumon* and *lyčman,* have the same origin, only the vowels **i** and **y** having been adapted to the particular languages. Supporting this in its own way is another meaning of the word *lik*—glitter, sparkle (Mikl.). Furthermore, in the Slovene dialect of Tolmin, *obličje* (from *lik*) is the same as a mask. And from time immemorial people have danced with masks (*likovati*).

k s(i)—Slov. *ki si*—you who are, as you are, in daily use also *k'si, k's* and *k's'*.

As we can see, this is a classic anagram in which there is a double meaning on the basis of homonyms. Actually the only homonym in this anagram is the word **lik (lyk)**. At one time it means a feast, at another time an image. The imperative **haji** (from **hajit**) has another meaning but only in a different context. The first meaning: Rest, if the feast of the earth is celebrated. The second meaning: Rest in the grave, you who are the image of the earth, and may evil spirits not disturb you.

There is still another possibility: this proverb could also be an incantation similar to the Christian commandment against working on feast-days.

The Helmets from Negova

Another important find with inscriptions are the 26 bronze helmets found in 1811 near Negova in Slovenske Gorice, Slovenia. Some of these helmets are kept in the National Museum in Ljubljana and the others in the National Museum of Art in Vienna. Jože Kastelic reported that up until the end of the war the prevalent opinion was that the most important and best preserved inscription on these helmets was a Germanic dedication in an alphabet similar to those from northern Italy, the Etruscan and the Venetic, and that the text is to be read as **HARIGASTITEIVAI**, which they word as **Harigasti Teivai**. Moreover, **teiwai** was to have been a deity.

I was able to accurately read this inscription only after I obtained an excellent photo of it from the Vienna National Art Museum (through mediation of I. Tomažič, for which I thank him here). Prosdocimi remarked that at the end of this inscription there were some letters which were not noticed by researchers. Of this I was quickly convinced by the very clear photograph.

When I was able to read these previously missing letters, the last word was obviously *vaijul* and not *vai,* as was formerly thought.

This inscription, which was according to German studies read as HARIGASTITEIVAI and worded as Harigasti Teivai, reads in reality as HARIGASTITEIVAIJUL and is to be worded as HARI GASTI TE I VAIJUL.

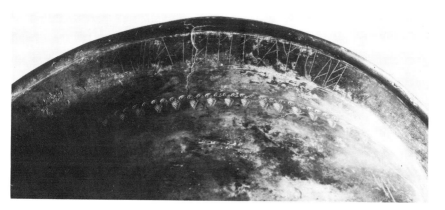

Helmet from Negova
Kunsthistorisches Museum, Vienna
Venetic language in Slovenia.

As we can see, the only thing that has changed is the last word. Earlier we understood it as an imperative, but now we are clear that it is a past participle: Old Slavic *voin,* Slovene *vojak*—soldier, *vojevati*—to make war which is the frequentative of *vojiti.* Of the same derivation are also: *voj* and *boj, vojnik, vojska* etc. Lithuanian *vejú; vyti,* imperfect *vajóti;* Old Indian *véti*—to conquer, persecute. The word is obviously of an onomatopoeic origin: *ojiti* (from the cry *oj!*) which had initially the meaning to cry out. This can be confirmed by the OCS *oiminъ*—soldier (see Leskin). From *oiminъ* developed *voiminъ,* same as *vogl* developed from *ogel*—corner. *Vaijul* is the same as *vojeval,* more similar still is Lithuanian *vajoti.* The fact that the inscription is found on a soldier's helmet also tells us that we are dealing here with the same meaning.

The other two words, *hari* and *gasti,* also have a military character.

hari—beat (aor. 3rd per. sing.); Slov. *hariti* and *harati*—to beat, flog (Pleteršnik, Miklošič), Kajkavian *hariti*—to strike, to beat (Skok).

Concerning **gasti**: Originally I saw in this word Slov. *gostiti se*—to be entertained, imperative: *gosti se!* Now that I have the authentic inscription in my hands, I tend to agree with the view of Pro. Stanko Kotnik, who in a letter to me suggested I read this word as meaning enemies. *Hari gasti*— he struck the enemy. He based his suggestion on the fact that originally *gost* meant the same as Latin *hostis*—foreigner— only that with the Slavs *gost* had developed from "foreigner" into "guest", and with the Romans into "enemy". At the time when the unknown hand engraved the above inscription with the beautiful, slim letters in the bronze helmet, *gost* obviously had the meaning "foreigner"—unfriendly, dangerous, threatening.

Since **te** means "and" (Slov. *ter;* Serbo-Cr. *te),* and **i** means "also" (Slov. *in, i;* Serbo-Cr. *i*), we can easily interpret the inscription.

hari— he struck, he beat (aor. 3rd per. sing.).
gasti— the foreigners, the enemies.
te i— and also.
vaijul—drove out.
Thus:

HARI GASTI TE I VAIJUL
Tolkel je tujce in jih tudi pregnal.

English: He struck the foreigners and drove them out.

Hence, it follows that the inscription was made after the soldier's death, when the helmet was laid in his grave. Perhaps he was a commander who had distinguished himself in battle or was at least an unknown hero.

The German explanation of this inscription was taken so seriously by the Nazis that they even named a town after Harigasti Teivai where this "oldest Germanic inscription" was found. They chose to ignore the fact that the script was Venetic and not Germanic. Even the symbol λ instead of the usual $\uparrow$ is Venetic (see Lejeune, *La lingua venete, Tableau de signes*); the difference consists in the fact that the shorter line of the first symbol is directed towards the middle of the vertical line.

Among the other inscriptions there are still three that should be looked at. The longest (AS VI 1659) and the most interesting one is in continuo:

SIRAKUHURLIARINEISVI

If we divide it into words we get the following:

ŽIRA KUHUR LI ARINEI S BI
A soldier who sacrificed (to god), fought more valiantly.

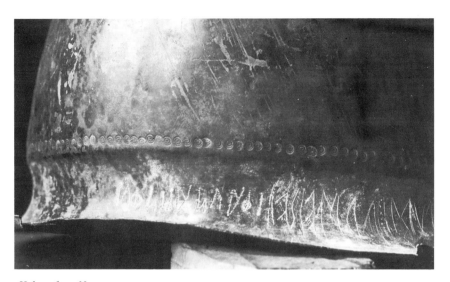

Helmet from Negova
Kunsthistorisches Museum, Vienna
Venetic language in Slovenia.

Let us have a closer look:

žira—he sacrificed; OCS *žirati*—to sacrifice: therefore *žrtva*—sacrifice, *žrec*—sacrificer etc.

kuhur—rogue; Slov. *kohar* (Plet.). In a figurative sense probably "soldier." Perhaps it is even related to the word *hariti*. Whoever would like to be *konjar*— horseman, must be a born *kohar* (Štrekelj, Plet.).

li—or, if, if possible; in regard to this meaning compare Chakavian: *li svak se razbiše, Jerolim osta sam* (Skok).

arinei—more valiant, literally "more insistent" he who more valiantly forces his way into the ranks of the enemy. This word is derived from the common Slavic and the OCS *rinoti* Slov. *vreči se (na koga)*—to throw oneself (on someone), to attack), Slov. *riniti*—to push, to press on, *-v ogenj*—into fire, *-v bitko*— into a battle, *-v koga*—into, onto someone. Regarding its form, **arinei** is a comparative. Collate the OCS *novei*—the newer, *mьnei*—the smaller; Slov. *manji, manjši, starji, starejši*—the smaller, the older one. The prefix **a** in **arinei** corresponds to OCS **a.**

s—oneself; Slov. *se.*

bi—he fought; Slov. *je bil* (from *biti, bijem*). The translation in more archaic

221

Slovene: *žrtvoval kohar li, vrinljiveje se bil*—when the soldier sacrifices, he fights more valiantly. Since in OCS *žreti* means the same as in modern Slovene—to gorge, we may translate the inscription accordingly: *Če žre vojak, je bojevitejši*— when the soldier gorges (himself), he is a better fighter. Or somewhat closer to the original with the help of archaisms: *Če kohar žre, vam raje rine v boj*—when the soldier gorges (himself), he is more willing to throw himself into the battle. Which of these translations is more acceptable? Considering that the inscription is found on a helmet, both translations would be acceptable. Everything indicates that many similar Venetic inscriptions had an ulterior import, which was often a parody of the first one. Anagrams were very popular, as I have shown with other Venetic inscriptions. Perhaps the ambiguity assured their perpetuation especially when engraved onto monuments or helmets.

The notion that one might be dealing with anagrams having a frivolous military meaning is confirmed by the inscription on the same helmet:

IWAUNAWINWUJ.

This inscription could, along with the others, be interpreted as an anagram. Whereas the first one is etched, this one is hammered in point by point, though of course by other hands at another time.

Let us first look at the original:

I WAUNA WINWUJ

In Slovene: In voljno se vojuj!
In English: And willingly fight!

i—and; OCS *i,* Slov. *in.*
wauna—willingly; Slov. *voljno;* Polish *wolno*—free.
The Venetic language had a close relationship with the Slavic north. In this inscription there is a similarity with the Polish where **l** before a vowel is pronounced as **ł** (w) at the beginning of a word; it was written in this inscription with the symbol ⟨Ⴤ⟩. Venetologists would like to interpret it as an **f.** However, this sound did not exist in Venetic, as we have already stated; this is still the case in other Slavic languages except in words borrowed from other languages.
winwuj—fight; Slov. *vojuj;* in my opinion it is a haplology (contraction) of **vij** and **voj** or **bij** and **voj.** It is an imperative, 2nd person, singular. Both **v**'s had been written with ⟨Ⴤ⟩, although somewhat differently from the previous ones. I have already written about the word **viti** as it is used in the sense of **vojiti.** Here

I would just like to say this: Its origin is, in spite of uncertainties, the same as that of *viti, vijem, zavijam,* (Slov. *volk zavija*—the wolf howls; Russ. *vitь, voju*—to howl; OCS *vyti.* All battles begin with a battle cry—howling. Also suggesting this is of course the OCS *oiminъ;* Slov. *vojak*—soldier. This shows that it must have originally been **ojiti.**

The fact that *vyti* is not the same as *vitь* does not contradict this etymology since the similar sounds **y** and **i** very easily merged. However, they most frequently became **oj,** that is, *voj, vojevati, vojak*—howl, to do battle, soldier. I suggest that the reader again look at the explanation for the word **vajul.**

I said it is possible we were dealing in this inscription with an anagram, a double meaning, which the soldiers had given to the official saying.

Another short inscription warrants our attention. In the front of a helmet—on the brim—is the following:

IERISNA

It is not out of the question that the word *juriš*—attack, raid, made its way to us in a similar way, and that the Slovene word *jeriti* is older, and indeed much older than the Turkish. This is confirmed by the Sanskrit word *jur*—to hurt and *jurni* f.—blazing fire, *jurvat*—to consume by fire (see Sanskrit English Dictionary, Oxford 1963). Accordingly, the various interpretations, from to strike, to hurt, and to rage, are closely related to the meaning of *juriti* or *jeriti* and *juriš.* Also to be included is Latin *ira*—rage, *irascor*—to be angry about. I think the Turkish word *juriš*(yoorish) is an Indo-European loanword from Persian.

In addition to this, another explanation is necessary. The letters which had been used as **s** were at the same time those with which **z** and **ž,** and the intermediate **ś,** had been represented. The inadequate distinction made between the sibilants, whether they are voiced or not, and the consonants (excluding l, m, n, ng, r) is typical not only of the Istrians but also of the Italians. The Veneti did not differentiate between them, as we do not today. This same incompleteness is also characteristic of the Etruscans, the contemporaries and neighbours of the Veneti and Italic people, and can be verified by a whole series of examples where the same word is written at one time with an **s** and at another time with a **ś.**

Consequently, the word *juriš*—aid, attack—is much older than previously thought. The inscription on the helmet from Vače substantiates this seemingly unbelievable hypothesis.

I would again like to emphasize that I do not consider any of the above interpretations as conclusive. At the same time, I will venture to say that none of them contradict that which we know about the development of Slavic languages.

The Palindromes

In an earlier chapter I mentioned that besides the anagrams the Veneti used the demanding form of the palindromes. The Latins called them the *versus carcimus*; the Greeks, on the other hand, *palindromos*; i.e., a word order that contains a word or a sentence which, when read backwards, still has the same meaning or yet another. For example, the place-name "Zali laz" means the same when read backwards. The place-name "Zali log", however, when read backwards reveals the place-name "Goli laz."

The Venetic inscriptions, which are mostly either ritual incantations or proverbs, also include masterful palindromes. As with the anagrams, the Veneti used the palindromes to make the incantations as mysterious as possible. They probably thought that only such sayings (as opposed to ordinary words and phrases) would be effective against evil spirits.

Es 89 (LLV)
Museo Nationale Atestino

After having thoroughly studied the Venetic inscriptions, I came to realize that several of them were palindromes. I will try to present the supportive evidence as clearly as I can.

Urn From Ateste

On the Ateste urn **Es 89** there is an inscription that caused me to think:

UKONAHAL K NOS

Anyone who wishes to examine this inscription more closely, will notice without difficulty that there is something visually wrong with it, because most of the letters stand on their heads when the urn is normally positioned, right side up. We would expect the inscription to run from right to left or from left to right, but it does neither. **UKONAHAL K NOS** can be read only if we stand the urn upside down. Did the person who drew the letters make a mistake? Or is this perhaps a suggestion? Are we to read the inscription also in the opposite direction? If we do that, we get an interesting result: **SON K LAHAN OKU.**

Joining the two parts of the palindrome into one unit, we get an unusually beautiful, thoughtful, and stylistically well ordered saying or spell:

UKONAHAL K NOS
Ukončal ki nas,

SON K LAHAN OKU
sen da lahan oku.

A more understandable transcription:

Slovene: Ti, ki si nas ukončal, daj da bo sen očesu lahak.
English: You who have put an end to us give the eyes an easy sleep.

Let us look at the individual words:
ukonahal—had finished; Slov. *ukončal*, from *končati*—to finish; arch. Slovene *konati* (Plet.). This means that the verb *konati* got a postfix -**ha.** Another interesting piece of information is the Latvian word *hal* which means death, end; this shows that the two words are closely related. Maybe it should be translated as:

UKONA HAL K NOS
Ukonča smrt ko nas
When death puts an end to us

nos—us; probably pronounced as **nəs**, just as in our dialects. Venetic **o** was also used for shortened sounds when these were not omitted.

Words in the opposite direction:

son—sleep; Slov. *sen* or *sən;* Russian *sonъ*; Lusatian *son;* OCS *sъnъ*; Old Slavic is the same. We find the word **son** with the same meaning also in other inscriptions.

k—that (conjunction); Slov. *ko*, same letter as for *ki*, but with a different meaning. Same as *ka*—that from eastern Styria. Kajkavian is the same.

lahan—light; Slov. *lahek,* also *lahen,* in general use in Slavic languages. In the 17th century also *lagan* as in Serbo-Cr. OCS *lьgъkь—levis*, lihgt.

oku—to the eye; Slov. *očesu*; in the Slovene dialect of Pannonia *oko, oka.* OCS *oko*.

The Boundary Stone

There is yet another piece that supports my interpretation. It is the inscription on an ancient rough stone, "hors des necropoles recounnues" (Lejeune), found outside of the known burial area, which had at one time served as a boundary marker between two pieces of land. Engraved on this stone is a saying whose meaning only becomes clear with the second reading, as a palindrome which creates two mutually completing verses:

ITU RIA MAK K NOS
Le to izrivši in maknivši, naj nosi

SON K KAMAJ RUTI
sen ko (je), kamen do groba!

In more understandable language:

In Slovene: Kdor izrije to in premakne,
    naj nosi v svojem snu, ta kamen do groba!
In English: Whoever digs it up and moves it,
    let him carry this stone in sleep to his grave.

Words from left to right:
itu—this; Slov. *to*, Russ. *eto*. Rezija dialect *ito*.

Es 21 (LLV)
Museo Nazionale Atestino

ria—had dug up; Slov. *izrivši*, a past tense participle. Comp. Russ. *hodja, govorja;* conditionally interpreted perhaps as: *ria (rija)*, Slov. *kdo to izril (bi)*— whoever would dig it up.

mak—has moved, has displaced; Slov. *premaknivši*, past part. from *makniti, premakniti*, OCS *makъ* from *maknǫti, mъknoti.* The most likely translation would be: Whoever digs it up and moves it (the stone)—will carry it in sleep to his grave (to his last day).

k nos—can carry; Slov. *naj nosi* , dial. also *ka nos(i)*. In Venetic there are many reduced forms of imperative.

Words from right to left:

son k—when sleep is here; Slov. *sen ko je* or *v snu*—during sleep.

kamaj—stone; Slov. *kamen*; OCS *kamy*; Lusatian *kamai;* Slov. dial. pl. *kameje, kamenje*—stones.

ruti—to the grave; Slov. *(k) ruti* ; arch. Slovene *rt*—high ground; Bulgarian *rъt*—mound; the OCS *rъtъ* means the same.

Whoever knows Slovene poetry will be reminded by this ancient Venetic stone, of the well-known poem *Boundary Stone* by Anton Aškerc, in which the neighbour Vid, who had secretly moved the boundary marker two spans, had to carry back this "cursed stone" for a hundred years. Both thoughts, the Venetic and the Slovene, are so similar that they are almost identical. We are reminded time and again of how deeply the Slovene roots reach.

The inscription **Es 21** has no special markings which would indicate that it is a palindrome, probably because the majority of these sayings or spells had their full magical power only when their double meaning was veiled in secrecy.

Interesting Evidence
from Idrija pri Bači

The two inscriptions on bronze bowls from Idrija pri Bači, Slovenia, convince us very strongly that we have here palindromes and not just anagrams.

Let us then examine the inscriptions **Is 1** and **Is 2** in reproductions from *La lingua venetica*.

Is 1 (LLV)
Naturhistorisches Museum, Vienna
Venetic language in Slovenia.

First we will look at the inscription **Is 2**. It is instantly clear what kind of ductus/image is here etched on the bronze vessel that accompanied the deceased. The letters are leaning forward, just the way we still write them today, which means that we have to read from left to right. In my transcription and interpretation the inscription reads as follows:

HATOR V HAN V(I)HAL

As this is a palindrome, we get the other half of the meaning by reading the inscription in the opposite direction:

LA HIVNAH V ROTAH

Is 2 (LLV)
Naturhistorisches Museum, Vienna
Venetic language in Slovenia.

The reader may wonder how we came to decide to read the inscription also from right to left. The letters themselves offer this approach; they are inclined forward but face backward—not all, but certainly four of them.

Our interpretation is confirmed (and this is the reason for its extraordinary importance) by the inscription **Is 1**. The direction of reading is unquestionably from left to right. When we read the inscription in this way we notice to our surprise that it is the same as **Is 2**, when this one is read in the opposite direction.

And now let us try to explain this palindrome. The contents of this inscription tells me that is has to be read in this way:

LA HIBNÁH V ROTÁH,
Le tu sem poginil (umrl) med rotitvami,

HATÓR V HAN V(I)HÁL
kateri (sem) v ogenj vehnil

In Slovene: Tukaj sem bil sežgan med zaklinjanjem zoper zle duhove jaz,
        ki sem omahnil v ogenj.
In English: Here I have been cremated with incantations
        (against the evil spirits)—I who have fallen into the fire.

I will explain each individual word:
    la—here; Slov. *tu, le-tu*. Everything indicates that the Venetic **la,** modern Slov. *le*, was still a locative adverb similar to the Polabian *laa, lā*, as is now in

Italian and French. In Slov. and Serbo-Cr. it had become a suffix of adverbs, expressing a movement toward the speaker: *sem-le, dotle*, etc. (Skok). As one of these suffixes, **le** also acquired an adverbial character. Accordingly, the Chakavian **la** in **andula** from Istria, is a remnant of the Venetic **la** and not a loanword from Italian.

h(i)bnah—vanished, disappeared (in the flames); Slov. *izginil*; OCS *gibnahъ*, an aorist. Compare **jekah** on the Ateste grammar tablets; Czech *hy(b)nouit*, Serbo-Cr. *gibnuh*.

v rotah—during oath, incantation; Slov. *v rotah, rota. V rotah* is locative pl. which is identical with arch. Slovene. This word is still used in *porota*—jury, *zarota*—conspiracy, *rotiti*—to swear to.

hator, or **kator**—which, who; **k** and **h** were often written with the same letter; Slov. *kateri*, Slov. dial. *kater* or *hter*; OCS and Russ. *katoryj*; Latv. *katars;* Lith. *katras.*

v han—into the fire; Slov. *v ogenj*. In the Slovene dialects this word is pronounced in a variety of ways: *ogn, o hn, o han, han*. The most informative for us are the *gon* or *hon* from the Slov. dialect in Friuli, Italy, where the first **o** is not used, and are therefore closest to the original Venetic **han**.

v(i)hal—he staggered, toppled into, collapsed, fell into; Slov. *omahnil*, also *vehnil, vehal*. Perhaps one must read the short line as an **i**, or rather the first vertical line in letter H is at the same time an **i**, that is—**ih**.

Now that we are familiar with the individual words, we can make a more exact translation into Slovene:

Le-tu sem poginil v rotah—jaz, ki sem v ogenj vehal. Or, in a more archaic language, taking into consideration the Slovene dialects:

le-tu gibnoh v rotah—kater v (o)gan vehal.

Without changing the meaning of the saying, the word **kator** offers another variation: **ka tor,** Slov. *ko trup*—when the corpse. The Slovene word *trup* is derived from *tor* with the help of the word-forming **p** (see Skok). We often find in the inscriptions **tor** with the meaning dust (in the sense of cremation ashes). A whole series of words have arisen from **tor** *treti, tarem*—to trample underfoot, grind, e.g., *toriti*—to carry a load (Plet.), more exactly: *utirati si pot*—to make a passage for oneself, Russ. *toritъ*, Bulg. *tor*—dung, dust.

If one compares the forms of the words in the above translation with the inscription itself, one will be able to observe that they are the oldest forms of the Slovene language which are still alive in the dialects. Furthermore, if one reads the original and the translation several times, one will notice a rhythm which calls to mind the meter of Slovene poetry and Alpine poetry in general.

In the incantation engraved on both receptacles, which were placed in the grave of the deceased, apparently the same wish is expressed—the same wish that is repeated in many similar inscriptions, namely, that the soul of the deceased might find rest. Contributing to this peace was of course the conviction that the ceremony of cremation be carried out in accordance with the prescribed ritual, that is, with incantations (**v rotah**) against the evil spirits as the corpse *tor, trup* fell into the fire—*v ogan vehal*.

Based on numerous (over seven thousand) relatively modest graves it can be assumed that the inhabitants of this area were not rich. This is the situation even today. The soil in this area is not fertile. Historians are of the opinion that the Veneti had begun to spread throughout the mountainous regions when the plain from the Adriatic Sea to the Alps had already been settled. This is probable. It is also not impossible that some of the Etruscans would have taken refuge in this secluded mountainous territory after centuries-long fighting with the Romans and ultimate annihilation in the 3rd century B.C. There are such minor differences between the Venetic and Etruscan alphabets that many experts (Mommsen was one of them) still consider several Venetic relics as Etruscan. Perhaps some characters (letters), such as $\emptyset$, h, for example, support this view. This letter appears very seldom in Venetic. It is found in the inscriptions from Padova and also in Idrija, as we have just seen. It is totally possible to ascribe this letter to the influence of the Etruscans, whether it be during the time when they were still powerful neighbours of the Veneti or later as they sought refuge from the Romans in the Venetic mountain territory.

A long time ago, when I still had no understanding regarding the connection between the Etruscans and our ancestors, I asked myself a question which was of particular interest to me; namely, where was the origin of the slender, graceful faces of western Slovenia, including those from the mountainous hamlets of the Tolmin area? The attractiveness of these girls reminded me of Toscana, at one time one of the most elegant Etruscan centres. Their culture survived until the Renaissance, which was a revival not only of Greek and Roman art, but also of the Etruscan. The great Tuscany artists, such as Michelangelo, were aware of this fact.

The feminine faces and also the faces of men from the southern slopes of the Alps remind us of the Etruscan portraits. The Etruscan artists specialized in extreme realism. The faces immortalized by them can still be encountered today on the streets and country roads of western Slovenia. The coming together of Slavic realism and exotic oriental stylizing shows that there was at one time on the Apennine peninsula a merging of two cultures: the northern Venetic or Proto-

Slavic and that of Asia Minor into one—the Etruscan. Numerous researchers maintain that the Etruscans came from Lydia, Asia Minor, where they had spoken the Hittite language. And there are numerous words in Hittite which are similar to or the same as Slavic, as Hrozny and Georgijev have shown. Such a merging of the two peoples would consequently not have been too difficult providing both had a similar language.

Sayings on the Rocks in the Carnic Alps

There were roads throughout the Venetic territory during pre-Roman times. One of these roads ran from Verona eastward to Tergeste, Postojna (in Slovenia), and on to Virunum in Carinthia (present-day Austria). The stopping places *(postaja* in modern Slovene) on this road, where the travellers could rest and refresh themselves, are still referred to in the same way. One of these is **Postojna** in Slovenia and the other is **Postioma** at the crossing of the ancient Venetic road and the present-day highway between Trevisio and M. Belluno. Postioma is in the native dialect **Postojma** (LLV). The name appears again several kilometres in the direction of Piave. Postojoma and Postojna are of course two different forms of the same word. In the dictionary of the Slovene literary language we also find the word *postoj, -oja,* which is the antiquated form of *postanek*—a rest stop. *Hoditi brez postoja*—to walk without rest. But the ancient Veneti did not travel without resting; they had the **postojomas** at intervals along the way.

The Roman name Via Postumia is a later name and should not be confused with Venetic place-names. It denotes the road connecting main Venetic towns, which was under the command of consul Spurius Postumius Albinus modified for military purposes and named Via Postumia. The reverse could just as easily be true; that is, the consul got his name after the place-name. Naturally, the name was adjusted to Latin usage and so, from **postojma** it became Postumia. According to the study *La via Postumia nella Venezia,* Di Plinio Fraccaro, *Beiträge zur älteren europeischen Kulturgeschichte,* Band I. Klagenfurt, Austria 1952, the place-names along the Roman road are not called Postoyoma, as claimed by Prosdocimi, but Postoima. This brings them yet closer to the Slovene Postojna.

The road that led from Padova to Postojna in the direction of Pannonia was in good condition but the road over the Carnic Alps, which the travellers followed on their way north and again when returning to their southern homeland, was quite different. It became narrower and more difficult the higher it wound into the mountains. There were no more *postojoma(s)*; the weary traveller had to seek shelter in some cave or rocky overhang.

It was a remote area where from time to time one encountered a traveller like oneself or possibly some robbers waiting to take all one's belongings.

The famous rock with numerous inscriptions by travelers crossing the Carnic Alps, Regional Museum of Carinthia, Klagenfurt/Celovec.

The southern merchants most often transported **amber** on their return trip from the Baltic area. (True amber is a fossil resin of extinct coniferous trees that flourished along the Baltic coast in Tertiary [Eocene] times, from 60 to 70 million years ago— Tr.). This precious, multicolored material was much sought after for jewellery making. It was also attributed with medicinal and magical qualities, presumably because it became electrically charged when rubbed.

But the amber was not able to protect the Venetic merchants; rather, it exposed them to danger as all things which are of value to men tend to do. In short, the wilderness of the Alpine highlands made them feel uneasy. To lighten their fears, they would write various spells or sayings on the rocks along the road. In the direction of upper Zilja Valley (Gailtal) below the Pleke (Plöken) Pass, there was a rock which was apparently a popular rest stop. The travellers became accustomed to writing sayings on this rock. These were probably common invocations and sayings (and not invented on the spur of the moment) used to help ward off misfortune, just as is still done today when God is invoked to protect from evil.

These inscriptions in the Venetic alphabet carved into this particular rock by the Alpine road, are so numerous that the rock is literally covered with them.

Not only did the travellers leave these messages during the time of the Veneti, but the habit of inscribing something on the same rock continued until a part of it was finally removed and brought to the museum in Klagenfurt, Austria. Most of what is written on it is illegible; nevertheless, some inscriptions in *La lingua venetica* are quite readable.

The word **bog**, Slov. *bog*—God, appears in these inscriptions, which is only natural. The fearful travellers on this dangerous road through the mountainous wilderness had turned to their god asking him for protection. This is also explained by the contents of these inscriptions. Let us look at some of them.

The first inscription **Gt 13** tells us:

GA VIRROVO TO BOG KOS
Ga varoval tu bog kdor že je!

In Slovene: (Naj bi) ga varoval tu bog, kdor že je.
In English: May god protect him here, whoever he may be.

ga—him, acc.; Slov. *ga.*

virrovo— protect; Slov. *varoval.* Because of the double **r** we could assume that it should be read as **virdovo** (aorist vardevo, vardeval from vardevati). The inscription probably originates from the time when the influence of the Latin alphabet was already noticeable; i.e., the **d** already being used as **d** and at the same time still as Venetic **r**. The word is generally Slavic and Balto-Slavic.

to—here; Slov. *tu, tod* . The semi-vowel in Venetic is very close to the short **o.**

bog—God; Slov. *bog*, OCS is the same. "The original adjective *bog* had already become a noun during the ancient Slavic times, meaning a deity who distributes fortune and earthly benefits according to his own good judgement" (Skok, Etim. rječnik). We find this word on the Ateste tablets, where it is without the letter **o** (**bga, bge, bgij**). This is nothing unusual. Even in OCS, as already mentioned, the **o** was often left out; e.g., in the Sinai Psalter: **bže** (*bože*), **bga** (*boga*), and so on.

kos—whoever; Slov. *kdor*; In Polish, *ktos*, abbr. *kos*. It was written as **cos** but since the **c** was more frequently a **k**, I transcribed it here as a **k**. The word is often repeated; one time it is written with **c**, another time with **k**.

Gt 16 (LLV)

An interesting inscription is **Gt 16**; in it the word **bog** is written as **bug:**

BUG OŠA SO VIŠAD
Bog o(b)šel to visoto!

In Slovene: Naj bi bog obšel to višavo! In dialect: bug ošo to višar!
In English: May the presence of God fill this highland!

oša—to have passed through, to pass around; Slov. *ošel, obšel*. Perhaps it is an aorist, or also *ošel*, OCS *ošьl*, Korčula Island *oša*.

so—this; Slov. *to*. The OCS demonstrative pronoun *sьo*—this, no longer exists in Slovene, except in words like *sinoči*—last night, and *danes*—this day, today.

višad—high place; Slov. *visota, višava*, OCS *viša*—high ground (Plet.). This word appears on the stone as **bišad**. The Veneti like the Slovene inhabitants along the Adriatic coast, have changed the **v** to **b** (betatism).

The following short prayer **Gt 14** is in its charm in no way inferior to the others:

BOG TIŠEJ ZIJAD TO
Bog utišaj zijad to!

In modern Slovene: Bog utišaj to zijat.
In English: God, restrain this gaping precipice (from claiming us).

bog was written in this inscription by the unknown writer as **vog** for the same reason as the word **višad** was in the previous inscription written as **bišad**.

tišej—alleviate, calm, comfort, imperative; the perfective verb *utišati, tišati* is also possible in Slovene (Plet.). *Tišej* is here written without an **i**. But since the lines of the preceding or following letters were used as **i** (in our case M equals Š) as we have seen in the Ateste tablets, it is correct to insert the vowel **i**. Vowels were sometimes left out.

zijad—precipice, chasm; Slov. arch. *zijat*—precipice (Plet.) compare also Slovene *zijalo*—one who gapes, *zijati*—to yawn; these have a parallel here.

Gt 17 (LLV)

There are also inscriptions that have no religious connotation. One of these is **Gt 17:**

TURAI B SIJTI
O, da bi potujočemu bilo priti dol!

In modern Slovene: O, da bi popotnik prišel spet tja dol!
In English: May the traveller succeed in coming down from these mountains.

The major part of this inscription is clear enough, although Pellegrini and Prosdocimi were not able to totally decipher it. The question is whether we should read *tuda i, todi i* or *turai* because of the already mentioned Latinization of the Venetic alphabet. Both variations are equally possible, yet I tend towards *turai*—travelling. In those days the travellers were of course mostly merchants who had to make their way over the rugged Alps. Slovene word *torati* means to carry a load (Plet.). In Russian *tor* means a cleared way, and in Chakavian it means a trail or track. The Russian *toritь* means to clear a way, a path; the root is *ter, teretь*—to break up; in this case to clear away debris, to clear a passage. This means that the most appropriate interpretation of this word is:

turai—travelling; it is a substantivized participle of the type **jekati** (see the Ateste grammar tablets).

b, read **bi**— often repeated, written with the same meaning as the aorist of *bit(i)* in the subjunctive. Slov. *biti*—to be, *da bi*—may it be.

sijti—to come down (as from a pass); Slov. *iziti*; OCS *sьiti;* Russ. *sьiti.* A long infinitive. Perhaps the travellers came from an area where the long infinitive had still been used. The interjections on the rocks along the road remind us of the well-known **Bug vas primi, gralva Venus**—with these words had Duke Bernhard Spannheim and his Carinthian nobility greeted the Styrian poet Liechtenstein, who often used Slovene words in his poems, as he was travelling through the country in the year 1227. Compared with **gralva,** *kraljeva*—royal, the inscriptions on the rocks are undoubtedly much better in regard to orthography.

When I look at these markings carved with clumsy hands into the living rock, probably before the traveller continued on his way in the direction of the pass, the question arises regarding the time period of their origin. They are certainly very old, for the letters are typically Venetic, like the ones we know from the inscriptions from the central Venetic regions, such as Ateste (Este),Padova and Cadore. I still have the feeling that they might date from the time period when the Venetic language was already influenced by the Latin alphabet of their Roman conquerors. I said earlier that **d** in these inscriptions is no longer only an **r** but also a **d** under the influence of the already predominant Latin alphabet. An inscription from nearby Gorina/Gurina in the Zilja Valley (Gailtal) proves that this view is correct. We are here considering the inscription **Gt 1:**

A TTO DONASTO AISUM
A to darujem bogovom.

In English: And this I offer to the gods.

a—a, and; Slov. *a, in.*

tto—this; Slov. *to;*

donasto—I offer, bring; Slov. *darujem, donašam.*

aisum—to the gods; Slov. *bogovom, "ajsom",* Etruscan **aison**—gods (Pallotino TLE, p. 100, no. 804).

In this inscription, the letters look just like those found on other copper plates from Gurina, i.e., Venetic. The letter **d** is no longer an **r,** but a **d.** The word

donasto, which appears frequently in the Venetic inscriptions is a clear indicator. Others read it in the same way. Even the **m** which normally reads as š (sh), according to Lejeune, is in all probability already an **m.** In view of this, I think we can sometimes read the **d** in the inscriptions from the rocks in Carnic Alps as a **d** and not as an **r.**

There are probably many more inscriptions (similar to those described so far) in our territory which are still undiscovered. If our archaeologists would begin to search in areas designated by Venetologists, they would doubtless discover many more. Places such as Vrem, Vremski Britof, Vranje, Vranja peč, Vranički vrh, Vranoviči, Vremska Gorca, Vranke, Vransko, Verače, and Vreme were probably former Venetic cemeteries. At that time the deceased were not buried, but rather cremated and the ashes placed in urns, *virati*—to place into; these were most often interred on a mountain-side or a steep slope. Vremski Britof i.e., Vrem cemetery, is in this respect a very interesting example. The original meaning has been preserved, although dimly, which is why they later added the word cemetery. Most of these place-names derive from the verb **virat,** which means in several Slavic languages to insert (Mikl.); in Russ. it is *verat.* In the Slovene language this word no longer has this meaning, but it has survived in words like *za-virati*—to obstruct, *vereje* or *vranj*—plug (Plet.). The Venetic phrase **virem a istna,** which we often find on the Ateste tablets, is clearly related to the cremation ceremony; **virem**—place through; **istna**—the oven opening. It is fairly certain that the word **istna** is related to the Slovene word *isteje*, or *istanje*—the vaulted masonry opening to the oven or fireplace.

Tergeste

Now let us return to our merchants, no longer up in the lonely and dangerous mountain passes, but rather south of the Alps in the upper Piave River Valley. But before we meet with them in a Venetic tavern, I would like to mention something else.

The reader will probably be interested to know that a Venetic merchant was called **tergitio.** We can also tell you that the settlement where he sold his wares was called **oterg, otergij** or **otergie**—market town—and the market place itself where his store **tergovla** stood was called **tergeste.**

Let us consider these words individually. They all originate from the same root, **trg**—market, which we Slovenes still use every day. It is also used by other nationalities from Scandinavia to Albania.

Somewhere in the city of Scarbantia there lived a Venetic merchant who was still so attached to his language that he used it in a message on his gravestone, where we are told what he had done during his life. This is the inscription **CIL, III, 4251** and it reads as follows: **B. Domatius Tergitio negotiator.** We are apparently dealing here with something bilingual; Venetologists also think so. Negotiator is the same as Tergitio, which is only the older form for **tržeči,** somewhat more accurately **tergitiǝ.** Since there was in the written Venetic language no symbol for the silent vowel, they used the **o** instead, which is why **tergitiǝ** was written as **tergitio.** There are in the Slavic languages words with this same ending. The Slavic word *vojnik* is in Hungarian *voinikio* (Mikl.), which indicates that it sometimes sounded this way in OCS, at least to foreign ears.

Another word is **tergeste,** from which Trieste is derived. Since the majority of linguists do not want to recognize the Slavs as a nation that had already existed a long time in the Adriatic area, they proclaim Tergeste to be Illyrian, although they can no longer deny that it is the same as **tržišče,** Old Slav. *tržište*—market place, or they simply say that it is a Veneto-Illyrian name with the understanding that the Venetic could not be equivalent to Slavic.

The third word is **oterg**—market town. As is commonly known, lead projectiles (glans missilis plumbea) were used during Roman and pre-Roman times. The combatants had the habit of scratching various inscriptions into the lead. This is what an Etruscan marksman had written on his projectile (CII 2635):

strevc, a truly remarkable inscription. In Slovene **strevc** means marksman, written *strevec* or *strelec; strevc* in dialect.

The Veneti had the same habit as the Etruscans; that is, to sign their names on projectiles. A Venetic soldier had scratched on his projectile in Venetic letters: **oterg** (Museo di Ascoli); another, likewise in Venetic letters: **otergie** (Museo naz. Romano). These puzzling inscriptions which have for a long time troubled Venetologists were found in Ascoli Piceno. How did they get there? The puzzle is solved by the third projectile, on which we see in Latin letters the following: **optergn** (see photograph).

Museo Nazionale Romano and Museo di Ascoli

After comparing the inscriptions, it was determined that they originated from a Venetic village called **Opitergium** (present-day Oderzo, east of Piave) during the Roman times. The soldiers from this town **Oterg** (*Otrg, Otržje*) participated in the battle for Ascoli which was besieged for several months in the year 89 B.C. They were certainly Roman soldiers, though still aware of the fact that they were Veneti, otherwise they would not have written on their projectiles the name **Oterg** in Venetic letters. However, another man who did not consider himself any longer strictly Venetic, wrote in Latin letters **optergn** (Slov. *obtržen*); i.e., the projectile was **optrg**enized or from Obterg indicating special danger.

The next word is **tergovla,** from which the name of the city of **Tergolape** derives. This means that the shop (Slov. *trgovina)* of the Venetic *tergitio—* merchant—was called **tergovla.** Even Pellegrini and Prosdocimi include it among the toponyms derived from **terg.** This city is not in Northern Italy, rather in Noricum where Venetic people lived and still live to this day. Where does the name Tergolape come from? The answer is found in the Russian word **torgovlja—** trade. Because the word has many archaisms it is more than likely that the Veneti who had maintained trade relations with the East Slavs had used the same word for the store. The place where the **tergovle** was carried out was called *Tergolavlje*, from which *Tergolabje* is derived, pronounced by foreigners as *Tergolape*. Two more words not yet discussed which were most probably used by the **tergitio**— merchant—are **otergec**—small market—and **tergit** or **tergti** and **tregti**; i.e., to carry on trade.

Former **Oterg** was Latinized to Opitergium. Apparently the Latin name did not take hold since the Veneti continued to use **Oterg**. The city gradually declined and fell into ruin. From Oterg came its diminutive, **Otergec**—small market; from this later developed in Italian dialect the name **Oderzo**.

That the above interpretations of **tergitio**—merchant, **tergil**—raded, are correct is shown also by Albanian lexicon. The presumed ancestors of modern Albanians, the Illyrians, adopted this word as well as a series of other words from the Venetic language.

How did I reach this conclusion?

The Illyrians, about whom the discussion has not yet ended, were neighbours of the Veneti. Many words which Illyrians borrowed from the Veneti are today found in the Albanian vocabulary. Among them is the word **tregti.** However, words with the infinitive ending in -**ti**, -**t** are Slavic (Venetic) loanwords as far as can be determined.

Let us look at some examples: **Veselit**—to eat one's fill, to be content with the food, Slov. *veseliti se*—to rejoice, to be happy; **zbavit**—to entertain, Slov. *zabavati*—to entertain; **zbyth**—to pound together, Slov. *zbiti*—to pound or nail together; *vozit*—to travel by boat, Slov. *voziti*—to travel or carry things in a wagon or other conveyance; **vertit**—to turn, Slov. *vrteti*—to turn.

Also **tregti**—to trade—is to be included among these words. These examples are enough to disprove the theory that **Tergeste** is not of Slavic origin (G. Meyer, H. Krahe, etc.).

Now let us leave our friend from the **Oterg**, who was proud that he was a **tergitio**—merchant, and **tergil**—traded, in his **tergovla**—store, in the **tergeste**—market place who knows for how many years, and ask ourselves this question: Can the view maintaining that the Illyrians gave the name to Trieste, *Tergeste* (Old Slav. *tržište*) really be defended when we know the Slovenes gave the closely related name Tržič to a nearby town? Whoever can still believe the theory about the Illyrian connection to the name *Tergeste,* even after the discovery of the Slovene morphology on the Venetic grammar tablets, might as well believe it. However, I am convinced that the majority of readers cannot rely on this theory because it contradicts common sense, especially if we take into consideration the fact that the adjective **tržaški** and the phrase **na Tržaškem** clearly indicate that the language of the inhabitants was closely linked to the meaning of the name **Tergeste.** How would this have been possible had there not been a continuity in the population and its language?

If the above examined words were Illyrian, then we could justifiably wonder what kind of language Illyrian was. At that time it must have been related to the Venetic to the point that it could not very well be distinguished from it. Some experts are of the opinion that it would be hard to draw a line between them. Could Illyrian therefore have been an ancient Slavic language? If not, then it must have been under strong influence from the Venetic language. This is clearly shown by the fact that there are many Slavic words in the Albanian language. Among them are words which must have entered the Albanian language only later, after the arrival of the South Slavs on the Balkan peninsula.

Along the Venetic Roads
The Taverns

Everything indicates that there were taverns or inns along the Venetic roads, perhaps even with better service than today when one considers the inscriptions on various wine jugs. For example, one of these is called **La situla di vale (Ca 4)** because it was found by accident as the ground was being excavated for the foundation of a new house in the easternmost region of the Cadore Valley on the upper Piave. This jug is characterized by its playful quality. On the inside of its mouth, overlaid with lead, the innkeeper had scratched letters with such a strong hand that they are still visible today even though the vessel is damaged.

My transcription follows the official method of reading the various letters, except for the punctation which I have left out (as discussed earlier) because Vetter's explanation is not convincing to me and thus unacceptable. The inscription reads:

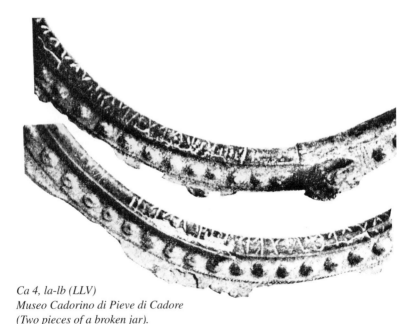

Ca 4, la-lb (LLV)
Museo Cadorino di Pieve di Cadore
(Two pieces of a broken jar).

EJ, K GOLTANOS DO TOLO, UDERAJ KANJEJ!

In Slovene: Ej, ko goltneš do tu-le, udari po konjih!

In English: Hey, if you drink to here (i.e., to this mark on the jug), hit the horses— move on!

I believe the translation is in harmony with the original which was dedicated to drinking, and also with the location of the inscription, namely at the top. If the guest had it filled to the top and drank it down, he would have had enough, for the jug is just a little less than thirty centimetres high and the rim a little more than two centimetres.

The explanation of the words is not difficult since they are already commonly known in the Slovene language:

Ej—hey; Slov. *ej.*

k—when, as soon as; Slov. *ko.*

goltanos—you drink down; Slov. *goltneš, pogoltneš*; compare Slov. *goltanec*—throat, gullet.

do tolo—up to here, this far; Slov. *do tu le;* compare Ukrainian *dotola* and *dotol.* Variations in Slovene dialects are also close to Venetic, and even the literary form *tod.*

uderaj—hit, whip; Slov. *udari*, also *uderi, udri* and *udrihaj* (from *uderihaj).* The general opinion of scholars indicates the root **der-**.

kanjej—horses; Slov. *konje*; Russ. *konjej* (pronounced *kanjej).* The genitive pl. is here instead of the acc., as is the case in archaic Slovene.

So let us again read the translation of this inscription on the bronze jug found beside this Venetic road:

English: Hey! If you drink to here, hit the horses! Enough! Ride on!

And how do other Venetologists read it? As usual they see only names: **eik Goltanos doto Louderai kanei.**

The difference is in the division of the words which are written without spacing. Based on the Slovene language there arises from my grouping of the letters a sentence full of meaning which is also in harmony with the circumstance.

There is something tragic about the discussions by western scholars of the inscriptions whose language is unintelligible to them. The inscriptions are invaluable statements telling us something about Europe of the first millennium B.C.—invaluable but only if one can read them, which is impossible without the knowledge of Slavic languages and even the Slovene dialects as well as the Chakavian and Kajkavian dialects.

There still remains one unexamined possibility. The interjection **Ej, k (o)** could be interpreted in another way; it could be read as **Jeik** meaning *jezdec—* rider. Much has already been written about the etymology of the Slovene word *jezdec,* and I believe that Bezlaj came the closest to the matter by deriving it from the Old Slavic *e(d)ti.* This could explain both forms, the Slovene *jezdec* and the Venetic **jeik.** We can approximate this word with the Czech *jeti—*to ride. Also the Lithuanian *eiti—*to go—is interesting in regard to **jeik** *jezdec—*rider. In this case it would be possible to read **d oto lo,** Slov. *da od tu—*yes, you drink from it. **Oto,** Old Slav. *otь—*from.

Every researcher and translator of ancient texts often finds himself in a similar dilemma. When I was translating Shakespeare, there were times when all commentaries left me in a lurch, each maintaining its own version; finally, I had to decide in favour of one of the possibilities. In the present case, the support for interpreting **jeik** as *jezdec—*rider—is the word **kanjej** *konji—*horses—and they belong together. Supporting **Ej k** is the playfulness of the inscription.

The Drunkard from Kanjevoj

Now let us move on! Where else but in the direction of *Kanjevoj* or Canevoi di Cadola, as it is called today. It unintentionally reminds us of the previous inscription.

This village is on the upper Piave River. There they found a bucket **(Bl 1)** 30cm in height, made of lead. Next to it was its handle, 15cm wide. Unfortunately the bucket and the handle have since been lost; but we know how they looked and what was written on them, thanks to the canon Lucio Doglioni, from Belluno. He is the author of several studies about the inscriptions of Belluno. The Etruscologist, Elia Lattes, was the first to publish the drawing of this bucket. Here is the picture of the drawing:

The drawing of the bucket from Canevoi di Cadola (Lattes, "RIL" 1901)

I have seen such concave buckets during my childhood, on the dusty road near Celje, Slovenia; the wagon drivers used them for watering their horses. The road is still there, black-topped now, but the wagons with the buckets hanging on them are gone. Is it possible that the shape of those buckets had originated in the distant past? Why not?

And what causes me to conclude that this bucket is related to the driver and the wagon? Have only a little patience, it will become clear.

As the reader has probably noticed, this inscription is different from the others in that the letters are already Latin but the language is still Venetic. The inscription must have come about in a time when the Veneti had abandoned their customs, among them also the alphabet, but still maintained their language. Nevertheless, they wrote the Latin letters somewhat differently from the Romans; dots were also used in their own way, not to separate words, but rather to separate syntax and phrases. It was similar to how simple people write today, sometimes dividing a word into two parts, and sometimes connecting two or even three words together.

The inscription on the bucket from Canevoi di Cadola is in this respect certainly very close to Latin. As concerns the dots, however, they are still not in agreement with Latin writing.

With the appropriate separation of the words, my transcription reads as follows:

(J)ENO NI ON TEJ APPIOJ, SE L(E) BOJ, SE L(E) BOJ AN DETIC OBO S(E) (J)EKUPETARIS.

In Slovene: In zdaj ob tej opit, se le boj se le boj, celo otrok ob sebi
           peketaje okrog.
In English: And now, drunken as you are, have fear, have fear even of children
           around you, when you travel.

As can be seen, I have added the letters **e** and **j** in parentheses according to my reading.

The translation of the individual words is very interesting:

jeno—and; Slov. arch. *ino,* in the 18th century also *jenoj* (Pohlin) and *jenu* (Gutsman). Another possibility is *E noni on tej,* which would be equal to the Russ. dial. *noni, nyne*—now.

ni—now; OCS *nyne,* Pol. *ninie,* Alb. *ni,* Latv. *nu,* Lith. *nunc.* This word is repeated often with this meaning.

on—near; Slov. *ob, o,* from Old Slavic **o,** *o-dolь, o-vozь.*

tej—this one, on this one; Slov. *tej*.

appioj—inebriated, drunk; Slov. *opit, pijan*. Compare OCS *blagoj, lokavoj, svetoj*. Thus, OCS could be *opioj*, here because of the vowel change, *appioj*, perhaps imp. **apioi!**—drunk!

se le boj—have fear; Slov. *se le boj*. It is repeated because it is a playful warning. Even today something like this is said.

an—also, and; arch. Slov. is the same, *an*, e.g.: *s teboj an s tvojim bratom*...(Pleteršnik).

detic—small child; Slov. *detec*, gen. pl. from *detece*.

obo s—about oneself; Slov. *ob sebi*, OCS *obъ;* Russ. *obo s*, the **s** is a shortened **se**.

jekupetaris—travelling by horse. The meaning of this word can be established by a whole series of inscriptions where it is found. Since the drivers would gladly have lightened their spirits with a few drops of wine, one had to entreat them to be careful. Such a warning, rather comic, is written on our bucket telling the driver who would drink too much that he must be cautious even of small children when trotting around in such a condition.

In order to understand the relationship of the word **jekupetaris** through the Slovene language we must analyze the word itself, which apparently consists of two parts. First there is **jek** and then **kopitat(i)**. Both words are Slovene. We have already discussed **jek** in connection with the alphabetic tablets as we looked at the verb **jekat**. *Kopitati,* which can be found in the Slovene dictionary, means to kick or dig with the hoof; *kopito*—hoof; Russ. *kopitetъ*—to wildly ride a horse. The Slovene language not only has *kopitati* but also *peketati,* which has a similar meaning. Everything indicates that the Veneti had allowed these two words to merge into one (haplology). The modern Slovene word *peketat(i)* was perhaps at one time *jekupetat(i)*. The same Venetic form **(j)epetari(i)** (LLV, vol. 1, 654), or **jeppetaris** (LLV, Pa 3 bis) also originates from this.

Jekupetarit, would mean in its parts: *jek, jekoma*—with resonance, *kopitati*—to trot, to travel by horse.

Some of my companions on this Venetic expedition will want to ask me which grammatical form **jekupetaris** actually belongs to, because it sounds somewhat foreign to the Slovene language. This is correct: considerable time has passed since it has been in daily use. However, with the help of Old Slavic morphology the explanation is not difficult. It is the perfective participle of the verb **(j)ekupetarit,** Old Slavic *jekupetar's;* it could, however, also be the participle of the reflexive verb *jekuptar'i s(e).*

And what have Venetologists discovered on this container which is nothing more than a water bucket? Again they discovered only names.

Those experts maintain that this is an epitaph since in the inscription, as also on epitaphs, there appears the phrase *ekupetaris*. Yet, as we were able to see, *jekupetaris* means the same as riding a horse. Therefore, it is not unusual that this word was sometimes written on objects other than the gravestones; e.g., on a bucket where the meaning did not exactly have anything to do with the transporting of someone into the next world, but rather about a simple ride in this world.

The assumption that the inscription on this bucket is an epitaph is refuted not only by the unambiguous Slavic text, but also by another very interesting and significant fact. The already mentioned canon, Lucio Doglioni (died 1804), whose credibility noone doubts, writes that besides this bucket, which he himself found, "there are two more, similar ones, found near a mill in Cimolaisu in Friuli, both having the same inscription as I had seen on mine. I am certain of this." (...avevano pure ambedue la stessa iscrizione che vedessi nella mia. Di ciò io sono certo... Pellegrini-Prosdocimi, *La lingua venetica*, page 450). The canon's report causes great problems for Venetologists because it is difficult to explain—if it were an epitaph for a certain person, why had it been written in three copies and found in various places?

For us it is proof that it was not an epitaph, but rather a humorous epigram warning drinking friends not to drink wine out of the water bucket as they travelled through the world.

Perhaps one can maintain that **jenoni** is contained in the **jeno ni,** and that it is a name, and that it is also found in other inscriptions. We could maybe consider Jenoni as a name in the sense that Johnny is a name for any man or boy (slang) but certainly nothing more than that.

If we take another look at the inscription and read it out loud, we will find that it has a rhythm. And if we write the silent vowel ə in the last two verses with **e,** as the Slovenes still do today *(e.g., m*ə*gla—megla),* we will see four verses:

Jeno ni on tej apijoj,
Se le boj, se le boj
An detic obo s(e)
Jekupetari s(e).

Still another corroborating fact tells me that I have correctly interpreted the inscription.

If we take a look at the photo, we see that there is another short inscription on the handle. It is composed of four letters: **PIIS.** As we have already seen, the Veneti used these two lines **II** as **je** (yè) or **ije** (iyè), comp. **otergje.** As they began to adopt the Latin writing, they were still using (as is fairly obvious from a number of indicators) the Latin **II** as **ije.** If we read the **PIIS** in this way, we have the word **pijes** or **pijeś,** since Latin did not have a š sound. If we look on page 36, we find the following: **pijež,** m., a playful word for a drunkard. Hence the inscription on the water bucket. It was addressed to just such a *pijež.*

Marriage Triangle

No less amusing is the inscription on a stone (**Pa 6**) found in Padova as late as 1962.

As one can see, the script is no longer Venetic; the inscription belongs to the Roman period. Italian Venetologists would like to know whether this is the last example of a dying tradition or the beginning of a new tradition. If we take a look at the text the answer is not difficult. This stele is not a gravestone but rather a parody recalling the fall of the Venetic culture.

Venetologists themselves have said that there is no example to be found among the ancient Venetic relics where the driver takes two people at the same time into the next world.

Then what is this relief supposed to represent?

The man who is driving the wagon is not in a good mood, though he is strong and confident. Standing next to the heavy, obstinate woman with a familiar headgear, is obviously the husband in this triangle which is portrayed with ingenious realism.

The inscription surrounding the relief is, as already mentioned, written in Latin script with some Venetic features, above all the dots next to the two letters with which the dots almost always appear in the Venetic writing. With **I,** only one, as is usually the case in the Venetic script, and **F.** The F is not an f but rather a **v.** Another Venetic or Etruscan characteristic must still be mentioned; that is, the omission of the vowels. In our example the vowel between **S** and **T** in *Fostiale* was not written. And here the **S** is a **z** (non-existent in Latin).

With this in mind, we can read the inscription as follows:

NIMU VOZTIALE GALLEN
Njemu je vozataj samec.

JAJE JEKUPETARS
Jojme popotujoč.

In Slovene: Njegov voznik je samec. Gorje potovati na istem vozu.
In English: His driver is a bachelor. Woe is me, travelling in the same chariot.

Pa 6 (LLV)
Museo Civico di Padova

And now the individual words:

nimu—to him; in Slov. *njemu.*

voztjale—the driver; Slov. *voznik;* arch. *vozataj* is certainly the derivative of *vozetjale;* OCS *vozataj;* Alb. *vostar*—the helmsman, and *vozetarem*—to row is a loanword from Venetic. Concerning the ending **e** comp. Slov. *otroče, niče* etc.

gallen—unmarried person; Slov. *samski;* arch. Slov. *golen*—immature (Pleteršnik); Czech *holomek*—unmarried young man.

jaje—oh dear, Slov. *jojme.*

jekupetars—"jekopitarec" (see earlier explanation).

The relief itself corresponds very well with the inscription. Was it a journey into the next world or even hell? Or is it merely a comic representation? Or perhaps only a satire on feminine faithfulness.

Was this stone at one time on a grave? In contrast to Christian customs, the Etruscans depicted and included frivolous objects on their graves and in their tombs. Had perhaps the Veneti, their contemporaries and neighbours, also done the same, at least later during the Roman period?

The Traveller with a Duck

In the inscription of this stele it is obvious that the θ (O with a dot in the middle) is the letter for **t** as in Greek usage θ (theta); this is demonstrated by **ekupetaris,** already familiar to us, where the θ is a **t** and not an **o.** Consequently, it is not very consistent of LLV to transcribe the first θ as **o.**

Furthermore, I must draw your attention to two more items in regard to this inscription. The first item is the second letter from the left as seen in the photo. The LLV maintains that this is a **k;** however, I am of the same opinion as H. Rix, who says that this is not a **k** but a ⟩ which can be nothing but a **c** when viewed in the direction of writing, from right to left. The second item is the questionable **i** before ekupetaris, which is to be represented by a part of an intersected line. I do not think there is a letter **i** there.

With these corrections my transcription of the epigram is as follows:

PUPTNEI JEGO RACO JEKUPETARIS
Popotniku njega raco za na pot.

In English: To the traveller his duck for the journey.

Pa 1 (LLV)
Museo Civico di Padova

puptnei, read **pupǝtnei**—to the traveller; Slov. *popotnemu, popotniku.* Similar to the Carinthian words *dedej, čarodej, sedej, mislej,* and perhaps *vidij, videj* in the grammar tablets from Ateste.

jego—his; Slov. *njega, njegovo.* This word is often repeated with this meaning in many Venetic texts.

raco—duck; Slov. *raca* (acc. *raco);* Friulian *razze;* Triestian, Venetian, augmentative *razzone;* Alb. *rosé.* If an **i** is also to be read here, we have a somewhat different sentence: To the traveller **also** his duck for the journey. The Slovene and generally Slavic **i**—also.

Comparing our translation to what we see on the stele from the 5th century B.C., we have a convincing confirmation. The matron is giving the man, who is holding a staff in his hand, a duck to take along with him on his journey. ("La donna tiene un volatile sulla mano destra..."comments LLV). In contrast to the previous discussion of parody in similar Venetic representations, not to mention the warning to the travelling *"pijež"*—drunkard—we have here perhaps a real gravestone, except that it is rather different from the majority of steles where we usually see portrayals of battle scenes.

A Song at the Loom

Very interesting and entertaining is the inscription on a clay loom weight. Venetologists do not know where to begin with this inscription, and yet, on the basis of the Ateste grammar tablets, it is totally understandable.

On this weight made of clay there are two beautiful verses:

O PATE SPEŠ TI TIKOAOJI
Ob petlji speš (hitiš) ti tkaje,

LOV(E) KLOKATU, APAJA VOLTIOM
lové klekelj, pojoč vitezom.

In contemporary Slovene: Sedé ob petljah speš ti tkaje,
Klekelj lovè, viteze opevajoč.
In English: Between the warps with speedy bobbins,
You weave, and sing your songs of heroes.

a pate—by loop; Slov. *petlja*—loop, *o petlji, predivu;* making loops of woof or weft around the warp; *petlja* is also the basic unit in knitting. Russ. *patla*—a

Es 119 (LLV)
Museo Nazionale Atestino
(First half of the inscription on the loom weight).

quantity of fibre, such as wool, ready for spinning, OCS *pęti*—to stretch.

speš—you hurry; Slov. *speš, hitiš;* Russ. *spešitь*—to make haste.

ti—you; Slov. *ti.*

tikoaoji—weaving; Slov. *tkaje.* Compare OCS *tъkati, istykati,* similar to Slov. *vtikati;* Czech *tkviti.*

lov(e)—pursuing; Slov. *lové;* OCS participle *lovъ.*

klokatu—bobbin; Slov. *klekelj;* Russ. *klok*—a clump of hair or wool.

apaja—singing; Slov. *opevaje,* Slov. dial. possibly also *opojaje* from *pojati.* Apaja is an adverb, comp. Russ. adverb *govorja,* Slov. *govoré.* Perhaps **a paja**—with song.

voltiom—to the princes, heroes, knights; Slov. *vitezom, volotom, vlatom.* This word is very common in the Venetic inscriptions. Voltiom is obviously dat. pl. from *volt(io).* Old Russ. *volotъ*—knight.

255

Es 119 (LLV)
Museo Nationale Atestino
*(Second half of the inscription on
the loom weight).*

Another translation of these charming verses:

Sedé ob petljah speš ti tkaje,
Klekelj lové, viteze opevajoč.

The weft you swiftly pass through warp,
And sing of gallant knights and heroes.

A Troublesome Diphthong

In reference to an article in *Naši razgledi* (Ljubljana), by Fritz Freiherr Lochner von Hüttenbach (Graz), I would again like to explain a pair of Venetic words which apparently give said author unnecessary difficulty.

Although I have explained the word **ego** several times, I will do it once more. The key to understanding this word is that it must be identified with the Slavic *jego* (yego)—his—and not with the Latin *ego*. I have shown that the Venetic **e** at the beginning of a word was pronounced as **je** (ye, as in yes) similar to Russian. Only this interpretation of the pronoun **jego,** written **ego,** gives us a comprehensible and logical reading of the Venetic inscriptions where this pronoun appears. *In all of the almost twenty inscriptions where this pronoun is found, there is not a single case where one could say that it does not mean the same as in Old Slavic.*

Following this **ego** is usually the word **voltii** (also **volti**), which is the dative of *voltie,* an aristocratic title or simply a word indicating respect derived from the Proto-Slavic *voltu.* Miklošič reconstructed the Old Slavic *vlatъ* as Old Russian *volotъ,* and in dialect *volotъ* or *bogatyrъ*—an aristocrat, a knight; Slov. *vitez.* **Jego voltii** thus means the same as "his lordship", in Slov. *njega veličju;* in dialect: *jega veličji,* and in some dialects even *jego veličji.*

The archaic Slovene word *boljci,* sing. *boljec*—a distinguished person—must also be mentioned here. Since both words *bolji* and *velik* are related, as is evident from the Russ. *boljšoj,* Slov. *velik*—big, great—it is quite possible to see in *boljci* the ancient **volti.**

From among the inscriptions which begin in this manner, I will here only mention one example, **Es 1:**

JEGO VOLTI GENEI VESONI

In Slovene: Njega veličja ženi Vesoni.
In English: To his lordship's wife Vesona.

Or as an anagram:

JEGO VOLTI GENEI VE SONI

In Slovene: Njega veličja ženi v snu.
In English: To his lordship's wife in (eternal) sleep.

genei—compare the Old Ind. *gena,* and the Old Prussian (Baltic) *genna.* (In Baltic as in Venetic there was not yet a palatal change from **g** to **ž,** or **k** to **č**). Comp. also Lat. *genus.*

ve soni—in sleep; Slov. *v snu,* arch. *v sni;* Old Ch. Slavic (OCS) *sъnъ;* Russ. *son,* Bulg. *son.* **ve**—in, Slov. *v;* (OCS) *vъ.*

Vesoni is the dative of Vesona (Vesna—a feminine name).

The diphthong **oi** is also giving Lochner von Hüttenbach difficulties. Since he does not have any conception of the Slavic morphology as it is revealed in the Ateste grammar tablets, he explains several linguistic characteristics found in the Venetic inscriptions all too simply. The diphthong **oi** is a good example. Al-

Es 1 (LLV)

though the Venetologists are aware of the reconstructions based on the Indo-European languages, they are profoundly convinced that in all **oi**'s we have to see the final syllable of the dative singular. They do not consider that it could be something else; e.g., nom. sing. of adjectives, of which there are many. I will mention here two of these adjectives which are very troublesome to Venetologists: **vivoi** and **murtuvoi.** Without a fine sense or feeling for the living language, as Venetic at one time was, they see two datives in these two words ending with **oi.** Even Lochner von Hüttenbach states that these two syntagmas are unclear to him. In reality these are not only syntagmas, but also sentences,—actually a saying—carved into the stone found in 1971 not far from Monselice, and kept in the Museo Civico of Padova (Lejeune). The saying is as follows:

VIVOI OLIIAL KVE MURTUVOI ATISTEIT

In Slovene: Za živa alil je, ko mrtev bo, se otešča.
In English: While alive he sang intoxicated, dead, he will be sober.

vivoi read **bivoj**—live, living. At first glance the word seems similar to the Latin *vivus.* Its roots, however, lie in the present participle *biv*, in OCS *byvъ.* With regard to the **v** one must take into account the betatism (v-b), and perhaps also the Oscan (Old Italic dial.) *bivus.*

oliial—had sung intoxicated; this word is of onomatopoeic origin and is still found today in several languages. In Slovene *aliti, alim*—to sing poorly, as those who are intoxicated, is significant. A second and just as acceptable interpretation would be: *olijal, oloval,* in modern Slovene *se nalival*—to pour oneself (full of wine).

kve—who; from **k** and **ve**; comp. the Istrian *ni-kvi, ne-kvi*—it is not known whether this is a haplology (contraction) of *nikakav, nekakav.* Concerning the particle **ve,** there are the examples: *do ve*—up to here, *tam ve*—there; however also *ve* as a pleonasm: *ve je prišel, ve je to le malo,* etc. (Plet., Mikl.). It is not impossible that one must read **k be** Slov. *kdor že bil*—whoever was, since **be** is an aorist, OCS *kъby.* Another possible interpretation, no less appropriate, is **k ve** Slov. *kot mi*—like us, in Old Russ. *vě* is the same as *mi*—we; the same is true in Old Czech.

murtuvoi—dead; Slov. *mrtev;* OCS *mrъtvъ;* Russ. *mertvyj.* Everything indicates that in Venetic the accent fell on the last syllable and as a result the silent vowel changed into an **o.** Compare OCS *svetoj, blagoj.* A similar thing happens in the Russ. adjectives of the type *živoj.* Accordingly, *murtuvoi* must be written as *murtuvoj* in that the two short **u**'s are similar in sound to the silent vowels.

atisteit—to regain one's senses, to be in one's right mind again; OCS *tъštъ*; Slov. *tešč*—empty stomach, sober, as for example: *na tešče, o(d)teščati se*—to eat something on an empty stomach; figuratively, to regain one's strength. **Atisteit** is 3rd per. sing., which would be OCS *otъstitъ* or *otъštajitъ*.

The saying is rhythmic; actually there are two verses which are to be read in the following way:

Bivoj alial kve,
murtuvoj atišteit.

As one can see I have written the **oi** as **oj**. Why? Because in Venetic the forms of the determinative adjective ending in -**i** had already changed into -**oj**. Earlier I mentioned several examples where the -**oj** is a suffix denoting the imperative. For example: **torjoj, stijoj, uherijoj.** Here the imperative is very clear since we are dealing with an incantation. In the same inscription (uherijoj) -**oi** is a suffix of the substantive **renioj**—at a trot. Just such a suffix was used consistently by the Slovene poet Anton Aškerc: ljubicoj, rokoj, not to imitate Russian, but simply following the dialect of his native region (Rimske toplice).

We can see that the arguments of those who would like to find traces of Latin in the Venetic language are very weak.

Trotting into the Next World

The following three steles **Pa 2, 3, 3 bis** represent battle scenes, as is evident from the drawings in *La lingua venetica* (LLV). Let us begin by looking at the inscription that surrounds the chariot with the two warriors wildly driving a pair of horses.

But first a short comment. I am not at all in agreement with Pellegrini and Prosdocimi, who omitted the initial letter .|. , while at the same time making allowance for an equally poorly visible .|. at the end of the right vertical line for the **i** symbol.

To the text of **Pa 2** I have added two silent vowels and two vowels, since the Veneti had sometimes omitted them, probably because of a lack of space, which is what we find in Latin inscriptions. I have also included accents which show

Pa 2 (LLV)
Museo Civico di Padova

that we are dealing with a verse that has a very lively rhythm imitating the wild movements of the horse-drawn vehicle. Here is the inscription:

I POLETÉI, VÉ, I GENÓJ
KARÁ N MENIJÓJ
JÉKUPETARÍ JEGO!

In Slovene: In poletevši, (ali) opletajoč z bičem, daj, i žêni,
    na bitko misli zdaj, v peketu dirjajoč!
In English: And rushing in, (or) brandishing the whip, simply drive him,
    think of the battle now, in this galloping race!

i poleti—and rushing in; Slov. *in poletevši, polet*—flight; OCS part. pres. act., e.g., *živei, gredei* (Leskin, para. 70). It could also be **pletei;** Slov. *opletajoč z bičem*—brandishing the whip; Russ. *plet*—braided whip.
ve—only, simply; Slov. dial. *ve je prišel, ve je to le malo* (Plet.); Russ. *ved*—surely, indeed.
genoj—drive; imperative. Slov. *žêni,* from *gnati, goniti.*
kara—battle; OCS *kara*—battle; Old Persian *kara*—war; Slov. *karati*—to *reprove;* common Slavic *karati se*—to quarrel.
n—now; reduction from **na** or **ni;** Slov. Rezian dial. *nja;* OCS *nynê*; Lith. *nu;* Alb. *ni;* Pol. *ninie.*
menijoj—think; imperative. Slov. *meni, misli;* OCS *mniti;* Russ. *мнить.* *Menijoj kara*—think of the battle, with the object in the 2nd case.
jekupetaris—(See previous explanation).
jego—him; accusative, i.e., the horse. Slov. *njega;* Slov. dial. *jega* (without **n,** as in Russ. *jego*).

We can say again that this inscription corresponds well with the theme of the representation and with what our Slovene dialects and the Slavic languages in general have to offer. It corresponds also very well with the language of other inscriptions.

The next inscription **(Pa 3)** probably originated from the same workshop. In view of the similarity of its pictorial elements according to archaeologists, it is closely related to the Alpine situlas **(Vače, Magdalenska gora).** This inscription is similar to the previous one; partly obliterated and marked by time, yet in good enough condition (except for the first letters) to be read in the photo published by the LLV. But we must keep in mind that in the photo the **f** (i.e., **v**) before **ugerijoj** is clearly visible, whereas the authors of the LLV did not notice it while in the museum (often the case due to poor lighting).

Pa 3 (LLV)
Museo Civico di Padova

...TER O PEJA VUGERIJOJ JEKUPETARIS JEGO

In Slovene: Ter pojoč vegaj se s konjem peketajoč.

In English: And singing, sway (with the chariot) as you ride along.

ter—and; Slov. *ter,* dial. *te;* Serbo-Cr. *te.*

o peja—singing, with song; Slov. *ob petju*—with song, *peti*—to sing, *poje*—sings, (3rd person), Bulg. *peja.* Slov. dial. also *pojati*—to sing. Comp. Greek *paian;* in Slovene littoral *pèan*—a happy thanksgiving song, comp. also **apaja (Es 119).**

vugerijoj—to sway; to dodder; Slov. *vegati se*. The iterative would be *vegariti*. A remnant of this form is probably *vegrast, vegast* (Plet.). It might also be *vugeriti*—before the change of **g** to **z**—to travel by horse and buggy or wagon, wagoning.

In any case, what is expressed by the epigraph is communicated to us by the relief itself. Whereas in the previous depiction the warriors are riding wildly, we cannot say the same for these two, although they are probably sitting in the chariot. Unfortunately the one on the right is—at least in the photo—almost totally obliterated, yet if one of them is singing it is certainly this one. The other one sitting next to him has already sung. He is napping; one can see on his face the bliss of someone who has had much to drink.

The third representation **(Pa 3 bis LLV)** is again war related. In contrast to the other two, here is only one warrior-rider with a spear in his hand who is galloping on the horse. Since the letters carved into the stone are undamaged, the inscription is clearly visible.

Pa 3 bis (LLV)
Museo Civico di
Padova

The inscription reads:

JÉNO GENÉIE NETIJÓJ
JEPPETARÍS A LVÁ RENIJOJ

In arch. Slovene: Ino goneje podnetuj, peketare kot lev rene.
In Slovene: Spodneti ga da bo drvel, peketajoč v boj kot lev!
In English: Drive him so he will gallop into battle, racing like a lion.

jeno—and; Slov. *in, ino.*
geneie—driving; Slov. *ženoč, geno(č), genoč.* Comp. OCS *živeie,* also the Old Slavic *živei, edei* (Leskin para. 70), which we found in **poletei (Pa 2).** The difference is justified by the fact that this work did not come from the same workshop as the other two.
netijoj—rouse; imperative. Slov. *neti!* literally to inflame, to rouse, to stir up.
jeppetaris—see jekupetaris.
a lva renijoj—running like a lion; Slov. *ob levjem teku;* **a lva** is my transcription of **a lba** since I suspect betatism here. However, one could also read **a lba renijoj**—running head-on; OCS *lьbъ*—forehead, face of a mountain.
renijoj—in the running, in the race; Slov. arch. and in dial. *renem, reni,* instead of *ženem* from *gnati*—to drive; even today in Bela Krajina and Brkini: *renem krave*—I am driving the cows. Noteworthy is also the German *rennen*—to run, to race.

As I looked at the reliefs, whether they were those depicting scenes of daily life or those representing warriors, I resisted the thought that these were all gravestones. Yet I cannot overlook the fact that the majority of them were found where urns and other objects placed in graves have also been found.

Consequently, it is possible to think that the riders and warriors in the chariots represent the journey into the world beyond, as the archaeologists maintain.

Warning on a Stone from Mt. Pore

A unique stone **(Ag 1),** with an inscription which had earlier been considered as Rhaeto-Etruscan, has been found on the western slope of Monte Pore (2405m), some 300m below its summit, along the ancient road from Colle Santa Lucia to Andrazzo (Andraž), where there must have been a border at one time. Monte Pore is to the west of upper Piave, not far from Cortina.

Before we begin with the explanation of the text, it should be mentioned that this road is still known as *Strada dei morč* (of Friulian origin acc. to LLV) or the "Road of the Dead", since the dead used to be carried on it from Santa Lucia to Andrazzo. There might have been some other reason too. According to the inscription on the stone, the road had always been dangerous. We will soon see why.

As in most other cases, the Venetologists have tried to discover names in the inscription on this stone, although it could not possibly be a tombstone, as it was found in an area where no burial ground had ever existed. There is no wonder that no names were established as they have no place in an inscription on a boundary stone.

This inscription serves, among other things, as a proof that dots and lines were primarily employed as decorations marking less visible letters and filling blank spaces and it reads as follows:

DO STIDZEI MEZDEI VOLAICOS
Slovene: ob tej stezi meje kdorkoli že

NISI CARIKOJ
(če) ni uradnik (pisar)

S NICO KA PROZOR
se uniči kot ogleduh.

In English: Along this border path whoever
(if) he is not an official (a scribe) shall be destroyed as a spy.

Next to the inscription there is a number, probably an official codex number; on the other side there are markings of a sort of crossroads or boundary direction, which can only represent a sign for a border crossing.

Let me repeat the inscription in an understandable translation: Anybody found on this border path, except authorized officials, shall be destroyed as a spy.

do—at, to, by; Slov. *pri, do.*

stidzei—path; Slov. *steza;* OCS *stьza* (reconstruction by Mikl.). In this case the letter Ⱶ is the same as Ӿ (acc. to LLV). As presented in the chapter on alphabet, this grapheme which is used as **s** and **z** in Etruscan, is pronounced as a dental **d**. Sometimes however, it was also used for **d'** or **dz**. This could serve as a reasonable explanation why the letter representing **z** for Etruscans was chosen to represent **d**; this was done simply because **d** is similar to **dz**.

Ag 1 (LLV)
Museo Civico di Belluno

mezdei—borders; Slov. *meje;* OCS *mežda.* Together: **do stidzei mezdei**—
do steze meje, ob mejni stezi (at the border path).

volaicos—anybody; compare Slovakian *volakdo, vol'akto* (acc. to Mikl. from
vola and *kdo*). *Vola* is Slovene *volja*—will, who, or the original imperative *volaj-
kdo.* The Venetic **volaicos** is composed in the same way. Instead of *kdo* or *kto*—
who, there is (as often found in inscriptions) **cos** or **kos.** Polish *ktoś,* Ger.
irgendwer—anybody (Mikl.). Lithuanian *kás*—who.

267

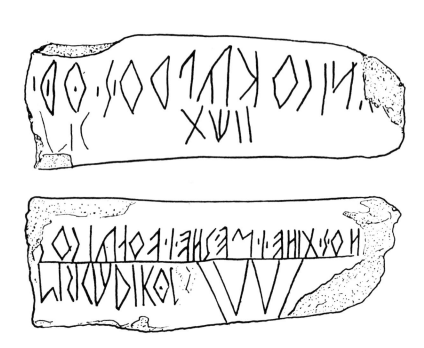

Ag 1 (LLV)

nisi—if he is not; it is possible that the inscription had already been influenced by the Latin language, as it probably stems from a later period: *nisi*—unless.

carikoj—an official, a scribe; read *čarikoj*. Literally Slov. *črkar,* somebody who can write letters, who knows the letters (Slov. *črke*). This same word appears again in the inscription **Ca 64: zdeili cariko,** *zadelj čark, s čarno močjo*—with magic power. As known from other cases, the ending **o** is silent.

s nico—is to be destroyed, shall be destroyed; Slov. *se (u)niči; ničiti, uničiti*—to destroy. Slovakian *ničit,* the verb comes from *nič*—nothing. We must also take into account the Latin *neco*—I execute. As **nico** is the third person singular, the infinitive (Venetic) would be **nicot,** and with the prefix *za zanikat(i)*—to deny.

ka—as; Slov. *kot,* east Styria, *ka*.

prozor—a spy; from *prozirati*—scan, monitor; Serbo-Cr. *prozor*—window, or a loophole in a sentry tower.

As it was mortally dangerous to linger in the border area near the top of Mt.

Pore, we should not wonder why the former *steza meje*—border path—is called Strada dei morč.

Judging from the inscription and its contents, the border station must have been somewhere on the pass where the stone was found. This supposition is more than confirmed by the word **čarnica**—border post (Šavli: *Veneti naši davni predniki* p. 48; *Unsere Vorfahren die Veneter* p. 48; I VENETI progenitori dell'uomo europeo p. 54). In the Etymological Dictionary by Skok we find the interesting word *carina* which is not the same as the younger "carina"—customs office, from *car*—tsar, but rather a "fence around the village communal land"; also south Ukrainian *carina*—an enclosed pasture. In its meaning it clearly coincides with *čarnica*—frontier post. In both cases it represents something which divides two properties. In addition, *carina* is a very frequent toponym. The origin of the word is unknown. Considering the Venetic inscriptions, we can now assume that it is of the same origin as **carikoj** (čarikoj), Slov. *črkar*—an official, a scribe—a derivative from *čarka, čara* Slov. *črka, čar*—a letter, magic. The borders of village land must have been likewise marked with such "črke" or "čarke", whereas on the state borders there were "čarnice".

It is of vital importance to know that Old Slavic *čъrto, čersti,* meant the same as to cut. It seems that markings *črteži* on the limits of pastures were cut either in the trees or on the stones. Bezlaj is of the opinion that Slov. *črta*—line—is a borrowed word; however, he contradicts himself saying that "*smreke črtati*"—to mark the spruce trees—is certainly Slovene.

Inscription on a Natural Stone

A stone of volcanic origin **(Pa 13),** which has not been shaped or worked, was discovered at a place where no burial grounds are indicated. The circumstances of discovery are also unknown. In spite of the fact that Venetologists do not think so, this stone is one of the most interesting grave markers. The shapes of the letters indicate that the inscription is of a later origin; the shape of the letter **N** is already more Latin than Venetic.

Although the second line is partially blurred, I presume we have here the inscription for a child.

Transcribed from the standpoint of the Proto-Slavic Venetic language it reads as follows:

I TO ZGEN TE I
In tu sežgan ter tudi

Pa 13 (LLV),
Museo Civico di Padova

MOLO N(V)ENNONI S
z molitvijo nedolžni si

TO SVE N NONI S
tu k svoji zdaj materi si

VIREM AIS
vložen. Gorje!

In modern Slovene: In tu sežgan z molitvijo, nedolžni,
si tu k svoji materi pokopan. Gorje!
In English: And here, cremated with prayers, innocent one, here you are buried
with your mother. Alas!

This inscription is engraved into a simple natural stone and is dedicated to an
innocent child. Let us take a look at the individual words:
i to—and here; Slov. *in tu;* Rezian dialect *i to.*
zgen—burnt; Slov. *žgan, sežgan;* OCS *žganъ.*
te—and; Slov. *ter, in;* OCS *te,* same in Serbo-Cr. and also in Slov. Styrian
dial.

270

i—also; Slov. *tudi, i*. Perhaps it should be pronouced **tei,** which is very close to Slov. *ter.*

molo—with a prayer; Slov. *z molitvijo;* Bulg. *molja.* Compare Slov. *molè*— praying, *molek*—prayer beads; in addition: *mol, mola, mel*—rock debris. Slov. *moliti*—to pray, and *mleti*—to grind (grain)—are probably of the same origin, although they differ in meaning; Rezian dial. *molo*—stone.

n(v)ennoni—innocent; Slov. *nedolžni*; Serbo-Cr. *nevini.* Acc. to Skok derived from *ne-vinьпь*. This adjective is rooted in OCS *vina*—cause, guilt—which disappeared due to homonymy with Slov. *vino, vinjen, nevinjen*—wine, intoxicated, sober. Venetic **n(v)ennoni, nevennoni** differs from *nevinьпь* in spelling only and confirms Skok's theory.

s—2nd per. verb to be; Slov. *si*; **i** has been dropped, as it often happens in Slov. as well, example: *kje s'pa doma?*—where is your home?.

sve—their own; Slov. *svoji;* compare *svekrovь* (mother-in-law). Skok places it among the words derived from Slov. *svoj*—its own (reflexive pronoun), see **svekrim (Ca 2).**

n—now; **noni**—mother. Serbo-Cr. and Kashubian (Slovincian) *nana, nena, nenia*—mother; Slov. *nona*— auntie, grandmother; Russ. *njanja* —wet-nurse.

s—Slov. *si* (see above).

virem—inserted, given over to the grave.

ais—alas; Slov. *ajs*—exclamation on touching something hot. It may be onomatopoeic or an interjection from Old Slavic participle *ois, oiti*—calling, yelling.

It is remarkable that the four lines of this inscription are verses. The reader soon acquires the feeling of rhythm when they are correctly accentuated:

I to žgen to i
molo, nvénnoní, s,
to sve ń noni s
virem, aís.

The question arises whether there is a possibility that **Nvennoni** is a name derived from **nevin**, much as its female form is Nevenka. In this case we would have discovered, apart from **Vessoni** (dative of Vesona, Vesna) and **Bojos**, another of the rare names in inscriptions which are usually of a general nature and include no names.

And another thing: I spell **N(v)ennoni** as it is spelled in the LLV (La lingua venetica), where **v** is presumed in the second place. Although the inscription is blurred there, I think it has been spelled correctly.

Inscriptions on Writing Tools

At the beginning of my paper, I spoke about my discovery on the lower part of the Ateste grammar tablets. I mentioned that besides this section which is dedicated to the morphology, that is, to the forms of the verb **jekat** and its derivatives, there is the middle part which deals with the phonetics and the alphabet; there is also a third, upper part.

Even a superficial look at the tablets will make every Slovene notice the word **vdan**—offering. It is found on three tablets and on three writing styles, what Venetologists call "chiodi"—nails—six times in all **(Es 27, 31, 32, 47, 51, 62)**. The styles were used by the Veneti at the holy places to write on wax plates, as was done by Greeks and Etruscans and later by the Romans.

Did **vdan** then mean the same as it does in modern Slovene? No, it did not. **Vdan** is not a word but a syntagma—**v dan**. The word **dan** is OCS *danь*, Slov. *davek, dajatev*; Pleteršnik interprets *dan,* (f.) as tribute, e.g., *dani,* subject to tribute. We also find the word *dan* in the dictionary of literary Slovene language, only here it is masculine in gender. For example, *plačevati danj*—to pay taxes; or *volk je pobiral krvavi dan*—the wolf collected a bloody tribute.

This **dan** was a **dan** of a special kind. If one looks into Miklošič's etymological dictionary one will find the explanation that the ancient Slavs had used it, that is, *danь,* as *vozarina*—freight toll, freightage.

But one may ask: to whom did the Veneti pay this *dan* or freightage or tribute? I found the answer right on the grammar tablets where the following is written: **V dan donasto... Reitijaj**. In Slovene: *V dan donašam... Reitiji*—I bring as tribute... to Reitija.

I will deal with the word **donasto** in detail later on. Here I will just say that I translated it with the Slovene *donešeno*, since I assume that it is related to *donesti*—to bring to. However, it is likely that **donasto** is the 1st person of **donast** Slov. *donest-i,* dial. *donost*—to bring to. But what kind of freightage? Could it not be for the journey into the life beyond?

Everything indicates that this is the case, as I examined all the inscriptions where **v dan** was found. Wherever it is written it is clear and undeniably **v dan donasto...Reitijaj**. Between the phrases **v dan donasto** and **Reitijaj** there appear different additions (mostly adverbial phrases) in the inscriptions **Es 27, 31, 32, 47, 51,** and **62**. Only one is partly effaced; the others are well enough preserved to be read without difficulty. All these inscriptions tell us that **dan** had been used on a special occasion, when the soul of the deceased who was cremated was setting out on its last journey. I would like to cite some of these examples without including too many annotations:

V DAN DONASTO VIREM A ISTNA REITIJAJ
V dan donašam vložen v isteje, Reitiji.

In English: As tribute to Reitija I bring it, and deposit it into the fire.

virem—placed or deposited into; Slov. *vložen*; Russ. *veratь*—to place into; in Slov. it is preserved in *zavirati, vereje, veriga,* etc.

a—in; Slov. *v;* OCS *a—(o)* (Mikl.).

istna—The Slovene *isteje* (also *istanje* or *mesteje*) means the vaulted masonry opening to the oven or the fireplace. Had the Veneti used special ovens for cremation? Did they call the opening through which they placed the corpse *istna*? It is not impossible that *istna* meant the same as the Greek *estia*—fireplace, or even funerary pyre.

Another very similar inscription is **(Es 47):**

V DAN VIUGIA URKLEI NA REITIJAJ DONASTO
V dan uoglené uречeni zdaj Reitiji donašam.

In modern Slovene: V dar za upepeljenca in svečenika zdaj Reitiji donašam.
In English: As tribute for the cremated and the officiant I bring now to Reitija.

There are two words here which require a special explanation:

viugia—charring, carbonizing; Slov. arch. *ouglene*. Of course today it is a seldom used word, since in the forests there are ever fewer charcoal kilns (*oglenica*) where wood is carbonized. The equivalent of **viugiat** in standard Slovene is *ogleniti* (to carbonize). But the forms in the dialects have remained much closer to the original. Since I spent my childhood years near Celje, *uogi* (also *uojgi*) is very familiar to me; Chakavian dialect *ugao*. *Viugia* does not mean fire since it is not a noun but a participle from *viugiat*—to char, to cremate. In our case it certainly has nothing to do with wood, but rather with the body of the deceased.

urklej—officiant; this **ur(e)klej** corresponds to the Slovene *urekli*. The fact that the **e** is missing is not uncommon in the Slavic languages, e.g.; Old Russ. *rkli,* also Slov. dial. (Rezian) *rkao.* As an incantation was intoned over the deceased (against the evil spirits that would be encountered in the life beyond) and the cremation took place, the tribute to the goddess (or god?) **Reitija** would be presented as an offering for the journey into her/his kingdom; the gender of Reitija is uncertain as that of justice. For that is what Reitija seems to signify: *pravični, urejajoči*—righteous, originator of order. Compare the Slovene word *red, redi*—order, may well be related to Reitija.

na—now; comp. Es 62.

Es 62 (LLV)

The third inscription **(ES 62)**, which is also found on a writing style (chiodo), is as follows:

V DAN KANTAMN K NA DONASTO REITIJAJ

In Slovene: V dan ob pokopu minulega doneseno Reitiji
In English: Offered as tribute to Reitija at the funeral.

kantamn—interred; Slov. *pokopan;* OCS *sъkatati*—to inter, from *konta* (Mikl.); Bulg. *kъtam*—to preserve; Slov. *konta*—rocky hollow, chasm.

k—who; Slov. *ki.*

na sometimes only **n**—now; OCS *nyne*; in Slovene Rezian dialect *nja.*

From these inscriptions engraved on bronze grammar tablets or on the sides of the bronze "chiodi" (styles), one can thus determine on which occasions **dan** was paid and also to whom; not, however, why this tribute called **dan** was paid. Almost certainly it was offered to Reitija in order to be protected while on the journey into the world beyond, where *tenje* and *bukke* were lurking. This tribute, of course, was not given directly into the hands of Reitija, but into the hands of her earthly representatives—the Venetic *verkoni* or *urklej* (priests).

On what do I base this conclusion?

In one of the inscriptions **(Es 43)**, found on a writing style of the Ateste writing school near the Reitija's shrine, we read:

274

MEGO DO TO VERKON DARNANJE R(E)KA IM

In Slovene: Dal (zato) da bi svečenik darovanje izrekel jim.

In English: My contribution, so that the priest will intone the ritual for them.

Es 43 (LLV)

mego—mine, my; Slov. *mojega. Brižinski Spomeniki*—The Freising Manu-scripts, have the same form: **mego** instead of *mojego, mojega.* **Mego** is treated as a nominative in Venetic. Comp. Ital. *me;* French *moi.* **Mego** means I.

do—gave; comp. Chakavian *do, dálo, dâlo,* (Jurišić, *Rječnik govora otoka Vrgade*/Dictionary of the Dialect of Vrgada Island).

to—this; Slov. *to.*

mego doto—my contribution, I give. Compare the Slov. genitive in syntagmas like these: *mojega medu, mojega sadu*—of my honey, of my fruit—instead of: *moj med, moj sad*—my honey, my fruit.

verkon—religious, priest; Russ. *vrakun* means babbler. However, this word first acquired a negative meaning only after the introduction of Christianity. It can also be found in Holder's *Altkeltischer Sprachschatz:* **Vercondáridubnó-s.** In view of the fact that the writing is Latin, this word could possibly be made up of *verkon* and *daritovanj;* Slov. *daritev* (offering). In Venetic this would be **daritovn** or even **daritobn. Vercondáridubnó-s** was "... the first priest of the altar of Rome and August in Lyon," which is what it says in the text. The Venetic (Slavic) sounding word should not surprise us since the relationship between the Veneti and the Gauls has not yet been researched. Furthermore, another name is very significant and informative, namely, **vercombogi-o** and also **vercombogi(us)** on one of the Latin monuments in Noricum (Carantania). In this arrangement the Slovene word *božji* (divine) is easily recognizable: **verkon bogio,** Slov. *vrakun božji*—priest of god.

darnanje—sacrificing; Slov. *darovanje.* As opposed to *daritev*—sacrifice—**darnanje** is the act of sacrificing. In Slovene there is also the word *darina*—offering, presentation, e.g.; *na darino se shajati* (Plet.)—a gathering for present-ing gifts, as a bridal shower. Therefore, **darnanje** could be derived from *darinanje.*

But the words *darnati, darinati* have, like the word **verkon,** undergone a change in meaning: Slov. *darnati*—to suck intensely (Plet.).

r(e)ka—to command, name, call; aorist from *r(e)kat* with the optative meaning; Slov. *rekati.* Comp. *ur(e)klej.*

The family of the deceased gave the offering to the **verkon** (priest) so that through the pronouncement **(r(e)ka)** of the sacrifice **(darnanje)** solicitation would be made to Reitija for the safest possible journey into the next world.

On another surface of the same writing tool there is one more inscription:

MEGO DOTO VIOUGONTA MOLDNAJE B(E)

Slovene: Dal to, da upepeljena ob molitvi bi bila.
English: Have given this, so that during the prayer she would be cremated.

viougonta—cremated, burned, from **viougonot**; Latv. *ugonot*—to illuminate. There will be more later about this very significant Venetic derivative from **ogon** or **ougon.**

moldnaje—praying, at prayer, from *moldnat*; Slov. *moliti;* Old Slovene has three roots: *mold-, modl-,* and *mol-* (Mikl.). Compare: *moledvati, moledva.*

Someone had to pay for the deceased to be cremated (viougonta) during the prayer, *"moledvaje"* as one would say in Slovene, although today this word has another meaning, namely to ask for kindness. The deceased could probably also have been cremated without prayer, but that would have been to their disadvantage regarding the journey into the afterlife.

The Veneti had, according to my interpretation of the inscriptions, a primordial fear (one could maybe call it an Indo-European fear) not of dying, but of not dying, and also of the life after death and the journey from one to the other where they would finally be united with the spirit of Life.

And what was this destination called? This too is evident from the inscriptions, and namely from those of the Ateste writing school where there were not only writers and **vetiji**—learned men, but also poets. They were indeed poets of a very special kind, for they could write the most concentrated verses possible.

But before I say anything more about this, it would be useful if I say something about the religion of the Veneti.

One could say that the religion of the Veneti, in view of their belief in **Reitija** and **Trumužijad,** was highly spiritual. In Slovene one could say Tromožjad or Tromožje (literally three men, triad, trinity). **Trumužijad** is probably the Venetic synonym for god, after whom our Mt. Triglav (three headed) was named and which has from time immemorial been in people's imagination associated with the divine. A representation of the Tromožjad with three heads is still preserved in the museum in Cadore where long ago one could have been healed with the miraculous water at the Tromužijad.

One of the most common details of ornamentation or symbol of the ancient Lusatian culture and the Urnfield culture is the circle with a dot in the middle. These eyelets or dots within circles must certainly be very old because they were found on the ancient idols in the Banat region, Yugoslavia. They are considered to be older than those of Mesopotamia. We also find them on the wagons in which the seemingly happy deceased travel into the world beyond. There are many of these symbols not only on the horse-drawn wagons but also on other articles. The experts who would like to blur the connection between the southern and northern Veneti as much as possible are embarrassed by these circles. For this reason they interpret them as ornamentation from an earlier period which has nothing to do with the Lusatian eyelets (LLV). I, however, believe that this is not the case, and that these circles with the dot in the middle not only embellish the carriages and other articles but are also a symbol that is basic to the Venetic religion. Perhaps this circled dot even represents what we today still call paradise. We received this word from the Greeks, and they got it from Persia: **Pairidaeza.** This compound word actually means an enclosed **circular area** or space. According to Petar Skok, it must have given rise to the shaping of the conception about "the island of the souls"; that is, about heaven.

Is this symbol then a recollection of earlier times when the Indo-European community was still unified? Did the journey of the Venetic souls into the next world and through it have something in common with soul migration of Hinduism? This migration in the after-life is deeply imbedded in the consciousness of the Hindus. Is it perhaps connected to the message of the Venetic **verkoni?**

The Oval Porphyry Stones

Pa 7. From the book *I Veneti antichi*. The reader will notice that the **o**'s in this inscription are round. The **o**'s with a dot in the middle are **th** and should be read as **t**. This inscription is an anagram:

1. HOSTI KA BO STO U PEJO
gostov ko bo sto jih zapoje,

2. HO STIHA BO STO UP JEJO
ko utihne, tedaj sto upov z njo.

Pa 7 (from the book I Veneti antichi*)*

In modern Slovene: Gostje ko bodo, jih bo sto pelo,
ko stihne (za vedno), sto upov z njo.
In English: One hundred guests, when present, will sing;
when song is over (forever), a hundred hopes depart with it.

1. Individual words:

hosti—guests; Slov. *gostov*, genitive. Compare suffix **i** in "ljudi"—people (gen.).

ka—when; Slov. *ko.*

bo—will; Slov. *bo.*

sto—hundred; Slov. *sto.*

u—in; Slov. *v.*

u pejo—into a song; Slov. *v pesem*; Bulg. *peja*; Slov. *pojem*—I sing. **Sto u pejo**—Slov. *sto u pesem (se jih spusti)*—a hundred of them join song.

2. Individual words:

ho—when; Slov. *ko.*

stiha—becomes silent, dies; Slov. *utihne, umre.*

bo—then; OCS *bo* (Leskin).

sto—hundred; Slov. *sto.*

up—hopes; Slov. *upov.*

jejo—with her; Slov. *z njo*; OCS *jejo.*

The inscription **(Pa 9),** from the book *I Veneti antichi*, is on a porphyry stone and is one of the most beautiful anagrams:

Pa 9 (from the book I Veneti antichi)

PIL POTEI KU PRI KONIOJ
plamen poti, ko pri koncu (je)

PIL POTEI KUPRIK ONIOJ
Plamen poti gomila umiri (naj).

In modern Slovene: Plamen življenske poti, ko pri koncu je, naj ga gomila umiri.
In English: The flame of life's path, when at the end,
     let it be calmed by the grave.

pil—a flame, ardour, glow; Slov. *plamen, vnema, žar*. Known in almost all the Slavic languages except in modern Slovene, unless the word *pal*—fire in the trees—is of the same origin. Miklošič thinks that Slov. *pepel*—ashes, arch. *popel,* comes from *po-pel*; i.e., what is left over after "pel." Russ. *pyl* means dust and flame.

potei—a way, a path; Slov. *poti*; OCS *poti*; Russ. *putej* gen. pl.—ways.

kuprik—a mound; Ukrainian (Gogolj) *kuprik*; Lith. *kaupra*—a small hill, *kauparas*—a mound.

onioj—calm down! Slov. *umiri!* Russ. *unyti*—to calm down; OCS *unyti.*

If the first **pil** is interpreted as Slov. *prah*—dust, ashes—we get a different anagram:

The dust of life's path, when at the end,
the flame of path is calmed by the grave.

Recently there was discovered another oval stone (**Pa 33**) which bears a very short inscription:

LANTEJ A KLON
pahnjen v grob

In English: Pushed into the grave.

What led to this conclusion?

The Slovene language had numerous archaisms which have already disappeared; however, some had survived as late as to the time of Pleteršnik and in some dialects to this day. One of these Old Slovene words is *laniti—to rush, kaj si lanil name?* (Plet.)—why did you rush at me? Its meaning closely corresponds to our inscription and is still in use in Vrsno near Kobarid; i.e., in the west, where the Venetic elements have been best preserved.

And how was he pushed—*lanit, lanjen*—into the "klon" (grave)? He was pushed with **lanitei**—connected to Slov. *lanča*—lance. Dalmatin and Megiser still write it in that way (lanzha). The word exists in other Slavic languages and in Italian. It is based on Latin *lancea* (Bezlaj), which is supposedly of Celtic or Illyrian origin (Bezlaj). I am not sure about this. If we consider the meaning *laniti*—to push—it is almost certainly of Venetic origin. It is probably related to Rezian *lanita* as well. *Lanita* means a jaw, a jaw of a beast that rushes at the enemy—semantically close to the spear.

klon—a grave; Slov. *uklon* actually means submission (Plet.) The original meaning can be detected in the Baltic words; e.g. Lithuan. *klono* (bottom). Thus the words present a double meaning:

LANTEJ A KLON
sunjen v uklon

LANTEJ A KLON
s sulico v grob (klon)

In English: Pushed into submission and
with a spear into the grave.

The Upper Part of the Ateste Tablets

I said that some inscriptions are not continuous sentences and only represent individual syntagmas, phrases, or instructive sayings. It seems that the inscription (**Es 23**) on one of the quite well preserved tablets is of the latter type. The already familiar initial phrase **mego donasto** is followed by a folk saying:

E B VIABAITSA PORAJ
in čeprav je bil vojvoda mogočen,

OPIOS ROBOS
opivši se, je robavs.

In English: Even though the chieftain was great,
when drunk he becomes a brute.

Here is the translation of the individual words:
e—and; Slov. *in*. Here, the teacher had the opportunity to explain that there were two **e**'s, and that the other is pronounced **je**, Slov. *je*; OCS *je* or *jestъ*.

b—would be; Slov. *bi*. In vernacular this *bi* is reduced to *b'*, same in Russian *by*, *b*. It is an Old Slavic conditional; OCS *bi* (maybe from aorist *by*), which has been retained in Serbo-Cr.

viabaitsa—duke; Slov. *vojvoda*. Slov. *vojevit* (Plet.)—combative; it is a word composed of two elements found in Lith. *viti*—bekriegen, nachjagen (Mikl.), to conquer, to pursue; Latv. *vaijat*, means the same; it is also in Slovene *vojd*—a village head; Beloruss. *vojt*; Russ. *voit*. The headman of the village was at the same time also its military leader; *viabait* (voje-vojd); when the ending was lengthened—**viabaitsá,** the leader must have had a higher rank. We should note in this connection the Slov. surnames Vratuša, Gostiša, or *zastavonoša*—standard bearer, and Russ. *junoša*—a boy. Under the influence of Miklošič, the official etymology to this day derives the old word *vojd* for a village headman, from *advocatus* which is supposed to have been transferred through Pol. *vojt* into other Slavic languages and even into Lithuanian; this explanation is certainly daring. If the Germans once wanted to prove at any price that their *der Vogt*—village head— did not originate in Slavic (since in this case they would be forced to admit that some of their own village order came from the Slavs), one would think that such misconstructions in favour of former Germanic masters should have been revised long ago. But that is not the case. Vasmer still explains *viot* from *advocatus, vocatus*.

poraj—powerful, mighty; OCS *pora*—force, power. Comp. the word **porai**—getting drunk, in **(Es 45)**, Slov. *opivši se.*

opio—aorist of **opit**. Comp. **appioj**—intoxicated (Slov. *opit)* on the vessel from Beluna **Bl 1.**

robos—a crude, uncivilized man; the meaning is the same, although it must have been even more pejorative in the Venetic language. Comp. OCS *robъ* a slave, a commoner; Serbo-Cr. *robijaž* a prisoner on forced labour; Slov. *robiti, robim, zarobiti jih, robantiti, zarobljenec*—to bluster, to speak rudely, a crude person.

In a single sentence the teacher had quite a number of words at his disposal to explain the grammar.

The official Venetologists read the above inscription as a dedication: e b (?) Fabaits a Porai op iorobos...The possibility that this inscription is an anagram, or a word play with a double meaning, should not be excluded.

It is easy to imagine the astonishment of the pupils when the teacher presented both meanings of the anagram to them. The anagrams should be looked for in frequently repeated phrases and syntagmas. I do not preclude the possibility of a hidden meaning in a number of inscriptions.

In the next inscription after the usual **mego donasto,** we find the following words which can be read with the slightest change, as follows:

E B VIABAIT ŠA PO RAJ
in bil vojvoda, šel v raj,

O PJO ROBOS
ali zaničevan rob

In English: Were he a chieftain or a despised slave, he should go to heaven.

The individual words:

e—and, is; Slov. *in, je.*

viabait—a duke or a chieftain; Slov. *vojvoda.*

ša—went; Slov. *šel*; OCS *šьlъ;* Rezian *šal;* Korčula Island *oša.*

po raj—into heaven; Slov. *v raj*; comp. Slov. *po raju*—into the heaven, *po konja*—(to get, fetch) the horse, *po gobe*—(to go) mushroom picking etc. The Slov. **raj**—heaven, is usually **rej** in the inscriptions. Comp. Sanskr. *raj*—to reign, meaning to wear a garment of light, glory; *raj*—shining, glowing.

o—or; Slov. *ali*, may be related to Italian *o* (or); Dalmatin wrote *oli.*

pjo—despised. Acc. to Mikl. the word might be related to Slov. *pljuvati*—to

282

spit—before it was substituted by *plju, pju* . The Venetic **pjo** confirms that.
robos—slave; Slov. *rob, suženj.*

Tablet **Es 25:**

ME GO DONASTO
jaz ga darujem

MEGO DONASTO
jaz darujem (donašam)

FOLTII OMNO SI
duše se spominjajoč

I UVANT ŽAR JUN S
in ventan žar mlad ta (je)

ŠAJNATEI REJTIAI
Šajnati Rejtiji

In English: I present it, I present (bring), remembering the soul, and this
destroyed young [life in full] glow—to the shining Rejtija.

The individual words:
me—I; Slov. *jaz.*
go—him; Slov. *ga* (jego).
mego—I; Slov. *jaz.* The teacher had a chance to explain that **mego** has a
shorter form **me** as well, as is the case with **jego (go).**
donasto—I bring, I present, presented; Slov. *prinašam, donašam v dar, dani.*

Here we have as it seems, only a few syntagmas and phrases in connection
with cremating and burial, that is, placement of urns into the grave. These
syntagmas and phrases served as a teaching aid with syntax and stylistics, and at
the same time the samples as in **Es 24** served as models for inscriptions on urns
and gravestones where they often appear. An example is inscribed on the gravestone **Es 4, Es 28: voltiji omnoj.** This can be an imperative (or an adverbial
adjective: compare OCS *svetoj, živoj, blagoj, svetyj* etc.) of **omnit,** whereas, on
our tablet, **omno si,** omne se—remembering—is a participle. It could be a noun
as well: **omnoj** (a monument), **Es 4.**

These syntagmas appear in large numbers in the inscriptions. Most often they
are in the imperative form: **omnoj!**

And now the remaining words:

voltiji—soul; Slov. *duše, duši.* More about it in notes to **Es 34** and **Es 44: op voltijo leno**—in a gentle mood; Slov. *blage volje.* From the OCS point of view, it may be a genitive, or it could possibly be a dative when interpreted in archaic Slovene dative: *poletje, poletji*—summer, *vpitje, vpitji*—shouting, *pitje, pitji*—drinking, or *poletju* which corresponds to **voltijo,** as **u** often represents **o.**

omno si—remembering; Slov. *spominjajoč se.* Compare Slov. *omeniti*—to mention, and *opomniti*—to remind.

si—are; Slov. *si, se* (reflexive pronoun); it may belong to the participle in front of it: **omnos,** spelled **omnosi;** compare Old Slavic participle hvalj-ьs (see Leskin para. 69).

i—and; Slov. *in.*

uvant, pronounce **uvanət**—bewitched, destroyed; Slov. *ventan, urečen, uničen.* See notes to **Es 24,** where it is without **u**—**vant.** I will add only this: the Slov. *ventan* (vanət) could be explained as east Styrian *fanta*—revenge. In addition *fantati*—to revenge, *fentati se*—to kill oneself. In modern language, Slov. *fentati* or *ventati*—*uničiti, pokončati*—to destroy; Slov. *kar prime v roko, vse fenta*—he ruins everything he touches; or the second meaning, to kill, to murder: *fental ga bom*—I will kill him—is still generally used in the lower strata of vernacular; it is still a fully living word (see Bezlaj, ESSJ). As already mentioned above, the meaning of Slov. *ventati*—*fentati*—to destroy, *ventan, fentan* destroyed—is essential if we are to understand this part of the inscription: the meaning of **uvant** in this case was not only "bewitched" but also *ventan*—destroyed; namely, **žar jun**—a young [life in full] glow.

žar—glow; slov. *žar*; the word *žar, žareti*—glow, to glow, beam, is known in all Slavic and Baltic languages in similar usage.

jun—young; Slov. *mlad*; Slov. *jun, juna, junec*—young ox, *junak*—a hero; Russ. *junyj*—youthful; Latin *iunior*—younger; the goddess Juno; Ger. *jung*—young.

s—this; Slov. *ta;* OCS *sъ;* Rezian *sej.*

With the help of various dialects the inscription would read in archaic Slovene: **i ventan žar jun sej.** Here I would like to add that although **i,** Slov. *in*—and—is a conjunction in the western Croatian dialect, Pleteršnik's Dictionary specifies it as a Slovene word as well. *Sej,* OCS *sъ,* is a demonstrative pronoun from Rezija Valley. Slov. *ta*—this (Plet). The rapport between the ancient Venetic and surviving Slovene dialects is quite remarkable.

This is also shown by the last ritual syntagma: **ŠAJNATEJ REJTIAI**—Slov. *sijajni Rejtiji*—to the splendid, shining Rejtija.

Šajnat, is a Slovene word. It appears in Pleteršnik side by side with *šajnast*—

shining, splendid—without a note specifying German origin. I think Pleteršnik came to the correct conclusion stating that it is derived from OCS *sijati, sij, sijajnat*—to shine, shine, shining, later *šajnat* (due to haplology). It is also in accord with the Rezian, e.g., *tu w ti hudej, w ti dobrej*—in bad and in good. The suffix is fully retained in Russian: *horošej* (dat. and loc.).

Tablet **Es 28** differs from others. It carries only three lines of the text in boustrophedon, whereas the lower part (**jekat**), the consonant forms and lowest line are missing. Judging from the similarity of letters to those on the tablet **Es 29** the experts place it in a later period. This is only a difficult to check supposition, as the letters on the tablet are badly blurred.

To some extent they are blurred on this tablet as well, but not enough to prevent us from reading the inscription quite reliably on the basis of technical reconstruction according to LLV.

MEGO LEME TOR VIRAT JEREI DONASTO
Jaz gline prah pokopat duhovnu donašam.

BOIJOS VOLTIJI OMNOJ
Bojos, duše se spominjajoč

Translation: I bring the dust of clay (ashes of the deceased) to the priest, so that he may place them into the grave. Bojos, remembering the soul.

mego—I; Slov. *jaz.*

leme—clay; Slov. *gline* (gen.).

tor—dust, ashes; Slov. *prah, pepel.*

virat—insert, place; Slov. *vložiti*; Russ. *viratь* Ger. *einstecken*—insert, (Mikl.); compare **virem**—Slov. *vložen* m., **virema**—Slov. *vložena* f.—deposited with the urn into the grave.

jerei—to the priest; Slov. *duhovnu;* Slovene dialect from Venetian Slovenia (Friuli, Italy) *jer*—a priest, also *jerej, jerov.* Rezian dialect *joerö.* More in the notes to **Ca 24.**

donasto—I bring, I give; Slov. *donašam, dajem.*

Bojos—Bojos, one of the few names; however, the appearance of a personal name is not strange in this tablet, as it was not used for didactic purposes. It is possible that it should be read: **bojo s**—Slov. *boje se*—being afraid, as "in the fear of God" in which case **bojo** would be a participle; **s**—Slov. *se* (reflexive pronoun).

voltiji—soul; Slov. *duše* pl.—**voltije.**

omnoj—remembering; Slov. *spominjajoči se,* literally, *omenjajoči.*

This inscription was from a later period and was probably not a votive inscription; the subject 3rd person singular is missing. It must have been instead a request to the priest stating that he should bury the remains of the relative in accordance with the religious custom. The Venetologists presumed that this inscription meant Lat. *fraterei,* because of the digraph **vj** which they pronounce as **f.** At the most, instead of *fraterei* we could make allowances for *viraterei* or *braterei;* OCS *bratrь*—brother.

As all the words except **virat** (infinitive of **virem**) occur repeatedly, their detailed interpretation was omitted here. The reader will find them in other inscriptions.

This inscription is subject to the same general remark I made elsewhere; i.e., that other interpretations are possible. But I am confident the result of my analysis is not far from the original meaning.

Es 32:

V DAN DONASTO VIREMA VIREM
V danj donašam vložena, vložen (v grob)

A ISTNA REJTIJAJ
v istanje Rejtiji

OP VOLTIJO LENO
ob volji blagi (blagovoljno)

In English: As an offering I bring her, him, placed into the fire,
  to Rejtija in a gentle mood (willingly).

As I already mentioned in my earlier explanation of the third part of the grammar tablets, there are no continuous and concluded sentences, but mainly individual syntagmas and phrases used as examples in teaching of grammar (syntax, phraseology). They are found in various inscriptions on urns and gravestones. In this way they served two purposes: pedagogical and magical-ritualistic.

As we are already familiar with some of the words, I will not repeat the explanation here.

dan—freightage, or road toll; Slov. *danj, dajatev za prevoz, prevoznina;* OCS *danь.*

virema, virem—deposited, placed, f. m.; Slov. *vložena, vložen.*

In the opinion of Venetologists who read **vi (vj)** as **f** and **virem** as **frem,**

Frema Fremaistna is, according to their reading, a name. I would not object, had this inscription not been on a grammar tablet. What would the names be doing there? Were they votive objects? Perhaps they were during the period of general decline of the Venetic culture when the customs and the language had already been forgotten. But these tablets originate from the period when the Venetic culture was at its highest point. This is evident from the careful form of letters and the general appearance of the tablet. Apart from that, a few too many of these "frems" appear in various Venetic inscriptions—no less than **nineteen.** The rule of probability alone says that it could not be a name. This explanation is further confirmed by the fact that **virem** and its derivatives are to be found on urns and other objects as well.

The male form of the participle **virem** on this tablet is complemented by its female form: **virema.** This is an interesting proof that in the upper part of the tablets morphological and other peculiarities were often stressed, although phraseology prevailed.

a istna—through the vaulted opening of an oven or fireplace; Slov. *v isteje;* Slovene language has also *m'steje, istanje, istnice.* The latter form is vital for our research as it indicates existence of an older *istne, istna.*

virema virem a istna—placed f., placed m., through the opening into the fire; Slov. *vložena, vložen v isteje.* For the second meaning: Slov. *istna, istina*— truth, see chapter "Anagrams".

a—in; Slov. *v.*

op voltijo leno—of a gentle mood; Slov. *ob blagi volji;* Latin *libens merito.* This Latin saying known from votive inscriptions (see **Es 44**), is written down in the present grammar tablet as well. For this reason, I think, we can assume that the meaning is equal to that of **op voltijo leno,** a phrase, connected to **donasto.**

op—at, by; Slov. *ob, o, pri;* OCS *obъ;* it occurs in all Slavic languages. Veneti wrote it phonetically.

voltijo—will, soul; Slov. *volji, duši;* dative of *volэtije.* In modern Slov. the verb *voliti (komu kaj)*—to will, to bequeath—and the noun *volilo*—a will—are still in use, whereas *voltje* has been completely lost. I myself could not trace it in our dictionaries. Nevertheless, another form with the same meaning has been retained and that is *volitev* Plet., *zadnja volitev*—the last will. And this is precisely the meaning it has in our present formula. As already seen, **volэtije**—Slov. *volja,* also denoted a soul.

leno—gentle; Slov. *blago, milo;* Slov. *leno*—lazy, has a different meaning although the word is the same. Semantically equal to Latin *lenis*—gentle, and Latvian *lens*—gentle. The difference is very interesting and strange: to a Slovene, a gentle man was first of all a lazy man.

In its form the word was already Old Slavic but it still retained its Baltic meaning. It should be noted that the above **op...leno** is a locative (dative) masc. of **len.** It represents a nominal declension of adjectives which disappeared in the Slovene language. It still exists in Serbo-Cr.: *dobar čovjek, dobra čovjeka, dobru čovjeku*—a good man, of a good man, to a good man. Due to the transition of **u** into **o,** we could read it as **op volətiju lenu.** This is a frequent case in Upper Carniola where **u** is often converted into **o;** instead of *mojemu staremu bratu,* we have *mojmo starmo brato*—to my old brother. In my opinion this **o** is a remnant of old Venetic and not, as maintained by our dialectologists, a later development in the form of transformation of **u** into **o** (in declension of pronouns and adjectives).

The above inscription is not a unified and concluded sentence; it contains individual syntagmas and phrases employed by scribe-priests for teaching their pupils, endeavouring to explain some rules of grammar at the same time. These phrases have been selected in such a way that they can be combined into sentences for exercise in syntax and stylistics.

The tablets also carry individual interconnected phrases and syntagmas, for example **Es 24:**

MEGO DONASTO VANT S MOLDONKEO
Jaz darujem ventan z molitvijo

KARAN MN S REJTIJAI
na zle duhove misleč, Rejtiji

In English: I bring (a tribute), protected by prayer,
mindful of evil spirits, to Rejtija.

vant pronounce **vanət**—protected by a spell against evil spirits; Slov. *ventan.* Srednja vas in Bohinj—Tine Logar, *Slovene Dialects: "Samo tistmo, k je znou ventat, niso (coprnce) mogle do živga"*—only him who knew how to cast spells, were they (the witches) unable to get at. In Lower Carniola *vanati se*—protect oneself; in White Carniola *vanati*—to cheat; in east Styria *vancati*—divining for water; *vančati*—to pay attention (Plet.). All these words have semantic connection with the Venetic word occurring ten times in various inscriptions; always with the same meaning—to cast out a spell. For example **vanti conis**—protected (against evil) you end; Slov. *ventan končaš,* **Es XLI** (already in Latin).

s moldonkeo—with a prayer; arch. Slov. *moledva, moledovati*—to beg, to beseech. Bezlaj (ESSJ) also mentions *moledkovati,* which is even closer to the

Es 24 (LLV)
Museo Nazionale Atestino

Venetic word. Although not preserved in written form, the word *moledvanka* must have existed or still exists in some Slovene dialect.

s (z)—with; Slov. *s, z;* in OCS *sъ* served as an accompanying preposition only. In our case **s moldonkeo** can be considered as one unit: the prayer and the praying congregation. All this together was called *moldonka. Z moldonkejo pokopan*—buried with a prayer.

karan evil spirit which punishes the soul on its way to the **van** (heaven); Slov. *karati* means nowadays to reproach mildly; in OCS, however, it still meant to punish (Mikl.). The Bulgarian *kara*—to pursue is even closer. The word is to be found in all Slavic and Baltic languages as well as in some other Indo-European languages with a similar meaning; e.g., in Old Persian *kara*—army. Slov. *karati*—to reproach—derives from the noun *kâr*—reproach, punishment, fight—as a result of long vowel gradation (iterative), *koriti*—to reproach, *pokoriti*—to subdue. The Slovene carnival mask called *kurent* or *korant* is with its horrifying, otherworldly

289

image distantly related to, and impersonating the ancient Venetic **karans** who pursued the souls of the departed.

mn s—abbr. of **mené se**—thinking, believing, imagining; Slov. *meneč se*; Slov. authors of 16th century used *mneti, mnim* in the sense of: to believe, to think, to have opinion. The modern Slovene word is *meniti*. In OCS *mniti*—to believe, to have opinion. In Venetic this word was connected with genitive; in this inscription **mn s** is a participle.

Rejtijai—to Rejtija. The OCS dative of *žena*—a woman—was *ženě* and not *ženi* as in Slov.; the diphthong **ai** is in perfect agreement with the **ě** in *ženě*, since the OCS letter jat **ě** developed from **ai**. In the chapter on relations between Latvian and Slovene dialects I mention that this *ai* is still used in Slovenia. The Inner Carniolan *maisit, mainit* etc.—to knead, to believe.

In archaic Slovene the above inscription could be translated as follows: *Jaz donašam, ventan z moledvo, za korante mne se, Rejtiji.*

Venetic: **Mego** or **me go donasto vant s moldonkeo karan mn s Rejtijai.**

We have already mentioned that the first word can be either **mego** (I), or **me go** (I-him). The teachers certainly warned their pupils about it.

The tablet **Es 31** is badly damaged so that most of the inscription is illegible. Nevertheless, the part of the phrase **V DAN DONAS(TO)**—I bring as a tribute, Slov. *v dan donašam*—is clearly visible.

Inscriptions from the Upper Piave Valley

For a researcher of the old Venetic world and language, the area around the upper Piave River is particularly attractive. The name itself is reminiscent of Old Slavic *plavъ*—boat, ship, and Slov. *splav*—raft. Both words are derivatives from *plu-ti, plovem, plavam*—to sail, I sail, I swim. This word is very old. It is found in Lithuanian: *plau, plauti;* in Latin: flumen, fluo; in Sanskrit: *plava* (a boat, a ship).

One might argue that the name Piave (blue, Slov. *Plava*) was not given to the river by the Veneti, but by Indo-Europeans. I do not think the Indo-European theory would be successful here if considered without prejudice. There are several obviously Slavic names in this area from Valle Sella, Slov. *sela*—a settlement, a village—to Lozzo, Slov. *laz*—cleared woodland—from Pusteria to Pekol, Slov. *pekel* (literally hell)—a rocky depression. The only question is whether the Slavs named those places in a later period (as they no doubt lived around the upper Piave River), or are the names of ancient Venetic origin, later to be Latinized by Romans? It was not possible, however, to Latinize all the names, although the inhabitants were also Latinized, or Friulinized or Germanized to some extent; yet, the original Slavic names were pronounced as they were in the olden times. The same applies to all toponymy that fell under the influence of Rome. The Venetic territory in northern Italy was no exception. In all probability the pressure to Latinize the names was rather strong because of the relative proximity to Rome. The proper noun Carni (Carns) was, in my understanding, no other than the Latinized Slovene name Gornji—upper (Venetic, **garni**). The Latinized toponym at Belluno Carnius is nowadays Kargnach (Ger. for Slovene village of Gornje, v Gornjah).

I find this short introduction necessary because our suppositions are well substantiated also by other names from the surroundings of the famous archaeological site on the bank of the Piave River that are in direct connection with Lagole di Calalzo, the old Venetic hot springs.

The springs were discovered only after the Second World War. Yet, there still lingers among the people the tradition that the area was once an important hot spring and that the waters of Lagole are miraculous.

We do not know whether the spring was in reality miraculous or not, but we certainly know that in this case the voice of the people was the voice of God. It has now been proven that at this very site people used to pour warm water over themselves with brass dippers, several of which have been discovered in addition to figures of soldiers and deities, various cups, etc. The unusual element of the dippers is their very long handles, engraved with inscriptions in old Venetic letters.

There are also a number of brass plaques. One of them is particularly impressive; it has a perfectly preserved image of a horse, showing us that the Veneti, who were the neighbours and contemporaries of the Etruscans, had a highly developed artistic sensibility.

The inscriptions on these works of art show that they were not imported. In addition, they suggest that the water was curative for both the humans and the horses. As is generally known the horses were held in great esteem by the Veneti.

The fact that Lagole di Calalzo used to be a thermal health centre is further substantiated by the archeological findings in this area, as explained by Pellegrini and Prosdocimi in LLV. The area is partly covered by the lake of a later origin. There are still springs of the supposedly curative water; there are also a number of caves in the area, some of which are of natural origin and some which appear to have been man made.

According to the above authors, the name Podie, as this area is called, proves that these observations are correct. Although the two authors try to connect it to the Latin *putidiae* from *puteus*—a cave, a well—we think that it is simply a misspelled *vodje*—waters. It has been pronounced as *bodje* due to betatism which is a common feature in Venetic texts; compare the place-names in Slovenia: Bodovlje, Bodešče. Vodje, Bodje, was easily turned into Podie in a foreign language.

The name of the place itself, Lagole di Calalzo, is of interest from the etymological point of view. Lagole is obviously nothing else but a translation of *kal* or Kalce—a pool. We know that *kal* in Slovene is a pool; in OCS *kalъ;* Latin *lacuna* (Mikl.). The Slavic version has been retained in Calalzo (Kalce). In OCS *kal* has a second meaning—mud. It is mud of a consistency suitable to be smeared on the body, Slov. *kaljati se*—to smear oneself with something. The waters in this pool must have been muddy Slov. *kalna* (like for example in Topusko spa for rheumatism), and certainly warm, thermal.

It is interesting that one of the dipper handles of Lagole bears the name of this place. The handle itself is damaged, but the inscription **Ca 48** is quite clear:

KALO DIBA

Ca 48 (LLV)

Considering betatism as well as the fact that **o** often denoted a silent vowel which usually was not written, except in the case of well-known sayings and toponyms, this inscription reads:

KAL DIVA

It is not necessary to be a great expert to explain this name on the basis of our previous knowledge: **kal** is Slovene *kal*—pool, OCS *kalъ* (even nowadays this word is used to describe a muddy pool) whereas **diva** is genitive sing. of OCS *divъ*—wonder, miracle; Serbo-Croatian *div*—a giant (a Balkan Turkism of Persian, i.e., Indo-European origin); Latin *deus*; Lith. *dievas*. In spite of some etymologysts to the contrary, e.g. Jagić, I think Slov. *deva*—maiden—is of the same origin as Old Ind. *devi*—goddess, or Latin *dea*—goddess. So, *deva* is best translanted as goddess, and *div* as god.

It is also of interest that the inscriptions tell us the name of this god.

Among the various objects used for healing is one which is very special and rare to quote LLV: "una plachetta con la raffigurazione stilizzata di tre teste"—a plaque with a stylized representation of three heads, pp. 475, 484. The authors of the book *La Lingua Venetica* placed a question mark after the description.

A confirmation that it really concerns three heads, i.e., a deity with three heads, also appears in the inscriptions on the handles of the dippers. It is called **Trumusijat Ca 6,** or in my transcription, Trumužijad. Taking into account that in the inscriptions from Lagola di Calalzo only one letter "**X**" is used to write **t** and **d: tonasto, donasto,** we may also read **Trumuzijad,** or Trumužijad, as the Veneti made very poor distinction between **s** and **š,** or **z** and **ž.**

This sounds very close to our Slovene language, though. It is true that instead of *možjad* we say *moštvo*—a team—nowadays, but there is no reason why the Slovene language would not once include the word *možjad* when we still use words like: *srnjad, otročad,* etc. for a group of deer or children. Then it was also able to form compounds, and **Trumužijad** was easily one of them.

Anyone who speaks Slovene will recognize the two component words at once: Slov. *mož*—man; OCS *mužъ;* Russ. *muž;* Serbo-Cr. *muž* etc. and **tru**—three. The **i** easily turns into **o** in compound words; e.g. Slov. *trojen, trojica*—triple, threesome; Venetic **tru** instead of **tro.**

Div (god) from Kalalce (if we are allowed to reconstruct the name for Lagole) who had three heads, was called Trumužijad. He had two other names as well. Some people called him **Trumuškad,** which is exactly the same, except that the second part of the name is formed from *moški, muški*—male, manly—and not from **mož.**

293

The official Venetologists, who were trying to clarify the Venetic language with the help of Latin, could have given us an equally detailed explanation; unfortunately, they would not even think of an etymology as presented here. And why not? I suppose it is impossible to give detailed explanation of Proto-Slavic, Venetic words on the basis of Latin. The other reason is, because in two places, **Ca 9** and **Ca 59,** another version of this name is found: **Tribusijatin.** As you have already guessed this is the dative plural of **Tribusjati,** with final **m** transformed into **n.** Such transformations are quite common in Venetic and in other languages as well as in Slovene dialects.

But the reader may ask: why suddenly **trib** in place of **trum?**

They are not, as maintained by Pellegrini and others, two forms of one word but two different words. A sanctuary like this dedicated to Šajnata Trumužijad, was called **trebnikъ**—*delubrum* or *trebište—altare* (Mikl.) by the Slavs. In Slovenia there are numerous toponyms like Trebnje, Trebija. That is where **Tribusjati** comes from. It may also be connected to Trobožje—tri-god, trinity.

So much for the hot springs of Lagole, taking into consideration all the archaeological and linguistic data. Correct reading of the inscriptions on the dipper handles fully confirms these findings.

This data also tells us some other facts. People came to this hot spring to cure their rheumatism or Slov. *kostenica* which was then called **kostonasto, kostoler, or** maybe **kostr.** At least one inscription includes **kostonasta** which is a feminine form.

How do we know this? From the inscriptions on the dipper handles. As already mentioned, the dippers were used for scooping the healing water and were afterwards left there as votive objects. I had this supposition confirmed through Italian experts, e. g., S. Ferri who says: "Judging by the present knowledge of the circumstances, we can say that the healing water was scooped with a dipper of a normal size with a long handle. After treatment the dipper became a votive object. Numerous caves around the springs testify to a cult in the very remote past." (LLV p. 476).

Those who are trying to explain these unusual testimonies of a forgotten culture are deeply convinced that the engraved inscriptions are the names of the pilgrim donors. After all, this would have been quite normal if it were not for an unexpected, interesting and noteworthy fact opposing it.

Whoever wants to make the effort to count the "names" of the donors (patients and others) will wonder why all the names end with a suffix -kos: **Arspetijakos, Ametikos, Pitamnikos, Aplisikos, Trišikos, Buticakos, Klutavikos, Brojcokos, Eneicos, Dejcilarikos, Voltolarikos, Fouvonicos, Inicintikos, Dillikos,** etc.

294

Handles with inscriptions and two bowls.

It would be difficult to object to these "names" if we did not notice yet something else: the Venetic names with suffix -**kos** are nonexistent, except in Lagole. We should ask who these people were who made the pilgrimage to recover their health in Lagole or Kalce. It would seem by a miraculous coincidence, only those whose names ended in -**kos.** Is this possible?

The only answer which can satisfy us is that they were not names at all. They were constructed as such by the Venetologists who were convinced that anything ending in -**kos** is a name. But is their assumption correct?

Not at all. This -**kos** is not a suffix of a surname; most frequently it is an ending of the 2nd pers. sing. present tense of verbs like **spitamnikos,** Slov. *spitaš*— you feed, **sossokos,** Slov. *osušiš, posrkaš*—you dry up, you sip it, **šutavikos**— you are making merry. Sometimes they are personal pronouns like **kos**—anybody; Pol. *ktoš;* Lith. *kas;* here and there a conjunction **ko** Slov. *ko* followed by **s** (a reflexive pronoun) combined into a single word with a verb still in use in modern Lith., or the demonstrative pronoun **s,** OCS *sь.* Several times it is the first syllable of **kostonasto.**

A more detailed study of the inscriptions on these dipper handles shows a tendency to play with words similar to that of the Ateste school of scribes in the temple of the shining Rejtija. This tendency to play with words had, in my view, a magical purpose and meaning.

Every inscription contained a kind of advertisment calling for the sick to get healed at the shining Tromožjad, the word **donasto** or **doto**—I bring, I give, I present—and also the name of the sickness Tromožjad was most capable of healing, although other sicknesses were not excluded.

I have already mentioned that the Veneti called the rheumatism **kostonasto** and **kostonasta** besides other expressions, and that all derive from **kost;** this is the same word as Slovene *kost*—bone. Slovenes still use *kostenica, kostnica,* and *koščenica* for rheumatism, which is very close to the Venetic expressions.

The word **kostonasto** and related words, engraved on the handles of the dippers confirm that this interpretation is correct.

The official theory, that most of these remains of Venetic language are nothing but names, has already been criticized in connection with other inscriptions, especially those from Ateste; but the dippers from Lagole finally completely disprove this theory, and take from it the last remnants of credibility.

For easier understanding, I would like to mention that the inscriptions include another syntagma with a double meaning which is frequently repeated. It is **donom Trumuskatei** and its primary meaning is: with a present (make a pilgrimage) to Tromožje; Slov. *z danjem, danom, darom* (romaj) *k Tromožju.* The other hidden meaning is: scoop the water at Tromožje or, closer to Venetic, *dojemi* "trumuškate" (that was the name of the water). In the anagram, **donom** is the imperative of the verb *donimatь, donjatь* in Russian. In modern Russian it means to bother, but this is already in a figurative sense, in the abstract. In the beginning it meant to bother somebody until you get what you are asking for; Slov. *zajel, dojel.* Some of this original meaning is still partly visible in the phrase: *jego ničem ne dojmešь*—you cannot get close to him. In other words: it is impossible to get anything from him (donjatь).

In Slovene this word is used only in its abstract connotation. Slov. *dojemamo*—we comprehend—is connected with a spiritual taking. Slov. *tega ne morem dojeti, to je lahko dojeti*—I cannot comprehend this, this is easy to comprehend. Thus the meaning is equal to that in Venetic, except that instead of water, we scoop thoughts. After all, it would not be very unusual in Slovene if you said: *dojemi še enkrat vode s tem korcem*—scoop the water once more with this dipper.

A Hot Spring for Rheumatism

The inscription **Ca 7** is on both sides of the handle and is very well preserved. It is particularly important as it tells us that the Three-men were also called Trumuzijati. This can be deduced from **Trumuzijatin,** dative plural. Replacement of **m** by **n** is common. The inscription should really read Trumuzijati**m** or as we would say in Slovene—Tromožjatim. The inscription is additionally interesting as it introduces two new words:

SUROZ RESUN KOSTONASTO
Nesreča resna kostenica (je)
A misfortune serious rheumatism (is)

TRUMUZIJATIN!
K Trem možem!
To the Three-men!

In modern English: Rheumatism is a serious misfortune,
therefore go to the Three-men (who will heal you).

Ca 7 (LLV)

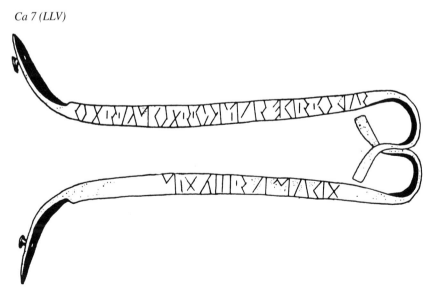

suroz—a misfortune; Russ. (Siberian dialect) *suraz* (Vasm.) connected to *rezatь*; Slov. *rezati*—to cut; OCS *rězati*. See **Ca 24** Russ. *srazit* Slov. *poraziti*—to defeat.

resun—serious; Slov. *resen;* OCS *resьnъ—verus, certus.* If we take into account the archaic and dialect form of the word in Slovene which cannot be declined, *res*—truly—the translation could be as follows: Truly, rheumatism is a misfortune. Therefore go to the Three-men!
kostonasto—rheumatism; Slov. *kostenica.* The word hides the verb **donasto** (written **tonasto**). Anagram: **donasto Trumuzijatin,** Slov. *darujem Tromožju*— I offer to the Three-men.
Trumuzijatin—to the Three-men.
The inscription **Ca 9** is short, very clear and interesting. The third version of the same word appears here: **Tribuzijad** in addition to the earlier **Trumuzijat** and **Trumuskat.** And not only that, the function of the word in the inscription shows it to be in dative plural, as in the above inscription. It reads as follows:

VOTOZNAJ S ON KOSTONASTO
Pritožujoči se nad kostenico

TRIBUZIJATIN
K Trem možem!

In English: Those complaining of rheumatism.
To the Three-men!

votoznaj—complaining; related to Slov. *otožen*—gloomy, from the root **teg-** which is unusually fruitful in Slavic languages. Comp. Slovene: *otež, togota, tezati* (Mikl.), *otežiti, otežen*—weight, anger, to strain, to weigh down, weighted down.
s, se—reflexive pronoun.
on—above; Slov. *nad;* Old Slavic *on* (Mikl.).
kostonasto—rheumatism; Slov. kostenica. Comp. *koščenasta*—bony.
donasto (tonasto), contained in **kostonasto.**
The inscription **Ca 15** is on both sides of the handle, and is very interesting as it proves what the archaeologists established about the hot springs at the Three-men.
My transcription differs from the official interpretation of individual graphemes only in two instances: I read the initial **H** as **h** not as **f,** and |< which I read as **k** and not as **ij:**

298

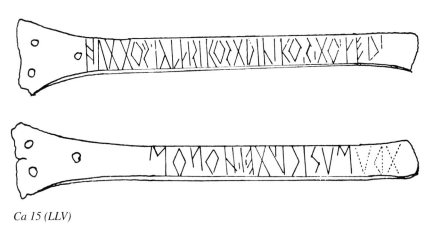

Ca 15 (LLV)

HUTTO SALLISIKOS TRIKI KOSTOLER
Kdorkoli si mažeš tročo kostenico

TRUMUSKATEI DONOM
K Tromožju z danjem (danom)!

In English: Whoever you are, massaging youself with ointment when oppressed by rheumatism, go to the Three-men with your offering!

Ca 19 (LLV)
Museo Cadorino di
Pieve di Cadore

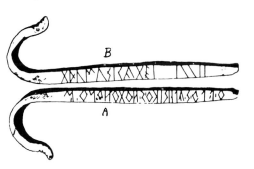

hutto—anybody; OCS *kъto;* Slov. *kdo.*
sallisikos—you grease yourself, you massage yourself; Russ. *salitьsja*—to grease oneself; Slov. *salo*—fat; see **Ca 19,** LLV.
triki—to rub; Slov. *troči*—rubbing; Latv. *trit;* OCS *tryti.* Slov. *treti*—to rub.
kostoler—rheumatism; Slov. *kostenica.*
Trumuskatei—to the Three-men.
donom—with a present, offering; Slov. *z danjem* (danom).

The inscription **Ca 12,** although short, represents a good example of language still heard in our dialects as well as in literary Slovene. Its special characteristic is **u** in place of **o** in **kustuler;** otherwise **kostoler.** From this we might deduce that **o** has been replaced by **u** in **kui** and **cuta** as well.

According to the valid orthography of the time, this inscription should not read:

KUI CUTA AME TI KUSTULER

Rather it should read:

KOI COTA AME TI KOSTOLER
Slov. Kdor čota, ome ti kostenico.

In English: He who limps (to the Three-men) sweeps away his rheumatism.

Ca 12 (LLV)

kui—whoever, one who; Slov. *kdor, ki;* Serbo-Cr. *koji;* Old Slavic *kъj, kyj.*

cuta read **čota**—to limp; Slov. *čotati;* It. *ciotto.* Pleteršnik believes it to be borrowed from Italian, but everything points to the contrary; i.e., that it is a Proto-Slavic (Venetic) loanword in Italian.

ame ti—to sweep away; Slov. *omete, omede ti,* namely the illness from the body. A phrase which could still be employed nowadays. Slov. *ome ti kostenico.*

Ougon

Analysis of the inscriptions on the writing styles has already convinced us that they often include various forms of the word **ougon** Slovene *ogenj,* Sanskrit *agni*—fire. In view of the importance of this word, I would like to examine it more closely.

This word appears unusually often, more than twenty times. It is found several times on the urns which contained ashes; i.e., the remains left behind by the **ougon**. This detail alone should be enough to let us know that the word **ougon** is not a proper noun as maintained by official Venetologists. Consider other words related in their meaning to cremation, for example: **istna**, Slov. *isteje, istanje*—the vaulted opening of a fireplace; **pozed**—hearth; Slov. *ognjišče,* Rezian dial. *pozid;* **viugsija**—dying down (as fire dies down); Slov. *ugasnivši.* The assumption that these are names is ever less probable. No one could maintain that these words, which are in their meaning very closely related to the content and purpose of the urns, had been repeatedly written down by chance in different localities on different urns. This interpretation seems still less probable when we recognize how extremely well **ougon** and its derivatives fit and agree contextually and grammatically in a variety of sentence connections.

Prehistoric man worshipped fire as a deity, similar to the sun. Fire was his friend when he knew how to use it; otherwise it could also be his terrible enemy. The chief god, at one time called Jupiter, at another time Zeus or Perun or Tinia (Etruscan), punished man with fire, while at the same time fire was sent to earth in order to subdue the icy winter. Fire demanded respect, for it would require effort to rekindle it if extinguished. Among primitive people, only the priests were allowed to rekindle the fire. The Roman vestal virgins, the priestesses of the goddess Vesta whose task it was to watch over the eternal fire in her temple, call to mind the most ancient of man's worries, namely, that the fire might go out.

The fire that was advantageous to man during his lifetime was also helpful to him in death. The dead were cremated not only because it was the easiest way to prevent decomposition, but also to ensure peace for the deceased himself through the special funerary ritual related to cremation; at the same time it ensured that he did not trouble the living.

We can easily imagine that the Veneti too used their own incantations or prayers at their funeral ceremonies, though they did not leave behind any records of them. Just as in the distant past, today we think that the soul of a man will not find rest in the hereafter if it has not departed in the prescribed manner, which includes prayer correctly formulated and intoned by the priests. Undoubtedly the prayers would not have the desired effect if they were not pronounced according to the prescribed usage. The European experts are mistaken when they maintain that the old sayings only represented incomprehensible babbling. They were incomprehensible only to the later people who no longer understood the original language. Not even the priests of later times, who were still using these ancient sayings, understood them. But this does not mean that they were meaningless.

One of these sayings reads **arse uerse,** which was the same as "Averte ignem" during the Roman times; that is, beware of fire. This saying comes from the Etruscans: Pallottino, TLE, p. 102. These are two of the few Etruscan words whose import we know through Greek and Latin authors.

The saying was interpreted as **Var'se, ver'se!** Slov. *var(uj)se, (pre)veri se* (e.g. Jager). That is, beware of, be careful of (the fire). If one reads the Etruscan from the position of Slavic languages, Jager's interpretation is illuminating even from the standpoint of the phonetics. All the texts show that Etruscan, similar to Venetic, had vowel reduction. The objection to this interpretation appears in the statement of the Latin author, Placidus, who writes: "Tuscorum enim lingua arse averte, verse ignem constat appellari." That is, the Etruscans say *arse* for "beware of" and *uerse* for "fire". However, it is most probably a question of an incorrect interpretation of the Etruscan letters. For if the translation is correct, then with respect to the word **uerse,** we know that its root is **ver-** from which the OCS *vьreti* is derived. In Slovene *vreti* means to boil, cook; in Serbo-Cr. *var* means glowing coals and *varnica* means spark.

Why had the Latins written **arse** instead of **varse** (var se), and yet at the same time **uerse** (ver se)? The answer is found in the inscription itself. In all probability the Etruscans pronounced the initial **v** as bilabial **u,** as is still common among the Slovenes. Among Latin speakers this was not the practice, at least not at the beginning of the word. The word **uerse,** however, provides evidence that it was bilabial. If it had been the dental **v,** the Latins would likewise have written it as such, since it also existed in Latin. Thus, at the beginning of the word **varse,** the bilabial pronunciation of **v** was no longer used, whereas it was retained in **uerse** in order to separate the two **e**'s for easier pronunciation.

As is commonly known, the word **ougon** belongs to the Indo-European vocabulary, whereas the Venetic **ougon** has a totally Slavic form. The Slovene **ogenj** or **ogәn** and other Slavic forms such as **oganj, ohon, ogonь, vogen,** are so close to the Venetic **ougon** that there is no substantial difference.

Anagrams

In the first chapter of this study I remarked that the Ateste grammar tablets were the key to the language, from which the dialects and the written Slovene language later emerged through the influences of the Slavic north, east and south. I should have said that there are several keys contained in these grammar tablets. One of them has already been discovered by other linguists; namely, the consonant groups in addition to the alphabet, which I think are not that important but do provide evidence that the Venetic language was a Slavic language. The consonant groups characteristic of Slavic languages are **pn, tn, tl, dn, sl, gn**.

We have already dealt with the second key, the Slavic morphology, and we have also examined the phraseology of the upper part of these unusual grammatical documents. But now we should investigate a third key of the "tablets of Reitija", which is officially still not uncovered, in spite of the high level of present day linguistic sciences. We could rightly call it the **magic key** because it unexpectedly expands and enriches the Venetic vocabulary.

In order to get right to the core of the issue, let us first read what is found on page 95 of the often quoted book *La lingua venetica*: "Particolare della stipe l'uso della scrittura, utilizzata non solo per le dediche ma ogetto, secondo l'evidenza, di speculazione magica"—meaning: The specialty of the subject is the use of the script, not only for dedication but also as the object of magical speculations (meditations), as it would seem. The authors Pellegrini and Prosdocimi have a presentiment of the truth, but only a presentiment. The object of magical specualtions is not only the graphiology (scrittura), but the actual words. The tablets have their magical power primarily and precisely because of the mystery and ambiguity of the words.

The majority of the syntgamas and phrases which we find in the third part of the Ateste tablets have the character of anagrams; e.g., the already familiar formula:

V DAN DONASTO....REITIJAJ

which could also be read in the following way:

vdan do nas to...rei ti jaj.

In Slovene: Vdan ob (do) nas tu...v raj ti pojdi
In English: Put in here with us (interred).... go to heaven, paradise.

vdan—to add to, put into; Slov. *vdan* in its original meaning *vdati, vdeti.*
do nas to—with or to us here; Slov. *ob, do nas tu.*
rei—to heaven; without preposition, as is still the case in Slavic languages;
Slov. *v raj;* Carinthian dialect *rej*—to heaven.
ti—you; Slov. *ti.*
jaj—travel, go; Slov. *jahaj, potuj;* Latv. *jat;* Old Ind. *yati.*
All these anagrams are taken from the third part of the grammar tablets. Each
form has its own meaning (vdan—v dan, donasto—do nas to, Reitijaj—rei ti jaj).
Included in the principal clauses are various adverbial elements which are themselves often ambiguous. Among them is **virem a istna** which besides its principal meaning can also be read as—sworn to the truth; Slov. *verjen istini* or
zaobljubljen resnici.
virem part. pres. pass.—to give promise, to swear to; Slov. *veriti se* (Plet.).
a—Old Slavic *a,* nasal; this preposition has already been dealt with several
times.
istna—truth; Slov. *resnica,* Old Slov. *istina;* Ukrainian *istnyj,* without **i** similar to the Venetic **istna;** OCS *istaja vera*—true faith.
There is a whole series of such anagrams. The writers from the Ateste writing
school made certain that their grammar tablets were as instructive as possible, as
well as being rich in sayings and prayers of a magical nature for use by other
verkoni in the Venetic region.
These diagrams in the third part of the Ateste tablets confirm my view that
the lower row, which supposedly contains the Venetic vowels, is a saying with its
own import. They also show that those archaeologists who maintain that these
inscriptions on the gravestones speak about the journey into the hereafter are
right. If **v dan** stands in direct relationship to this journey, then the phrase **rei ti
jaj** is even more intimately revealing and related to the hereafter.

Were the Scribes Also Poets?

Am I perhaps attributing to the Veneti too much depth of thought and poetic
subtlety? And where is the proof of these fine qualities? I find it in their sometimes rather exuberant and wise poetic sayings which are preserved for us on
various objects, particularly urns. I would like to mention only some of these
sayings; those related to fire, the element most closely associated with the ritual

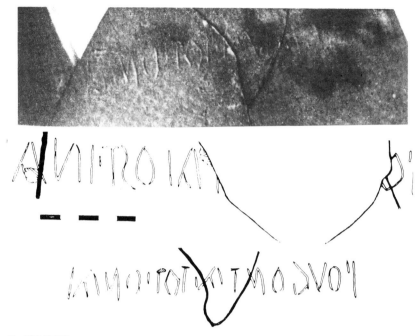

Es 106 (LLV)
Museo Nazionale Atestino

of cremation. On the Ateste urn **Es 106** we find written in Latin characters the following:

> **V ÓUGON TAJ, O, STINÁJ**
> **V OUGON TAJ, TOT I ONAJ**

In Slovene: V ogenj ta mi o iztli, v ogenj ta kot bomo vsi.
In English: Into this fire, oh, you fade, into this fire, just as we all will!

v ougon—into the fire; Slov. *v ogenj.* I interpret the Latin **F** as **v.** See earlier explanations.

   taj—this; Slov. *ta, taj* (Plet.); Serbo-Cr. *taj.*

   stinaj read **sǝtinaj**—to die out; Slov. *tleti* and *tinjati*—extinguishing, (Plet.); Serbo-Cr. *stinjati*—to burn.

305

tot i onaj—this one and that one; Slov. *ta in oni;* Slov. dial. *tot;* Ukrain. *tot, tota, toto* (this, m., f., n.,); Russ. arch. *tot.*

In the inscriptions on these urns, **ougon** is not the only word that is used in direct relation to its contents. Let us look at the two verses on the Ateste urn **Es 105:**

V OUGON TAJ VUGISON JAJ
BRIGDINAJ JEGO

In Slovene: V ogenj ta, ugašene, naj gredo, brige in skrbi njegove.
In English: Into this fire, extinguished, let them pass: His cares and sorrows.

vugison—died out, quenched; Slov. *ugašen.*

brigdinaj—daily cares; a confirmation of Lehr-Spławiński's theory that Proto-Slavic is a Baltic language as it is changing into Venetic, which means that Venetic is closer to Slavic than Baltic. There is the word **brig-dinaj**—daily cares. Latv. *bridinat* from *brig-dinat* meaning to care for, to take responsibility for something; *bridinajums*—care and sorrow—is probably the same as the Venetic **brigdinaj** without the velar **g**. Compare Slov. *direndaj, ringaraj, vodostaj.* Latv.

Es 105 (LLV)
Museo Nazionale Atestino

dienet means to serve, similar to Slov. **dnina**—day's wages—hence *brige-dnina*—concern for the day's recompense or daily concerns.

jego—his; Slov. *njega, njegovi;* Slov. dial. *jega;* Old Russ. *jego;* Russ. *jego.* This word with the same meaning is found at least seven times. See earlier comments.

In any case, this inscription is very beautiful, especially when one considers the fact that the word *ugašati*—to burn down slowly, going out slowly—in Slovene and in other Slavic languages had, and still has, the metaphorical meaning "to die" and that during antiquity the word fire meant not only fire, but also a deity. In order to make things clearer, let us look at another inscription. Etched into one of the "chiodi"—styles—**Es 40** is the following:

VI OUGON TAJ VIOUGONTNA
DONASTO REITIJAJ

In Slovene: V ogenj ta, upepeljenca donašam Reitiji.

In English: Into this fire, I bring, that which must be cremated, to Reitija.

donasto—See earlier explanations.

viougontna—to cremate the body; from **viougonat**—to burn, to cremate. Here we have a derivative of **ougon**—fire; Slov. *ogenj.* Except in the Slovene Rezian dialect, this word has been lost in Slavic languages. However, it has survived in Latvian with the meaning "to illuminate". It would be appropriate to also consider this meaning (to illuminate, to brighten) in the above inscriptions, whereby the deceased not only dies but is, figuratively speaking, illuminated. According to all indications, the Veneti believed that in the fire, along with the mortal remains being destroyed, the evil within the person would also be burned and cleared away. If it was not destroyed by fire, it would be a hindrance to the person on his/her journey into the afterlife. In this connection the priests (the verkoni) certainly had an important role during the cremation ceremony, as the deceased (whose corpse was considered a kind of tribute to Reitija) departed in accordance with their beliefs.

In the Slovene language the verb form of **ougon**—fire—does not exist, except in the Rezian dialect, *ognjiti, onjevte tarine*—burned grass; Slov. *ožgane trave.* The verb *gonobiti,* with imperfect aspect, could have appeared only later, after *ugonobiti* had lost its initial meaning. In the modern Slovene the word *ugonobiti* means to destroy. For fire not only illuminates, but also destroys.

As a result of the syntagma, the above quoted verses conceal two other verses which consequently give the inscription its fullest meaning:

VI OUGON TAJ VI OUGON TNA
DO NAS TO REI TI JAJ

In Slovene: V ogenj tajn, v ogenj tenj ob nas tu pojdi v raj!
In English: Go into mysterious fire into fire of shadows,
from us away into the paradise!

Here are two more words that need some explanation:
taj—secret, mysterious; Slov. *tajn,* also *taja* (Plet.).
tna—outline, silhouette; Slov. *tenj* from the same root as *tema*—darkness.

The strange beauty of these verses, written on the brittle and yet durable urns is not to be overlooked. If Walzel is right in explaining the German word *dichten*— to compose, with—to join, to unite—then it is hard to imagine more skilful and capable writers than the Veneti.

It is unfortunate that we do not have an opportunity to examine additional urns to find out if on their clay, made black over the centuries, there are more of such lyric poems.

What if someone should ask: is this poetry only a product of your imagination? If this were indeed the case, I would gladly admit it. The reader who has accompanied me thus far into Venetic prehistory along the difficult roadways of words, recognizes that there are just too many of these inscriptions where the second meaning—which gives their magical power—can be recognized without too much imagination.

Venetologists are convinced that on all Venetic, Etruscan and Roman urns there are only names. But this is not true. The Veneti, as all indications show, were primarily concerned that their journey into and through the hereafter would proceed safely. That is why they did not engrave names on the urns with the ashes of the deceased; rather, they engraved prayer epigrams, which they had obtained from the Ateste school or from other schools. Then what happened to the names? Perhaps they were written on the perishable glaze or on wood attached to the urns. More likely, in accordance with their beliefs (which were related to Hinduism), the Veneti did not record any names. This can be surmised from several inscriptions which bid the deceased to pass away; i.e. give up the attachment to existence.

There are several indications that this was the case. I would like to mention a particularly noticeable one: the ritual incantations of the Ateste tablets are also found on urns. There is no doubt that these tablets were primarily of a didactic nature. Of course, there was no purpose for names on tablets and the same could be said for the triangular writing styles, which had the same function as the tablets, namely, instruction in the language and ritual incantations. Furthermore, the inscriptions on the urns show that they are related to the content and purpose of the urns; e.g. **ougon**—fire, **vugison**—died down, **viugia**—charred, **viougonta ivir**—burned splinters of wood; in Slovene: *iver,* also *ivir* (Plet.), or *iverje.* **Ivir** and fire have always been related to one another. Man was equated with the **ivir** which the fire destroyed, consumed (ugonobi).

In addition the language of these inscriptions, similar to the Ateste tablets, shows that the Proto-Slavic language existed at a time when the Balto-Slavic language was changing into Slavic. In some cases it is more similar to the former, and in other cases to the latter.

Since we are now examining the word **ougon,** let us look at several forms of one of its derivatives, the verb **vougontat:**

VIOUGONTA moldnaje b(e)
May she be cremated during the prayer.
VIOUGONTAJ...urkleioj
The cremated...(is) under a spell against evil spirits.
vantej VIOUGONTIOJEGO
Urns of the cremated.

We could add a whole series of other participles (adjectives) to those already mentioned, as for example **viugiajemu,** Slov. dial. *ouglenemu*—to the cremated; **urkli,** Slov. *urekli, urečeni*—he who is under a spell; **murtuvoj,** Slov. *mrtvi*—the dead. These words are taken from the books *La lingua venetica* and the *Manuel de la langue Venete.* The form **urkli** (without e) is also found in some Slavic languages and the Slovene Rezian dialect.

There are no names on the early Venetic urns. They first appear during a later period under the influence of Roman culture which gradually displaced the Venetic. After that we find urns with names engraved on them. However, since the Venetic traditions were not yet totally wiped out (in spite of progressing Romanization), the Veneti continued to write their ritual sayings in addition to the name and sometimes the sayings were written even without the names. We have already cited several examples of this in connection with the word **ougon.** Many were also in use during Roman times, particularly those related to fire. I have already mentioned that to the Veneti as well as other nations, fire was seen as having divine characteristics.

The various still remembered ritual sayings written in Latin were those most often added to the names of the deceased; e.g., CANTA, KONJA, FREMA, RUTUBA, FUXS, FUXSIAE, FOVGO. Of course, for the Venetologists, all these words are only names. In reality, they are something else, as we can see if we take a closer look:

CANTA aor.—was interred f., OCS *sъkǫtati*—to inter.

NERCA aor.—was interred f., OCS *nreti*—to let oneself in; Russ. *nyrkatь, nyrjatь*—dive into something; Slov. *nora*—cave.

KONIA—concluded; OCS *konati*—to conclude.

FREMA—laid into the grave, (from the Venetic **virema**); at the same time also an anagram. As already mentioned, the Venetologists read the Venetic **vi** as **vh,** out of which (under subsequent influence of Latin) evolved the **f,** thus **virema**—**vrema**—**frema.** On a fragment of a small painted bowl is written **frem,** which is supposed to be an "abreviazione di un noto personale venetico". In reality, it is nothing more than the adjective, m. of **frema.**

RUTUBA—grave, mound; OCS *rъt*—ridge; Slov. *rt*—spit of land or a formation extending out from the main body. Suffix **-uba,** comp. with Slov. *poguba, obljuba,* etc. Bulg. *rъt*—mound, hill.

FUGISONIAI—extinguished; same as in the familiar sentence **v ougon taj, vugison jaj**.

FUXS—this would be an interesting name if the word were Latin. However, since it is Venetic it is not a name but a substantive, meaning extinction; Slov. *ugas* (Plet.), Venet. **vugos.** The Veneti had used the Latin X for their palatal fricative. **FUXS TITINIA** is therefore the extinction of Titinias—his ashes.

FUXIAE, (vugəsje)—extinguished; Slov. *ugas.*

FOUGO read **VOUGO**—at the end of the name L. Ennius P.F. is not an additional name; rather, it simply means "cremated" (aorist of the verb that is already familiar to us in connection with the urns.

MOLTISA—pray for; Slov. *moliti za,* the name follows.

Into the Heavenly Van

The "names" we examined above and similar ones found on the urns are not names, but rather a reminiscence of former ritual sayings and incantations. They are from the period when the Venetic culture and its art of writing inscriptions had already been lost. Of all the sayings this one is probably the best preserved:

I VAN TE JAJ

In Slovene: In v van te(daj) pojdi!
In English: And into paradise then go !

310

The preposition **v** is missing before the word **van** because it merged with the first letter. The sentence means the same as "rei ti jaj". Wherever the Venetic word **van** appears, either on gravestones or urns, it has the same meaning as **rej**; i.e., paradise. In the Slovene language *van* has almost fallen into oblivion, though it is still mentioned by Pleteršnik. He writes: "van, m. Die Entäusserung"—parting with, and next to this: "vanati se—verzichten, sich auf den Weg machen"—to give up, to leave. It is mistakenly interpreted as being a German loanword (**Es 4**).

JEGO VOL(E)TIJO M(I)NOJ
I U VAN TI JAJ!

In Slovene: Njegova duša mini, in v van potuj!
In English: May his soul pass away, and travel into paradise!

This ritual verse is repeated in a whole series of inscriptions, although during Roman times when the Venetic language had fallen into disuse, it was distorted in a number of ways: IVANTEIAI, IVANTIOI, IVANTINA.

The Veneti called the soul **vol(e)tio, volja**—will; Russ. *voloть*—knight, and the Slov. *veleti*—to command, *voliti*—to choose—are all related. Does then the word **voltijo** really mean both knight and soul? This troubled me, but not anymore. Both words probably have the same root, and the Slovene word *volja*—will— probably developed from **vol(e)tio** and is related to Latin *volentia*—will. There is no doubt that we have here a homonym; i.e., the same word with two meanings. The Venetic ritual formula **op voltijo leno,** Slov. *ob volji blagi,* means the same as the Latin votive phrase *libens merito.* On this I am of the same opinion as Venetologists. That we are dealing here with a word that has two meanings is also confirmed by the Ateste tablets. According to ancients—perhaps this is an Indo-European belief as well—the will or "vol(e)tio" was inclined to evil. The Veneti would entreat the soul at death to put an end to whatever was still alive within, and to move on into the "van" where it would be immersed in something which was greater than personal existence.

When I looked into the Sanskrit dictionary (given to me by Dr. Aleš Bebler who followed my Venetic research with great interest), the whole thing became even more meaningful. The word *van* (Vana) in Sanskrit means, among other things, a foreign and distant land, a cloud in the sky shaped like a ship, a yearning. The Slovene phrase *v božji van*—into God's paradise—is very close in its meaning to Sanskrit.

What a strange and mysterious connection (probably from a common Indo-

European substratum) between the supernatural *van* and the ancient Hindus who, in their yearning for holiness, parted with worldly affairs and entered into solitude. The Mahabharata is full of descriptions of just such undertakings. The Venetic **van** certainly represented something very similar, the yearning for the distant: the sky, heaven, paradise.

When I think of all that is concealed in these words, and how by comparing them something can suddenly become apparent which no historiography or philosophy can reveal, I see my undertaking as consistent with my predilection for poetry. Ultimately, even poetry attempts to free itself of the mundane to arrive at the truth, which always seems so distant though we may diligently aspire to it.

Where is the Slovene "van" today? Only in the old dictionaries and certainly in our national subconscious, which comes to light in the subtleties of our lyric poetry. It is still expressed in Slovene songs from the Rezija Valley. The "van" is also present in the letters engraved in the blackened clay and bronze. It went deep into the life of the people, the Slovene people, who in part still possess the ancestral land and who still speak a modernized version of the ancient Proto-Slavic, Venetic language.

Slovene Inscriptions on the Ducal Throne

To return long denied historical memories to Slovenes we have to review many areas, particularly those which under the pressure of foreign rule and foreign history writing have been discarded by Slovenes themselves as historically untenable.

The inscriptions on the Ducal Throne at Gospa Sveta (Maria Saal) in Carinthia must be part of this reassessment. Urban Jarnik, a learned Carinthian Slovene recorder of folk traditions, explained the inscription along the west seat as **MA • SVETI VERI**—Has Holy Faith.

Although his interpretation limped a little linguistically, Slovenes accepted it with enthusiasm. The interpretation was at first also acceptable to Germans; after all, the investiture ceremony on the Prince's Stone and the presentation and judicial proceedings at the Ducal Throne were all conducted in the Slovene (Venetic) language. It was therefore understood that the inscription was in Slovene.

The materials for the Ducal Throne came from the ruins of the nearby Roman city of Virunum, which served during the entire Middle Age as the local quarry. The throne is constructed relatively simply. It has two seats, one facing west and the other facing east; in the middle there is a common backrest.

Regardless that three experts, Kumpf 1818, Eichorn 1819, and the state-appointed Rudolf Graf Goes 1834, all confirmed Jarnik's three-word interpretation (the only difference was that Goes saw a colon in place of the dot), there were soon objections. The later version of Theodor Mommsen received the seal of official acceptance. He included it in his *Corpus inscriptionum Latinarum* as MANSUETI VERI although there is no N in the inscription.

To those who were afraid to see Slovene inscriptions on the Ducal Throne, this was a welcome relief. Now they were certain that the Slovene claim had been defeated. Hieronimus Megiser, who first presented this inscription along with the general description of the western seat of the throne, read it as **MASVETIVER;** he did not see the I as it was covered by the ground and discovered only at the beginning of the last century by Kumpf.

Those who wanted to prove that the inscription could not be Slovene voiced objections to the vertical direction of the writing, and the shape of the letters which was the same as those found at Virunum; therefore, how could it be "eine slavische oder windische Inschrift"—a Slavic or Slovene inscription?

Ducal Throne at Gospa Sveta (Maria Saal), Carinthia which is, besides the Prince's Stone, the only symbol of Slovene law and statehood.

Max Ritter v. Moro insisted that Slavs did not write vertically, but he obviously had in mind the East Slavs as this is not true of the West Slavs. It was characteristic of Veneti to chisel their inscriptions into such and similar pillars either up or down, or from left or right. These customs were not completely discarded when the Veneti accepted Latin script.

The rural population of northern Italy and the eastern Alps was Venetic from antiquity. Why should we then be surprised to find a Venetic (Slovene) inscription on the Ducal Throne? There are important Venetic finds from Slovene Gurina, Zilja Valley (Gailtal), Carinthia.

The history of the area has not been well researched. Pellegrini in his *La lingua venetica,* p. 609, says: "Tutto un capitolo di storia dell' espansione paleoveneta resta da impostare, come pure resta da dare una fisionomia al Norico pre-gallico o non-gallico che manifesta un preoccupante vuoto linguistico sotto l' etichetta 'illirico'." An entire chapter of history of Proto-Venetic expansion remains unresearched. We must also develop the image of pre-Celtic and non-Celtic periods of Noricum, the periods that are recorded under the term "Illyrian".

In the 4th century the Roman population was ordered by Emperor Constantine to accept the Christian faith. Noricum was included, which means that some of the indigenous Veneti, mainly those living in the cities, were also converted.

The western seat of the Ducal Throne

The shape of the letters of the inscription along the western seat is, according to experts, the same as was in use during the first centuries A. D. The word **VERI** in the front part of the inscription is in the style used during the 1st century, and **MA SVETI VERI** is from the 4th century, although the shape of the letters is from the 2nd or 3rd century, suggesting that in remote Noricum the style of lettering changed slowly.

We have three explanations: **VERI** on the front was written during the pagan period, and later when Christianized they added **MA SVETI VERI.** Jarnik came very close to the meaning of the inscription, but he probably did not know that Veneti used boustrophedon. The second possibility is that the letters were carved at the same time by two different craftsmen. When we read the two parts together we have:

VERI MA SVETI VERI.

Slovene: Prisegaj, ampak pri sveti veri (novi, krščanski veri).
English: Swear, but by the holy faith (new, Christian faith).

veri—swear; Slov. archaism *veriti se,* modern Slov. *prisegaj!*—to swear, to testify, to believe. Ger. *betheuern.*

315

ma—but; Slov. *ampak, a, vendar;* **ma** as an adversative conjunction. It is common in the Slovene littoral, Dalmatia, Montenegro, Herzegovina, western Bosnia and northern Croatia. Skok says that it is difficult to think that the word *ma* would be of Italian origin; it appears in too many locations. It should also be compared with Slov. *mar.*

sveti veri—by the true faith; Slov. *sveti veri* dative. It was a caution to witnesses and all who were called before the throne.

German historians, later joined by Slovene historians, insist the inscription got there by chance; i.e., when stones for the throne were chosen, the pillar with inscription was part of the selection—nothing more.

Whoever examined the Ducal Throne either on site or in photographs knows that the word **VERI** is very visible. Big, strong letters take up the entire front of the right side of the western seat. We know that the ceremony at the Ducal Throne was very precise (contrary to the opinion of Slovene historian Bogo Grafenauer); it is impossible to imagine that the construction of the Throne was careless and that a stone with Latin inscription was chosen. There were plenty of other stones in the ruins of Virunum to select from. The inscription is Venetic (Slovene) and was carefully formed and engraved.

Across the top of the eastern seat of the Ducal Throne there is another inscription, which Wolfgang Lazius, the first to write about it (*Geographia*

The eastern seat of the Ducal Throne

316

Pannoniae), read as **DN DUX DOMIT** or **DUX DOMITI**. He wrote from memory—the word DUX is actually at the end. Megiser read it as **RUDOLPHUS DUX**. This reading received official approval at least among German experts, who added that in 1360 at the time of investiture of Duke Rudolf, the inscription RUDOLFUS DUX replaced an older inscription. What older inscription? Probably the one seen by Lazius.

The eastern seat of the Ducal Throne (detail)

Austrian experts were/are under official pressure to find solutions which would deny the Venetic (Slovene) origin of the inscriptions, although all official procedures at the Ducal Throne were conducted in the Slovene language even later when German dukes were invested. Megiser, as we can see from his biography, was not very reliable. He deliberately distorted certain facts, and rechiselled the inscription. What caused him to do this last? Emperor Rudolf was his benefactor, and Megiser received the title *Comes Palatinus* from him. It was obviously out of gratitude that he "discovered" the emperor's name on the famous Ducal Throne.

When I examined the inscription at the site, I instantly saw two letters which could not be L and F but were very far from it. The one read as F is the Venetic ʮ ; next to it is the same letter in upright position which is a common practice in Venetic script. It should not be ruled out that it is an ᛙ, only that the short line on the right is connected to the following V—such connections are frequent in Venetic script. The original inscription was at least partially in Venetic letters. There are several inscriptions with a mixture of the two scripts from the time when Latin had almost replaced the native Venetic script.

Besides the Venetic ʮ and ᛙ, the letters VDO on the left are also clearly visible; on the right there are again V and DUX. Only two letters are unclear, or

317

completely chiselled over, the first one on the left before V and one on the right of the second V.

All above letters were also Venetic with the difference that D was read as R and under Latin influence it was written and read as D. From the Gurina inscriptions we also know they were interchangeable during the transitional period; that is, D was read as D or R.

Of the two completely chiselled-over letters, the first one was, in my opinion, T and the second II; that is, Venetic JI, IJ or Latin E. Other letters suggest this. The inscription thus reads:

TU DON MUJI DUX

Slovene: Tu doni moj duh!
English: Here resounds my spirit!

tu—here; Slov. *tu.*

don—resound, resonate; Slov. *doni,* dial. *don,* imp. of *doneti.*

muji—my, mine; Slov. *moj* dial. *muj.* Czech *muj* locative or dative of *moi* (Skok). For this reason *muji* not *moj.*

dux—spirit; Slov. *duh;* Veneti also at times used Latin X for H. (They did not know xi).

In different words, the inscription reads:

Slovene: Božji duh pravičnosti naj doni s tega sodnega stola.
English: Let God's spirit of righteousness resound from this seat of justice.

The Origin of the Name Veneti

The theory about the autochthony of the Slovenes, advocated by Davorin Trstenjak, was rejected by historian Fran Kos with the observation that Roman and Greek writers (Herodotus, Polybius, Livy, Tacitus and Strabo) nowhere mention that a Slavic people lived between the Adriatic and the Danube. That is correct. These writers neither know nor mention the name "Slavs". It is common knowledge that this name in its Greek form "Sclabenoi" first appeared in documentary sources during the 6th century A.D. But does this mean that there were no Slavs or Proto-Slavs between the Adriatic and the Danube (if we limit ourselves to this area) at that time? By no means. We know that these writers were talking about the Veneti. Ptolemy, who was not only an astronomer and mathematician but also a geographer, calls the Slavs "Venedi".

Does this mean that the Slavic tribes, with whom these historians and geographers came into contact, had not called themselves Slavs or Sloveni?

The Polish Slavist, Leszek Moszyński, published several years ago an exceptionally interesting study *"Ist der Name Sloveni tatsächlich ein nomen originis?"—* Is the Name Sloveni actually a *nomen originis?* It appeared in Slovene translation in the journal *Jezik in slovstvo/* Language and Literature; 1978/9, pp. 5–6. This study signified a reinstating of the older etymology which derives the name "Slovenes" from "slovo—word. This etymology originated with Dobrovski who equated the *-ĕn* in *Slovĕn* with the ending *-ĕnin.* But more recent etymologists disagreed with Dobrovski, using the argument that the so-called "nomen originis" with the ending -ĕnin could only be formed from toponyms. Or more simply: Only those names which derive from place-names, e.g., Derevjani, Derevljani, Poljani, Ločani, were formed with this ending. Consequently, the explanation for the name "Sloveni" as having derived from *slovo*—word—(although self-evident) fell into disrepute. In its place a whole series of etymologies was produced. Even Šafařik tried his hand at it; he developed a derivation from the Lithuanian *salava.* From among the assortment of derivations, the one that was the least plausible gained acceptance (as is usually the case with historians) since its complexity made it seem the most scientific. It relates the name "Sloven(e)" with the root **k'leu, k'lou,** from which the Latin *cloaca*—sewer—is derived. Moszyński finally put things again in their proper order. With a very precise analysis he demonstrated that many scientists equate the suffix in the name "Slovan" (Slav), Sloven(e), with the suffix -j-ěnin. We find this in various other tribal names arising from toponyms, whereas in the name **Slovan, Sloven(e),** no trace of this epenthesis (inserted -j-) has been found until now.

Based on this and on an analysis of Proto-Slavic systems of tribal and ethnic names (in addition to the oldest historical documents which contain the name **Slovan** including OCS texts) Moszyński comes to the conclusion that the primary form "Slověni, Sloveni, Slovani" cannot be equated with the group of source names, which would mean that the name was not a "nomen originis". It was the appellative of the type "bratěnъ, bratenъ, bratanъ," and it stood for linguistic "relative" (pobratime), as opposed to those called "Nemci" (the mute ones), whose language was not understood. Not a single Proto-Slavic tribe called itself "Sloveni"; this expression was used for themselves and linguistically related neighbouring tribes when their actual names were not used for some reason. They are our "slověni". We and they are "sloveni". We speak a common language "slovenьskъ". One could not say: we are Sloveni, without having another, linguistically related group with which to compare oneself.

There have been quite a few things written about **the origin of the name Veneti,** yet none of the interpretations has become generally accepted. I think the etymologists could have done a better job. They completely overlooked one of the most important leads to the solution of this problem; that is, the name Veneti may well be nothing more than the Greek adaptation of Sloveni and especially the endearing forms: Slověnьci, Slovenьci, Slovaci, Slavonci, or Slovinci.

As is commonly known, there is no **sl-, slo-** in Greek or Latin. In order to facilitate the pronunciation of **sl,** the Greeks inserted a **c,** resulting in **scl** or **skl.** Also, neither of these two languages had the Slavic silent vowel. Furthermore, the Slavic **c** before the letter **i** was also foreign to them; on top of that the **v** was absent in Greek. As you can see, Greeks had good reasons to make the changes they made.

It appears that the **c,** before the silent vowel **ə** and other vowels, was made into a **t** for easier pronunciation. This is also the case in the *Brižinski spomeniki*— Freising Manuscripts; e.g., *imot'i.*

If along with Sloveni and Slovani, the name **Slo-venьci** had also been used (and it probably was), then how would it have been pronounced in Greek?

The name **Slo-venьci**—which could also be written **Slo-venьt'i,** since there is only a minimal difference between the letters **c** and **t'**—had caused difficulties for them. In it there are four phonemes which were foreign to them and difficult to pronounce. This is why they simplified the name: They discarded the first syllable and the last one they changed into **Henetoi** or **Uenetoi.** Because the **v**

320

was a foreign sound to them it was dropped. In its place they used an **e** with an additional spirant, **h** or **u.** Latin has the **v** so it changed the name into **Veneti.** The name survives in this form, as do several variations thereof: Venedi, Vinedi, Vendi, Vindi, etc.

Pliny (L III. 24) mentions that there was a village in Noricum called **Solvense.** Everything indicates that this is merely a reshaped **Slovence.** Pliny had written Solvense because the consonant group **sl** was foreign to him. Others simply omitted the first syllable (slo) but he kept it, though in a Latinized form with the **o** placed before the **l.** He also translated the Slavic **c** (mistaken for a **t** by foreigners) more accurately with an **s,** since the Latin **c** could either represent the English **ch** (before **e** and **i**) or **k.** Regarding its form, **Slovence** (Slovense) is accusative, replacing the nominative in many topographical names. For example: Šmarje and Medvode, etc. In Outer Noricum during Roman times, when the Slo-venetic people were forced into anonymity, there were several villages with names compounded from Wend-, Vind-, named after them; e.g. Vindobona (present Vienna). Pliny's original form survived in the name Solvense (Slovence). This name is also mentioned by A. Linhart in his historiography. He suggested that the name was a derivative of Solva or Salva. The hypothesis that Solvense might be a contracted form of **Solva mansio** is as superfluous as it is pointless. Linhart of course could not see it any other way; he was a great devotee of the official line which maintains to this day that Slovenes settled in the Alps only in the 6th century A.D.

The different groups of Sloveni had also used the name Slovani amongst themselves, the endearing form being Slovanьci. This explains another form which was used for the Slavs, namely **Anti.** Slo-vanьci was probably already reduced to Slovanci, from which Anti (not Vanti) was derived. As already mentioned, the Greek does not have a dental **v,** barring some exceptions in dialects.

An interesting confirmation of the above hypothesis is represented by the Scandinavian form **Ven, Van** for Slavs. As we can see, **Ven** does not stem from Slo–venьt'i as did Veneti; rather, it is an abbreviation from Slo-ven, Slo-van.

No less convincing is the fact that the name Veneti was never used by Slavs to describe themselves. They were called thus only by their neighbours who had changed the names Sloveni, Slovani, Slovenьci, Slovanьci into Henetoi, Uenetoi, Veneti, Vends, Antes, Vens, Vans, etc.

The name **Windisch,** still used for Slovenes by their German speaking neighbours, can also be very adequately explained by the above hypothesis.

It should be mentioned that the name Slovan first appears in historical documents in the Greek form **Sklabenoi** during the 6th century. Why this form? Everything indicates that the earlier form **Slovenьci** had been gradually displaced by the shorter Sloveni or Slaveni. This then became the Latin **Sclavus** which, as a result of the prisoners from Slavic countries, came to be synonymous with slave.

Someone may wonder about the shortening or reshaping of the names. This is of course nothing special; it is done all the time. Let the reader look closely at an example he is grammatically familiar with, and he will have no problem understanding what I mean. Here are three names from Slovene usage, sometimes the first part of the name is used: **Vladimir—Vlado**; the letter **i** was exchanged for an **o** in order to make it sound right. Sometimes the second part is used: **Miro**; here an **o** is added. In case of **Valburga** we have **Vali** or **Burga**; and in case of **Valentin: Valens** or **Tine,** etc. Letters were removed or added in order to comply with Slovene usage. Such and similar name shifts also happen with tribes and nations.

The *Vita St. Columbani* (618) also confirms the fact that during the beginning of the 7th century **both names, Sclavi and Veneti, had been used synonymously.** There it is written how Saint Columban intended to journey to the land of the Veneti, also called Slavs. Since there had not been a settlement in the Alps in the 6th century, the two names clearly refer to the West Slavic Veneti, the predecessors of modern Slovenes. The chronicler understood that these were one and the same people with two names.

Summing up: As long as the name **Slovenьci** and **Slovanьci** were in use, the Greeks and Latins transcribed them as **Henetoi, Uenetoi, Anti, Veneti.** Later, when the shorter form derived from the first syllable became common, the name **Sclavi, Sklabenoi** became prevalent among foreigners. After this time, in the northern part of Europe, there emerged from Slo-ven and Slo-van the names **Ven** and **Van.** The Germans continued to use **Wenden** and the adjective **Windisch**, though the form **Vind** (from Slovinьci) is common.

I would like to note that F. Jeza also found a similar explanation for the name Veneti, but he associated it with his theory about the Scandinavian origin of the Slovenes. He deduced the name Slovenes from *Solvendi—*turned to the sun. To validate his etymology, all Slavs would have to be of Scandinavian origin since the name Slovani was common to all of them. Also, the similarities between Scandinavian and Slovene words can all be explained by the influence of the Venetic language on the whole area where it was spoken, from the Adriatic to the Baltic and to some degree in Scandinavia.

It is clear that the various forms of the name **Sloven(e)** have corresponding forms which adapted to the languages of non-natives during the course of history. I became aware of this etymology years ago, but I did not dare advance it until I discovered the morphology on the Ateste grammar tablets. Since we now have evidence of Slavic origin and character of the Venetic language, this explanation becomes very meaningful; it accords with Slavic, Greek, Latin and German phonetics.

As a result of this effort to show the gradual development of the **name Veneti** (which was widespread in many regions of Europe during antiquity), I think there will be a better understanding of the presence and contribution of the Proto-Slavic Veneti in the history of Europe. It will also reflect on the position of their descendants, the Slovenes.

Similarity of Slovene, Latvian and Breton Words

I am convinced that long before the Christian Era, there existed a connection between the Adriatic and Baltic regions; that is, between the Adriatic and Baltic Veneti. I base this conviction not only on a series of characteristics in the western Slovene dialects, but also on a comparison of the Baltic vocabularies, especially Latvian and Slovene. I found a whole series of words which exhibit sameness or similarity. Allow me to cite some of them here. The Latvian words were taken from a book on orthography; they are followed by the corresponding Slovene words and in parentheses the same words in one of the Slovene dialects. Particularly striking is the sameness of the Latvian words to those in the Slovene dialects. The literary Slovene exhibits slight variations due to its more rapid development.

Sagrabt—zagrabiti (zagrabt)
pagrabt—pograbiti (pagrabt)
sagriezt—zagristi (zagriest)
saest—zajesti (zajest)
sasalit—zasoliti (zasalit)
sadurt—zadreti (zadrt)
sarunāt—zaravnati (zarunat)
jemt—jemati (jemt)
maisit—mesiti (maisit)
mainīt—menjati (majnit)
samainit—zamenjati (zamainit)
paiest—pojesti (pajest)
pasedet—posedeti (pasedet)
paiet—pojti (pajet)

paržaget—prežagati (paržaget)
izmezt—izmesti (izmest)
vartit—vrteti (vartit)
paškielet—poškiliti (paškilet)
pazabt—pozabiti (pazabt)
parstat—prestati (parstat)
parstavet—prestaviti (parstavet)
pardot—predati (pardat)
pardurt—predreti (pardrt)
pariet—prijeti (parjet)
parnest—prinesti (parnest)
dunet—doneti (donet)
vienmer—venomer (vjenmer)
vienkop—venkup (vienkup)

Here are a few more Latvian words that are identical or are in close agreement with words found in Slovene dialects:

parvaret—prevarati (prvaret); **parziemot**—prezimiti (parzimet); **pekle**—pekelj(peklo); **parverst**—prevreč (parverzt); **parspet**—prespeti (prehiteti Plet.); **parradit**—preroditi (parradit); **parnest**—prinesti (parnest); **parliet**—preliti (prelit, parlit); **paziti**—paziti (pazit); **sadurt**—zadreti (zadrt); **parlit**—priliti (prlit, parlit); **pariet**—preiti (preit); **pazit**—paziti (pazit); **pazvanit**—pozvoniti (pazvanit); **parbegt**—prebegniti (parbegnt); **parlit**—priliti (prlit, parlit); **parvest**—prevesti (prvest, parvest); **sadurt**—zadreti (zadrt).

It is amazing how close these words are in their meaning, phonetics, and morphology to Slovene words. The written Latvian words cannot be distinguished from spoken words in Slovene dialects. The majority sound as if they came directly from Inner Carniola, Slovenia. What was thought to be exclusively ours turns out to be equally at home elsewhere, far from us among the Latvians in the Baltic.

Now let us look at another group of words which are also either the same or very closely related to literary Slovene and the surviving Slovene dialects, as well as other Slavic languages. We will visit Brittany in France. This is the land which was known in Caesar's book *De bello gallico* as the "land of the Veneti". The Bretons themselves call it **Breizh** (f.), while the residents of this land are called **Breizhiz** (Brejžic), a word still familiar to Slovenes as a proper noun. Considering that it refers to a people that live on the seashore, these names have meaning. In Slovene *breg* means coast, shore, and *brežan* is the coast dweller. **Breže** and **Brežice** are common place-names in Slovenia. Breton is still spoken in the once Venetic land along the Atlantic coast. The following Breton words and their French equivalents are from *Dictionnaire Breton-Français* by Roparz Hemon, 2nd edition, Brest 1948:

mennout—penser, vouloir; Slov. *meniti*, dial. *menət*. Both meanings (penser, vouloir) correspond to the Slovene *meniti*—to think, to believe.

meneg—mention; Slov. *omemba*—mention, still more obvious is the noun *omenek*—that which is mentioned. Pleteršnik has also *menek*—opinion—which is in every regard the same as the Breton.

yar—poule; Slov. kokoš, but also *jara, jarica* (pullet)—a young chicken, common Slavic.

iskriv—étonnant; Slov. čudovit—wonderful—is very similar to *iskriv, isker, iskrec*—lively, sparkling.

c'hoantaat—désirer; Slov. *kvantat* —talking obscenely.

c'hoant m.—désir, envie; Slov. *poželenje*—longing, desire, related to *hót, hóta*—pohotnost—desire (Plet.).

fretenn f.—cercle de fer; Slov. *železni obroč*, comp. with *vreteno*, dial. *vreten*.

venaat—s'affaiblir; Slov. *oslabiti*—to enfeeble and *veneti* dial. *venet*—to wilt.

marc'h—cheval; Slov. *konj*—horse and *mrha, marha*—old horse (Plet.).

donaat—approfondir; Slov. *poglobiti*, from *don, dno*—floor, bottom, Old Slav.

dno; dniti—to install the floor (Plet.); Lith. *dunet.*

skasek—qui marche gauchement—one who walks clumsily, identical to Slov. *skazek.* Also the Franconian word *skakkja* could be the same as Slov. *skaza*—deformity; OCS *kaziti.*

tec'h—fuite; Slov. *beg* and *tek*—flight, run.

yac'h—sain; Slov. *zdrav* dial. *jak*—healthy, strong.

yac'hat—guerir; Slov. *ozdraviti* dial. *jačati, jačat*—to make strong.

motet—rendu inconscient; Slov. *omotičen, omoten,* from *motiti*—dizzy, giddy.

pegat—lutte; Slov. *boj* fight; also *pehanje* from *pehati,* dial. *pehat*—driving hard, a horse.

mouez—humide; Slov. *vlažen* and *(pre)močen*—damp, soaking wet.

hiraat—(s')allonger; Slov. *hirati, hirat*—becoming frail, weak. *Hir*—consumption (Plet.).

rozellat—ramasser avec le rouable; Slov. *rožljati, rožljat*—to jingle, with money or clanking with weapons.

ozhac'h—homme marié ayant des enfants; father; Slov. *očak, očanc*—a fatherly older man.

palich m.—bâton pour abattre des fruits—a stick, a pole, Slov. *palica* or *palika* (Plet.).

palichat—abattre à l'aide d'un bâton—to beat with a stick; Slov. *paličat(i)* (Plet.).

abafaat—rendre ou devenir timide—to frighten; Slov. *prestrašiti* and *obavat(i) se* (Plet.). The adjective **abaf,** timide, is derived from **abafaat;** Slov. noun *obava*—fear (Plet.).

abretaat—avancer—to prosper; Slov. *napredovati, pridobivati;* Russ. *obretatь* pronounce *abretatь;* Old Slav. *obretati*—iterative of obresti. The root is *ret-* from which are derived numerous Balto-Slavic words; e.g., *obrest, obrsti, srečati* and Bulg. *sretnja,* etc. This word also belongs to the Slov. Rezian dialect: *obrietla*—she has found; i.e., gained. See Logar, *Slovene Dialects.* It is unlikely that **abretaat** would correspond to the French *apprêter*—to prepare—since the Breton **abretaat** and the OCS *obretati* (Russ. phonet. abretatь) are much closer in their form and meaning.

Caution is advised with French, Celtic, Anglo-Saxon and Italian words. Hidden in many of them is a Venetic substratum that entered either directly or through the Gallic or Frankish languages. The etymology of such words is usually designated as "unknown" or "uncertain" since no one has considered a Venetic origin.

maritell—tracas, souci—worry; Slov. *skrb,* and *mora*—nightmare, *moritelj* for *morilec*—killer (Plet.), in dialect *maritel.*

yez—langue;—language; Slov. *jez-ik*—tongue; Old Slavic root jez-, jez-ykь,

326

comp. OCS *kamy, kamikъ; jezykъ* was developed in the same way from the Proto-Slavic root *jezy-*. **Yez** was preserved in Breton. Interestingly, Vasmer does not mention the Breton **yez** as a parallel to *jezykъ*.

youc'h m.—cri, exclamation, plainte—call, cry; Slov. *juhu, juhej-sati, juhniti* (Plet.).

marvet—mourir—to die; Slov. *umreti, mrleti.* The adjective of **marv** is Slov. *mrtev*—dead.

mar adv.—tellement, si—so, so very; Slov. *tako* and *mar* with similar meaning, e.g., *mar je tako*—is it so; **mar** sub.—doute, incertitude; Slov. *mar*—concern, worry (Plet.), and *nemar*—carelessness, inattention.

kern f.—cime, sommet; Slov. *krn*—mountain peak, rocky summit. We have in Slovene a good explanation for this particular meaning of the word; the Old Slavic *krъnъ* is in the verb *krniti, okrniti,* from which the adjective *okrnjen*—reduced in size, shortened—is derived. The Celtic **kern** was also probably a mountain peak, truncated, reduced in height, since Druid temples were located there. However, the attempt to explain the Slovene *krn* through Celtic influence is rather meaningless since the word is common Slavic. The Russ. *kornatь* means to shorten; Slov. *krnit(i).*

ragellat—bavarder—to gossip; Slov. *regljati,* dial. *reglat* e.g. *babe regljajo*—the women chatter, gossip.

bistro adj.—lait qui file—milk that flows. This word is very interesting because the Slovene *bister, bistra, bistro* (Old Slavic bystrъ) means: fast, lively, active and at the same time also clear. "Along with the concept of quickness, there is also the association of the concept of clarity" (Plet.); for example, *bistra voda*—flowing, clear water. We also find both of these subtleties of meaning in Russian. With regard to the Breton **bistro** in the French etym. dictionary there is the remark "mot obscur". However, if we explain it on the basis of parallels with the Slavic and Slovene lexicon, "bistro" is no longer an obscure word. It means a bar where service is fast and clean.

pellaat v.—(s')éloigner—to move away; Slov. *peljati, (od)peljati se,* Slov. dial. *pelat*—to carry, to drive. In addition to Slovene this word exists only in Slovak and Serbo-Cr.

peurc'horet—très chaud, brûlant—very hot, burning, comp. Slov. *pregoreti*—to burn through.

nak m.—refus—no, refusal; Slov. *nak.*

nakaat v.—refuser—to refuse; Slov. *nikati* (Plet.); *zanikati*—to deny; *nakat* does not exist as a verb in Slovene, though it would be entirely in accord with the structure of the language.

hud m.—magie; comp. Slovene *huda* from *hud*—evil; there are numerous derivatives like *hudina*—evil, *hudič*—the devil, *hudoba*—wickedness, etc.

huderezh—hurlement; Slov. *tuljenje, rjovenje*, comp. Slov. *hudoreči*—to curse, insult (Plet.).

hudour m.—magicien; Slov. *hudir*—the evil one, the devil.

venaat—(s')affaiblir—to weaken; Slov. *venet(i)*, also *venot(i)* (Mikl.), Old Slavic *venati, venoti.*

skarsaat—diminuer, raccourcir—to diminish, to contract; Slov. *skrčiti(se)*, dial. *skarčit. Krčiti* is common Slavic.

skarn—décharné—lean; Slov. *shujšan*, Carinthian Slovene *skuren*, meaning horrible, shameful (Plet.). Comp. *skurne štorije* (Messner). The Russ. *skvernyj*—bad, repulsive, improper—shows that it is not a Celtic loanword. According to Mahek, says Vasmer, this word could be associated with the Slov. and Serbo-Cr. *kvariti*—to damage, spoil, and **kvar**—to harm.

sed—voici—here is; arch. Slov. *sod* and *tod*, Old Slav. *sьde*, Russ. *zdesь*—here.

serc'heg—amant—sweetheart; Slov. *srček, ljubček.*

serc'h—concubine; Slov. *srčce, srčece* (Plet.)—mistress.

tri—trois; Slov. *tri*—three.

tanavaat—(s)amincir, (se) raréfier; Slov. *tanjšati (se)*, Bret. **tanav**—Slov. *tanek*—thin, delicate.

reuziad—infortune, malheur—misfortune; Slov. *revščina*, from the root *rev-*. From this comes the Bret. **reuziad** and **reuz;** Slov. *revež, "revšad".*

preizh m.—proie; Slov. *plen*—plunder, *preža*—ambush. Also **preizher**—pilleur; *prežar*—he who lies in ambush, dial. *na prež* and *na preži*—lying in ambush. It is related to the Old Slavic *oprezati*, Slov. *oprezati, oprezovati*—to be on the lookout.

draen m., **drein**—épine; Slov. *dren*—cornelian cherry (Cornus mascula, a European shrub).

garan f.—grue (oiseau), crane; comp. *gavran*—raven.

derv—colloq.—chénes; Slov. comp. *drevo*—tree, *drevje* pl., dial. *drev.*

gor m.—chaleur—warmth; Slov. *gorkota* from *gorek*—warm. Bret. **goriñ**—chauffer; Slov. *greti*—to heat.

gorre m.—surface, partie supérieure; Slov. *površina* and *gornje, gorenje*—upper. Of interest is the designation Gorre-Breizh, Haute-Bretagne; Slov. Gornje Brežje (Upper Brittany). Just as significant is the word **gorreenn** f.—surface déterminée; Slov. *gorenje*, i.e. (omejena) *površina*, comp. *gornina* and *gorna*—mountain meadow; *goren*—the first floor, upstairs (Carinthian dialect).

gouyezh f.—dialecte; in eastern Styria, Slovenia, *golč, guč*—speech, Old Slavic *gučati*—to speak (Plet.).

gouelec'h—désert; Slov. *golež*—barren mountain, *goliš* m.—barren area (Plet.).

taravat—frotter; Slov. *tarem, tareš* from *treti*—to grate.

What conclusions can we draw from all this? Is it possible that these identical language forms came about by chance in lands geographically so distant from one another as Slovenia, Brittany, and Latvia? Does the similarity not suggest that these peoples and their languages must have been at one time very closely related? If so, when could this have been? Certainly not in recent times; that is, around the 11th or 12th centuries A.D. when, according to dialectologists, the diphthongization of the vowels began. We must also remember that, between the Latvians on the Baltic and the Slovenes on the Adriatic, there was all of central Europe and there was no known tribal migration of Latvians or Slovenes during that period or later.

These two languages must have already been in contact with each other before this period, in a much more distant past. Indeed they were. It was during the time when the language spoken in the specified area of Europe was the common Proto-Slavic language—the Venetic language.

The above presented words are a strong confirmation of this view. They are characteristic of the Venetic language inasmuch as it is known to us from the various inscriptions. Our conclusion is also supported by the fact that the Old Slavic letter jat (ě) was still the diphthong **ai,** and let us not forget reduction of the vowels.

What is the situation with the letter jat (ě) in Slovene dialects? Was it present in our dialects, such as those from Ribnica and Notranjska (Inner Carniola)? Judging from the following examples, it is quite certain that our dialects did not have it. The Latvian infinitive **maisit** is Slov. *mesiti,* dialect *maisit*—to knead. Likewise, Latv. **mainit** is Slov. *meniti,* dial. *mainit*—to think, to believe; or **maina,** Slov. *mena,* dial. *maina*—change. In Latvian the diphtong **ai** has survived directly from the Indo-European past, whereas the **ai** in Inner Carniola had a different course of development. Initially, it was **ai** (maisit); then it changed into jat **ě** (měsiti), only to revert to **ai** later on, where it has remained to this day.

If we consider that the Venetic substratum has with its linguistic peculiarities survived much better in the remote, mountainous areas, then we have a simple and logical answer: The Latvian **maisit** and the Slovene dialectal **maisit,** or **mainit** and **maina,** identical in every respect, have retained their identity because they both represent a remnant of the Venetic language which was not influenced by Old Slavic as we know it through Cyril and Methodius.

My ideas may surprise some people but they are a logical development; anyone willing to closely examine the above details will see that I am not far from the mark. Anyone unencumbered by traditional or official theories about the development of the Slavic and Slovene languages will certainly think about these problems very much along the lines I have. It is impossible to assume that identical words in such geographically remote languages as Slovene and Latvian came about by chance.

I would like to mention here that last year a very interesting study was published by Prof. Dr. Vojislav Nikčević, *Slovenački jat i venetski jezik*/The Slovene jat and the Venetic Language, *Zbornik radova*, num. 9, 1986 Cetinje, Yugoslavia. He presented in this study a broadly based, critical analysis of the Slovene jat in regard to the previous theories about it. He completely substantiated my views on this subject.

In regard to the Breton words which are at the same time Slovene, we might speculate that they could simply be the remnants of Celtic language on our soil, nothing more; however, this assumption is disqualified by the fact that the majority of these words are Slavic in general; i.e., they are also native to those Slavic regions where the Celtic influence did not reach. It is also true that the listed words are very productive in Slavic languages with respect to their derivatives. An exception might be the word **pellat,** Slovene *peljati,* which exists only in Slovene, Slovak, and Serbo-Croatian, and which Miklošič attempts to explain differently. This word could indeed be a Celtic remnant.

This comparison of three languages so geographically distant from one another as are Slovene, Latvian and Breton, gives as a fairly good idea what the linguistic map of Europe actually was during the first millennium B.C.

The knowledge that the Slovene dialects contain an abundance of linguistic proto-elements and even whole words which were already in use during the distant past should be an incentive to the linguists to devote more attention to these dialects before it is too late. The influence of school, radio and television is today very strong and the dialects are disappearing more and more; however, there are characteristics which are not subject to the changes brought about by the literary language. Among them are the ancient Venetic and Indo-European diphthongs and the reduced or silent vowels. These things are frequently not as modern as Ramovš and his students (myself at one time included) have maintained.

When I came to the end of this study, I found an essey by R. Rotković *Slovenski krugovi i mi u njima*—Slavic Circles and We Within Them *(Ovdje,* Feb. 1989). He mentions the Cronicle of Trajekt (Utrecht, 1477) the original text of which he personally examined in Amsterdam, where he discovered reference to Slavs on the Atlantic coast in antiquity: "Dagobertus perdomuit omnes Frisones et Slaves et Wiltos...". Rotković also mentiones the book *Le Slave et le Breton* by Feliks

Mihalovski (1861), who lived in Brittany. In his book he presents many Slavic words used by Bretons: mast, oslabit, lezuh (ležuh), jenih (ženih), ulavyza (ilovica), kazat, ploniet (planiti), obilje, plodovi, debelit, krasit, vrutz (vroč), bos, put, etc. All these words are still in daily use in the Slovene language. Rotković says that no one continued this research. Obviously, he has not as yet seen my comparative study on this subject.

Conclusion

At the conclusion of this study of the Venetic language, I would like to review some of my thoughts and summarize my position. I do this because some official historians and media people, who are more devoted to political expediency than anything else and who know nothing about things I have been examining, have already tried to distort and falsify my findings.

I began my investigation of the Venetic language on the advice of one of the most respected Slovene linguists. He would not have counselled me to do this had he not seen a possibility that the Venetic language, surviving in written form only in inscriptions on monuments, urns, and a few other objects, could be of Slavic origin. He thought that a poet trained also in linguistics might find something in these inscriptions which would not be apparent to a scholar with different training.

After many years of research, I discovered a number of important elements. On the Ateste tablets from the 5th century B.C. I found Slavic morphology and phraseology. The project became more and more attractive as I worked on the inscriptions found in the regions where we, the Slovene people, still live today. There is something in the human heart which gives rise to an emotion of well-being and even joy when we discover something of our past, regardless whether it is the past of two generations or the past of many generations.

I knew that my findings were not without significance. If the Veneti were Proto-Slavs—and the Ateste tablets not only confirm this but also provide an unambiguous proof thereof—then the official theory that our ancestors came in the 6th century to the area where we live today must be rejected, and we must return to the earlier understanding that the Slovenes are an indigenous, autochthonous people.

Based on my discoveries on the grammar tablets, I began to examine various inscriptions in order to determine whether they corresponded to one another. It turned out that they harmonized very well. I was unable to find a single inscription that could not be deciphered on the basis of the Slavic languages and the surviving Slovene dialects, above all the Slovene archaisms. The Kajkavian and Chakavian dialects were also of considerable help.

The Slovene language has its roots deep in the Venetic language; later, in the course of centuries, it developed into a literary language, in part as a result of contact with other Slavic languages to the north, east, and south. The criticism that my writings are founded on biased Slovene separatist motives are too absurd to justify a response, but I note that many historians do not oppose Poles, Czechs and Slovaks in their claim of being indigenous to their regions (i.e., being West Slavs and direct descendants of the West Slavic Veneti). The same historians find the mere thought that Slovenes are indigenous people and descendants of the Veneti degenerate and almost blasphemous. I cannot understand such glaring bigotry on the part of academically trained historians.

There are also archaeologists who say that there is no proof of continuity of population and culture in the eastern Alps and northern Italy. I would venture to say, however, that if we do not yet have archaeological proof, it does not prevent us from understanding that we are West Slavs and that we are direct descendants of the Veneti. There is enough evidence in other branches of research. The Slovene place-names for example, particularly in the Alpine region, reach as far as eastern Switzerland and are clearly of pre-6th century origin. Another example is the whole series of Slovene words in northern Italian dialects (mainly in the provinces of Veneto and Friuli) and the names on Roman monuments throughout the former Venetic territory. We cannot forget the similarity or sameness of such a large number of words in Slovene, Breton, and Latvian languages. It would be very strange indeed if we assigned any other than Venetic (Proto-Slavic) origin to these languages. Much of the language, especially in Brittany, was later Celticized, whereas the Slovene dialects retained their original Venetic form, characterized by vowel reduction and diphthongization. The Proto-Slavic Venetic language in the west developed faster then the Old Slavic in the east. There is much evidence that the farming culture of Slovene villages is indigenous Slavic culture, predating Romans and Celts. These are admittedly some very far reaching conclusions, yet they must be addressed and we must come to terms with them.

The criticism that the linguistic forms on the Ateste tablets are too modern is not valid. The majority of the modern forms of the verb *delati* also existed in the Old Slavic that **Cyril and Methodius** wrote. The forms of the verb *delatъ*—to work (supine), *dêlavъ, dêlaj, dêlahъ, dêla* (aorist), *delaję* (part. pres. act.)—did not change for close to two thousand years. The verb **jekat** also belongs to the same group, and the forms *jekat, jekal, jekav, jekaj, jekah, jeka, jekaje* fully correspond to the above forms of the verb *delati*. **The only difference between Venetic and Old Slavic is their alphabets.** The Veneti did not have letters for reduced vowels and nasals, and neither do we Slovenes, which makes the similarity between the two languages even more striking, especially when the Venetic is transcribed into our Latin script. Thus, the criticism that I do not take into account the principles of language development is far-fetched. I constantly keep them in mind and I also keep in mind the fact that development of the western Proto-Slavic language was different from that of the eastern Slavic. The critique which states I have forgotten the 3000 years that separate Slovene from Venetic makes no sense. **The language which was written by Cyril and Methodius** did not begin with them, but in fact originated centuries earlier. The chronological difference between the Ateste forms of the verbs and the modern forms in Slovene and other Slavic languages encompasses a time span of 2500 years. Yet the chronological difference between the Old Slavic forms which brothers Cyril and Methodius first wrote down, and the Venetic from Ateste is much shorter, perhaps only a few hundred years, for we have no proof that the Slavs in the east had not spoken the same language centuries earlier as they had during the time of Cyril and Methodius. I suggest to such historians and linguists who would condemn my work that they examine all these details in a scientific manner.

In analyzing the Venetic inscriptions I have tried to examine each word from as many angles as possible; moreover, I based my work exclusively on well-known etymologists. Yet at the same time, I often came to new findings which were not possible before the discovery of the Ateste tablets. During the course of my research I was naturally very pleased whenever I discovered a word in our language that survived through the many centuries in an almost unaltered form.

There is a certain amount of objection to Slovene toponyms in northern Italy; the opposition insists that they are due to a migration of Slovenes into Friuli in the Middle Ages. A few names could perhaps be explained away in this manner, but this hypothetical settlement is a question in itself and cannot in the least explain the whole series of places named after the Slavs. In the Euganean hills southeast of Padova there is a place called Schiavanoia, and west of here Schiavicone, north of Padova Schiavo, a Po River tributary called Schiavenna, and southeast of Este (Venetic Ateste) a place called Schiavonia and so on.

The Slavs were obviously present in the western Alps and northern Italy during Roman and pre-Roman times, otherwise where did these names come from: Golliaz (Goljač), Blatta (Blata), Otemna (Otemna, from *tema*), Voza, Dogliani (Doljani), Susa, Cozie (Kozje), Osiana, Meia, Bersezio (Vršič), Nova lessa, Razor, Verigo, Sasseglie (Zaselje), Selle, Selzach (v Selcah, north of Turin), Ornavasso (Orna or Gornja vas), Salessio (Zalesje), Olessio (Olesje), Prelaz (in the Alps north of Turin), Rodin, Verzel (Vrzel), Bersac (Vršac), Gora (near Ligurian coast), Vissoie, Saloka (Zaloka)?

The Venetian chronicler, Martin da Canala, wrote something concerning the **derogatory term Sclavons used by the Genovese when referring to Venetians** (*Etim. riječnik*/Etymological Dictionary, Skok). These names were after all not just names; they were related to actual people. They show us very simply that the Veneti and their descendents the Venetians, were Slavs and were considered to be Slavs. The Venetians themselves did not like to talk about their Slavic predecessors, but their rivals and enemies made sure that it was not forgotten.

It is understandable that the Venetians were not happy about being reminded of their "Schiavonian" origin, since they did not know that they were heirs of a great culture, a culture centuries older than that of the Romans and comparable to the Greek and Etruscan. The Venetic culture was not simply an extension of the Etruscan; it had a status of its own. Its artistic expressions were uniquely Venetic; its language, although related to the Etruscan, was as distinct as one Slavic language is distinct from another. The difference between the Veneti in the eastern Alps, the Slovene Littoral and Dalmatia and the Veneti of northern Italy is that the latter allowed themselves to be Romanized, while the former were able to maintain their language and customs, perhaps because they were a greater distance from Rome and were able to secure more favourable terms from the Romans. Later, after the collapse of the Roman Empire, new Slavic influences from the north, east and south also helped to preserve Slavic language and traditions.

As already mentioned, **the Veneti and the Etruscans were related, and they both came from the north.** The Etruscans later mixed with another people but their northern origin was never completely lost.

The relationship of the Veneti on the Adriatic's east shore to those on the opposite shore is a chapter in itself, but since they were skilful mariners we can be sure there was no lack of exchange, friendly or unfriendly. We know that in regard to deciphering the Etruscan language, the dialect of Vrgada Island in the Adriatic is of major importance. There are similarities between the two languages; the diphtong **oa** is a specialty of Vrgada which is also regularly found in the Etruscan. Regarding the association with the Illyrians, it can be safely said that the Veneti were on a higher cultural level. Evidence can be gleaned from the Venetic loanwords in the Albanian language which developed on the Illyrian foundation. These loanwords are mostly from the upper strata of the language representing concepts which accompany civilization.

All remnants of Illyrian language—with the exception of a very short, three-word inscription from Shkodra, Albania—were found on the opposite side of the Adriatic in Calabria and Apulia, Italy. These are the so-called **Messapian Inscriptions.** They are known to us mainly through the book *Die Sprache der Illyrier/* The Language of the Illyrians, Hans Krahe (1955). There are some 250 brief inscriptions and three longer ones in Messapic language. The longer texts are presumably public documents and the short inscriptions are funerary and votive in nature. This language was spoken by a people who invaded southern Italy from Illyricum around 1000 B.C. I recognized at first sight some words in the inscriptions that are in structure obviously Slavic, while the names on the gravestones are non-Slavic. In the inscriptions there are syntagmas like **plastas molda**— Slov. *plačaš mlada*—you pay young (f.); **bilia**—Slov. *bilje, življenje*—life. What can we conclude from this? If the names on the gravestones are Illyrian but other inscriptions are Venetic, then Venetic was the language presumably spoken and written by the ruling class. Were the Messapian Illyrians subordinate to the Veneti or perhaps to the Etruscans, who spoke a language similar to Venetic? Who knows?

Who were the Veneti in northern Italy and the eastern Alps? What were their relations with other peoples of their time? These things cannot be known unless we take into consideration a wider area, at least in this part of Europe. I am totally convinced that the Slovene people are indigenous to this region regardless of the very strong opposition from official historians. The classically trained intellectuals are terrified at the mere thought that history did not start with Romans and Greeks. The conservative element among our Slovene intellectuals is also convinced that we became civilized only after our contact with the Latins. This is obviously not so. The cosmic clock was working even before the Romans and Greeks.

A theory that is breaking new ground is in danger of being used for any number of low, dishonourable purposes. My own work did not escape this kind of treatment. Particularly offensive and backward is the attitude of the Slovene historian Bogo Grafenauer, who made special effort to malign and discredit my discoveries. His fanatical devotion to the official Serbian point of view has made him intellectually insensitive. He did everything in his power to invalidate and disprove my work even before he examined it. My thesis on the origin of Slovenes did not fit in with his total dedication to the Serb dominated establishment. All important elements of Slovene history and culture were adjusted in a way that pleased the Serbian bosses of his department.

The intention of my research was from the very beginning to uncover that part of our history which has been denied us by official historians for political reasons. Our history was written and dictated by foreigners who had, and still have, designs on what is left of our ethnic territory. I wrote in 1941 when the forces of Fascism and Nazism launched their massive assault on Slovenia, that the trees become aware of their roots only when a powerful storm is raging over the forest. At that time I did not know just how deep our roots were; I did not know they went as deep as the very beginnings of European culture.

Now that I have come to the end of this study, I would like to say once more that I do not consider my interpretation of the individual words or texts of Venetic inscriptions to be definitive. There will be perhaps other, more competent linguists who will be able to discover additional details; nevertheless, anyone wanting to approach the Venetic language will not be able to ignore the Ateste grammar tablets. **Their Slavic morphology cannot be removed or doubted or refuted.**

* * *

I wish to thank all who helped me in any way, or stood by my side during my Venetic "adventure", among them Anuša Sodnikova, my wife, who helped with copying and ordering the many strange and difficult words, and Alojz Wagner who assisted in gathering a variety of literature and other sources. Special thanks to Ivan Tomažič who made the printing of my Venetic studies possible in the German, Slovene and Italian languages.

337

Bibliography

Considering that my study is also a critique of the existing Venetological research, I am using classifications of individual inscriptions as found in *La lingua venetica* by Giovani Battista Pellegrini and Aldo L. Prosdocimi Padova 1967; and in *I Veneti antichi* Fogolari and Prosdocimi Padova 1988. These two works are to date the most detailed presentations of the Venetic linguistic heritage.

The individual inscriptions are numbered and lettered as they are found in the above two books, guided by the locations and districts of archaeological sites: Es—Este, Pa—Padova, Vi—Vicenza, Tr—Treviso, Od—Oderzo, Bl—Belluno, Ca—Cadore, Ag—Agordino, Is—Isonzo, Ts—Trieste, Gt—Gailtal, Ad—Adria. The inscriptions from Slovene areas are listed under Is, Ts, Gt. Inscriptions from Negova are not listed in LLV. One inscription is taken from Fabretti's "glossarium Itallicum", and one from Lajeune.

All objects, with longer but mostly shorter inscriptions are preserved in the northern Italian museums, in towns as annotated in the *La lingua venetica*. They are: Museo Nazionale Atestino (Este); Museo Civico di Padova; Museo Civico di Vicenza; Museo archeologico del Palazzo reale di Venezia; also in the Museo civico di Treviso; Museo Montebelluna; Museo di Storia Naturale di Verona; Museo Maffeiano di Verona; Museo civico di Adria; Museo Cadorino di Pieve di Pieve di Cadore; Museo civico di Oderzo. Those from Slovene lands are mostly in the Kärntner Landesmuseum in Klagenfurt/Celovec; the Naturhistorisches Museum (Prähistorische Abteilung) and the Kunsthistorisches Museum (Prähistorische Sammlung), Vienna.

La lingua venetica (abbreviation LLV) by Giovani Battista Pellegrini and Aldo L. Prosdocimi (Instituto di glottologia dell' Universita di Padova, 1967).

This excellent book is the most important source for Venetological studies. The inscriptions are introduced with clarity and care and were the basis of my research, although my interpretations differ partially from those of other Venetologists. Part Two of the book is not very interesting; it is devoted to the interpretations of individual words and "names". The reproductions in LLV of the inscriptions and objects on which they are found, offer everyone an opportunity to examine my work and join the study.

338

Albansko-srpsko-hrvatski Rečnik, 1981.

Alföldi, Geza: *Personennamen in der römischen Provinz*, Heidelberg, 1969.

Alföldi, Geza: *Noricum.*

Berlot, Anton: *Eine studie der Sprache der Rassenen oder Etrusker*, Zürich, 1966.

Bezlaj, France: *Etimološki slovar slovenskega jezika*, Ljubljana 1976–1982, I, II.

Bezlaj, France: *Slovenska vodna imena*, Ljubljana, 1956.

Bezlaj, France: *Eseji o slovenskem jeziku*, Ljubljana, 1967.

Courtenay, Bauduin de: *Materialy dlja južnoslavjanskoj dialektologiji i etnografiji*, 1895.

Dennis, George: *The cities and cemeteries of Etruria*, I, II.

Dicziunari rumantsch, latin-tudaisch, Switzerland, 1979.

Fabretti, A.: *Corpus inscriptionum italicarum*, 1867.

Fogolary—Prosdocimi: *I Veneti antichi*, Padova, 1988.

Georgijev, Vladimir: *Etruskische Sprachwissenschaft*, Sofia, 1970.

Georgijev, I. V.: *Dešifriraneto na etruskija ezik*, Sofija, 1971.

Holder: *Altkeltischer Sprachschatz*, Graz, 1962.

Irish-English Dictionary, Dublin, 1932.

Islandsko-russkij slovar, Moskva, 1962.

Jabornegg: *Kärntens Römische Alterthümer*, 1870.

Kiekers, Ernest: *Einführung in die indogermanische Sprachwissenschaft*, München, 1933.

Kos, Milko—Ramovš, Franc: *Brižinski spomeniki*, Ljubljana, 1937.

Krahe, Hans: *Die Sprache der Illyrier*, 1955.

Latviski-angleska vardnica, Goeppingen, 1946.

Lejeune, Michel: *Manuel de la langue Venete*, Heidelberge, 1974.

Leskin, A.: *Handbuch des Altkirchenslavischen*, Heidelberg, 1922.

Logar, Tine: *Slovenska narečja*, Ljubljana, 1975.

Mayani, Zacharie: *Les Etrusqes commencement a parler*, Paris, 1961.

Megiser, H. and J. Stabej: *Slovensko-latinsko-nemški slovar*, Ljubljana, 1977.

Miklošič, Franc: *Etymologisches Wörterbuch der slavischen Sprache*, Wien, 1886.

Miklošič, Franc: *Altslovenische Laut und Formlehre*, Wien, 1850.

Nikčević, V.: *Slovenački jat i venetski jezik*, Zbornik radova, Nikšić, 1968.

Onomastica jugoslavica, glasilo medjuakadem. odbora za onomastiku, Zagreb.

Pallottino, Maximus: *Testimonia linguae etruscae*, Firenze, 1968.

Pauli, C.: *Corpus inscriptionum etruscarum*, Roma, 1864.

Pellegrini, G. B. and Prosdocimi, A. L.: *La lingua venetica*, Padova, 1967.

Pleteršnik, Maks: *Slovensko-nemški slovar*, Ljubljana, 1894.

Rječnik govora Vrgade, Zagreb, 1973.

Roparz, Hemon: *Dictionaire breton-français*, La Daule, 1948.

Sanskrit-English Dictionary, Oxford, 1963.

Skok, Petar: *Etimologijski rječnik hrvatskog i srpskog jezika*, I, II,III, Zagreb, 1971.

Stowik, J.: *Die Slaven*, S. Mórton, 1908.

Vasmer, M.: *Etimologičeskij slovar russkogo jazika*, Moskva, 1964.

Wahring: *Deutsches Wörterbuch, mit einem Lexikon der deutschen Sprachlehre*, Berlin, München, Wien, 1975.

Slavic Elements in the Etruscan Language

The Etruscan, Rhaetian and Yapodic Inscriptions

Matej Bor

Introduction

In the earlier chapters of this book we saw that the Venetic (Slovene) toponyms are spread over a wide area of south-central Europe, including northern Italy (Etruria) and eastern Switzerland (Rhaetia). In Yapod country (Istria), the ancient language has been retained and is used in its modern form to this day. As is commonly known among paleographers, the Etruscans, Rhaetians and Yapods used a script almost identical to that of the Veneti. Is it possible that their languages were related?

Although we inherited inscriptions from these three nations, linguists have so far not been able to decipher them. There is one exception though. Anton Berlot decided to study them with the help of the Slovene language and he was relatively successful. The Etruscan, Rhaetian and Yapodic inscriptions are (officially) still considered an insoluble puzzle, and the reader may well question the possibility of deciphering them with the help of the Slovene and other Slavic languages. However, we were in a very similar position in regard to Venetic inscriptions, and we succeeded to a fair degree.

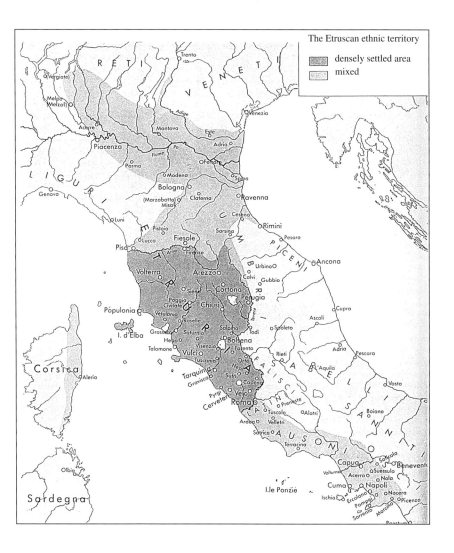

The Etruscan ethnic territory

densely settled area

mixed

Slavic Elements in the Etruscan Language

The Etruscans were a people originally closely related to the Veneti; they came from the north and in course of time merged with another people which eventually influenced also their language. Their oldest inscriptions can be deciphered like those of the Veneti; however, their later inscriptions are increasingly influenced by a language which descended, as it seems, from the Hittite and are therefore undecipherable through Slavic languages.

Dr. Vladimir Georgiev, a well known Bulgarian scientist and Etruscologist, published a study *Altetruskische Inschriften/* Old-Etruscan Inscriptions, Sofia 1970. Unfortunately, he made a big error by trying to explain the Etruscan inscriptions including the oldest (which can be deciphered only with the aid of the Slovene and other Slavic languages) exclusively through the Hittite language.

Another attempt to clarify this problem is very interesting and instructive. The French archaeologist Zacharie Mayani—who is also mentioned in Berlot's book on the Etruscans—believed that the Etruscan language was related to the Albanian, *Les Étrusques commencent à parler/* The Etruscans Began to Speak, B. Arthaud, 1961. He proceeded to decipher it following this theory, but eventually came to the conclusion that the majority of the Albanian words he used for deciphering the enigmatic Etruscan language were actually of Slavic origin—they were **Slavic loanwords**. We know that these loanwords were not introduced into the Albanian language after the settlement of the South Slavs in the Balkans in the 6th century A. D.; they were borrowed many centuries earlier from the language of their West Slavic neighbours—the Veneti. I mentioned earlier the particular importance of the Vrgada Island dialect in regard to deciphering the Etruscan language. On this island we find the best preserved archaic Slavic dialect of all the islands in the Adriatic, the so-called Chakavian and Ikavian dialects. One of the outstanding peculiarities of these dialects is the diphthong **oa** in words such as **doar** and **moariti**. This diphthong is also a common feature of the Etruscan language.

Our suggestion that the Slavs lived in the Balkans in antiquity, before the arrival of South Slavs in the 6th century, is strongly supported by a forgotten excerpt from the writings of Mojsij Korenski (born in 370 A.D., died in the second half of the 5th century), in which he acknowledged their presence in that area at that time. Dr. Ivan Mužić, who pointed this out to me in his letter, quoted this section from a Venetian edition. The same was quoted by M. Premrou in his *Monumenta Sclavenica*, Ljubljana, 1919: "The Slavs dwelt in the 'vast land' of Dacia. When it was conquered by the Goths, they (the Slavs) migrated to Thrace, Macedonia, Achaea and Dalmatia."

Let us return to the Veneti and the Etruscans. As far as we know, they were contemporaries. Their writing was so similar that the paleographers often find it difficult to establish which of the two people should be credited with a certain inscription. In the nineteenth century, the Venetic inscriptions were generally attributed to the Etruscans. The German historian Momsen, an authority in his time, was of the opinion that the Veneti were northern Etruscans—a plausible theory, since the Etruscan towns of Bologna and Spina (to mention just two) in the estuary of the Po and Adria Rivers were north of the Apennines. Yet, on the basis of subsequent discoveries, Momsen's thesis could be also seen from the opposite perspective. We could say that the **Etruscans were southern Veneti**. It is known that they called themselves **Rasenna** (according to Dionysius of Halicarnassus). The Greeks called them Tyrsenoi or Tyrrhenoi. Their country was called Tyrrhenia in Greek and Tuscia, or Etruria in Latin. Although there is a theory which considers them to be migrants from areas north of the Alps, there is no explicit evidence of their Slavic origin in a direct European line. All evidence has disappeared in the course of time, largely due to the Romans who, after centuries of war against them, finally defeated the Etruscans—their teachers— and subjugated them. It is known that Emperor Claudius wrote a history of this nation in several volumes; unfortunately, the work was not preserved. It was probably destroyed by successors of Claudius who wanted to remove every trace of information about the Etruscan people who gave the Romans their culture and were in turn destroyed.

The ignoring and belittling of the Etruscans has continued through history. Researchers have been unable to prove that the Etruscan language was an Italic dialect and have decided, for fear of loss of the "Latin identity", that it stemmed from a prehistoric language group; as such it could not be deciphered or interpreted by means of any known language. Out of this developed the so-called hermetic method through which some researchers tried to decipher the Etruscan from within itself. This has taken them nowhere and the study of this language has ended in a blind alley thanks to the unscientific approach.

Some Italian experts were especially troubled by the possibility of a connection between the Etruscan and Slavic languages. The West Slavs were, to a large extent, either driven out of their traditional territories or assimilated by other nations. For a long time they have been looked upon as an inferior race; therefore, all traces of their presence had to be removed. This attitude is still very much alive and I would like to expose it with the aid of evidence preserved in the language of the Rasennes.

The wave of the Venetic (Proto-Slavic) settlers which spread over the Alps to the northern Adriatic in the 2nd or 1st millennium B.C. did not stop there, but proceeded over the Apennines, across the Italian peninsula, and in limited numbers as far as Sicily.

Perhaps the best way to start this inquiry is to look at some words whose meaning is known to us through the ancient Greek and Latin authors, or those associated with drawings and objects on which they are inscribed.

It is known that Maecenas Caius Cilnius, who was the teacher of certain Roman poets, among them Horace, descended from the Etruscan tribe **Silni**—powerful, strong; Slov. *silen.* Livy, (X, 3), who mentions this name in the Latinized form **Cilnium** and **Cilnii,** also tells us that this tribe was a *gens potens.* This would by itself not serve as proof for the connection between the Slavic and Etruscan languages, but there are a number of other words known and preserved.

A good example is the surname **Markezič,** even now present in Slovene and the languages of South Slavic nations. In a senate committee of Trst (Trieste) a member named Markezič (Ital. Marcesic) fought for the rights of the Slovene language. This surname descended from the Etruscan; it is written in the vault *dell Orlo* (probably from the 4th or 3rd century B.C.) and is so well preserved that it cannot be overlooked. In the *Testimonia linguae etruscae,* Maximus Pallottino, (TLE) p. 32, inscription **84,** it is copied out exactly, but in the index he changed this name into *Marcesi,* just as was done under the fascist regime when the Slovene names were Italianized. Similarly treated was the name **Marcešič** (see *Index patronymique, Catastre national de l'Istrie*—Index of Surnames, National Land Register of Istria, Sušak, 1946). To minimize or hide the offence, he added to *Marcesi* the number of the inscription and after that in brackets the letter **c.** Why this roundabout method? Did he fear that unless things were distorted, the Slavic origin of this undeciphered language would be discovered? He did the same with the name **Matvešič** (Istrian, Matešič) and other words testifying to the Slovene or Slavic elements in the Etruscan. Another example is **puliac,** which he correctly transcribes in the text, but in the glossary records as *pulia* with the inscription number and the letter **c** in brackets. He used this same method in the word **Aninaic,** which was changed to *Aninai.*

The surname **Matvešič** has also been falsified in Pallottino's glossary in *Testimonia linguae etruscae* (TLE). It is found in the "vault of inscriptions" from the 6th century B.C. in its unchanged original form **Matvesic.** He copied it correctly in the text but not in the glossary; there the letter **c** was not included.

The Etruscan word **velznalc** has undergone the same procedure; the letter **c** is still present in the transcription but is omitted in the glossary (TLE 138). The meaning of the word **velznalc**—man of learning—has been preserved in the Slovene language to this day.

Veliak is also an old Etruscan word; in Slovene *veljak*—a worthy. It is found in four inscriptions (**TLE 326, 560, 561, 630**) written as **veliak** and once as **veline**. In his glossary Pallottino removed the final **k**. The too obvious similarity or sameness with the Slovene *veljak* was too disturbing to Pallottino. There is very little doubt that **vel** had the same meaning in Etruscan times as it has today in Slovene and other Slavic languages; i.e., a great man. This is also reflected in a bilingual inscription giving some old Etruscan words in translation: *violens* in the inscription **605** referring to **velimen**.

As we can see, the obvious Slavic character of these words was tampered with. If we consider this and Pallottino's introduction to his *Testimonia linguae etruscae* (TLE), it is obvious that for Italians the issue is far from unimportant. History tells us that the Romans and Italians respectively, are obligated to the Etruscans for a great part of their spiritual and material culture; therefore, it was important to determine where the origins of the Etruscan culture were. To prove that these origins were Slavic, at least in part, would evoke strong disapproval and opposition from some Italian researchers. It would also cause the Italian identity to lose some of its splendour, at least in the minds of certain segments of Italian society.

It is a known fact that long before the invention of gunpowder, lead missiles were used for combat, *glans missilis plumbea.* Various short inscriptions were engraved onto these objects. One of them (**TLE 784**) bears the word **strevc.** It is a Slovene word, still used, *strelec,* colloquially *strevc*—marksman. After many similar examples we cannot dismiss this as a coincidence. So, someone had written the word *strevc* on a missile. Similarly a Venetic soldier made the inscription on another missile: **otergin** Slov. *otržan,* after the village of **Oterg** (see *La lingua Venetica,* Pellegrini/Prosdocimi).

The meaning of the Etruscan words is unknown to us, but there are dozens of words whose meanings have been passed to us by Greek and Latin authors. Pallottino compiled them in his book on pages 101 to 107 together with the original explanations of the ancient authors.

One of these words which should have long ago attracted the attention of linguists is **droŭvna,** same meaning as the Old Slavic *drevьno*—ancient. The form and meaning of this word have been preserved in several Slavic languages, the only difference being the vowel **e** in Old Slavic and modern Slavic languages in place of the Etruscan **o**. Experts in Old Slavic grammar and phonetics know

347

that the word *drevъno* and examples like *devet, kleveta* are an exception to the rule. The letter **e** in front of **v** turned into an **o**. The Etruscan form is thus even more correctly Slavic than this form in modern Slavic languages, and belongs to the type of words like *slovo* or *plovo*.

The Etruscan month of March in Latin transcription was called **velcitanus.** If we take away the suffix **us** and bear in mind that the letter **t** was sometimes exchanged with **d,** we get *velci dan.* In Serbian *velik dan* means Easter. This is the festival of spring, the time when the day grows "big" (in Slovene, *velik*). The same words are found in Old Russian, whereas in Lithuanian Easter is called *velikos.* There obviously exists a connection between the Balto-Slavic and the Etruscan (Venetic). The letter *c* in *velci dan* could be taken for a *k,* or perhaps the Etruscan language and the Venetic of the later period, already included palatalization.

The month of October was in the Latin transcription called **xosfer,** which has to be read as **gosber,** although the Etruscologists usually—without a good reason—read the letter *b* as *f.* **Gosber** leads us to the comparison with the Serbo-Cr. *gozba*—feast. This word has the same derivation (see Skok) as *gost*—guest, in Czech, *host.* When the guests arrived, there was a *goz-ba* (feast). The best occasion for *gozba* or *gosber* was in October at grape-harvest time in Etruria.

The Etruscan name for Ulysses was **Nanos.** *"Pará Tursenoís Nános kaleítai"*— Ulysses was washed ashore. What should we think of this? What is the connection to the Slovene *nanos* (something which is washed up or deposited by water)? **Mt. Nanos** in Inner Carniola (Slovenia) is a crumbling, eroded formation, its gravelly sides resembling something that has been deposited by water. The similarity of the two terms is remarkable. The Etruscan **Nanos** and the Slovene mountain have the same name.

Subulo—a piper; *"subulo tusce tibicen dicitur"* is obviously of Slavic origin. Common usage on the Krk Island: *sopele.* Also used in Slovene: *sopilo*—a wind instrument. *Sopela,* in the dialects of the Croatian coast, derives from *sopiti, sopeti, sopsti*—to blow (as into a wind instrument). The Lithuanian is *sapelka.* The Latin transcription should perhaps be *supulo.* Pipers are often portrayed on Etruscan objects.

An ancient report tells us (see TLE, p. 102, no. **814**) that the Romans inherited houses with *atria* (among so many other things) from the Etruscans. The *atrium* was the central space in the early Roman house; it had a hearth and a smoke hole in the roof and it served as the kitchen and the family room. The Old Slavic word *otrъ or atrъ* (acc. to Miklošič) is very close to it. We must note that *atri-um* is a Latinized Etruscan word which originally read *atrij.* Whether the **a** was pronounced nasally is not known.

The word **capyas**—hawk's claws—could be related to the Slovene *skobec*—hawk—and also *kopje*—spear.

A goddess in the Etruscan as well as in Latin was called *dea*. Some linguists object (without any apparent reason) to its connection with the Slovene *deva*—maiden. The Lithuanian word *deva*—goddess—speaks in favour of its Slavic roots. In Sanskrit *devi* also means goddess.

The word **baltea** also shows the proximity of the Etruscan and Balto-Slavic languages. The only thing we are told about this word is that it was a *"tuscum vocabulum"* Etruscan word. The Balto-Slavic *baltas,* originally *balto*—mud—is closely linked with it.

Another word of Etruscan origin is **histrio**—actor—which is no surprise since the Roman theatre was influenced by the Etruscan stage. This word has parallels in Slavic languages. In Russian and Ukrainian *hist* means artfulness, skill; it can also mean talent. In Berneker's opinion *hist* is connected with *hitit, hitrij* and further with the Slovene *hiter*—swift. In Russian the word *hitrij* has a different meaning—shrewd, cunning.

It is known that the Etruscan state leaders performed the function of religious authority. In Latinized transcription they were called **lukumones.** Where does the word originate? Perhaps from the Old Slavic *likč*. According to Miklošič the Ukrainian *lyčman* also developed from it. In the course of time **i** changed into **y,** which had a **u** sound, and was consequently written as **u,** since the Etruscan alphabet (similar to the Venetic) did not have a special symbol for **y.** In Ukrainian *lyčman* means the oldest herdsman or shepherd, an outstanding person. In Etruscan language it was probably the same but on a higher level, a secular and religious shepherd.

The Etruscan word **lanista** (gladiator) may well be related to the Slovene *(p)laniti*—to dash upon. The relation between *laniti* and *lanča* needs to be better understood. *Lanča*—lance—was used in Slovene in the 16th century. It is common also in other Slavic languages (Serbian and Croatian). Its derivation is not known. "It derives from the Latin *lancea*—lance—of unknown, perhaps Celtic or Illyrian origin," writes Bezlaj. Oddly enough he does not mention its possible derivation from the Etruscan. It is a historical fact that the Romans took many words directly from the Etruscans; **lanista** is one of them.

The most interesting toponym is **Popluna,** which was changed by the Romans in the spirit of their language into Populonia. Archaeological research shows that in Etruscan times this place was the centre of ironworks and was built on thick layers of slag. In need of coal during the First World War, the Italians began to melt the Popluna slag which still contained 35–40 percent iron due to the less advanced Etruscan technology. The grenades made of this iron were in

1917 killing Austrian soldiers, the majority of whom were Slovenes. This was written by Werner Keller in his book on Etruscans *Denn sie entzündeten das Licht/* For They Kindled the Light. Why the name Popluna? From Miklošič's etymology we know that the modern Slovene word *pepel* formed out of the Old Slavic *popelъ*. The root is *pel,* which developed into *pal, palež*—burning—and *po* means after. Together they mean the leftover of burning, the residue of burning—ashes, slag. The place built on the *popel*—slag—was thus named Popluna. Taking into account Etruscan orthography, this would read Popeluna (Populonia).

A word whose meaning is known to us from Greek records is **moutouka** (thūmós) or lust for life, impulse. Trying to interpret it we cannot ignore the Old Slavic *motati se*—to move. It has been preserved in various Slavic languages. In Slovene *motati;* in Russian *motatь*—to move. In the Greek transcription the first diphthong might be a mistake and the word should possibly be spelled *motovka.* **Moutouka** is Slavic in form, including its ending.

Keeping in mind that the words so far examined are unequivocally Slavic, I think I am not going to offend science if I try to interpret as Slavic more words.

On at least two stone sarcophagi there is the word **kamna** (TLE 135, 138). What does it mean? Presumably the stone coffin itself was called **kamna.** It could still be called so now in the Slovene language. In both inscriptions it is actually written as **kamnas;** the context allows us the conclusion that **s** is not a suffix but rather a demonstrative pronoun. In Old Slavic *sъ* stood for—this—therefore: this **kamna,** this sarcophagus. Between punctuation marks the Etruscans wrote not only words but also syntagmas; although it is self-evident the official linguists have not taken this into account.

Two other sarcophagi bear the inscription **kamoi** instead of **kamnas.** In Polabian (Elbe-Slavic) the word for stone is *kamoj,* as in Etruscan. I have to mention that I read **o** containing a short vertical line as **o.**

The Etruscan word **meiani** (TLE 99) is the same as Slovene *mejaši*—those sharing a common border. They could also be called *mejani.* Similarly **mena** could have the same meaning as the Slovene *mena*—change of moon phase. One tomb bears the inscription **mena me kana** (TLE 730). In Slovene *mena me konča*—the change of the moon phase finishes me. The older Slovene for *končati*—to end, to finish—still found in Pleteršnik is *konati.*

I will examine a few more words which are of Slavic origin. They are found mostly in the older inscriptions when the language was still predominantly Venetic (Proto-Slavic). The Etruscan **lad,** sometimes **lado** with its semi–vowel **o,** was identical with the Slavic *ladъ*—harmony, concord, agreement. In Russian the word *láda* colloquially means sweetheart, beloved. In its verbal form, *ladati*—to sing—is found in the White Carniola region of Slovenia and in the Kajkavian dialect of Croatia. In modern Slovene language it is hidden in the words *lagoden, lagoda*—leisure.

The word **lud** is identical to the Old Slavic *ludъ*—insane, crazy. It is a common Slavic word still used in the same form in Serbian and Croatian. It is quite possible that the Latin word *ludus*—game, fun, jest—stems from the Etruscan, as the Romans had usurped many games from the merry or "ludicrous" Etruscans.

It would be superfluous to continue with these examples which will be found in the detailed examination of the Etruscan texts. I would like to look now at the difference between the official reading of some of the Etruscan letters and my reading.

The Etruscologists believe that the Etruscan language did not know the vowel **o**. On the basis of some comparisons between Etruscan and Latin inscriptions, we can safely say that the **o** was included in the Etruscan alphabet. If it had not existed then it would not be included in the Latin transcripts of the documented Etruscan words: **valado, korovis, lukumon, Nanos, subulo, gosber,** etc.

The Etruscans knew **o** and used it in their writing as they used other vowels. This can be confirmed through numerous inscriptions. It is true that some of these contain only an **o** with a dot or a crosslet in the middle (see the alphabetic plate from Marsigliana d'Albegna, various pitchers and other objects). Nevertheless, it is questionable whether this grapheme really stands for **th** as some researchers want us to believe. Might it not, as in the Venetic language, stand for the letter **o** to which was added a dot, a line or sometimes a small cross? The Etruscan inscriptions were engraved, cut, or written (judging from the result) by illiterate craftsmen. Perhaps they found the letter **o** too blank and graphically too dull and chose to improve it according to their own fancy. This led to confusing **o** with the Greek letter which has a dot in the middle, the **theta,** and is pronounced as **th.**

As long as Etruscan was a living language, those who read it were probably not too troubled by such creativity, although they might have scolded an engraver now and then. When the language died out in the course of time, nobody spoke it anymore and chaos ensued. Due to its similarity to the Greek *theta,* the letter **o** was progressively read as **th,** regardless whether it had the dot in the middle or not. This has been the case to the present. The confusion is all the greater as in some examples of Etruscan alphabet **o** with a dot in the middle actually represents the dental **t** or a similar consonant, perhaps even **t'** or **th,** since the difference between the Indo-European **th** and **t** was to a certain extent still felt at the time. When the writers were unable to distinguish between the two sounds any more, they wrote it indiscriminately either as **t** or as **o** with a dot. In my transcription the consonant **t** is used in both cases.

My opinion also differs in regard to the letter **D.** The official Etruscologists propose to read it as **R.** This letter has undergone a mutation as had the letter **o.** The Etruscan alphabet included the letter **D** as well as **P** (see Pallottino, TLE p. 13, and other records). I write these two graphemes here from left to right for easier reading.

The illiterate engravers often created confusion between the letters D and P; this is seen in numerous inscriptions. Sometimes they drew the body of the letter P low enough to make it look like a letter D. The reverse was also done; the bow of the letter D was joined to the ascender so high that a letter P was created. It is difficult for a scholar to distinguish between the two; however, if one approaches the inscriptions from the standpoint of similarity between the Etruscan, the Venetic and Slavic languages, then one can establish from the context how to read a particular grapheme.

Perhaps the Etruscans were not much bothered by such inexact writing methods since their **r** and **d** were very similar. The **r** was a retroflex consonant where the rotation of the tongue was barely perceptible or had gradually completely disappeared, as in Swedish or English, where the **r** merges with **d** into an apical pre–palatal retroflex. I have already described the changes of the letter **r** into **d** in the later period under Latin influence in the chapter *Spells and Sayings on the Rocks in the Carnic Alps,* in the inscriptions from Gurina.

The phonetic value of the letter **d** can be explained only within a particular context. For example the Etruscan scholars advocate that the word written in Latin as *lart* or *Lart* is a proper noun and is the Etruscan **larth.** One could possibly accept this reading, but the word **lad, lar,** appears too frequently. The word is clearly linked to the Slavic *lad*—peace, harmony.

In spite of the fact that official linguists prefer to read the word as **Larth**, it should be read in my opinion as *lado,* notwithstanding the Latin *Lart*. To the Latin ear the Etruscan **d** sounded as **r,** owing to the rotation which was still used. The final **o** which would in this case be a semi-vowel with a distinct o-sound, was increasingly omitted as too weak and alien to the Latin pronunciation.

Scholars insist that the Etruscan language did not know the voiced plosives **b, d, g.** I differ also in this case. It did not know the vocal plosive **g,** but used the voiced spirant instead. In transcription it corresponds to gamma γ and was also similarly written Ⴤ Ⴥ . This letter was also used for the voiceless velar spirant **h.** In my transcription Ⴤ denotes **h** or **g** depending on the text, and is a grapheme for the voiced spirant. The letter ⊢ ⊨ correctly read by scholars as **h** also served for the spirant **g** (gamma) in some inscriptions.

The letter **D** has been discussed above. B can also be found in the Marsiglian alphabet which is considered a variation of the Greek alphabet, and which was supposedly adapted by the Etruscans to their own needs. Some of the preserved alphabets do not have a B, but we should not overlook the fact that these do not include a **D** either. Does this mean that the *r* as such did not exist in the Etruscan or that there was no corresponding grapheme for it? This is most improbable, since **D** exists in other examples of the Etruscan alphabet and, of course, in the inscriptions.

Regarding the consonant **b**, it can be legitimately stated that it was often exchanged with **v** (betatism), as with the Veneti and to this day in the Tolmin area, western Slovenia. In certain word groups it was then written as **v** ⅂. One of the alphabets, which does not include the letter **b**, gives the similar looking number eight (8) instead, and is read by scholars as **f**, but this is clearly the second grapheme for the labial **b**.

The merging of **d** into **r** can be observed in other languages as well, and was mentioned in my Venetic study. Here I would like to give only two examples: the Latin *meridies* derived from *dedidies* (medium—the middle) and the Slovene place-name *Mirna peč* from the *mi(e)dna peč*, courtesy of Koštial.

One more remark: the Etruscan **e** sometimes reads **je**; *e.g.,* **pe—pje, e—je** (estь), similar to the Venetic **ego—jego** *(yego)*. The Etruscan language also had diphthongs which are written in various ways, although no special graphemes exist for them. Usually they are written as **ei, oa,** etc.

My conclusions are contrary to the official Etruscology:

1. The Etruscan language had five (not only four) vowels.
2. The consonants included **l** and **r**; **m** and **n**; **s**, **ś** and **z (ž?)**; **c (k)**, **t** and **p**; **v** and **h**; **b**, **d** and **g (γ)**; and **c** (affricate). It did not, however, include **f**, simply because the Old Etruscan was like the Venetic, a Proto-Slavic language (**f** is foreign to all Slavic languages). The Etruscan language possibly already had **č (ch)**, written as **c**. It also had diphthongs **ai, au, ei, oi, ui** and **oa**. Possibly it knew **j**, but did not develop a special letter for it and used **i** instead, similar to Latin which developed from the Etruscan alphabet. Very rarely does the grapheme ϙϕⅅ occur. Pallottino explains it as the Greek **ph**. I read it as a sound similar to consonant **b**, but close to w. It is known in the Slovene dialects.

The language of the Etruscan inscriptions, which I tried to decipher and translate, is very close to the Venetic and proves that the Rasennes and the Veneti were not only neighbours and contemporaries but also relatives. After the Rasennes had merged with a highly civilized people from Asia Minor, the languages also merged. The historians have not as yet been able to identify this newly arrived people. Some think that the newcomers came to the Tyrrhenian coast from Lydia, a kingdom in Asia Minor with the capital at Sardis. They rely for this information on "the father of history", Herodotus, the Greek who lived in the 5th century B.C. Most of the ancient authors accepted his explanation, with the exception of Dionysius of Halicarnassus who maintained that the Etruscans were the native, aboriginal people of Italy.

Who is in the right? I suppose both, each in his own way, inasmuch as Etruscans were the result of a union of two people. Herodotus was perhaps wrong to take the Etruscans for Lydians. Some scientists, among them Etruscologist Georgiev, believe that they were of Hittite origin. There exists a certain affinity between the Hittite and the Lydian languages , but the former is considered the older of the two. It seems they both originated from the old Indo-European. This hypothesis was well researched by Bedřich Hrozny, with his precise deciphering of the Hittite language.

Did the Hittites and the Veneti meet in the Apennines? Did the Etruscan language develop from the Hittite and the Proto-Slavic Venetic languages? These questions should be dealt with at length, and there should be a parallel and thorough investigation of this as yet mysterious language. When did their meeting occur? Who were the earlier settlers on the Italian territory, the Hittite or the Veneti? Were the Veneti there when the Hittites occupied the Tyrrhennian coastal area? About the relations of the two people one can only make a guess, but judging from the inscription below, they were not especially friendly. It reads as follows:

CENA
KALAT U RUS B APJE NAS
C JEME CU HETIE

In translation: Anyone drinking with him who is a Hittite, offends the Rasennes.

A more detailed interpretation of this inscription on a wine jug can be found among the texts. Here I would like to draw your attention to three words only: **Rus** (Rasenne); **Heti** (Hittite, also called Hati, Geti, the Egyptians called Cheta); **Cena**—this word is included in the Bezlaj's Etymological dictionary of Slovene language, meaning a tribe, a race (western Slovenia, Tolmin area.) **Cena** is also found in Štrekelj's dictionary.

That Herodotus and Dionysius of Halicarnassus were both right is also the opinion of P. Kretschmer (Glotta XX, 219 sgg). He reviewed the older findings of C.O. Müller, and thinks that the Rasennes represented the indigenous population of the area and that in the beginning of the first millennium B.C. the Hittites arrived from various Aegean lands and overpowered the Rasennes.

It would appear that the Hittites, who were speaking a language structurally and idiomatically at least partly Indo-European, did not find it too difficult to communicate with the indigenous population; eventually they merged with them. The Hittites were different from the Greeks in that they did not stay in their trading posts, but penetrated the hinterland (see Johannes Lehmann, *Die Hetiter/ The Hittites*, Vienna, 1986). As heirs to the more advanced cultures of the Near East, they changed the landscape and customs wherever they went. They founded cities, traded, dried marshy land and introduced various improvements that had never been thought of by the natives of the Apennine peninsula. The Veneti too contributed a great deal to the culture now known as Etruscan—among others, probably the alphabet. The Hittites traditionally used cuneiform writing and hieroglyphics, but soon adopted the Venetic alphabet, the origin of which is as yet unknown. Pallottino and other linguists are of the opinion that it developed from the Marsiglian alphabet, that is, via western Greeks; this has not been proved. Another possibility is that the Greeks and the Veneti both got their alphabet from the same source.

At the Vinča excavation site in the middle Danubian area, Prof. Dr. Radivoje Pešić discovered on various excavated articles all graphemes known in the Etruscan language; however, *the Vinča finds are several thousand years older than the Etruscan.* This brings to mind the possibility that the Indo-Europeans known as Veneti were on the Apennine peninsula much earlier than what the official historians allow (and if they were not, it is still entirely possible that they brought their alphabet with them). So far there is no counterevidence. This part of European history is still shrouded in darkness.

As I said earlier, the oldest Etruscan inscriptions found on jugs, mirrors, lamps and tombs can be deciphered on the basis of Slavic morphology. The surnames, professions and designations of non-Slavic origin, written on some sarcophagi, are a matter apart; they already show later influences. But there are still some traces of the Venetic language in the later inscriptions. The proverbs and admonitions are clearly a heritage of the Venetic (Slavic) past.

In my interpretations of the Etruscan texts, there are certainly things that could be explained differently. I nevertheless maintain that some of the anacreontic inscriptions on jugs which are mostly of Greek manufacture are linked with the object—the jug, the wine, the drinker—so logically that my translations cannot be effectively contradicted. They often explain the engraved images; e.g., Hercules nursing at the breast of the goddess. This led me to the decision that the joyous elements—song, music, dance, and play—on the Etruscan remains (even on the sarcophagi) are of Venetic (Slavic) origin.

The purpose of this study is to show what kind of linguistic neighbours the

Veneti had to the west, south and east. As we discovered through detailed analysis of the preserved words and texts, there was essentially no difference between the Veneti and their neighbours in this respect. They all spoke Slavic with some dialect variations. Pallottino's opinion, shared by many linguists, that non-Indo-European was spoken in the western part of the Italian peninsula and Indo-European on its eastern side, is poorly documented. In regard to the difference between the Rhaetian and the Venetic, we can say on the basis of the evidence we have that there was no substantial difference between them. The very name *Retia,* which is a deity among Veneti and a hunter among Rhaetians, is closely linked to the Slavic word *retiti*—to pursue intensely. Since the Rhaetians in their mountainous region lived mostly from the hunt, it is probable that *retijan* originally meant a hunter and later developed into the *nomen ethnicus,* the name of the people.

The Old Etruscan language—I repeat— was Slavic in its structure and meaning; so, all the older inscriptions can be unravelled with the help of Slavic vocabulary. Later, when it mixed with the Hittite (or Lydian), the situation changed. Since my field of interest is mainly the Venetic, as the language of the predecessors of the Slovenes, and its neighbouring related languages, my involvement with the Etruscan has been limited to the oldest inscriptions in which the Slavic elements prevail.

In my Venetic studies I stressed that the Slovene language with its surviving dialects and the Croatian Kajkavian and Chakavian dialects are of the utmost importance to these studies. These can be considered the key to the earliest written communications of European culture. A doubting Thomas should carefully read at least those Etruscan words whose meaning is known to us from the ancient writers; words like *velznalc, strevc, veljak, Markezic* and so on. To turn a deaf ear to these and similar words means that one has no aptitude for the language—even worse, it points to a certain lack of logic. It can be compared to the geologist who finds fossilized shells, snails or fish in the mountains, but stubbornly denies that the sea ever existed at that elevation.

As we continue with the examination of the Etruscan language, the reader will gradually shed any doubts; it will become obvious that the Slavic words in the Etruscan give a clear indication who these people were. Anyone who gives this study serious consideration will have no problem understanding that there is an organic connection between words and people. Like the geologist up in the mountains, if he is at all attentive he will recognize that indeed the area was at one time under the sea, namely the sea which nourished the particular species. The same can be said about a dead language like the Rasennian. When you find in it Slavic words which are still in use, and some which are typically Slovene, you cannot but view the Etruscans, their language, history, and origin from a completely new perspective.

On the basis of the analyses in my Venetic study, I came to the conclusion that the Veneti were one of the Slavic people who once inhabited the regions between the Baltic and the Adriatic Seas. The study of the Etruscan language equally strengthens the theory that the Rasennes were also of Slavic origin, and suggests that the Proto-Slavic Veneti, the bearers of Urnfield Migration in the 13th or 12th centuries B.C., spread not only to the northern Adriatic and along the Dalmatian coast, but also farther southward across the Apennine peninsula and in some instances as far as Sicily.

The Etruscans still remembered and related their history long after they had settled on the Tyrrhennian coast, and Herodotus is known as the first author who wrote about their origin. According to him they came from Asia Minor, from the Lydian kingdom with the capital at Sardis. During the reign of King Krez (noted for his great wealth) the kingdom was overtaken by a famine. The people had patiently suffered for eighteen years but then could not endure any longer; they searched for a way out of their distress. The king divided his people into two halves. The first half was to remain in Lydia and the second half was to move out. They cast lots; the king stayed in their homeland, and his son Tyrsenos led the others who would seek their fortune in some foreign land. In Smyrna they built their fleet, loaded it with provisions for the journey and sailed in a westerly direction. They experienced many hardships and met many nations and finally settled in the land of the Umbrians. They built their cities and were still living there at the time of Herodotus. They called themselves Tyrsenians after their leader Tyrsenos.

Herodotus dated their settlement back to the time of Homer (9th century B.C.). His report was believed to be reliable and was generally accepted. But Dionysius from Halicarnassus, a Greek in Roman service, was opposed to it. He maintained that the Etruscans were an indigenous people who lived in Italy from time immemorial. The validity of their views has been a matter of dispute to this day. Herodotus was almost half a millennium older than Dionysius, but he was not reliable as a historian. He followed mostly oral traditions; travelling across Greece, along the Black Sea, through Asia Minor, Syria, Babylon and Egypt he wrote down what people told him. Since he knew only Greek and probably needed interpreters, the credibility of his records is questionable. Dionysius was sounder as a scholar; however, it is possible that he knew less about the Etruscans than Herodotus who was their contemporary. Whose report should we accept as reliable; who is right? You will probably be surprised, but in my opinion they were both right. They complement each other perfectly.

What led me to this conclusion? Above all it was the Slavic, Venetic elements in the Etruscan language. These elements stem from those Etruscans who (in the opinion of Dionysius) were the indigenous, ancient people in the area. However, he is only partially right about this. The Etruscans with Slavic roots—the Rasennes—also came as settlers to the Apennines, but considerably earlier (according to Herodotus) than the people who came by sea from Asia Minor.

Most of the oldest Etruscan inscriptions on jugs, mirrors and other objects can be understood with the help of Slavic languages. Later inscriptions, however, which already contain a strong admixture of the language of the newcomers from Asia Minor, resist such interpretations. They include too many elements which have nothing in common with Slavic languages. Possibly they were linked to the Indo-European in the distant past, but had in the course of time undergone strong influences from other Asian languages.

The question of the origin of the newcomers remains unsolved. Were they really Lydians? Some researchers, among them the Bulgarian scholar Georgijev, believe that these settlers were Hittites. This would not be unusual from the linguistic standpoint. We know that the Lydian was a branch of Indo-European which was related to the language spoken in some regions of the Hittite empire. Georgijev tried to interpret the Etruscan inscriptions, but without success. Firstly, he presumed that all the official evaluations of the Etruscan letters were correct. Secondly, he approached all inscriptions from the position of the Hittite language. In my view, there were two stages in the development of the Etruscan language. During the older phase the Slavic components prevailed; and during the younger the Slavic elements decreased, especially in regard to technological and administrative terms introduced by the Hittites (or Lydians?) who came from a more advanced background, the highly developed Asia Minor.

At the same time we should not reject the probability that the Rasennes already had a relatively developed civilization when the Hittite settlers arrived on the Tyrrhennian coast. It is probable that for a certain period both languages were used, each for specific purposes. The building of tombs was a novelty brought by the newcomers; this becomes obvious when Etruscan tombs are compared with other oriental tombs along the Mediterranean coast. Although most of the inscriptions found on and in the Etruscan tombs are written in Hittite and cannot be deciphered on the basis of Slavic languages, the exceptions are the sayings added to names, surnames, professions, functions or decorations which have been bestowed upon the deceased. Why was the Rasennian language used especially for philosophical or patriotic inscriptions on the tombs of the soldiers who died in combat? There are also some inscriptions where the original Slavic components predominate; e.g., the inscription dedicated to the above-mentioned Markezič:

Interiors of two Etruscan tombs in Cervetera, 7th and 4th centuries B.C. The majority of priceless artifacts of the renowned Etruscan culture were preserved in underground tombs which were only recently discovered.

Lad o jale, k legniesi, Markezič! Kalja teži mɘnj zle, nakn voja si oamce le(s). (See the interpretation under **TLE 80.**) Here I only wanted to give the translation and note that the transcription corresponds to TLE with two changes: instead of **Markezic** I have Markezič, and instead of **mun** I have *mɘnj*, as is still pronounced in colloquial Slovene; the silent vowel sounds like a short *u*. The inscription reads: *Mir* (**lad**) *v jalovini* (**jalu**) *zdaj, ko si se ulegel, Markezič. Sramota* (**kalja**) *teži manj hudo* (**zlo**), *ko po boju počivaš tukaj* (Peace in this wasteland, now that you have lain down, Markezič. Disgrace is less burdensome, as you rest here after the battle). A typical inscription for a soldier. It can be wholly understood only on the basis of Slavic terminology. The same holds true for the inscription on the tomb **TLE 730: mena me kana;** in Slovene: *mena me konča, kona;* in English: (the change in) the moon phase finishes me. The Slavic languages include the archaic form *konati;* the modern Slovene is *končati*—to finish, to terminate.

359

The Etruscan and the Venetic both used the change of **o** into **a;** in some Slavic dialects this is still a common practice. The Etruscan form **kana** is intelligible in the spirit of the Slavic phonetics. (See the detailed interpretation below.)

The thesis that the Etruscan was a combination of two languages is supported by the vocabulary in some of the oldest inscriptions on Etruscan objects, mostly jugs. The reader will be convinced of this when examining the translations and explanations of the texts. The most persuasive are the inscriptions which accompany the illustrations. One of the most interesting texts is unquestionably that on a mirror (Fabretti, *Terzio supplemento,* No. 394/137*)* portraying a well known mythological motif of Minerva emerging from Jupiter's head. There is also the text on a bronze mirror showing Hercules nursing at Juno's breast. The inscription on this mirror can be deciphered without any problem on the basis of Slavic philology.

The relations between the Slavic Rasennes and the newcomer Hittites around the 8th century B.C. (during the early period of their coexistence before they established a united cultural entity) may be clarified to some extent on the inscription **TLE 65.** They were, presumably, not very friendly, which is to be expected. The inscription says: "It would be a shame if one of us drank in the company of a Hittite." This suggests that the Rasennes had certain reservations about the Hittites. Later developments show however, that the more advanced Hittites gradually absorbed the Slavic Rasennes, perhaps without too much hostility.

On the basis of these findings I have allowed myself to try to interpret some Etruscan texts, mostly those written on jugs and mirrors. I also interpreted both inscriptions on the famous Pyrgian tablets where there is also a Punic text next to the Etruscan; that is, in the Phoenician language spoken in Carthage. This was thought to have been a translation of the Etruscan text, but that is not the case; the Punic inscription is similar in contents only. As was stated earlier, it is of interest to our research that the majority of the inscriptions we will examine belong to the oldest period. This corresponds well with the hypothesis that the Proto-Slavs (Veneti) had inhabited the Apennine peninsula long before the settlement of the Hittites (Lydians).

The merging in Italy of the two people belonging to two different cultures and races is also evident in Etruscan visual arts: the heads and faces of stylized portraits show a strong oriental influence, while the realistic, non-stylized representations are typically European, the kind that you can still meet on our streets.

Someone will perhaps raise an argument against this interpretation, saying that the images on the Etruscan situlas are similar if not the same as those we know from the Venetic situlas. That may be so, and why not? After the arrival of the Hittites, the Venetic craftsmen accepted some new, oriental influences. The various centres of production were after all not so completely isolated from each other that we could not expect some merging of styles and fashions. I also think that regardless of the style of images, they show us authentic scenes from the daily life of the Veneti and the Etruscans: the realistic depiction of Venetic imagery, like the stele representing a carriage with a man, his wife, and her lover or the one of a matron giving to her elderly man a duck as travel provision. These pictures bear no trace of orient; yet, they remind us of the old Etruscan style on ceramics and stone reliefs. In other words, the Proto-Slavic elements are strong in the Etruscan.

To this analysis of the Slavic elements in the Etruscan or Rasenne language, I am adding a few texts or inscriptions whose meanings are supported by drawings on the same objects. In addition to these, I enumerate some inscriptions where the similarity between the Slavic languages and the Rasenne is very much in evidence. They are all from the older period of the Rasenne culture, with the majority of their vocabulary deriving from Slavic morphology and syntax.

Ivory tablet from 7th century B.C. engraved with the 26 letters of the Etruscan alphabet. The shallow depression was for wax which was the writing surface. (Museo Archeologico, Firenze)

361

The Etruscan Inscriptions
The Pyrgian Tablets

In the Museum Villa Giulia in Rome are preserved three gold tablets discovered a few decades ago during excavations 13km from the ancient Cere in Pyrgius on the Tyrrhenian coast. There, in a bay now embellished by Castello di Severa, one can still see from a boat in good weather the square stone blocks of the ancient harbour of Cere. But that is not all. Since the end of 1957 excavations have uncovered an ancient temple consisting of two buildings with extraordinarily rich archaeological finds. Three gold tablets represent the most precious items— precious because they have long inscriptions. One is Punic in Phoenician letters, the other two are Etruscan and remarkably well preserved. In addition, there is a badly damaged copper tablet. See Pallottino **TLE 873–876.** Exceptionally good colour reproduction is in the book *Le citta etrusche,* Mondadori, 1973).

It is known from historical references as well as from the contents of the Etruscan inscription that a temple was built in Pyrgius by **vojevadjej Velianas** (Slov. *vojvoda*—duke), in honour of goddess Uni (Juno), called Ashtart by the Phoenicians. This temple was demolished by Dionysius, the Greek tyrant of Syracuse, in the first half of the fourth century B.C. Since its treasury was empty, he launched a raid against the rich Etruscan towns on the Tyrrhenian coast. Pyrgius and its surroundings were completely destroyed and Cere never recovered from this blow. Later the Itals (Romans) took advantage of the destruction and desolation and occupied Etruscan lands. The Etruscans erected a monument dedicated to this event. The holes at the edge of the tablets show that they were fastened to a stone or wooden wall. The fact that one of them is written in Phoenician (Punic), as was then spoken in Carthage, shows that the Etruscans and the Phoenicians, who had colonies in the area, organized a common defence against the Greek aggressor.

The Punic inscription carefully avoids any mention of Latins, which is understandable; two allies have the same enemy, yet, in battle and in other matters they adopt different attitudes towards him. In the Etruscan text there is no caution in this regard, as far as can be judged by comparing the two inscriptions.

In my view the Etruscan text is not a dedication of Duke Velianas, but actually something much more interesting; it is a narration of Etruscan history, which is probably not found in their other inscriptions. I use the word "probably" on purpose, because I was not able to decipher the inscriptions from the later period when the Slavic language elements were already lost within the dominant Hittitic.

Pyrgian tablets with Etruscan inscription.
(Museo di Villa Giulia, Roma)

The Phoenician colony was isolated on the Tyrrhenian coast and had no wish to expose itself, especially since the power of the Romans was growing. This was possibly the reason that historical events were left out of the text.

Both Pyrgian gold tablets are listed in Pallottino's transcriptions of the Etruscan inscriptions under numbers **874** and **875.** Mondadori's colour picture of the tablets is so clear that almost every letter can be seen in detail; our copy is not as good, but it will suffice to show the reader just what these tablets are like.

As we have here the original, there is no need for Pallottini's transcription; instead I will present my own. There is at times a difference between my version and Pallottini's, as was already explained in the introduction where I dealt with individual graphemes and explained how my reading differs from the official Etrurology.

Before I go into the actual transcription of the text I would like to make a short comment.

The data provided by the present inscription accords well with our historical knowledge of the attack of Dionysius of Syracuse on the Etruscan coast and his booty which was exceptionally rich. We also know that the Romans took advantage of the weakened Cere and occupied its territory. This conquest did not, however, take place at once; fighting between the Etruscans and Romans lasted for a long time. The second part of the inscription tells how the Duke Veliunas (he could have been son of Velianas, but certainly his successor) won against the enemies again and beat them totally and forever. This is at least what the Pyrgians thought. At that time the Temple of Consolation must have been rebuilt and the three golden tablets mounted.

As is known from mythology, the Phoenician goddess **Ashtart** was called **Una** by Etruscans. The two names are joined in this inscription with the conjunction **al;** Slov. *ali*—or. The same **al** appears twice more, first in the case of **žilac al selje;** Slov. *žitelj ali selje*—inhabitant or settlement—and then as a conjunction, **al**—but—in a syntagma **al zase nas;** Slov. *ali zasede nas*—but he occupies us.

There is only one point that is not in agreement with known historical circumstances; Dionysius of Syracuse attacked Cere in 384 B.C., whereas archaeologists presume that the tablets are older, originating from the end of the 6th or the beginning of the 5th century B.C. If this is true, the inscription does not apply to Dionysius of Syracuse, but to one of his predecessors who attacked the Tyrrhenian coast. It is also possible that dates are not accurate; after all, there is a difference of a hundred years or so.

Pyrgian Inscriptions in my Transcription

1.

Etru. ITA TMIAJ KAK DERAM AZVA VATIEHE
Slov. Ta tempelj je kot hram ozval utehe

UNI AL ASTRES OJEMIA SA MEH OUTA
Junone ali Astarte, prijemši za meč ovod (tu)

OJEBADEJ VELIANAS SAL CLUVENI AS TURUČE
vojvoda Velianas sel slovenji, ko ga je postavil.

MUNI STAS OUV ASTA MERESCA ILAKVE TULE
Ponosna stavba ta je ostala. Morsko Ilakve, zavetišče

RASE NAC CI AVIL HURVAR TE ZJAME ITALE
rasensko, ko je umrl, gusar tedaj zajame, Ital

ILAKVE AL ZASE NAC AT RANE S ŽILAC AL
Ilakve pa zasede. Od te nesreče sta žitelj in

SELJE ITALA AK NA ZVED S I TA NIM
selje od Itala. Kakor je razvidno i ta nam

HERAM VE AVIL JEN JACA POLUMHVA
hram je, glej, uničil in jako polomil (poškodoval).

2.

NAC OJEBADIJE VELIUNAS O AMUCE CLEVA
Nato ko je vojvoda Veliunas po omoč (pomoč) klical

E TANAL MASAN TIUD UNI
Je udarila silna volja Junone

AS ZELACE VA KAL TMIAL
da je zločince v kali zatrl,

AVIL HVAL(E) AMUCE
uničil zahvaljujoč omoči (pomoči)

POLUMHVA SNUJAV.
in porazil dokončno.

365

Translation

1.

This temple was built and named as the Temple of Solace of the Goddess Juno or Astarte by Duke Velianas, Clovenji (Slovene?) prince, when he was preparing for battle. This proud building still endures, whereas Morsko Ilakve has been taken by the pirate (Dionysius), and Ilakve has been taken by the Itals. Since this misfortune, the inhabitants and the settlements are Italic. As we can see, he ravaged and severely damaged this temple as well.

2.

Then Duke Veliunas (the successor to Velianas) called to goddess Juno for help. And her powerful will struck out so that the criminal aggressors were nipped in the bud, and thanks to the help, permanently defeated.

Text of one Etruscan and one Punic inscription

Glossary

ita—this; Slov. *ta;* Russ. *eta;* Slov. eastern Styria dialect *eta, eto* meaning *ta*—this (Plet. and Mikl.).

tmiaj—a temple. The word is a postverbal form from arch. *tmiat;* Old Church Slavic (OCS) *ašče ktoь тьтьт*—if someone kills; the root *тьт* is compared to Greek *temno*—I kill (Miklošič, Vasmer). It might be related to Old Slav. *тьпǫ, tęti*—to kill, to beat. Slov. *ubiti, tolči.* As we know, animals were sacrificed (killed) in temples. The Slov. word *uteti* of the same origin is no longer used; that is, in the meaning cut off—*abhauen* (Plet.). Slov. *oteti*—to rescue, and *tnalo*—a chopping block—are still in use, whereas *naton*—a place for chopping (Bez., Plet.)—has been forgotten.

kak—like, as; Slov. *kakor, kot;* eastern Styria *kak.*

heram—temple; Slov. *hram, or božji hram*—sanctuary, house of God. OCS *hramъ*—domus (Mikl.), *templum;* Sanskrit *harmyam* (a fortification, a castle); Ger. *feste Gabäude, Burg* (Machek, Skok); these would suggest Etr. **heram** as a fortified temple. The Hittite *karimmi* (Machek) speaks in favour of the hypothesis that the Slavic part of the Etruscans later mixed with Hittites.

azva—proclaimed; Slov. *oklical, ozval.* See Plet. *ozvati*—verkünden, ausrufen. Slov. *ozval ga je za kralja*—he proclaimed him king. The same word as in Slovene, except for the common change of **o** into **a.** OCS *zvati, zvataj*—to call, a caller; **azva** is aor. 3rd prs. sing.

vatiehe—consolation; Slov. *utehe* (gen. sing.) from *tih, utišati*—silent, to silence; OCS *utěha.* We should also note that **vatiehe** has a prothetic **v.** Compare Slov. *ogenj, vogenj*—fire; *uho, vuho*—ear; *osel, vosu*—donkey, etc. Such **v** is found in Slovene dialects and also in Lusatian Wendish.

Uni al Astres—Juno or Astres. The Phoenician name for Uni was Ashtart. The two names are joined by the conjunction **al;** Slov. *ali,* dialect and vernacular *al*—or; OCS **a** and **li.** That this is no coincidence is also shown by the Etruscan **žilac al selje**—inhabitant or settlement—and an adversative **al** in the same inscription, **al zase**—but he occupies. These two meanings of **al** are the same as in Slovene. Goddess Uni (or Una?) was in Etruria one of the twelve principal deities; Greeks called her Hera and Latins, Juno.

ojemija—embracing; Slov. *objemajoč, objemaje,* we would now say: *stiskajoč*—pressing (his sword). OCS *jьт, jьтǫ* (Mikl. *jemǫ, jamem, objamem*). Letter **b** has been discontinued in Etruscan. **Ojemija** is pres. part. act. For ending compare OCS *delaję.* Slov. *delaje, jemaje, objemaje*—working, taking, embracing. Russ. participle *čitaja,* and even more so *projdja* (perfective verb), come closest to the Etruscan ending.

sa—for; Slov. *za.*

meh—sword; Slov. *meč.* OCS *mьčь*; Greek *mahe*—battle, *maheire*—sword. It may be that the Croatian word *mahir, maher* (Hvar Island)—a large butcher's knife—is also connected to **meh.** Slovene *meč* is then of the same root as Etr. **meh,** and both of them are from *mahati*—to wave, to brandish, to swing. Still in use in Slovene language: *mahali so si, dober zamah*—they waved to each other, a good swing, etc. A distant connection would be Georgian *maxva* and Sanskrit *meh*—sword. It is semantically incorrect to derive *meč* from *mekь (kь);* i.e., something pressed and soft (Bez.).

outa—here; Serbo-Cr. *ovde;* Slov. dial. *ovda* (Mikl.). Considering that the silent **t** was used for the voiced **d** in writing and possibly also in pronunciation, *outa* and *ouda* are unusually close. In this respect the Styrian *dovta, gorta*—down there, up there—is of interest; also the Rezian *ta: ta po ti potá, ta po ti gorá* (Matičetov, *Rožce iz Rezije), ta na Kosiginej* (Bez.); in this instance *ta* means here, or there.

ojebadjej—duke. As the official Etrurologists read my **b** as **f** and my **o** as **th,** there is a substantial difference between their and my interpretation of this word: instead of their **Thefariei,** I have **ojebadjej,** Slov. *vojevodja, vojvoda*—duke. The word is Old Slavic and undoubtedly onomatopoeic; originally *oiti, vojiti, ojevati.* This is substantiated by OCS *oimin*—soldier, pl. *oimi* (Leskin para. 50). *Oimi* were soldiers; they were shouting "oili" during the battle. One of the basic elements of a battle used to be shouting, which served to frighten the enemy and encouraged the fighters. It applies to animals as well as people. Dogs snarl during a fight. *Volčje vijo*—wolf's howl (Plet.). The original *oiti* evolved with a prothetic **v** into *vojiti, vojin, vojvoda;* also further into *vojd*—village chief (Plet.). It has been borrowed by the Germans—*der Vogt*—and by the Hungarians—*vajda.*

Velianas—a name.

sal—messenger, envoy; Slov. *sel.* An envoy, maybe to the assembly of twelve Rasenne city-states. OCS *sьlь;* Serbo-Cr. arch. *sal*—nuntius (Skok). Identical to Etr. **sal;** Russ. *posol*—envoy.

cluveni—named, called. Later in the text there is also **cleva**—he called. This is aorist of arch. **clevat.** The word is an older form of *sloveti,* (sloviti)— to be renowned. At the time when these inscriptions were made, the conversion of **k** (kentum) into **s** (satem) had not yet been completed. What was this consonant like? Apparently something between **k** and **s:** *çluva* and *çluveni.* As in Sanskrit *çravas;* Slov. *slava*—fame. The Etruscans were not too particular regarding the pronunciation of **s** and **š,** most frequently resulting in **ś.** That seems to have been the case with **c** and **k** as well. This phenomenon is also known in Latin: it is unknown to this day whether the pronunciation was "Cicero" or "Kikero". **Sal cluveni** could therefore mean either the envoy called, or Slovene (adj.) envoy. The ancient name for Slavs (Sloveni, Slovani) appeared for the first time. I allow for the latter possibility and have employed it in my translation. **Cluveni** has a common origin with Greek *kleos*, dial. *klefos;* Slov. *slava, sloves*—fame. Old Irish *clú*—fame.

as—when; comp. Czech *as*—around, approximately. Old Russ. *ače, aci, acě;* Ukrainian *až;* OCS *ašče.* Comp. Eng. as—when, like.

turuce—set up. In Slavic languages this word occurs repeatedly in various meanings and forms. The closest to the Etruscan is Bulg. *turjam, turem*—I set (a thing) down, I lay (a thing) down (Mikl.) Pleteršnik has *turati*—to push this way and that way. The word **turuce, turce** is often repeated. Most of the time it appears on various sculptures with the meaning: this man set up this sculpture.

muni—splendid, shining; pronounce munji, as in "slovenji." Serbo-Cr. *munja*—lightning, *munjevit*—of lightning. OCS *mlьnii*—shine, lightning. Old Slavic arch. *mlьni* (Vasmer). With regard to Icelandic *mjollnir*—lightning, the hammer of god Tor and Lith. *mulna*—the hammer of god Perun; Skok supposes that the word is of mythological origin. It is interesting that Uni or Juno was Jupiter's consort, and Tor and Perun are Germanic and Balto-Slavic equivalents of Jupiter.

stas—a place; OCS *stasь*—regio pastorum (range lands), an area where shepherds gathered (including shepherds of souls). In our case the priests of the goddess to whom the place was consecrated. Serbo–Cr. *stasina*—porticus, a courtyard—offers an additional meaning to the Etr. **stas;** the Slov. word *stas* is of the same origin, but has a different meaning.

ouv—this; eastern Styria, Slovenia *ov*—this; Ger. *dieser* (Plet.); *ov den*—this day (Mikl.); OCS *ovъ*—this.

asta—(he) stayed; Slov. *ostal (je),* aor. 3rd prs. sing. from arch. *astat.* Serbo-Cr. *osta.* OCS *stati, ostati.* In OCS this could be: *stasь ovъ osta,* almost exactly as in Etruscan.

meresca—of the sea; Slov. *morsko.* OCS *morьsko.* In the meaning it corresponds to present Slov. *primorsko. Priobretoсь odъ morьske zemlje* (Skok). Ending –a in **meresca** is the result of the common change of **o** to **a.**

Ilakve—the name Ilakve. The Etruscan name for Pyrgius is unknown; however, as we learn from this inscription it must have been **Ilakve.** The word reminds us of the Latin *ilex*—an evergreen oak. This oak has another Latin name as well—quercus cerris, in Slov.—*cer* (Plet.). Numerous places have been named after it: Cêrna, Cêrno, Cêrnik (Skok), Cerovica, Cerovlje, Cerovce (Bezlaj).

Cere probably acquired its name from this variety of oak and **Ilakve** from the Etruscan form *ilex*—a rather interesting connection. It seems that the Latins took both names from the Etruscans. Noteworthy is also the Albanian word *ilque* for evergreen oak, which is very close to the Etr. **Ilakve.** Slov. *jelka*—balsam tree—is similar as well; Greek *eláte*. It would appear that at the time, the Bay of Cere must have been overgrown with oak (cer), and the nearby place was called **Ilakve** after the synonym for *cer.* It may be that the oak tree ilakve (L. ilex) was a subspecies of "cer" which grew in Cere.

In the opinion of Miklošič (quoted also by Bezlaj), *cer* is a loanword from Latin (cerris); however, as it is widespread in Slavic languages this etymology is incorrect, particularly as it was already used in OCS, *cerь*. As "cer" grows in rocky terrain, connection with Slov. *čer, čeri*—cliff, cliffs—should not be excluded.

Ilakve could also be interpreted through *lokva*—bay. Due to the obvious connection between *ilex* and *cer,* the above interpretation seems more appropriate.

tule—shelters; Russ. dial. *tula*—a shelter, a sanctuary (Vasm.). It occurs in OCS as *toulь*—quiver; Slov. *tul, tulec;* Old Slav. arch. *tulь*. It occurs in various forms in all Slavic languages. Apart from *tul, tulec,* the Slovene language also includes other words of the same origin, which explain the etymology of *tul* as is demonstrated in Russian where the word *tulitь*—to hide, to put away, to cover—is still in use . The same verb is used in other Slavic languages with similar meanings. In Slovene: *tuliti—roža svoj cvet tuli*—flower hides its blossom; *tuliti otroka k sebi*—to press the child to oneself; *stuljenik, stulina*—ein zusammengeschrumpftes Ding—a shrunken object (Plet.). Other Slovene words of the same origin: *stuliti se, stuljeno hoditi, stuliti*—to bend oneself, to walk stealthily, to crumple. In Rezian dial. *tuliti se za kom*—to sneak after somebody, to move in a sneaky manner after somebody, to stalk.

Concerning Etr. **tule**—it is possible that the word is the same as the Slovene *tla,* Serbo-Cr. *tle;* which is the same word as *tule,* except for spelling. Letter **u** was used to denote a short **ŭ** or semi-vowel, as in *jer* and *jor,* as they did not distinguish between them. OCS *tьlo, tьlja*.

Rase—"Rasenia" (gen. of Ras or Rasa) was the name the Etruscans or Rasennes used for their country. The word is repeated in other inscriptions.

nac—then; Serb. *nakon;* arch. also *nak,* in the meaning—after, *naksjutra*—after tomorrow; Miklošič connects it to Slov. *vznak*—on one's back; OCS *vьznakъ*. The word **nac** pronounced **nak,** frequently occurs in Etruscan inscriptions.

ci—who; Slov. *ki, kateri;* OCS *či, ci* (Mikl.), equal to Etr. **ci**—pronounce *či* or *ci*.

avil—died, to have ceased; found in numerous inscriptions on tombs. OCS *ubylъ* from *ubyti—deficere,* to die (Mikl.). To cease being. The Etr. **a** at the beginning is there due to the uncertainty of pronunciation of the semi-vowel **ŭ**. Although this word no longer exists in Slovene the memory still lingers; e.g., Slov. *glas se ubije, vino se je ubilo*—a voice gets dull, the wine loses flavour. This verb has its roots in *biti, sem*—to be, I am—rather than *biti*—to kill. The **v** is there in place of **b** due to common interchangeability. Comp. Slov. dial. *vil* in place of *bil.*

hurvar—pirate, whoremonger; Slov. and Croat. also *kurbar* and *kurvar* (Plet., Skok); the meaning is the same regardless of spelling. It fits the context very well, since **kurbar** applies to Dionysius who robbed the Etruscans of a part of their territory. Some linguists think this word derives from an ancient relationship with Ger. *Hure.* Loeventhal is of the opinion (acc. to Skok) that it derives from Old Slavic *kurъ.* The consonant **h** perhaps speaks for its relationship with Ger. Hure.

Etruscans had reason enough to nickname Dionysius as they did; however, there is a possibility that *kurvar* and Greek *koursares* have merged into a single word—OCS *hurъsarъ*—or in Slovene *gusar*—pirate. The only difference between *hurvar* and hursar is the consonant **s**. In either case, Dionysius earned the title.

te—then; Slov. *tedaj; dial. te* (Plet., Mikl.). OCS also *te*—then, Ger. *dann* (Mikl.).

ziame—he dips; Slov. *zajame.* Also *zajme* from *zajeti* Ger. *in Besitz nehmen, occupieren, umringen, umzingeln*—to take possession of, to occupy, to surround (Plet.). OCS *jęti, jemati, jemljǫ* (Mikl.). The form *ziame* resulted from combining *zajame* and *zajme.*

Itale—Ital (nomin. from vocative); comp. Slov. *niče*—a nothing. Serbo-Cr. *sine*—son.

al—or; Slov. *ali* in the meaning "but". See note to **al** above. Obviously, **al** was employed simultaneously as a conjunction "or" *ali bi šel?*—or would you go? Also as a preposition "but" *ali tega ne bom storil*—but I will not do it. This similarity between Etruscan and Slovene is a fairly clear indication that to study Etruscan through Slovene and other Slavic languages is only logical.

zase—he occupied; Slov. *zasedel, zasel je.* The question is whether **zase** is an aorist or present tense.

nac—then; Slov. *nato, nakar.* (See above).

at—from; Slov. *od.* OCS *otъ*—pronounce *atъ.*

rane s, at rane s—since this misfortune, since this calamity. In OCS *rana* means a blow, a misfortune, and as in Slovene it also means a wound. It has identical meaning in Czech. The final **s** is a demonstrative pronoun **sъ**. The second format could possibly be read as **at dane s**—from this day on; Slov. *od tega* *dne,* as it is not always clear whether to read the Etr. Ⴃ as **r** or as **d.** It is useful to know at this point that the genitive is written with -**e** as it is still done in Slovene, *od tega dne*—from this day.

žilac—inhabitant; Slov. *prebivalec, žitelj.* Russ. *žilec,* from *žiti*—to live; Slov. *živeti.*

al—or, but; Slov. *ali.* (See above).

selje—a settlement; Slov. *naselje.*

Itala—Itala; gen. of Ital. (See above).

ac (pronounce *ak*)—like; Czech. *jak;* OCS *akъ.*

na—on; Slov. *na;* OCS *na.*

zved s—evidence; Slov. *zvedek, zved;* **ac na zved s**—as it is evident. Slov. arch. *kakor je na razvedek, razved.* In Slovene *razved* has been lost and only *razvedek* has been retained (Plet.). There is also *poizved*—inquiry (Plet.). Russ. *razvedka.* The **s** at the end (which must have merged with the *razved)* is a demonstrative pronoun **sъ.** Slov. *danes*—today. (See above).

i ta (ita?)—also this; Slov. *i ta, tudi ta.* Maybe **ita** (as at the beginning of the inscription) unless we should have read **i ta tmiaj** there as well. This would mean that the temple of Uni was not the only temple Velianas had built.

nim—us; Slov. *nam.* Vowel **i** in place of **a** can be explained with OCS *ny*—accus. us. We can consider the above form, if not a proof, at least a hint that at one time dat. pl. had been *nym.*

heram—a temple; Slov. hram. (See above).

ve—look, know! Slov. *glej, vedi!* The word is also Slovene, Mikl. and Plet. give two meanings: 1. *ve je prišel* Ger. er ist ja gekommen—he did come; *ve je to malo*—yet there is so little of it (conj. *but*). They compare it to Russ. *vedъ*—but, anyway, nevertheless. 2. Slov. *do ve* Ger. bis hieher—this far; *tam ve, tu ve* (tu-le)—there, here. Also *ve*—now, *baš ve*—just now.

avil—destroyed, damaged, demolished. It seems OCS *ubyti* and *ubiti* merged into one word due to their similarity, particularly after the difference between **y** and **i** had been done away with. Thus, **avil** can mean both—he died, or he destroyed, killed; Slov. *ubil.* (See notes for *ubylъ).*

jen—and; Slov. *in;* dial. *jen;* arch. literary form also *jen.*

jaca—strongly, very; Slov. *jako, zelo.* OCS *jako.*

pulumhva—damaged, broke; Slov. *polomil, poškodoval, polomastil.* Regarding **u** instead of **o** comp. Polabian *lümit*—to break, and regarding suffix comp. Russ. *lomychatъ* (Mikl.). The final Θ is transcribed as **v** (a sound between **v** and **b,** still known in western Slovene dialects).

372

2.

nac—then; Slov. *nato, nakar.* (See above).

ojebadije—a duke; Slov. *vojvoda.* (See above).

Veliunas—a name. Probably a descendant or even a son of Velianas. Veliunas could have been a nickname for veli-junak, vele-junak—great-hero.

o—for; other contexts *about;* Slov. *o, ob.*

amuce (pronounce *amučje*)—help; Slov. *pomoč.* Pleteršnik also has *omoč* which is a Slov. form of **amučje**—*omočje.*

cleva—he asked, he called. (See above).

e—is; Slov. *je;* OCS *e* and *estъ.*

tanal—he hit; Slov. *udaril.* OCS *tьnal* from *tęti.*

masan—strong; Slov. *močan;* Sansk. *mahan*—great. Possible connection with Slov. *mahati*—to wave. Slov. *zamášen*—weighty, soaring; Ger. wuchtig, schwunghaftig (Plet.). Serbo-Cr. *mašiti* and *mahati.* Slov. *mašiti* Ger. werfen— to throw (Mikl.). The Russ. *masa* means very big.

tiud (tjud ?)—wonder, will; Slov. *čudo, volja.* OCS. *čudъ*—mos, voluntas. Slov. *čud*—nature, an inclination, character. This is another example of **t** (t') not yet wholly converted into ć, (č).

Uni—of Juno; gen. of Una. (See above).

as—when; Czech. *as*—when.

zelace pronounce **zelače**—culprits, villains (accusative); Slov. *zlikovce;* from *zloben, zel*—evil. OCS *zъlъ*—evil.

va—in; Slov. *v;* OCS. *vъ;* Russ. *vo;* also Slov. dial. *vo.* Compare *vanj*—into him.

kal—bud; Slov. *kal. V kali zatreti*—to nip in the bud. Old Slavic. *kolъ* and *kъlъ* (Bez.).

tmial—killed, beat; Slov. *ubil, pobil.* OCS *tьтеть*—to kill. *Ašče kto tьтеть dъlžьbita*—if anyone kills... The root *tьт* is compared to Greek *temno*—I kill. The word could be related to *tьnǫ, tęti*—to kill. (See the explanation accompanying **tmiaj).**

avil—destroyed; Slov. *uničil.* (See above).

hval(e)—thanking; Slov. *zahvaljujoč.* OCS *hvalъ*—thanking, past participle, active form. Also *hvalé.*

amuce—help; Slov. *pomoči, omoči.* (See above).

polumhva—he defeated, destroyed; Slov. *porazil, polomastil, uničil.* (See above).

snujav—extort, to obtain by force; Slov. *izsilivši.* Slov. *znujati*—Ger. *abdringen* (Plet.). Slov. participle could then be *znujav-ši.* In my opinion the final symbol Ө is a sound between **v** and **b**, still in use in the dialects of the Slovene littoral. **Znujav** is act. past participle.

Translated into a modern, only slightly archaic Slovene language it reads as follows:

Nato je vojvoda Veliunas klical (Junono) na pomoč. In posegla je vmes njena silovita volja, tako da je zelače v kali zatrl, uničil, in zahvaljoč Junonini pomoči znujavo polomastil.

In English: Then Duke Veliunas prayed to (Juno) for help. And her powerful will asserted itself; he was able to nip the culprits in the bud and destroy them, and thanks to Juno's help defeated them permanently.

A Wise Counsel

A pitcher found in Capua bears a short but interesting inscription (**TLE 774**); in my transcription it reads:

KA	**PJE**	**MUKA**	**TEZA**	**KA**	**PJEŠ**	**SLI**
Ko	pijoč	muka	teza,	ko	piješ,	zlij!

In modern Slovene: Ko piješ in te muka teži,
to, kar piješ, izlij!
In English: When you drink and troubles weigh upon you,
pour out what you are drinking!

ka—when; Slov. *ko.* Slovene dialects also *ka.*

pje—drinking; Slov. *pijoč.* In Slovene it could also be *pijé,* although in this particular case this form of participle is not in use. Other cases are Slov. *stojé, sedé, hodé*—standing, sitting, walking. Comp. Russ. *pitь, pju, pješ.* OCS *piti.* I read **e** as **je,** as in Venetic inscriptions.

muka—torment; Slov. *muka;* OCS *mǫka;* Lith. *muka.* This word is generally Slavic and Baltic.

teza—to weigh, to stretch; Slov. *(na)teza.* Plet. *tezati* Ger. ziehen, recken—to draw, to stretch. Dalmatian *teza*—to torment. Old Slavic root *teng.* In Slovene several derivatives are still in use: *natezalnica*—a rack, *natezati*—to stretch, *težiti—to weigh on, teža*—weight, *poteza*—a move, etc. A large number of derivatives are found in all Slavic languages.

ka—when; Slov. *ko.* Possibly also *kar—what* from *ka–že.*

pješ—see **pje.**

sli pronounce **zli**—pour out; Slov. *zlij, izli.* Root *lí,* consequently *lьją (lьjó)* (Mikl.). OCS *sъli.*

Bronze cup (Museo Nazionale, Tarquinia). Cups and jugs were often decorated by Etruscans with images and inscriptions.

An Invitation to Drinking

TLE 19. A pitcher.

CU PJEŠ CAR PUNIES MI
Da   piješ kar   polniš   mi

In modern Slovene: Pij tudi ti, kar polniš mi (meni).
In English: Drink also yourself, what you pour me.

cu read **kǝ, kŭ**—that, let; Slov. *da;* eastern Styria *ka.*

pješ—you drink; Slov. *piješ,* from *piti.* OCS *piti, ty pijoši.* See TLE: **ka peš sli**— what you drink, pour away; Slov. *kar piješ, zlij.*

car—what; Slov. *kar.* OCS *kъ, ka* etc.

puniš—you fill; Slov. *polniš.* OCS *plъniti, plъniši.* Western Slov. dialects *pun;* Serbo-Cr. *pun, puniti, puniš.*

mi—to me; Slov. *mi,* dative.

If this inscription were transcribed a little closer to the western Slovene dialects it becomes virtually identical with the original: *k pješ, kar puniš mi.*

The Advantage of Being Elderly

TLE 20. A pitcher.

CU	PJE	LADI	ŠA
Da	pije	miru	se,

H	VUIUOUT	UMLEDŚIJE
ko	vojujejo	(se) mlajši.

In modern Slov.: Naj se pije miru, medtem ko se mlajši vojujejo.

In English: Let us drink to peace, while the younger (men) do battle.

This is an interesting inscription showing the prevailing attitude of the Etruscans to their battles with the Romans which were fought intermittently for centuries.

cu read **kŭ**—that, let; Slov. *da,* eastern Styria *ka.* OCS *kъ.*

pje—is being drunk; Slov. *pije (se).* OCS *piti, pijǫ.* Polabian *pait;* Russ. *pjet.*

sa pronounce **śa**—reflexive pronoun *se;* OCS *se;* Russ. *sja.*

h—when; Slov. *ko.*

vuiuout—they battle, they fight; Slov. *vojujejo.* OCS *vojevati, vojujǫtь* (3rd prs. pl. pres.). Etruscan used to have the old suffix -*ǫtь.*

umledśije pronounce **umledšije**—younger. Slov. *mlajši.* OCS *mladъ.* For **e** comp. Slov. dial. *mlęš*—hired hand, farm hand, junior. The root is *mel* and *mol* and spread by the formant **d**—*mledan.* **Umladšije:** Serbo-Cr. (Montenegrin dial.) *omlad, omladan, omladiti, omladina*—youth. The inscription is followed by number XXII; separately, **ACVE.**

Advice to Drinkers

This inscription is found on the base of a clay pitcher and consists of four verses. The Paulus's CIE (8413) contains a hand-made copy which endeavours to be true to the original. The verses are curved, rounded, and form a spiral. Below is my Slovene transcription and interpretation. Since the text is versed, I added the diacritical marks. The verses are iambic octosyllables.

MI	ÁLIKV	A	UVÍL	JESÍ
Če mi	žejen	in	zbit	si,

ÁLE	SPURÁ	TE	V	NALETJÁ
a	spodbode	te	v	nalet

IN	PEJN	MLEDÚŠI	ATEDÍ
in	pijan	malodušno	otodi,

MLAHÚTA	ZÍHUHE	MLAHTÁ
mlahota	zdihujoč	mlaha.

ANA	ZINACE
En	izrek.

The inscription runs from left to right. It is divided by colons which, as already mentioned, do not serve only to divide the words. Sometimes the colons are omitted and whole syntagmas can be found between them. Translated into modern Slovene and English it reads as follows:

Če si mi žejen pa zbit,
If you are thirsty and tired,

Te pijača (ol) spodbode v polet,
The drink will inspire you to soar,

Medtem ko pijan malodušno otodi,
But inebriated, from here in dejection,

Pijanec (mlahota) zdihujoč mlaha.
The drunkard is staggering, sighing.

En izrek.
A saying.

This text is on a wine pitcher. It recommends drinking if you are tired and thirsty, as it will refresh you and give you new enthusiasm; however, drinking must be moderate, otherwise the opposite results. There are several other, similar inscriptions on Rasennian pitchers. The following is my explanation of the individual words:

mi—me; Slov. *mi* dative, *mi greš s poti*—get out of the way (for me); *ne hodi mi od doma*—do not go away from home (for my sake); Etr. **mi** probably also I.

alikv—thirsty; Slov. *žejen;* OCS *alčnyj* from *alkati*—to be thirsty, desirous of. Slov. *lakota*—hunger, *lakom*—greedy, *lačen*—hungry— are also of the same origin.

a—and; Slov. *in, a;* Czech *a*—and; Slov. dial. sometimes *a* means "and". Rezian *tri a tri*—three and three (Bez.).

uvil—weary, tired; Slov. *zdelan, zbit;* OCS *ubylъ*—deceased, also tired, exhausted; from *ubyti, byti.* Etruscan **uvil** and **avil** in the meaning of deceased, dead, destroyed. In both cases **v** instead of **b** (betatism).

jesi—you are; Slov. *si;* OCS. *jesi;* the same in Serbo-Cr.

ale—beer; Slov. arch. *ol, olej*—beer; OCS *ol;* Lithuanian *alus.*

spura—to prompt, to inspire; Russ. *sporyj*—quick, successful, profitable. Arch. Slov. *spor* (Ger. ausgiebig)—abundant (Plet.). *Žito je sporo*—grain is abundant. This word *izpora*—violentia (Mikl.)—impetuosity—is found in many languages. Lithuan. *sperus*—quick; Ukrain. *zaporati* Ger. zurecht machen—to prepare (food) (Mikl.). Serbo-Cr. *oporavit se*—to get stronger, to recover (health).

te—you; Slov. *te.*

v—in; Slov. *v;* OCS *vъ.*

naletja—acc. pl. flight; Slov. *v polete; v naletja*—in flight. *Nalet vode*—onrush of water; *nalet snega*—snowfall. Regarding suffix comp. Slov. *smet, smetje*—rubbish sing. and pl.; *cvet, cvetje*—flower, sing. and pl.; *poletja*—summers; *doživetja* experiences.

in—and; Slov. *in.*

pejn— drunk; Slov. *pijan;* Slov. dial. *pjen, pjэn.* OCS *piti;* Polabian *pait;* Russ. and Ukrain. *pju, pitь.*

mleduši—dejected; Slov. *malodušen, (o)mledušen, mleden, omleden. Mledna hrana*—tasteless food. Old Slavic root *mla-, mled* (Mikl., Bez.).

atedi—from here; Slov. *otodi, od tod;* OCS *otъ-todu;* Slov. dial. *tedi, (tedaj)*—then.

mlahuta—flabbiness; Slov. *mlahota. Mlahuta* is a personification; here it means a drunkard. Regarding the suffix comp. *dobrota*—a good man; *grehota*—sin; *potrata*—waste, etc. It stems from the same root as *mleden*—dejected.

zihuhe—sighing. Slov. *vzdihujoč, vzdihuje*. Comp. Slov. *ohati, zlovoljno je ohal*—he grumbled hatefully; Slov. *ihtati, hlipati*—to sob. The origin is onomatopoeic.

mlahta—he staggers. Slov. *mlahá; mlahta* is also possible: *Glej ga, kako jo mlahtá*—look how he is staggering. The inscription consists of four verses. At the end there is a short postscript: **ana zinače.** Slovene *en znak*—a saying, an utterance. **Zinače** is a vocative which became nominalized. Similar Slov. *maček, mače*—a cat; Serbo-Cr. *junak, junače*—a hero. The origin of **zinače** is from *znati*—to know, or *ziniti*—to utter; OCS *zinǫti*. *Znakъ* is in the OCS the postverbal from *znati*. Comp. Slov. *ziniti, katero ziniti*—to utter, to utter some words.

Ana zinače with the same meaning in inscriptions TLE 27, 28, 49, is also found in Rhaetian inscriptions on horns.

Condemnation of Drinking

TLE 865. A pitcher of unfired clay. Below each Etruscan word there is the Slovene equivalent:

MI	**NA**	**TES**	**K**	**TUM**	**PÉTI**	**ČINÁŠ**
mi	na	tešče	ki	tam	peti	začneš

A	**OINEÓJ**	**AP**	**TALÁ**
a	vrč	ob	tla.

Translation: You begin to sing to me on an empty stomach, and the pitcher (you throw) to the floor (to the ground).

mi—to me; Slov. *mi*, e.g. *mi greš spod nog!*—Will you get from under my feet, get out of my way!

a tes—on empty stomach; Slov. *na tešče*. OCS *tъštь*.

a—on; Slov. *o, na*. Already familiar OCS *a* (see Mikl.).

tum—there; Slov. *tam*. From Old Slavic *tŭ;* Slov. dial. *təm*.

peti—to sing or maybe to drink; Slov. *peti* or *piti*, maybe both. OCS *pěti, pojǫ*.

činaš—you begin; Slov. *začneš;* OCS *čьnǫ, četi*. Slov. *začeti, počinjati* (Mikl.); Serbo-Cr. *činiti*.

a—but; Slov. *a, toda*.

oienoj—Etr. form for Greek *oenochoe*—a pitcher of a special form. (The inscription is found on an "oenochoi" pitcher).

ap—by, next to, to; Slov. *ob*. OCS *obъ, ap* due to vowel change.

ap tala—to the floor, to the ground; Slov. *ob tla*. OCS *тьlo, тьlja*. Slov. gen. pl. *tal*.

Note: see **pevas ni k jesi u piku** (Museum of Padova)—you are singing now when you are at the top; Slov. *Poješ (pevaš) zdaj ko si na višku.* This inscription on "oenochoi" is of great importance for several reasons. First, it is Slavic; this becomes obvious as soon as we take a look at a few words like **peti**—to sing, **cinas**—to begin, as well as **tala**—the floor, the ground—and get acquainted with their forms. Second, the inscription is very much in harmony with the pitcher which is called **oineoj** in Etruscan.

Finally, I would like to call your attention to the meter of this inscription composed of the two unrhymed verses. In order to make it easier for the reader to feel the rhythm, I added the necessary accents.

And something else. Pallottino reads the 7th letter from the left (in Latin transcription) as **q;** I think it is actually **th,** to be pronounced as **t.** As the pitcher is not available to me, I cannot say who made the mistake—the Etruscan scribe or the copier. The difference in pronunciation is important though; if we read it as Θ, we have a clear Slavic word: *тьštь.* Even if I were wrong, the form **teskv (tesq)** corresponds to the Old Slavic *tŭsk*—on empty stomach (Mikl.); Slov. *tešč.*

Avleš Beluskeš

One of the oldest Etruscan inscriptions (**TLE 363**) has been found in Vetulonia. It is supposed to have originated in the 7th or 6th century B.C. and is written on a gravestone representing an armed warrior with a helmet holding a battle–axe in his right hand and a shield in his left. The inscription runs down the right side, then continues along the lower edge and ends on the left side.

In transcription, first the Etruscan and then the Slovene:

AVLEŠ	**BELUSKEŠ**	**T**	**USNUT (J)E**
Avleš	Beluskeš	tu	uspavan je

PANAL	**AŠ**	**MINIMUL**
Vladal,	dokler ni	preminil

U	**VANI**	**KE**	**HIR**	**UMI**	**ABERSNA**	**H**	**SE**
v	vanu	ko (bo)	hir	uma	obrsne	naj	se.

Translation: Alveš Beluskuš is asleep here. He ruled until he passed away. When
in heaven, may the troubles of the mind clear up.

Let us look at the individual words:

Avleš—a name. There is a possibility, however, that it might mean "the late"
connected to *avil*—died. OCS *ubylъ*—ceased to be, died. Swedish *avlida*—to
die. Compare Pyrgian tablets **TLE 874, 875.**

Beluskeš—a surname. Official Etrurology reads Feluskeš, but the grapheme which
is very similar to number eight is obviously a **B** (See Introduction).

t—here; Slov. *tu.*

381

usnunt—put to sleep; Slov. *uspavan;* Russ. *usnutь*—put to sleep. Also to pass away, to die.

panal—to rule, to govern; Slov. *vladal.* Pol. *panovac*—to rule, from *pan*—master in Czech, Pol., Lusatian. Lithuanian *panas*—lord.

aš—until; Czech *až*—until.

minimul—passed away; Slov. *preminul.* The word is found in some other inscriptions in the same meaning; e.g., **TLE 57, 59.** The Etruscan language must have had a shorter and a longer version of this verb: **minimat** and **minit.** The latter is often found in the form **mini** (aorist or present tense?).

u vani—in heaven. The word frequently occurs in Venetic inscriptions. Pleteršnik: Slov. *v božji van, tja v van*—into God's heaven, into heaven. Probably from *vъnь*—out; Sans. *vana.*

ke—when; Slov. *ko, kadar.* Slov. dialect also *ke.*

hir—trouble, distress; Slov. *tegoba.* OCS *hyrъ*—illness. Slov. *hirati*—to ail. In Etruscan **hir uma** means trouble and not mental illness. Slov. *hir*—tuberculosis (Plet.). Basque *hiraat*—becoming frail.

abersna—to clear up; Slov. *razjasni, obrsne.* Slov. *Nebo se obrsne*—the sky clears (Plet.). Perhaps connected to Slov. *brisati, obriše*—to wipe, wipes.

h—may; Slov. *naj, da;* actually *k.* In Venetic **k** and **h** are often interchangeable. In Slov. *k* turns into *h* before *g* and *k.* The exchange is understandable as both *k* and *h* are velar consonants, *k* being a plosive and *h* a spirant.

se—reflexive personal pronoun; Slov. *se.* OCS *sę.*

This inscription is one of the oldest. It is no surprise that all the words and grammar can be explained on the basis of Old Slavic as well as modern Slavic languages. Among the words, however, there is one which is found only in Slovene—**abersna.** Today it is an archaism, maybe still used in some dialects. The dictionary of Pleteršnik contains it. In another meaning, *obrsniti*—to scratch lightly—it is found in the *Dictionary of Slovene Literary Language.*

The contents and the meaning of the inscription harmonize well with the figure on the stone. His authoritative and proud bearing shows that the man buried there was no mere soldier, but a commander or even a ruler. The inscription is in agreement with the gravestone.

It is interesting that the Etruscans, who could be called the southern Veneti, used inscriptions on their gravestones whereas there are none on the Venetic stones. It would seem that having more contact with the East, where reverence for the dead, the ancestors, was widely practised, the Etruscans adopted some aspects of this tradition.

Inscription on the Back of a Snake

A snake coiled around a pitcher (aryballos) carries the inscription (**TLE 331**) without breaks between the words *in continuo*:

**hefmašuveitesalevarearavapeisnislarekasiais
emal...udikemaluvekavisiazilizixina ein sudueas**

Jug from the 7th century B.C. with an inscription on the back of a snake. (Museo di Villa Giulia, Roma)

This is a transcription by Pallottino who is usually (not always) dependable; therefore we will use it as well, naturally taking into account my interpretation of some letters (d, r, b, t). What do we get from these seemingly hopeless lines of letters? Let us take a look:

	HEMBAŠ	**UVEITE**	**ŠALE**	**VARE**	**ADA**
Slov.	Zbijaš	uvite	šale	vare(č)	jada

	VA	**PEISNI**	**SLADE**	**KA**	**SJAIS**
Slov.	v	pesni	slade,	ko	sijajiš.

	JE	**MALU**	**DIKE**	**MALU**	**VEKA**	**VI**	**SJA**	**ZILI**
Slov.	Je	malo	dike,	malo	veka	v	tem	žitju,

	ŽIGINA	**JE**	**IN**	**SUTU**	**JE**	**AS**
Slov.	užgano	je	in	zasuto	je	že.

Translation: You strew your witty banter, brewing poison
Into sweetness of the song, while yet you brightly shine.
So little fame, and little time is in this life,
No sooner lit, it is already buried.

Anyone who reads these verses carefully—the inscription is versed—can feel the rhythm. Let us write this four-verse poem once more, this time with diacritics and punctuation:

Hémbaš uvéite šále, varé adá
Va péisni sláde, ka sjaíš.
Je málu díke, málu véka vi sja žíli,
žígina je in sútu je as.

Let me explain the individual words:
hembaš—to beat, to pound; Slov. *zbijaš*. This word is related to the OCS *hebat*—to copulate. In Old Czech the meaning is different, *hebati*—to kick, to beat; the word may also be related to Slov. *hibati*—to find fault, to blame; *hiba*—a flaw, a defect (Plet.).
uveite (**ei** pronounced as diphthong)—twisted, wound up; Slov. *uvit, zvit*. Comp. Slov. *uvijati*—turning motion. Also *uviti (kožo na muževni vrbi)*—to loosen the bark on a willow branch (to make a whistle). This is done in the spring

when the sap is flowing. A branch without knots is selected and the bark on it is loosened by a twisting motion, then it is slid off the branch in one piece, undamaged; from the branch itself a mouthpiece and the stop for the far end are made. This completes the whistle. In the novel *Trotamora* by V. Habjan (which is full of Slov. Carinthian words), *uvit* means the same as *zvit*. The phrase **uveite šale** means twisted jokes, jokes with double meaning.

šale—jokes, pranks; Slov. *šale*. The word *šala* is generally Slavic as well as Old Slavic, but there are differences in meaning: OCS only has *šalenъ*—(mad, loud); Slov. *besen, bučen*. The meaning varies from joke to anger to deceit.

vare, varé, from **variti**—cooking, to cook. Participle of OCS *variti*—to cook. Slov. *variti, kuhati;* Russ. *varitъ*. The phrase "*variti strup*"—to brew poison—appears frequently in Slovene legends.

ada (gen. sing.)—poison; Slov. *jad, strup.* Polish *jadъ*—poison. Russ. *jadъ*—poison; OCS *jadъ*. There may be a roundabout connection between the Greek *Had* and *jad*.

va—in; Slov. *v.* (See under *vi).*

peisni—songs; Slov. *pesmi.* OCS *pêsnь.* Ukrain. *piti*—to sing. An inner etymological connection between to sing and to drink is not to be excluded. Comp. diphthong in **uveite (šale)** and diphthong in **peisni (slade).**

slade—sweetness pl.; Slov. *sladkosti,* also *slad,* gen. *slada*—a sweet, Ger. *die Süsse* (Plet.).

ka—when; Slov. *ko, kadar.*

sjajiś—you shine; Slov. *siješ, sijajiš.* OCS *sijajǫ, sijati.* Comp. Old Russ. *sinecъ*—the devil (Mikl.). From Slov. *sij,* gen.—a glimmer. Slov. *siniti*—first light (of the day).

je—is; Slov. *je.* OCS *jestъ, je* (Leskin 87).

malu—little; Slov. *malo.* OCS *malъ, mala, malo.* From Old Slavic *malŭ.*

dike— adornment, fame; Slov. *dike,* gen. of dika. The word is used in Croatian only, whereas in Slov. and Hung. it is a borrowed word. Strangely, etymologists fail to see a common origin of this word and the OCS *dikъ*—wild. The transition between the two meanings is Lith. *dykas,* meaning free, (Skok).

malu—little. (See above).

veka—time, gen. sing.; Slov. *veka, časa.* OCS *vêkъ* Ger. Kraft, Lebensalter—age, power, period of life, years. Lith. *veikti*—to work. In Etr. both meanings, power and age merged.

vi—in; Slov. *v.* OCS *vъ.* Slov. dial. *ve, vo, va.* The same in other Slavic languages; Russ. *vo.*

sja—this; Slov. *tem, tej* f.—**vi sja žili.** Russ. *vsja*—all f. (the entire life).

žili—in life; Slov. *(v) življenju,* arch. nom. *žilje.* Russ. *žitъ*—to live. It seems that this verb developed into a post-verbal *žilje*, which is otherwise not known in the meaning "of life" in Slavic languages. Slov. *življenje*—life—is probably only a longer version of *žilje*. Comp. Slov. *silje, siljenje; zdravje, zdravljenje*. Comp. Pyrgian tablets: **žilec i selje.** Slov. *živec*—Ger. *ein lebendes Wesen* (Plet.)—a living being. Also *živelj, žilje*—Ger. die Adern—veins (Plet.). *Žilo*— Ger. *die Speise*—food, etc.

žigina je—it is burnt, it is lit; Slov. *užgano je, zagori.* Comp. Slov. *užigati.* OCS *žegǫ* (from *žьgiti, žešti*). Slov. *žgan*—burnt, *žganje*—brandy, *sežiganje*—burning, *sežigati*—to burn.

in—and; Slov. *in.* OCS *i*—*et* (Mikl.).

sutu—covered with earth; from Slov. *suti, spem*—to strew. OCS *suti, sъpǫ.*

as—already; Slov. *že,* arch. *uže.* Slovak *už;* Old Slavic *ožь* (Vasm.). Another possibility is Czech *as*—probably; Slov. *bržčas*—probably, Czech *až*—until, *až do smrti*—until death. It would seem that "already" is the most suitable translation.

Minerva and Jupiter

Based on the already proven data of this language, which was called Rasennian by the Etruscans themselves, I would like to further elucidate with a few more inscriptions, particularly those where the verbal content is accompanied by an illustration. I think this will be useful.

In ancient mythology there is a well-known myth about Minerva's birth from Jupiter's head. The Romans acquired Minerva from the Rasennians who called her **Menrva;** on the other hand, the Etruscan Jupiter is known as **Tinia** in Rasennian. It would seem that **Tinia** was the supreme deity of the Rasennian pantheon and **Menrva** was the goddess of wisdom, art and war, similar to the Greek Athena.

If we take into account everything we know about Minerva and Jupiter, it will be very interesting to examine the Etruscan mirror found in Palestrina (Preneste) in southern Italy. The engraving on this mirror represents the birth of **Menrva** who is rising, in full armour, from Tinia's head (Fabretti, *Terzio supplemento*, no. **394**, p. 137).

The accompanying inscription explains the situation:

TANR TINIA MENRVA JETA USVA

Slovene: Znotraj Tinija Minerva ujeta je ušla.
English: Inside Tinia Menrva, caught, has escaped.

This is an easy inscription; its individual words are translated as follows:
tanr—therein, inside; Slov. *tam notri;* in the Slov. dialect of Rož Valley, Carinthia, *tantre, tantr* (reduction from *tam notri*—inside); OCS *vъnǫtrъ.* **Rasennian tanr** is obviously a distortion of **tantr** which is derived from *tam* and *ǫtrъ.* After the change of **m** to **n:** tantre, particularly as the Rasennian **o** sounded more like **a** (similar to OCS—acc. to Mikl.). There is a possibility that **tanr** was formed before the change of **an** into nasal **on.**
Tinia—Tinia, Jupiter.
Menrva—Minerva.
jeta—caught; Slov. *ujeta.* Even now in Slov. *jetnik, ujetnik.* OCS *jęta, i.e. ujeta.* From the verb *jęti.*
usva—she escaped; Slov. *ona je ušla;* OCS *ušva.* Did the Rasennians have the **l** which was written as **u** (v), and did they already pronounce it as **u**? In Upper Carniolan dialect the **l** is frequently changed (at the end of the word) into **v**; instead of *ušla,* we have *ušva.* It could be that this particular pronunciation is a remnant from those far off days when the Proto-Slavic Veneti, the distant ancestors of the Slovenes, first settled in the Alps and northern Italy. If we consider everything we know about the Venetic language, this is I think, a logical assumption.

Juno and Hercules

Inscription **TLE 399;** (Buonamici EE 390, tab LIV—NRIE 288, Speculum aeneum. Iunonis Herculi lac praebentis imag. exhornatus).
On this bronze mirror there is a representation of Juno offering milk from her breasts to Hercules.
Let us look at the inscription. First of all the excription from TLE—**eca : sren : tva : ihnac : hercle : unial : clan : θra : sce.** Taking into account that periods and colons were employed to separate words and syntagmas, my transcription reads as follows:

	ECA	ZREN	TVA	IH	NAC
Slov.	Eto	zrenje	tvoje	njih:	potem ko

	HERCLE	UNIAL	CLAN	ORA	SCE
Slov.	Herkul se je	utrudil,	človek	boginjo	sesa.

Translation: Observe the scene of the two of them:
when Hercules becomes tired, the goddess nurses him.

The above text is an exact description of the engraved image.

eca pronounce **eka**—this; Slov. *eto;* Lat. *eccum.* It is hard to say whether the Latins adopted this interjection (or adverb) from the Etruscans or the other way around. Ital. *ecco* (eko) is in conversational use in Slovenia along with the Slov. *eto.*

zren—scene; Slov. *zrenje, prizor.* From *zreti*—to observe, look at; i.e. here is

Mirror, 4th century B.C. Representation of an act from Etruscan mythology. Tired Hercules nurses at goddess's breast, symbolizing his being adopted as her son. One of the participants is holding tablet with the inscription (Museo archeologico, Firenze). Bronze mirrors were decorated with images and inscriptions on one side; they were polished on the other side.

388

something worth seeing. OCS *zьrěti*—to observe, to look at. This word is found in several inscriptions in various forms. Lithuanian *žereti*—*to shine* (same origin)—the root is *zer;* Slov. *žareti, videti, gledati*—to shine, to see, to watch.

tva—your; Slov. *tvoja.* See **TLE 747.** Lat. *tua.*

ih—them (two); Slov. *njih.* OCS *ih.* Slov. dialect *jih.* This word is often found in Venetic and Etruscan inscriptions.

nac pronounce **nak**—after, whereupon; Slov. *nakar;* Serbo-Cr. *nakon,* dial. *nak.* (See **TLE 874**—Pyrgian Tablets).

Hercle—Hercules.

unial—became tired; Slov. *se utrudil;* OCS *unyti;* Russ. *unjat*—to calm down. Participle *unjal.*

clan—man; Slov. *človek.* (See below).

ora— goddess; Greek *ora*—goddess. Albanian *ore*—a mythical being.

sce read **sǝče, sǝśe**—(he) suckles, nurses; Slov. *seše, sesa;* OCS *sьsati, sьsǫ;* generally Slavic. Russ. dial. *ssatь, ssu.*

Until I analyzed this inscription, I was certain that **clan** could mean only a member (of a family), a clansman, a relative, as it appears innumerable times in tombs next to the family name. I thought it was the same as the Slavic word *član*—member; however, the above text explains that the man or male child is nursing at the goddess' breast. This indicates that **clan,** Slov. *član*—member—must have meant a male, a man. The word is probably derived from *čelo*—forehead, **celan,** written as **clan** after the vowel omission. The forehead distinguishes humankind from other beings, therefore, this may have played a role in naming us. The Old Slavic etymology for the word was *čelověkъ,* a compound of *čelo* and *věkъ,* later reduced to *čьlověkъ.* So, *čelověkъ* meant a being who gets its power from its forehead. We can assume that the Rasennians did not know this compound. A man was *čelan,* **clan.** Vek(a) has the same meaning in the inscription: **Je malu dike, malu veka**—there is little fame, little power (TLE 331). In Slovene, *vek* means an era, a time, a century; although its primary meaning in modern Slovene is—a lifetime. The OCS *věkъ* meant power, primeval power. The Slovene Protestant writers still used it as power: *Ti si moj vek!*—You are my power! (Dalmatin); *On bo ljudem moč ino vek dal*—He will give the people strength and power (Trubar). Today this meaning is still retained in some dialects. In White Carniola they say: *človek na stare dni nima veka*—a man does not have strength in his old age.

The objection that Hercules was a demigod and not a man is not valid. He was made a demigod only later. When Juno nursed him he was still a child. Juno did not know that the child's father was her own husband, Jupiter (Zeus); in that case she would never have offered him her breasts, as she was wildly jealous. Actually it was Pallada Athena who persuaded her to nurse him. Consequently, the inscription on this Rasennian mirror is quite accurate: See the goddess who is nursing a child!

Celebration with Orpheus in the Grove

Inscription **TLE 474** (Buonamici EE 393—NRIE 293, Speculum aeneum. Orphei vaticinantis inter iuvenes et mulieres imag. exhornatus). The inscription is on a mirror which features Orpheus surrounded by young men and maidens. Below is my detailed interpretation:

	PIR	**HE**	**UN**	**RUAMIEL**	**U**	**GAJEH**
Slov.	Pir,	hej,	in	ramovš	v	gajeh

	BA	**IM**	**LASIDA**	**JEHA**	**S**
Slov.	Bila	jim	veselica	divja	to.

Translation: Hey, there was a feast and a bustle in the grove,
it was a wild celebration.

pir—feast, celebration; Slov. *pir, pirovanje;* OCS *pirъ*— a feast. From *piti* (Mikl.).
he—hey; Slov. *hej, he*—an interjection.
un—and; Slov. *in.* See other examples and corresponding entries where it is also spelled **an.** Slov. dialect *jən* comes the closest to **un.** There are a number of variants in Slovene.
ruamiel—noise, hustle, bustle; Slov. *vrvež, ramovš, ramuš, ramuh*; Ger. *das Getöse, der Lärm.* Pleteršnik fails to give *der Rummel* which is certainly related to Etr. and Slovene. There is also Latin *rumor;* Slov. *ramovš*—noise.
u gajeh—in the grove; Slov. *v gajeh.* OCS *gajь.* The word *gaj* is generally Slavic.
ba—was, imp. 3rd p. s. or a haplology of *bila*—was; equal to OCS *bo*—for, because. Compare Upper Carniola *bua.*
im—them; Slov. *jim;* OCS *imъ.*
lasida—boisterousness, festivity; OCS *laskati;* Russ. *lasyj*—desirous, craving. Czech *laska*—love. Lat. *lascivus*—lascivious. Old Ind. *lasati*—wishes (Vasm.).
eha read **jeha**—evil, wild, lewd (See note on **jege** in the Glossary); related to

Ukr. *jahyj*—evil; Ger. *böse;* Slov. *jaga baba,* and *divja jaga* (from a Slovene folk tale).

There is not a single word which is out of place or is in disagreement with my translation; also the pictorial representation itself closely coincides with the text, and offers additional evidence that my translation is very much in harmony with the original.

A Humorous Inscription

TLE 645. A mirror.

The first part of this inscription is blurred, but the second part is quite clearly visible:

MIZKAT NA SVEH
NA SVEH S NAROA

Slovene: Mežikati vsem (na vse), iz vseh se norčevaje.
English: Winking at everyone, making fools of all.

mizkat, miscat, mižkat—to wink; Slov. *mežikati, mežkati* (Plet.).
na sveh—at everyone; Slov. *na vse* (note: **mižkat** was followed by a genitive).
s naroa—teasing, making fool of; Slov. *se norčujoč, se norčevaje;* also *noriti*—Ger. narren, bethören, anführen, betrügen (Plet.).
As the inscription is on a mirror, its meaning is particularly appropriate.

The Rasennians and the Hittites

TLE 65. A pitcher. Scyphus geom. In my transcription:

	CENA				
Slov.	Pleme.				

	KALAT	**U**	**RUS**	**B**	**APJE**	**NAS**
Slov.	Blatiti		Rasensko	bi bilo,	če pije	naš

C   JEME   CU   HETIE
Slov. ko z   njimi,   ki so   Hetitje.

Translation: It offends the Rasennes,
if one of our men drinks with those who are Hittites.

The contents of this inscription suggests that there was unfriendliness between the Rasennians and the newcomer Hittites before they merged into a single Etruscan nation. The inscription begins with the word **cena** which is somewhat separated from the rest of the text.

cena—a tribe, a race; the word *cena* is included in Bezlaj's *Etymological Dictionary of Slovene Language* meaning a tribe, a race (western Slovenia, Tolmin area). It is also found in Štrekelj's Dictionary, with the same meaning. Bezlaj dealt with this word also in his *Essays on Slovene Language;* there he looks for a connection between *cena* and the Old Kimb. *cenetl*—a tribe. He derives both from the root **ken–** which is to be found in Slov. *začeti, činiti, končati*—to begin, to do, to finish. In Venetic and Etruscan inscriptions **konat** occurs most frequently; Slov. *končati* and *konati.*

kalat—literally, to throw mud at, to offend; Slov. *blatiti, kaljati* (Plet.). Related to words *kal, kalen, kaluža*—mud, muddy, a muddy pool. Russ. *kaljat.* OCS *kalъ*—mud. The word is also found in other Etruscan inscriptions; e.g., **Kalia teži mun zle...** Slov. *kalja (sramota) teži manj zlo*—Disgrace (shame) is less burdensome...

u—at, with; Slov. *pri, u; u nas*—at our place, with us. *U okna*—at the window. OCS *u boga*—with the God.

u Rus—with the Rasennians, or in Rasennia. The Etruscans called themselves Rasenna. Innumerable statements have been written about the etymology of the name *Rus.* The Arabs, for example, called the Normans "Russians". Skok states that it is not certain that the "Russes" were only a Swedish tribe; he thinks this was just an idea developed by Miklošič. The origin of the name *Rus* is probably much more involved. It is possible that the Swedes borrowed the word from the Russians, and that it is related to OCS *rusъ*—reddish brown; Slov. *rus*—red, reddish brown. Pleteršnik cites Lat. *russus*—red—in this connection. It seems that the word is Proto-Slavic (Venetic) and that the Latins acquired it from the Rasennians (Etruscans). Russia is the modern term for *Rusъ.*

b—would; Slov. *bi;* OCS *bi,* a conditional.

apje—drinks; Slov. *opije;* OCS *piti*—to drink.

naš—our; in the meaning "our man".

c—when; Slov. *ko,* dialect *k.* It is not clear how the **c** was pronounced, but most likely somewhere between **c** and **k.** It seems that this conjunction follows the verb: **apje naš c...** instead of **c apje naš...**

jeme—with them; Slov. *z njimi.* OCS *imi.* Slovene dialect *jimi.*

cu—who; Slov. *ki,* dial. *k.*

Hetie—Hittites. Their own terms for themselves were **Heti, Geti, Hetie** pronounce Hetje. See the introductory study about the relationship between the Hittites and Rasennes. When they moved into the Rasennian territory in Italy, the Hittites brought with them various skills and the terminology related to such skills from the highly developed Asia Minor. Later on after the two languages merged, the Etruscan language was left with numerous Hittitic expressions from the areas of technology, agriculture, crafts and government administration. However, the Rasennian language has been preserved in relative purity—without Hittitic admixture—in poetic expressions.

The Name "Marcesic"
in the Vault of dell Orco—Tarquinia

I will quote here a few short inscriptions which confirm their Slavic origin, although they do not come from the earliest era.

One of them is published in **TLE 84.** In Pallottino's transcription it reads as follows:

larthiale : hulxniesi : marcesic : caliathesi : munsle : nacnvaiasi : oamce : lex...

In my transcription and interpretation:

	LAD	**O**	**JALE**	**HU**	**L(E)GNEŠI**	**MARCESIC**
Slov.	Mir	v	jalovini	ko	legneš,	Marcesič.

	KALJA	**TEZI**	**MUN**	**ZLE**
Slov.	Kalja	teži	mun	zlo

	NAKN	**VAJA**	**SI**	**O**	**AMCE**	**LE(S)...**
Slov.	po(nakon)	voja	si	na	omoči	le(tu)

Translation: Peace in this wasteland, now that you have lain down, Markezič.
Disgrace is less burdensome,
As you rest here after the battle.

Explanation of individual words:

lad—peace, harmony, tranquility; Czech harmony; Ukr. agreement. Related to Slov. *lagoda*—die Ausgelassenheit (Plet.)—ease; Russ. *lad, -a*—agreement, harmony. There are a number of derivatives from **lad**. In Zagorje and eastern Styria region, Slovenia, *ladati*—to sing (in harmony), *ladarice*—female singers. Russ. and Serb. *lada*—a spouse.

o—about, in (see Pyrgian tablets); Slov. *o, v.*

jale, o jale—wasteland, in this wasteland; Slov. *v jalovini.* OCS *alъ*—*nequitia. Slov. jal* also envy, infertility.

hu—when; Slov. *ko* (k to h). Compare change of **k** into **h** before **k** and **g**.

legneši—you lie down; Slov. *legneš* from *legniti* (Plet.). The ending -**ši**, is OCS, compare *hvališi;* Slov. *hvališ*—you praise. The word is generally Slavic and Indo-European. OCS *legǫ—I* lie down; Slov. *ležem, legnem;* **legneši** (2. per. pres.)—you lie down, Slov. *ležeš.*

Marcesic (Marcesič or Markešič)—a surname. It is not necessary to stress that it is a typically Slavic surname; same and similar forms of it are still found in Slovene and Serbo-Croatian. The original Etruscan form of this surname is **Marces, (Markeš).**

kalja—mud, in the sense of shame, disgrace; Slov. *kalja*—der Schmutz am Leibe—dirt on body, Bodrež, Gorica/Gorizia region (Plet.). Related to *kalja* is *kal*—a pool. OCS *kalъ*—mud; generally Slavic, Indo-European. Compare **kalat,** TLE 65.

tezi—it weighs down; Slov. *teži,* from *težiti.* OCS and generally Slavic.

mun—less; Slov. *manj;* in Slov. dial. and vernacular mǝn(j). Comp. OCS *mъne, mъnij.* Since there was no separate letter for either the soft or the hard semivowel or silent vowel, the **u** was used; it was a short sound.

zle—bad, very; Slov. *hudo, zelo*—adv. Czech *zle.* From OCS adjective *zъlъ*—badly, very. Generally Slavic. **Mun zle**—less badly. Slov. *manj hudo (zelo).*

nakn—after; Serbo-Cr. *nakon;* arch. Serb. *nak.* (See Glossary to the Pyrgian tablets).

vaja—of a battle; Slov. *boja, voja*—gen. sing. **Nakn vaja**—after the battle. Slov. *po (nakon) boju;* also *voj, vojak, vojna*—battle, soldier, war (Plet.). OCS *voj, vojinъ.* Lith. *vaina.*

si—stay, sojourn; Slov. *bivajoč;* OCS *sy* (gen.) *sǫšta.* Comp. Ital. *essendo.* This

394

part. pres. of *byti* disappeared from Slavic languages. As shown, the Etruscan language still had it. Nevertheless, the forms *sem, si, smo, ste, so*—I am, you are, we are, you are, they are—have been retained. At present, *sy* is translated with a subordinate clause.

o—on, about; Slov. *o.* (See Glossary to Pyrgian tablets).

amce—help, invigoration; Slov. *omoč, pomoč* (Plet.). Here in the meaning of rest. (See **o amuce** in the Glossary to Pyrgian tablets). In our case the vowel **u** is missing. Together with the preposition it should read **o amuce**, lit. on rest; i.e., at rest, recuperating. **Nakn vaja si o am(u)ce** therefore means: when after the battle you take a rest here. Marcesič was obviously a soldier whose feelings were badly hurt by shame when the Etruscans lost the battle. Comp. TLE 875: **o amuce kleval**—he called for help. Slov. *na pomoč klical.*

le(s)—here; Slov. *semle, le-tu.* **Le** was not only a particle, but an adverb of place; later, the emphasis shifted to *tu*. It is hard to say what followed **le** as the inscription is not complete. Maybe it read **les** instead of **le**. *"Prid, zidar se les učit"* (Vodnik)—Come mason here to learn!

The Veteran's Pitcher

This inscription is on a pitcher, **CIE 8411.**

	ÁLI	**KE**	**A**	**PUMIN**	**KARÁ**
Slov.	ola	da	v	spomin	bitke

Slovene: Da (popijemo) ola (piva) v spomin bitk!
English: Let us drink beer in memory of the battle!

áli—beer; OCS *olъ*—beer.

ke—that; eastern Styria and Kajkavian *ka*—yes. Also Venetic.

a—in; OCS *ǫ* as an adverb, as is *vъ*.

pumin—memory; Slov. *spomin*. Arch. *pomin* Ger. die Erinnerung—memory. Also, *na pómin se imeti*—sich in Acht nehmen (Plet.)—to be on one's guard.

kará—of a battle; Slov. *bitke*—gen. sing. Slov. arch. *kar* (m.)—a quarrel (Bez.). It is also possible that *kara* is gen. pl., because *kara* still in OCS means "battle" similar to Old Persian *kará*—army. Also in Venetic inscriptions, (Pa 2) **kara**—of battles.

Every Feast Has an Ending

This inscription is on the brass rim of a pitcher in the Museum of Padova and can also be read from the Slavic-Venetic viewpoint. It is written *in continuo:*

PEVASNIHJESIUPIKUTIUTISAHBILIPIPERISNATI

If we take a close look we can see that two of the words are interconnected semantically, grammatically and syntactically. They are: **PEVAS,** 2nd pers. of the verb **pevat**—to sing; OCS *pěvati, peti* (compare **TLE 865**). The second word is **UTISA,** 2nd pers. aorist of the verb **utihat**—to become silent; Slov. *utihniti.* When we take this into account, it is not difficult to understand the seemingly incomprehensible inscription:

	PEVAS	**NI**	**H**	**JESI**	**U**	**PIKU**
Slov.	Pevaš	zdaj,	ko	si	na	višku (piku),

	TI	**UTISA**	**H**	**VILI**	**PIPERI**	**SNATI**
Slov.	Ti si	utihnil	ko	bile	pipeli	(so) snete.

Translation: You are singing now, when at the top,
But fell silent when the pipes were taken down.

Note: As is known the bagpipes (pipeli) are worn over the shoulder, and are taken down when the playing is over. Comments on individual words:

pevas—you are singing; modern Slov. *poješ.*

ni—now. This word has disappeared from Slovene; however, it can be found in the meaning "now" combined with various suffixes or without them; e.g., OCS *nynje, nynja;* Lith. *nu;* Alb. *ni* (from *nu); Czech *nyni;* Lat. *nunc,* etc.

jesi—you are; Slov. *si;* OCS *jesi.* Serbo-Cr. *jesi.*

u—in; Slov. *v.*

u piku—at the top. Comp. Russ. *pik*—mountain top. There must be some link with the following words: *pikniti, pičiti, navpik*—to pierce, to sting, vertically. There is also the mountain of Špik, Slovenia.

ti—you; Slov. *ti.*

vili—were; Slov. *bili.* We still find in Slovene Littoral dialect, due to betatism, *vili* instead of *bili.*

piperi—pipes, bagpipes; Slov. *piščali.* OCS *pipela,* plural, *pipeli*—*sambuca, tibia* (Mikl.)—pipe, pipes.

snati—to take down; Slov. *sneti.* Russ. *snjatь;* OCS *sъnjati.*

The Rhaetian Inscriptions

The relationship between the Venetic and the Etruscan languages involves also the relationship between the Rhaetian and Etruscan. The official Etrurologists have established certain similarities, at least in script. The two scripts are the same with the exception of a few minor differences; there is for example in Rhaetian a double **s,** leaning against a vertical line.

In his book *The Etruscans* (Penguin Books, 1956), Pallottino considers the Rhaetians and the Etruscans as non-European, whereas the Veneti were in his opinion Indo-European and linguistically close to the Italic group. As is well known, my views about the Venetic language are different, and I also disagree about the Rhaetians and their language.

The museum in Este preserves the Rhaetian inscriptions. They are engraved on deer horns, actually on short terminal sections of horns. Most of the inscriptions are in excellent condition. The only defect in a few samples is what seems like a word missing; we are not certain whether this is indeed so in every case. However, our main aim is to determine if the language of these inscriptions is related to the language of the numerous ancient toponyms in the area of the former Rhaetian region in the Alps. Even though the inscriptions are not all preserved in their entirety, they offer enough material for our purpose.

What could the contents of these inscriptions be? The horns have a hole on the thin end. This gives us—besides the language—strong evidence that they were worn by hunters as amulets, and that they had a magic significance. Their maximum length is 10cm, just the right size for the purpose. We can expect that these inscriptions were actually spells and warnings against the dangers of hunting in those wild mountains.

The Rhaetian Inscriptions on Deer Horns

1.

RITANIM VLKA

Slov. Lovečim volka

Translation: To wolf hunters.

ritanim—to the hunters, to those who pursue (animals). Old Ind. *rtis* f.—attack, fight. Old Russ. *retь*—a fight, eagerness. Serb. *rat*—war—is of the same

397

origin. **Ritanim** would therefore be dat. pl. of **ritan*—one who hunts, a hunter. This word is repeated in other forms several times in these inscriptions. It could be that the Slov. *retiti*—to damage, to hurt, Ger. *verletzen* (Plet.)—is related. All of these words originate in **ritat (ritanim).** Latvian *rietet*—to go down, to lay down; *riet*—to bark, to growl. In addition to **ritat* also **rietet, *ritet.* (See other inscriptions).

vlka—a wolf; Slov. *volka.* OCS *vьlka.*

2.

This inscription has very clearly etched letters and reads as follows:

...RITAL ELE MAJ S ZINAKE

Rital ele maj s zinake

As shown by the dots (and the photograph), something could be missing on the left side. In my opinion, something is missing. However, supported by the rest of the inscription, the missing part can be assumed to be: You who will go... or You hunter who will go... If we consider this assumption the translation of the entire verse reads as follows:

Slovene: Ti, ki boš šel... lovit jelene (jelena), imej ta znak pri sebi.
English: You, who will go... to hunt deer, keep this charm (amulet) with you.

rital—(you will) hunt, follow; participle of **ritat.** Slov. *lovil, zasledoval, šel nad.* In the first inscription a noun derivative **ritanim,** dat. pl. of **ritan.**

ele pronounce **jele**—deer; Slov. *jelen.* Various etymologists trace *jelen* to Old Slavic **ely* (ele?); gen. *elene;* Russ. *ólenь;* Ukr. *ólinь.*

maj—have; Slov. *imej;* Serbo-Cr. *imaj.* Slov. vernacular *mej, mam.* OCS *iměti, imamь.*

s— this; Slov. *to, ta.* OCS *sь* has been retained in words like: **si**-*noči, dane*-**s.**

zinake i.e. **zinaxe, zinache, h** and **k** were often interchangeable—a charm, amulet (with magic powers). OCS *znakъ*—a sign, Ger. *Zeichen* (Mikl.). Latv. *zinat—Kunde geben* (Mikl.)—to announce. The root is zen-. It is interesting that the same word with the same meaning is also found in three Etruscan inscriptions: **TLE 27, 28, 49.**

3.

This inscription also involves a wild animal—a lynx. There is uncertainty whether all the words have been preserved here. It appears that the beginning is missing; however, the part that has been preserved is understandable:

RIZI	**V**	**KED**	**RINA**	**KE**
Slov. Risu	v	brlog	rine	ki

Translation: To him, who pushes his way into a lynx's den.

Rizi v ked rina ke

I will explain how I arrived at this interpretation:

rizi—to the lynx; Slov. *risu* (arch. *risi*). Why **z** instead of **s?** Because the lynx got his name from his colour, which is for example in Russ. *ryžij*—red–haired. Perhaps the double **s** which is a peculiarity of these inscriptions should be pronounced as **s.** In this case the word for the lynx would be identical to that in OCS *rysь. Ryžij* actually comes from *rysь–ij* or *ryzij.* Also in Slovene there is a word of the same origin *rus*—red; sometimes *rs, rsa*—ox, cow (Mikl.). Latin *russus,* Ital. *rosso* etc.

v—into; Slov. *v;* OCS *vъ.*

ked—into the den, shelter, cover. Bezlaj's *Etymological Dictionary keta*—a shelter built of woven branches and plastered with clay—wattle and daub, especially in vineyards in eastern part of Slovenia; its etymology is unclear, probably from *kъta Indo-European *keut—to cover. The purpose of an animal den or a human shelter is to provide cover against bad weather or enemies.

rina—he pushes; Slov. *rine,* from **rinati;* Slov. *riniti*—to push forward. OCS *rinǫti*—to throw oneself upon (someone or something); Ukr. *rinuti*—to run hard. This word appears in several Slavic languages including the Venetic.

ke—who; Slov. *ki.* In Venetic and Etruscan languages the pronouns often follow the predicate.

4.

As we shall see, this inscription too has a magical meaning; it protects the hunter from danger.

	S	**TU**	**VATI**	**NAGE**
Slov.	Ta		ureče	kače

Translation: This (one) casts a spell on snakes.

s—with; Slov. *s, z; s tu*—*s to;* OCS *sъ.*

tu—this; Slov. *to.*

vati—bewitch, cast a spell (imperative). In OCS *vě-, větъ*—pactum—agreement, contract; *větovati*—loqi—to speak. *Vetij*—rhetor, speaker—is from the same root. Serbo-Cr. *vještica, veštica*—a witch. If our explanation is correct, **a** in **vati** is a reflex for OCS jat (ě), similar to some examples in Etruscan; OCS *bě,* Etr. **ba.** Compare Latin *vates*—*a prophet.* Also *vatus.* Did the Latins acquire this word from the Etruscans, who were famous soothsayers?

nage—snakes. Vasmer considers the Slov. word *nag*—naked—as related to Sanskrit *nagas*—a snake. Considering that *nagas* also means an elephant, i.e., a naked animal, this linking of meaning is justified. The Rhaetians would in all probability call a snake **naga.** Considering that in Slovene there are many words which are completely identical in phonetics and definition with the Sanskrit, it would not be unusual if the Veneti in Rhaetia and elsewhere used the same word for snake as did Sanskrit. The question arises whether the explanation for Slov. *gož*—a grass snake—is correct. *Gož* is considered to be related to Latin *anguis*—a snake, or Lith. *angis*—snake, an adder. It sounds more probable that *gož* is derived from Slov. *gol*—naked—particularly since there is in Slovene also *golž,* i.e., *golež*—naked; this is also supported by *gadolas*—*schlangenhaarig*—bald (Plet.).

5.

On one of the horns there is a very clear inscription which reads:

VALTE ONA
Slov. zvalite ovna!

Translation: Roll down the ram!

Valte ona

valte—roll down! Slov. *zvalite!* In Rhaetian **i** is reduced as in Slovene dialects and vernacular: *zvalte ga po tleh*—roll him to the ground! OCS *valiti, valь.*

ona—a ram (acc.); Slov. *ovna.* I think this word should be pronounced **ovna,** since **v** (u) was already omitted in speech of the time. Maybe **o** crossed with a line was pronounced as **ou?** This interpretation offers itself in part because most of these inscriptions are connected to hunting. To conclude, let me add: the word **ouvna**—a ram—Slov. *ovna* and the adjective **ovoni** Slov. *ovnji*—of the ram—also occurs in Venetic inscriptions (see **Es 55, Ca 62, and Ca 66**).

6.

The following inscription is in content very similar to the previous one. It is partially broken on the right side, but still legible:

> **RITIEI   KNI   RISA**
> Slov. Loveč   končaj   risa!

Translation: Hunting, finish the lynx!

ritiei—hunting, following. From **ritit (ritet). Here part. pres. act. In OCS we find the same ending: *živei, gredei;* also in the Venetic language.
kni—finish; Slov. **konaj!* Old Slavic *ken–*. From this root, after transition of **e** into **o: конь.** Czech *do kna* (dial.)—to the end. Venetic *keni*—finish! (**Es 57**).
risa—a lynx (See inscription no. 3).

7.

> **REITEMU JUSI   NAGE**
> Slov. lovečemu   preganja   kače

Translation: It chases away the snakes for the hunter.

Reitemu jusi nage

reitemu pronounce **reitjemu**—for the hunter, dat. sing. (see explanations to no. 1 and 6).
jusi—chases away. Russ. *jusit, suetitьsja*—to run excitedly around, to get excited. See Russ. *jus*—a quick one, a cunning one (Vasm.). In Venetic, the verb is not reflexive as in Russian; it applies to the subject in accusative.
nage—snakes (see explanation to no. 4).

8.

This inscription—a very short one—is not a spell, but advice:

TRPAEI IS(I)

Because I read **ě** in the middle of the word as **je** (ye), and because I think that the line after **s** should be pronounced as **i,** my approach slightly changes the reading of the two words:

TRPAJEI	**ISI**
Slov. Potrpežljivo	išči (divjad)

Translation: Patiently search (for game).

trpajei—patiently. Same form as **ritiei**—hunting (see no. 6). OCS *živei, gredei.* In Venetic there is identical part. pres. act. Informal was probably ***trpait.** OCS *trъpěti*—to suffer; Lett. *terpit*—to endure. In some Slavic languages it has the meaning: to bear patiently. In Russ. *терпеть*—to suffer, to bear patiently. Slov. *po-trpeti,* in addition to *potrpežljiv,* also *trpežljiv* (Plet.)—patient. In Serbo-Cr. archaism *trapiti* (Mikl.). The above-mentioned infinitive ***trpait** could have been iterative of ***trpet, *trpit.**

Another possibility: **TRPA(J)EJ S**

Translation of this has essentially the same message: Be patient. Hunt patiently! Compare Slov. *strpeti se*—to endure. *Nisem se mogel strpeti*—I could not hold out.

isi—look for; Slov. *išči.* I have not concluded this simply on the basis of Slov. dial. *iši, iš;* Sanskrit *isati*—he seeks, looks for (Vasmer, Bezl.).

9.

This inscription is also of a magic character. It is a spell:

KNL	**SES**	**U**	**SILU**
Slov. (Naj bi) kanil	ta	v	sili

Translation: This will help in difficulty.

knl read **kanil** or **konil, konal**)—to intend; Slov. *ukanil*—he deceived, he misled, *kanil* (Vodnik)—he intended. The vowels are missing because the Rhaetian inscriptions were more affected by the Etruscan than the Venetic. Old Slav. root *ken–*. The word is of the same origin as *konati, končati* or *čęti*. Serbo-Cr. *činiti, činim* (Mikl.)—to do; OCS *konь*—to finish; *čьnǫ, četi*.

ses—this; duplication of demonstrative pronoun **sь**—this. Russ. *sesь*. **Ses** (this) refers to the amulet.

u—in; Slov. *v.* OCS *vь.*

u silu—in difficulty; Slov. *v sili*. Serbo-Cr. *silje, nasilje*—trouble, violence, from *sila*—power; 16th century (Vuk, Skok). It seems that **lь** hardened into **l,** as in Upper Carniolan dialect.

10.

This inscription is another warning to the hunter:

LASTE	**BL**	**KI**	**GINA**
Slov. Počasnè	bil	ker,	poginil

A more readable Slovene: Ker je bil počasnež, je poginil.
Translation: Because he was a laggard (slow-foot), he died.

laste—slow-foot, a laggard. This assumption is based on the Slovene archaism *last, lasti*—easiness, slowness (Plet., Bezl.). When we consider the form, we see that it is possible that **laste** is identical to a laggard or slow-foot; i.e., a noun. Serbo-Cr. *lastan*—easy-going.

bl read **bil**—he was; Slov. *bil;* OCS *byl.*

ki—because; Slov. *ker;* Slov. dial. *k' je.* As we have seen, the pronouns sometimes followed the verb.

gina—died; Slov. *poginil, ginil,* 3rd prs. aorist. OCS *gynǫti*—to die; Slov. *giniti, poginiti.*

Does **laste**—a laggard—refer to the beast or the hunter? Probably to the hunter, as this is an encouragement to the hunter to be quick.

11.

A magic spell with the help of the amulet (zinake).

	E	**S(E)**	**S**	**TU**	**ATELL**	**A**	**GINU**
Slov.	In	se	s	to	otel	pred	poginom!

Translation: And with this (amulet), saved himself from death!

e—and; this has sometimes the same meaning in Venetic.

s(e)—himself; Slov. *se.* OCS *sę*—himself.

s—with; Slov. *s;* OCS *sъ.*

tu—this; Slov. *to.* A shortened form of OCS *tojǫ*—with this.

atell—saved himself; Slov. *otel, se otel. Oteti se.* As early as the Freising Manuscripts (Brižinski spomeniki) *oteti.* Found also in other Slavic languages. Old composite *otъ-mo.* **Atell** is an example of vowel change from o to a. And why two **l's?** It is possible this was their way of recording the hard **l** which is still in use in Polish and Russian.

a—from; OCS *ǫ.* According to Miklošič this nasal **o** was due to a common vowel change pronouced as **a;** the same change is observed in Venetic.

a ginu—from death; Slov. *pred poginom.*

12.

This inscription is very clear and it appears to be complete.

	RITIEM	**V**	**TINU**
Slov.	lovečim	v	močvirju

Translation: To those hunting in the swamps.

ritijem—to those who are hunting, dat. pl. of **ritija*—hunter—one who pursues, tracks animals (see notes to no. 1). OCS *retiti*—to strive, to fight.

v—in; Slov. *v.* OCS *vъ.*

tinu, v tinu—in the swamp. OCS *tina*—swamp, mud (*borboros,* Vasm.). Russ. *tina*—swamp.

This charm or amulet had magic power against the dangers of hunting in the swamps, not only against wild animals, but probably against evil spirits inhabiting such places. Clearly, hunting in the swamps was associated with difficulties;

that is why this special precaution.

The following examples prove that the Rhaetian inscriptions on deer horns have the character of hunting charms or spells.

Padova 221:

RITAMNE H (J)ELANU
Slov. Lovcu   na   jeleno (košuto)

Translation: To a doe hunter.

Padova 224:

RITIEI KUŠITU
Slov. Loveč   košuto

Translation: Hunting a doe.

Košuta is an OCS word known in all Slavic languages. It seems that the Venetic and Rhaetian had two expressions for a female deer, **košuta** and **jelena.** In Slovene *košuta* means a doe and *jelen* means a buck. It is entirely possible to use *jelena* for a doe; this was probably the case in by-gone times. One remnant of this is found in western Slovene dialect in the Tolmin area where *jelena* is still used for the name of a cow (Plet.).

Padova 239:

LASTE VU TIHINU
Slov. Počasi   v   tišini

Translation: Slowly in silence.

laste—slow. (See notes to no. 10).

Laste vu tihinu

406

vu tihinu—in silence; Slov. *v tišini.*

Religious Advice

On the pallet from Padova (Pre-Italic Dialects no. 244) there is an inscription which is justifiably considered Rhaetian. It reads as follows:

	ET	**SUA**	**LEUTI**	**KU**	**KAIAN**
Slov.	Od	svoje	grešnosti	da	pokajan
	From	his	sinfulness	let	repentant

	NAKI	**NA**	**TARI**	**SAK**	**VIL**
Slov.	naj	na	tari	vsak	bi bil
	should	on	deathbed	each	be.

In readable English: Let every man on his deathbed be repentant of his sins.

et—from; Slov. *od.* OCS *otъ.* Slov. dial. also *əd.*

sua—his (own); Slov. *svoje.* The possesive pronoun has not as yet merged with the demonstrative pronoun **j.** It was probably indeclinable.

leuti—sinfulness, envy, anger, malice. All these concepts are comprised in the word *lud* (which is found in most Slavic languages); its predominant meaning now is "crazy". The vowel **u** was formed from the diphthong **ou** in the root leut- (Skok).

ku—when, since; Slov. *ko, da.* Kajkavian, and east Styria *ka.*

kaian read **kayan**—repentant; Slov. *spokorjen, pokajan.* Serbo-Cr. *kajati se*— to repent; same in east Styria. Slovene archaism *kajba*—repentance—Ger. *Die Reue* (Plet.).

naki—should. Various forms in Slavic languages. Serbo-Cr. *neka;* Slovak *nak*— should (Bezl.).

na—on; Slov. and generally Slavic *na.*

tari, na tari—on deathbed, in death pains. *Tara*—Ger. *die Marter, die Plage, die Pein* (Plet.). The same meaning in Venetic. The word is a postverbal of *treti, tarem*—I grind, I crack, I triturate. OCS *treti,* from *ter-ti.*

sak—each; Slov. *vsak.*

vil—was; Slov. *bil.* A common change of **b** into **v.** Compare Slov. dialect from Soča Valley where *vil* and *bil* are interchangeable.

The meaning of the inscription has been explained correctly, I think, and it provides important data on the Rhaetian as well as Venetic and Etruscan religion. The dimension of repentance was of great importance, just as it is in Christianity. It ensured merciful treatment in the next world. This inscription shows that Rhaetians (Veneti) placed stress on the necessity that each man should be cleansed of the evil within himself before his death. Only then will his journey to the **van** be undertaken in comfort.

The Yapodic or Messapic Inscriptions

East of the Veneti in Istria was the home of the Yapods. But they also lived on a long strip of coast in present Apulia, Italy. History has very little to say about them, and linguists (Pallottino, Krahe) are of the opinion that their language was Indo-European with certain "Illyric" peculiarities. Pallottino says that linguists do not as yet know what meaning to ascribe to the word "Illyric", particularly as the present Albanian dialects which are supposed to be derived from it, "have nothing in common with old Venetic or Yapodic." (*The Etruscans*, p. 29).

We would have no knowledge what language was spoken by the Yapods in Istria if they had not also lived on a fairly long stretch of coast in present-day Apulia. They left a number of inscriptions—not many, but most significantly rather talkative. They are known as "Messapic" inscriptions. There can be no doubt that the language of the Yapods of Apulia was either identical or closely related to the language spoken by Istrian Yapods, as well as to that spoken by the people mentioned in the Umbrian text of the Iguvine tablets. They were called Yapuzci, which is only another name for Yapigs or Yapods. Their homeland was the coast south of Ravenna.

These names lead us to the conclusion that they were the same people. There is no data on when and why they were separated, but it is clear from the inscriptions that their language was close to Venetic (Proto-Slavic). We can safely assume that they came from the north as one of the Venetic tribes and settled the eastern and the western Adriatic coasts in the second millennium B.C. The texts on the Yapodic inscriptions are Proto-Slavic. The language of the inscriptions is Slavic, but the names are not—E. G. Aprodita is almost certain to be Greek Aphrodite. Such names as Tabara, Theotorias, and Etos Trohandes on the gravestones sound completely foreign to the Slavic ear.

What does this mean? Are those the names of some nation which had been Venetized (Slavicized) by the Yapods of Apulia, or are they Illyrian? If they are Illyric it would mean that the Veneti, who had their own script for a long time, lived alongside the "Illyrians". As they were the more civilized of the two, their language prevailed, but the subject people kept their old names. This is a common practice. Cemeteries in Slovenia of 150 to 200 years ago have many gravestones inscribed in German, but the names, although deformed, remained Slovene.

The Yapodic language must have been a branch of Venetic, as shown by words like **plastas**—you pay; Slov. *plačaš; OCS plaštaš;* **molda**—young; Slov. *mlada,* Old Slavic *molda;* **bilia**—existence, sojourn; Slov. *bivanje,* OCS *bylije;* **blazit**—to soothe, to appease; Slov. *blažiti;* OCS *blažíti;* Russ. *blažitь;* **agolizei**—naked, poor, barefoot; Slov. *ogoličeni;* **prevezivana**—carried from place to place, transported; Slov. *prevažana;* OCS *vesti, vezo, prevesti;* Latv. *vezums*—a ride. There is an interesting inscription on a pitcher which ends with: **Iliriai la ziovaj**—long live Illyria; in modern Slov. *Živela Ilirija.* We will return to this inscription later.

Some readers may ask why the Veneti on the Adriatic and in the Alps did not inscribe the names of the deceased on their gravestones, whereas Yapods in Apulia engraved only names on some of theirs. In my opinion this is a result of the influence of Eastern culture, which led both the Etruscans and Yapods or Messapians in their ways of preserving the memory of their dead.

In his book *Die Sprache der Illyrier/* The Language of Illyrians 1977, Hans Krahe writes: "The inscription PID. II, 368 bis (Ruvo), is written in the Greek script, but in some mixed language. The only discernible word is **damatura** which is Messapo-Illyrian; everything else is uncertain because the inscription is written *in continuo.*" That may be so, but if we examine it from the standpoint of the Venetic, i.e., the Proto-Slavic language, then it is possible to recognize the words and understand them. As a result of detailed analysis, I have transcribed this inscription so that the reader may have a better look; it reads as follows:

SON RUKA, DAMATURA, TOU
E BUGEI MAKEI KONA LON
T OUNDE TA VA SUTE ATURENA

Slovene: Sin narical, Damatura, je tvoj,
in z božjo (po)močjo končal (upepelil) je truplo.
Potem je bilo tja v grob odpeljano.

English: Your son mourned, Damatura,
and with god's help finished (cremated) the body.
Which was thereafter taken to the grave.

A careful examination shows that each word and its meaning clearly fit the Venetic and Old Slavic language systems.

son—son; Slov. *sin;* OCS *synъ;* Lith. *sunus;* Sans. *sunu;* Ger. *Sohn.*
ruka—mourned, intoned a dirge; 3rd prs. sing. aorist of **rukat.* In westernmost

Slov. dialect *rkao* (Mikl.). Russ. dial. *urkli.* Venetic *urkli,* etc. The common root is *rek-* (Mikl.). Compare also Slov. *jelen ruka*—a buck calls. Slov. verb *naricati*—to intone a dirge.

Damatura—the name of a goddess.

tou—yours; Slov. *tvoj,* "derived from vowel change (ablaut) *tue" (Skok).

e—and; Slov. *in.*

bugei—with god's (help); Slov. *z božjo.* From **bog-ji,* before palatalization (see Venetic **bugenija**).

makei—with power, with help; Slov. *močjo, (po)močjo.* Lett. *makts*—power; Lith. *macis;* Russ. dial *magu, magti*—I can, can.

kona—he completed, he finished; Serbo-Cr. *dokonjati*—to execute, to do, *perficere.* Miklošič maintains that the Old Slavic root *ken-* becomes through vowel change *kon-.* Ukrainian *konati.* Compare Venetic **pri konioj**—at the end; Slov. *pri koncu.* Grammatically, **kona** is an aorist 3rd prs. sing.

lon—*viaticum,* travel provision for the deceased. See Irish *lon*—food, travel ration. *Lon* (with a short **o**) is a black bird which reminds us of death.

t(e)—and; Slov. *ter.* Slov. dial. eastern Styria, also *te.*

ounde—then; Serbo-Cr. *onda.* This **e** must have been pronounced very broadly, close to **a**.

ta—there; Slov. *tja*—an adverb of place.

va—into; Slov. *v.* Istria *va.* Russ. *vo.*

sutje—a grave; Slov. *suti* has the same root; it is a frequent word on the Etruscan gravestones.

aturena—taken away, carried away. Compare Slov. *torati*—Ger. *schwer tragen* (Plet.)—to carry a heavy load. In its form **aturena** is an adjective (from a participle). Serbo-Cr. *terati.* The word is widespread with diverse meanings in Slavic languages and the Venetic.

A helmet from the Basilicate in Lucania has a most interesting inscription. It has been reprinted by Krahe on p. 37, with a remark stating that its linguistic origin is controversial. It is in Greek script *in continuo.* If we begin to consider its Slavic elements we soon realize what it says, although the language is very ancient. It is a mixture of Old Slavic and Veneto-Slavic but already has some elements which can be defined as Slovene and Croatian.

In my transcription:

	VETE	**PISE**
Slov.	Veče	piše

411

	AGAN	**ASMETA**	**PONTI**	**NAS**
Slov.	ogenj	osvete	poti	nas

	S	**UPME**	**DI**	**KI**	**AIAO**	**VEARE**
Slov.	z	upi,	da se	kdor se je	vojeval	prebije

Translation: The assembly writes:
The fire of vengeance leads us
with hopes that he who fought frees himself.

vete read **vetje**—assembly, senate; OCS *vešte*—senatus, from *vê-tje* (Mikl.), *veštati* derives from it. Serbo-Cr. *većati*—deliberating in the assembly. Miklošič thinks this word is connected with *obetati*—to promise. The variations of this word are widely diffused in all Slavic languages. Ukrainian *viče*—gathering of people. Baltic Prussian *vaitat*—to speak. Serbo-Cr. *veće*—senate.

pise pronounced **piśe** or **piše**—he writes; Slov. *piše*. The word *pisati*—to write—is used in OCS. There are in OCS also other words without 3rd prs. sing. endings; for example, *povine, blĕdĕje, ubeži* etc. (see Leskin para. 87). In this particular case the word **pise** probably means it (assembly, gathering) sends a written message.

agan—fire; Slov. *ogenj.* Compare Venetic **ougon.**

asmeta—of vengeance; Slov. *osvete* (genitive sing.). The word is of the same origin as *osveta*—vengeance. Skok says that this word has almost completely replaced OCS *méstъ.* This assumption is confirmed by **asmeta,** a genitive sing.; its nominative must have been **asmet.**

ponti nas—lead us; Slov. *vodi nas, napoti nas,*póti nas* (Plet.). It seems that the inscription came into being before transition of *on* into *ǫ* (a nasal), provided, naturally, that the Messapic or Yapodic ever had it. OCS *pǫtь, razpǫtije.*

nas—us; Slov. *nas.* Compare Venetic, Etruscan examples.

s upme—with hopes; Slov. *z upi.* Compare the ending (instrumental) with *s potmi, z možmi* etc. Etymology of this word is uncertain. Slov. *upati, (ob)upovati*—to hope, to despair. Polabian *opam*—hope. The instrumental with preposition (s) is a relatively new phenomenon in certain Slavic languages. It seems that Yapodic already had it. Compare with Venetic.

di—that; Slov. *da,* dialect *de* and *d'.*

ki—who; Slov. *ki.*

ajao—he fought (in battle); Slov. *se vojeval.* Considering OCS *oiminъ, voinъ*—soldier—we may assume that the word is of onomatopoeic origin and is derived from the verb *ojiti*—to shout. Attacking soldiers shout. Compare with Venetic **oleal**—he shouted, and Slovene dial. *aliti*—drunken singing. Also compare the ending -**ao** to Serbo-Cr. participles ending with -**ao** and Slov. -**al** (pronounce au).

veare—he breaks through (to the victory, from the fight). This word is connected to OCS *oriti—evertere* Ger. *fallen machen*—to turn over, to destroy, to kill (Mikl.). Serbo-Cr. *oboriti.* I think we should consider prefix **vy** instead of **ob.** So we have **vyore** and when the **y** changed into **e** the result was **veare**—from, out of. In some Slavic languages *vy* (from) has been retained; e.g., Zilja Valley, Carinthia dialect. Slov. *v vigred*—into spring, literally "exit"; i.e., the time when everything is rising out of the earth. According to Skok it is related to the source producing the sound, and is of the same origin as Slov. *oriti se*—to resound.

Note: the Messapic did not have an **f;** hence, the Greek **f** was written as **v.**

I would like to alert the reader to the rhythm and harmony of the inscription; for this reason I present it here with appropriate accents:

Agán asméta pónti nas

s úpme di kǝ ajáo,

vearé...

This may well be a quote from a heroic or epic poem.

A pitcher from Manduria has a most instructive inscription. It is written in Etruscan script in the usual style without division into words (in continuo), and transcribed by Krahe p. 33, as follows:

asstazallies

ilirailaziovai

In my transcription and interpretation:

AS S TA ZALLES
Slov. Ko s to zaliješ

ILIRAI LA ZIOVAJ
Slov. Ilirijo tu zovi!

Translation: When this (drink) you pour
Call to Illyria! (Drink a toast to Illyria).

as—when; Czech *až* (Mikl.).

s—with; Slov. *s.*

ta—this; Slov. *to* (instr.), **s ta;** Slov. *s to* (vowel change)—with this.

zalles—you pour; Slov. *zaliješ*. The double **l** here probably means **lj.** OCS *lijati, lьjǫ*—to pour, I pour.

Ilirai—to Illyria; "Illyrios, forefather of the pre-Roman Illyrians, Illyricum..." (Skok). Final -ai is a diphthong which rhymes with **ziovaj.**

la—here; Slov. *tu, tule, le-tu.* See Venetic **less**—here. Slov. *les* is an abbreviation of *le sem*—this way, here.

ziovaj—call; Slov. *zovi, vzklikni.* Imperative 2nd prs. sing. OCS *zvati, zovo*—to call, I call. Slov. *zvati, zovem.* It seems that the Messapic form is iterative like the OCS *zivati. Zivaj,* Slov. *pozivaj* changed into **ziuvaj** and later into **ziovaj.** It is very interesting and instructive that this patriotic Yapodic verse to hon our Illyria was written in Slavic.

The inscription on the brass tablet from Ruvo belongs to those Messapic inscriptions written in Greek script (PID II, 350, Krahe, p. 35). In my interpretation and transcription it reads as follows:

> **ARTOS   ATOITOS**
> Artos   Atoitos

> **TAJ   DO   ITAJ   GUNAK**
> Slov. Ta(j), da,   ta je   junak,
> This one, yes he is a hero

> **HA   I   PEN   SKLEN**
> Slov. ki   tudi, ko   glava je   sekana
> who also as the head is being cut

> **DUGA   VE**
> Slov. dolg (svoj)   ve.
> knows his debt.

In a more readable language: This one is a hero,
He knows his debt (to his country),
Even as his head is being cut.

This translation can be substantiated by the assumption that we are not certain whether the Messapic fricative **j** (y) was written by the Greek letter gama. It

414

is also possible that both letters theta are actually delta. The inscription is probably not very well preserved, as various interpreters explain some words each in his own way. Some, for example, read **n** in **gunak** as **m,** and some read the last two words as **oupave** or **thugave.**

Artos Atoitos—a name and a surname.

taj—this one; Slov. *ta, taj.*

do—yes, that; Slov. *da.* The OCS conjunctive *da* was sometimes, by way of exception, written as *dó* (dó i ućenici tvoji vidętь děla tvoje).

itaj—this one; Slov. *taj, itaj.*

gunak read **junak** or **hunak**—a hero; OCS *junъ, junakъ.* Generally Slavic and Indo–European. Slov. *junak;* Lat. *iuventus;* Ger. *jung.*

ha—yes; Slov. *ka* in the meaning *da* as in eastern Styria, and in the Kajkavian dial. **h** is often interchangeable with **k** in Venetic.

i—also; Slov. *tudi, i.* OCS *i.*

pen sklen read **pen seklen**—beheaded. The Breton *penn* means head. Taking into account the similarity of Breton, Slovene and Venetic words, the latter being closely related to Yapodic, I allow myself to interpret **pen** as the Breton *penn.* This interpretation is also suggested by the next word.

s(e)klen—cut; Slov. *sekan.* The root *sek-* is generally Indo-European and features strongly in Slavic languages. **S(e)klen** is a passive past participle of

s(e)klet; Slov. *sekljati*—to cut into small pieces.

duga ve—knows his debt; Slov. *dolg (svoj) ve.* OCS *dlьgъ.* It seems that at the time when this inscription was made, the OCS *dlьgъ* had already changed into *dug* as in Etruscan and later in Serbo-Cr.

ve—knows; Slov. *ve,* 3rd prs. sing. of *vedeti*—to know, OCS *věděti* (Mikl. identifies the same root as in *videti*—to see). The word **ve** has the same meaning as in Slovene and Chakavian dialect.

We do not know where this inscription was originally located. Was it on the grave of someone who was beheaded and whose name was Artos Atoitos? Or perhaps a quotation from a poem or saying etched on a copper plate? Such plates engraved with sayings and verses were known and used among Etruscans.

On the altar in Valesio (Krahe, p. 33) there is an inscription in writing which is very similar to the Etruscan. Krahe said in 1955 that all endeavours to explain this inscription had failed.

I considered the writing very carefully, and offer it here in my transcription and translation:

HALOTI	**TA**	**OTORITA**
Slov. Golota	tvoja (naj bo)	skrita,

OL	**NE**	**IDI**	**VA**	**RIS**	**LA**	**OHO**
Slov. ali	ne	idi	v	ris	tu	okoli!

This is a warning to the believers: Your nakedness must be covered; else, do not enter the sacred circle surrounding the altar!

haloti—nakedness; Slov. *golota* pl. *golote.* Compare with OCS *golъ*—naked. A fricative **h** in place of **g,** same as in Slov. dialects; we also have the common vowel change from **o** to **a.**

ta—your; Slov. *tvoja.*

otorita—hidden; Slov. *skrita,* something that is inside. OCS *otrъnъ*—inside. Probably adj. of *otorit*, or an adverb like Slov. *notrika* (dialect from Goriška Brda).

ol—or; Slov. *ali.* In the 16th century it was written *oli.*

ne idi—do not go; Slov. *ne idi.* Same in Serbo-Cr. and OCS.

va—into; Slov. *v.*

ris—magic or sacred circle; Slov. *ris.* The sacred circle still surrounds the altars of today, though this pagan word is not used in the ritual language of Christianity.

la—here; compare Slov. *le sem, semle*—this way. *Le* was originally a locative adverb, same as Italian *la.*

oko—around; Slov. *okoli,* Serbo-Cr. *oko;* **la oko,** here around.

The following inscription is on six stones from the altar of Vieste near Monte Garganu (PID II, Krahe, p. 26). Examining it I recognized that there are not only words but also sintagmas. This we must not forget during the analysis of the text.

AGOL	**ZONVE**	**LDA**	**AJAJ**
Slov. Oholost	plevela	ljudi	(pre)vejaj!

DIVA	**DAMATRA**	**OPAKALE**
Slov. Čudežna	Damatira	ničvredne

DA	**NA**	**KLA**	**TORI**
Slov. da	na	tla	stare (potepta)!

DEIVA	**DAMATIRA**	**PREVEZIVENA**
Slov. Boginja	Damatira	prevažana

DIVA   DAMATIRA
Slov.   čudežna   Damatira

BLAŽIT   AGOLICEI
Slov.   blaži   ogoličene (gole in nage).

The meaning of this inscription is religious. First it asks of goddess Damatira to winnow out the chaff of pride from people, then to trample to the ground the wicked, and lastly, to soothe the fate of the poor, the naked.

agol—pride, arrogance; Slov. *oholost.* In the 18th century it was written *ohôl,* Ger. *die Hochmut* (Bezl.) meaning arrogance, pride. Vowel change from **o** to **a.** Messapic **g**—γ (h).

zonve—of the weeds; gen. sing. of **zonva.* In Slov. we have today *zona,* meaning dread, horror; Ger. *Der Schauder* (Plet.). In the 19th century *zona* also meant any weed seed and immature grain removed during winnowing (Mikl.) It seems that in Messapic the word had the suffix **va (zonva).**

lda—of people; Slov. *ljudi.* OCS *ljudъ;* Latin *populus* (Mikl.). Slov. *ljud, ljuda;* Ger. *das Volk.* Polabic *l'eedi, l'eude, l'eudai.* Latv. *l'iadi.* Old High German *liut.* In Messapic **lda** (gen.) the letter **u** was reduced as in Slov. *ldi,* or simply omitted in written form, following the Etruscan example.

ajaj—winnow; Slov. *vejaj, (raz)vejaj* (imperative). OCS *vějati;* Ger. *wehen.* Slov. *vejati*—winnowing (grain). Czech *vati* (from *vъjati*) is closest to the Mess. **ajaj** (imperative). Unless it is older than the Slavic form, this Messapic word developed from *vějati, vajati*—**ajat.**

diva—miraculous, holy; OCS *divo (diva)*—wonder, marvel, *divьnъ*—wonderful. Serbo-Cr. *diviti se*—to wonder—and the adjective *divan*—wonderful; Czech *divny.* Compare the Venetic **kal diva** (Ca 49).

Damatira—name of a goddess; in the original **Damatra,** vowel **i** was omitted.

opakale—miscreant, scoundrel; OCS *opako, opaky*—retrorsum, contrarium—backwards, opposite; Slov. *napak,* from *na opak,* upside down, contrary. Serbo-Cr. *opak*—turned the wrong way, Ger. *verkehrt, schlimm* (Mikl.). Slavic and Balto-Slavic. Messapic **opakale** is an adjective. (Comp. Czech forms).

da na—that onto; Slov. *da na.*

kla—ground; "OCS *tlo, tla*—pavimento. Slov. *tlo,* pl. *tla,* from this *kla...*" (Mikl.). It seems the Messapic (Venetic) **tla** changed into **kla.** Compare *tlačiti, klačiti*—to tread upon. This change from **t** to **k** is very common in Slovene dialects; it is an old phenomenon. Compare also Rumanian *klake, kalake,* which derives from Slavic *tlaka.*

417

tori—pound, crush; Slov. *stre, stare, tre.* Old Slavic **terti.* OCS *tьrǫ, trěti.* Vowel change e to o. Slov. *utor,* Russ. *tor,* Slov. *utrta pot*—a well trampled path; *zator, zatreti*—to trample under foot, to suppress. The word is very frequent in Venetic. Skok thinks *truplo, trup*—corpse—is of the same origin.

prevezivena—carried, transported; Slov. *prevažana.* OCS *vesti.* Slov. *vesti, prevesti.* Goddesses were—as nowadays—transported or carried in processions from place to place.

blažit in the inscription **blasit**—to soothe, to console; Slov. *tolaži, blaži* (3rd per. sing. pr.), *blažiti*—to soothe, to make happy (Plet.), Ger. *glücklich machen.* OCS *blažiti*—to bless (benedicere), *blagъ.* According to Miklošič's reconstruction of Old Slavic *bolgъ,* the metathesis took place by the time of this inscription. However, considering **molda** (*mlada*), found on a tombstone (Krahe, p. 24), I doubt this transposition. It is probable the two inscriptions belong to separate time periods.

agolicei read **agoličei**—naked, bare, poor; Slov. *gole, ogoličene, siromake.* OCS *golъ*—naked. Compare the endings in Slov. noun *ljubej,* pl. *ljubeji.* Compare also *ogoličiti, ogoliti*—to strip naked, to rob someone. Particularly interesting is *ogoluzniti* (Plet.).

A grave marker made of Leccian stone (PID 396, II, Krahe, p. 24) carries an inscription which contains at least three words recognizable at first sight as Slavic: **plastas**—you pay; OCS *plaštaš;* **molda**—young, Old Slavic *molda;* **bilia**—existence, life, OCS *bylije.* These three words suggest an interpretation of this short inscription on the basis of Slavic terminologies:

plastas
moldatthehiai
bilia ettheta
hipades Aprod(i)ta

In my transcription based on the interconnectedness of the above three words, the meaning is as follows:

     PLASTAS
Slov. plačaš

MOLDA	**T**	**THE**	**H**	**JAJ**
Slov. mlada	ti	tja	ki	greš

BILIA ET DETA
Slov. bivanje od deteta

HIPADES APROD(I)TA
Hipades Aprodita

English: You who are leaving
(to the other world)
You paid young (with your life)
for a child, Hipades Aprodita.

plastas pronounce **plaštaš**—you pay; Slov. *plačaš*. The Yapods, similar to the Etruscans and Veneti, did not distinguish between the consonants **s** and **š;** the Istrians do not even now make this distinction.
molda—young; Slov. *mlada.* Old Slavic *moldŭ* or *moldъ*—young. It seems that in Yapodic the change from **mold** to **mlad** had not as yet been accomplished.
t the h jaj—a sintagma, meaning: you who are to go there, that is, to the other world; Slov. *ti tja ki idi—ti, ki ti je iti tja.* Similar syntactical peculiarities are shown also in Slovene—use of imperative instead of 3rd per. singular. Regarding **h** it is probable that it was pronounced as **h** and as **k**—the two were similar.
jaj imperative of **jat**—to go; Slov. *iti.* Compare Baltic and Venetic. Slovene *jahaj*—ride, meaning "go". Lithuanian *jati*—to go.
bilia—existence, life; OCS *bylije.* Slov. *bivanje.* **Bilia** is probably plural.
et—from, of; Slov. *od.* OCS *otъ.* Slov. dial *ed,ǝt.*
deta—of the child or infant (gen.); Slov. *deteta.* OCS *děte;* derived from Indo-European *dhei*—to nurse. Slov. *dojiti.* The suffix -te had not yet existed at the time. Comp. Slov. *oko, očesa,* but Serbo-Cr. *oka.*
Hipades—surname
Aprodita—name. Greek Aphrodite.
There is another characteristic inscription (Krahe, p. 25) on a piece of Leccian stone—obviously a grave marker. This inscription is short but illustrates the language well.

In my interpretation:

ATHIDA
Odide

PLATOR
Plator

LAHON
Lahon

HA DIVE
k bogu

Translation: Plator Lahon has gone to god.

athida—has gone (3rd per. sing.) of *othidat. Slov. *odšel je*. Regarding **th**, it seems that Slavic **t** (otъ) which was pronounced close to **d** (od) was written with theta (th). The initial **a** is a result of vowel change.

Plator—a name.

Lahon—a surname.

ha—to; Slov. *k*. Eastern Styria and Kajkavian *ka*. The changeability of **k** and **h** is already familiar.

dive—to the god, deity; Slov. *divu*. The same word with the same meaning is frequently found in Venetic. The ending **e** is also found in Russian. **Dive** could—considering **diva Damatira**—be explained as a dative of *diva* (goddess). The word *div* is connected to OCS *divъ* and *divij*. Bulgarian *div*—wild. OCS *divъ* means miracle as well as wild. There is a connection to Lithuanian *dievas*—god, and Latin *deus*—god. Of the same opinion are Meiilet, Bernecker, Bezlaj and Vasmer.

420

PART THREE

Review and Commentary

Ivan Tomažič

Introduction

Important innovations always provoke not only approval but also disapproval and criticism. Our interpretation of early European history, the so-called **Venetic theory,** was received in the same way. There was enthusiastic acknowledgement, but there was also strong opposition. The main reason for the opposition and resistance is the fact that the Venetic theory exposes the falsehood created by official historians and linguists regarding the origin of European nations and languages and the arrival of Slavs in central Europe in the 6th century A.D.—and particularly the arrival of Slovenes in the Alps and the northern Adriatic area at that time. The Venetic theory is a guide to an entirely new understanding and a new vision of European prehistory and later socio-political developments in central Europe.

When I first presented these thoughts in the *Glas Korotana/* Voice of Korotan, Vienna 1982, I had no idea that from this modest beginning there would follow books in different languages dealing with the problem. I challenge intellectuals, particularly Slovene intellectuals, to recognize how little we know of our past, and how mistaken the official theories are. This challenge is open to all friends of history; let them spend some time examining these new findings.

Approval of the Venetic theory came from those intellectuals who were not bound by ideological or personal considerations. However, professional historians, particularly in Slovenia, responded largely with contempt considering us, the three new Venetologists, to be meddling amateurs. They were unable to admit that their views about the early history of central Europe were untrue and badly outdated; but at the same time they had no qualified counter arguments, and this irritated them. Their responses were a display of discomfort embellished by personal opinions and imagined connections between events which had nothing whatsoever in common. Thus began a long and heated controversy. It is not yet over.

In this part of the book I will be reviewing and repeating some details in hopes of elucidating at least part of the controversy and allowing the reader to consider the simple fact that the Venetic theory is based on evidence which cannot be manipulated or disregarded.

In reality, we are not presenting a new theory, but rather substantiating those historical and linguistic facts which have already been studied and reported by

422

Mt. Triglav, 2864m, in the Julian Alps is the highest mountain in Slovenia. Its massive form symbolizes the old Slovene god "Triglav", who was related to the Venetic Trumužijad (with its sanctuary in the Carnic Alps, Lagole di Calalzo).

other researchers. From among Slovene authors who contributed to this cause I would like to mention several, starting with the learned reformer Adam Bohorič who flourished in the 16th century; then, historian Martin Baucer and Janez V. Valvasor, who was a member of the British Royal Society; Dr. Janko Grampovčan, Davorin Žunkovič, Henrih Tuma, Davorin Trstenjak, Anton Berlot and Ivan Rebec. I also mention the Italian researcher Giuseppe Sergi from the turn of the century who, like the above authors, considered Slovenes to be indigenous inhabitants since prehistoric times and descendants of the Proto-Slavic Veneti. The principal aim of this book is to transmit these discoveries.

423

Veneti Through History
From Ancient Slavs to Veneti

The question of the pre-Indo-European language in central Europe has been largely neglected. I will introduce in a separate paper at the end of these chapters the thesis that Proto-Slavic was the original language of central Europe. But now I would like to consider whether the Venetic language can be considered the beginning of Slavic languages.

Some answers to this question will be found within the developments of the **Indo-European** process itself. Europe changed its image after the arrival of Indo-Europeans not only in its material culture, with the transition from Linear-pottery and Nordic cultures to Corded-pottery culture, but also in social conditions and language. Giacomo Devoto compares the origin of Indo-European languages with the development of Latin-based languages (*Origini indoeuropee,* p. 161) because of well-known internal and external conditions. In regard to the Indo-European process, we do not know the internal conditions; what is acknowledged is the strong influence of invaders from the Russian steppes and the Caucasus area. The presence of these newcomers with their Kurgan or Mound-grave burial was proven in Europe from the time of the appearance of Indo-Europeans. Their Battle-axe culture imposed itself on a variety of predominantly agricultural groups in central Europe. The languages of indigenous people and newcomers influenced each other, developing new expressions.

After these events (around 2000 B.C.) new languages began to evolve on the foundation of the indigenous Proto-Slavic language. Those which developed early contained more of the old, indigenous elements. The Venetic language, a blend of the old and new, could be considered the beginning of this process, and has therefore best preserved ancient Slavic elements in their original form.

During the developmental process, from the beginning of Indo-European presence to Lusatian culture, was formed the **first nation**, called by German researcher Erich Röth Proto-Illyrians (*Sind wir Germanen?/* Are we Germans? p. 266). Since then, science has established that there were no Illyrians in central Europe, and that Lusatian culture must be equated with Venetic culture (P. Bosch-Gimpera, J. Filip, *Enzyklopädisches Handbuch zur Ur- und Frühgeschichte Europas/* The Encyclopaedic Handbook of Prehistory and Early History of Europe, p. 688, Prague 1969). The first nation which formed in central Europe from

Archaeologist Marija Gimbutas regards the Urnfield culture as a central European culture. Its bearers were Veneti. They spread their culture during the Urnfield migration, and were thus the first known nation of central Europe.

merging of the indigenous and newcomer Indo-Europeans was the nation of Veneti.

Later offshoots of this process were the Illyrians, Thracians and Balts. The German language is, according to Röth (p. 264), two-thirds derived from the Venetic, which he calls Illyrian. Other original Indo-European languages developed under a variety of influences; they also received the stamp of the Venetic language, which was present even at the most remote Indo-European location— India. Etruscan and Celtic cannot be counted among the independent languages; they developed directly from Venetic.

The Veneti were the central factor in the formation of new Indo-European

425

languages. Their own language developed from ancient Slavic before the onset of Urnfield culture, and gradually progressed within Corded-pottery culture. This development continued in **Únětice** culture where Indo-European components dominated, including Kurgan or Mound-grave burial. There was a major change when Únětice culture changed into **Lusatian**, in which prevailed original pre-Indo-European elements, including language and agricultural lifestyle. Here, also, the dead were cremated, expressing a new vision of life and death (G. Devoto, p. 135). In Lusatian culture the new Slavic language, Venetic, reached its full development.

Cremation of the dead and burial of the ashes in urns marks the beginning of the famous **Urnfield culture**. The Veneti were its bearers, and they spread their religious message and language through much of Europe.

The Name Veneti

The original name of the Veneti is unknown to us; however, considering their descendants, we can safely say that the basis for the name was the ancient Slavic term *slovo*—word. From it developed the adjective Slovenet or Sloveneti (pl.) to designate people of the same word, people of the same language.

The bearers of Urnfield culture reached the Black Sea and Asia Minor. Homer (8th century B.C.) knew of them and immortalized them in his *Iliad* as **Eneton** (Enetoi). And why not Slovenetoi? Because the Greek neither had the consonant pair **sl** nor the letter **v.** Much later this abbreviated name became known among speakers of Latin, who did not have the **sl**, but had the **v**—thus the name **Veneti.** The Veneti probably called themselves Sloveneti or Sluveni as we have discovered on Etruscan and Venetic inscriptions. Pliny the Elder recorded the name **Solvense** (Slovence); he moved the letter **o** forward to conform to Latin pronunciation.

About one century before Christ, Latin became the language of the Veneti in Italy, and they themselves adopted the name; however, we know that earlier they used the name Slavon or Sloven, as shown by the wide distribution of the toponym "Sclavon". The letter **c** was inserted, as was done by the Byzantines, who used the term Sklabenoi (Lat. Sclavi) which later became synonymous with the word "slave".

With the expansion of the Roman Empire the name Veneti spread, especially towards the north. Among Germans they became known as Winedi or Wenden (Wends). In 615 A.D., the Slovenes in Carantania were known as Veneti (Vita S. Columbani), and in 623 and 631 A.D., they were named Winedi (Fredegarii Chronicon).

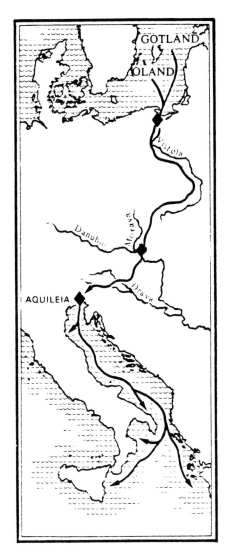

The Amber Road—the main Venetic artery between the Baltic and the Adriatic Seas. The other two important routes were the Danube, which connected central Europe with the Balkans and Asia Minor, where Veneti are reported by Herodotus and Homer (Paphlagonia), and the Atlantic coast where Veneti are historically proven (Brittany).

The Gothic historian Jordanes (551 B.C.) used the name Veneti as a general term for Slavic people. The Italian researcher Pittioni (Alteuropäische Sprache und Urgeschichte, p. 203) says: "The name Veneti belongs only to the bearers of the Urnfield culture." Also German linguists finally admitted the independent character of the Venetic language (H. Krahe). Until 1950 they considered the

427

Illyrians to be the pre-historic population of central Europe. Ptolemy (2nd century A.D.) was first to use the name Veneti as a general term for Slavs.

Although all Slavic languages derive from an original, common language, we cannot say that all Slavs descended from Veneti simply because they received the Venetic language from the bearers of Urnfield culture, which they variously incorporated and preserved through history. Referring to the *Manual de l'antiquité slave* (Niederle) and other sources, Devoto (p. 353) says: "The Slavic languages distanced themselves least from their common beginning." We could consider in the same spirit his ensuing words (p. 123): "The Venetic language is that remainder of the Indo-European community after the Greeks, the Hittites, the Iranians and the Indians developed their own national characteristics." This suggests that the Venetic language, based in ancient Slavic, was the principal element in linguistic development in Europe.

The name "Slovenes" in Venetic inscription. The Venetic inscription **Ca 62** is on the handle of a dipper at the sanctuary of Trumužijat in the hotsprings at Lagole di Calalzo in the Carnic Alps. Michel Lejeune and Aldo L. Prosdocimi read the inscription as names; they did this simply because they did not have the key to the interpretation of Venetic inscriptions. In their view, the inscription, when read from left to right, contains the following names:

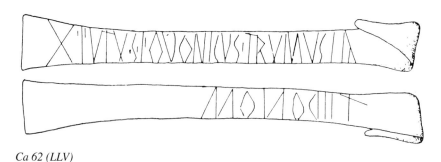

Ca 62 (LLV)

FUTUS. FOVONICUS. TRUMUSIA... DONOM

First of all, we must ask why they bypassed the first letter **X** (T)—at times also hard **H** or **K**—and why they read the second letter, the I with punctation lines as an F, although Veneti did not have the letter **F**.

ti or **ki**—you, who; Slov. *ti*; a personal pronoun; **ki**—who, which; Slov. *ki, kdor.*

It is found in several Venetic inscriptions.

utu—from; Slov. *od;* OCS *отъ.* In Slovene dialect from Rezija Valley *ut.*

slouonicu—Slovenes; in dialect Slovencu, correct form Slovencev—Slovenes. The second **o** has been retained in the name of the region of Slavonia, and in the Italian Schiavoni.

s—this; a demonstrative pronoun. Slov. *ta,* or verb (3rd per. sing.) *si*—are.

trumusia—Trumusiatei, name of the deity; the last three letters are not readable on the handle, but there is no doubt about them.

donom—with gift, with present; Slov. *z darom,* a similar Slovene word is *donos*— gain. The resemblance with Latin *donum* originates in Etruscan and hence in common Indo-European root.

jit—to go; Slov. *iti,* in dialect *it, jit.* The same word with the same meaning is also found in **Ca 31** and **Ca 67.**

TI	UTU	SLOUONICU	S	TRUMUSIATEI	DONOM	JIT
Ti (kdor)	od	Slovencev	si, k	Tromožju z	darom	iti (moraš)

English: You (whoever you are) of the Slovenes,
   go with a present to the Trumusiatei.

A special meaning of this inscription could be related to historical information that the Romans wanted to replace the Venetic deity with their god Apollo. The inscription is in harmony with the location and the time; it encourages the Slovenes (Veneti) not to forget their own god.

Veneti in the Este Culture

Were the Veneti and Slavs the same people? Are these two synonyms or two different concepts? We have to consider the term Veneti in two dimensions. First, we must regard the Veneti as that component of the ancient Slavs who within Corded-pottery, Únětice, and Lusatian cultures gradually adapted to the new European reality. The ancient Slavic language was enriched with new elements by the Veneti. This new language, which has survived with major or minor changes, they carried into various areas along with their Urnfield culture. In this sense we can consider Veneti as the beginning of Slavs, not genetically or ethnically, but linguistically.

The second dimension of the term Veneti is the formation of the Venetic family; i.e., those groups who felt most closely linked to the bearers of Urnfield culture, whether through regular contact (for example the Amber Road, or along the sea coast from the Baltic to Brittany) or because of the numerical strength of the bearers of this culture, who settled in particular locations such as the middle

Danubian area or Paphlagonia in Asia Minor. Some of these groups have been known as Veneti since Homer (9th century B.C.).

In the course of centuries, Urnfield culture transformed itself into new cultures which, to some degree, retained the old traditions. In central Europe Hallstatt and Etruscan cultures are the most important. But the most genuine heritage in Urnfield tradition is recognized in the **Este culture**—the present understanding of the term Veneti is associated with it. The Veneti followed the Amber Road towards the end of the 2nd millennium B.C. as far as the Adriatic Sea. In Slovene territory (Ruše near Maribor and the vicinity of Ljubljana) strong settlements of the bearers of Urnfield culture have been proven since 1200 B.C. The Amber Road from the Baltic through Poland, Bohemia, Austria and Slovenia to the Adriatic could be named the "Venetic road", and these nations as Veneti heirs.

From Slovenia the Veneti came without difficulty to the areas which are now part of Italy. The lands on both sides of the northern Adriatic became their new home. Two important Italian historians, Giuseppe Sergi and Giacomo Devoto, acknowledge that the Veneti came to Italy from the north, and the best and most natural passage for them was through Slovenia.

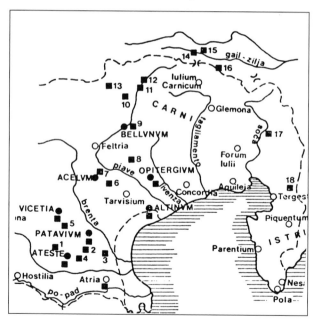

The most important archaeological sites of Este culture, which are also found throughout Slovenia as far as Negova near Maribor and farther north in the Slovene ethnic territory.

Situla from Novo mesto, Slovenia. The distribution of Este culture in Slovenia is well documented by inscriptions, situlas, and many other artifacts.

The Veneti became particularly well established in the area between the Po River and the Alps. Their largest centre was Ateste (now Este), a very well documented site with numerous finds. The most important finds are inscriptions on bronze or stone, suggesting a very high cultural standard, not only on the material level but also socially and spiritually. Above all, they disclose the ethnic origin of the people. Venetic script itself, brought to Italy by the Veneti, originated in Vinča culture. Few inscriptions were preserved—which is also true of Etruscan inscriptions. The oldest Venetic inscriptions known to date are from the 6th century B.C., indicating that they learned the script much earlier.

In Italy the Veneti expanded into various areas. Their earliest settlements are archaeologically confirmed in northern Italy around 1100 B.C. One hundred years later they expanded through Villanova culture as far as Tuscany. Villanova culture is named after a village near Bologna, and differed from the Urnfield only in the shape of some urns and the custom of burying urns in cemeteries rather than open fields.

Veneti and the Formation of Celts in the Hallstatt Culture

As with any other great culture, Venetic Urnfield culture in time evolved and branched out. Besides the Este, Hallstatt and Etruscan cultures developed between the 9th and 8th centuries B.C.

From the very beginning, central Europe was the stage for the creation and development of the Veneti. Hallstatt culture can be attributed only to them. It is noted for the presence of the Urnfields, and reached from Bavaria to Austria and Slovenia. One of the principal activities of this culture was salt extraction and its resulting trade.

A special feature of the Hallstatt is the appearance of the Celts and their La Tène culture. They were the most often-mentioned people of antiquity, although no one knows with any degree of certainty who they were. Historians usually place them among the first nations that developed from the Indo-European event, but this is a misconception. There were no Celts before the first millennium B.C.; they appeared around 600 B.C., and through La Tène culture, were known only since 500 B.C. They arrived mysteriously and in the same way disappeared in the first century B.C.—after they had ruled various lands of Europe. The Celts survived longest in France, but when they were finally conquered there in 58-52

Ceremonial wagon, 7th century B.C. (Hallstatt culture), from Strettweg near Judenburg, Austria. (Landesmuseum der Steiermark, Graz)

B.C. by Julius Caesar, they merged with the indigenous population. Also in the British Isles they were assimilated into the local population. Because they left no inscriptions, their language and ethnic affiliation are unknown.

In regard to ethnic origin and language of the Celts, we can extract some information from known events. First, they appeared in the western region of Hallstatt culture. Since their culture originates from the Venetic Urnfield, we can assume that their language was Venetic. The Celts were nowhere indigenous; that is, tied to the land as farmers. Among the rich displays of Celtic heritage there are no farm tools, which would indicate that they came out of a nation as a special class or group. Another noteworthy detail is that the Celts had good relations with the Veneti, whether it was in Italy, Austria or Slovenia. They also spared the Etruscans, which suggests kinship.

There is a guarded linguistic recognition of Celts only in a few toponyms but even this is uncertain; the toponyms in question are probably Venetic. The most often cited word of supposedly Celtic origin is **Alps**, but it could just as easily be Venetic and originate in the Old Slavic word *lob,* which means a steep hill. A group of hills or mountain peaks was called *alobje* or *albje* (albye); for those unfamiliar with the language, like the Romans who transmitted to us the name, Albye and Alpes not very different. There are other toponyms considered to be Celtic, which can be explained through Venetic association; those with the compound *-durum* we are told correspond to Irish *dor*—door—but it could just as easily derive from the Slovene word *duri*—door.

There are in the new-Celtic language some Venetic elements. I will cite only a few. The word **tolm** means deep water, pool, the same meaning as the word *tolmun* in the Slovene language. Celts had at least ten words for water. **Sora** and **dobra** are two new-Celtic words that mean water—in the Slovene setting both of these are river names—and **sava,** which means water current, is the name of another river in Slovenia. **Trent** is a stream or river that often floods; it corresponds well with the name of a valley in western Slovenia—Trenta—where floods are a common occurrence. Someone will say that Celts left these names in Slovenia—improbable. Their stay was far to short. Besides, the names of rivers in Slovenia are older then the Celts themselves; the meanings of these names are found in Sanskrit, suggesting that the Celtic language was Venetic or very similar. This is best clarified by yet another new-Celtic language, the Breton, which has so many Venetic/Slovene words as to present a difficulty—is it Celtic or Venetic? Julius Caesar considered Bretons to be Veneti. Detailed comparisons between Breton and Slovene languages are found in Part Two.

Veneti and Celts in Noricum

Just a passing note about a very unusual representation of history: I am refer-ring to the manner in which Austrian historians present the Celts, glorified and raised to a position which was never theirs. Many conventions and professional gatherings were dedicated to them, and many books written about them. They are treated as the first known nation who, with "Celtization", improved the na-tive population and became the founders or fathers of Austrian history—a view totally inconsistent with reality.

The Celts spread through a number of European countries with their La Tène culture during the 5th and 4th centuries B.C., but all we know about them is what can be gleaned from archaeological finds and a few scanty reports. They left no written records.

After much travel around Europe, the Celts finally came to Noricum in the 3rd century B.C. They never settled or ruled Noricum, and we cannot be certain about the archaeological finds; probably more than half of what is attributed to the Celts belongs to the Veneti. The Celts settled only along major roads, impor-tant commercial centres, and other strategic locations. There are virtually no traces of La Tène culture in the eastern Alps (see Part One, chapter Noricum). The continued survival of Venetic Hallstatt culture suggests a peaceful coexistence between the two groups.

That the Celts cannot be considered an indigenous people of central Europe is explained by the example of Bohemia. There the Celtic Boians took over the rule and named the land after themselves (Bojerheim, Boeheim) yet, when they were driven out by Germans at the beginning of the first century B.C., the Celtic king and his people required only a small territory between Bratislava and Hainburg, thus indicating that they were only a small group, an occupying force. The native Slavic population continued to flourish in Bohemia.

There are a number of inaccurate historical references about the Celts in Noricum. Several stories by Livy (d. 17 A.D.) have to be regarded with caution; they describe events that took place two hundred years previously when the Ro-mans had no idea who the "populi alpini" were, and could easily have mistaken them for the "Gauls". Only around 150 B.C. was the name "Taurisci norici" used in reference to "populi alpini" in order to differentiate from Taurisci in Slovenia, although both were of Venetic stock.

There are no historical records that can prove Celts were Noricum's popula-tion. The few Roman reports about Norici do not tell us much, as there was not a clear understanding with respect to the Alpine population; they did not distin-

Statuette from fired clay, called Goddess Mother (Stadtmuseum Wels, Austria). Although attributed to Celts, its style suggests Venetic origin.

guish between the Celts and the Veneti. First they used the general term "populi alpini", and then Taurisci and Gauls. Of some interest is their naming of southern Bavaria as Vindelicia and not Gallia, regardless of the fact that their Celtic La Tène culture completely displaced Venetic Hallstatt culture. Even in Great Britain, Celtic Wales was named Venedotia by the Romans. But the most striking example is Armorica, present-day Brittany. Julius Caesar called its inhabitants Veneti. If they were Celts as historians think, it is clear that for Romans there was not much difference between Celts and Veneti.

Livy mentions a king of "Gauls" called Cincibilius, but this Latinized name does not help us understand to whom it belongs. It is possible that, like other Celtic tribes the Celts in Noricum had a king, but we must not confuse him with the king of the "Taurisci norici" whose existence is known because of King Voccio, from 60 B.C. Who he was is explained by the name itself, VOKK, preserved unaltered on a Norican coin. It is a Venetic name still in use in the Slovene language as a surname, Vovk.

The Celts were mentioned one more time by Caesar in association with the siege of Noreia in 60 B.C. (not to be mistaken for the battle at Noreia in 113 B.C.); the attackers were Celtic Boians. After this event there was no more mention of Celts in Noricum.

The names of various peoples appearing on two dedication tablets found on Mt. Štalen (Magdalensberg), Carinthia—Norici, Ambidraves, Ambilici, etc.—do not represent Celtic tribes or independent nations. They were all Veneti listed according to their districts, Norici from Noreia, Ambidraves from Drava River region, Ambilici from Bela or Bila River region. Naming of people according to their districts is a common practice among Slovenes to this day: Carinthians, Carniolans, Styrians and so on.

As proof that Celts settled Noricum or that the Norici (Taurisci) were Celts, some place-names are cited; yet we do not even know what kind of language Celts spoke because there is no known document written in continental Celtic. Welsh, Irish and Scottish of the British Isles are probably Celticized languages of the original inhabitants, adopted by the Celts when they settled. The Celticists are of the opinion that the Island Celtic had a different course of development from that on the continent, and that it is impossible to reconstruct continental Celtic from the few surviving words. We could perhaps get some understanding of this problem through the Breton. In Brittany on the Atlantic coast there is historical proof of Veneti as they are described in some detail by Caesar. If they were one of the Celtic tribes, as many researchers think, then we have to say that continental Celtic was a Slavic language. Slavic elements in Breton are easily recognizable.

Not only in the Alps, but also in the fore-Alpine areas north and south, where Celts are historically proven through archaeological finds and written sources, there are virtually no Celtic place-names. Among often cited names is Bregenz in Bavaria on Lake Constance; but the word *bregec* is the diminutive of the Slovene word *breg*—shore or hillside. Similar names are found in Brittany and even more frequently in Slovenia. Another name cited is Hallstatt as well as Hall and Hallein, mentioned in relation to salt deposits. The word for salt in new Celtic is **hal, halann, haloin,** and in the continental Celtic it was **sal, salann, saloin**—as in modern European languages. This indicates that when the Celts arrived in the British Isles they adopted the language of the native population, and also the older word **hal.** In Venetic and continental Celtic languages, the change from *hal* to *sal* occurred before the Celtic conquering campaigns in the La Tène period;

Situla from Kuffarn, Austria, 4th century B.C., substantiating the presence of Venetic culture in Noricum during the La Tène period.

this change did not reach some peripheral areas like Greece and the British Isles. We must also remember that the word **hal** was considered by linguists not as Celtic but Illyrian—the earlier term for the Venetic language (e.g., E. Röth *Sind wir Germanen?/* Are we Germans? p. 135). This older form has been retained in the Vedic Sanskrit. The names Hallstatt, Halein, Hall are therefore of pre-Celtic origin.

Notwithstanding the apparent linguistic kinship between Celts and Veneti, we have to consider the Celts in central Europe as an independent nation. Their society was established mainly along military lines; besides soldiers it included craftsmen, miners and merchants, but no farmers.

What became of Celts in central Europe? In Italy they had a century of battles with Romans, and when they were finally defeated, they gradually disappeared from central Europe—mainly under German pressure. Any trace of them was gone from Noricum even before the arrival of the Romans in 15 B.C.; they either withdrew or merged with the local Venetic population. The name of a Celtic tribe, Volcae (according to Caesar), German Welschen, Slovene Vlahi, was used for Romanized Celts. It was later used for all Celts, and still later for Romans and Itals in general. Welsch Tyrol is the name for the Italian speaking South Tyrol. In Slovene vernacular, the term Vlahi or Lahi now means Italians.

If Noricum were Celticized as Austrian historians claim, then the principal language in Noricum would have been Celtic at the arrival of the Romans. That arrival was not hostile; the main concern of the Romans was to have free passage to the Danube. They had no particular interest in Latinizing the population. The acceptance of Roman military presence by the natives allowed continuation of social and cultural structures under the leadership of their own ruling class.

What do we find at the end of the Roman occupation? Was there widespread use of the Celtic language? No, there was not! There were no traces of it. On the contrary, as soon as Inner Noricum became independent after the departure of the last occupying force (the Byzantines), we find the Slovene (Venetic) language was the official and common language of the land. This linguistic development is a very strong argument that Noricum remained Venetic during the La Tène period, and as "Regnum Carantanorum", started its new history.

Until now, these discoveries were jeopardized by the official theory of the 6th century migration of Slovenes. But, since the continuity of the Veneti in the Slovene nation has been proven, the history of the Veneti can no longer be ignored. Austrian historians make every effort to present the Celts as the inhabitants of Noricum before the arrival of the Romans. They do this for one reason only: to avoid indisputable evidence that the Veneti were the indigenous inhabitants of Noricum, and that the Slovenes are their direct descendants.

Veneti and the Etruscan Culture

The Etruscans were till now a complete puzzle for historians and linguists alike, but the deciphering of the Etruscan language by Matej Bor has put an end to the mystery. We also have to credit Anton Berlot and Ivan Rebec for their contribution in the discovery of Slavic elements in Etruscan inscriptions, although their work lacks a professional study of individual words.

Since antiquity, a great deal has been written about the identity of Etruscans,

438

Etruscan woman on the lid of an urn, Perugia, 4th century B.C. (Hermitage, St. Petersburg)

without anyone being able to explain who they were. The well-known Etruscologist, Maximus Pallottino, came perhaps the closest when he stated that Etruscans were a nation made of a number of different ethnic groups, but the question who and from where these groups came remains unsolved. The most important clue for identification of the first of these groups is **Villanova culture**, a branch of Urnfield culture. The Villanovans were accomplished metalworkers and controlled the rich copper and iron mines of Tuscany. The native inhumation burial custom was gradually replaced by cremation, and by the 8th century B.C., the custom of cremation was the prevailing burial practice. At that time urns were no longer buried but were deposited in large underground tombs. This custom was retained even after several centuries when cremation ceased.

The bearers of Villanova culture were Veneti. Their merging with the indigenous population of Tuscany marks the beginning of Etruscan culture with the Venetic language predominating. Later, the Hittites from Asia Minor whose kingdom in Anatolia was destroyed around 1200 B.C., took advantage of this symbiotic relationship. They united with the existing population and contributed their oriental customs. Thus begun the Etruscan culture of the latter period. The languages amalgamated and Etruscan gradually lost its original Venetic character but the Venetic/Etruscan script survived unchanged.

The general view is that the Etruscans received their script from the Greeks, and later imparted it to the Veneti and Rhaetians. This is difficult to reconcile with a number of other events, particularly in regard to linear writing which, we are told, was invented by the Phoenicians around 1200 B.C. The Greeks received it from them in the 9th century B.C., and the Etruscans from the Greeks. However, Etruscan inscriptions are known from the 8th century B.C. when the Greeks began to settle in parts of southern Italy (*Universalgeschichte der Schrift*/Universal History of Writing, Campus Verlag 1990, p. 290). It is difficult to imagine that the script would have reached the Etruscans without a time lag. The identical form of Etruscan and Vinča scripts also indicates that Etruscan script is much older than what official linguists concede, and that it was probably brought to Italy by the Veneti.

Etruscan and Este cultures developed at approximately the same time. West of the Este culture were the Melaun and Golasecca cultures. The bearers of these were the Rhaetians, who had the same script as Veneti and the same or a similar language. All these nations, Veneti, early Etruscans and Rhaetians, are descendants of the same Venetic Urnfield culture, which included Switzerland and Bavaria. Throughout these areas there are many Venetic toponyms.

Veneti in the Roman Empire

The legend about Romulus and Remus tells us that Romulus established Rome in 753 B.C. But archaeological finds from 1977 show that the city of Ruma (Roma) existed a long time before that. Its original inhabitants were the Sabines, an Etruscan tribe; the name is probably a family name. The first rulers of Rome were Etruscan kings who advanced the city politically, economically and culturally. After the migration of many people from neighbouring Latium into Rome, the Etruscans promoted an agreement on joint rule. Henceforth, the rule alternated between the Etruscan and Latin kings. There were many confrontations between the two groups, until finally the Latins won. The decisive year was 509 B.C., marking the end of Etruscan influence in Rome. The patricians overthrew the monarchy and created the republic. The Roman senate at once established a strong army, thus laying the foundation for the Roman Empire, and the Romans implemented their powerful expansionist interests without delay. First, they overtook the small states of Latin population and then the Etruscan city states. In the course of several centuries with barbaric wars and mass murder campaigns, the Latins (Romans) destroyed the Etruscan nation—in gratitude for the culture and advancement bestowed by the Etruscans.

Latins learned from Etruscans not only building skills and good management of resources, but also literacy. The oldest, but unreadable Latin inscription is from the 5th century B.C., yet there is an older Roman stone with inscription (6th century B.C.) called "lapis niger"—black stone—found in 1899. Its language is archaic Latin, but the script is Etruscan. The Latin language is recognizable in inscriptions only after the 3rd century B.C. when the Latins formed from the Etruscan and Greek alphabets a simpler writing system. The Iguvine Tablets are from that period. They are read from right to left and half of them are written in Umbrian script (an offshoot of Etruscan). At that time the Romans began to systematically destroy all remains of Etruscan culture and literacy, as reported by Livy in his description of events in Rome at the end of the 3rd century B.C. (T. Livius XXV, 1, 12).

The invasion of Celts into Italy opened a new historical chapter for Venetic lands. The Celts first settled in the Po River plain around 400 B.C. From there they continued their campaigns, reaching Rome in 387. After many wars, the Romans finally defeated them in northern Italy in 175 B.C. and ruled in Venetic lands. The Veneti did not meet the powerful Romans with armed resistance.

Lapis niger (black stone) with the oldest Latin inscription. The letters are Etruscan.

It is of some interest to us that the Celts did not first occupy Noricum which was nearest to them; instead they forayed along the Danube to the north and to the south. Another group moved into France, and from there to Italy and Spain. Only in the 3rd century B.C. did they arrive from Greece over the Balkans to present-day Slovenia and into Noricum, where they disappeared in the 1st century B.C.

When Romans fought Celts in central and northern Italy, they also intruded upon and colonized the Venetic lands. One of the most important Roman colonies, established in 181 B.C., was Aquileia (Slov. Oglej). Because the Veneti were thus effectively prevented from initiating armed resistance, the transition to Roman rule was peaceful in Venetic lands south of the Alps. The Romans were extending their control methodically. In the major Venetic religious centre at Lagole di Calalzo they replaced the Venetic god Trumužijat with Apollo. In the cities Latin gradually prevailed, but in the countryside the Venetic language survived—in some areas till the Middle Ages. As we are told by several historians, the Slovene language was still in use in Friuli during the Aquilean Patriarchate, which explains why there are so many Slovene words in present-day Friulian. The city of Aquileia was destroyed by Huns in 452. After that the patriarch moved to the town of Grado/Gradež.

Much harsher treatment was received by the neighbouring Venetic lands of Istria, Yapodia, Pannonia and Dalmatia; Rhaetia and Vindelicia must be included —although independent, they too had a Venetic population. The Greek geographer Strabo (born in 63 B.C.) considered Venetia, Istria, southern Pannonia, Noricum and Dalmatia as part of northern Illyria (De Geographia VII, 5); this means he saw a unity, which could have existed only in regard to language and ethnicity. In reference to Venetia he is more exact, stating that in the west it bordered on Rhaetia, and in the east on Pannonia and Dalmatia, meaning that entire present-day Slovenia was included. Archaeological finds in Istrian fortifications (castellieri) are related to Venetic culture as is evident at the archaeological site at Most na Soči, Slovenia.

The Romans met fierce resistance in Istria. In the first war against that land in 178 B.C., they assembled an enormous force. Romans put into battle four legions with approximately 37,000 men, 1800 cavalry, and 30 warships. We can imagine the brutality of the attack and the desperation of the defenders. The Romans next undertook a campaign against the Yapods (from southern Slovenia to Dalmatia), and against the Carns in 171 B.C., against Pannonia in 156 B.C., followed by another attack on the Carns, Taurisci and Liburnians in 129 B.C., and against Dalmatia in 119 B.C.

In 89 B.C. the Romans extended their legal system to the lands between the

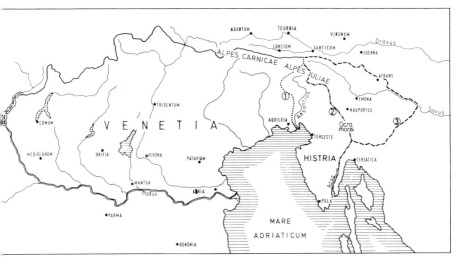

The tenth Roman province "Venetia et Histria" until the downfall of the empire.

Po River and the Alps, whereby Venetia was incorporated into the Roman state. With the new division of Italy into regions, Venetia and Istria became the tenth region in 27 B.C. At that time (58–52 B.C.), Julius Caesar victoriously completed his campaign in Gaul. In Brittany, he also conquered the Veneti whose bravery he admired.

In 25–13 B.C. the Romans initiated war against Alpine nations known under their common name, Rhaeti. A strong opposition was organized, but after much bloodshed the Romans were in full control. The land of Rhaetians reached as far as Lago Maggiore and Piave River to Lake Constance/ Bodensee —Lacus Venetus. It was divided into small autonomous states, whose names were inscribed on the "Tropaeum Alpium" mentioned by Ptolemy. The monument displayed the names of all conquered Alpine nations, among them also an indubitably Slovene name—**Isarci.**

After Rhaetia, the Romans attacked Vindelicia. They now had a clear passage from Italy over the Alps to the Rhine Valley. We can imagine the barbarity of these wars from the words of the Roman historian Cornelius Tacitus (Annales II, 18) when he writes: "Although this victory was very important to us, it was ghastly. From the fifth hour in the morning till night, bodies of the enemy and weapons covered a distance of ten thousand paces." (Approximately eight kilometres.)

Let us now turn to Noricum, the only independent Venetic land bordering on the Empire. Its rulers recognized that a war with the Romans would destroy their land; to prevent this they came to an agreement with the intruder. The Romans wanted a free passage to the Danube, where they intended to build the famous *limes*—the defence line against possible attacks from the north. They were also interested in the high quality Norican steel, which they could not produce themselves. This may have been the reason for sparing the Norici.

Noricum signed a treaty with Rome, which allowed Roman military presence, but retained an independent internal administration. However, in 45 A.D. the Romans proclaimed Noricum to be a Roman province and established their own capital—Virunum. The indigenous population continued to use its own language and customs. In the southern part of the Alps a neo-Latin language, Ladin or Rhaeto-Romance, developed at that time. Its territory stretched from Friuli to Switzerland and beyond, forming a language boundary between Latin south of the Alps, and remnants of the indigenous language from Vindelicia and Rhaetia through Noricum and Pannonia to Istria and Dalmatia.

Veneti after the Fall of the Roman Empire

In 476 King Odoacer of the Heruli invaded Italy and gave the final push to the Western Roman Empire by deposing its last Emperor, Romulus Augustulus. Outer Noricum (Noricum ripense) north of the approximate Salzburg-Vienna line was by then already in the hands of Germanic conquerors, to whom Odoacer finally relinquished it in 488. But Inner Noricum (Noricum mediterraneum) south of this line, including part of Slovenia, remained connected to Italy for almost another century. When Odoacer was in power in Italy, Inner Noricum was part of his kingdom. However, in 493, Ostrogoths under the leadership of Theodorik defeated Odoacer and ruled Italy and Inner Noricum. The Byzantine emperor decided to again unite the eastern and western parts of the Empire, and in 535 his army attacked the Ostrogoths in Italy. For greater defence efficiency, the Ostrogoths transferred Inner Noricum to Frankish rule. Finally, after a long war, the Byzantines defeated the Ostrogoths in 555. They also forced Franks out of Inner Noricum and established their own rule. In 568 the Langobards occupied Italy and the Byzantines left Inner Noricum.

In the second half of the 5th century, when the Empire was already disintegrating, the Rhaetians became independent; but in 493 they were attacked and conquered by Ostrogoths. This was the second time the Rhaetians suffered major destruction in their push for independence. Rhaetia, which had earlier many Roman colonies, was now occupied by Germanic people; but the Rhaetians did not die out completely. As late as the 8th century, historian Paulus Diaconus (II, 15) used with emphasis the expression "true Rhaetians" which means there were still some natives who used their own language.

Other Venetic lands, particularly present-day Slovenia and Istria, were a thoroughfare for a variety of military movements, but they were mostly under Byzantine rule, and in matters of religion were subject to the Aquilean Patriarchate.

The fate of Inner Noricum is of special interest to us, because events at this time show clearly that Slovenes were the indigenous people and an uninterrupted continuation of the Veneti. Of great importance now are two questions: who governed Inner Noricum after the departure of the Byzantines in 568, and who were the people who lived there at that time?

Let us review the most important dates and events:

—476 Odoacer took control in Italy and Inner Noricum.

—493 The Ostrogoths defeated Odoacer and ruled in Inner Noricum.

—535 The Ostrogoths transferred Inner Noricum to the Franks.

—555 The Byzantines defeated the Ostrogoths and forced the Franks from Inner Noricum.

—568 The Byzantines left Inner Noricum because of the Langobard invasion of Italy.

Roman ruins in Celje, Slovenia.

There is no historical report about an invasion of Inner Noricum after the departure of the Byzantines but it is certain the land was not without government. We can infer that it was the indigenous population which assumed control and established its independence. This will be easy to understand if we remember that the Romans never dealt forcefully with Noricum; they left internal rule to the natives. The civil administration could change into a political or military force under the right conditions. The events in Rhaetia show a desire for independence, but the Rhaetians were overtaken in war with the Ostrogoths. The Norici waited for more favourable conditions to put their ambition for independence into action, and were only thus more successful.

Two attacks by Bavarians after the departure of the Byzantines show that Inner Noricum was not without rule or defence. The first Bavarian attack (with intention to plunder) was in 595 and they carried away much loot. Encouraged by their success they undertook a second attack the following year (596) but this attempt was foiled and they were soundly defeated. The report of Paulus Diaconus about these events is most revealing. He writes that the attacks were on "sclaborum provincia"—Slavic state. This means the attacks were not against a transient or newly-arrived people but on a state, called by him "provincia", the same term used by the Langobards themselves to describe their own kingdom in Italy (see Enciclopedia Universale, XII, Milano 1970, p. 304).

Diaconus mentions the people of this state by their name; that is, the name most commonly used at that time in Latin, *Sclavi*—Slavs. The name was used in the Middle Ages for Veneti (Slovenes) in Friuli. An important document from 615, *Vita S. Columbani,* mentions Slavs, meaning Slovenes, besides their regular name Veneti.

Thus, in the year 595, Inner Noricum was an independent state; the principal name of its inhabitants was Veneti and their secondary name was Slavs (Sclavi). Diaconus was, as a Langobard born in Friuli, accustomed to using the name Sclavi, but there is no doubt these inhabitants were Slovenes, who established an independent state after the departure of the Byzantines. There is no historical source that can tell us anything different. There is no historical documentation or proof of an arrival of Slovenes in Noricum and the Adriatic area. All opposing claims by official historians are falsifications of historical reality. To those who have any doubt or objection, I will give further explanations and evidence in the following chapters.

Noricum at the end of the Roman Empire. Noricum ripense (Outer Noricum) was occupied by Germanic tribes, and Noricum mediterraneum (Inner Noricum) remained connected to Italy until 568; thereafter it became an independent state—Carantania.

Designations of Toponymy
Ancient Slovene Place-names

In the second part of this book, Bor dealt with the name **Tergeste** and its derivatives, and there are many other names from Roman or pre-Roman times which demonstrate that the Venetic language was related to Slovene, and that the Veneti were the predecessors of Slovenes.

Postojna is the name of the Slovene town famous for its caverns. The town lies adjacent to difficult mountainous terrain to the north which eventually leads to the Ljubljana basin, making this a natural resting place. In the distant past the name meant a roadside resting station, a post, on the road from Aquileia (Oglej) to Pannonia, but this was gradually forgotten. When German occupation forces wanted a German name for the town, they discovered that the same word (postojna) also means kestrel, a small European falcon which can hover in the air against the wind—windhover. Thus the place was named Adelsberg.

Postojna is not mentioned in Roman sources, but we can assume that it developed gradually around the roadside station. The road linking Venetic towns from Verona to Aquileia had a similar name; historians claim it was named after its Roman builder, Consul Spirius Postumius Albinus, who lived in the second half of the 2nd century B.C. The Veneti must have had a good road connecting their most important towns. Spirius Postumius probably only adapted the old Venetic road for Roman military needs after they had taken over Venetic lands. It is possible that he adopted his second name from the name of the road (he considered it his lifetime project), although the name of the town Postojna in Slovenia and other place-names with the same meaning are certainly independent of the *"Via Postumia"* of the Roman consul. This is demonstrated by two other places of the same name. One is **Postojoma** near Treviso, the name being pre-Roman, Venetic; according to Venetologists the original name was **Postoima** (Di Plinio Fraccaro, *Beiträge zur älteren Europäischen Kulturgeschichte,* 1952), which is almost the same as present-day Slovene pronunciation. Farther along on the same road is the second Postoima, giving a strong indication that these were indeed roadside stops.

Pola is a well-known Roman town in Istria with a pre-Roman name which in Slovene very appropriately means fields; the town is still surrounded by large fields. Romans renamed the town Pietas Julia, probably on the basis of the first

Trst/Trieste, a pre-Roman trading centre of Venetic (Slovene) origin.

letter of the old name. Nonetheless, the name never took hold; for the people the fields remained Pola. There is a town with a similar name in Friuli, **Redipulia,** called Rodopuglum in a 14th century document, the name being a Latinized form of Rodno polje—native field. Similar place names are all over former Venetic, now Italian territory. From the Slovene word *poljana*—a relatively level, visually pleasing field f.—we have **Poiana** near Vicenza, **Poiana** near the town of Este, the former Venetic centre, and **Poiano** near Verona. There are other similar names. From the Slovene (Venetic) word *raven, ravna*—even, flat, level—are names such as **Ravenna,** formerly Ravna (see Historical Atlas, National Geographic 1987). Similar names of the same origin are also found in German speaking areas: **Raven, Ravensburg, Ravenstein,** etc.

Gurina is another name from ancient times. It belongs to a place in Carinthia, where during excavations they found a Venetic inscription. Gorina or Gurina means elevated, high—it is a very suitable name for this settlement. There is also in Slovenia a village called Guranja vas close to a hill called Gura (gora—mountain) near Sežana, north of Trst/Trieste.

Soča River (Ital. Isonzo) was called Aesontius by Romans (it has no meaning in Latin) and in old records Sontium, very close to Slovene Soča, which again is very close to Sanskrit *socati*—to shine, to sparkle—and *suca* clean (Sanskrit **c** is pronounced as Slovene **č**). Soča is in fact a clean and sparkling river.

Timavus (earlier Temavus), Slovene Timava, has been a well-known river since antiquity. Most of it flows through limestone caverns, including the world famous Škocjanske caverns, where it appears very briefly in a deep chasm. When

449

it flows above ground and through the caverns, it is simply called Reka—River. But when it comes into daylight near Trst it is Timava. Why? Venetologists Prosdocimi and Pellegrini (La lingua venetica, p. 581) say that the meaning of the name is unknown. Of course it is unknown—for those unfamiliar with the Slovene language. Actually, in Slovene Timava means it flows from darkness, *tema*—darkness. This interpretation needs no support, but there is another river in Slovenia, which also flows from an underground cavern; its name is Temenica.

Isarcus is the Latin name of a river west of the Dolomites. The name originates in Slovene *izaro, izarci*—lake, small lakes. A similar name is **Isar,** a tributary of the Danube in Bavaria. There is also **Isarci,** from the Tropaeum Alpium—name of the inhabitants of the Isarcus River Valley.

Livenza is the name of a river in Friuli, as in Slovene *livnica,* vocative of the verb *liti, razliti*—to pour, to spill. The Romans renamed it Liquentia, which is an exact translation of the Venetic (Slovene) name. Since Livenza is pre-Roman, acknowledged even by Prosdocimi and Fogolari in *I Veneti antichi,* p. 393, it could not have originated in the Latin. The people preserved not the Latin but the older Venetic form of the name and adapted it to Italian pronunciation.

Saloca is on a Roman map (Tabula Peutingeriana) a place-name on the road north of the Karavanke range towards Virunum. This Slovene name demonstrates that the population of this area was Slovene during Roman times. Zaloka, (Latin Saloca) or simply Loka is also now a frequent place-name, a compound of *za*—beyond, and *loka*—wet, swampy meadow. The village of Zaloka in Carinthia is still there, and is equated with the ancient Saloca by Slovene historian Linhart.

Bodensee (Lake Constance) is the name of the lake on the border of Austria, Germany, and Switzerland in former Vindelicia. The name originates in the Slovene word *voda*—water. As in many other words, betatism changed the letter **v** into **b.** The Roman name for this lake was **Lacus Venetus,** indicating that the indigenous population of that area was Venetic, and for this reason the old Venetic name was preserved. Since Germans no longer understood the word, they thought the lake received its name from a village named Bodman. It is more probable that the village was named after the lake. There is also in Austria a small lake called Bodensee. German researcher Hans Bahlow enumerates many streams with the name **Bodenbach**. Many similar names substantiate our view that the name evolved from the Slovene word *voda*—water—in pre-Roman times. There are many names in Slovenia deriving from *voda, boda*: Vode, Vodice, Budine, Bodenci.

Windischgarsten is a well-known resort in the centre of Austria; the "Windisch" in its name reminds us of Slovenes. Romans called this small town **Gabromagus,** a compound of Gabro and *magus* which suggests that the pre-

The world-famous caverns at Postojna.

Roman name was Gabrov or Gabrovo, which is a distinctly Slovene or Venetic name. The Slovene word *gaber* means elm, a common tree in the area. There are many place-names in Slovenia derived from this word: Gaber, Gaberje, Gabrovo, to name a few.

Grado was an important city in Church history as early as the 6th century A.D. Located on an island of the same name near Trieste, its Slovene name means a fortress, a fortified place. Similar names are scattered here and there in the once-Venetic areas of Italy. For example, **Grado** on the Tagliamento River, **Gradisca** (Slov. Gradišče) near Lago di Garda. Even more of them are in Slovenia: Grad, Gradec, Gradež, Gradišče, Podgrad, and so on.

Patavium is Latin for **Padova** (renamed Padua), one of the most important Venetic cities. The name comes from Slovene *potovje*—junction of roads. Padova was an important junction in antiquity, and was probably then called Patavia or Potovje. The same could be said of the Latin name **Poetovio** for the Slovene city of **Ptuj,** also a major road junction in antiquity and now. Its name Potovje during Venetic times is almost identical with the Latin Po(e)tovio.

Longaticum is the Roman name for the Slovene city of Logatec. The name originates in the Slovene word *log* or arch. *long*—meadow by a body of water.

The Romans as usual adapted the Slovene name to their usage; yet, historians tell us there were no Slovene people in this area during the Roman period.

Ad Pirum in the mountains of **Montes Venetici** is the Roman name for the Slovene town Hrušica, at one time on the major route to Emona/Ljubljana. The original name was Krušica—a mountain of crumbling rock, shell. The name was too difficult for Romans to transform; instead they translated it using the colloquial Hrušica—small pear (Ad Pirum). Later, when the mistake was discovered, the correct name for the crumbling geological formation was established—**Ocra mons.** Thus, the place is historically recorded with two names.

Adria is a town on the Adriatic coast near the mouth of the Po River; it has been known since antiquity, and gave the name to the Adriatic Sea. The Old Slavic word *adro* means bay. Adria was on a bay two thousand years ago, but silt deposits gradually accumulated and now the town is a distance from the sea. The name has no connection to Latin which uses *sinus* for bay. From the Slavic (Venetic) word *adro* developed the place-names Adro near Brescia and Adrano near Bergamo.

Padus is the Roman name for the Venetic **Paduša** or **Po** River. In modern Slovene we would say Padana, a river on the plain into which flow (fall) tributaries, Slov. *padati*—to fall. The Venetic name Paduža is mentioned by Polibius who said: "Padus a fontibus uno continuoque fluit alveo: ubi vero ad Trigabulos, quos vocant, pervenit in dua scinditur partes, quorum alterius ostium Padusa, alterius Olana vocatur." Both names are feminine as is customary in the Venetic and Slovene naming of rivers, while Latin river names are masculine. The name Padus is an adaptation to Latin form. The word *Trigabulos* is related to the archaic Slovene verb *gabati*—to ford.

In his book *Komu nismo tujci* published in 1995, Leopold Verbovšek presented many Slovene names. They are known from antiquity not only in Slovenia but also in northern Italy, Switzerland and Bavaria, speaking of the great age of the Slovene language.

There are many toponyms in Switzerland which originate in the Venetic language. Someone may ask, how is that possible? Rhaetians lived in that country. That is true, but who were the Rhaetians and what language did they speak? We get a clear answer from their inscriptions which can be translated with the help of the Slovene language, as revealed in the second part of this book. The same is true of toponyms; they too substantiate our view that the Rhaetians spoke a Venetic language. Although our view has been well documented in earlier chapters, I will add a few toponyms which have not been discussed.

Sihltal Valley is west of Zürich with a river named Sihl, the same name as that of the Slovene **Zila** River in Carinthia. The name originates in the pre-Indo-

European (i.e., ancient Slavic) root *sil* meaning "water flows" and is also reflected in Sanskrit *Sila* with a similar meaning.

La Derotchia is a river in canton Valais. The name is an adaptation of a very common Slovene expression *deroča*—fast flowing; the root is *der-,* the verb *dreti* or *derti*—to rush, to flow fast. The name Drava, a fast flowing river in Austria and Slovenia, has the same root meaning. That is why Piccolomini, later Pope Pius II, wrote about it as "praecipuus Dravus". Drava is an archaic word, but *deroča* is still used in the Slovene language. In the area of the Venetic Slovincians (Kashubians) in Poland there is the **Drawo** River.

There are in Switzerland also many names compounded from the Slovene word *gor, gornje*—upper; for example, **Gornergletscher, Gornergrat, Gorneren**. The name **Gurin** in canton Ticino also belongs to this category; it is the same name as Gurina in Carinthia, known since pre-Roman times. In Ticino the name is now **Bosco-Gurin;** i.e., an old name to which a new one was added.

A number of Slovene names are found in Liechtenstein on the Swiss border. The mountain above the city of Vaduz is called **Gora,** a common Slovene name meaning mountain. There are other distinctly Slovene names in Liechtenstein: **Gritsch,** an Alpine meadow area; **Samina** a valley; **Göra** and **Obergöra** are two plateaus.

The name for people living in Wengen, Switzerland, is **Gertsch,** interesting because in Slovene *grča* means knot, gnarl. Around Bern they still have a saying in regard to Gertsch people from Wengen: "Das isch öppis für Gertschen," meaning, "This kind of heavy work is for sturdy, strong people." In Slovene folk idiom *grča* means strength, endurance.

Another old name which tells us of the presence of the Venetic language in the distant past is **Stein am Rhein,** the village where the Rhine River flows from the Bodensee. The Latin name was **Stenium ad Rhenum.** If this name had come from the German word *Stein*—stone—it would have been transcribed into Latin as "Steinum". However, Stenium is from Slovene *stena*—wall, cliff. The high, precipitous cliff at this location is topped by **Hohenklingen** castle. This name also comes from Slovene; *klin* is a wedge, a sloping, angular mountain crest. Many names in the Alps derive from *klin*.

All these ancient names, unquestionably connected to the Slovene language, reveal that in the past there lived in these areas a nation of the same language group, and this could only have been the Veneti. Their ancient language has been preserved in its modern form by the Slovenes, while in Switzerland, Bavaria and Austria it was replaced by German and in Italy by Latin and later Italian and the Friulian languages.

As an additional point of interest, I draw the reader's attention to the many compound names with the term **Windisch-** not only in Austria, but also in Switzerland and Bavaria, in spite of the fact that modern Slovenes never occupied these areas. The majority of these names were formerly in Austria, but only a few remain. Windisch means Slovene (see Duden's German dictionary) and is directly related to the adjective "Venetic". In Italy and especially in Friuli placenames such as Sclavons, Sclavani, Scavi have the same meaning, and have been preserved since the early Middle Ages when this name came into general use.

Windischbergerdorf near Cham, Bavaria
Windischbuch near Mergentheim, Württemberg
Windischbuchen near Miltenberg, Bavaria
Windischbach near Ohringen, Württemberg
Windischenhaig near Kulmbach, Bavaria
Windischenlaibach near Bayreuth, Bavaria
Windischenbach near Bayreuth, Bavaria
Windischgrün near Hof, Bavaria
Windischhausen near Weissenburg, Bavaria
Windischletten near Bamberg, Bavaria
Windisch near Baden, Switzerland

In addition, there are in these regions many names with **Wend-, Wenden-,** and **Wendisch-,** which refer to the ancient Venetic inhabitants and their descendants, the Slovenes.

The Message of Toponyms

Toponyms tell a story about ancient peoples, their customs, language and origin. The naming of a mountain, a hill or a place was of much greater importance for the ancients than it is today. Their naming was a description, a road mark, a warning, a remembrance. The French Historian Gallois said long ago (1903) at a congress in Rome: "Let us for a moment put all our books aside and turn to the message that can be drawn from the land itself." This suggests that we can get a clearer image of a nation through toponyms—if we know how to read them—than from archaeological remains.

If we examine a place-name in this light, we can gain not only the message from the name itself and its location, but also a much wider network of information. The geographic and ethnographic messages contained in a particular name have implications that go far beyond linguistic values. Let us look at the name

Ljubljana, capital of Slovenia (Ital. Lubiana, Ger. Laibach). There is also Lubiana near Verona, Italy, and Windischenlaibach in Bavaria. We know that the name originates in the Old Slavic word **lob** or **lub** with the same meaning as in Russian, *lobъ*—forehead, steep hill. Since antiquity there has been a settlement under the steep hill that is now occupied by a large castle. In the Slovene language the word *lob* is preserved in *lobanja*—skull—from which derive place-names such as Lobnik, Lubel (Ljubelj), Leoben in Austria. There are in the mountain chain Adamello two peaks, Lobia Alta and Lobia Bassa. The name Ljubljana is clearly of Slavic origin, but during Roman times it was better known as **Emona,** although this Roman town was a short distance south and on the opposite bank of the river on the site of an ancient fortification, or stronghold. The Latin verb "emunio" means to build.

Another name that has challenged linguists is that of the present-day town of Vrhnika on the road between Postojna and Ljubljana. The Romans called it **Nauportum.** The name has no meaning in Latin aside from the suffix -um. However, the mystery vanishes at once when we examine it from the standpoint of the language that has long been used in the area. In Slovene it means **Na odprto**—into the open. At that locale the traveller leaves the mountains and forests behind and emerges onto the open, moorish plain that stretches as far as Ljubljana.

When the name **Apennines** is closely examined, we discover that it has no meaning in Latin or Italian, while in Slovene the meaning is clear. It tells us about the type of rock this mountain range is formed from; namely, limestone. Slovene word *apno*—lime, *apneni, ap(e)nini hribi*—limestone mountains; Latin *calx*. It tells us also of the first Indo-European settlers on the peninsula, the Venetic Urnfield people.

There are many names in northern Italy and Slovenia which originate from the Slovene words *graditi* and *gradišče,* the first meaning to build, and the second a structure, a stronghold—**Gradisca, Gradišče, Grado.** Regardless of the present border these names send a message that is still clearly understood in modern Slovene, indicating that the first proven language of northern Italy, Venetic, has survived in the Slovene language. The place-name **Belgrado** in Friuli has the same meaning, made up of two words *vel* (betatism) *bel*—large, and *grado*—stronghold. Inasmuch as the city of Grado was established in the middle of the 5th century A.D., it is a clear indicator that there has been an uninterrupted presence of a Venetic (Slovene) population in that area. The Veneti cannot be dismissed as a vanished race and separated from their descendants, the Slovenes—official theories notwithstanding.

Some readers will perhaps object to this detailed clarification of single names and words, but history is full of misunderstandings which have been built around words, words deliberately distorted or inadvertantly misunderstood. In regard to Slovene history the Trans-Carpathian theory, which nearly destroyed Slovenes as a nation, was based on such deliberately misshapen words. The greatest German nationalistic historian, Gustav Kossinna, used such methods to prove that Slovenes had no right of domicile in central Europe. One of his petty word-plays was to prove that Slovenes must have come from the swamps of Pripet because they borrowed the word "bukev" (Ger. Buche) from Germans when they came to central Europe. It is an old Slovene and generally Slavic word. In Slovene it has numerous derivatives: *bukev, bukati se, buka, bukač, bučati, bučela,* showing it is a basic word, which German *Buche* certainly is not; it is most likely a loan-word from Venetic. The same is true in toponymy. Much can be learned if place-names are understood and are not distorted for political reasons.

Slovene Traces in Friuli

The Rhaeto-Romance language group to which the Friulian belongs, extends from Switzerland to South Tyrol and Friuli to the Adriatic. The change from the original language to Latin and later to Romance was imposed for political and economic reasons and steadily progressed towards the Alps. In Friuli, this transition lasted into the latter half of the Middle Ages. Friulian historians themselves, who consider Slovene to be the native, indigenous language, write about this evolution. Here I would like to offer a few examples.

Giacomo Baldissera wrote in his book *La pieve di Tarcento* that a regulation existed as late as 1497 which required that the villages in Tarčent area be sent Slovene priests, indicating that Slovene was the language of the area. It has been completely suppressed since then. Important information is also given by **Marcantonio Nicoletti** (+1596), a lawyer in Čedad (Cividale), who wrote in his *Costumi e leggi* that Slovene was used besides Friulian in the medieval Friulian parliament. He also wrote that in the villages Slovene was spoken more than Friulian, which was not yet completely formed. Some seventy years later **Giovanni Francesco de gli Olivi** noted in his *Historia della provincia de Friuli* (Udine 1660) that in earlier times the Slovene language was spoken in the villages and Friulian in towns. This is the typical progress of a new language which establishes itself first in cities and towns and then gradually penetrates the country-side.

Paulus Diaconus wrote in his *Langobard History* (IV, 44) about an event through which we can assume that the majority of the population in Friuli still spoke Slovene around the year 600 A.D. Diaconus described the arrival of Slavs

*Albrecht Dürer: Una Villana Windisch—
A Slovene Village Woman—in the area
of the Brenner Pass at the beginning of
the 16th century.*

in many boats from Dalmatia in the Langobard Duchy of Benevento, where they
attacked the Langobards. Historians place the event in 642. The Langobard Duke
Aio was killed in this battle. His successor Rodoald developed a novel method of
dealing with the invaders: he spoke to them in their own language and created a
sense of trust, then unexpectedly attacked them and drove them out. Our interest
is in Rodoald's knowledge of Slavic language. From the date of the battle we can
infer that his childhood years passed around 600 A.D. when the majority of
Langobards were still in Friuli; there, as a child in the company of local children,
he learned the Slavic language.

The large number of Slovene toponyms in Friuli reflects the language of the
past. Šavli mentions a large number of them in the first part of this book. Equally
important are Slovene remains in the Friulian-Romance language. I will limit
myself to a few words; the Friulian is followed by Slovene and the translation:

scuote *skuta*—milk curd; **govet** *govedo*—cattle; **ranizze** *oranica*—field; **cespe**
češpa—plum; **razze** *raca*—duck; **clanz** *klanec*—ascent or descent (on a road);
boc Slov. dial. *buč*—beehive; **breon** Slov. dial. *brjon*—heavy plank; **britule**
britva—razor, pocket knife; **clocie** *kloča, koklja*—mother hen; **molzi** *molzti*—to
milk; **pacie** *paša*—pasture; **plancie** *planka*—board; **racli** *rakla, prekla*—bean-

pole; **radic** *radič*—chicory; **renzi** *renčati*—to growl; **ronc** *ronek*—the foot of a hill; **ruta** *ruta*—kerchief; **scrin** *skrinja*—chest, coffer; **scudiele** *skodela*—cup; **stangie** *štanga*—bar, rod; **struzze** *štruca*—long loaf; **trop** *trop*—herd.

Slovene toponyms and micro-toponyms are present in the plain as they are in mountainous areas. Regarding Slovene words in Friulian language, they are mostly simple everyday words from family life and work; that is, the most enduring words which could not be uprooted are mainly from the Slovene dialect. They offer a clear indication of the presence of the Slovene language in Friuli in the distant past.

In the upper reaches of the Piave River there is **Calalzo**, a settlement with a Slovene name. Calalzo is the Italianized Slovene word *kalce* diminutive of **kal**—pond, small lake. This is supported by the full name of the place "Lagole di Calalzo"; *lagole* is Italian for *kalce*, a tautology. Here, Veneti had an important sanctuary dedicated to Trumužijat. They came to cure their ailments in the thermal waters of the ponds, and attributed the miraculous cures to the presiding deity—the Trumužijat. When the Romans occupied the area they replaced Trumužijat with Apollo and gradually removed Venetic customs and culture and language. In Friuli, wherever the Slovene language is still spoken, this process of demolition continues unabated. During fascist rule the language was brutally persecuted. But even now in the 1990s, the Slovene minority in Friuli has virtually no rights—a sad comparison with rights the Italian minority enjoys in Slovenia.

In order to recognize the original language of the area in question, it is essential to know the **geographic direction** of the language movement. When we compare Friuli with Slovenia, we can see that the Venetic language was steadily pushed from Friuli towards Slovenia and never in the opposite direction. There is a gradual disappearance of Slovene from Friuli. Whether from the toponyms or from the Friulian language itself, this is a clear indication that the original language of Friuli was Slovene. We cannot develop this kind of comparison in Slovenia. No language, be it Latin or any other, has been gradually pushed outward; the movement has always been in reverse. The Slovene language territory has been steadily encroached upon, from all directions. When the Romans withdrew at the fall of the Empire, the indigenous Slovene language reasserted itself, and the only reminder of Roman occupation are a few names of colonies and fortifications. The only exception is the coast of Istria where the Romans were not only rulers but to some extent residents. Everywhere else the toponymy is exclusively Slovene. The Vremska Valley near Trst with its Slovene toponymy and its important archaeological finds from all periods, including an interesting Venetic inscription, proves an uninterrupted presence of Slovenes in that area.

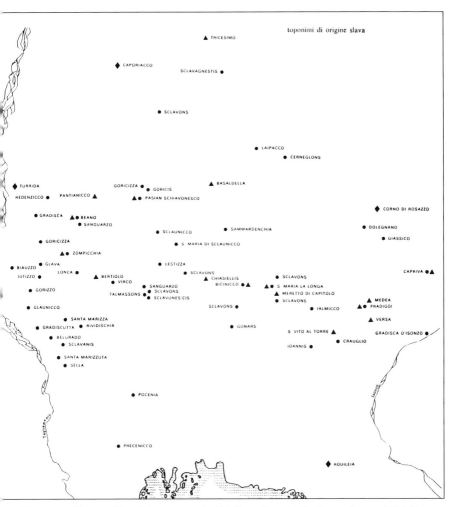

Numerous Slovene (Venetic) toponyms in Friuli confirm the findings of several Friulian historians showing that Slovene was in use there until the Middle Ages.

There is also no trace of Latin in the Slovene language, which would not have been possible if Slovenes were settling in a land where Latin was in general use—especially when the Latin would have been on a much higher cultural level than the language of the newly-arrived, backward Slavs from Trans-Carpathia. To bypass all this evidence and assert that the Slovenes arrived in the 6th century A.D. is preposterous.

459

Historic Evidence
Sparse Written Records

Historian Bogo Grafenauer admits that "regarding the time of settlement of Slavs in the eastern Alps and upper reaches of the Sava River Valley, we have no direct documentation"—comment in the translation of Diaconus's *The History of Langobards*. Then he endeavours to validate his own theory about the arrival of Slovenes with a self-willed interpretation of three historical sources. **The first source** is records from the Aquileian Patriarchate which state that by the end of the 6th century, there were no Roman bishoprics in Noricum. Grafenauer presumes the arrival of Slovenes at that time and charges them with the destruction of bishoprics, but his presumption is contradicted by known data. It is apparent from the biography of St. Severinus that the Romans left Noricum gradually. Because the bishoprics were inherent in Roman colonies they disintegrated, which is why the Aquileian records make no reference to a violent overthrow or arrival of a new people.

The second source is the letter from Pope Gregory the Great to the Bishop of Salonica in the year 600, where he mentions with concern that the Slavs had begun to enter Italy through the Istrian gate. Grafenauer incorrectly interprets these words to mean settlement of Slavs. The settlement of a people would not have disturbed the Pope, but the Slavic and Avar attackers did not come to settle; they came to plunder and wear down Byzantine military power. That these attackers had no intention of settling is proven by the fact that Slavs together with Langobards and Avars again attacked the Byzantines in Istria in 603, which means they did not settle earlier in the area. In 611 the Slavs attacked again. But the Byzantines stayed on in Istria, as did the indigenous Slovene inhabitants, whom we cannot liken to those Slavic soldiers (probably Balkan Slavs) who were in Avar employ in 603 when the Avar king sent them as reinforcement to the Langobards during the siege of Cremona.

The third source and the most important one for Grafenauer is *The History of Langobards* by Paulus Diaconus, in which there is no word about a supposed arrival of Slovenes. Grafenauer obstinately interprets (to suit his own views) several sentences by Diaconus which have an entirely different meaning. (See below).

We cannot avoid speculating: How is it possible that the big changes that would have occurred with the arrival of Slovenes in central Europe were not

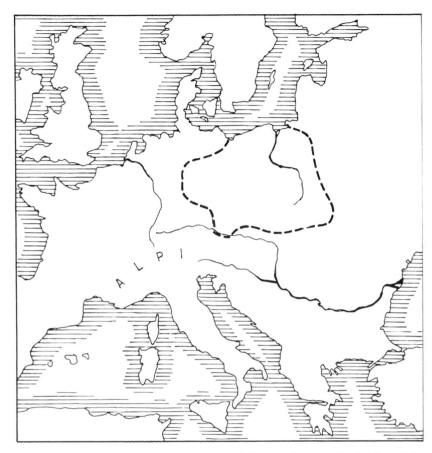

The Lusatian culture, 1300 B.C., encompassed the area between the Baltic and the Danube.

recorded in any historical source? The migrations of Gotts and Langobards, who were eventually assimilated by the indigenous population and disappeared as nations, were recorded. But that Slovenes could have occupied central Europe from the Adriatic to the Danube, including the formidable Alps, without historical record is impossible. Did the Slovenes come as conquerors? Whom did they battle with? Whom did they conquer? What happened to the conquered? What happened to the native inhabitants? Did the Slovenes kill them? Did the natives flee? Where? Nothing is known about these details. Did the Slovenes come peace-

461

fully and settle among the native population, which must have been a much larger nation? How is it possible that the language of the newcomers completely displaced the language of the indigenous population? What was their language like? How is it possible that the newcomers from Trans-Carpathia assimilated the indigenous population with its higher cultural standards and development in farming, trade and commerce? Why are there no historical reports about these changes?

Inasmuch as there is no historical documentation about the arrival of the Slovenes, Grafenauer says, "the meaning of toponymical and philological analysis is that much greater." The message of toponymy and philology has been widely discussed in earlier chapters.

It is true there is no historical documentation about the arrival of the Slovenes, but there are some, though scanty, records from the Roman period which indicate their indigenous status.

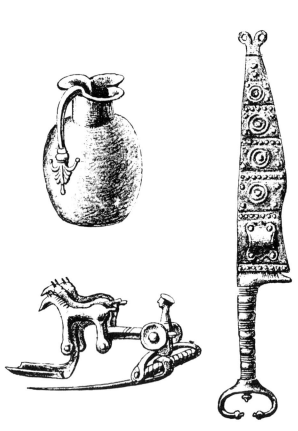

A few of the numerous finds from Most na Soči, Slovenia (Lucia Group). The place was an important trading centre of the ancient Veneti.

St. Jerome and St. Columban

These two noteworthy men from antiquity, one a theologian and writer and the other a missionary, are important witnesses.

St. Jerome was one of the greatest teachers of the early Western Church. Jerome was born circa 347 at Stridon, in the Slovene littoral (according to Encyclopaedia Britannica, near modern Ljubljana, Slovenia). Jerome's parents may have been Roman settlers, but he could have been just as easily of native descent. His education, begun at home, was continued in Rome. Most of his life was spent in Rome and Palestine. At the request of Pope Damasus I (366–384) he translated the entire Bible into Latin, the *Vulgate*. He also wrote a number of biblical, ascetic, monastic, and theological works.

A fibula in the form of a peacock, 7th century A.D., Bled, Slovenia. As a Christian symbol, it confirms the presence of Christianity among Slovenes of that area at an earlier period than is commonly considered by historians.

In his *Commentary to Paul's Epistle to the Ephesians,* he refers to the name **Tychicus** and gives an explanation of it in the following words: "Tychicus enim silens interpretatur" (Patrilogiae latinae tomus XXVI; Commentar. in Epist. ad Ephes. Liber III, cap. IV, Migne edit. 1866). There was no need for an explanation in the text; it seems he simply wanted to intimate that he knew the language from whence the particular word came. In Slovene the name would be Tihik from the word *tih*—silent. Jerome's translation is correct when he says: "Tychicus actually means silent." This suggests that he knew the Slovene language and above all it proves that Slovene (Venetic) was spoken during his time in the area of present-day Slovenia.

There is a book written in Glagolitic script attributed to St. Jerome (not proved), twenty-two pages of which have been preserved. In the 15th century the book was heavily illuminated as a relic of St. Jerome. Davorin Žunkovič explains in his *Die Slavische Forzeit/* The Slavic Prehistory, that the book had different owners. The Glagolitic script is very old, its origin unknown, but it probably predates St. Jerome. Some linguists think it is a continuation of the Venetic script, although its letters are round. That the Glagolitic is related to St. Jerome is evident from the attitude of Pope John X (910–928) who was opposed to Slavic Liturgy, be it that of Ciril and Methodius or the Glagolitic, which was in use in Istria and Dalmatia. When it was explained by priests of Glagolitic Liturgy that it originated with St. Jerome, he withdrew his opposition. The explanations must have been substantial to convince the Pope.

We can presume with certainty that St. Jerome knew the Slovene language, and from this we can conclude that the indigenous population of his birthplace was Slovene.

The biography of **St. Columban** (543–615) is an important document. It contains evidence that the Slovenes were called Veneti around 600 A.D. It was written in northern Italy where Veneti were well known, and no mistake could have been made concerning the name and the people to whom it belonged. As the most important representative of Irish missionary activity in Europe, Columban arrived in France in 591 with twelve disciples; he established monasteries. Around the year 600 he was doing missionary work in Bavaria near Bodensee (Lacus Venetus) and later in Switzerland; his biography reports that in 612 he was staying at Bregenz (on Bodensee). From there he wanted to move his mission to the Veneti in Noricum, but the angel of God told him that this nation was not ready for the Gospel. Hence, he moved to Lombardy to the small town of Bobbio (south of Milan) where he founded a monastery. He died there in 615.

His biography was written by his disciple and successor, Abbot Jona Bobbiensis. There we find a description of how St. Columban intended to travel to Noricum, whose inhabitants he called **"Veneti qui et Sclavi dicuntur"**—the Veneti who are also called Slavs. This means the principal name of Slovenes was Veneti. The name Slavs was secondary and was disseminated from Byzantine areas as Sclavini or Sclavi. The writer of the biography did not know them as recent settlers.

St. Severinus

The biography of St. Severinus is one of the important historical documents of the last period of the Roman Empire during the second half of the 5th century. The writer of the document was Eugippius, a Roman like Severinus. His intention was not to write a historical account, but rather to describe the life and activities of St. Severinus in terms of saintly legends with an interweaving of miraculous events. Scattered here and there are also descriptions of other events in Noricum.

The document presents a fairly clear picture of the attitude held by the remaining few Romans towards the indigenous population, always referred to as "barbarians" (common term for all who were not Romans). More detailed are the contacts of the Romans with Germanic tribes who by then occupied Outer Noricum—the principal area of Severinus's activity. They are usually mentioned by their tribal names: the Rugians, the Scirians, the Alemanni, etc. The Roman Empire existed at least nominally until 476, but had virtually no influence in Noricum in the last few decades. It is easy to understand the hardships of the remaining Romans. St. Severinus was to minister to their religious needs and to alleviate their social difficulties.

Reading his biography, one notices the distance between the Romans and the natives, who were clearly not Romanized. Romans were always a small part of the population concentrated in towns, and they moved for reasons of safety from one town to another with greater security. With the fall of the Empire they found themselves isolated and threatened, not so much because of the presence of Ger-

St. Severinus came to Noricum as a monk in 450 A.D. and worked there till his death in 482.

manic troops in Roman employ, but because of the indigenous population. Of interest is the report about the two monks sent by Severinus to Inner Noricum. They returned after several months, glad to have escaped the "barbarians" (chap. 36). The incident indicates that the population of Inner Noricum was not Romanized.

Who the indigenous people were is not stated; they are always referred to as "barbarians". In chapter 20 we read that after the fall of the defense line in the north, the city of Patavia continued to maintain its military force. When a few of these defenders went on the road to Italy to collect pay for themselves and their comrades, they were killed by the "barbarians". From this and other reports we see that the relationship between the Romans and the indigenous population was by this time hostile. Although the native population is not named, it is clear from place-names that it was Slavic (see chap. 18). For example, the Roman name Patavis was followed by the native name **Baszowa**. In chapter 3, we find the name Danubium (Danube) followed by the native name **Tunawa**; the modern Slovene name is Donava. In chapter 15, a place named **Chunizen** is mentioned, very close to the Slovene Konjice. Nearby was a river with the name **Businka;** in Slovene we would say Božinka. These and other names speak of the native population of Noricum which was, as we know, Venetic.

St. Severinus died in 482, six years after Odoacer deposed the last emperor of the western Roman Empire and assumed the rule himself. In 488 Odoacer transferred the rule of Outer Noricum to Germanic tribes. At that time the last Romans moved from Noricum to Italy and took the remains of St. Severinus with them.

Jordanes, Procopius and Emperor Julian

The Gothic historian **Jordanes** was a bishop in southern Italy. He wrote in 552 the book *De Getarum sive Gothorum origine et rebus gestis,* in which he mentions Slavs a number of times by the names Windi, Sclavini and Anti. According to him Sclavini existed earlier, but under different names. He equates them with Windi and Anti, indicating that they were all Slavs. He also called Windi Veneti. This linkage of names indicates that Jordanes did not differentiate; for him Veneti and Sclavini were Slavs.

The Byzantine historian **Procopius** wrote a report in 555 about the building projects of Emperor Justinian. He wrote about newly built and restored fortifications in the Balkan provinces. There were a large number of old fortifications which he restored, and interestingly, nearly all of them had Slavic names. Ivan Gorenc collected over forty of these names (Venetic Tribune Jan. 22, 1995,

Grossvenediger, 3674m, a famous mountain of former Noricum which reminds us of Veneti who lived at its base.

Ljubljana). I will mention only one of them in Illyricum, a fort named **Millareka, Mila reka,** meaning gentle river. In some transcriptions it is **Mala reka**—small river.

The names of these forts speak of the presence of Slavic people in these areas much before the arrival of the South Slavs. This is another reason for the inadmissibility of claims that Slovenes came into the Alps in the 6th century.

In the writings of **Emperor Julian** from 358—when according to official historians the inhabitants of Friuli, Istria and Pannonia were all Romanized—we

467

find a statement about Aquilea (Oglej) in Friuli: "In reality here are administered the Mysians, Pannonians and the Italici who live in the interior. These (last) were earlier called **Eneti**; even now when the Romans occupy their towns, they maintain their original name by adding a character which they call **ou** which is often used by them instead of beta. This is I think, because of a pronunciation peculiarity native to their language."

Tabula Peutingeriana is a Roman road map of Noricum used by their legions and merchants. The Slovene (Venetic) place-name Saloca (in present spelling Zaloka) is on the map (See Ancient Slovene Toponyms).

Emperor Julian was a native of Thrace, but wrote in Greek. From his writings we glean important information. First, that in the 4th century the Veneti still had their own language, and second, that Romans occupied only their cities. It is not clear whether the name Veneti applied to all nations mentioned or only to the Veneti in Friuli. In English translation the word "last" is added, limiting the name Veneti to the inhabitants of the "interior". This word is missing in the original and also in French translation. Nonetheless, the most important discovery for us is that in the 4th century the Veneti in Italy and the outlying areas around Aquileia spoke their own language, while their cities were occupied by Romans. This finding conforms with statements of some already mentioned Friulian historians. If even in Italy the Venetic lands were not completely Romanized, we can be certain that Romanization was far less advanced in lands toward Pannonia; i.e., Slovenia and Noricum.

Paulus Diaconus and Slovenes in
The History of Langobards

Paulus Diaconus, the most important historian recording events in central Europe during the 6th and 7th centuries, wrote primarily about the history of Langobards, but he also mentioned other important events of that period. There is no doubt that if Slovenes reached the border of the Langobards at that time it would have been considered a major event and would not have been ignored by Diaconus; yet, there is no report about such arrival in his *The History of Langobards*. He mentions Slavs only in regard to particular events, but never in regard to a settlement. The peaceful indigenous people are not mentioned because history writing is mainly concerned with military exploits. The Langobards had little contact or trouble with the people in the Alps (Noricum), and in the

Paulus Diaconus, a Langobard who wrote The History of Langobards *around the year 783 in Montecassino, Italy.*

direction of Istria and Slovenia they were confronted with attacks from Avars and Balkan Slavs. The native Slovene population was not involved in these events.

Defenders of the theory that the Slovenes arrived in the 6th century consider *The History of Langobards* to be their most important piece of evidence. Therefore, we have to examine it closely and see what is actually written there. We have to allow that the events related to Slovenes as described by Diaconus occurred 200 years previously; hence, we cannot expect from him the accuracy of a chronicler. His is a description of events he found in other sources.

The most important reference to Slovenes, whom he calls Sclavi—Slavs—is the report of the two Bavarian attacks on the Slovene state (Noricum). In the year 595, King Tassilo of Bavaria attacked the Slovene state (Sclaborum provinciam) and returned home with much booty: **"And he soon thereafter invaded the province of Slavs, overpowered them and returned to his homeland with much loot." (HL, IV, 7).** It is unclear where the attack took place, probably not in the difficult-to-access Alps. Since the attackers came from the direction of Salzburg, we can presume the event occurred somewhere in the Inn River Valley. We must take note of the important word "provincia" (Enciclopedia Universale, XII, Milano 1970, p. 304); to Langobards it meant an independent state with defined internal organization and defence. If the Slovenes just arrived and occupied the area as we are told by official historians, how could they have had such wealth as to entice the Bavarians to plunder? If the Slovenes had arrived to conquer the land, they would have been the aggressors, but that was not the case. The report states that they were attacked and ransacked in their own land.

The second Bavarian attack the following year (596) with similar intentions was foiled with the help of Avars: **"When in the same days the Bavarians came to attack with an army of up to two thousand men, the Slavs with the help of the Avar kaghan killed them all." (HL, IV, 10).** The location of this attack is also unknown. That the Avars were involved in this battle with the Bavarians suggests that the battle took place in an area where the Avars felt threatened, perhaps somewhere in the northeastern part of Carantania. Some historians think it may have taken place in western Carantania near the Drava River source; but that should not be taken too seriously. Would the Bavarians, after ransacking Slovene settlements, wait until the Avars marched the breadth of the land in order to have a battle with them? Probably not.

The Slovenes are next alluded to in the 24th chapter; the area is Istria. In 601 the Byzantines again attacked the Langobards. As result, the latter allied themselves with the Avars and the Slavs, and attacked Byzantines in Istria with united force: **"Meanwhile the Langobards with Avars and Slavs attacked the land of Istria and destroyed everything with fire and pillage." (HL, IV, 24).** There

470

is no mention in the text of a settlement of Slavs. From where these Slavs came is unknown. They were not the indigenous Alpine Slavs (Slovenes); rather, they were South Slavs who were in the employ of the Avars, as is evident from the following report of the Avar king sending Slavs as re-inforcement to the Langobards who were besieging the city of Cremona: "**For this reason King Agilulf in the month of July left Milan and besieged the city of Cremona with Slavs, who were sent to him as re-inforcement by the kaghan, the king of the Avars.**" (**HL, IV, 28**). These Slavs who were also fighting in Istria had

Langobards and their neighbours, the Slovenes, from Istria to Carantania.

nothing to do with any kind of settlement there. They arrived and departed according to Avar military strategy.

In 603, the Langobards agreed on a cease-fire with the Byzantines. As a result, the Slavs alone attacked the Byzantines: **"King Agilulf concluded peace with the emperor for one year and later for another year; he also renewed peace with the Franks. In spite of this the Slavs in this year killed soldiers in Istria; they also ransacked the country."** (HL, IV, 40). The Avars even attacked the Langobards in Friuli: **"Around that time the king of Avars whom they call in their language kaghan invaded the province of Venetia with an enormous crowd."** (HL, IV, 37). This Avar attack in which the Langobards were defeated, was described by Diaconus in an especially colourful style. The Langobard Prince Gisulf of Friuli (Forum Julii) fell in this battle. The defence of the capital (Forojulianum oppidum) was assumed by his wife Romilda. Diaconus blamed her for the defeat, accusing her of treason. In his unbelievable story, he presented her as a harlot who watched the Avar king from the city ramparts and fell in love with him. To accomplish her intention she let him take over the city, its residents and defenders. The king massacred the population and destroyed the city.

This tale and others that follow, describing the fate of Romilda, suggest a particular purpose on Diaconus's part. It is possible that Romilda was not a Langobard, and was thus blamed for all the troubles. She could have been of Venetic (Slovene) background; the following story hints at just such a possibility. Her two sons had properties among Slovenes in Carantania. Diaconus writes: **"As we said, when the Friulian Duke Gisulf died, his two sons took over the governing of the duchy. The two took into their power Slavs in a district called Zellia, as far as a place called (Mederia) Meklarija."** (HL, IV, 38). Historians claim that the Slovenes had just arrived and were breaking through the Istrian gate, but from the above description we see that such was not the case. The natives among whom the Langobard princes had their land-holdings were Slovenes. Zila (Zellia) and Meglarje (Mederia) are well-known Venetic (Slovene) place-names which could not have been created instantly, but must have been there before the arrival of the Langobards.

In connection with these attacks of Slavs on Byzantines, the letter of Pope **Gregory the Great** (600) to Massimus, the Bishop of Salonica, is especially meaningful. This letter is much cited by defenders of the official theory regarding the arrival of Slovenes, and is considered by them to be an important piece of evidence. In question are the following words by the Pope: "quia per Histriae aditum iam ad Italiam intrare coeperunt" meaning "because through the Istrian gate they started to enter Italy." He was speaking of Slavic soldiers who were attacking the Byzantines about whom the Pope was concerned and on whose presence he relied; they were his allies. These events were not attempts by Slavs to settle; there is not a word about settlement. It is a description of the military actions which Balkan Slavs and Langobards undertook against Byzantines. The theory about the settlement of Slovenes is an invention. The indigenous population of Istria and the surrounding areas remained unchanged and it could not have been any other than Venetic, Slavic.

It is very naive to depend on Diaconus as proof of Slovene settlement in the 6th century; two examples from *The History of Langobards* will provide clarification. Grafenauer states in his commentary: "Slavs settled the later Slovene territory on the west bank of the Soča River (Goriška Brda and Venetian Slovenia) only after new battles against Friulians in 705. In 720 they tried to take the Friulian plains but without success." The following two incidents are cited as evidence.

The first incident (HL VI, 24) describes a fictitious attack of Slovenes on Friulians, an attack solicited by the Friulian Duke Ferdulf himself. The description of the battle is so fantastic that the reader at once recognizes the event took place only in the imagination of the writer. During this battle "all Friulian nobility was butchered". Of course, if this were true, there would have been no further obstruction and Slovenes could have taken Friuli if they so chose. Diaconus's intention was to show through this imagined battle the dangers of strife and disunity—this thought he expresses very clearly in his closing words.

In the second incident (HL VI, 45) the intention was to glorify young Langobard noblemen, who were schooled and housed by Duke Pemo himself. "When under his care they reached adolescence, the duke received a message that an immense horde of Slavs was on its way to a place called Lauriana." Pemo "attacked with the young noblemen and defeated the Slavs; on the Langobard side no one was killed except Siguald who was already advanced in age." This description too reads like a fairy-tale. Is it believable that a handful of adolescent boys killed an "immense horde" of professional soldiers, yet did not suffer one casualty? Is it probable that the old man Siguald was killing Slavs "as he wished" without consequence until he welcomed death voluntarily?

In both scenes Diaconus invented a heroic image to set before the Langobards as an example. In the first scene it was "Munikis who showed there his bravery and manliness" when he, with shackled hands, killed and conquered the enemy.

In the second scene it was Siguald, who killed Slavs "as he wished" and then said: "Now I will gladly accept death if she comes." This type of story-telling is very common with Diaconus; his historical accounts are generously interspersed with legends and inventions meant to entertain or moralize. That historians accept every account as an actual event says something about their research skills.

The Venetic Inscriptions

The Slavic character of the Venetic language is clearly shown by ancient Venetic inscriptions. They reveal that the Slovene language is its continuation, which should not surprise anyone; the Este culture included present-day Slovene territory. In the book *Narečna struktura praslovanskega jezika v luči južno-slovanske leksike/* Dialect Structure of the Proto-Slavic Language in the Light of South Slavic Lexicon (Ljubljana 1992), Lyubov V. Kurkina says that the western area of Slovenia (Tolmin) preserved the most archaic of all Slavic dialects. Nearby, at Most na Soči, is the site of the largest Venetic finds in Slovenia, where more than seven thousand urn graves were found. A large variety of artifacts were discovered along with the pottery burial urns. The discovery also includes several important inscriptions.

I will later examine two inscriptions, one from western Slovenia and one from Italy. But first, I would like to have a close look at the grammar tablets on which Matej Bor found very obvious indications that Slovene is a continuation of the Venetic language.

Mystery of the Ateste Tablets

Among numerous archaeological finds from Ateste, modern Este, 31 km southwest of Padova (now Padua), there are several bronze tablets from the sanctuary of Reitija where there was a school for writers or scribes (scuola dei scrittori). The tablets usually have two parts; in the upper part there is a verse of some kind, and in the lower, rows of letters. Consequently, they are called alphabet tablets by Venetologists.

There is no doubt that the tablets were used as teaching aids, but there is still a question whether they were really alphabet tablets. Venetologists say that the characters in the lowest row were consonants, and those in other rows were vowels which are repeated for the entire row. But why is the consonant **K** among the vowels? Venetologists say it is there to spell AKEO, which to them means "alphabet". But why would the same word be repeated sixteen times? For magical effect, they say. One may also ask why the vowels **I** and **U** are missing. And why is there also an **E** among the consonants? In **Es 26** there is an **A**, and in **Es 25** an **II**; that is, two **I's**. And why not include in the reading the bottom letters, which are clearly in the same column with other letters? Prosdocimi stated in his book *I*

Veneti antichi that, because of so many open questions, there is doubt whether these tablets can be called alphabet tablets.

Why have official Venetologists never tried a different approach? Was there a secret motive behind their insistence on a Latin-based solution? Would it have been politically inexpedient for them to find a fundamental solution to the problem? They already suspected that the Veneti were a Proto-Slavic people. At any rate, Bor recognized that the answers can be found only through Slavic languages and especially Slovene and its dialects, and he was able to solve the mystery. He also changed the direction of reading—from the top down; he included the bottom line of letters which actually became the key to understanding the total meaning of the lower half of the tablet.

If we look at tablet **Es 26** (see Part Two for tablet illustrations) we find in the middle a row of symbol ◇ which is in the opinion of Venetologists an **o,** but the real **o** is vertical ◇. Only in **Es 23** does the fifth row from the bottom appear as letters **o;** on every other tablet it is smaller than the real **o** and is horizontal. It is usually in line with other graphemes but not always. On tablet **Es 24** there are more of them than other letters. Thus, the row of horizontal symbols is considered an ornament dividing the lower from the upper half of the tablet. There are instances in other inscriptions where letters are used as ornaments; for example, **Es 45** (see Inscriptions on Writing Tools) where **X** (T) is repeated nine times as an ornament. I should add that if the horizontal symbol were read as **o,** it would not change the meaning of the graphemes and words on the lower half of the tablet.

The various tablets are damaged, but **Es 23** is not. We will use it for this short examination. The letter **E** needs some explanation. In Venetic it is pronounced as **ye** (**ye**llow) at the beginning of the word, also true of **e** in Slovene dialects: *eno—jeno, belo—bielo*. In Friulian the **e** is still pronounced as **ye**: *esolâ—jesolâ, entrâ—jentrâ, emplâ—jemplâ*. The same is true of Russian; the **e** at the beginning of the word is often pronounced as **ye**. The pronunciation of the letter **e** as **ye** is also validated by other Venetic inscriptions. The statement by the noted linguist Pokorny that the Venetic language is closely related to the Balto-Slavic, means that the comparisons between Venetic and Slavic languages as done by Bor are correct.

E	E	E	E	E	E	E	E	E	E	E	E	E	E	E
K	K	K	K	K	K	K	K	K	K	K	K	K	K	K
A	A	A	A	A	A	A	A	A	A	A	A	A	A	A
E	H	B	T	IS	R	Š	P	N	M	L	K	ITI	J	D	V

From left to right: **jekaje, jekah, jekab, jekat, jekais, jekar, jekaš, jekap, jekan, jekam, jekal, jekak, jekaiti, jekaj, jekad, jekav.** The majority of these derivatives from the verb **jekat**—to echo, to resound—are still in use in Slovene. In dialects **jekat** also means to cry. (See Part Two for detailed explanation and illustrations).

Sayings (not names) on Gravestones

The Venetic inscription **Es 6** is on a gravestone from Este. It was found in 1920 in Morlongo on an estate called **Staro**—old; this is a distinctly Slovene micro-toponym. There are, from the time of the ancient Veneti, many such toponyms in the areas surrounding Padova.

This inscription confirms our understanding that periods in Venetic script are ornamental, associated with some letters and not used to divide text into words. We also find our views in regard to the Venetic word **ego** vindicated—it is not the Latin *ego* (I). The same spelling of the two words has misled Venetologists into thinking they had uncovered a Latin connection in Venetic inscriptions. The inscription is from the 3rd century B.C. or older, when Latin was not yet known among Veneti.

.e.xo.o.s..tiio.ie.xe/.s.tiio.i.
(Museo Nazionale Atestino)

476

To correctly understand the Venetic **ego** we must apply the same rules used in explaining the pronunciation of the word **ekat**. The meaning of the Venetic word **ego** is the same as in Old Church Slavic (OCS) and in Russian *ego*—him.

What word did the Veneti use for "I"—first person singular? We know from other inscriptions, e.g., **Es** 57, that it is **mego**. It is possible that the abbreviation **mi** was used conversationally as among the Etruscans. Even now *mi* is used as "I" around Trieste in Slovene and Italian; the same is true of former Venetic areas in Italy. It is possible that the speakers of Latin received the Venetic **ego** indirectly from the Etruscans. In Latin it is an isolated personal pronoun, while in the Venetic language this form is repeated.

Venetologists divided this inscription into the following words: **Ego Ostioi Egestioi**. The first word they interpreted as Latin meaning "I", the second and third words as names in dative. Why names? Because official Venetologists did not understand these inscriptions, they assumed that all inscriptions were names. It was an easy way out of their embarrassment. If the word **ego** really meant "I", then it could not relate to the names which are in dative; Venetologists say the grave is speaking. Perhaps. But let us look at Bor's transcription and translation:

E . GO . O . S . T I I O . I . E . GE . S . T I I O . I .
jego   ostijoj   jege   stijoj

Slovene: (Od) njega ostankov zli duh stoj proč.
English: (From) his remains evil spirit stay away.

jego—him, from him; Slov. *njega, od njega.*

ostijoj—remains; Slov. *ostanki.* Although written with **i** the pronunciation is more like the Slovene *j.*

jege—this is a mythological word preserved in Slovene as *jaga;* (for example *divja jaga*—wild hunt). Arch. *jega* with the meaning of an evil spirit. The beginning **e** is **ye**.

stijoj imperative from **stati**—stay away, do not come near, do not touch it; Slov. *stoj, ostani*—halt, stay away.

All four words are still known in Slovene, offering us a good translation which is in perfect harmony with the gravestone and the attitudes of people at that time.

Interpretation of Venetic Inscriptions

We will take a look at one of the Venetic inscriptions from Slovenia, from Idrija pri Bači, 1st century B.C. on a bronze tablet (8X2cm). On each end it had a hole through which it was attached with nails to a wooden or ceramic container in which perhaps some food was stored, and thus came to the grave of the deceased. It is now preserved in the Museum of Natural History in Vienna.

Before Bor no one was able to explain this inscription, which is only natural. No one tried the logical approach; i.e., to read it with the help of the language of the area—the Slovene. Venetologists used their standard procedure, looking for more names. The inscription is in two lines.

LYK Z(E)MELIN K S
HAJI ČOS KA B(I)

In Slovene: Kadar je ta praznik zemlje
                počivaj, pa naj bo karkoli.
In English: When there is this feast of the earth,
                rest, no matter what.

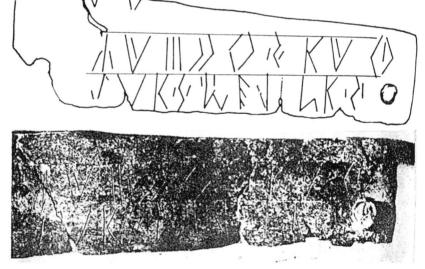

Is 3 (LLV)

478

Let us examine Bor's division of this *in continuo* inscription and his explanation of individual words:

lyk—celebration, dance, feast; OCS *likъ*—choir (Miklošič). Ukrainian *lykovati*—rejoicing, dancing (Mikl.). In the Slovene language this word has been preserved to describe something pleasant; *olika*—good manners; *likati*—to improve speech; to describe the goodness of a person the word *lik* is used (*lik človeka*).

z(e)melin—of earth; the first **e** was left out (possibly because it was not accented) after the custom that came from the Etruscans, who received it from the Semites. This omission of vowels was in a small way practised also in the Venetic language. Now we say *zemljin* because the second **e** has been dropped. *Zemlja*—earth, *zemljin*—of earth. In one of the Etruscan inscriptions on a mirror there is the name of the goddess **Semela,** indicating the word was used by the Etruscans.

k—if, when; Slov. *ko*, in dial. *k*, which equals the Venetic **k**. In the Slovene language we have a number of words consisting of a single consonant, particularly common in dialects.

s—this one; Slov. *ta, to, tu;* OCS *sь*.

haji—rest; Slov. *počivaj*, in dial. also *hajaj* and *haji*, from *hajati, hajam, haj ga*—let him be (Plet.), Russ. dial. *hajatь*, and *nehaj*—let it be. Now it is used in Slovene only with some prefixes like *ob-hajaj*—celebrate. In a Tyrolean Christmas song "haji" is used with the meaning rest, sleep (child), probably a relic from the old Venetic language. Slovene mothers still put their child to sleep with: *ajati, ajaj!* meaning rest, sleep!

čos ka—whatever; Slov. *kar, karkoli*, Czech *čos*—some.

b(i)—would; the Venetic silent vowel **i** was often left out. In colloquial Slovene we also often say *b* instead of *bi*.

Against this interpretation there was an article in *Delo* Mar. 31, 1995, Ljubljana, by Prof. Jan Makarovič. We can see how unfounded are the objections of those who dismiss the interpretation of the Venetic inscriptions on the basis of the Slovene language.

First of all, he cites the authority of the well-known Venetologist Michel Lejeune, who interpreted the inscription as three names: **Luks Mel(i)nks Gaijos.** It is understandable that Lejeune tried to explain the inscription in this manner; he had no knowledge of the Slovene language, and therefore could not reach a better conclusion.

Next, we are reprimanded for our interpretation of the second letter (u) as **y**; we did this because the Venetic language does not have a separate letter for **y**. That the word is read as *lyk* and not *luk* is evident from the OCS; there, this word is written as *lyk*. Since we do not have the letter **y** in the Slovene alphabet, we write the word with **i** (lik). Anyone familiar with Slovene knows the difference.

He also says that we have written the word **smelin** with a **z** instead of **s.** This is true, but only because Slovene orthography requires in this case a **z** for correct pronunciation. The Veneti used the same character **s** for two very similar sounds.

Etruscan mirror, representing "Phuphluns", "Semele", and "Apula"—Bacchus, Semele, and Apollo.

480

The Italians and Germans also do not have a separate character for the Slovene **z;** they would write the Slovene word *zemlja* as *semlja.* Perhaps there is meaning also in that the first **s** is written in reverse.

A special problem for Lejeune is the letter **č** which is written as double **c.** Since he does not know what to do with this **cc,** he simply skips it.

From the first four letters Lejeune makes the name **Luks** with the explanation that it corresponds to Latin *Lucius,* but his explanation is hypothetical. He has no way of knowing that this is a name or that it is a Latin name. The second name is **Mel(i)nks.** To facilitate the pronunciation he adds the letter **i.** The third name **Gaijos** also has a pronunciation problem; we could perhaps say Gajos (Gayos) but not Gai-jos. There are three **i**'s which cannot be overlooked, and they harmonize with the word **haji.** There is also a question of whether the sound is **g** or **h.** They are very similar and the Veneti used the same character for both. In Tolmin area a sound between **g** and **h** is used. In Rhaetian script, which is almost the same as the Venetic, this character meant only **h** (see *Die Räter als sprachliches Problem/* The Rhaetians as a Linguistic Problem, Ernst Risch, Chur 1984). For a stronger **h** approximating the German **ch,** the Veneti had a different grapheme.

After Lejeune conjured up the three names, he had three letters left over and did not know what to do with them. If he had known the Slovene language he would have at once understood that they are two words: **ka** *kar* and **b** *bi.*

Bor's interpretations on the basis of the Slovene language and its dialects and other Slavic languages are difficult to contradict. They are well researched. Matej Bor made far-reaching discoveries which will challenge linguists for some time to come.

Opinions and Responses
Bogo Grafenauer and His Theories

Dr. Bogo Grafenauer is the most important theoretician involved in developing and establishing the theories about the late origin of Slavs, and the settlement of Slovenes in the area of the northern Adriatic and the eastern Alps in the 6th century. He presented his views in great detail as a supplement to the Slovene translation of *The History of Langobards* by Paulus Diaconus. I will bypass his philosophizing about historiography, the scientific methodology, and the unprofessional dilettantism of his antagonist, and look at the actual material he uses to support his views and theories.

1. **The beginning.** In Grafenauer's view the Slavic language formed as late as the 1st century A.D. In his opinion the Slavs are recognized as a people as late as 2000 years after the beginning of the Indo-European era. This view is sharply contradicted by the best historians, who consider Slavs as part of Indo-European development from its inception; e.g., Giacomo Devoto, *Origini indoevropee,* 1962. But even his interpretation falls short. In my view the Proto-Slavic language existed before the arrival of the Indo-Europeans, and was the basis on which the later central European languages developed.

2. **The Slovenes.** Even less acceptable are Grafenauer's assertions about the Slovenes, whom he recognizes as a nation only after the late Middle Ages. He considers them to be a tribe which came to the Alps in the 6th century. Against this image of history we posited the thesis—which we can defend—that the Slovenes are one of the oldest nations of Europe and have resided uninterruptedly in their land as descendants of Proto-Slavic Veneti. Grafenauer is using a variety of homespun props in support of his theories.

3. **Linguistic evidence.** The linguist, R. Nachtigal, claimed that palatalization in the Slovene language of **k-g-h** to **c-ž-s** started only in the 3rd century A.D. Grafenauer's conclusion is that the Veneti could not have brought this language with them 1000 years earlier. It is fairly certain that Veneti and Etruscans knew the softening of consonants; yet, if the softening started later, it is no proof that the Slovene language did not exist in earlier periods. We must also emphasize special characteristics of the Slovene language which speak of its ancient origin; for example, the **dual,** which could not have begun in the 1st or 3rd century. On the contrary, by then most languages had already lost it. The exceptions were Sanskrit, Lusatian Wendish, and Slovene.

4. **Archaeological sources.** Grafenauer denies the Slavic character of Lusatian

An excerpt of Frank J. Lausche's speech of November 28, 1967, in the United States Congress, stating that according to research by Dr. J. Felicijan in the Genesis of the Contractual Theory and the Installation of the Dukes of Carinthia (Koroška), *Thomas Jefferson initialed a page in Bodin's* Republic, *describing the Slovene ceremony of the investiture of dukes of Carinthia.* (The Slovenians from the Earliest Times, *Draga Gelt)*

culture. He is relying on the Czech archaeologist, Jury Neustupny, who claims that the bearers of Lusatian culture were related to the historical Celts. This is incorrect simply because of the commonly accepted view that the Celts have been known only since 500 B.C. Equally erroneous is his view that bearers of Urnfield culture were connected to the development of the Celts and Germans. Grafenauer rejects linguistic unity of the Urnfield culture on such a large territory. But his rejection is meaningless if we recognize that at least in some areas, the diffusion of Urnfield culture occurred on the foundation of the existing ancient Slavic language.

5. **The name Veneti for Slavs in the Baltic area.** Grafenauer states that there were some Veneti in the area who were assimilated by Indo-European groups, from which later evolved Slavs. The name Veneti was given to them by the Germans for this reason. It is difficult to understand his views. Slavs are documented

as the indigenous population in Germany predating Germans themselves, and the naming of Slavs as Veneti is a relatively late practice among Germans.

That Slavs existed in Germany in prehistoric times is substantiated by Lusatia and its ancient culture. There is other evidence. Firstly, between Berlin and Hanover there lived till the last century the indigenous farming population of Slavic Wends. A few were found and described by Joachim Berger in *Wendländisches Wanderbuch,* 1983. Secondly, the historian Nikolaus Haas *Geschichte des Slawen-Landes an der Aisch und den Ebrach Flüssen,* 1819, reports about Slavic population between Würzburg and Nürnberg, saying that they were the original population of Germany in the opinion of scholars. Thirdly, under the caption "Wenden" are a variety of reports in *Allgemeine Deutsche Real-Enzyklopädie für die Gebildeten Stände,* Leipzig 1855, about Slavs living (not just arriving) in several localities in 6th century Germany. They had a number of names. He mentions in the area of Mecklenburg Botriten (Bodrici) "ein mächtiges Volk" (a powerful people) who had their own kings. Wilzens lived along the sea, and there were the "Rhetarians whose ruling house was since 1181 related to Germany". The German historian Erich Röth justifiably advances the question on the title page of his book *Sind wir Germanen?/* Are we Germans? He answers with the subtitle *Ende eines Irrtums/* The End of a Fallacy. He considers the Veneti, whom he calls Illyrians, to be the oldest nation of Europe.

6. **Written sources.** From among written sources Grafenauer cites Roman historian Tacitus, who mentions the Veneti as a people who lived from the Carpathian Mountains to the Baltic Sea, but he is not sure whether to count them among Germans or Sarmatians; this suggests his knowledge of the area was minimal. The only other source mentioned is the geographer Ptolemy (2nd century A.D.) who refers to the Veneti as "a very big nation" on the "Venetic Gulf". This is all he offers from ancient sources. What do we learn from this? We learn that

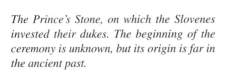

The Prince's Stone, on which the Slovenes invested their dukes. The beginning of the ceremony is unknown, but its origin is far in the ancient past.

484

both authors called a big nation in the north "Veneti". This was probably because they knew about their relation with the Adriatic Veneti through the Amber Road, or the connection on the sea between the Baltic and Brittany where Caesar mentions Veneti.

In 1902 Niederle wrote: "Those Baltic Veneti/Wends from ancient sources are unquestionably Slavs, but only those on the Baltic." His opinion was accepted by all historians without question. Can they prove that only Baltic Veneti are entitled to their name?

The next report about Slavs presents them with their own name (Greek: Sklavinoi, Latin: Sclaveni) and belongs to the 6th century A.D. Grafenauer states that Procopius mentions Slavs along the Danube in the first half of the 6th century. Does he not know that Procopius mentions many old fortifications which were ordered restored by Emperor Justinian? Among them were several Slavic names, although adapted to foreign pronunciation: Bregedaba (Breg deber), Gribo (Hrib), Borbreg (Vrh brega), Bre (Breg), Debre (Deber), Rakoule (Rakovlje), Millareka (Mila or Mala reka). Obviously, there was a Slavic speaking population in the area much before that time regardless of whether they are called Veneti or Illyrians. The claim that Slavs resided till the 6th century only beyond the Carpathian Mountains is meaningless.

Historian Jordanes, who wrote around 550, mentions the Veneti and Slavs with names Sclavini and Antes. Grafenauer knows about the Slavic community from Romania to the Visla River, but he is silent about Jordanes's "Sclavini" who settled in the area between the mouth of the Sava River and the Danube delta. In addition, Jordanes does not make a distinction between Sclavini and Veneti, and states that the people who were called Sclavini existed earlier under different names. Grafenauer should take this into account; he should not look for them only under the name Sclavini.

The most important source for Grafenauer is *The History of Langobards*, in spite of the fact that he never mentions the arrival of Slovenes or Slavs. Grafenauer's views are based on erroneous interpretations of some of Diaconus's texts.

There are other historical sources from the time of the supposed settlement of the Slovenes but they are carefully avoided by Grafenauer. I will remind the reader only of the biography of St. Columban. Its writer is an abbot, a learned man; he writes in northern Italy where the Veneti were well known, so there could have been no mistake about the people and the name. When he mentions the Slovenes of Noricum, he calls them Veneti, whose secondary name was Slavs, "Veneti qui et Sclavi dicuntur". This statement is so convincing that all arguments presented by Grafenauer and his co-workers have very little meaning.

7. **Toponymy.** Grafenauer admits the value of toponymy only when it is subjected to microscopic analysis. Clear and direct connections of toponyms to a particular language are for him unacceptable, presumably for fear they may undermine his theory. He asks: "How is it possible to expect a language and the names developed therein to remain unchanged through the space of three millenniums?" Why not? What about the Basque language? Are not the similarities between Sanskrit, Slovene and other European languages very old, yet provable? Even more easily provable are the many Slovene toponyms from pre-Roman times; however, this is systematically avoided by Dr. Grafenauer for fear that it would irrevocably damage his theory. The true intention of our historian is clearly indicated by his insistence that the toponyms can be compared only to the language of those people who are historically proven for the given area. According to his theory, there were no Slovenes in northern Italy, so there must be no Slovene toponyms in that area regardless of how obviously Slovene they are. For the Roman period he admits only Venetic toponyms in northern Italy, in Dalmatia the Illyrian, in Noricum and Slovenia the Celtic, although he does not know any of these languages.

8. **The name Veneti/Wends.** Grafenauer has no explanation for the name Veneti, but he rejects having any connection with Slavs, except those along the Baltic coast. As proof he mentions Caesar, who considered Celtic Bretons to be Veneti. According to Grafenauer these can be counted among Veneti, but Slavs cannot. There is a good reason for this—if Slavs were admitted, then Slovenes would have to be admitted and that he wants to prevent at any cost. Yet, it was precisely the Slovenes who were called Veneti in 615 (Vita St. Columbani). We should note that the Romans did not differentiate between Celts and Veneti; they named the large Bodensee Lacus Venetus, although it was in the centre of the Celtic cultural area. The report by the Greek historian Polibius (2nd century B.C.) that the Celts spoke a different language than the Veneti should not be taken too seriously; he probably knew neither of them. It is also probable that after three centuries of roaming around Europe the Celts developed their own dialect, in spite of the fact that they originated in the Venetic culture.

Grafenauer's insinuation that the name Veneti is not related to Slavs in origin or meaning we answer with the thesis that Veneti were the source of Slavic language in the new Indo-European form. I add that unless due consideration is taken for the time and place of the first appearance of the name Veneti, we cannot resolve its fundamental meaning. Homer was the first to use the name; later it was diffused (through the Romans) in its Latinized form first among the Adriatic Veneti and later in central Europe. There is no evidence that the name was known in central Europe before the advent of the Romans.

One of the old Slovene customs was the deliberation of village elders under the linden tree. (G. Caprin, Alpi Giulie, 1985)

9. **Many "nations" in the eastern Alps.** To draw attention away from the Venetic (Slovene) population in the eastern Alps, Grafenauer speaks of the many nations of this area. He makes extensive efforts to prove that there were no names in the eastern Alps which could be linked to **Slavs** or **Veneti.** The dedication tablets from Štalenska gora (Magdalensberg) Carinthia contain names of eight groups of inhabitants which are considered by our historian to be separate tribes with separate ethnic backgrounds, although it is clear that the names represent localities and not tribes or nations: **Ambidraves** from the Drava River region, **Norici** from Noreia, the capital and its environs, **Ambilici** from the Bela or Bila River Valley, **Ambisonti** from the Soča (Aesontius) River Valley, **Taurisci** from Upper Carniola, and **Carni** from eastern Friuli, and so on. It is incredible that Grafenauer thinks that every valley was a separate nation with separate language. In reality they were all Veneti listed according to their districts.

10. **The destruction of Church organization in Noricum** was for official historians an obvious proof of the arrival of Slovenes. Two written sources are presumed to speak of this. In the synodal record of 579 at Gradež/Grado there are signatures of Bishop Johannes from Celeia, and Bishop Patricius from Emona; signatures of bishops from Poetovia and Virunum are missing. Grafenauer concludes that the two dioceses perished in the first thrust of Slavs from the north. Ten years later, in a report about religious conflicts in Istria, Bishops Johannes

and Patricius are mentioned, but without dioceses. According to Grafenauer this means the bishops were refugees, their dioceses Celeia and Emona having fallen in the meantime to the advancing Slavs.

These are no more than personal interpretations. There is no doubt that the mentioned dioceses collapsed, but the reason was the gradual withdrawal of the Romans, who represented the bulk of Christian congregations in Noricum. When the Christians departed, the dioceses dissolved. The two sources present the case very well. There was no violent persecution of Christians and subsequent fleeing of bishops—such violence would have been recorded. Silence is the most eloquent proof that dissolution of the dioceses cannot be attributed to an arrival of pagan Slavs, but is rather a proof of normal developments at the time when the Romans were leaving Noricum. In Istria, where the Byzantines ruled, the dioceses remained intact.

11. **The destruction of old cities of Noricum** cannot prove the settlement of a new nation; there are too many possible causes for their destruction. We should not forget the many armies that passed through the area, such as the Gotts and the Huns, who certainly would not have spared Roman cities. The excavated city of Carnuntum near Vienna reveals the layout of the cities of that period; they were relatively small centres, not comparable to a modern concept of a city. The cities served only the occupation forces. The native population had no need of them—it had its own centres.

12. **The indigenous population**. Historians have tried in a variety of ways to explain the question of indigenous population. Some have insisted that after the withdrawal of the Romans to Italy all these territories were unpopulated, and others state that the indigenous people at the same time fled to Italy and Bavaria, but they have no evidence. Yet others state that inasmuch as there is no trace of native population, it must have been annihilated by the Slovenes. Grafenauer's theory is a mixed bag so to speak; according to him part of the indigenous population fled, and part stayed to ensure the cultural and economic continuity. The latter were to have been the Ladins (Romanized Celts) called Vlahi or Lahi (Ger. Welsche). Slovenes know the word through a few place-names, but mainly through the naming of Italians. When this term came into use is unknown. It is possible that our predecessors used this name for Romans who stayed in Slovene lands. It is certain the name Vlahi did not belong to the indigenous population; if that were the case, Vlahi would be considered as the indigenous population of all Germanic and Slavic lands where the name is used. Its origin is the Celtic tribal name Volcae.

The German historian Gerndt states in his *Vierbergelauf,* p. 109, that in Carinthia the village population preserved its native non-Romanized language through the centuries of Roman rule. As an example, he offers the history of the Carinthian folk custom "Vierbergelauf", which has been preserved from antiquity.

Regardless of contrary evidence, our historian Dr. Grafenauer continues to present Vlahi as the indigenous inhabitants of Slovene lands; in his words, they "had a very important place in the cultural development of Slovenes." Just how remote from reality this statement is can be seen in the fact that the Slovene language has virtually no words of Latin origin; yet, wherever newcomers established themselves they could not avoid adopting elements from the indigenous population. The Langobards completely disappeared in the indigenous population, and Hungarians who occupied part of Slovene Pannonia took on many Slovene words. It is impossible to imagine that the highly developed Roman culture or indigenous Romanized population would succumb to the primitive Slavs.

Objections of a Historian

The Slovene historian, Dr. Rajko Bratož, made an effort to contradict the indigenous status of Slovenes and their descendancy from the Veneti in the *Primorske novice* Oct. 28, 1994. To make open statements for the media is rare for an opponent of the "Venetic theory". I responded in the same paper on Feb. 17, 1995:

Dr. Bratož: We have not even one document in the Venetic language from late antiquity.

Answer: It is not necessary that there be documents from that particular period when we have many from the earlier period, which clearly show the presence of the Venetic language in Slovene lands. The inscriptions from Idrija pri Bači and Negova are very important evidence. From a later period, we have interpretations of Slovene words from St. Jerome, and pages of the book that were in all probability written by Jerome himself in the 4th century in the Slovene idiom spoken in the Karst and Istria areas at that time. To this we should also add the document from Čedad (Cividale), Friuli; that is, the inscription of the Langobard King Ratchis, written in old Venetic style *in continuo,* and understood only on the basis of the Slovene language.

Dr. B.: The inhabitants of these areas were literate, and left us some literary works and inscriptions in the Latin language.

Answer: These literary works were not left by the population; rather, they were left by men of distinction from among the Roman colonizers, including their bishops. The population was mostly illiterate, and what was written for home use on perishable materials could not survive.

Dr. B.: Nothing—and this I would like to underline twice—has been preserved in the Venetic language.

A helmet from Negova near Maribor, Slovenia, with a Venetic inscription which can be read only with the help of Slovene, a clear indication that the Slovene language was present in that area during pre-Roman times.

Answer: The important thing here is the question of why nothing has been preserved—although, as I already stated it is not true that nothing has been preserved. If there were no inscriptions in Venetic, it would only mean that Latin was enforced as the language of public use, a condition that held sway in all of Europe even after the fall of the Roman Empire.

Dr. B.: If the "Venetic theory" were true, and if we had an ethnic relationship of culture and language here, then in late antiquity, after several centuries of development, a literary language would have emerged.

Answer: Instead of saying, after several centuries of development, you should have said, after several centuries of oppression. How could the Venetic language have developed when Latin was imposed and enforced? Culture and literature can develop only in freedom.

Dr. B.: Theoretically, we would have had in late antiquity Venetic translations of the Bible, and Venetic religious writings, such as happened for example in Egypt and Syria.

Answer: Impossible. At that time, the liturgical and Biblical language in Europe, besides Greek and Hebrew, was Latin. These three languages were sanctified, as it were, and there was no possibility that yet another language would be permitted. We are well aquainted with the difficulties of Saints Cyril and

Methodius as late as the 9th century. In the Middle East, where Christianity spread earlier, the norms were different.

Dr. B.: The 4th century was in a way the spring of nations, when the various ethnic groups—who had their own culture and tradition—also affirmed their literature. We know nothing about the Veneti in this regard.

Answer: What spring of nations? Slovene lands were still under the iron hand of the Roman legions, whose duty was to keep the rebellious indigenous population in subjugation. In those conditions ethnic groups had little or no opportunity for cultural advancement.

Dr. B.: Besides, the "Venetic theory" rests on the assumption that the Veneti remained pagan, and that they drove the Christianized Romans out of the cities while they lived in the countryside and persisted in their pagan traditions.

Answer: The "Venetic theory" does not rest on this assumption, but on the reality that Slovene is the continuation of the Venetic language. The Veneti did not drive out the Romans; they left on their own accord, a fact well-illustrated by the biography of St. Severinus.

Dr. B.: This is a totally incorrect picture. The Slovene lands were in late antiquity completely Christianized.

Answer: Not true. Not even Italy was at that time completely Christianized. Regarding Slovenes, we have to distinguish between Noricum and other territories. When St. Valentine came around 440 to do missionary work in the area of Passau, he was driven out by the local people. After Noricum's independence in 568, the indigenous population re-established its own religion, and Christianization began only around 750. Circumstances were different among Slovenes south of the Alps under the Aquilean Patriarchate; there, Christianization continued as it did in Friuli. For this reason, there was no explicit missionary activity among our people south of the Alps—which would have been present if the Trans-Carpathian Slavs had arrived in this area in the 6th century.

Dr. B.: If there were still pagans around, they were in the cities among the intellectuals. The middle and lower classes were Christianized.

Answer: The opposite was true. The Christian faith established itself first in the cities. The word pagan *paganus,* is from *pagus*—village—and came into use during late antiquity. The pagans were therefore village people, people from the countryside.

Dr. B.: The "Venetic theory" is in direct opposition to the discoveries of our archaeology and history sciences.

Answer: On the contrary, archaeology gave us the Venetic inscriptions, the remarkable remains of the Slovene language from before two thousand years ago, and the valuable situlas—the pride of our ancestors. And history tells us that after the year 568 when the Byzantines left Inner Noricum, no one but the indigenous people ruled that land. Twenty-five years later these same people were able to repel the plundering intrusions of the Bavarians. History (Paulus Diaconus) tells us that at the end of the 6th century the Slovenes had their own state which was the envy of Bavarians. I would like to ask the historians who insist that the Slovenes came in the 6th century, did they come as a band of gypsies or as conquerors? If as gypsies, then how could they have established in such a short time a state that was the envy of their neighbours, and if they came as conquerors, with whom did they do battle? What happened with the previous inhabitants? How were they able to populate the large area from the Adriatic to the Danube in the span of one generation?

Dr. B.: The reference to the influence of German research is not very useful here, because the results of French, Italian, and English research are the same.

Answer: Who invented the Trans-Carpathian theory? Who started to denigrate the Slavs? Who destroyed the indigenous Venetic people in central Germany? The French, the English, and other history writers merely copied German anti-Slavic inventions; however, there were also some true researchers, like the Italian Giuseppe Sergi, and the German Erich Röth. Our deepest respects go to them; they were the pioneers of the "Venetic theory". Our thesis is in full agreement with their views.

Dr. B.: Your theory, if I understand it right, embodies a wish to establish in Slovene lands an affirmation of its history and Slovene presence from the beginning of civilization.

Answer: Yes, absolutely, and more! The essence of the "Venetic theory" is to correct the wrongs committed against the Slovene nation—the disfiguring of its origin and its early history.

Dr. B.: As a historian of antiquity, I am familiar with the various inscriptions on the gravestones from that period, and it seems to me that the translations of some inscriptions into Slovene—especially when considering the contents—are bordering on the absurd.

Answer: Could Dr. Bratož give us a different, yet authoritative translation? If he cannot do that, then his objections are meaningless. The texts have to be translated as they are. Some of Bor's translations are even supported by pictorial representations on the gravestones themselves. Besides, the Venetic inscriptions are found not only on gravestones, but on numerous other articles.

Dr. B.: I am afraid that foreign observers will consider the "Venetic theory" as a reflection of some cultural complex of ours.

Answer: The most portentous complex the Slovenes have is the Trans-Carpathian theory. Whoever rejects it is raising the confidence of the Slovene nation. This has been proven by the latest articles, written by distinguished Italians on the occasion of our presentation of the Italian edition of this book *I Veneti progenitori dell'uomo europeo* in Padova, Vicenza, and Verona. The receptions in the three cities were extremely cordial. I thank Dr. Bratož for this opportunity to respond to some objections, though only briefly, due to lack of space.

Objections of a Linguist

As a representative of the linguists who oppose the relation of the Slovene and Venetic languages, Prof. Rado L. Lencek of New York (Columbia University) responded with the article, *The linguistic premises of Matej Bor's Slovene-Venetic theory* (Slovene studies 12/1, 1990, p. 75–86). Below is Bor's reply, originally printed in the book *Z Veneti v novi čas,* Ljubljana 1990.

"What should I say regarding this criticism from New York? Above all, that its negative position does not differ from those written in Ljubljana. The only difference is in the tone; it is written in an academic and decent language. This I cannot say about all reviewers in Ljubljana. Unfortunately, Lencek is not considering my studies in their logical and investigative approach; rather, he views them mostly, or even entirely, from the position of agreement or disagreement with official Venetology. Since there is disagreement, except in some particulars and in the evaluation of the majority of graphemes, Lencek cannot accept my work as worthy of a thorough study.

That Lencek did not find it necessary to thoroughly examine the work he was reviewing as a linguist is obvious; many instances show this. Let me look at a few of them.

In the book *Veneti naši davni predniki,* I wrote that the Veneti seldom left out vowels, as Etruscans did. Yet, on the Ateste grammar tablets we find, for example, **bga** instead of boga (gen. sing); this particular abbreviation was used also in the Old Church Slavic. There is also **pširiš** instead of poširiš. My critic includes among these abbreviations **jaj**, convinced that I see in it the Slovene *jahaj*—not so. In my interpretation jaj belongs to those words I consider close to Baltic languages: the Latv. *jat*—to ride (on horseback), to go. A similar vocal (not graphic) abbreviation we find in some Serbo-Cr. dialects *jaat*—to ride; Slov. *jahati*. In Russ. *jehatь*—to travel, to ride.

The next instance is in regard to the word **mak**, which is in my view act. past participle of to move, to displace; Slov. *premaknivši*. Lencek says that I came to this interpretation "presumably, by way of an incorrect analogy with the pattern of Russian *mjaknut*—to soften (Slov. *omehčati*, note M. B.), past indicative *mjak,* etc."

In the glossary of words I give only the Slovene translation, but if he had looked at the linguistic analyses appended to the texts, he would have seen next to the word **mak**—*premaknivši, makniti, premakniti.* He would have discovered that the active past participle was in full agreement with the form and meaning in this palindrome and the same participle in the OCS *maknǫti, makъ;* Slov. *premakniti, premaknivši;* same as *dvignǫti, dvigъ;* Slov. *dvignivši.* In the written form the difference is only in the OCS letter ъ which was of course not used by the Veneti.

The explanation is clear and comprehensive, yet, Lencek inserted the Russian word *mjaknut*—to soften. I wonder why. Did he want to inform the reader about my "unprofessional" method? If this was his intention he has obviously missed the mark. I think this is simply a lack of knowledge of the material on his part. If this represents his professionalism, then I would rather stay as I am—"unprofessional".

As an example of my "naive" explanations, my critic offers the Venetic **kolassiko** (Ca 1), which I translate into Slov. *koleselj*—type of carriage. But he does not mention *koleska,* which can be found in Pleteršnik as well as in my commentary (Slov. edition of *Veneti naši davni predniki,* p. 319).

Besides **kolassiko** there is in the inscriptions also its synonym (instr. sing.) **kala(s)ijoj** (Es 122 bis). In the Venetic this word was fem. with a fem. suffix **kalasija*.

The next example is the Venetic **vesces,** which I translate as—up; Slov. *kvišku.* I also give its Slov. synonym *viškej.* This can be found in Pleteršnik and in my glossary. But this is not all. I also gave the obvious synonym **vesce,** and next to it the Slov. *viški, kvišku;* this too is from Pleteršnik with the meaning: *in die Höhe, aufwärts*—height, upwards. In Slovenia this is an archaism now, but Bohorič (16th century) still used it. So did Megiser.

There is also dissatisfaction on Lencek's part with my explanation of the inscription on the bronze situla from Škocjan: **osti jarej**—Stay young! Stay well! Slov. *ostani jar, mlad, zdrav!* He objected that the root **sti** discovered by Miklošič along with **sta** in **stati** could apply to the Venetic **osti.** Also my reference to *oprosti* is unacceptable to him. In regard to the word **jarej,** there is no reason to presume that the Venetic adjective **jar** (yar) did not have the suffix -**ej.** We have in Carinthia words like *dedej, sedej, ljubej,* etc. It is true these are nouns (also adjectives), but why could **jarej** not be a noun? Vigorous, healthy, young—*jar,* "jarec"—although, I think this is not a noun, but rather an adjective with a suffix, required by the short word **jar.** At any rate, what could be more natural than to read on a wine jug or bucket "Stay well (young)!" particularly when I offered a detailed and comprehensive account of each word—as in all my transcriptions— which my critic has obviously not read?

Regarding betatism or interchangeability of **v** and **b**, it is true that in Slovene dialects of the coastal areas, this change occurs only at the beginning of the word; however, the Venetic language knew betatism also before the last vowel.

Since betatism is unknown in the dialect of Upper Carniola, we can presume that the place-names **Bodešče**, **Bodovlje** in the northwest part of Slovenia are of ancient Venetic origin. Bodešče was once Vodešče from *voda*—water; this is substantiated by the location of the place at the confluence of Sava Bohinjka and Sava Dolinka Rivers. The same is true of Bodovlje from Vodovlje which is by the Sora River.

We know that betatism was used in the 4th century in the area of Aquileia. In the ruins of a basilica from that period a mosaic floor has been preserved. It contains an inscription dedicated to one of the donors: **CYRIACE VIBAS**— Cyriac lives in God. The Latin *vivas* was written vibas. As betatism is unknown in Latin and Celtic, it must have entered from the local Venetic language. Betatism has been preserved in western Slovene dialects to this day.

There is no need to talk about the "puzzling" **jekupetaris**: I gave a detailed explanation earlier that it was a Proto-Slavic active past participle from **jekupetarit**. "Die auf -i- auslautenden Verbalstämme haben aber in den ältesten Quellen gewöhnlich die Form auf -sis; ihr **i** geht vor dem Formans in -j- über..." *Handbuch der altkirchenslavischen Sprache*, para. 68, Leskin. The form **jekupetaris** is then from the period when the **i** before the formant had not yet changed to **j**. I interpret this word as being a compound of the still familiar **jek**

Etruscan stone with three heads from 5th century B.C., Orvieto. The meaning of the sculpture may well be linked to the Venetic Trumužijad.

and **petati**; they are both ours and recorded in Pleteršnik. **Jek** is of the same origin as **jekat**. This interpretation is supported by several variations of this verb, particularly **jepetaris**. My critic thinks the word is related to Latin *equus*. There is no need to make additional explanations regarding the Venetic punctation. But I will say that there are too many exceptions to fit punctation "law" as expounded by Vetter; besides, it is obvious that dots and short lines were added to less conspicuous letters, and sometimes to empty spaces between letters, and now and then to separate a syllable or preposition. This has been explained in the book. Lencek does not offer any explanation regarding his opposition to my interpretation; he merely refers to the established authorities and repeats their views. He does this as if my views regarding punctation were not part of the investigation of this particular problem.

Although Prof. Lencek knows the Slovene language, he blindly believes R.S. Conway and others who say that the diphtong -**oi** is always a suffix for different genitives, or as some think, datives. However, no one thought that at times this diphtong is actually a suffix -**oj**; for example for various imperatives, or a suffix for the nominative sing. -**oj** in some Slavic languages, or a suffix for instrum. sing. in adjectives and nouns. The Slovene poet Anton Aškerc used these suffixes regularly, not under the influence of the Russian but his native dialect. (See *Unsere Vorfahren Die Veneter*, p. 282). As evidence that the case with -**oi** is much more involved, I will present an instructive and interesting inscription (discovered in 1971) which confuses Venetologists a great deal. If it is a votive object then the giver must have a nominative suffix, but according to official explanations it does not because it ends in -**oi**, the same as the accusative. Who is the giver and who is the recipient? If we follow the official theory the inscription cannot be explained, but following my views it can be explained with relative ease. The official interpretation: **Vivoi alialekve murtuvio atisteit.** In my interpretation:

BIVOJ OLIAL JE K BE
Živ   prepeval je   kdorkoli

MURTUVOJ ATISTEIT
mrtev se   iztrezni

In Slovene: Kdor je živ prepeval (alil) pijano, se mrtev iztrezni.
In English: While alive he sang intoxicated; dead, he will be sober.

bivoj (betatism)—live, living; Slov. *živ, bivajoč*, from *biti*.
olial—sang intoxicated; Slov. *aliti, alim*—to sing poorly, as those who are intoxicated (Pohorje), Bezlaj, Etim. Dic.

496

je (from beginning **e**)—is; Slov. *je.* This form is known in OCS *estъ.*

k in many inscriptions **ki**—who; Slov. *kdor, kdo.*

be—he was; 3rd per. imper. OCS *be.* Possibly an interjection **ve** preserved as an archaism in Slov. (jetzt, Plet.). *baš ve* (ravnokar)—just now, or **kve**—who; Slov. kdor, kdo.

murtuvoj—dead; Slov. *mrtev;* Russ. *mertvyj* (dial. mertvoj).

atisteit—to regain one's senses, to be in one's right mind again; Slov. *se strezni;* OCS *tъštъ;* Slov. *tešč*—(on an) empty stomach, sober. Ger. *nüchtern, nicht betrunken* (Wolf dict.).

This is according to Lejeune's *Manuel de la langue Vénetè,* Heidelberg 1974, p. 75, slightly more detailed, as Lencek evidently did not read the exposition of this inscription.

Another of the many examples showing that the inscriptions are not only names as Venetologists claim, is the one I entitled "Drunkard from Kanjevoj" (Bl 1). It is on a lead bucket. As explained by Canon Lucio Dogliono: "There were, besides the bucket I found, two more similar ones, found near a mill in Cimoláisu in Friuli, both having the same inscription as I had seen on mine. I am certain of this." (Pellegrini—Prosdocimi: *La lingua Venetica* p. 450). It is questionable that there would be the same names on three buckets found in different places.

There is another indication that speaks against the hypothesis that only names appear on jars, even wine jars. There are too many of some names as compared with others; for example, those in connection with **ougon** (officially Fougon) or **virem** (officially Frem). There are dozens of them.

Let him not be offended, but I find no satisfaction or necessity to continue to relate his opinions and his "thorough" examinations. He disappointed me not only with his professional bias and the way he familiarized the reader with the author's material, but also how he approached the document which means so much to Slovenes and other Slavs—the Ateste alphabetical tablets, or as I call them (due to their contents), the grammatical tablets. It seems Lencek is the only Slovene linguist who tried to examine them. Unfortunately he did it through Conwayan glasses, thus, he was unable to see in them anything of importance; however, what we can forgive a Conway or Pellegrini or Lejeune, we find difficult to forgive a linguist who is a Slovene. How is it possible that sixteen variations of the verb **jekat**—which is still in use today—tell him nothing? Lencek's concerns about the beginning **je** (**ye**s) are totally without foundation if we suppose that the Venetic was a Slavic language, and there is no doubt about this as we can see from the Ateste tablets and numerous other inscriptions. It is typical for Slavic languages that very few words start with **e**—mainly in foreign words. This means my reading of the beginning **e** as **je** is justified; compare Russian **e** at the beginning of many words.

Further, as we know, the Ateste tablets were of a didactic nature, and cannot be considered as votive objects. They were produced in the classical period of Venetic literacy as revealed by their exceptional graphic form, the finely shaped letters obviously written by skilful hand. At that time the Veneti knew the importance of these tablets; they made copies in wax or clay impressions, indicating a considerable interest in these tools of literacy. Later, due to decadence, it is possible they became objects invested with magical properties by illiterate people. The tablets from Ateste were originally intended for educational purposes as we can see from the contents. It is for this reason that I ask myself whether it is possible that names were written on these objects. That we find similar or same words also on gravestones is not unusual. The texts on the tablets were composed to meet the need for ritual sayings related to burial ceremonies and grave sites. In other words the similarity or sameness of words does not equate with same names; rather, it means similar word units, syntagmas and phrases.

The mildly ironic statements about what I have uncovered in various inscriptions, which according to Lencek are names, is a typical response from official historians and linguists. But I have good reasons for my hypothesis. There is no mistaking an appropriate inscription, be it on a wine jug or burial urn, whether it is a word of inspiration to the thirsty traveller or a ritual saying to protect against evil spirits. The Veneti very rarely used names in their inscriptions; in their burial customs they were quite different from their neighbours, the Etruscans.

The inconsistency of phonologists who read the grapheme of one vertical line **I,** sometimes as **h** and sometimes as **i**, does not disturb Lencek, but he is bothered by my reading of the grapheme which is very similar to Greek gama as voiced sibilant ϑ and the very similar unvoiced **h** as it occurs today in western Slovene dialects.

I wonder why Lencek finds my reading of ✗ as **d** strange; the official Venetologists read it as such. They transcribe it as **z** but read it as **d**. For example: **zoto**, read **doto**. The same grapheme was in my opinion also used for **dz**. For example: **do stidzei**—to the path (Ag 1).

The word that convinces linguists and my critic about the Latin origin of the Venetic language is **ego**. This is understandable; official Venetologists consider **ego** to be identical with the Latin *ego*. I am not the first linguist who doubted that this was a Latin word, but I am probably the first to discard the Latin connection. The Russians write this word exactly as was written by the Veneti, **ego**, and pronounce it as **jego** (yego)—him. The word is Proto-Slavic. There are to date more than twenty known examples of the word **ego**, and they all have the same meaning. I used letter **g** in transcribing Venetic soft-palate voiced sibilant γ to facilitate reading, as the study is intended also for the layman. Perhaps I should have

Reminding us of the Venetic belief in trinity is the ritual stone excavated at the top of Mt. Štalen (Magdalensberg) Carinthia.

collected all examples and printed them together; the reason I have not done so is lack of space. However, what I was not able to complete will be done by someone else when philology eventually frees itself of certain prejudices and the tendency to treat abstractly the living questions of language. Even a dead language like the Venetic, when approached without prejudice, yields a cross section of human verbal endeavour. There are sayings, spells, witty thoughts, at times with poetical meter and harmony and deep meaning.

The other word that disturbs my critic is **mego**. I confess that I too spent a considerable amount of time with it, but after a number of years of reading inscriptions with this word countless times, and comparing them with each other for meaning, contents, and syntax, I finally came to the conclusion that this is a nominativized accusative of the original personal pronoun **me** Slov. *jaz*—I— with a suffix -**go**. I was led to this conclusion by the thought that the original, Proto-Slavic nominative was not **az** (jaz) but **me**, which is found to this day in the Slovene language in all cases other than the dative. Later, for unknown reasons **az** replaced **me**. The Italian *me* and the English *me* are related to it.

I could go on and say more in support of my theory, but that will do no good when the critics are unable to examine the breadth of their own discipline with a fresh look. Instead they merely repeat what others have "discovered". The answers to Lencek's objections are found mainly in Part Two of this book, but also in a number of articles.

I presented a few criticisms to show that his understanding of the material is inadequate and especially that his opinion is biased. My linguistic thesis on the transition of the Venetic language from the Balto-Slavic and Proto-Slavic into

Slavic with Slovene elements, which should have represented the bulk of his response, was mentioned by Lencek only in a footnote in Slovene—without translation. This act represents in a nutshell the essence of his method and his attitude. He also failed to recognize that I did not consider the Venetic language from the middle of the first millennium B.C. to be Slovene. The latter developed from the Venetic and in the course of time received additional influences from the neighbouring Slavic peoples to the north, east and the south. In spite of this, the Slovene language is what it is, independent, with its own peculiarities precisely because it inherited elements from their Proto-Slavic forebears, the Veneti. To research the Venetic language in depth will be a considerable undertaking, and can succeed only when there is a new generation of linguists able to think openly, independently, and free of intellectual blinders."

A Mistaken Memorandum

After the independence of Slovenia in 1991, a group of Slovene historians published a memorandum to inform the world about the brave Slovenes who dared to resist the Yugoslav army and disabled it in ten days. Unfortunately, included in this memorandum were also pieces of information which do not correspond to reality. We find: "The hour of birth of the Slovene nation began in the second half of the 6th century, when the newly-arrived Slavs started to mix with the remnants of the Romanized local population. Around 630 there formed within the eastern Alps the oldest known Slavic state, Carantania. The Slovenes were known from the 9th to the 13th century as Carantanians—their earliest name."

Unbelievable! How is it possible to concentrate so much error, untruth, and misrepresentation of history in three sentences?

It is not true that the predecessors of Slovenes were Slavs who arrived in the 6th century from the Pripet Swamps or anywhere else. There is no proof and no historical record of this.

It is not true that these Slavs mixed with remnants of the Romanized indigenous population, because there was no Romanized indigenous population. Who could this Romanized indigenous population have been?

It is not true that Carantania was formed around 630. At that time King Samo's kingdom was formed—probably at Carantania's initiative.

It is not true that the earliest name for the Slovenes was Carantanians—and that only in the 9th century.

Let me briefly explain. The arrival of Slavs in the eastern Alps and the upper Adriatic in the 6th century is a fabrication by those who are ignorant of true history and those who want at all cost to deny the Slovenes the right of domicile in central Europe, in spite of the evidence that they resided since the Bronze Age on the lands they occupy now. Even the Italian researcher, Sergi, has recognized, on the basis of archaeological and linguistic research, that Slavs had been in Italy since the Bronze Age. This recognition is in complete agreement with the well-known distribution of Venetic Urnfield Culture.

The occupation of the eastern Alps and the upper Adriatic by Slavs in the second half of the 6th century would not have been possible simply because at the time the area was ruled by the Byzantines, who left the eastern Alps (Inner Noricum) in 568 due to the Langobard westward move. What happened in Inner Noricum at that time? Why was it not occupied by Bavarians? Probably because the Norici utilized the opportunity and declared independence, just as was done by the Rhaetians (without success—they were destroyed by the Ostrogoths).

Only 27 years after the departure of the Byzantines there is recorded in Inner Noricum a state with the name **Sclaborum provincia**. Who were the citizens of this state which was later called Carantania? The name itself tells us they were Slavs, but this does not mean there were no national distinctions among Slavs. In the biography of St. Columban from 615 these famous words appear: **Termini Venetiorum qui et Sclavi dicuntur**—the land of Veneti who are also called Slavs. This means their principal name was Veneti. The name Sclavi (Slavs) was secondary. The very important Fredegarii Chronicon from that time calls the Slovenes several times (!) Veneti or with the German variation **Winedi**, **Wenedi** or **Winidi**; we can see that "Carantanians" was not the earliest name for Slovenes.

Another question involves the Slovenes in Pannonia, in Lower Carniola, and in the Slovene littoral who did not belong to Carantania. When was the hour of their birth? And who were the people living in the littoral before the supposed arrival of the Slavs? Were they also only remnants of the Romanized population? If the backward Slavs mixed with the locals of high Roman culture, then the result should have been a mixture imbued with Roman culture and its language. But we know that in the Slovene language and culture there are no traces of Romanization.

The puzzle is solved by numerous remnants of the Slovene language from Roman and pre-Roman times, including the Venetic inscriptions. A good example is the inscription **osti jarej** (see Part Two). The other important element is the direction of the movement of the language boundary. If the Slovene language were moving with new invasions and settlement into Italian territory, then we would find numerous traces of indigenous language in Slovene territory and in the Slovene language. But that is not the case; the exception is a few toponyms from the time of Roman occupation, and even those are usually translations from the original Slovene (Venetic).

Meije—this mountain range is west of Monte Bianco; it constituted the approximate boundary of ancient Rhaetia. Its name has no meaning in the languages of the area, but in Slovene it means border. A similarity of meaning was transmitted through the Venetic language which was related to Rhaetian. The highest peaks in the range are Grand Pic de la Meije, 3987m, and Pic Central de la Meije. (Photo F. Francou, Briancon, Schrollverlag).

But there is a surprisingly large number of Slovene toponyms throughout northern Italy; and, while the Friulian Romance language was being formed, Slovene was the language of Friuli.

I think this is proof enough that the Slovene language existed in pre-Roman times; but with Romanization of the Veneti in Italy, the Slovene language was gradually moved towards the present language boundary between Slovenes and Italians. All this is easy to comprehend if we recognize that the Veneti were the predecessors of modern Slovenes.

If the Slovenes arrived at the doorstep of Aquilea (Oglej) in the 6th century A.D., it would have been a major event and it would have been reported, but there is no such report. Paulus Diaconus mentions Slavs who were in the service of the Avars and fought on the side of the Langobards in Istria (they were Balkan Slavs who were then under Avar rule), which means he is not writing about settlement of Slavs, but rather about soldiers and their campaigns against the Byzantines.

New Directions
The Ancient Slavs

When and how did the first signs of social life appear in central Europe; that is, social life that was above hunter-gatherer struggle for survival? When did man start producing his food by cultivating land and breeding domestic animals? The date of permanent settlement also depends on the answer to this question. Permanent settlement brings about new family relationships, social and economic progress and also new spiritual development, with a corresponding enlargement of vocabulary.

The earlier researchers placed the beginning of permanent settlement in central Europe in the Late Stone Age (Neolithic) about 3000 B.C., but later discoveries show social activities which suggest permanent settlement much earlier. I will mention only three discoveries.

In 1992 the archaeologists discovered in Bavaria near Abensberg on the Danube a large number of **flintstone mines**, dating from around 5000 B.C. Flintstone was the most precious raw material at that time; the best tools were produced from it. Large-scale trade in flintstone and tools resulted, which suggests permanent settlement and a relatively prosperous social life.

The second discovery is from 1993: the **body of a man found in the Tyrolean glacier Similaun** above the Ötz Valley, dating from 3300 B.C. His clothing and various objects found with him indicate a sophistication of social life impossible to imagine for that period. His tools show that he belonged to a small band of the Ramedello culture in the southern part of the Alps. However, the same tools were also found north of the Alps, which suggests communication between the two geographic areas.

The Ice Man's period corresponded with the end of the wide-spread central European Linear-pottery culture. Archaeology established for that period a transition into new forms of pottery, but this does not necessarily mean a change of population; the objects for daily use change from time to time within the same population. There is also the question of ethnicity and the language of Ramedello culture. The Ice Man belonged to the pre-Indo-European population in the Alpine region, which gradually moved with their herds higher into Alpine pastures, and was able to resist the assimilating forces of the Indo-Europeans. Their pre-Indo-European culture was the foundation for the formation of the Veneti in the Lusatian and Urnfield cultures.

The man from the Tyrolean glacier.

The Ice Man was affectionately named "Ötzi" by Austrians. The Viennese author Dr. Günther Nenning wrote in Viennese dialect in one of his articles: "Ötzi war a Slovene"—Ötzi was a Slovene. These words later became the title of one of the chapters in the book on the subject, *Der Mann aus dem Eis* (Verlag Orac, Wien-München-Zürich). He added: "The Veneti were—according to Slovene researchers—the ancestors of Slavs and particularly the ancestors of Slovenes."

The third discovery is the **Script from the Vinča culture**, 6000–4000 B.C.

From linguistic research we know that the original forms of a language stay for a long time even after another language has been superimposed. J. Pokorny *Substrattheorie und Urheimat der Indogermanen*/ Substratum Theory and the Ancient Homeland of Indo-Europeans, Vienna 1936, found in the Irish language a residue of Hamitic languages from North Africa. This indicates the possibility of a common language in the Middle Stone Age (Mesolithic). Danish linguist, H. Möller published in Copenhagen in 1911 the *Vergleichendes Indogermanisch—semitisches Wörterbuch*/ The Indo-European—Semitic Comparative Dictionary, in which we find many roots of words which are still in use in Indo-European and Semitic languages and which point to a pre-Indo-European connection between these languages. For this reason alone we should not exclude the possibility of finding traces of pre-Indo-European language in Europe itself; for example in the Linear-pottery culture. The language of that period, which probably had a limited vocabulary, was relatively wide-spread and could not have completely disappeared.

What language did the Ice Man and his contemporaries speak before the arrival of Indo-Europeans? So far no linguist has seriously examined this question. Is it for fear the results may be undesirable? My view is that in the millenniums before the arrival of Indo-Europeans, the principal language of central Europe was **the Proto-Slavic.** This can be inferred from the following evidence: the similarity between the Basque and Slavic languages, the similarity between the Sanskrit and Slavic languages, and the script from the Vinča culture.

The similarity of Basque and Slavic languages. Being a pre-Indo-European language, the Basque is in the best position to give us an insight into the period before the arrival of the Indo-Europeans. It has been archaeologically proven that Indo-Europeans did not cross the Pyrenees. Their Corded-pottery culture met strong resistance from the Bell-Beaker culture/ Glockenbecherkultur; thus, the Basques were able to keep their pre-Indo-European culture and language.

Various linguists have examined the elements of similarity between the Basque and Slavic languages, particularly the Slovene language, which has best preserved the ancient characteristics. Their studies were not limited to similarity of

From the 6th to 4th millenniums B.C. the territory between the Sava, Drava and Danube Rivers was under the influence of Vinča culture. At the beginning of the 3rd millennium Vučedol culture emerged in the same territory with the first appearance of the steppe people who initiated the Indo-European period. By the end of the 3rd millennium, the influence of Vučedol is proven as far as Trieste and Prague. A family or group grave from Vučedol culture was discovered in 1985 near Eisenstadt, Austria.

words, but included syntax and phonetics. Here I present only those words which will be accessible to the average reader without additional research. The Basque word is followed by the Slovene word with translation:

Aizkora sekira—axe
zaku žakelj—burlap bag
bota obutev—footwear
korru krog—circle
ata vrata—door
azkenez konec—end
bizi biti—to be
zitu žito—grain
tarratu trgati—to pick
zalicka žlička—small spoon
zapo žaba—frog
erreka reka—river
gar žar—glow
sara stara—old (f.)
zilbot život—body
xeekatu sekati—to chop
ganditu ganiti—to move
leka leča—lentils
pikarda pikčast—dotted, spotted

goritu goreti—to burn
gora gori—up
goren gornji—upper
izreka izrek—saying
lotu lotiti se—to start
masitu mazati—to oil, to smear
nagatu nagajati—to annoy
ixek jezik—tongue
ixekatu jezikati—to chatter
hiratu hirati—wasting away
pikatu pikati—to prick
elikatu olikati—to polish
oker okoren—clumsy
erditu roditi—to give birth
ondoren ondoten—of that place
eskatu iskati—to search
opor odpor—resistance
palanka planka—board

These similarities could have originated only in the period before the arrival of Indo-Europeans; there were no later contacts between Basque and Slavic languages, not even during the Urnfield Migration when the Proto-Slavic in Indo-European form was disseminated.

Some discoveries were made recently by Spanish scientists who found through genetic analysis a link between the inhabitants of Spain and North Africa. Through the study of the HLA gene, they discovered that the Basques and Berbers had a common origin. (Reported in the daily *El Pais*, Nov. 24, 1995).

The Berbers, numbering about 5 million, are the remnant of the original North African population which was not assimilated by the Arabs. Their distant kinship with the Basques is also suggested by archaeological discoveries. In the Middle Stone Age (Mesolithic) starting around 10,000 B.C., the cultures of central and western Europe and North Africa were uniform. The article in *El Pais* also mentions linguists who see similarities between the Basque and Berber languages. A place-name in central Morocco indicates this ancient connection between the two shores of the Mediterranean. The little town of **Zagora** can be identified with both Basque and Slovene languages: *gora* is generally Slavic and means mountain; *za* is a preposition and means beyond—the town beyond the mountain—which in fact it is. There are other names with Slavic or Slovene meanings:

zveza—connection, junction; **Golan** *gol*—barren, treeless; **Tabor** *tabor*—stronghold, open-air meeting. At the end of the Ice Age, the climate of the Sahara changed and many people were forced to relocate. Some went to Europe where they mixed with the survivors of the Ice Age (Berber/Basque connection). Gradually new languages formed. The similarity of the Venetic, Slovene, Basque, Breton and Sanskrit languages suggests there was a Proto-Slavic language in Europe in the very distant past, before the arrival of the Indo-Europeans. This also indicates that Slovenes are one of the oldest nations in Europe.

    The similarity between Slavic and Sanskrit languages. Bor mentioned this a number of times, but the most thorough examination of the subject I have found to date are the lectures by Joseph J. Skulj, Toronto. A few of his findings follow.

    Sanskrit belongs to the Indo-European language group, its final stages having developed only after the arrival of Indo-Europeans in India. Although it has been a dead language for a long time, its position remains the same as that of the Latin in Europe; it continues to hold a place of importance in the area of culture, and especially in religion. Hinduism has its roots in the Sanskrit books, the Vedas, which have preserved the original Vedic Sanskrit unchanged. The word Veda means the same in Sanskrit as it does in Slovene—knowledge. The most important and oldest of these books is the **Rig-veda**, generally considered to have originated at the time of the arrival of Indo-Europeans in India, circa 1500 B.C. Skulj discovered that the majority of basic words in Rig-veda are related to Slovene. His findings are supported by the *Chambers Encyclopedia* in which the Aryan languages of India are considered as "Indo-Balto-Slavic languages". It has been established that the Balto-Slavic languages contain the oldest forms of Slavic, and are for this reason closest to Slovene, which also has special characteristics of the oldest Slavic language.

    As an example of similarity between Sanskrit and Slovene languages (see Slovene pronunciation table at the beginning of the book), I will cite a few words. The Sanskrit root, and the verb in 3rd person singular present tense, are followed by the Slovene infinitive of same or similar meaning. The English translation is directly from the Sanskrit:

lubh, lubhati	ljubiti	to desire greatly
smi, smayáti	smejati se	to smile
bhī, bhayate	bati se	to fear
priyátva	prijatelj	beloved
resh, reshate	režati se	to howl
ajījivat	oživeti	restore to life

jña, jānāti	znati	to know
ru, rauti	rjuti	to roar, cry aloud
pricchya	priča	to be asked or inquire after
tap, tápati	topiti	destroy by heat
div, dívyati	divjati	to play, sport, joke
stu, stavīti	slaviti	to praise, extol
stáva	slava	praise, eulogy
dur	duri	door
veśá	veža	house entrance, lobby
vár	varuh	water, pond, protector
klath	klati	to hurt, kill
krath, krathati	krotiti	to hurt
klav, klavate	klavrn	be afraid
vah, vahshyati	voziti	to transport, to convey
bhiyās	bojazen	fear
jīv, jīvati	živeti	to live
bhága	bog	gracious lord, supreme power
dā, dāti	dati	to give
trai, trayáti	trajati	to protect
budh, budhī	buditi	to wake
beś, beśati	bežati	to go
i, éti	iti	to go, flow
vaśin	važen	having power or authority
vid, vedati	vedeti	to know
bhávat	bivati	being, present
sūdayati	soditi	to settle
vāsá	vas	abode
vas, vásati	vasovati	to dwell, live
dám/dáma	dom	house, home
kota	koča	shed, hut
vār	varuh	water, pond, protector
ghorá	gorje	horror, frightful, terrible
sthānú, sthalnu	stalno	stationary, firm
himá	zima	snow, cold, winter
dáy, dáyate	dajati	to give
agni	ogenj	fire
curu	črv	intestinal worm
cit, cetati	čutiti	to perceive, care for
math, mathati	motiti	to trouble, disturb

han, ghnate	gnati	to strike, beat
oshta	usta	lip
karpata	krpa	patch, rag
hod, hodati	hoditi	to go
śvit, śvetate	svetiti	bright, white
tamā	tema	night
bal, balate	boleti	to hurt
prabudh, prabudyate	prebuditi	to wake up
man, manyati	meniti	to think
hita	hiter	running, speeding
brū, brāvīti	praviti	to speak, say
kās, kāsate	kašljati	to cough
kup, kupyati	kipeti	swell, heave, boil with emotion
mātā	mati	mother
tātā	ata, tata	father
sūnū	sin	son
bhrātā	brat	brother
vidhavā	vdova	widow

The similarity of Sanskrit and Slovene is not limited to individual words; there is similarity also in morphology. For example, the Sanskrit has the dual which is characteristic of the Slovene language. The illustration is in first person dual:

Sanskrit:	**Nagnau**		**hladake**	**vode**	**plavavah.**
Slovene:	Naga	v	hladki	vodi	plavava.
English:	Nude	in	cold	water	we two are swimming.

In Slovene, *hladak* and *hladek* are old forms for *hladen*; *hladki* is dative f. of *hladka*.

This illustration is in first person plural:

Sanskrit:	**Svetam**	**karpatam**	**saha**	**sivanikya**	**sivyamah.**
Slovene:	Svetlo	krpo	s	šivanko	šivamo.
English:	Bright	patch	with	needle	we sew.

The likeness of Slovene and Sanskrit languages could have originated only in the time before the settlement of Indo-Europeans in India; that is, in the earliest period of the Indo-European era, indicating that the Indo-European language at that time was very closely linked to the Slavic, or even, that the Proto-Slavic was the principal element in the formation of Indo-European languages. The only explanation is that **Proto-Slavic was the language** which was widely distributed in Europe before the beginning of Indo-European development.

Inasmuch as Sanskrit remained unchanged for nearly 4000 years and is still understood, it can help us with the translation of some Slovene names, particularly river names. Excepting minor changes, river names have stayed the same for thousands of years; however, changes in the spoken language have caused the loss of the original meaning. Some names of Slovene rivers are still understandable to us; for example: **Drava** from *deroča*—fast flowing; **Timava** (earlier Temava) from *tema*—darkness, it flows from a cave. But the meaning of the names of several other Slovene rivers are best clarified by the Sanskrit. In this sample of seven rivers we have the name of the river followed by the Sanskrit and its translation (Sanskrit c is pronounced as Slov. č).

Sava	*savah*—flow, *savati*—to flow
Savinja	*savinī*—river
Soča	*śocati*—to shine, *sucá*—pure
Sora	*sora*—meandering, serpentine movement
Vipava	*vibhava*—strong, rich (source of river)
Zila	*sila*—vein, tendon, *sira*—brook, narrow stream
Mura	*murati*—to entwine, to bind, *murá*—rushing

Script from the Vinča Culture

In the middle Danubian area the **Vinča culture** flourished between the 6th and 4th millenniums B.C. It was named after the archaeological site 14km east of Belgrade, where the majority of the objects of this culture were found. Researchers have been studying this culture for many years, and found letters of a writing system at the earliest stages of excavation; later, Dr. Radivoje Pešić made extensive studies of this alphabet and was able to establish definitive conclusions. As a well-known Etruscologist and professor in Milan, Italy, he devoted himself mainly to research of the Vinča alphabet—the oldest linear writing in the world. His findings appeared in a number of publications including the *Grande enciclopedia contemporanea* (Milano). An early death prevented him from publishing his findings; fortunately, his sons have posthumously published the book *Vinčansko pismo/* Vinča Script, Beograd, 1995, on the basis of his writings.

History tells us that hieroglyphics were the first form of writing, followed by

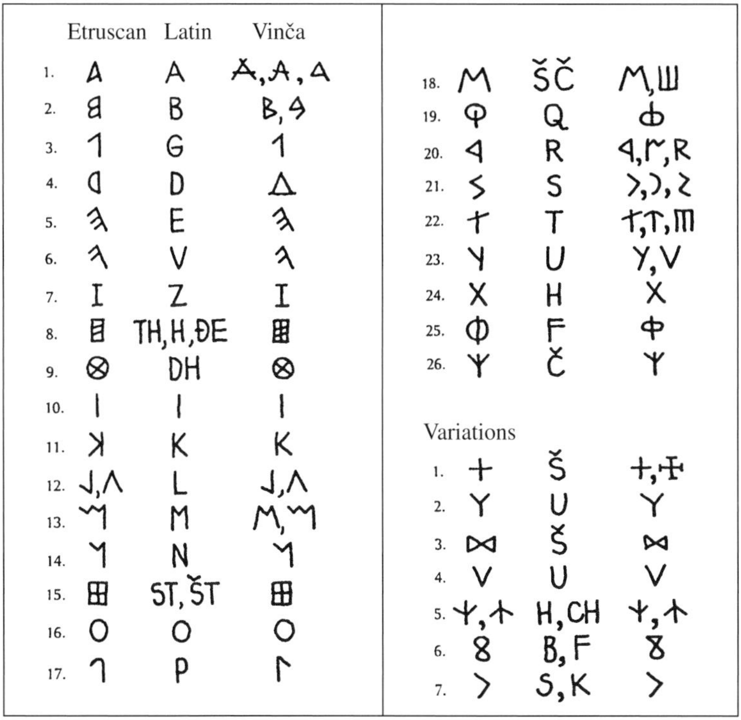

	Etruscan	Latin	Vinča
1.	A	A	Ä,Ä,Ä
2.	ꓭ	B	ꓭ,ꟼ
3.	ꓶ	G	ꓶ
4.	ꓷ	D	Δ
5.	ꓱ	E	ꓱ
6.	ꓥ	V	ꓥ
7.	I	Z	I
8.	ꓮ	TH,H,ÐE	ꓮ
9.	⊗	DH	⊗
10.	I	I	I
11.	ꓘ	K	K
12.	↓,∧	L	↓,∧
13.	ꟿ	M	M,ꟿ
14.	ꓸ	N	ꓸ
15.	⊞	ST, ŠT	⊞
16.	O	O	O
17.	ꓒ	P	ꓒ

	Etruscan	Latin	Vinča
18.	M	ŠČ	M,Ш
19.	Ψ	Q	⏀
20.	ꓤ	R	ꓤ,ꓩ,R
21.	ꓢ	S	�,〉,〈
22.	ꓔ	T	ꓔ,T,ꟿ
23.	Y	U	Y,V
24.	X	H	X
25.	Φ	F	Φ
26.	Ƴ	Č	Ƴ

Variations

	Etruscan	Latin	Vinča
1.	+	Š	+,ꝑ
2.	Y	U	Y
3.	⋈	Š	⋈
4.	V	U	V
5.	Ƴ,ꓕ	H,CH	Ƴ,ꓕ
6.	8	B,F	8
7.	〉	S,K	〉

Comparison of Etruscan letters with letters from various objects from Vinča culture, as presented by Dr. Pešić. Below is the earliest known Etruscan alphabet from the 7th century B.C.

the cuneiform, and lastly, the linear form of writing. The understanding until now has been that hieroglyphical writing developed around the 3rd millennium B.C., first in Mesopotamia (Sumerian), then in Egypt and on the Indian subcontinent, and linear writing in the 2nd millennium B.C. in the Middle East. The syllabic, representing spoken syllables rather than individual sounds, is presumed to have been the first form of linear writing. From this developed consonant writing; i. e., Semitic script from 12th century B.C. This was soon divided into three groups: Phoenician, Old Hebrew, and Aramaic. From Old Phoenician developed the Greek alphabet, which included vowels and is considered to be the origin of the writing systems of eastern and western Europe. This theory of the evolution of writing was turned on its head by the discovery of Vinča script, which already existed in the 4th millennium B.C. The process of research that led Dr. Pešić to his conclusions are presented with great clarity in the above book.

The first big surprise of Vinča script is the similarity or virtual sameness with Etruscan and Venetic scripts. To explain, we have to look again at what historians say about the Etruscans. Herodotus, the Greek historian, was of the opinion that the Etruscans came from Anatolia, in which case it would have been natural for them to bring the Phoenician alphabet with them. However, Herodotus's view was rejected by Dionysius of Halicarnassus, according to whom the Etruscans were an indigenous people. In that case, they could have received the script from the Greeks who started to settle in the 8th century B.C. in southern Italy. But

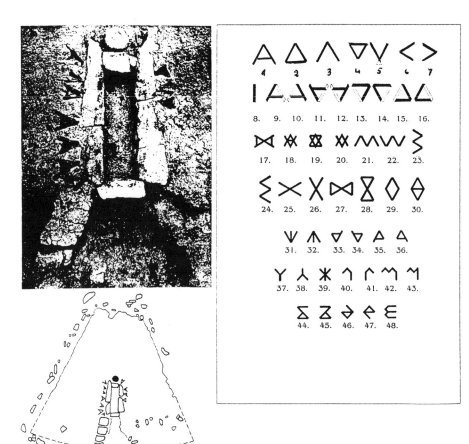

Stone structure from Lepenski Vir. From the three basic signs, 48 graphemes developed representing the foundation for all linear writing.

Etruscan inscriptions are already proven, which means that they could not have received it from the newly-arrived Greeks. Much more understandable is the view that the Etruscans came to Italy around 1100 B.C. as part of the Veneti, and brought with them the alphabet from Vinča culture.

The forerunner of Vinča culture in the middle Danubian area, dated around 7th and 6th millenniums B.C., was **Lepenski Vir culture.** Archaeological discoveries show this culture as being particularly sensitive to symbolism that expresses a relationship between the abstract and the realistic. We can imagine that within this relatively advanced culture there could have appeared not only pictorial but also graphical expression of thought. Dr. Pešić draws our attention to three basic symbols from Lepenski Vir $\mathsf{A} \triangle \wedge$ which are clearly visible in the picture of the altar or structure from Lepenski Vir. They could represent the first attempt or the starting point of all subsequent alphabets.

The Lepenski Vir graphemes can be considered a formative attempt to represent an experience or an object. Some researchers regard the graphic expressions of Lepenski Vir as being related to the graphic expressions and spoken language of the Middle Stone Age (Mesolithic) culture of central and northern Europe.

Vinča culture is of extraordinary importance because of its linear script, founded on the original symbols of Lepenski Vir. Research of Vinča culture has been continuing since 1908. On numerous objects archaeologists found unusual letter-shaped symbols, but they did not dare to see in them a writing system from the 5th or 4th millenniums B.C. Miloje Vasić saw the letters in 1910, and interpreted Vinča culture and its script to be more recent than Phoenician script.

Later, advanced research (carbon C-14 dating and other methods) established the Vinča culture period at between the 6th and the 4th millenniums B.C. Dr. Pešić established recognition of the Vinča script as the beginning of the world's linear writing systems. He selected 57 graphemes; from these there are 14 considered to be variations of vowels, which are with further analysis reduced to 5 vowel graphemes and their variations. From the remainder of the graphemes there are 43 which are regarded as consonants with their variations.

With the classification of all graphemes, Dr. Pešić came to the understanding that Vinča script had 26 letters, excluding the variations. The large number of objects with written symbols made a detailed analysis possible on all its demanding, professional levels. The inscriptions are clear and legible and in the majority of cases are the work of an experienced hand. The size of lettering conforms to the size of the object. There are around 1000 found objects with letters or inscriptions. Some are from the later period; for example, the amulet from 1250 and others from 1075 B.C. This means Vinča script survived an extraordinary length of time and was reaching out from its home base.

Phoenician		Latin	Vinča
1.	⊀ ALEPH	A	A,⊀
2.	�9 BET	B	B,9
3.	↖ GIRNEL	G	↑
4.	△ DALET	D	△
5.	⋧ HE	E	⋧
6.	Y VAV	V	⋏,Y
7.	I ZAYIN	Z	I
8.	⫴ HET	H	⊞
9.	⊗ TET	DH	⊗
10.	⋋ YOD	I	I,⋋
11.	⋋ KAPH	K	⋈
12.	L LAMED	L	⅃,∧
13.	⋎ MEM	M	⋎,M
14.	⋎ NUN	N	⋎
15.	⟊ SAMEKH	X	⟊,X
16.	O AYIN	O	O
17.	⌐ PE	P	⌐
18.	⊬ SADE	S	⋌
19.	Φ QOPH	Q	⊄
20.	⊿ RESH	R	⊿,⌐,R
21.	W SHIN	₷	W
22.	⨯ TAV	T	⨋

The Phoenician alphabet compared with Vinča script.

In comparing letters of later cultures with the letters of Vinča culture, Dr. Pešić found they all have a greater or smaller number of letters in common with Vinča script. For example, the Old Phoenician alphabet had 10, Old Greek had 12, and Etruscan had all letters in common with Vinča script. The Cyrillic and the Glagolitic alphabets also contain a considerable number of letters that are the same as those of the Vinča culture.

From the similarity of various alphabets we can consider the following course of development of linear writing; we recognize two directions of expansion. One stream of transmission flowed south to the Middle East, where it was received by Greeks, Phoenicians, Egyptians, etc.; the other, probably older, went to the north, and took the art of writing to central Europe. There it was received by the Veneti and taken during expansion of Urnfield culture as far as Italy, where it reached its highest development in Este and Etruscan cultures. Thus, Etruscan and Venetic

516

scripts originated with Vinča culture, which is a strong confirmation that the Veneti and Etruscans had a common origin in Urnfield culture.

The astonishing similarity of Vinča and Etruscan alphabets is, in Dr. Pešić's view, clear testimony that the Etruscans came from the area of Vinča culture. He also reminds us that the Etruscans called themselves "Rasenna" which could be related to the still-existing place-name Raša or Rašica in the area of Vinča culture. It is possible that a group of Vinčans moved from their home base through Pannonia and Slovenia as far as Tuscany and this may well be the explanation for the name "Rasenna". "Regardless of this," says Dr. Pešić, "it is very probable that the people of the Vinča language type covered a large area in Europe." This view is completely in harmony with our thesis regarding the origin of the Veneti (and Etruscans), and a Slavic substratum, on the base of which later evolved the

The drawing of a jar from Vinča culture has symbols which can be interpreted as an inscription. The wave-like decorations on the neck of the jar suggest interaction of Vinča and Linear-pottery cultures of central Europe. The drawing of an amulet from a later period (circa 1200 B.C.) shows an inscription with well-shaped letters.

517

Venetic within Indo-European structure, spreading with Urnfield culture into many areas of Europe.

Bibliography: *Die Lepenski-Vir-Kultur und der Beginn der Jungsteinzeit an der Mittleren Donau,* Köln-Wien 1971/ The Lepenski Vir Culture and the Beginning of the Late Stone Age in the Middle Danubian Region.
New Techniques in the Analysis and Interpretation of Mesolithic Notation and Symbolic Art, A. Marshack, Valcamonica Symposium, 1970.
A Study of Writing, The University of Chicago, Second Edition, 1963.

Dr. Pešić concludes his study by saying: "In this book we took a strong position that there was a writing system in the 4th millennium B.C. We showed with a number of tables the similarity of the oldest scripts with that of the Vinča script. We were not able to detect any difference between the Etruscan and Vinča scripts. They both have the same characteristics in the form of the letters, their phonetic values, the number of the letters, the presence of ligatures and punctations, and the direction of writing and reading."

"From this we must also derive some conclusions about the origins of the Etruscans," says Pešić. "It is impossible that the Etruscans were without an alphabet and a writing system at the time of the arrival of the Greeks in Italy; at that time the Etruscans must have known the numbers without which they could not have built their known architectural works. Knowledge of numbers means the knowledge of a writing system. We must also remember that the Greek alphabet lacked a number of letters which the Etruscan alphabet had, and that the Etruscan did not have certain letters that were included in the Greek alphabet."

Inasmuch as the Etruscans came from the north, it is fairly certain they brought the writing system which was known in the middle Danubian area. There is in reality no mystery about the Etruscans and their script. The mystery has been created by historians and linguists who have till now maintained that Etruscan is an unknown language. This was also pronounced by Strabo in the 1st century B.C. But his contemporary, Titus Livy, stated that the city of Cere, now Cerveteri, was in his time an educational centre where young Romans studied philosophy, literature, and rhetoric—in the Etruscan language.

Voluminous literature on the Etruscan language and script has not answered key questions. In his analysis of the Etruscan language, Pallotino depended on Latin, English, French, Swedish and Finnish. Other researchers compared the Etruscan with yet other languages, but to no avail. A marginal connection was seen in the similarity between the Latin and Etruscan languages due to partial

518

derivation of Latin from Etruscan. This similarity is insignificant and does not resolve the larger question—the origin of the Etruscan language.

In his book *The Vinča Script*, Dr. Pešić expresses his view on this subject: "The most important contribution in the search for identity of the Etruscan language is the study of the Venetic language by Matej Bor."

An Overview of Slovene History
In Place of Conclusion

The Slovenes as a people began in the prehistory of central Europe, in the 13th century B.C., when their predecessors, the Proto-Slavic Veneti, evolved within Lusatian culture. The Veneti were the bearers of Urnfield culture which spread over many areas of Europe. Around the 8th century B.C. between the Alps and the Adriatic Sea, they developed the important Este culture; its numerous inscriptions can still be understood through the Slovene language.

The earliest incontrovertible documents found to date, referring to the Slovenes as "Winidi" or "Veneti", apply to the period following the departure of the Byzantines from Inner Noricum. After the breakdown of the Roman Empire, the province of Inner Noricum (the southern half of present-day Austria and part of Slovenia) was for a short time governed by the Germanic King Odoacer, then by the Ostrogoths followed by the Franks, who were in the year 555 A.D. driven out by the Byzantines. In 568, the Langobards were on a westward move into Italy, leading to the sudden departure of the Byzantines from Inner Noricum.

What happened in Inner Noricum after the last of these occupation armies departed? Who were the indigenous people who inhabited Inner Noricum during these changes of rule? The answers can be found only through the events that followed. Twenty-seven years later an independent state emerged called "sclaborum provincia" (Slavic state), as recorded by Diaconus. What is important here is the word "provincia". It was used by the Langobards themselves to describe their own state, making it clear that "sclaborum provincia" signified a state with defined boundaries and defined internal organization.

We can conclude that, after the departure of the Byzantines, the indigenous people of Inner Noricum proclaimed themselves independent. Naturally, only the people inhabiting an area can found a state through an administrative act of this kind. It is obvious that the native people of Inner Noricum were Slavs because the village population of the area had not changed since pre-Roman times. More can be learned about these people from documentary evidence; e.g., Vita St. Columbani, which dates back to 615 in which they are explicitly called "Veneti" (their principal name) and also known as "Slavs" (Termini Venetiorum qui et Sclavi dicuntur). The Fredegarii Chronicon of 658 repeatedly calls Slovenes "Veneti" (Winedi). Just as explicit was Alcuin, a writer and contemporary of

Charlemagne. In addition to these sources, other evidence exists; for example, Venetic inscriptions can be read and understood with the help of the Slovene language. A great number of topographical names throughout what was once Venetic territory are undeniably Slovene. Many of these names come down to us from Roman and pre-Roman periods (see earlier chapters).

The relatively recent theory, which postulates the arrival of the Slovenes in their present territory at the end of the 6th century A.D., is completely in error, inasmuch as it is undocumented. First of all, where would all these people come from to occupy a huge territory from the Adriatic Sea to the Danube? Certainly not from the swamps of Pripet, as official historians claim. It would have been a very unusual swamp. Secondly, how could they have taken the choicest area in the centre of Europe, right next door to the Bavarians and Langobards, without a major war, and without a single historian writing one word about it? This is plainly impossible. Nothing of the sort happened. The only reason Slovenes were able to retain at least a small part of their original territory at that time, as now, is simply because they were indigenous to these areas from time immemorial.

Just when the Roman name "Noricum" was officially changed to "Carantania" is not known; they were most likely used simultaneously and when the Roman occupation ended, the indigenous Slovene name took the lead. In the year 623 under Duke Valuk, Carantania joined the large Slavic federation, the Kingdom of Samo, which extended far to the north and included Lusatia. After the death of King Samo in 658, this state disintegrated.

Thereafter Carantania remained an independent duchy. What must be mentioned here is that the investiture of Carantanian dukes was quite unusual. The ceremony was performed in the Slovene language even later, when German or Latin was in use elsewhere on such occasions. The contents of this ceremony demonstrated a high degree of democratic perception and was centuries later studied by Thomas Jefferson during the drafting of the Declaration of Independence of the United States of America.

Carantania was often threatened by the Avars. In a resulting war in 745, the Slovenes were helped by Bavarians. After they had defeated the Avars with joint forces, the Bavarians required Carantania to be annexed to the Frankish Kingdom of which they themselves were part. The Carantanian Duke Borut foresaw in this alliance future advantages for his people, despite the partial loss of independence. Under his successors, Gorazd and Hotimir, the Slovenes converted to Christianity through the missionary efforts of the Irish Bishop St. Modest, whose remains are entombed in the church he founded at Gospa Sveta near Celovec/Klagenfurt in Carinthia, Austria.

Soon after the death of Charlemagne (who was crowned in Rome as the first emperor of the Holy Roman Empire in the year 800) his own kingdom was divided. When the Hapsburgs came to power in 1335 in the East Frankish Kingdom to which Carantania then belonged, they took over its legacy but still had to be invested as Dukes of Carantania. The famous ceremony on the Prince's Stone (now in the museum in Klagenfurt) continued to be performed in the Slovene language. When after 1414 the investiture ceremony ceased (under German pressure), the occasion was limited to presentation before the Ducal Throne (the two-seat stone throne stands in the field at Gospa Sveta). This ceremony was also performed in the Slovene language and remained unchanged until the modification of the Constitution at the time of Empress Maria Theresa's ascendance to the Austrian throne in 1740. At that time the presentation before the Ducal Throne ended, and the Carantanian legacy was incorporated into the Austrian Constitution. The Slovenes had at that time the same status as Germans—as a community within the state. [In 1991 Austria prevented the Slovenes from using the Prince's Stone as their symbol of statehood]. Tr.

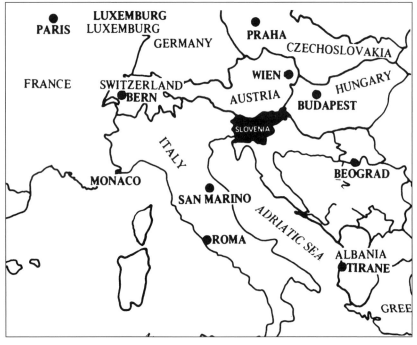

Slovenia, in the heart of Europe.

When the Pannonian region was freed from the Avars in 828, the second Slovene duchy—Pannonia—came into existence. It achieved special importance during the reign of Prince Kocelj (861–876). He is known for the support and protection he gave to the Slavic apostles Cyril and Methodius and for being a strong advocate of the introduction of native Slavic language in the liturgy. His contributions and endeavours in this field were given recognition more than a thousand years later during the Second Vatican Council. After Kocelj's death, Pannonia was annexed to Carantania. The Pannonian territory was ultimately lost to the Hungarians who invaded the area in 896–900. Nowadays, only a small minority in Hungary reminds us of the once-strong Slovene duchy.

From the 15th century on, the southern Slovene regions of the Hapsburg Monarchy (present-day Slovenia) were repeatedly victimized by Turkish raids. It was mostly the Slovenes—without outside help—who bore the brunt of those recurring invasions. It was the Slovenes who suffered and lost most, fighting in the first line of defence for the freedom of Europe.

The Slovene people also suffered a great deal under the burden of feudalism. Peasant uprisings were organized against brutal lords, but were ruthlessly suppressed. Especially noteworthy were the uprisings of Tolmin of 1478, 1515, 1573, and 1713. They represent a powerful struggle by the Slovenes for their social liberation. The effects of this struggle were also felt beyond the borders of Slovene territory.

During the Protestant Reformation (started in 1517), the Slovenes were part of the whirlwind of contradictory events but were able to advance their cultural position and status. One of the most important milestones was the printing of their first books. In 1584, the entire Bible was translated into Slovene and printed, representing an achievement which few nations could afford at that time. They also advanced culturally during the Catholic Counter-Reformation. In 1597, a Jesuit college was established in Ljubljana. It was an institute of very high standard listed in international registers as the origin of Ljubljana University.

During the 19th century the Slovenes were not subject to violent nationalistic pressures, but the steady advance of Germans from the north and west relentlessly moved the language boundary closer and closer to the present-day state border in southern Carinthia. It is worth mentioning here that a painting by Albrecht Dürer, painted somewhere in the area of the Brenner Pass in 1505, is entitled: Una Villana Windisch—A Slovene Village Woman; the subject was probably his hostess. This suggests that there were Slovene settlements in Tyrol at that time. Many toponyms and place-names in that region are of Slovene (Venetic) origin.

Napoleon also left his mark on the Slovenes. In 1809, he founded the Province of Illyria which included most of the Slovene and some of the Croat terri-

Venetic horse from the situla of Vače, Slovenia. From the images of this beautiful situla, sculptor Oskar Kogoj created a distinct, lightly stylized form of the horse which has become a symbol of the Veneti. This sculpture of natural size was cast in the finest bronze, and placed in 1994 in front of the palace of the United Nations in Geneva—a monument to the first nation of central Europe which, with its Urnfield culture, initiated the formation of European community.

tory. After Napoleon's defeat in Russia in 1812, the Province of Illyria reverted to Austrian dominion.

The revolution of 1848 had its impact on Austria, bringing about an important awakening of national consciousness. The Slovenes developed an aspiration for a united Slovenia within the framework of the monarchy. This, however, proved to be unattainable. The idea was Utopian, considering the circumstances; the powers at that time did not want a united Slovenia. Divide and rule was the preferred method then as it is now.

Meanwhile, the frontier between Slovenes and Croats was consolidated and, in 1866 in the west, the Slovene region in Friuli (the Venetian Slovenia), a territory which was ruled by the Republic of Venice until 1797, had to be relinquished to Italy by Austria.

At the end of the First World War, the Slovenes placed their aspirations in the right of self-determination of nations. They hoped that President Wilson of the

United States would support them in their struggle for a united Slovenia. However, they were bitterly disappointed. The new borders were drawn in such a way that more than one-third of Slovene-speaking territory was carved out and awarded to Austria, Italy, and Hungary. The remainder was incorporated into the newly-founded state of Yugoslavia. The dominant Serbs did not acknowledge the Slovenes as another nation with their own culture and language, and the Slovenes knew that Yugoslavia was not their true homeland.

During the terror of the Fascist regime in Italy, the Slovenes found themselves under heavy oppression; the same was true for Slovenes in Austria. Yet, they organized themselves as best they could, and their struggle represents the first resistance in Europe against Fascism and Nazism; for this they were relentlessly persecuted and many were brutally murdered.

World War Two brought more of the same. There was the occupation of all Slovene territory, followed by persecution, killings, and deportations. It is difficult to imagine the tragedy that befell this small nation. Nevertheless, the Slovenes developed a powerful resistance on all their ethnic territories and expected that after the war they would be granted the right to gather all their regions into a single, united entity, which would have represented a glorious chapter in their history. However, at the end of the war, the dominant powers, the U.S.A. and Britain, chose otherwise. Carinthia was again handed to Austria and Venetian Slovenia and Trst/Trieste to Italy, while Slovenia itself was consigned to the Yugoslav Communist dictatorship.

It is no surprise that the Slovenes were the primary contributors to the dismantling of Yugoslav Communism. The ten-day war in Slovenia against the aggression of the Yugoslav Army astonished people all over the world and aroused admiration for the small nation which fought so bravely for its freedom.

After 1247 years, since the annexation of Carantania to the East Frankish Kingdom in 745, Slovenia has finally joined other democratic countries of Europe as an independent state.

Ostani jar—Stay well!
(Toast on the situla from Škocjan, Slovenia).

Index